THE OXFORD HANDBOOK OF

CANADIAN POLITICS

D1281407

THE OXFORD HANDBOOK OF

CANADIAN POLITICS

Edited by

JOHN C. COURTNEY

DAVID E. SMITH

OXFORD
UNIVERSITY PRESS
2010

OXFORD
UNIVERSITY PRESS

Oxford University Press, Inc., publishes works that further
Oxford University's objective of excellence
in research, scholarship, and education.

Oxford   New York
Auckland   Cape Town   Dar es Salaam   Hong Kong   Karachi
Kuala Lumpur   Madrid   Melbourne   Mexico City   Nairobi
New Delhi   Shanghai   Taipei   Toronto

With offices in
Argentina   Austria   Brazil   Chile   Czech Republic   France   Greece
Guatemala   Hungary   Italy   Japan   Poland   Portugal   Singapore
South Korea   Switzerland   Thailand   Turkey   Ukraine   Vietnam

Copyright © 2010 by Oxford University Press, Inc.

Published by Oxford University Press, Inc.
198 Madison Avenue, New York, New York 10016

www.oup.com

Oxford is a registered trademark of Oxford University Press.

All rights reserved. No part of this publication may be reproduced,
stored in a retrieval system, or transmitted, in any form or by any means,
electronic, mechanical, photocopying, recording, or otherwise,
without the prior permission of Oxford University Press.

Library of Congress Cataloging-in-Publication Data
The Oxford handbook of Canadian politics / edited by John C. Courtney and David E. Smith.
p.   cm.
Includes bibliographical references and index.
ISBN 978-0-19-533535-4
1. Canada—Politics and government.   I. Courtney, John C.   II. Smith, David E., 1936–
JL15.O94 2010
320.971—dc22   2009023189

1   3   5   7   9   8   6   4   2
Printed in the United States of America
on acid-free paper

CONTENTS

....

PART VI CANADA IN THE WORLD

PART VII MAJOR ISSUES OF THE TWENTY-FIRST CENTURY

CONTRIBUTORS

....

YALE D. BELANGER is Assistant Professor, Department of Native American Studies, University of Lethbridge.

STEPHEN BROOKS is Professor, Department of Political Science, University of Windsor, and Adjunct Professor, Department of Political Science, University of Michigan.

R. KENNETH CARTY is Professor of Political Science and Director of the Centre for the Study of Democratic Institutions, University of British Columbia.

JOHN C. COURTNEY is Professor Emeritus of Political Studies and Senior Policy Fellow, Johnson-Shoyama Graduate School of Public Policy, University of Saskatchewan.

WILLIAM CROSS is the Hon. Dick and Ruth Bell Professor for the Study of Canadian Parliamentary Democracy, Department of Political Science, Carleton University.

ELISABETH GIDENGIL is Hiram Mills Professor, Department of Political Science, McGill University, and Director of the Centre for Democratic Citizenship.

MICHAEL HART, a former federal official, now holds the Simon Reisman Chair in Trade Policy at Carleton University's Norman Paterson School of International Affairs.

JANET L. HIEBERT is Professor, Department of Political Studies, Queen's University.

MICHAEL HOWLETT is Burnaby Mountain Professor, Department of Political Science at Simon Fraser University, Burnaby, British Columbia.

JANE JENSON holds the Canada Research Chair in Citizenship and Governance, Département de science politique, Université de Montréal.

RICHARD JOHNSTON is Distinguished University Scholar and Professor of Political Science, University of British Columbia, and former Professor of Political Science and Research Director of the National Annenberg Election Study, University of Pennsylvania.

SIMA JOSHI-KOOP is a Doctoral Candidate in the Department of Political Science, Simon Fraser University.

JAMES B. KELLY is Associate Professor, Department of Political Science, Concordia University.

WILL KYMLICKA is the Canada Research Chair in Political Philosophy, Queen's University, Kingston.

HARVEY LAZAR is Adjunct Professor, School of Public Administration, and Senior Research Associate in the Centre for Global Studies, University of Victoria.

CHRISTOPHER P. MANFREDI is Dean of the Faculty of Arts, McGill University.

GREGORY P. MARCHILDON is a Canada Research Chair in the Johnson-Shoyama Graduate School of Public Policy, University of Regina, and Fellow, School of Policy Studies, Queen's University.

ÉRIC MONTPETIT is Associate Professor, Département de science politique, Université de Montréal, and Director of the Centre de recherche sur les politiques et le développement social.

PAUL NESBITT-LARKING is Professor and Chair, Department of Political Science, Huron University College.

DAVID R. NEWHOUSE is Associate Professor and Chair, Department of Indigenous Studies, Trent University.

ALAIN NOËL is Professor in the Département de science politique, Université de Montréal.

BRENDA O'NEILL is Associate Professor, Department of Political Science, University of Calgary.

JONATHAN ROSE is Associate Professor of Political Studies at Queen's University in Kingston, Ontario.

PETER H. RUSSELL is Professor Emeritus of Political Science, University of Toronto.

ANDREW SANCTON is Director of the Local Government Program and Professor of Political Science, University of Western Ontario.

DONALD J. SAVOIE holds the Canada Research Chair in Public Administration and Governance, Université de Moncton.

F. LESLIE SEIDLE is Senior Research Associate, Institute for Research on Public Policy, Montreal.

GRACE SKOGSTAD is Professor of Political Science, University of Toronto.

ELINOR SLOAN is Associate Professor of International Security Studies, Department of Political Science, Carleton University.

DAVID E. SMITH is Professor Emeritus of Political Studies, University of Saskatchewan, and Senior Policy Fellow, Johnson-Shoyama Graduate School of Public Policy, University of Regina.

STUART SOROKA is Associate Professor and William Dawson Scholar, Department of Political Science, McGill University.

PAUL G. THOMAS is the Duff Roblin Professor of Government, St John's College, University of Manitoba.

JENNIFER M. WELSH is Professor in International Relations at the University of Oxford and a Fellow of Somerville College.

CHRISTOPHER WLEZIEN is Professor of Political Science and Faculty Affiliate in the Institute for Public Affairs at Temple University.

LISA YOUNG is Professor of Political Science, University of Calgary.

THE OXFORD HANDBOOK OF

CANADIAN POLITICS

CHAPTER 1

INTRODUCTION: TRANSFORMATION OF AN UNNATURAL COUNTRY

JOHN C. COURTNEY
DAVID E. SMITH

MORE than sixty-five years ago, Bruce Hutchison, a leading Canadian journalist, wrote an early popular history of Canada. He called it *The Unknown Country* (Hutchison 1945). The adjective was well chosen. Although at the time a major contributor of personnel and material to the Allied cause and to ultimate victory, Canada had yet to establish in its own eyes, or in the eyes of others, an independent character, be it measured politically, economically, or culturally. It is customary to cite the Statute of Westminster, 1931, as marking Canada's constitutional coming of age. Under the terms of that British Act, Canada and other Dominions, such as Australia and New Zealand, achieved legislative autonomy in law, as they had for a long time—in fact, from the imperial Parliament. Depression and war delayed for a decade and a half peacetime assertion of Canada's maturity, and even then it took another decade and a half for the imperial legacy to exhaust itself.

The Suez debacle of 1956 revealed rather than precipitated the separation that had developed with the mother country. What at the most public level was a disagreement over foreign policy and military strategy, subjects that during the 1950s vestigially bound Canada to Great Britain, permeated Canada's sense of itself as well and drove home the realization that the British tie had unraveled. Harold Macmillan's metaphorical "wind of change" speech in 1960, although directed at events in Africa, was felt across the Atlantic. Canada's first Canadian-born governor general, Vincent Massey, was appointed in 1952. A strong anglophile, his autobiography, *What's Past Is Prologue*, appeared a decade later (Massey 1963). By then, such a prediction could hardly have been more inaccurate than when applied to the new Canada in the making.

The chapters in this book deal with subjects and policies that illustrate the transformation that has occurred in Canadian politics in the past half century. A list of some of the topics discussed makes the point: the Quiet Revolution in Quebec after 1960; the Canadian Charter of Rights and Freedoms, entrenched in the Constitution Act, 1982; the adoption of official bilingualism in 1969, of multiculturalism in 1971, the Medical Care Act (universal medicare) in 1966; the emergence of Aboriginal peoples from the shadows into the historical, legal, and political consciousness of nonAboriginal Canadians; a similar consciousness-raising in the South about the North and the Arctic; an appreciation of the central role that natural resources, particularly those located in western Canada, will play in the future prosperity and security of the country as a whole; the implications of global economic trends and communication technology on national integration; and the movement from peacekeeping in Cyprus and the Middle East four decades ago to defending the homeland against terrorists and fighting an armed conflict with escalating casualties in Afghanistan today.

Of course, Canada is not alone in experiencing rapid and widespread change in recent decades. What sets it apart from other nations, at the very least in the minds of Canadians themselves, is the belief that Canada is not a natural country. Extreme climate, immense area, sparse population, with a superpower as a neighbor—no wonder it feels vulnerable; no wonder a repeated theme of Canadian literature, in whatever language, is (in the title of Margaret Atwood's popular guide to Canadian literature) *survival* (Atwood 1972). As another Canadian intellectual, Northrop Frye, observed, Canada is "a country divided by...great stretches of wilderness, so that its frontier is a circumference rather than a boundary" (Falardeau 2004, 83). Here is why transportation (canals, railroads, highways, pipelines) and communication (radio, television, satellites) are so central to Canadian history. They annihilate distance and transcend divides, be they mountain ranges, oceanic straits, or linguistic differences. A simple way of visualizing Canada, and at the same time contrasting it to the United States, is to look at one's hand and to see the palm as the United States and the fingers as Canada, or, more accurately, Canada's pronounced regions set apart by geography or culture.

Canada is a small country by every measure, except size. Michael Hart (chapter 22), says much the same, only epigrammatically, when he writes that the Canadian reality is "too much geography and too little demography." Although the population, more than thirty-three million in 2008, is small, it is more than double what it was in 1951. The signal features of the interrelationship of people and place are a population huddled along (that is, within 200 miles of) the U.S.–Canada boundary; overwhelmingly concentrated in the two large central provinces, and in a handful of regional centers, such as Vancouver, Calgary, Edmonton, Winnipeg, Ottawa, Quebec City, and Halifax; distributed very sparsely over the northern half of all provinces, except Prince Edward Island, and throughout the three northern territories—Yukon, Northwest Territories, and Nunavut; increasingly urbanized, as a result of both rural-to-urban migration everywhere and a vast influx of immigrants from overseas into metropolitan centers. In the prairie provinces of Saskatchewan and Manitoba, the total populations of which have grown very slowly, a large part of the urban migration is composed of Aboriginal peoples who have chosen to leave native reserves in the northern parts of the provinces and move to the city.

Canada's comparatively small population relative to its size is, for all practical purposes, made smaller still by linguistic and ethnic cleavages. Not only has postwar immigration diluted assumptions and priorities that once dominated English Canada, but, as Alain Noël demonstrates in chapter 6, the ambition of French-speaking Quebecers to assert mastery over affairs in the province of Quebec, seen, for example, in the promulgation of language laws to promote the use of French in the workplace—and a reciprocal desire on the part of the federal government to make Canada a linguistic home for speakers of English and of French—has had the effect of fragmenting the national cohesion the earlier English-language regime had implicitly imposed. In addition, and for reasons set out by David Newhouse and Yale Belanger in chapter 19, the concerns of Aboriginal peoples have now become the concerns of Canadian governments. Once again, the effect of this new perspective is to throw doubt upon earlier assumptions of cultural uniformity.

As opposed to some countries, such as Ireland perhaps, which might be said to have too much history, modern Canada could be said to have too many histories. At the very least, and in marked contrast to its Anglo-centric past, there is more than one master narrative. In chapter 17, Will Kymlicka describes and analyzes the kaleidoscopic nature of Canadian society, notes the speed with which this has occurred, and distinguishes Canada's situation from other countries—for example, Australia and the United States, with which Canada is usually compared. Possessed with this knowledge, the appeal of the Canadian Charter of Rights and Freedoms (adopted in 1982) to individual Canadians from coast to coast to coast may be readily understood.

One of the most widely used history books of the postwar era was *Colony to Nation* (Lower 1949). The Whiggish-inspired title says it all—the course for Canadian evolution was encoded, predetermined. As the preceding paragraphs suggest, that assumption was not to be realized. Indeed, during the 1960s, conflicting interpretations of the word "nation" and *nation* (in French), roiled Canadian politics and threw into question, at least in some quarters, the belief in what Canada had become. What happened to alter that development, why, and with what consequences is a recurring theme of the chapters that follow. The authors do more than touch on that, however. If Canada is no longer Hutchison's "unknown country," it is still not known terribly well abroad or at home. Although each of the thirty-five authors furthers understanding of some aspect of Canadian life, together their singular achievement is to paint a many-hued portrait of a country and people (or peoples) extravagantly blessed by providence.

The chapters in this book were written in 2007 and 2008. All were completed before the federal general election in October 2008. That election saw the Conservative government led by Stephen Harper returned to power, but still without a majority in the House of Commons. This was the third minority government (that is, a government that did not command support from a majority of members in the elected lower chamber of Parliament) in four years. The previous elections were in 2004 (which produced a Liberal minority government) and 2006. It is important to make this point, because with elections now occurring at less than two years apart, and in light of the time required to publish a volume such as this one, it is not feasible to have, even for a short time, current electoral data in the hands of the reader. If any consolation is to be had from this deprivation, it is that dramatic swings in voter support for Canadian political parties have not been evident during the past decade, and that returns of the last-but-one election are not confounded by the most recent returns.

Canadians may well have to accept the likelihood that minority, as opposed to majority, governments will be around for some time. Minority parliaments have become familiar fixtures on the political landscape in the recent past. From the time of Confederation in 1867 through to the end of 2008, Canada held forty federal elections. In the first ninety of those 141 years, only two elections (one in 1921 and the other in 1925) produced minority parliaments. Since 1957, however, fully 50% (nine of eighteen) of the federal elections have led to minority parliaments.

Apart from the Unionist government that brought Conservatives and some Liberals together during World War I, and in contrast to the great majority of European parliaments, Canada has had no experience of interparty coalition government at the federal level. It is as if, as Ken Carty and Bill Cross explain in chapter 11 (this volume), when minority parliaments are elected in Canada "the parties' basic instinct is to amplify and sharpen partisanship in the hope that the next election will return the system to 'normal.'"

The likelihood of majority parliaments becoming the "norm," at least for the foreseeable future, is slim. Canada's "national party" system, in which one party (typically the Liberals for most of the twentieth century) would regularly gain a measure of support and elect members of Parliament from all regions of the country, is now a thing of the past. Since the early 1990s, when the party system became deeply fractured in the wake of the collapse of the Meech Lake Accord, minority parliaments have become "the new norm" (Cross 2009). If this continues to be the case, the possibility of coalition governments composed of two or more parties cannot be ruled out in the years ahead.

This handbook is made up of twenty-eight chapters (eight of the chapters are co-authored). Sixteen of them deal with the institutions and processes of Canadian government and politics. In that last sentence, "Canadian" encompasses federal, provincial, and local governments. The subjects analyzed are Parliament, Constitution, courts, cabinet, Charter, federalism (fiscal as well as political), political parties, elections and voting, interest groups, public opinion, and the media. The remaining chapters discuss aspects of Canadian demography, Canada's external relations and international trade, four public policy areas (social, health, science, and the environment), defense and security, and, last, democratic reform.

By inference, a handbook makes large claims for completeness. Still, not every subject can be covered. To take as one example, no chapter has been explicitly devoted to the North—that is, that expanse encompassed by Yukon, Northwest Territories, and Nunavut. If one purpose of this publication is to make known what is unknown, to fill in the blank spaces, so to speak, then omission of the North is a large void. Northern resources, security and defense, and governmental innovation (Nunavut, for instance, is an Aboriginal political unit where there are no political parties and where government is formed and run on the basis of consensus) are arguments for inclusion. The counterargument (that is, for exclusion) is that the northern territories comprise only three of Canada's fourteen jurisdictions, or, if a regional perspective is adopted, one of five or six regions of the country. Except for chapter 6, on Quebec, there are no chapters devoted to single provinces or regions. Admittedly, although it may be second best, the functionally oriented chapters that follow, such as those by Elinor Sloan (chapter 27) on security and defense, Michael Howlett and Sima Joshi-Koop (chapter 26) on the environment, or David Smith (chapter 5) on federalism, regionalism, and the provinces, incorporate issues relevant to the North to the same extent that they incorporate issues relevant to Atlantic Canada or British Columbia.

Two illustrations of topics denied their own chapter are monarchy and the Senate of Canada. One reason for omitting them is that to do otherwise would be to grant both more attention than they normally receive. Few Canadians pay attention to monarchy other than as a British institution. There is not now, nor has there ever been, strong republican sentiment in the country. Moreover, monarchical government has well served Canada's strong regionalism and cultural pluralism. At the same time, the Crown as the first principle of Canadian government, evident in the operation of Parliament, the bureaucracy, the courts, the provinces, and more, remains invisible (Smith 1995). In any case, absence of a separate chapter in no way ignores the Crown's presence in Canadian public life, as such chapters as those devoted to the Constitution (chapter 3); Parliament and legislatures (chapter 9); and first ministers, cabinet, and public service (chapter 10) demonstrate. It is also a feature of chapter 28, on democratic reform, for opposition increasingly expressed to prime ministerial power is in reality often opposition to the prime minister's exercise of prerogative power inherent in the Crown. This is evident when, in the absence of parliamentary consent or even consultation, appointments are made by the governor general on advice of the prime minister; when the government unilaterally makes foreign policy decisions, including the deployment of troops abroad; and when the prime minister on his own initiative advises the governor general to dissolve or summon Parliament.

Like Mark Twain's aphorism about the weather, there is a tradition in Canada of talking about Senate reform but never actually doing it. To be more precise, within the political and academic classes, there is perennial discussion of the topic, which on occasion produces some concrete proposals, but nothing more than that.

Between them, Paul Thomas (chapter 9) and Leslie Seidle (chapter 28) explore the options for reform. These range from making the upper chamber a House of the Provinces, the members of which would be selected by a variety of methods to promote its representative capacity, to keep it much as it is except for introducing terms in place of appointment until age seventy-five. In other words, the proposals run the gamut from the megaconstitutional to the minimalist. It is the plethora of options on offer and the lack of agreement on any one of them that disqualify the Senate from having its own chapter in this book. There is no agreement in Canada on the form of an improved upper house, because there is no agreement on the function such a body should play. Until there is a consensus on the role of the Senate in Canada's Parliament and in the federation, reform of the Senate will remain a parlor or seminar pastime.

The criterion of choice for the policy chapters needs to be specified. More cryptically, the question is: Why these policy subjects and not others? For instance, at one time it was not possible to talk about public policy in Canada and not mention agriculture. Grain was the country's major export, the fourth in a succession of staple goods—the earlier ones had been fish, fur, and timber. The requirements of the grain industry determined the location of rail lines and, in turn, the settlement of the prairie provinces. More than that, grain was the crop for which the collection and transportation to ports influenced the growth of Vancouver and the modernization of the St. Lawrence Seaway. It is important to note that compared with other grain-producing countries of the world, all of which have year-round, warm-water ports available to them, Canada's crop must be hauled 1,000 or 2,000 miles to port, of which only those in British Columbia are open all year. James G. Gardiner, a former federal minister of agriculture, once told the Montreal Board of Trade that had it not been for western grain, which passed down river en route to Europe, that city would still be the Indian settlement of Hochelaga. That economy, just as an Anglo-centric Canada that once looked to Great Britain for cultural and political cues, now seems as if it were from another country. Although important, grain and farming in general have declined in political significance and as a share of the gross domestic product, along with the decline in the country's rural population. One index of that decline is the virtual absence of any reference to agriculture-related topics in the general election campaigns of recent decades.

One exception to this statement is the high-profile debate that surrounds the subject of plant biotechnology as it concerns genetically modified crops and foods. Canada remains one of the world's major exporters of food. The Canadian government has taken a lead role in the search for improved quality and quantity of food exports. Here is the source of its interest in genetically modified foods. At the same time, it is highly sensitive to critiques to plant biotechnology coming from potential purchasers abroad. In its examination of this debate, and other science-related subjects such as reproductive technologies, Grace Skogstad's chapter 25 demonstrates the breadth of change that has transpired in agriculture from a time when the popular image of that industry was of the man and the plow, or even the combine. It may be an exaggeration to say that, except for uncertain markets, the rhythm of agriculture was as predictable as the growing seasons; but it is only an exaggeration. As chapter 25 illustrates, the politics of agriculture and of other science-based activities today is about uncertainty, as defined by issues of risk, regulation, research, and public relations, where the public in question may as easily be non-Canadian as Canadian. This is a conclusion reinforced by the comparative analysis Éric Montpetit presents of interest groups and social movements in chapter 14.

Like agriculture, the timber and fishing industries no longer have a stronghold on national political or public attention. Although important to all Canadians, they are especially important for the well-being of specific provinces. Indeed, it is a feature of the Canadian economy that one or at most a few provincial governments act as powerful advocates and defenders of specific industries—examples include Ontario for automobile manufacturing or the financial sector, Alberta and Saskatchewan for the oil industry, and British Columbia for timber. Canada is a country that still depends upon its natural resources for a large measure of its prosperity. At the same time, a substantial proportion of that natural resource activity flows into international trade. From the perspective of this handbook, the activities of and challenges that confront these industries constitute a major dimension of international trade. For that reason, they are most appropriately discussed in Michael Hart's chapter (chapter 22) on trade and globalization.

Social policy, health care, science and technology, and the environment have been selected as specific policy areas for analysis in part because they are not jurisdictionally fixed. At one level they do have a strong provincial provenance. Property, education, and the provision of social service are matters that the Fathers of Confederation appear to have agreed should be provincial concerns. But over time, and especially during the postwar era, as an acceptance of national standards grew, they ceased to be so jurisdictionally privileged. This was made possible by the growth of the government's spending power. Increasingly, Ottawa designated funds in policy areas where it could not constitutionally legislate alone. In chapter 7, Harvey Lazar makes it abundantly clear that "substantial concurrency is achieved in areas of provincial legislative competence by the federal government exercising its 'spending power.'" It is through this mechanism that medicare, originally a program introduced by the provincial government of Saskatchewan, became a national program with national standards. The story of medicare, which Canadians repeatedly say is the most important service government provides them today, is discussed by Greg Marchildon in chapter 24.

A distinguishing feature of federalism is its capacity to enable one jurisdiction to try out institutional arrangements or processes different from those of other jurisdictions. James Bryce, then British ambassador to the United States, was one of the first to have noted more than a century ago in his classic study of American government that "federalism enables a people to try experiments in legislation and administration which could not be safely tried in a large centralized county" (Bryce 1891, 344). The transfederal diffusion of medicare in Canada is illustrative of Bryce's point, starting as it did in Saskatchewan then spreading to the federal level and all provinces. A more formal expression of Bryce's pronouncement is found in contemporary political science theory. The "diffusion of innovations" theory helps to explain why reforms instituted in one federal jurisdiction often make their way into others (Poel 1976).

Certainly this has been the case with a number of the laws governing the conduct of elections in Canada. Elisabeth Gidengil describes those reforms in chapter 13. Originally adopted by a single province, laws establishing independent electoral boundary commissions, election expenses, and party financing regulations, and granting the vote to women, First Nations people, and prison inmates, all started in one province and spread, with time, to others.

In each of the policy chapters, one theme that transcends the specific policy under review is the dispersion of policy effect or influence. Social policy, health care, science and technology, and the environment—these affect Canadians locally, provincially, federally, and internationally. Global travel, instant communication, the recategorization of issues—from localized pollution to global climate change—place in question the concept of boundaries, which is traditionally deemed essential in the study of federalism. There once was a time when, in the words of a much-quoted opinion of the Judicial Committee of the Privy Council that dealt with the location of the treaty power under the Canadian constitution, provinces were compared with watertight compartments. The role of provincial Crown corporations, particularly in energy production, be it hydro- or thermal-based electricity, was premised on the idea of provincial priorities and development. Today, the integration of economic activity between and among provinces and with foreign countries, particularly the United States under the Canada–U.S. Free Trade Agreement and, more recently, Mexico under the North American Free Trade Agreement, renders the concept of hermetically sealed provinces antique.

It does more than this, however, for it conflicts with the thesis of Canada's being a "double federation" (chapter 5). Both the cultural dualism of English and French Canada on the one hand and the horizontal territorial federation of provinces on the other seem remote sometimes from the world Canadians inhabit at home—concentrated urbanized populations that are multiethnic in character—and poorly placed to prepare Canadians for the world they encounter abroad. That external world is discussed by both Jennifer Welsh in chapter 20 and Stephen Brooks in chapter 21. In some respects, federalism offers a distorted prism through which to examine modern Canada.

Canada is the world's original parliamentary federation. Few studies of federal systems ignore its experience. Readers of this handbook will be reminded a number of times in a number of contexts of Canada's complex federal arrangements. None is more distinctive than the unique combination of federalism, parliamentary government, and, since 1982, the Canadian Charter of Rights and Freedoms. The chapters by James Kelly and Christopher Manfredi (chapter 3) and Janet Hiebert (chapter 4) discuss the interrelationship of the Constitution, the courts, and the Charter, as well as the strains and conflicts that exist among them. As an example, federal government is about the dispersal of powers; its force is centrifugal. By contrast, parliamentary government in any system patterned on the Westminster model is about the concentration of power; its force is centripetal. This last point is elaborated by Donald Savoie in chapter 10 in his assessment of first ministers, cabinet, and public service within the context of a system that combines parliamentary government with federalism. Add to these contradictory forces the Charter's guarantee of a range of rights to Canadians regardless of where they may live, and the tension that already exists between center and periphery, as a result of the workings of the first set of institutions, is compounded by the tension set up between citizen and governments.

Note the plural of that last word, for the Charter limits provincial governments as well as the federal government, and in that respect it is viewed by some critics as an enactment with an effect that undermines both federalism and parliamentary government. That is to say, provincial values and priorities are no argument for exceptionalism from the provisions of the Charter. Nor is parliamentary supremacy, to the extent that this concept is understood in a federation in which legislative powers are divided, in any way privileged. As Janet Hiebert notes in chapter 4, "at one time rights were thought of as protected by, not from, parliamentary sovereignty"; no longer is this true in Canada. Parliament and the government still have a role; they must see that proposed legislation conforms to the values enunciated by the Charter. They must do this or the courts will be called upon to intervene to see that the rights and freedoms specified in the Charter are upheld.

A study of legal and political science publications of the past twenty-five years—since the adoption of the Charter—reveals a continuing concern about the prejudicial effects of so-called judicial activism arising from Charter litigation on the health of parliamentary democracy (Mitchell et al. 2007). In its guarantees, the Charter recognizes certain classes of persons—the disabled and minority language groups are two examples. Distinguishing some Canadians over others in such a fundamental document as the Charter is only part of the complaint. Equally troubling from this perspective is that rights claims enfeeble politics and the traditional political process. No longer are disputes resolved through accommodation and compromise. Instead, courts deal with individual cases with a specific set of facts. According to this argument, the consequences are detrimental to healthy politics, which in this interpretation includes a vigorous federal system. James Kelly and Christopher Manfredi (chapter 3) explore in more detail the tension that has arisen following the introduction of a higher law into the Canadian Constitution.

Like other countries that share the Westminster system—Great Britain being the paramount case—the concept of "the Constitution" is ambiguous in Canada. For some, the practice of responsible government, whereby the cabinet or political executive must command the support of a majority in the House of Commons, is the essential feature of the Constitution. If that is the case, then an equally remarkable feature of the Canadian case is that nowhere in the principal written document, the Constitution Act, 1867 (originally entitled the British North America Act), is this practice described. It is almost totally based on convention, the understood but also usually unwritten practices of parliamentary government, transferred to the colonies that later became Canada. The 1867 Act concerns itself largely with the structure and terms of Confederation. As Andrew Sancton notes in chapter 8, this focus on federal and provincial worlds confined institutions as central to Canadian life as those of local government to an extraconstitutional (and vulnerable) existence.

This book is not simply a study of public policies; or of legislative, executive, and judicial institutions; or of the Constitution and Constitution making; or of electoral and political practices. However unintentionally, it is also testament to the scope of consultative processes in Canada, of which one type stands out: the Royal Commission of Inquiry. Federal and provincial governments have turned to Royal Commissions countless times to investigate important questions of public policy, to pave the way for major policy changes, to gauge public opinion, and to lay out courses of action for possible government implementation.

Appointed under executive (which is to say, cabinet) order, commissions of inquiry have enabled governments of all stripes to seek policy advice from experts and the public. The range of subjects they have been assigned at the federal level is impressive, as is obvious from the commissions alluded to in chapters by Peter Russell (chapter 2), David Smith (chapter 5), Alain Noël (chapter 6), Paul Thomas (chapter 9), Stuart Soroka and Christopher Wlezien (chapter 15), Will Kymlicka (chapter 17), Brenda O'Neill and Lisa Young (chapter 18), David Newhouse and Yale Belanger (chapter 19), Jane Jenson (chapter 23), Greg Marchildon (chapter 24), Grace Skogstad (chapter 25), Elinor Sloan (chapter 27), and Leslie Seidle (chapter 28).

Collectively, these authors draw our attention to several federal Royal Commissions whose ambitious reports, in many instances, profoundly influenced public policies and public opinion in Canada. Among them are inquiries whose very title captures a turning point in Canadian history: Dominion–Provincial Relations (1940); National Development in the Arts, Letters and Sciences (1951); Health Services (1964); Status of Women (1967); Bilingualism and Biculturalism (1969); Newspapers (1981); National Security and Intelligence (1981); Economic Union and Development Prospects (1985); Reproductive Technologies (1989); Electoral Reform and Party Financing (1991); and Aboriginal Peoples (1996).

Not only have Royal Commission recommendations often shaped subsequent public policy, but the comprehensive research tasks they have assigned to academicians and other experts have led to the publication of many invaluable and, in some cases, timeless studies in their respective field (Wherrett 2008). One of the contributors to this book, Jane Jenson, assigns in a separate article a significant and positive role to Canadian Royal Commissions. Established often in response to crises or uncertainties about the direction that public policy should take, commissions have a demonstrated potential to generate "new representations of history, of the present community, and of available futures that both educate and may very well empower" (Jenson 1994, 48).

As consequential as Royal Commissions were in ushering in a number of nation-building initiatives (ranging from the Canadian Broadcasting Corporation and the Canada Council, to medicare and the Canada–U.S. Free Trade Agreement), they have clearly fallen out of favor. Prime Minister Trudeau (1968–1979, 1980–1984) appointed forty-five Royal Commissions (quite possibly a record number); Prime Minister Mulroney (1984–1993), sixteen. But in the fifteen-year period between 1993, when Jean Chrétien's Liberals came to office, and the reelection of the Harper Conservatives in 2008, only seven commissions were established. The decrease is possibly explained by the obvious fact that few "megatopics" were left to be explored after the spate of inquiries in the period after the Great Depression and the end of World War II.

But more plausibly, the explanation lies in a different direction. For one thing, the mechanism for consulting the public over vital issues of policy has moved from the confines of commission hearings and commission-generated surveys to the ballot box. Referendums were at one time extremely rare in Canada. This has not been the case in the past two decades. Referendums have been held recently on a variety of issues and have, in many instances, generated widespread public interest and citizen participation levels that exceeded those of general elections. Their subjects have been diverse: a restructuring of the country's Constitution (the Charlottetown Accord, 1992), Quebec's secession from Canada (1995), First Nations Treaty Rights in British Columbia (2002), secular and parochial schools in Newfoundland and Labrador (1995 and 1997), video lottery terminals in New Brunswick (2001), and replacement of the plurality vote with some variant of proportional representation (British Columbia, 2005; Prince Edward Island, 2005; and Ontario, 2007).

Two contrasting approaches to public consultations have also defined the shift away from Royal Commissions of the past decade and a half. On the one hand, citizens' assemblies (described by Leslie Seidle in chapter 28) have been convened in both British Columbia and Ontario for the purposes of studying the electoral system and recommending, if deemed appropriate, its replacement with another method of voting.

On the other hand, it is conceivable, at least at the federal level, that the unquestioned concentration of power in the Prime Minister's Office in the past fifteen years or so has dampened the enthusiasm of senior political officials for Royal Commissions, in that they could well fear forfeiting control of an issue to an extra-parliamentary consultative body. In their place, carefully structured focus groups and frequent government-sponsored public opinion surveys have found favor. They have replaced the open public hearings of Royal Commissions, just as outside consultants contracted by government departments and agencies for targeted research and recommendations have replaced the commissioners once called to head public inquiries.

A cardinal characteristic of a Constitution based on convention is its malleability. That claim is supported by other chapters in this handbook by Ken Carty and Bill Cross (chapter 11), Richard Johnston (chapter 12), and Elisabeth Gidengil (chapter 13) on political parties, elections, voting, and the electoral system. That said, and certainly compared with the past, parties are now institutions that are statutorily recognized and subject both to parliamentary regulations and court rulings. In addition, the conduct of elections is strictly governed by laws relating to such matters as broadcasting and election expenses (Courtney 1978; 2004).

In chapter 15, Stuart Soroka and Christopher Wlezien raise the possibility that, in contrast to the separation of powers that is one of the defining features of American government, Canada's parliamentary system may well have become less responsive to public opinion over time. They quote political scientist James Mallory's observation that "the mass of citizenry is perhaps as far away from the real decisions of government as they were two hundred years ago, and the cabinet system provides strong institutional barriers to the development of more democratic ways of doing things" (Mallory 1974, 208).

If true, the "distance" between cabinet government and citizen might well be added to the list of social, political, and technological developments that collectively are said to have contributed to the decline in levels of political trust and to an increase in negative attitudes toward parties and government by Canadians. George Perlin (2007) has identified four possible reasons for the heightened level of popular discontent (what he labels the "malaise of Canadian democracy") with politics and government in Canada. They are the changing post–World War II economic conditions prompted by the introduction of new technologies and the opening of domestic markets to international competition; a substantial decline in individual participation in networks of social groups, a phenomenon forcefully described in Robert Putnam's "bowling alone" thesis (Putnam 2000); the effect of television in portraying politics and election campaigns in a largely negative and image-focused style; and the increasingly ineffective and inconsequential role that political parties play in connecting citizens to government.

To these might be added, most markedly with respect to younger voters in Canada, declining levels of voter turnout over the past two decades. Canada, of course, is not alone in this regard. Ken Carty and Bill Cross (chapter 11) observe that comparative studies suggest that "younger, postmaterialist voters are rejecting traditional, hierarchical forms of political participation in favor of more direct, egalitarian methods." But with respect to Canada in particular, Elisabeth Gidengil notes in chapter 13 that some critics of Canada's new voter registration system have put part of the blame for declining voter turnout on the replacement of door-to-door enumeration at election time with the so-called "permanent" voters' list. Although that criticism of the voter registration system remains to be empirically demonstrated, concerns have continued to be voiced about shifting the onus to register voters in Canada from the state to the electors themselves.

Earlier it was said that monarchy and the Senate were not given separate chapters in this handbook because to do so would grant them more attention than Canadians usually give them. When it comes to Quebec, that rationale has to be turned around. Not to give Quebec its own chapter would depreciate one of the most distinctive forces in Canada's history and politics. There is, in Canadian political and academic worlds, an unresolved debate regarding whether Quebec is a province like or unlike the other provinces. Those readers familiar with Canadian history will know that this question has never been far below the surface of the country's politics, and as several contributors to this volume note (see Alain Noël, chapter 6; Peter Russell, chapter 2; and Janet Hiebert, chapter 4), it has been very much "on the surface" in the past twenty-five years as political leaders have sought through mega-constitutional negotiations to make the Constitutional Accord of 1982—which Quebec governments continue to reject—acceptable to the province.

Much of the debate has centered on discussions, disagreements, and, at times, controversies over whether Quebec is a distinct society. The federal government's policy of official bilingualism and the Canadian Charter of Rights and Freedoms may be seen as initiatives to deprovincialize loyalties associated with claims to Quebec's distinctiveness that, when taken to their extreme, become arguments for separation. These positions are analyzed by the authors of the chapters noted previously, and are subjects of a wide body of literature elsewhere. As important as they are to the future of Canada as a united federation, there is, nonetheless, a disadvantage to focusing on these matters alone.

To begin with, Quebecers themselves see beyond the "national" question. The Quiet Revolution was about breaking with the past, about modernizing, about catching up with North American political practices—for example, with escaping from a patronage-ridden government and with secularizing Quebec society. As becomes clear from any close reading of recent Quebec history, the province not only "caught up," but surpassed the practice of other jurisdictions when it came to instituting high standards in the conduct of elections, politics, and bureaucracy. Quebec society has changed, too. Nowhere is this more evident than in the role of women. It is worth recalling that the Quiet Revolution and the feminist revolution were coterminous. One might say the same of the transformation of youth culture.

This point is made because, rather than distinctiveness being the hallmark of Quebec, in these areas there is comparability with the rest of the country. Brenda O'Neill and Lisa Young (chapter 18) demonstrate this convergence of interests and concerns, as do Jane Jenson (chapter 23) and Greg Marchildon (chapter 24), but only to a degree. In the words of the title of chapter 23, what is at issue in matters of this kind is "Canada's social architecture." This metaphor cries out for elaboration. In an introductory chapter, however, it is enough to say that the structure that is the Canadian federation has many rooms, some the same and some different. Similarity seems to be truer in the realm of policy than of politics.

One explanation for the contrast is suggested by Stuart Soroka and Christopher Wlezien. In chapter 15, they distinguish between the public's policy preferences and government's (federal and provincial) responsiveness. The degree of policy diffusion among provinces or between federal and provincial governments is a matter of some significance in a federation. So, too, is knowledge of the factors that are conducive to this diffusion. One answer offered by Jonathan Rose and Paul Nesbitt-Larking (chapter 16), is technology. For a variety of reasons, not least space—there is so much of it—Canadians have put a premium on the importance of communication. Although not unusual in the rest of the world, it is unexpected being located right next door to the United States for Canada to have established a public broadcasting network (radio in the 1930s and television in the 1950s). Private broadcasting plays a major role in the transmission of information and programs, but public broadcasting, in English (the Canadian Broadcasting Corporation) and French (Radio-Canada), and in Aboriginal languages in parts of the country, testifies to the dual belief in the integrative capacity of transcontinental programming and in the requirement to recognize the place in this enterprise of the English and French languages.

The production of satellites is only the most recent technological development to influence the spread (and speed) of communication in Canada. Language is a sensitive issue in a bilingual country. Communication, especially its regulation, is equally sensitive. In the modern world of iPods, e-mail, and the Internet, technology may be viewed as either a boon or a bane. What it cannot be is dismissed. It is a truism that technology democratizes. The big question in Canada is whether, at the same time, it promotes similarity or difference. Returning to Quebec, it would seem that when the issue is policy, the effect is the first; when it is politics, the second.

Acknowledgment. We thank Ursula Acton for her administrative assistance in the preparation of this book.

REFERENCES

Atwood, Margaret. 1972. *Survival: A Thematic Guide to Canadian Literature.* Toronto: Anansi.

Bryce, James. 1891. *The American Commonwealth*, 2nd ed. London: Macmillan.

Courtney, John C. 1978. Recognition of Canadian political parties in parliament and in law. *Canadian Journal of Political Science* 11(1): 33–60.

——. 2004. *Elections.* Vancouver: UBC Press.

Cross, Bill. 2009. And the future is: Coalition. *Globe and Mail.* January 26. http://www .theglobeandmail.com/servlet/story/RTGAM.20090123.wcocoalition26/BNStory/ specialComment/.

Falardeau, Jean-Charles. 2004. Roots and values in Canadian lives. In *Visions of Canada: The Alan B. Plaunt Memorial Lectures, 1958–1992*, ed. Bernard Ostry and Janice Yalden, 75–98. Montreal: McGill-Queen's University Press.

Hutchison, Bruce. 1945. *The Unknown Country: Canada and Her People.* Toronto: Longmans, Green and Company.

Jenson, Jane. 1994. Commissioning ideas: Representation and Royal Commissions. In *How Ottawa Spends 1994–95: Making Change*, ed. Susan D. Phelps, 39–69. Ottawa: Carleton University Press.

Lower, A. R. M. 1946. *Colony to Nation: A History of Canada.* Toronto: Longmans, Green and Company.

Mallory, J. R. 1974. Responsive and responsible government. *Transactions of the Royal Society of Canada*, Fourth Series, XII: 207–225.

Massey, Vincent. 1963. *What's Past Is Prologue: The Memoirs of the Right Honourable Vincent Massey.* Toronto: Macmillan.

Mitchell, Graeme, Ian Peach, David E. Smith, and John D. Whyte, eds. 2007. *A Living Tree: The Legacy of 1982 in Canada's Political Evolution.* Markham: LexisNexis Canada.

Perlin, George. 2007. The malaise of Canadian democracy: What is it? How is it to be explained? What can we do about it? In *Political Leadership and Representation in Canada: Essays in Honour of John C. Courtney*, ed. Hans J. Michelmann, Donald C. Story, and Jeffrey S. Steeves, 154–175. Toronto: University of Toronto Press.

Poel, Dale. 1976. The diffusion of legislation among the Canadian provinces. *Canadian Journal of Political Science* 9(4): 605–626.

Putnam, Robert. 2000. *Bowling Alone: The Collapse and Revival of American Community*. New York: Simon and Schuster.

Smith, David E. 1995. *The Invisible Crown: The First Principle of Canadian Government*. Toronto: University of Toronto Press.

Wherrett, Jill. 2008. The research agenda of RCAP. *Canadian Public Administration* 38(2): 272–282.

PART I

THE CONSTITUTIONAL ORDER

CHAPTER 2

CONSTITUTION

PETER H. RUSSELL

CANADA'S FOUNDING CONSTITUTION

Canada is one of the oldest constitutional democracies in the world. Its founding Constitution, the British North America Act (BNA Act), was enacted by the British Parliament in 1867.[1] Although the name, status, and method of amending the founding Constitution have changed, and additions have been made to Canada's Constitution (most importantly in 1982, when the Constitution was "patriated"), the substantive provisions of the original Constitution have changed very little since 1867. Indeed, among countries with written Constitutions, only the United States and possibly Switzerland can lay claim to being governed under the same constitutional text for a longer period than Canada.

The fact that there has been relatively little change in the founding Constitution does not mean that Canada's constitutional system has been frozen in time. Quite to the contrary, Canada's constitutional development has been a story of evolution and adaptation. Most of the changes that have occurred through this evolutionary process have been effected not by formal constitutional amendment, but by less formal instruments of constitutional change. These include "unwritten" constitutional conventions, changes in political practice, judicial decisions interpreting the constitutional text, and ordinary legislation establishing institutions and regulating governmental practice. The net result of these informal changes is to evolve Canada into an independent, continental federation that its founding fathers would scarcely recognize.

The BNA Act united three of Britain's North American colonies—Canada, New Brunswick, and Nova Scotia—into a federal union of four provinces, called the *Dominion of Canada*. The colony of Canada was created in 1840, when the colonies of Lower Canada and Upper Canada were joined together. In the federal union created by the BNA Act, these two parts of Canada were separated into the provinces of Quebec and Ontario. Representatives of the colonies of Newfoundland and Prince Edward Island took part in the meetings that led to the Confederation in 1867, but declined to join the new Dominion at that time.

The BNA Act was an Act of the British Parliament and reads much more like an ordinary piece of legislation than the constitution of a new state. It is devoid of ringing phrases and packed with small technical details. The only statement of fundamental principle comes in the opening words of the Act's preamble: "Whereas the Province of Canada, Nova Scotia, and New Brunswick have expressed their Desire to be federally united into One Dominion under the Crown of the United Kingdom of Great Britain and Ireland, with a Constitution similar in Principle to that of the United Kingdom..." That short statement of principle, although obscure, is fundamental to how Canada would be governed.

It must be assumed that the most important part of this obscure statement refers to the practice of responsible government that had begun in colonial Canada in the 1840s, and a little earlier in Great Britain (Buckner 1985). Responsible government means that the executive powers of government that are formally vested in the Queen must be under the direction of ministers who are responsible to the elected house of Parliament. Responsible government is clearly the key to democratizing parliamentary government. Yet nowhere in the BNA Act are the requirements of responsible government spelled out. Canada's founders simply accepted it as part of their constitutional heritage. Sections of the BNA Act set forth the size and shape and important procedural aspects of Canada's legislatures. However, the fundamental rule that federal and provincial governments are to be directed by political leaders who command the confidence of the legislative chamber that the people have elected is left to the unwritten conventions of the constitution.

Although Canada's founding Constitution was an Act of the British Parliament, its key terms were negotiated by political leaders of Britain's North American colonies in meetings in Charlottetown, Quebec City, and London. The politicians who took part in these meetings were the true architects of Canada's Constitution and are known as the *Fathers of Confederation.* There was no expectation in the Canada of that day that the product of their constitution making would be submitted to the people for approval. The seventy-two resolutions agreed to at the Quebec conference in 1864 covering all the important elements of the constitutional plan were submitted to a full debate in both houses of the Parliament of the colony of Canada and approved by a vote in each. Referred to as the *Confederation Debates*, they constitute the fullest account of the issues and ideals that stirred Canada's constitutional founders and, in that respect, are comparable with the Federalist Papers in the United States (Ajzenstat et al. 1999). There was no similar legislative debate or approval of the Confederation in the other two founding colonies.

The federal character of the political union they were forming was most challenging to the Fathers of Confederation. The only federation they knew well was the American, and it seemed to be coming apart in a civil war just as Canada's constitution makers began their work. A federal constitution was adopted, not because of any belief in the intrinsic merits of federalism, but as a political compromise. John A. Macdonald, who was to become Canada's first prime minister, and other English Canadian leaders preferred a legislative union to federalism, which they thought was a weak form of government. But the sine qua non for the leaders of French Canada was a province, Quebec, in which their people would be a majority with legislative power to protect and nurture their distinct language, laws, and religion (Silver 1982). Nor were Maritime leaders willing to hand over all legislative power to a far-off Canadian Parliament in which they would be a minority.

EVOLUTION OF THE CONSTITUTION

The BNA Act contained no amending provisions. The assumption of all concerned was that as an Act of the U.K. Parliament it would be amended by the U.K. Parliament. The Fathers of Confederation readily accepted this arrangement. This did not mean that the imperial Parliament would impose its will on Canada. The Fathers of Confederation were leaders of colonies that, for a generation, had enjoyed self-government in their internal affairs. They fully expected that the U.K. Parliament would, as was evident in the Confederation process, deal with Canada's Constitution only in response to requests from Canadian authorities.

In fact, during the long period from 1867 to patriation of the Constitution in 1982, thirty amendments were made to Canada's Constitution. Most of these amendments were technical in nature or were made to accommodate the addition of provinces to the federation. In the early days, Ottawa did not make a practice of consulting the provinces before submitting a constitutional amendment for enactment in Britain, even when the amendment affected the structure of the federation by, for example, empowering the federal Parliament to create new provinces, or restructuring the Senate to form a new section out of the four western provinces.

During the twentieth century, the growing strength of provincial rights sentiment began to affect the amending process. In 1907, Prime Minister Laurier held a federal–provincial conference and obtained the consent of all the provinces except British Columbia before requesting an amendment to the subsidies paid to the provinces. The federal government sought and obtained the consent of all the provinces before requesting the 1940 amendment giving the federal Parliament exclusive jurisdiction over unemployment insurance, the 1951 amendment making old-age pensions a concurrent field of legislation with provincial paramountcy (unlike the other two fields of concurrent jurisdiction—agriculture and immigration—in which there is federal paramountcy), and a 1964 amendment adding supplementary benefits to that jurisdiction. Provincial consent was secured for a 1960 amendment providing for compulsory retirement at age seventy-five of judges appointed by the federal government to the provincial superior courts even though it did not relate to provincial powers.

In 1949, the federal government, without provincial consent, secured an amendment to the BNA Act that amounted to a mini patriation of the Constitution. The amendment gave the federal Parliament the power to amend the BNA Act—except for certain sections—without going to Britain and without the consent of the provinces. The exceptions included the exclusive legislative powers of the provinces, denominational school rights, and the right to use English and French in federal, Manitoba, and Quebec institutions (Favreau 1965, 21–23). This power of the federal Parliament to amend the BNA Act unilaterally was used just five times—three times to change representation in the House of Commons and twice to alter the Senate (compulsory retirement at age seventy-five), and to add one senator each for Yukon and the Northwest Territories. The 1949 amendment was only a temporary solution to the lack of a full all-Canadian constitutional amending process.

The expansion of the federation began in 1870 when the province of Manitoba was carved out of the vast western and northern territories earlier, transferred from the Hudson's Bay Company, and added to Canada. The colonies of British Columbia and Prince Edward Island joined Canada in 1871 and 1873, respectively. Canada became a nine-province federation when the provinces of Alberta and Saskatchewan were carved out of the Northwest Territories in 1905. Newfoundland, at one time a self-governing British Dominion, became Canada's tenth province in 1949.

Today Canada is a ten-province federation with three northern territories—Yukon, the Northwest Territories, and Nunavut. The latter was severed from the Northwest Territories in the 1990s as part of a land claims settlement with the Inuit people who constitute more than 80% of Nunavut's population. Although the three northern territories do not have provincial status or full control of their natural resources, their elected legislatures have extensive powers and their governmental leaders have become full participants in intergovernmental relations in Canada.

As provinces joined the Confederation, they did so on the basis of terms of union, each of which had its own distinctive form and clauses. The terms of union of Ontario and Quebec are found within the Constitution Act, 1867; for the prairie provinces, they are in statutes of the Parliament of Canada; for the other provinces, except Newfoundland, they take the form of British orders-in-council. By contrast, Newfoundland's is found in an Act of the U.K. Parliament (Hogg 1977, 31–35).

All of these terms of union are entrenched in the Constitution. Section 43 of the Constitution Act, 1982 provides that changes in these terms of union must be authorized by the federal Parliament and the legislative assembly of the province concerned.

With regard to content, there were differences, too. For instance, the Acts of the Canadian Parliament that created the three prairie provinces retained for the federal government (until 1930) the natural resources of those provinces alone. Similarly, the historic rights of language and denominational schools written into the BNA Act in 1867 do not apply evenly across the country. Manitoba was the only new province with terms of union that contained the right to use English or French in its legislature and courts. The right to denominational schools in section 93 of the BNA Act became applicable to British Columbia and Prince Edward Island when they were admitted to Canada. Slightly different versions of section 93 were negotiated for Manitoba, Saskatchewan, and Alberta, and a much more extensive and complex guarantee of denominational school rights was part of Newfoundland and Labrador's terms of union (Hogg 1977, 824).

Although the historic constitutional school and language rights apply differently among the provinces, there is no constitutional variation in the legislative powers of the provinces. Section 94 of the BNA Act provides for the possibility of the "common law" provinces (that is, all the provinces except Quebec) handing over to the federal Parliament their power to make laws relating to property and civil rights. However, section 94 has never been used and is, in effect, a dead letter. In terms of the formal constitutional division of legislative powers, the Canadian federation is symmetrical. However, differences arising from various intergovernmental agreements and the different capacities of the provinces mean that, at a less formal level, there are many forms of asymmetry in the operation of the Canadian federation (Milne 1991).

Canada's transformation from a British colony to a self-governing nation-state occurred along an evolutionary path that was relatively without conflict and, until 1982, without major constitutional restructuring. Canada enjoyed full autonomy in its internal affairs from its earliest years. The governor general's power to reserve a federal bill for consideration by the U.K. government and that government's power to disallow an Act of the Canadian Parliament fell into desuetude in the 1870s—although these marks of imperial authority have yet to be removed from the text of the Constitution (Russell 2004, 38). Autonomy in foreign affairs came more slowly. The principal turning points came in the 1920s, when Canada established its own Department of External Affairs, and culminated with the Balfour Declaration of 1926 (Dawson 1937). The Balfour Declaration, issued at the conclusion of the Imperial Conference of 1926, in effect, marked the transition of the British Empire to the British Commonwealth. It recognized Australia, Canada, Eire, Great Britain, New Zealand, and South Africa as "autonomous Communities within the British Empire, equal in status, in no way subordinate one to another in any aspect of their domestic or external affairs, though united by a common allegiance to the Crown, and freely associated as members of the Commonwealth of Nations" (Russell 2004, 53).

The Statute of Westminster, enacted by the U.K. Parliament in 1931, gave legal expression to the principle of Dominion autonomy by declaring that no British Act would apply to any of the self-governing Dominions unless expressly requested by the Dominion concerned. However, a special Canadian clause had to be inserted in the Act, because there was no agreement among the federal and provincial governments on how the BNA Act was to be amended in Canada. Thus, section 7 of the Statute of Westminster retained British legislative supremacy over Canada's Constitution.

By the 1930s, Canada's status as a sovereign independent state was almost complete. The British monarch remained Canada's head of state, but the Crown's powers in Canada are exercised (on advice of Canada's prime minister) by a governor general who was now appointed by the sovereign, also on the advice of that prime minister (Smith 1995). Two forms of subordination to the United Kingdom remained. One was the need to go to the U.K. Parliament to amend the Constitution. The second was that a British tribunal, the Judicial Committee of the Privy Council (JCPC), remained Canada's highest court of appeal. The federal Parliament had created the Supreme Court of Canada as a general court of appeal for Canada in 1875; however, the Supreme Court's decisions could be appealed to the Privy Council in London and often were, particularly in cases dealing with the constitutional division of powers. After passage of the Statute of Westminster, the Canadian Parliament appeared to be in a position to terminate Privy Council appeals. In the 1930s, Parliament did end appeals to the Privy Council in criminal cases. However, it was not until 1949 that Parliament amended the Supreme Court Act to make the Court supreme in law as well as in name. At that time, the Court's bench was expanded from seven to nine justices.

As Canada was evolving to the status of a fully sovereign state in the international community of nations, it was at the same time evolving internally into a federal state in which sovereign powers were divided between the central government and the provinces much more than had been contemplated by some of its founding fathers. Indeed, the irony of Canada's federal development is that, although its Constitution was designed to provide for a more centralized federation than the American, the reverse occurred. The Canadian federation became one of the most decentralized federations in the world—despite the text of its Constitution. Two factors primarily account for this. One is the political strength of the provincial rights movement; the other is the interpretation of the Constitution by the JCPC.

Although Quebec's francophone majority has always harbored a strong allegiance to Quebec as the French Canadian homeland, provincial loyalties and identities have been strong in the other provinces, too. The first province to elect a secessionist government was Nova Scotia—a year after Confederation. The movement was quelled by offering the province better financial terms and its leader, Joseph Howe, a place in the federal cabinet. It was the Premier of Ontario, Oliver Mowat, the winner of six consecutive provincial elections, who led the fight in the courts to defend provincial powers against perceived federal encroachments (Armstrong 1981). In 1887, an interprovincial conference, hosted by Quebec premier Honoré Mercier and attended by the premiers of the three other founding provinces and Manitoba, called for a constitutional restructuring to strengthen provincial powers.

Constitutional decisions of the JCPC, the body of British Law Lords that until 1949 served as Canada's highest court, gave legal backing to the provincial rights movement (Pierson 1960). When appeals in constitutional cases began to come before the JCPC in the 1870s and '80s, the British judges quickly made it clear that they would not take the centralist approach shown in the Supreme Court of Canada's earliest decisions. As members of the highest court of the British Empire, their constitutional jurisprudence was animated by a spirit of liberal imperialism that cast them in the role of guardians of minority interests in Britain's far-flung Dominions

(Greenwood 1974). Their decisions confined use of the federal Parliament's general power to make laws for the peace, order, and good government of Canada to emergencies such as famine or war; restricted the federal trade and commerce power to the regulation of economic activities that are entirely interprovincial or international; and elevated the provinces' property and civil rights power virtually to the status of a residual power (Cairns 1971; Russell et al. 2008).

The culmination of the JCPC's constitutional jurisprudence came in the 1930s, when it was called upon to review federal legislation addressing the social and economic consequences of the Great Depression. Mackenzie King's Liberals questioned the constitutionality of this legislation when it was introduced by the Bennett Conservative government. When King returned to power in 1935, he asked the Supreme Court of Canada to rule on the constitutional validity of the entire suite of New Deal legislation (McConnell 1968). The Supreme Court, by this time faithfully following JCPC precedents, found much of the federal legislation unconstitutional. Most of the Supreme Court's decisions were upheld on appeal by the JCPC. Among the laws struck down in these New Deal decisions was legislation establishing a national system of unemployment insurance and implementing labor standards that Canada had committed to in a convention it signed as a member of the International Labor Organization. In the latter case, the JCPC ruled that when the Canadian government signs an international treaty, legislation giving domestic legal effect to such international commitments must comply with the constitutional division of powers between the two levels of government. Lord Atkin summed up the significance of this for Canada in a memorable sentence: "While the ship of state now sails on larger ventures and into foreign waters she still retains the watertight compartments of her original structure" (Judicial Committee of the Privy Council 1937, 354).

The difficulty Canada experienced in responding effectively to the social and economic problems of the Depression prompted Mackenzie King's government in 1937 to establish the Royal Commission on Dominion—Provincial Relations, commonly known by the surnames of its cochairmen, Rowell-Sirois (Canada, 1940). The one immediate positive result of Rowell-Sirois was the 1940 constitutional amendment giving the federal Parliament exclusive jurisdiction over unemployment insurance. However, in a more general way, the commission heralded a strengthening of the federal government's role in the federation. This was evident not only in Ottawa's wartime leadership, but also in its role during postwar reconstruction and its assertion of control over the main sources of taxation (Corry 1958).

The end of JCPC appeals in 1949 gave the Supreme Court of Canada an opportunity to take a more independent approach to constitutional interpretation. Supreme Court justices gave new life to "inherent national importance" as a test of what could be brought under the federal peace, order, and good government power (Supreme Court of Canada 1952), and adopted a more pragmatic interpretation of the federal trade and commerce power, allowing the federal government to regulate commerce that is primarily, although not exclusively, international and interprovincial (Supreme Court of Canada 1971). To maintain its legitimacy as a creditable constitutional umpire, the Supreme Court of Canada has been careful not to push centralizing interpretations too far (Baier 2006).

PATRIATION

The last remnants of Canada's constitutional subordination to the United Kingdom and provision of an all-Canadian process of constitutional amendment finally occurred in 1982. That it took so long to "patriate" Canada's Constitution had nothing to do with obstacles put up by the United Kingdom, but was entirely the result of political differences within Canada.

The political differences that made patriation such a difficult struggle were of two kinds. First was the question of the locus of the constitution-amending power in Canada. Deciding who should have custody of a country's or a people's highest law—in effect, deciding where constitutional sovereignty should be lodged—is as profound a challenge as a constitutional democracy can ever face. Failure to agree on that question prevented patriation from occurring when the Statute of Westminster was enacted in 1931. Meetings of federal and provincial leaders in 1935, 1950, and the early 1960s failed to produce agreement (Russell 2004, 57). Second, underlying the difficulty of reaching agreement were fundamental differences in the very nature of Canada as a political community. The differences ranged from those in English Canada, who envisioned the country as a single democratic nation with a Constitution that should be amenable by a majority in its national Parliament, to French Canadians who understood Canada to be a union of two founding peoples and insisted that Quebec, the one province with a francophone majority, have a veto power in the constitutional process. In between were those who believed that the provinces must have a role in amending the Constitution, but one that does not inflict on the country the straightjacket of unanimity.

In October 1964, the amending formula issue seemed, finally, to be resolved. Guy Favreau, justice minister in the Pearson government, announced that the federal government and all ten provincial governments had reached agreement on an amending formula developed by his Conservative predecessor, Davie Fulton. Under the Fulton–Favreau formula, constitutional amendments to the division of powers or to the use of the English or French language would require unanimous consent of the provinces and the federal Parliament, whereas most other amendments would be subject to a 7/50 rule—consent of the federal parliament and seven legislatures representing 50% of the population (Russell 2004, 72). Just as the amending formula issue appeared to be resolved, a second source of difficulty arose. Quebec, as a condition of agreeing to patriation, now wanted changes in the Constitution to recognize its special status in Confederation. Quebec's constitutional aspirations reflected the spirit of the Quiet Revolution—the transformation of the province, extending over a generation, from a rural Catholic society to an industrial, urban, and predominantly secular society. Quebec governments now sought additional powers for Quebec that would enable its people to be *maîtres chez nous* (Cook 1986; McRoberts 1988).

Quebec's insistence on substantive constitutional change as part of patriation opened up the agenda of constitutional politics to an expanding array of constitutional proposals. Soon after Pierre Trudeau became leader of the Liberal Party and prime minister of Canada in 1968, he put forward constitutional proposals aimed at countering the decentralizing thrust of Quebec's proposals. At the center of Trudeau's constitutional vision was a Charter of Rights and Freedoms that would, as he put it, "define the common thread that binds us together rather than respond to the forces of self-interest that tear us apart" (Russell et al. 1982, 36). Trudeau also proposed restructuring the Senate and the Supreme Court to make them more legitimate institutions of the federation.

With Quebec and federal government proposals on the table, it was not long before the other provinces began to push for their constitutional reform priorities. As the federal and provincial governments became embroiled in constitutional discussions, leaders of Canada's Aboriginal peoples, another source of deep constitutional discontent in the country, sought to gain access to the constitutional game. The constitutional struggle became even more intense after the Parti québécois (PQ), under the leadership of René Lévesque, came to power in Quebec in 1976, with a commitment to hold a referendum on Quebec becoming an independent country loosely associated with Canada. Thus it was that, beginning in the late 1960s and on through the '70s, Canada's political leadership became deeply engaged in "mega" constitutional politics—mega both in the breadth of the constitutional change agenda and in the prominence of constitutional debate in the public affairs of the country (Russell 2004, 74–76).

In 1971, a constitutional resolution seemed in sight, when all of the first ministers in a meeting in Victoria agreed to a package of constitutional reforms that included an amending formula, a mini charter of rights, some increases in provincial powers, and a provincial role in the appointment of Supreme Court judges (Simeon 1972). But the Victoria Charter died when Quebec Premier Robert Bourassa came under blistering attack for accepting an agreement that gave so little to Quebec, and withdrew his support for it. Again at the end of the decade, a series of federal–provincial meetings seemed close to reaching agreement on a broad set of proposals. It is questionable, however, whether René Lévesque would ever have agreed to constitutional reforms that fell short of Quebec independence. Also, by this time the constitutional agenda had become extremely complex, with many cross-cutting interests. This attempt at a resolution of constitutional differences through elite accommodation ended in failure in February 1979 (Cairns 1985; Romanow et al. 1984).

It was Pierre Elliott Trudeau who unlocked the door to patriation. After the Liberal victory in the February 1980 election, Trudeau immediately girded for battle in the Quebec referendum (May 1980) organized by the Lévesque government, which sought a popular mandate to negotiate sovereignty and association with Canada (Dufour 1990). Trudeau's leadership was crucial in defeating the sovereignty association proposal by a 60% to 40% margin. Trudeau's promise that he would lead a process of constitutional renewal was a crucial factor in the federalists' referendum victory. When a process of federal–provincial negotiations on a broad constitutional agenda again failed to produce agreement, Trudeau announced, in October 1980, that his government was prepared to proceed unilaterally with patriation and a few constitutional changes, dubbed the "people's package."

The part of the package with the most appeal to the people was a constitutional Charter of Rights and Freedoms. Through fall 1980 and winter 1981, a parliamentary committee conducted fifty-six days of televised parliamentary hearings on the Charter that resulted in the adoption of a number of amendments submitted by civil liberties groups (Sheppard and Valpy 1982). Despite the Charter's popularity, Trudeau and his government came under attack from a "gang of eight" provincial premiers for leaving them out of the constitutional process. Using the reference case procedure, Quebec, Manitoba, and Newfoundland challenged Trudeau's unilateralism first in their provincial courts of appeal and then on appeal in the Supreme Court of Canada. In September 1981, the Supreme Court ruled, seven judges to two, that as a matter of law, the federal government on its own without provincial consent could request the U.K. Parliament to pass legislation that would patriate Canada's Constitution with a Charter of Rights and Freedoms added to the Constitution. However, the Court also ruled, six judges to three, that unwritten constitutional convention required the federal government to have the support of a "substantial number" of provinces for submitting such a request to the U.K. Parliament (Russell et al. 1982).

Trudeau respected the Supreme Court's ruling on constitutional convention. In November 1981, he entered into yet another negotiation with the provincial premiers. This resulted in the insertion of a legislative override in the Charter (section 33, the notwithstanding clause) and changes in the amending formula that strengthened the role of provinces and abandoned national referendums as a deadlock-breaking device. Nine provincial premiers—all except Quebec's René Lévesque—agreed to this amended package (Romanow et al. 1984). With a few more changes prompted by public pressure to protect women's rights better and to recognize Aboriginal rights, this package of constitutional changes went forward to London and was enacted into law by the U.K. Parliament in March 1982.

The British Act of Parliament that patriated Canada's Constitution was the Canada Act. It was a short and simple Act that stated: "No Act of the Parliament of the United Kingdom passed after the Constitution Act, 1982 comes into force shall extend to Canada as part of its law." The Constitution Act, 1982 was attached to the Canada Act as schedule A. It contained all the substantive changes that the patriation package made to Canada's Constitution. One serious concern is whether Canada's Constitution in 1982 achieved what constitutionalists call *autochthony*—a root in the country itself (Hogg 1985, 45). The authority of Canada's Constitution did not come directly from the people themselves. The provincial premiers firmly rejected Trudeau's proposal for a referendum. Both houses of the federal Parliament passed resolutions supporting the patriation package, but there was no systematic effort to secure the support of the provincial legislatures or of the Aboriginal peoples. Quebec's National Assembly, the one provincial legislature that voted on the patriation resolution, passed a decree rejecting it by a vote of seventy-eight to thirty-eight.

The Constitution Act, 1982 did not give Canada a new Constitution. What it did do was repackage the original Constitution (now entitled Constitution Act, 1867) and its amendments, and make some additions to the Constitution. The main additions to the Constitution were the Canadian Charter of Rights and Freedoms, recognition and affirmation of the rights of Aboriginal peoples, a commitment of federal and provincial governments to the principle of fiscal equalization, and a set of rules for amending Canada's Constitution. The Constitution Act, 1982 also added to the list of provincial powers in section 92 of the Constitution Act, 1867 a new power to make laws with respect to the management and taxation of nonrenewable natural resources that might enter into interprovincial trade—providing such laws do not discriminate against other provinces or conflict with paramount federal law.

The Canadian Charter of Rights and Freedoms is a comprehensive bill of rights that includes civil liberties similar to those found in the constitutions of many western liberal states (see chapter 4, this volume), but it also has some distinctive Canadian features. The most controversial of its distinctive features is a legislative override clause that Trudeau accepted to secure the support of provincial premiers who were concerned that the judicial enforcement of rights would undermine parliamentary democracy (Weiler 1984). Section 33 permits the federal Parliament and provincial legislatures to insulate a law from a court challenge based on certain sections of the Charter. The sections to which it applies are those covering universal rights such as the fundamental freedoms of religion, expression, association, and assembly; due process legal rights; and equality rights. It does not apply to voting rights, mobility rights, the right to use English and French as languages in communicating with government, or minority language education rights. The legislative override can be used for a five-year period and can be renewed.

The legislative override clause has never been used by the federal Parliament, and in only a handful of cases by provincial legislatures (Leeson 2001). The most controversial use of the override came after a 1988 Supreme Court decision overturning Quebec's French-only sign on the grounds that it violated the guarantee of freedom of expression in the Charter. A few years later, Quebec brought its sign law into line with the Supreme Court's decision by requiring that French be the prominent, but not the exclusive, language on outdoor signs (Russell et al. 2008, 213). The very sparse use of the legislative override reflects politicians' fear of public backlash and the popularity of the Charter in all parts of Canada.

The Charter has propelled Canada's judiciary into the political limelight as never before. The legal profession, strong legal-aid programs, and an array of civil liberties organizations provided a strong infrastructure for making use of the Charter (Epp 1998).

After 1982, Charter cases flooded into the lower courts and, in 1984, began to reach the Supreme Court of Canada. From the outset, the Court made it clear that it would not shy away from giving effect to section 52 of the Constitution Act, 1982, which explicitly states that "the Constitution of Canada is the supreme law of Canada, and any law that is inconsistent with the provisions of the Constitution is, to the extent of the inconsistency, of no force or effect." Between 1984 and the end of 2007, the Supreme Court decided 489 Charter cases—22% of its caseload (Russell et al. 2008). During that period, the Supreme Court overturned federal legislation criminalizing abortion and denying prisoners the right to vote, but has upheld anti-hate propaganda laws and legislation legitimizing same-sex marriage.

The recognition and affirmation of Aboriginal rights is provided for in section 35 of the Constitution Act, 1982—a section that lies outside the Charter. To obtain provincial government consent, the word *existing* was inserted as a qualification of the "aboriginal and treaty rights" recognized in section 35. This led to a series of conferences between 1983 and 1987 at which Aboriginal leaders tried, unsuccessfully, to secure from federal and provincial first ministers acknowledgment that Aboriginal peoples' inherent right to govern their own societies was among the existing rights recognized in section 35 (Hawkes 1989). The first of these meetings in 1983 resulted in the federal government and nine provinces agreeing to an amendment to section 35 that made it clear that "treaty rights" include rights secured through modern land claims agreements. The 1983 constitutional amendment was the first use of the new constitution-amending formula (Canada 1983).

Aboriginal peoples in Canada have sought to assert their rights in the courts as well as through the negotiation of agreements with federal and provincial governments. In its 1990 decision in *Sparrow*, its first case dealing with section 35, the Court indicated that it would take a broad and liberal approach to interpreting "existing aboriginal rights" (Supreme Court of Canada 1990). Subsequently, in an important 1997 decision, the Court recognized common-law native title giving Aboriginal peoples ownership of unceded traditional lands, including subsurface minerals (Supreme Court of Canada 1997). Supreme Court decisions also upheld Aboriginal harvesting rights secured in historic treaties that cover much of Atlantic Canada, Ontario, and western Canada (Supreme Court of Canada 2004). The negotiation of modern land claims agreements that began in the 1970s was opened up in the 1990s to include self-government arrangements. In the agreement with the Nisga'a people, approved by the federal Parliament, the British Columbia legislature, and the Nisga'a people, the Nisga'a secured paramountcy for their laws on matters vital to their cultural identity over federal or provincial laws (Canada 1998). To date, fifteen agreements on land and self-government matters, with the status of constitutionally protected treaties, have been negotiated in the northern territories and several provinces. Negotiation of such agreements continues in many parts of Canada (Penikett 2006).

The constitution-amending formula set out in sections 38 through 49 of the Constitution Act, 1982 is complex. Section 38 sets out the "general procedure," the 7/50 rule—approval by the federal parliament and legislatures of two thirds of the provinces that have at least 50% of the population. The general procedure covers amendments to the division of powers, the Charter of Rights, and, with a few exceptions, to the House of Commons, the Senate, and the Supreme Court. As a gesture to Quebec, with legislative powers that are not protected by the 7/50 rule, a province can opt out of an amendment that derogates from its rights, and if such an amendment transfers power over education or other cultural matters to the federal Parliament, can receive "reasonable compensation." Section 42 lists five matters that require the support of the federal Parliament and legislatures of *all* the provinces: the office of the Queen and her representatives in Canada, the guarantee to all provinces that their representation in the House of Commons will never be less than their representation in the Senate, English and French language rights, the composition of the Supreme Court of Canada, and the amending formula itself. Some flexibility is provided by section 43 that permits the federal Parliament and the provinces concerned to made amendments in relation to matters that apply to one or more provinces, but not all the provinces, and by sections 44 and 45 that retain a limited power for the federal Parliament and provincial legislatures to make amendments in relation to their own institutions.

Postpatriation Developments

Since patriation, little use has been made of the new all-Canadian process of amending the Constitution. As noted earlier, the 7/50 rule has been used only once. The only other formal amendments to Canada's Constitution since 1982 have all been made under section 43 (Russell 2004, 249). A 1993 amendment made New Brunswick Canada's first officially bilingual and bicultural province. In that same year, the Constitution was amended to permit a bridge to replace the constitutional guarantee of continuous ferryboat service as Prince Edward Island's link with the Canadian mainland. The other two amendments removing guarantees of religious education in Quebec and Newfoundland and Labrador reflected a shift to a more secular society.

It is not for want of trying that so little use has been made of the new constitution-amending procedure. The driving force behind the continuation of megaconstitution politics was the unwillingness of Quebec governments to accept patriation as a satisfactory response to Quebec's constitutional aspirations. Although the Supreme Court had ruled that support for the patriation package by Quebec's National Assembly was not legally required, the Conservative Mulroney government, which came to power in 1984, nonetheless took the position that Canadian unity required bringing Quebec back "into the constitutional family." The first major effort to accommodate Quebec was an agreement reached by Prime Minister Mulroney and the ten provincial premiers at a federal government retreat at Meech Lake in April 1997 (Cohen 1990; Monahan 1991). The Meech Lake Accord embodied what Quebec's Liberal premier, Robert Bourassa, put forward as the minimum terms on which Quebec would accept the patriation package. Most controversial was a proposal to recognize "that Quebec constitutes within Canada a distinct society." Other clauses would give Quebec and other provinces a key role in selecting Supreme Court justices and more power in relation to immigration, to set limits on the federal spending powers, and to increase the types of constitutional amendments requiring unanimous provincial consent. Because the Meech Lake Accord included changes in the amending formula, it required the consent of the federal Parliament and all the provincial legislatures, not just their governments, and that consent had to be obtained within three years. The need to obtain legislative consent opened up the constitutional debate as never before. The Meech Lake Accord died when the three-year time period ran out in June 1990, without approval of the Accord by the legislatures of Manitoba and Newfoundland.

After the death of the Meech Lake Accord, Robert Bourassa's Liberals joined the PQ in organizing a broad consultation of the Quebec people on Quebec's constitutional future. The result of Quebec's *estates général* was an ultimatum that Quebec would hold a referendum on the sovereignty of Quebec, unless by October 28, 1992, it received an acceptable offer of constitutional accommodation from "the rest of Canada." In response, the rest of Canada, led once again by the Mulroney government, began to develop yet another package of constitutional proposals. This time, the package included proposals to meet the concerns of other provinces, of the Aboriginal peoples, and of the many Canadians who had opposed the Meech Lake Accord because of its focus on Quebec's interests. The result was a veritable smorgasbord of constitutional proposals put together through the most participatory constitutional process Canada had yet seen—a process that included a citizens forum, parliamentary hearings, and mini constituent assemblies across the country (Russell 2004, 164–189).

By July 1992, leaders of the federal government, Aboriginal peoples, territorial governments, and all the provinces except Quebec agreed to a large package of proposals. The final round of negotiation took place at Charlottetown in late August 1992 where Robert Bourassa, Quebec's premier, after obtaining some modifications of the package to better meet Quebec's concerns, agreed to put the amended package of proposals to a referendum in Quebec. By this time it was inevitable that the rest of Canada would also vote on the Charlottetown Accord. Federal legislation had been prepared for holding such a referendum, and two provinces—British Columbia and Alberta—had legislation requiring referendums before submitting constitutional proposals to their legislatures (Boyer 1992).

On October 26, 1992, nearly fourteen million Canadians—75% of eligible voters—voted in Canada's first countrywide referendum on constitutional matters. They were asked to vote yes or no for the Charlottetown Accord, a package of sixty proposed constitutional changes to virtually every part of the constitution. The Accord included a Canada clause recognizing Quebec as a distinct society within Canada, but also the equality of all provinces and their diverse characteristics; increases in provincial powers, balanced somewhat by proposals to strengthen Canada's economic and social union; a role for provinces in appointing Supreme Court judges; an elected Senate with equal representation of the provinces but reduced powers; a guarantee that Quebec would always have 25% of the seats in the House of Commons; and recognition of the Aboriginal peoples' "inherent right to self-government within Canada" (Russell 2004, 275–301). The referendum resulted in a rejection of the Accord by 54% of the voters. A yes win was recorded in only four of Canada's ten provinces: Newfoundland, New Brunswick, Prince Edward Island, and Ontario. The vote against the Accord in Quebec was led by those who thought it gave Quebec too little, whereas the vote against it in the rest of Canada was led by those who thought it gave Quebec too much. Given the need for unanimous approval of the package by the federal Parliament and all the provincial legislatures, the referendum was the end of the Charlottetown Accord.

By this time, the only group left in Canada with an appetite for constitutional restructuring were the Quebec sovereignists. In 1994, the PQ returned to power and moved quickly toward a referendum. On October 30, 1995, five million Quebecers, 94% of the eligible voters, participated in Quebec's second referendum (Drouilly 1995). This time, they were asked whether they agreed that "Quebec should become sovereign, after having made a formal offer to Canada for a new Economic and Political Partnership." The result was much closer than it had been in 1980. The no side took 50.6% of the vote, a margin of just 64,000 votes over the yes side. The Canadian federation seemed to have come within a whisker of a breakup.

Although the PQ government remained in power until its defeat by the Liberals in the April 2003 Quebec election, it did not press for another referendum. The PQ had operated on the assumption that a vote of more than 50% for the yes side, no matter how small the margin of victory, gave Quebec a right to secede unilaterally from Canada. Two developments at the federal level set up new hurdles to this approach to Quebec secession. In 1998, in response to questions referred to it by the federal government, the Supreme Court rendered a lengthy decision on the constitutional rules governing secession of a province (Supreme Court of Canada 1998).

That decision held that neither under international law nor Canadian constitutional law did Quebec have a right to secede unilaterally from Canada on the basis of a simple majority referendum vote for Quebec sovereignty. However, the Court also held that, if a Quebec referendum results in a clear majority on a clear question to pursue sovereignty, the federal government and the other provinces are obliged to negotiate in good faith with Quebec on the amendments to Canada's Constitution that would facilitate Quebec's separation from the Canadian federation. The Court left it to "the political actors" to determine what constitutes a "clear majority" and a "clear question." In 2000, the federal Parliament passed the Clarity Act, stipulating that the House of Commons would decide whether a provincial referendum is "a clear expression of the will of the population of a province that it wishes to cease to be part of Canada and become an independent state." If a referendum passes the clarity test, then secession must take place by amending the Constitution of Canada through negotiations that consider, among other things, the division of liabilities and assets, changes in provincial borders, the rights and interests of Aboriginal peoples, and the protection of minority rights (Canada 2000).

One other fallout from the 1995 Quebec referendum that made the constitution-amending process even more difficult was legislation introduced by Liberal Prime Minister Jean Chrétien to honor the commitment he made in the referendum campaign to restore Quebec's constitutional veto (Canada 1996). This legislation commits the federal Parliament to support amendments under the 7/50 rule only when they are supported by legislatures or referendums in British Columbia, Ontario, Quebec, at least two of the prairie provinces with 50% of that region's population, and at least two of the Atlantic provinces with 50% of that region's population. In effect, this legislation gives each of Canada's five regions a veto over constitutional amendments. Although the federal legislation adding the five-region veto to the 7/50 rule is not constitutionally entrenched, it would take a very bold government to override it.

The end of the era of megaconstitutional politics has not meant that Canada has gone into a constitutional deep freeze. Since the 1995 Quebec referendum, Canada's constitutional system, like that of most long-established constitutional democracies, has continued to evolve through piecemeal rather than wholesale changes. Formal constitutional amendments have been confined to those that do not affect the federation as a whole and can be done under section 43. Fear of returning to the turmoil of a larger constitutional agenda makes political leaders reluctant to attempt constitutional amendments under the general procedure. Most changes occur through the more fluid processes of constitutional development. These include a steady stream of judicial decisions interpreting the constitution. Changes in the operation of the constitution have also come about through political practices such as including representatives of Canada's three northern territories in intergovernmental meetings and political agreements such as the 1999 Social Union Framework Agreement, which set rules for federal spending in areas of provincial legislative responsibility (Canada 1999). Finally, legislation such as the 1996 federal statute adding five-region veto to the constitutional-amending process and the Clarity Act regulate how governments will use their constitutional powers. Other statutes have made important changes in the institutions of government. A leading example are statutes enacted by British Columbia, Ontario, Saskatchewan, and the federal Parliament establishing fixed election dates for their parliamentary elections (Russell 2008, 134–142).

Unless there is another Quebec secessionist crisis, and as long as there is considerable fear of provoking such a crisis, Canada's constitutional development will proceed as it has through most of its history: through incremental changes along an evolutionary path.

NOTES

....

1. In this chapter, Constitution in the uppercase is used when referring to the Constitutional text or its amendments. When reference is being made to the whole

constitutional system, including constitutional conventions and judicial decisions, constitution is written in the lowercase.

REFERENCES

Ajzenstat, Janet, Paul Romney, Ian Gentles, and William D. Gairdner, eds. 1999. *Canada's Founding Debates*. Toronto: Stoddart.

Armstrong, Christopher. 1981. *The Politics of Federalism: Ontario's Relations with the Federal Government, 1867–1942*. Toronto: University of Toronto Press.

Baier, Gerald. 2006. *Courts and Federalism: Judicial Doctrine in the United States, Australia and Canada*. Vancouver: University of British Columbia Press.

Boyer, Patrick. 1992. *Direct Democracy in Canada: The History and Future of Referendums*. Toronto: Dundurn Press.

Buckner, Phillip. 1985. *The Transition to Responsible Government: British Policy in British North America*. Westport, Conn.: Greenwood Press.

Cairns, Alan C. 1971. The judicial committee and its critics. *Canadian Journal of Political Science* 4(3): 301–345.

———. 1985. The politics of constitutional renewal in Canada. In *Redesigning the State*, ed. Keith Banting and Richard Simeon, 92–145. Toronto: University of Toronto Press.

Canada. 1940. *Report of the Royal Commission on Dominion—Provincial Relations*. Ottawa: Queen's Printer.

———. 1983. *Constitutional Amendment Proclamation, 1983*.

———. 1996. *Statutes of Canada, 1996*, chap. 1.

———. 1998. *Nisga'a Final Agreement*. Ottawa: Indian Affairs and Northern Development.

———. 1999. *A Framework to Improve the Social Union for Canadians*. Ottawa: Ministry of Supply and Services.

———. 2000. *Statutes of Canada, 2000*, chap. 26.

Cohen, Andrew. 1990. *A Deal Undone: The Making and Breaking of the Meech Lake Accord*. Vancouver: Douglas and McIntyre.

Cook, Ramsay. 1986. *Canada, Quebec, and the Uses of Nationalism*. Toronto: McClelland and Stewart.

Corry, J. A. 1958. Constitutional trends and federalism. In *Evolving Canadian Federalism*, ed. A. R. M. Lower, F. R. Scott, et al., 92–125. Durham, N.C.: Duke University Press.

Dawson, R. MacGregor. 1937. *The Development of Dominion Status, 1900–1936*. London: Oxford University Press.

Drouilly, Pierre. 1995. An exemplary referendum. *Canada Watch* 4: 25–27.

Dufour, Christian. 1990. *A Canadian Challenge*. Lantzville, B.C.: Oolichan Books.

Epp, Charles R. 1998. *The Rights Revolution: Lawyers, Activists and Supreme Courts in Comparative Perspective*. Chicago, Ill.: University of Chicago Press.

Favreau, Guy. 1965. *The Amendment of the Constitution of Canada*. Ottawa: Queen's Printer.

Greenwood, F. Murray. 1974. Lord Watson, institutional self-interest and the decentralization of Canadian federalism in the 1890s. *University of British Columbia Law Review* 9: 244–279.

Hawkes, David C. 1989. *Aboriginal Peoples and Constitutional Reform: What Have We Learned?* Kingston: Queen's University Institute of Intergovernmental Relations.

Hogg, Peter W. 1977. *Constitutional Law of Canada*. Toronto: Carswell.

————. 1985. *Constitutional Law of Canada*, 2nd ed. Toronto: Carswell.

Judicial Committee of the Privy Council. *Attorney-General for Canada v. Attorney General for Ontario* (1937) A.C. 326.

Leeson, Howard. 2001. The notwithstanding clause: A paper tiger? In *Judicial Power and Canadian Democracy*, ed. Paul Howe and Peter H. Russell, 297–327. Montreal: McGill-Queen's University Press.

McConnell, Howard. 1968. The judicial review of Prime Minister Bennett's New Deal. *Osgoode Hall Law Journal* 6: 38–86.

McRoberts, Kenneth. 1988. *Quebec: Social Change and Political Crisis*. Toronto: McClelland and Stewart.

Milne, David. 1991. Equality or asymmetry: Why choose? In *Options for a New Canada*, ed. Ronald L. Watts and Douglas M. Brown, 285–307. Toronto: University of Toronto Press.

Monahan, Patrick. 1991. *Meech Lake: The Inside Story*. Toronto: University of Toronto Press.

Penikett, Tony. 2006. *Reconciliation: First Nations Treaty Making in British Columbia*. Vancouver: Douglas and McIntyre.

Pierson, Coen G. 1960. *Canada and the Privy Council*. London: Stevens.

Romanow, Roy, John Whyte, and Howard Leeson. 1984. *Canada...Notwithstanding: The Making of the Constitution 1976–82*. Toronto: Carswell/Methuen.

Russell, Peter H. 2004. *Constitutional Odyssey: Can Canadians Become a Sovereign People?* 3rd ed. Toronto: University of Toronto Press.

————. 2008. *Two Cheers for Minority Government: The Evolution of Canadian Parliamentary Democracy*. Toronto: Emond Montgomery.

Russell, Peter H., Tom Bateman, Janet Hiebert, and Rainer Knopff. 2008. *The Court and the Constitution: Leading Cases*. Toronto: Emond Montgomery.

Russell, Peter H., Robert Decary, William Lederman, Noel Lyon, and Dan Soberman. 1982. *The Court and the Constitution: Comments on the Supreme Court Reference on Constitutional Amendment*. Kingston: Queen's University Institute of Intergovernmental Relations.

Sheppard, Robert, and Michael Valpy. 1982. *The National Deal: The Fight for a Canadian Constitution*. Toronto: Fleet Books.

Silver, A. I. 1982. *The French-Canadian Idea of Confederation*. Toronto: University of Toronto Press.

Simeon, Richard. 1972. *Federal–provincial Diplomacy: The Making of Recent Policy in Canada*. Toronto: University of Toronto Press.

Smith, David E. 1995. *The Invisible Crown: The First Principle of Canadian Government*. Toronto: University of Toronto Press.

Supreme Court of Canada. *Johannesson v. West St. Paul* (1952) 1 S.C.R. 292.

————. *Attorney General of Manitoba v. Manitoba Egg and Poultry Association* (1971) S.C.R. 689.

————. *R. v. Sparrow* (1990) 1 S.C.R. 1075.

————. *Delgamuukw v. British Columbia* (1997) 3 S.C.R. 1052.

————. *Reference re the Secession of Quebec* (1998) 2 S.C.R. 217.

————. *Haida Nation v. British Columbia* (2004) 3 S.C.R. 511.

Weiler, Paul. 1984. Rights and judges in a democracy: A new Canadian version. *University of Michigan Journal of Law Reform* 18(1): 51–92.

CHAPTER 3

COURTS

JAMES B. KELLY
CHRISTOPHER P. MANFREDI

THE judiciary plays an extremely important role in the maintenance and development of the Canadian constitutional system. In addition to maintaining the rule of law and the administration of justice, the courts and members of the judiciary are significant constitutional actors through their interpretation of the federal division of powers and the Canadian Charter of Rights and Freedoms. Understanding the evolution of Canadian federalism is incomplete without a consideration of the decisions of the Judicial Committee of the Privy Council (JCPC), Canada's highest court until 1949, and the Supreme Court of Canada after appeals to the JCPC were abolished. Similarly, the evolution of the Canadian Charter of Rights and Freedoms has been shaped by the Supreme Court of Canada and its approach to rights and freedoms.

This chapter provides an overview of the structure and functions of the court system and focuses, although not exclusively, on the Supreme Court of Canada. The first section outlines the constitutional basis of the court system in Canada and the division of judicial responsibilities between the federal and provincial governments. Although Canada is a federal system, the structure of the judicial system does not reflect this principle because of the dominant role assigned to the federal government. The second section considers the appointment of judges and the attempts at reform by the federal and provincial governments since the 1960s. Each level of government has attempted to reduce partisan patronage in the appointment process, but it remains an important determinant of those elevated to the judiciary. The third section focuses on the Supreme Court of Canada and discusses three critical events that structured this institution: the abolition of appeals to the JCPC in 1949, the elimination of most appeals as of right in 1975, and, finally, the entrenchment of the Canadian Charter of Rights and Freedoms in 1982. The final section considers the courts and their role in the evolution of Canadian federalism and the Canadian Charter of Rights and Freedoms.

THE STRUCTURE AND FUNCTIONS
OF THE COURT SYSTEM

Under Canada's federal constitution, both the national and provincial governments have responsibility for the establishment and administration of Canada's courts. In practice, this has meant the emergence of three types of courts, each named for the section of the Constitution Act, 1867 under which they fall. Section 96 courts are the superior courts of general jurisdiction found in each province. These courts are established and administered by the provinces, but the federal government appoints and remunerates their judges. The superior courts are divided into trial and appellate courts, with a jurisdiction that is unlimited with respect to subject matter, but is limited geographically to the province in which they are located. Section 101 courts are established and administered by the federal government, which also appoints and remunerates their judges. These courts include the Supreme Court of Canada (discussed later), the federal court of appeal, the federal court, and the tax court of Canada. With the exception of the Supreme Court, the jurisdiction of these courts is limited to the "laws of Canada," narrowly defined. Section 92 courts are established and administered by provincial governments, which are also responsible for the appointment and remuneration of the judges sitting on them. In addition to the jurisdiction they have over provincial laws, these courts have been given a significant role in the administration of Canada's criminal law.

The shared constitutional jurisdiction over these courts means that the relationship among them can be described as a unified, hierarchical pyramid, with the Supreme Court sitting at the top of the pyramid and exercising final authority over both federal and provincial law. Next in order of authority are the federal court of appeal and the section 96 provincial courts of appeal. At the next level, one finds the federal court, the tax court, and the section 96 trial courts of general jurisdiction. Last, the section 92 provincial courts form the base of the pyramid. One of the most enduring controversies about this relationship concerns the jurisdictional line between section 96 and section 92 courts. According to some observers (Russell 1987, 61–63), the desire to preserve elements of section 96 courts' exclusive jurisdiction against the expansion of section 92 courts has unnecessarily complicated certain areas of the law.

The structure of Canadian courts derives from their principal function, which is to decide particular cases rather than to resolve universal policy questions. As such, courts rely on an adversarial system that is generally bipolar, depends on historical facts about events that transpired between disputing parties, and seeks to implement retrospective remedies. By contrast, policy formation is multipolar, relies on social facts about ongoing phenomena, and seeks to regulate social relations prospectively. However, as courts have been called upon to exercise a greater policy-making function, they have attempted to deal with these differences by relying on interveners to represent better the range of social interests affected by its decisions, relying on extrinsic evidence for social facts, and exploring novel uses of its remedial powers. With regard to the general policy-making process, it is unclear, however, whether these measures satisfactorily compensate for the inherent limitations of adjudication within the adversarial system.

One of the most crucial constitutional principles governing Canadian courts is judicial independence. This principle is evident in several constitutional provisions: The federal appointment of provincial superior court judges under section 96 establishes a level of independence from local political influences, section 99 grants judges security of tenure, section 100 provides for security of salaries, and section 11(d) of the Canadian Charter of Rights and Freedoms guarantees the right to an "independent and impartial" tribunal for persons charged with criminal offenses. In 1985, the Supreme Court synthesized these provisions and articulated three minimal conditions for judicial independence: security of tenure, financial security, and independent control of a court's internal administration (*R. v. Valente* 1985). In 1997, in a highly controversial judgment, the Supreme Court used the financial security component of judicial independence to establish an entirely new mechanism for determining judicial salaries (*Reference re Remuneration of Judges of the Provincial Court [P.E.I]* 1997). The mechanism involved the establishment of judicial compensation commissions with recommendations that could be rejected by governments. The controversy derived largely from the fact that the Court made such rejections subject to judicial review, creating a clear perception of conflict of interest. In 2005, the Court retreated somewhat from its earlier position and clarified the principles governing the operation of these commissions (*Provincial Court Judges' Assn. of New Brunswick v. New Brunswick [Minister of Justice]; Ontario Judges' Assn. v. Ontario [Management Board]; Bodner v. Alberta; Conférence des juges du Québec v. Québec [Attorney General]; Minc v. Québec [Attorney General]* 2005).

JUDICIAL APPOINTMENTS

The appointment of judges in Canada is the formal responsibility of the governor general at the federal level and the lieutenant governor at the provincial level, because all power is vested in the Crown under the Constitution Act, 1982. However, because the Canadian Constitution is based on both written and unwritten rules, the governor general and lieutenant governors act on the advice of the federal and provincial cabinets when appointing individuals to the bench (Russell 1987, 112). Although judicial appointments are made by the cabinet at both levels of government, cabinets simply ratify the selections made by the minister of justice or provincial attorney generals, with the exception of the position of chief justice for all section 96 and 101 courts, which is selected by the prime minister (Russell 1987, 112).

Although Canada is a federal system, the appointment of judges departs markedly from the federal principle because the Constitution Act, 1867 provides the national government, through the governor general, with the power to appoint the senior provincial court judges. Instead of having an appointment process based on the federal principle such as the United States, and consistent with the division of powers, the appointment of Canadian judges is quasi federal because of the hierarchal nature of the judicial system and the dominant role assigned to the federal cabinet. Under the Constitution Act, 1867 the appointment of judges is authorized by sections 92, 96, and 101: Sections 96 and 101 judges are federal appointments; section 92 judges are provincial appointments (Morton 2006, 57). Although individuals chosen by provincial attorney generals represent the largest category, the most senior appointments are the responsibility of the federal minister of justice and the prime minister. For instance, section 101 courts include the Supreme Court of Canada, the federal court of Canada, and the tax court of Canada; section 96 courts include the courts of appeal and the superior courts in each province. In contrast, although the federal cabinet monopolizes judicial appointments at the highest levels, section 96 appointments are less senior and involve civil, criminal, and family law courts at the lower levels of the judiciary (Greene 2006, 7–10).

Peter Russell (1987, 114) argues that the submission of judicial appointments by the minister of justice to the cabinet accounts for the high level of partisanship in the Canadian judicial system that continues today, despite reforms to address partisanship in judicial appointments. Until 1967, there was a very strong connection between the party in power and individuals appointed to the bench (Riddell et al. 2007, 5). The attempt to reduce partisanship (but not to eliminate it) as a selection criterion for judicial appointment began with Pierre Elliott Trudeau after his appointment as minister of justice in 1967. Trudeau established a consultation system with the Canadian Bar Association that reviewed candidates for potential appointment to section 96 courts (Russell and Ziegel 1991, 5–6). As part of its responsibility, the Canadian Bar Association's consultative committee reviewed candidates submitted by the minister of justice and ranked them as qualified or unqualified (Greene 2006, 13–14). Although the minister of justice retained the discretion on whom to appoint, individuals ranked as unqualified by the Canadian Bar Association were rarely appointed by the minister of justice. Although judicial advisory committees were established to reduce partisanship in federal judicial appointments, recent studies suggest that "the screening committees had little or no success in insulating the appointment process from partisan consideration" (Riddell et al. 2007, 20). According to this study, nearly 36% of judicial appointees donated to political parties between 1988 and 2003, and 30% donated to the party in power (Riddell et al. 2007, 20).

Until 1978, a special advisor existed within the Office of the Minister of Justice with responsibility for compiling dossiers on potential nominees that were subsequently reviewed by the Canadian Bar Association (Russell and Ziegel 1991, 5). In an attempt to ensure the independence of the judiciary and to improve the appointment procedure, an Act of Parliament established the Office of Commissioner for Federal Judicial Affairs in 1978 as an arms-length agency with responsibility for screening candidates for appointment to section 96 courts and the federal court. Despite the attempts at reform throughout the 1960s and '70s, the Canadian Bar Association continued to criticize the presence of partisanship as a selection criterion for appointments. In 1988, the Mulroney government responded to these demands and expanded the mandate of the Office of Commissioner for Federal Judicial Affairs to include a solicitation function for section 96 courts, as well as to establish provincial and territorial judicial advisory committees that would review the qualifications of solicited candidates (Riddell et al. 2007, 7–8). Furthermore, in 1991, the ranking system was changed (from qualified or unqualified) to highly recommended, recommended, and unable to recommend (Greene 2006, 22). Under the Conservative government of Prime Minister Harper, this ranking system has subsequently been changed simply to recommended or unable to recommend.

At first, the membership of provincial and territorial judicial advisory committees was not disclosed to the public, but this practice ended in 2005. In addition, Irwin Cotler, then minister of justice, created a code of ethics for the judicial advisory committees, released the committee guidelines, and introduced an annual report by the Office of Commissioner for Federal Judicial Affairs outlining the activities of the judicial advisory committees. Initially, the judicial advisory committees were composed of seven individuals: three laypersons, three lawyers, and one judge. Under the Harper government, membership increased to eight, with the addition of a representative drawn from law enforcement agencies. The current composition for each provincial or territorial judicial advisory committee is as follows: one member of the Canadian Bar Association, one member of the provincial law society, one judge, one nominee by the provincial or territorial attorney general, one member of the law enforcement committee, and three nominees of the federal minister of justice who represent the general public (Office of the Commissioner for Federal Judicial Affairs 2007). The appointment of an individual to represent law enforcement was criticized by the Canadian Bar Association and the chief justice of the Supreme Court of Canada, Beverly McLachlin, as interfering with the judicial process and as an attempt to appoint judges more receptive to the needs of law enforcement.

Provincial governments began to reform the appointment procedure for section 92 courts during the 1980s, with Ontario taking the lead under former Attorney General Ian Scott, who established the thirteen-member Ontario judicial appointment advisory committee. Unlike the federal judicial advisory committee that simply solicits applications, the Ontario committee has a recruitment function and may advertise vacancies (Greene 2006, 20). Not all provinces have established judicial advisory committees, but several (Quebec, British Columbia, and Manitoba) have replicated the approach in Ontario, and Alberta has established a committee to screen judicial appointments (Greene 2006, 21–22).

The Supreme Court of Canada Act establishes the following regional—but not provincial—representation: three judges from Quebec, because of the province's civil law tradition; three judges from Ontario; one judge from Atlantic Canada; and two judges from western Canada (Ziegel 2001, 133–134). By custom, one judge is now appointed from the prairie provinces and one from British Columbia. The last appointment procedure to be reformed was that involving the Supreme Court of Canada. This occurred in April 2005, under former Prime Minister Paul Martin. In response to the hearings conducted by the Standing Committee on Justice and Human Rights, which recommended parliamentary and public participation in Supreme Court of Canada appointments, then Minister of Justice Cotler established an interim process that was subsequently modified by the Harper government.

Under the interim process, Justices Abella and Charron were appointed to the Supreme Court of Canada after a parliamentary hearing on their candidacies. This did not, however, constitute a confirmation hearing as in the United States, where potential candidates are scrutinized by the Justice Committee of the U.S. Senate before being appointed to the U.S. Supreme Court, because in Canada neither candidate appeared before Parliament. Instead, the minister of justice defended the candidacies of Abella and Charron in Parliament before a nonparliamentary committee that was composed of seven parliamentarians, one representative of the Law Society of Upper Canada (because the vacancies occurred in Ontario), and one representative of the Canadian Judicial Council. Although the committee did not directly scrutinize the nominees, it its final report was to be considered by the prime minister before the appointment was made (Minister of Justice 2005, 3–4).

For subsequent appointments to the Supreme Court of Canada, the minister of justice established the following process. First, the minister of justice would consult with the chief justice of the Supreme Court of Canada, the provincial attorney generals where the vacancy existed, the relevant law societies, and the Canadian Bar Association. This consultation would produce a shortlist of five to eight candidates. Second, an advisory committee composed of four parliamentarians, a retired judge, a nominee of the legal profession, a nominee of the provincial government where the vacancy occurred, and two laypersons would review the shortlist and produce an unranked list of three candidates. Third, the minister of justice would provide advice to the prime minister, who would submit the name of a candidate drawn from the shortlist to the cabinet for approval. Finally, the minister of justice would appear before the Standing Committee on Justice and Human Rights to justify the candidate, but only after this person was *appointed* to the Supreme Court of Canada on the advice the prime minister (Minister of Justice 2005, 10–11).

Before the Martin ministry was defeated in January 2006, a vacancy occurred in the prairie provinces and the minister of justice began the process for an appointment to the Supreme Court of Canada. Indeed, the advisory committee had produced a shortlist of three candidates, but the process was suspended because an election was called for January 23, 2006. Upon assuming office, the Conservative government accepted the shortlist produced by the advisory committee, but required the nominee to appear before Parliament to be questioned by the advisory committee. After this process was completed, the advisory committee reported to the prime minister, who then decided whether to appoint the nominee to the Supreme Court of Canada (Minister of Justice 2006, 1–2). This resulted in the appointment of Justice Marshall Rothstein of Manitoba to fill the vacancy created when Justice Major from Alberta retired in late 2005.

Although this is an important step in reforming the appointment process for the Supreme Court of Canada, it still does not constitute a confirmation hearing or a substantive parliamentary role. Indeed, the prime minister still retains the discretion whether to accept the views of the advisory committee when appointing an individual to the Supreme Court of Canada. Although the process has become more transparent, it has simply reduced the discretionary power of the prime minister, who previously had unfettered discretion in choosing a Supreme Court justice and must now choose from a shortlist produced by an advisory committee established by the minister of justice. However, with the unexpected retirement of Justice Bastarache in 2008, the minister of justice announced on May 28 a modified process for selecting a new judge from Atlantic Canada. First, a pool of qualified candidates would be identified by the minister of justice in consultation with the attorney generals and leading members of the legal profession from the Atlantic provinces. Second, a Supreme Court selection panel composed of five members of Parliament (two from the government caucus and one member from each of the three recognized opposition caucuses) would review the list of qualified candidates and produce a unranked shortlist of three candidates that would be forwarded to the prime minister and the minister of justice. Finally, the nominee would appear before an ad hoc parliamentary committee for a public hearing on their candidacy (Department of Justice 2008).[1]

Prime Minister Stephen Harper and Minister of Justice Robert Nicholson did not follow this modified process in the 2008 nomination of Thomas Cromwell from the Nova Scotia Court of Appeal. Arguing that the Supreme Court selection panel had failed to produce a list of candidates because the opposition parties refused to participate, the prime minister suspended the process and nominated Justice Cromwell (Office of the Prime Minister 2008). According to the prime minister, the appointment would not be finalized until "Mr. Justice Cromwell has the opportunity to answer questions from an ad hoc all-party committee of the House of Commons" (Office of the Prime Minister 2008). However, because this nomination occurred shortly before the governor general dissolved Parliament and set a federal election for October 14, 2008, it is unclear what the composition of this ad hoc committee would be or whether a minority or majority government will control the next Parliament—outcomes that have importance implications for the ad hoc appointment process of Supreme Court justices in Canada.

THE SUPREME COURT OF CANADA

In 1875, the Canadian Parliament exercised its constitutional authority to "establish a General Court of Appeal for Canada" (Constitution Act, 1867, section 101) and established the Supreme Court of Canada (Snell and Vaughan 1985). Originally composed of six justices, the Court's membership expanded to seven in 1927 and reached its current size of nine justices in 1949. As discussed in the preceding section, the Court's membership—both formally and informally—has throughout its history reflected the federal nature and regional politics of Canada. One important convention, which reinforces Canada's linguistic duality and which operated with only one exception over the past six decades, is that the position of chief justice alternate in a manner that reflects this duality.

As a "general court of appeal," the Supreme Court has jurisdiction over both federal and provincial law, but in no area does it function as a court of first instance. The one exception to this rule is found in what is called the *reference procedure*. Under the Supreme Court Act, the government can "refer" legal questions to the Court for an advisory opinion (and the Court can hear appeals from reference cases decided by provincial courts of appeal). Although nonbinding in principle, these opinions in practice have the same force as judgments emanating from the Court's resolution of disputes arising from ordinary litigation. The reference procedure has both advantages and disadvantages. On the one hand, it provides a "fast track" to the resolution of controversial issues; on the other, it can mean that consideration of those issues takes place without the discipline that comes from the full adversarial development of concrete disputes.

Although nine justices sit on the Court, five justices constitute a quorum for deciding cases. Full sittings of the Court became more common after 1973, but it is still not unusual for the Court to divide its work by forming panels of fewer than nine justices to hear and decide cases (Heard 1991). There are no particular rules for how these panels are constituted, and the chief justice has full discretion to assign justices to them. In general, however, there is an attempt to take regional concerns and subject matter specializations into account. The Court hears cases during three sessions, beginning in January, April, and October of each year. Hearings generally last two hours, and each side is given one hour to present its oral arguments. The Court may render its decision immediately after the hearing, but it is much more common for the Court to reserve its judgment to permit discussion among the justices and the preparation of written reasons. From 1997 to 2007, approximately 25% of appeals produced a split decision in which one or more of the justices dissented from the final outcome. The time between hearing a case and the judgment generally ranges between four and six months.

The Court's history has been marked by three critical turning points: abolition of appeals to the JCPC in London in 1949 (Snell and Vaughan 1985, 171–195), elimination of most appeals as of right in 1975 (Snell and Vaughan 1985, 233–253), and the establishment of the Canadian Charter of Rights and Freedoms in 1982.

Prior to 1949, the Court's jurisdiction was general, but it was hardly final. Until then, the Court was very much a junior partner to the JCPC. Not only could its decisions be appealed to the Law Lords in London, but by virtue of a procedure known as a *per saltum*, appeals to the Court could be bypassed altogether. Arguments that the Court's appellate jurisdiction should be final as well as general stemmed in large part from criticism of the JCPC's interpretation of the division of powers between the federal and provincial governments. In general, the JCPC interpreted these powers in a way that strengthened the provinces at the expense of the national government. For advocates of strong national power to deal with critical events like the Depression, these interpretations appeared to be the misguided judgments of a distant colonial power detached from, and uninformed about, the reality of Canada. After passage of the imperial Statute of Westminster, 1931, which recognized the legislative autonomy of countries like Canada and Australia, and after Canada's substantial contribution to the Allied victory in World War II, this criticism plus a growing sense of national maturity made abolition of JCPC appeals possible. A consequence of this evolution was to elevate the Canadian Court's reputation and prestige.

The second critical turning point in the Court's history occurred in 1975, when amendments to the Supreme Court Act eliminated appeals as of right in civil cases involving more than $10,000. These amendments left only two categories of cases in which there could be an appeal by right to the Supreme Court: criminal cases in which there was a dissent in the court of appeal and cases in which a federal or provincial law was declared beyond the authority of the legislature that enacted it. With the exception of these cases, the Court, through the leave (or permission) to appeal process, became its own gatekeeper. According to the legislation, the Court is empowered to grant leave to appeal whenever it is "of the opinion" that "the case involves a question of public importance or if it raises an important issue of law (or a combination of law and fact) that warrants consideration by the Court" (Supreme Court of Canada 2007). The decision to grant leave to appeal is made by three judge panels of the Court. On average, the Court receives about 600 applications for leave annually, and approximately 12% of those applications are successful (Supreme Court of Canada 2008).

The shift away from appeals as of right in civil cases toward a process dominated by discretionary grants of leave to appeal has had a profound impact on the Court's role. The Court is no longer the passive servant of individual, private litigants. It now sets its own agenda and, although the Court has no control over which issues enter the judicial process at the trial court level, it does decide which of those issues emerge from that process. This allows the Court to play a leading role not only in the development of law, but also in the development of public policy more broadly understood.

If the shift toward taking cases by leave rather than by right has given the Court discretion to set its own agenda, then the third critical turning point has expanded the potential scope of that agenda. After acrimonious negotiations between federal and provincial governments, punctuated by hearings before a special joint committee of

Parliament, followed by a crucial Supreme Court advisory opinion, the governments of Canada and nine provinces (excluding Quebec) agreed in November 1981 to patriate the Canadian Constitution from Great Britain and entrench within it a domestic amending formula and a judicially enforceable Canadian Charter of Rights and Freedoms. The Charter brought new opportunities to litigants and the Court to bring the judicial process to bear on a wide range of social and political issues.

The impact of this change on the Court's work has been both qualitative and quantitative. For example, in 1975, the Court offered the view that it had no role to play in the public debate on abortion; in 1988, the same justice who articulated this view declared that the Court had to assume an "added responsibilit[y]" of ensuring that legislative initiatives "conform to the democratic values" inherent in the Charter (Manfredi 1993, 19–21). The Court's impact has been felt in policy areas as diverse as the democratic process, sexual orientation, and health care. In quantitative terms, the Supreme Court of Canada has been more active in the post-Charter era than during any period of its history. From 1982 to 2007, the Court decided 489 Charter cases (about twenty per year). In 169 of those cases (about 34.6%), the Court upheld the Charter claim. As a result, the Court nullified eighty-four federal and provincial statutes, for a rate of 3.4 nullifications per year. Contrast this, for example, with the Court's activity under the statutory bill of rights, enacted by Parliament in 1960. From 1960 to 1982, it decided thirty-four bill of rights cases (about 1.5 per year). It upheld the claim on only five occasions (14.7%), resulting in the nullification of one section of one act: section 94(b) of the Indian Act was declared inoperative in *R. v. Drybones* (1970).

As the Supreme Court's role in Canadian politics and governance has increased under the Charter, so, too, have debates about the relationship between courts and democracy. These debates are not entirely new, because they were at the forefront of the movement to abolish appeals to the JCPC. Nevertheless, both the character and visibility of these debates have changed.

COURTS AND DEMOCRACY

In addition to protecting the rule of law and ensuring that political actors exercise their powers consistent with this principle, the courts have played an important role in the development of Canadian federalism and the protection of rights and freedoms. The contemporary importance of judicial review of public law is significant, because it was not provided for by the framers of Canada's original Constitution, the British North America Act, 1867. Judicial review of government action slowly emerged as Canada evolved from a quasi-federal colony within the British Empire to an independent federal state with the passage of the Statute of Westminster (1931), the abolition of appeals to the JCPC (1949), and finally, the patriation of the Canadian

Constitution in 1982. Indeed, domestic judicial review was conducted within a colonial framework, best characterized by the initial absence of the Supreme Court of Canada in 1867 (established in 1873) and its status as the second highest court until 1949, when appeals to the JCPC at Westminster were abolished. In fact, the Supreme Court of Canada would only become "supreme" in 1975, when it gained control over its docket and had the discretion to select which appeals to hear (Russell 1987, 344).

There are two important roles that the courts have played in relation to Canadian democracy and the constitution: first, as an umpire of federalism in relation to the division of powers between the two orders of government and, second, as the self-proclaimed "guardian" of the Constitution under the Canadian Charter of Rights and Freedoms. Both roles have important implications for the question of judicial power and whether the courts protect or undermine democracy. The first role performed by the courts, the umpire of federalism, continues to be an important aspect of judicial review, yet it has been overshadowed by the question of judicial power that resulted with the passage of the Canadian Charter of Rights and Freedoms (Baier 2006, 123–155). As the umpire of federalism, the courts have defined federal and provincial jurisdiction, and invalidated government action determined inconsistent with the division of powers. Although the umpire of federalism appears to be a neutral role, because it suggests the courts simply patrol the division of powers to prevent unconstitutional action, both the Supreme Court of Canada and the JCPC were criticized, at different times and by different governments, for distorting the BNA Act beyond the intentions of its framers.

In defining the meaning of critical powers granted to the federal government under section 91, such as trade and commerce, and the POGG clause (peace, order, and good government), the JCPC was criticized by supporters of the federal government as having a "provincial bias" that undermined the BNA Act as a strong, centralist constitution (Vipond 1991, 152). Similarly, after the Supreme Court of Canada became the highest court in 1949, the provincial governments experienced a series of defeats that strengthened POGG, established federal control over offshore mineral resources, and reduced provincial control over the export and taxation of natural resources.

Because of the weakness of the Canadian Senate as an effective federal institution, the regulation of intergovernmental conflict became an important role performed by the Supreme Court. Instead of simply patrolling the boundaries between the two orders of government, the Supreme Court of Canada became a significant constitutional actor because of the growing reliance on the reference procedure, which allows either level of government to submit constitutional questions for resolution to their highest court. For instance, the Supreme Court of Canada has been asked to determine the constitutionality of an attempt at unilateral patriation of the BNA Act by the federal government (*Reference re a Resolution to Amend the Constitution* 1981), whether the federal government could unilaterally alter the composition of the Senate (*Reference re Legislative Authority of Parliament to Alter or Replace the Senate* 1980), and, most recently, whether unilateral secession of a province was constitutional (*Reference re Secession of Quebec* 1998).

The perception of bias on the part of the Supreme Court of Canada resulted in provincial opposition to the Charter of Rights. Judicial review of rights, it was believed, would further contribute to the centralization of the Canadian federation (Laforest 1995, 124–125). The adoption of the Charter demonstrates the paradox surrounding the courts and democracy: To be effective, the Constitution Act, 1982 would have to provide the courts with a more explicit role than had existed under the BNA Act, and, second, the expansion of judicial power should not come at the expense of parliamentary democracy and federalism. A stronger role is provided by two new constitutional provisions: section 52(1) of the Constitution Act, 1982 and section 24 of the Canadian Charter of Rights and Freedoms. Under section 52(1), the Constitution is declared to be the "supreme law of the land" and any law determined inconsistent with the Constitution is "of no force or effect" (Kelly 2005, 10). Although the Constitution does not specify which institution declares acts "of no force or effect," section 24(1) provides that, in cases when a statute violates rights and freedoms, a court may apply remedies that are "appropriate and just in the circumstances," suggesting an empowered judiciary with the responsibility to declare acts unconstitutional under section 52(1) (Kelly 2005, 11).

The courts have provided several interpretations of section 24(1) and each demonstrates growing judicial power through the remedy clause. In addition to invalidating acts as unconstitutional, the courts have also adopted the remedy of amending legislation through judicial review by simply reading statutes as constitutional. This occurred in *Vriend v. Alberta* (1998), when the Supreme Court of Canada read sexual orientation into the provincial human rights code after determining that its absence rendered the act unconstitutional (see chapter 4, this volume). In contrast, the courts have also suspended declarations of unconstitutionality to provide the responsible legislature with an opportunity to amend a statute to ensure its constitutionality, as the Supreme Court did in *M. v. H.* (1999), when it determined restricting the definition of spouse to opposite-sex couples violated equality rights under section 15(1) of the Charter. Although the emergence of the courts as policy actors depends on the remedy used, with judicial amendment of legislation through the reading-in provision, the most policy-driven remedy, and suspended decisions most deferential to legislative choices of elected officials, the development of section 24(1) illustrates an important point—the discretionary choices of courts are the bases of judicial power.

In designing the Charter of Rights, the framers were conscious of the danger of judicial power and provided several mechanisms to ensure that judicial review advanced constitutional supremacy and parliamentary democracy. First, the Charter contains a general limitations clause, section 1, that allows rights to be limited if it is "demonstrably justified in a free and democratic society." As a result, rights are not absolute, but can be limited to advance valid public policy objectives pursued by Parliament and the provincial legislatures. Second, the Charter of Rights contains a legislative override clause, section 33, that allows Parliament or the provincial legislatures to override judicial decisions involving specific rights and freedoms (fundamental rights, legal rights, equality rights) for a renewable five-year period. Although the notwithstanding clause has been used infrequently, most important in *Ford v. Quebec* (1998), when the Supreme Court of Canada invalidated provisions of Quebec's French-only sign law, it represents an important check on judicial power that can preserve both constitutional supremacy as well as federalism when provincial governments determine Charter review centralizes areas of provincial jurisdiction.

The question of judicial power and the Charter of Rights is a central debate surrounding the courts in Canada. Judicial activism has been defended as a dialogue between courts and legislatures that ultimately provides the last word to legislatures because of the notwithstanding clause and the ability to justify legislation as a reasonable limit under section 1 (Roach 2001, 250–251). Alternatively, judicial activism and expansive judicial review have been criticized as undermining constitutional supremacy and facilitating the emergence of "jurocracy"—a term coined by Morton and Knopff (2000, 108) that refers to the "rights bureaucracy" composed of courts "but also administrative tribunals, human rights commissions, legal departments, law reform commissions, law schools, and judicial education programs." This debate will not be resolved, however, because it rests on normative positions regarding appropriate boundaries between courts and legislatures, contestable notions of democracy, and the legitimacy of judicial review.

CONCLUSION

The judicial system is a product of the constitutional structure and the unique features of Canada's federal system. Although the independence of the judiciary is constitutionally protected by the Canadian Charter of Rights and Freedoms, this principle has been essential to Canadian democracy since 1867. Although the structure of the judicial system reflects the federal principle, the political responsibility for appointing and remunerating judges departs from this, because the federal government appoints all provincial court of appeal and superior court justices. Furthermore, although the Supreme Court of Canada acts as the "umpire of federalism," the provincial governments have no role in appointing justices to this court, and this has led to criticism of the Court's having a federal bias when it adjudicates division of power disputes between the two orders of governments. With the passage of the Charter of Rights in 1982 and the increased scope of judicial review, the concern over centralization has intensified with the invalidation of provincial statutes as inconsistent with protected rights and freedoms. In turn, this has raised the specter of judicial power and concerns that the courts have transitioned from being legal institutions to political institutions because of the significant policy-making role provided to judges under the Canadian Charter of Rights and Freedoms.

NOTES

1. *Editors' Note*: To ensure the "full complement of nine judges" on the Supreme Court of Canada, and after consultation with the leader of the opposition, Prime Minister Harper announced in late December 2008 that the governor general had accepted his recommendation and appointed Mr. Justice Cromwell to the Court. The parliamentary consultation process was bypassed, adding further proof of the uncertain status of the appointment procedure reforms first introduced by the Martin government in 2005.

REFERENCES

Baier, Gerald. 2006. *Courts and Federalism*. Vancouver: UBC Press.

Department of Justice. 2008. "Minister of justice announces selection process for the Supreme Court of Canada." May 28. http://canada.justice.gc.ca/eng/news-nouv/ nr-cp/2008/doc_32258.html.

Ford v. Quebec (Attorney General) (1998) 2 S.C.R. 712.

Greene, Ian. 2006. *The Courts*. Vancouver: UBC Press.

Heard, Andrew. 1991. The Charter in the Supreme Court of Canada: The importance of which judges hear an appeal. *Canadian Journal of Political Science* 24(2): 289–307.

Kelly, James B. 2005. *Governing with the Charter*. Vancouver: UBC Press.

Laforest, Guy. 1995. *Trudeau and the End of a Canadian Dream*. Montreal: McGill-Queen's University Press.

M. v. H. (1999) 2 S.C.R. 3.

Manfredi, Christopher P. 1993. *Judicial Power and the Charter*. Toronto: McClelland and Stewart.

Minister of Justice. 2005. Proposal to reform the Supreme Court of Canada appointment process. October 20. http://www.canada.justice.gc.ca/en/dept/pub/scc/index.html.

———. 2006. Speaking notes for the minister of justice and attorney general of Canada, Vic Toews, Q.C., Ad Hoc Committee to Review a Nominee for the Supreme Court of Canada. February 27. Ottawa, Canada. http://www.justice.gc.ca/en/news/sp/2006/ doc_31772_1.html.

Morton, F. L. 2006. Judicial appointments in post-Charter Canada: A system in transition. In *Appointing Judges in an Age of Judicial Power*, ed. Kate Malleson and Peter H. Russell, 56–79. Toronto: University of Toronto Press.

Morton, F. L., and Rainer Knopff. 2000. *The Charter Revolution and the Court Party*. Peterborough: Broadview Press.

Office of the Commissioner for Federal Judicial Affairs. 2007. Judicial advisory committees. March 31. http://www.fja.gc.ca/fja-cmf/ja-am/com/index-eng.html.

Office of the Prime Minister. 2008. "PM announces nominee for Supreme Court appointment." September 5. http://pm.gc.ca/eng/media.asp?id=2265.

Provincial Court Judges' Assn. of New Brunswick v. New Brunswick (Minister of Justice); Ontario Judges' Assn. v. Ontario (Management Board); Bodner v. Alberta; Conférence des juges du Québec v. Quebec (Attorney General); Minc v. Quebec (Attorney General) (2005) 2 S.C.R. 286.

R. v. Drybones (1970) 2 S.C.R. 282.

R. v. Valente (1985) 2 S.C.R. 673.

Reference re a Resolution to Amend the Constitution (1981) 1 S.C.R. 753.

Reference re Legislative Authority of Parliament to Alter or Replace the Senate (1980) 1 S.C.R. 54.

Reference re Remuneration of Judges of the Provincial Court (P.E.I.) (1997) 3 S.C.R. 3.

Reference re Secession of Quebec (1998) 2 S.C.R. 217.

Riddell, Troy, Lori Hausegger, and Matthew Hennigar. 2007. Federal judicial appointments: A look at patronage in federal appointments since 1988. *University of Toronto Law Journal* 58(1): 1–36, 39–74.

Roach, Kent. 2001. *The Supreme Court on Trial.* Toronto: Irwin Law.

Russell, Peter H. 1987. *The Judiciary in Canada: The Third Branch of Government.* Toronto: McGraw-Hill Ryerson.

Russell, Peter H., and Jacob Ziegel. 1991. Federal judicial appointments: An appraisal of the first Mulroney government's appointments and the new judicial advisory committees. *University of Toronto Law Journal* 41(1): 4–37.

Snell, James G., and Frederick Vaughan. 1985. *The Supreme Court of Canada: History of the Institution.* Toronto: University of Toronto Press.

Supreme Court of Canada. 2007. Role of the Court. November 23. http://www.scc-csc.gc .ca/aboutcourt/role/index_e.asp.

———. 2008. Statistics 1997 to 2007. March 3. http://www.scc-csc.gc.ca/information/ statistics/HTML/cat2_e.asp.

Vipond, Robert. 1991. *Liberty and Community: Canadian Federalism and the Failure of the Constitution.* New York: State University of New York Press.

Vriend v. Alberta (1998) 1 S.C.R. 493.

Ziegel, Jacob S. 2001. Merit selection and democratization of appointments to the Supreme Court of Canada. In *Judicial Power and Canadian Democracy,* ed. Paul Howe and Peter H. Russell, 131–164. Montreal: McGill-Queen's University Press.

CHAPTER 4

....

THE CANADIAN CHARTER OF RIGHTS AND FREEDOMS

....

JANET L. HIEBERT

THE decision in 1982 to adopt the Canadian Charter of Rights and Freedoms has been appropriately characterized as the most radical break ever made with the nation's constitutional and legal traditions (Smiley 1983, 89). The Charter transformed a basic governing principle upon which the Canadian political system was founded: the supremacy of Parliament. Before the Charter's adoption, the decisions of Canadian federal and provincial legislatures were generally beyond judicial reproach, provided they complied with the Constitution's division of powers between federal and provincial legislatures, and were consistent with the rule of law. By including the Charter in the Constitution, courts are now authorized to review legislation for its consistency with rights and to provide remedies for breaches that can include the invalidation of legislation. The Charter also introduces a serious tension with Canada's other constitutional pillar: federalism. It does so by promoting pan-Canadian values that courts interpret in a context divorced from explicit consideration of an important rationale of federalism—the accommodation of diverse policy outcomes between provinces.

Yet, a bill of rights is neither a self-enforcing nor necessarily dynamic force for social or political change. Much depends on how it influences the assumptions and behavior of those who interpret it, or alters the strategies or claims of citizens and groups in their interactions with the state. For this reason, when the Charter was adopted, it was difficult to predict the extent to which it would affect the Canadian political psyche or influence political and judicial behavior. Although the Charter proved popular among citizens, it was only reluctantly accepted by most provinces, which would have preferred that it not be adopted at all. Moreover, public servants lacked clear direction about whether and how to reexamine policy assumptions, and the judiciary entrusted with its interpretation had a well-earned reputation for reluctance to interpret rights robustly, despite the earlier adoption of a statutory bill of rights in 1960.

The purpose of this chapter is to assess the Charter's impact on the Canadian political system since it was adopted in 1982. The Charter's intersection with federalism tells an important story of significant change arising from the promotion of identities based on "Canadianness" at the expense of "competing regional loyalties" (MacIvor 2006, 221–222), the homogenization of legislation (Laforest 1995, 135), and the defederalization of political culture (Laforest 2006, 70). This chapter considers another important political dimension of the Charter: its effects on the parliamentary character of Canadian politics. It does so by examining how three of the Charter's most important sections have evolved: the limitation clause of section 1, the notwithstanding clause of section 33, and, with a specific focus on social policy distinctions based on a traditional definition of spouse, the equality rights of section 15. All three sections played an important role in framing the kind of rights project the Charter would represent and each, in its own way, reveals how and why the Charter has come to influence legislation and political behavior. This assessment reveals that judicial influence on legislation is considerably broader than what could reasonably have been anticipated in 1982. This influence arises not only from more extensive judicial oversight of legislation than many would have expected, but also from bureaucratic and political reliance on judicial criteria in the policy process. Before proceeding further, it is helpful to review briefly how the Charter came into being.

Origins of the Charter

Historically, Canadian constitutional negotiations were influenced by the need to secure agreement about how to amend the British North America Act (BNA Act), now known as the Constitution Act, 1867. Although this legislation served as a core foundation of Canada's constitution, as an Act of the British Parliament, it could only be amended upon Canada's request to the U.K. Parliament. Even after Canadian sovereignty became a political reality with the passage of the Statute of Westminster in 1931, the omission of an amending formula delayed Canada's capacity to achieve full sovereignty. Although Canada amended the BNA Act nine times between 1930 and 1964, by 1964 it had become evident that the pragmatism that had earlier allowed for incremental constitutional changes was insufficient to address conflicting visions about what kind of political project the Canadian Constitution should reflect and promote (Russell 2004, 56–58).

Constitutional negotiations would now also have to confront conflicting nation-building projects, one reflecting a pan-Canadian version of nationalism (complicated by differing views on the appropriate balance of powers between the provincial and federal governments), and a very different nation-building project that emphasizes Quebec nationalism and seeks economic and political autonomy. However, a core element of the pan-Canadian project would prove particularly contentious: Pierre Trudeau's proposed constitutional bill of rights. As prime minister, Trudeau ensured the idea of a constitutional bill of rights would remain on the constitutional agenda from its first placement in 1968 until the Constitution was amended in 1982. Trudeau's intents were to protect individual rights and undercut claims for collective rights he opposed, and to promote a pan-Canadian identity that he hoped would transcend provincial and, in particular, Quebec identities. However, a constitutionally entrenched bill of rights was strongly opposed by the provincial premiers, who perceived it as an abrupt rupture to, rather than refinement of, Canadian constitutional principles.

The provincial premiers continued to express strong reservations about a bill of rights throughout the many rounds of constitutional negotiations held between 1968 and 1981. Not only did the premiers want to focus on other constitutional issues (such as refining and changing the relationship between federal and provincial powers that had evolved since 1867), but they were also highly reticent about altering the principle of parliamentary supremacy, which historically did not separate consideration for individual rights from the general apparatus of governing. At the time of these constitutional debates, conventional wisdom portrayed the question of whether to adopt a bill of rights as a choice between one of two rival Liberal constitutional models. One form, a more juridical model, was associated with the American political system, in which citizens can challenge the legitimacy of legislation from a rights perspective in court, and judges are empowered to grant wide-sweeping remedies, including the invalidation of inconsistent legislation. The other Liberal constitutional form, a more political version, was equated with the Westminster parliamentary model and emphasized the supremacy of parliamentary judgment. This is the tradition to which Canada subscribed until 1982. Under this tradition, rights were thought of as being protected by, and not from, parliamentary sovereignty.

The provincial premiers saw no need to depart from this tradition and rejected the idea that the Charter would significantly improve the quality of the Canadian polity. However, in the event of having to accept the Charter's adoption, the provincial premiers sought to mitigate the possible influence judicial review could exert on legislation. They rejected the federal proposal to state rights as if they were absolute (and rely on judges to determine their appropriate scope) and insisted upon the inclusion of a broadly worded limitation clause, constructed with the intent of influencing how courts evaluate legislation that is claimed to infringe upon rights. Their hope was to encourage judicial deference for legislation to permit legislatures broad latitude to pursue legislative agendas despite any adverse implications for these codified rights.

For more than a decade, federal and provincial officials debated various limitation clauses, all intended to assuage provincial premiers' concerns that judicial review would significantly constrain governmental capacity to define and defend the public interest (Hiebert 1996, 13–31). But, after the failure of yet another round of constitutional negotiations in September 1980, the federal government indicated it would seek unilateral patriation and reform of the Constitution. At this stage, only two provinces (Ontario and New Brunswick) supported its reform package. The federal threat of unilateral action had several unintended consequences that weakened the other provinces' political capacity to continue opposing the Charter. One was the unexpected role that parliamentary hearings had in promoting the popularity of the proposed Charter. The federal government had hoped to gain quick approval in the House of Commons for its unilateral strategy and to "shift the political limelight from the glare of intensive debate in the Commons to the more tranquil circumstances of committee consideration" (Romanow et al. 1984, 112). However, opposition to this federal intent to proceed hastily unwittingly created a national stage for boosting public support for the proposed Charter. Public interest in the Charter far exceeded expectations and extended significantly the duration of the hearings. The publicity attached to these hearings helped promote public awareness and interest in the Charter, whereas citizens' interventions helped shape many of the Charter's key provisions (Kelly 2005, 63–64). In short, this first experience of citizen engagement with the Constitution contributed to a strong sense of ownership of the Charter and transformed citizens' conception of their relationship to the Constitution (Cairns 1992, 62–95).

The growing public support for the Charter also altered the balance of powers in constitutional negotiations on the crucial issue of the Charter's adoption. The majority of provincial premiers who opposed the Charter now found themselves on the defensive for explaining why Canada should reject the Charter. But, their arguments to preserve parliamentary supremacy had little resonance in a public discourse that increasingly emphasized the protection of rights from legislatures. The growing popularity of the Charter also made it difficult for the provincial premiers to insist upon their preferred limitation clause. Faced with the stinging rebuke in public hearings that this clause rendered the Charter's promise of protecting rights little more than a verbal illusion, the federal government altered significantly the wording of the clause to its current form, and in so doing ensured that limits on rights would be harder to justify in court (Hiebert 1996, 22–24). The limitation clause provides the following: "The Canadian Charter of Rights and Freedoms guarantees the rights and freedoms set out in it subject only to such reasonable limits prescribed by law as can be demonstrably justified in a free and democratic society" (section 1).

This federal unilateral threat had one more consequence that helped facilitate agreement for the constitutional reforms that included the Charter. This threat provoked constitutional litigation, which culminated in a bold act of statecraft by the Supreme Court (Russell 1983, 213–238). By ruling that unilateral action by the federal government would be legal, but would not be constitutional in a conventional sense, this decision compelled the political actors to resume negotiations (*Reference Re Amendment of the Constitution of Canada* [1981]). This ruling made it difficult for the federal government to proceed unilaterally, but at the same time, it also made it unwise for any individual province to assume it could block constitutional reforms. A few weeks after the Supreme Court reference, negotiations were once again underway with an alliance of eight premiers firmly opposed to the federal proposals. However, late in the process, a compromise was reached to bridge the two sides. Ottawa would accept the provincial government's preferred amending formula, but without fiscal compensation for opting out, and seven of the eight opposing provinces would accept the Charter, but with a notwithstanding clause that would apply to fundamental freedoms, and legal and equality rights. The notwithstanding clause allows the provinces or the federal government to preempt or set aside the effects of judicial review of most sections of the Charter for renewable five-year periods. Although the notwithstanding clause had been discussed earlier, it became more important to those premiers critical of the Charter after the wording to the limitation clause was changed to its current version. As amended, the limitation clause makes it more difficult for governments to convince judges that legislative restrictions on rights are constitutional. Although the earlier version would have placed an onerous burden on citizens to demonstrate that legislation is unreasonable, the amended wording shifts the burden of persuasion to governments and requires that they demonstrate that limitations on rights are reasonable and demonstrably justified.

Quebec was the only province not to accept the constitutional reforms, and the consequences of this political decision to proceed without its consent continue to shape constitutional and federalism debates.

The Charter's Impact on the Political Process

As the Charter has evolved, a rich political science literature has emerged discussing its various dimensions of influence, including the Charter's effects on how citizens relate to the constitution (Cairns 1991, 108–138), its impact on federalism (Clarke 2006; Gagnon and Iacovino 2007, 37–43; Knopff and Morton 1985, 133–182; Laforest 1995, 125–149; LaSelva 1996, 64–98; Taylor 1993, 155–186), its influence on the strategies and objectives of social actors and groups (Hein 2000, 3–31; Manfredi 2004; Smith 1999), the conditions under which judicial rulings encourage social policy changes (Smith 2008), the Charter's effects on the language and tenor of political debate (Knopff 1998, 683–675), the Charter's influence on government litigation strategies (Hennigar 2004, 3–23), its effects on bureaucratic and executive behavior (Kelly 2005) or parliamentary behavior (Hiebert 2002), and its influence on election laws (Hiebert 2006, MacIvor 2004). Rather than address one of these specific issues, the remainder of this chapter focuses on how three of the Charter's most important sections have evolved (sections 1, 33, and 15), which provides important insights into what kind of rights project the Charter has become, and how and why it is altering the parliamentary character of Canadian politics.

General Limitation Clause of Section 1

As argued earlier, the provincial premiers who opposed the Charter hoped that if they could not prevent its introduction, they could at least influence its design in a way they thought would curb judicial influence on legislation. Their concerns would soon be echoed in scholarly debates about the Charter's potential to judicialize politics (a term that refers to the influence judicial rulings exert on political behavior and political culture). But, far from curtailing judicial influence on legislation, the inclusion of the limitation clause in the Charter has had the opposite effect. It has enhanced judicial influence on the legislative process and has done so in two ways. First, it has led to a broad interpretation of rights that triggers judicial review of legislation far more frequently than would likely have occurred without this clause. Second, as a consequence of the political apprehension arising from this frequent judicial oversight, public and political officials have adopted judicial perspectives on proportionality as relevant criteria when developing legislation in an attempt to reduce the likelihood that legislation will provoke Charter litigation or lead to its invalidation.

Bills of rights do not necessarily include a general limitation clause. When the Charter came into effect, it was uncertain how the inclusion of a general limitation clause would influence judicial review. In the early days of the Charter, some scholars argued that the Canadian courts should simply interpret the limitation clause as recognition of the obvious fact that rights are not absolute, and that internal or definitional limits will inevitably have to be defined (Bender 1983, 674–675). However, the Supreme Court has broached the section 1 limitation clause as warranting a distinct judicial method for interpreting the Charter. The Court has adopted a two-stage approach that separates the issue of whether a right has been infringed from the question of whether the infringement is justified. It has also decided to interpret rights broadly and to avoid imposing definitional limits that restrict the scope of rights, as are used, for example, by American courts. This decision to interpret rights broadly is clearly linked to the Court's decision to separate the issue of whether a right exists and has been infringed, from the determination of whether the legislation in question is constitutionally valid. By distinguishing these issues, the finding that a right has been violated does not have direct consequences for the judiciary's ultimate decision about whether the legislation in question is constitutionally valid, which is decided later in the process. However, by separating these issues, Canadian judicial interpretations of rights are not tempered by acute consciousness about how the finding of a right violation affects Parliament, despite this consideration being a persistent concern in most political systems where unelected judges have the power to alter the decisions of democratically elected legislatures.

Once the Court rules that a statute or a statutory provision violates a right, the government bears the burden of persuasion for demonstrating that the impugned legislation is reasonable and constitutionally justified. The Court has become extremely reluctant to declare the intent or goals of legislation invalid. Although the Court has indicated that only legislative purposes consistent with a free and democratic society can possibly be justified as reason to restrict Charter rights, its record indicates it is not prepared to veto regularly legislative objectives for being illegitimate under the Charter. A rare example of this blunt judicial veto was the court's rejection of a provision of the Canada Elections Act that denied prisoners the right to vote (*Sauvé v. Canada* 2002).

This reluctance of the Supreme Court of Canada to rule that the Charter prohibits a government's legislative objective outright has meant that the Court has had to focus on other criteria to sort out whether impugned legislation is constitutionally valid. These are proportionality criteria, which comprise (1) the need for a rational connection between the legislative objective and the means chosen, (2) a choice of means that impair the right as little as possible, and (3) a requirement that the deleterious effects of the legislative restriction be proportionate to the importance of the objective (*R. v. Oakes* 1986).

In short, the Court's interpretation of section 1 has turned the Charter into a very different rights project than many associate with a bill of rights. Judicial review of the Charter is not primarily about defining rights that legislatures cannot transgress, but instead is mostly concerned with reviewing the quality of how Parliament restricts rights. Thus, for government, the challenge has less to do with convincing judges that legislation is consistent with rights (and, in fact, governments frequently concede a rights violation has occurred) than it has with convincing judges that the means used to pursue rights-restricting legislation are consistent with judicial norms of proportionality. This distinctive approach to judicial review not only ensures the Charter serves a different function than might have been anticipated in 1982, but its two dimensions—the broad interpretation of rights and the focus on the quality of the means used to pursue a legislative goal—have important implications for the political process.

One obvious implication is that the more broadly rights are interpreted, the more likely it is that legislation will be found to have Charter implications, thereby requiring that Canadian governments defend legislation more often than they might otherwise be required. However, defending legislation is expensive, resource draining, and can place governments in the unenviable political position of having to defend legislation that is said to have violated rights.

A second implication of the Court's reluctance to veto rights-offending legislative goals, and to review instead the quality of legislative means, is that it has given legislatures wide berth to pursue legislative purposes that infringe upon rights, whether by effect or intent. Some might conclude that this way of interpreting the Charter contradicts the purpose of a bill of rights, which is to insulate rights from legislative incursions. They would argue that Canadian courts have it wrong by focusing on whether the means used to restrict rights are valid, if they have not first asked if it is appropriate to restrict rights at all. But others see this approach as facili-tating a beneficial dialogue between courts and Parliament. By rarely vetoing legis-lative objectives outright, legislatures are frequently given an opportunity to revise problematic legislation (Hogg and Bushell 1997). However, not all accept the utility of this dialogue metaphor, and suggest that it simply masks the perennial tension of judges reviewing the decisions of democratically elected legislatures (Petter 2007).

A third implication of the Court's emphasis on proportionality criteria arises from its treatment of the craft of designing social policy as having far more preci-sion than is appropriate. When a social problem has been recognized as warranting legislative redress, it is often difficult to conceive of effective ways to pursue legisla-tion that also satisfy criteria such as rationality or minimum impairment. Even with extensive knowledge and resources that can be drawn upon by public officials or others who influence legislation, what is often lacking is methodological capacity or full information to establish causality between intent and effects, harm and remedy, or the consequences of intervention versus nonintervention. Yet, such relational considerations are implied by a focus on rationality and minimal intrusiveness. Moreover, a strict judicial emphasis on proportionality criteria can constrain a gov-ernment's ability to achieve its legislative objectives, by encouraging the adoption of cautious means to satisfy judicial criteria, or even forgoing legislative goals that will not likely meet these tests. Examples of difficulties satisfying judges about propor-tionality are various versions of federal election finance legislation since the 1980s, all attempting to regulate individual and group advertising during electoral cam-paigns. Before the Supreme Court ultimately upheld this legislation in 2004, lower courts rejected the relevant legislation for failing to satisfy the minimal impairment criterion, and held out a test of rationality that would be exceedingly difficult to satisfy: proof that, without the legislative measures in place, money would corrupt or buy elections (Hiebert 2006, 272–285).

A related concern with the Court basing so much emphasis on the means used to pursue public policies is what this test entails for judges. If the development of legislation necessarily draws upon incomplete information, educated attempts to identify problems that could derail a policy, and lessons from other jurisdictions (in short, informed best estimates), the same subjective and discretionary qualities must also characterize others' assessments of legislation, including judges'. But judi-cial assessments are made even more challenging because judges lack specialized expertise to evaluate conflicting social science evidence, behavioral data, or schol-arly debates that are relevant to the social policy decision being reviewed (Hiebert 2002, 59–61). Nevertheless, reading Supreme Court Charter cases over the years sug-gests that the regularity of making proportionality assessments has decreased judi-cial sensitivity about the consequences of having to wade into the subjective terrain associated with evaluating the fit between legislative goals and their means. Although in earlier jurisprudence the Court was extremely reluctant to render judgment on matters for which there are no correct answers (*Reference re Public Service Employee Relations Act* 1987), the Court no longer seems to be particularly burdened by this possibility. No better example exists than in its review of the Charter implications of Canada's public health care system (*Chaoulli v. Quebec* 2005) (see chapter 24, this volume).

The basis for this Charter claim was that the failure of Quebec to allow private health care insurance for services covered by the public system violated both the Quebec and Canadian Charters. Review of this claim entailed a philosophical undertaking about whether individuals should be able to purchase faster and/or higher quality care on the private market, and about the possible impact a parallel private system would have on the public system (Choudhry 2005, 79). Although both undertakings were heavily value laden, the Court expressed little concern about its role in resolving these issues, or whether its involvement was consistent with an appropriate institutional division of labor for such a complex and contested policy issue.

A fourth and most significant implication of this judicial approach is its influence on bureaucratic and political judgments about legislation. The Court's broad interpretation of rights has meant that government and public officials regularly assess legislative initiatives conscious of their Charter implications. Political concerns about the prospects of litigation or invalidation have encouraged the development of a Charter screening process, in which Charter consistency is based on the Court's proportionality criteria and relevant case law.[1] In these prelegislative evaluations, governmental lawyers play a pivotal role in assessing the likelihood that initiatives will be subject to Charter litigation, and advising how to lower the risk of Charter litigation and invalidation (Hiebert 2002; Kelly 2005, 222–249). So important has awareness for Charter implications become in the policy process, that federal legislative initiatives cannot proceed to cabinet without a preliminary assessment of Charter implications, including a risk assessment. Thus, a change has been made to the Memorandum to Cabinet to require Charter analysis comprising "an assessment of the risk of successful challenge in the courts, the impact of an adverse decision, and possible litigation costs" (Dawson 1993, 53). Many provincial governments have developed similar processes (Kelly 2005, 214).

Although some might applaud this development, particularly if they equate this interpretation of Charter compliance with better legislation, the attempt to discern policy principles from existing case law can distort how policy initiatives are translated into legislative means. Courts generally articulate rules in the context of a specific legal dispute, but to elicit a rule from case X to govern situation Y is rarely straightforward. The difficulty is not simply determining the relevant rule. A different policy context might actually change how a court thinks about an issue. The changing composition of the court, or of the judges hearing a particular case, can also undermine predictability. Moreover, treating lawyers' interpretations of relevant rulings as the proxy for determinations of Charter compatibility denies the legitimacy of parliamentary judgment about how rights appropriately guide or constrain legislation (Hiebert 2002, 222–223). This focus on compatibility can also come at the expense of other relevant policy considerations. One former provincial attorney general had the following to say about this focus on Charter compatibility:

Charter compliance in the legislative process is inherently reactive, rather than proactive, as it requires government to approach policy making from the perspective of risk analysis rather than from the perspective of broader social and economic priorities or the balancing of differing societal interests. In other words, although the question "Is this legislation Charter compliant?" often leads to a different answer than the question "Is this legislation good public policy?," the former question often takes precedence in public policy analysis. As a result, risk management becomes the driver of the analysis. (Plant 2007, 4)

In summary, the clause the provinces insisted upon, inspired by hope that it would curb judicial influence on legislation, has had the opposite effect of what they intended. Not only has it led to a broader interpretation of rights that more frequently subjects legislation to judicial oversight than would likely have occurred had no limitation clause been included in the Charter, but the consequences of such extensive judicial oversight have led public and political officials to internalize judicial rules in the policy process as a defensive measure to avoid litigation or policy disruption arising from a negative judicial ruling. However, such bureaucratic and political reliance ensures that judicial decisions are more influential than Charter skeptics or supporters anticipated. Courts not only determine the constitutionality of specific legislative decisions that are subject to Charter challenge, but their decisions potentially influence the entire range of a government's legislative agenda.

Notwithstanding Clause

The notwithstanding clause is the Charter's most obvious concession to federalism. It allows legislatures to dissent from judicial decisions, or preempt judicial review altogether, for most sections of the Charter for renewable five-year terms, thereby accommodating the territorial-based diversity that federalism was intended to accommodate. The notwithstanding clause has been invoked sixteen times by a total of four governments—Yukon, Alberta, Saskatchewan, and Quebec (Kahana 2001, 256), but most of these uses occurred in the first few years after the Charter was adopted; the last usage occurred in 2000.

The notwithstanding clause has become so controversial that politicians have become extremely reticent to use it. Four reasons explain why it is viewed as having such questionable legitimacy. First, many consider the notwithstanding clause fundamentally inconsistent with the rights project they ascribe to the Charter. A common view of the Charter's purpose was to bring about two significant changes to the Canadian polity. One was to introduce a more legal form of adjudicating disagreements between citizens and the state whereas the second was to protect individual rights—in particular, those of minorities—from being adversely affected by the decisions of representative government. Many consider the notwithstanding clause inconsistent with both intents. It allows ordinary legislation to suspend the effects of a judicial ruling, and, by operating on a majority basis, it might not shield minority rights (Whyte 1990, 350–352).

Second, few Charter proponents accept the merits of differentiated interpretations of the Charter to reflect provincial public policy differences. The majority of Charter supporters, particularly in English-speaking Canada, embrace the pan-Canadian nature of rights that judicial interpretations typically promote. Unity for most means uniformity, at least with respect to the treatment of rights. Consequently, the idea that the notwithstanding clause could protect legislation that deviates from a national rights standard is antithetical to the kind of rights project most Charter supporters associate with the Charter.

Third, the Charter has altered citizens' perceptions of Parliament's competence for making value judgments that implicate rights. This is not a uniquely Canadian outcome. Citizens and politicians alike seem unable or unwilling to resist the equation of rights with legal interpretations. As Tom Campbell (2001, 87) says of the United Kingdom's Human Rights Act,

> interpretation is almost universally seen as the prerogative of the courts because it is part of adjudication, and that is taken to be their exclusive function. It is therefore not only politically difficult but also constitutionally questionable for parliaments to reject a court's particular interpretations or even question a court's interpretive methods. (Campbell 2001, 87)

Survey research confirms that a clear majority of Canadians believe that courts, not Parliament, should have the final word on decisions related to rights (Nanos 2007, 52–53).

The public perceptions that the Charter's value lies in authorizing courts to protect citizens from rights abuses by government, and that courts have greater legitimacy to interpret rights, have encouraged politicians to emphasize compliance with judicial Charter interpretations as the morally appropriate path to take. This is also a useful political strategy to renege on responsibility for contentious issues that divide a caucus or provoke the wrath of vocal or influential elements of a party's electoral constituency. Politicians can avoid controversy and responsibility by claiming that their hands are tied by the Charter from pursuing a controversial position. However, this strategy makes it difficult for politicians to defy openly a judicial ruling on which they disagree, as they would be doing by invoking the notwithstanding clause.

Finally, many politicians see utility in distinguishing their party from their partisan rivals in terms of alleged support for the Charter. An important element of this tactic is to criticize the notwithstanding clause. Soon after the Charter was adopted, politicians began exploiting public doubts about the clause's value for political purposes. An early example was Pierre Trudeau's (1987) criticism of federal political supporters of the proposed Meech Lake Accord for their failure to remove the notwithstanding clause when bargaining with the provinces. Then Prime Minister Brian Mulroney, the target of Trudeau's wrath, retaliated by blaming Trudeau for having agreed to a power he characterized as being so inconsistent with the idea of a Charter that it rendered the Charter "not worth the paper it is written on" (Trudeau 1987, 153). Claimed aversion for the notwithstanding clause has become a conscious political strategy, as was evident in the 2004 federal election. Trailing in the polls, the incumbent Liberal government tried to resurrect a faltering campaign by criticizing Conservative leader Stephen Harper for failing to rule out the possible use of the notwithstanding clause (Canadian Broadcasting Corporation 2004). Although the Liberals managed to preserve power in the 2004 election, albeit with minority status, this political strategy failed in the next election. Liberal leader Paul Martin pledged during the 2006 televised political leaders' debate that his government, if reelected, would remove the constitutional power of a federal government to invoke the notwithstanding clause (Canadian Broadcasting Corporation 2006). However, the Conservative Party prevailed during the 2006 election with a minority government.

Such political strategies as equating Charter compatibility with Supreme Court rulings and trying to score political points by criticizing the notwithstanding clause have long-term implications for political behavior. The more frequently politicians treat hostility for the notwithstanding clause as a sign of respect for the Charter, or portray an issue as beyond their institutional competence, the more difficult it becomes to assert shared responsibility with courts for interpreting the Charter. If citizens are routinely conditioned to accept that respect for the Charter precludes disagreeing with the Court, it will become extremely difficult for legislatures to invoke the notwithstanding clause, even if the legislation in question is inspired by a sincere belief that the legislative action is justified from a rights perspective and/or the relevant judicial ruling is perceived as harmful or unjust.

Equality Rights and the Transformation of Marriage

If asked to identify the most significant social policy change attributable to the Charter, the definition of marriage is an obvious answer. Before the Charter's adoption, the legal understanding of marriage was based on an 1866 common-law ruling that marriage "as understood in Christendom" is "the voluntary union for life of one man and one woman, to the exclusion of all others" (*Hyde v. Hyde and Woodmansee* 1866). As of 2005, Canada became one of only a handful of nations legally to recognize marriage between same-sex partners—a change attributable to cumulative equality rulings, their impact on political strategies by affected citizens, and political reluctance to defy judicial authority.

It would have been extremely difficult in 1982 to predict that within a generation of the Charter's coming into effect, the definition of marriage would change to allow same-sex unions. At the time, most politicians showed little sympathy for the idea that equality prevents discrimination on the basis of sexual orientation and, as a result, the Charter makes no mention of sexual orientation as a prohibited category of discrimination. But politicians were not the only obstacles in redressing this form of discrimination. Judges regularly invoked textbook definitions of marriage or spouse that relied upon an opposite-sex definition. However, within a decade of the equality rights coming into force (a delay of three years was intended to allow public and political officials to redress old legislation that violated equality), the Supreme Court signaled a fundamental change to how it viewed equality. The Court moved from its pre-Charter position of accepting the validity of policy distinctions that denied benefits or recognition to those in same-sex relationships, to one that characterized the hallmark of a tolerant society as its willingness to treat same-sex partners and relationships as equally worthy of respect and tolerance as traditional family relationships.

Four ideas have emerged in the Court's equality jurisprudence (*Egan v. Canada* 1995; *M. v. H.* 1999; *Mirono v. Trudel* 1995; *Vriend v. Alberta* 1998) that have had profound implications for social policies that implicitly or explicitly distinguish on the basis of sexual orientation. These ideas are that equality prevents discrimination based on personal characteristics such as those enumerated in section 15(1) as well as analogous grounds that include sexual orientation, tradition and custom do not justify the continued discrimination same-sex partners incur, costs and the scope of required changes are not justification for prolonged inaction, and, most important for the issue of marriage, equality not only prohibits unequal treatment in law, but also precludes laws from conveying a message that those in same-sex relationships are not entitled to equal concern and respect.

Within a few years of the most significant of these equality rulings, the 1999 decision *M. v. H.* (indicating that equality has both a substantive and symbolic element), provincial courts of appeal in British Columbia, Ontario, and Quebec ruled that the common-law definition of marriage violates equality. One of these rulings, *Halpern v. Canada* (*Attorney General*) (2003), issued a new common-law definition of marriage, allowing same-sex partners to marry. The federal government did not appeal this decision, and Prime Minister Jean Chrétien announced in June 2003 that his government would develop draft legislation to change the definition of marriage. The definition is as follows: "Marriage, for civil purposes, is the lawful union of two persons to the exclusion of all others." But political opposition (including a sizeable element of Chrétien's caucus) discouraged the government from immediately introducing the legislation and, in an attempt to silence critics, it launched a reference case with the Supreme Court. In its ruling, the Court confirmed that the federal government has jurisdiction over marriage, but refused to answer the question of whether a prohibition on same-sex marriage is unconstitutional (*Reference re Same-Sex Marriage* 2004). However, the Court's earlier indication that equality requires both equal treatment in benefits as well as in the messages and symbolism in the law, suggests that it would be difficult to defend successfully a definition of marriage that does not recognize same-sex partners.

As remarkable as this paradigm shift in jurisprudence has been the fact of political compliance with these rulings. Political opposition to these rulings could have been expressed in three different ways. The notwithstanding clause could have been invoked to delay the legal force of a judicial ruling. A government could adopt a minimalist approach to restrict the scope of legislative change to the bare minimum necessary to comply with a specific ruling. Or a government could seek a constitutional amendment to alter the scope of equality to preclude recognition of sexual orientation as a prohibited ground of discrimination. Even if this latter strategy proved unsuccessful, the political act of pursuing constitutional change would represent a significant political overture to critics of the new judicial rule (Smith 2008). However, despite initial reluctance and delaying tactics, Canadian legislators have enacted sweeping changes to human rights codes, adoption laws, pension schemes, indeed the entire range of provincial and federal laws that directly or implicitly make policy distinctions on the basis of sexual orientation, including marriage. This contrasts with the United States, where legislators actively tried to reestablish the heterosexual nature of marriage (Smith 2008).

An obvious question arises. What explains Canadian legislators' willingness to introduce substantial reforms to give effect to these rulings? Although the explanation for how and why judicial rulings affect political outcomes is complex (Epp 1998; Rosenberg 1991), the following two considerations go some distance toward an explanation for Canada.

Institutional context matters when explaining how pressures for social change are mobilized, where and in what form these pressures are exerted, and the relative constraints and limits that institutional actors have to resist these changes. Miriam Smith (2008) provides a persuasive account of why institutional context is so relevant in explaining the capacity of the gay reform movement to bring about changes in Canada, as contrasted with the United States. She argues that judicial rulings on gay and lesbian rights have had more influence on social policy decisions in Canada as a result of differences in the respective federal structures (jurisdiction in Canada on central issues affecting lesbian and gay citizens, such as marriage or criminal law, is federal and therefore not prone to decentralized and diverse treatment), differences between the parliamentary and separation of power systems (legislative changes under the Canadian parliamentary system are not as likely to encounter institutional obstacles as those arising within a separated system), and differences in the relationship of legislatures to courts (a stronger culture of compliance with judicial rulings exists in Canada).

A second consideration is whether and how a bill of rights influences the assumptions or attitudes of those in power. As argued earlier, the twin public perceptions, that the Charter's value lies in authorizing courts to protect citizens from rights abuses by government, and that courts have greater legitimacy to interpret rights, have made politicians reluctant to defend policy positions that are clearly contrary to judicial rulings. This sense that Parliament lacks authority to define the scope of Charter rights, and how rights properly guide or constrain legislative decisions, was not as apparent during the first few years after the Charter was adopted. For example, when equality rights first came into force in 1985, the federal Conservative government did not broach the Charter as establishing new normative standards that prevent political and policy considerations from being given effect, or as necessarily privileging judicial over political interpretations. Instead, the Charter was treated as a statement of principles with meaning and application that should be determined by Parliament. As the minister of justice stated in a discussion about equality: "It is the role of Parliament, which represents the people of Canada, to make policy choices among the various means of complying with the Charter" (Crosbie 1985, 33).

However, as the Charter evolved, and jurisprudence on same-sex benefits accumulated, this perception changed about Parliament having a valid role in determining whether and how equality constrains legislation. After the *M. v. H.* (1999) ruling, which provided strong reason to assume that hundreds of federal legislative provisions were also suspect for denying benefits and recognition to same-sex partners, the federal Liberal government defended comprehensive remedial legislation in 2000 as necessary to comply with the government's moral obligation to respect the Charter's core values, and made it clear it was the Court, not Parliament, that defined their meaning (Hiebert 2002, 214). Although different governments were in place during these two periods, this shift in perception about whether Parliament can appropriately determine how Charter rights should constrain policy decisions, likely has less to do with partisanship than with declining confidence in Parliament's authority to make value judgments that implicate rights, particularly when these collide with judicial rulings.

Conclusion

Despite initial uncertainty about its potential effects, the Charter has changed the parliamentary character of Canadian politics in ways that are profound. One of the most significant of these is the extent and breadth of judicial oversight of legislation, a consequence of the Court's broad interpretation of rights. Another significant change is how this judicial oversight influences legislation. The idea that the Charter would influence political priorities is not particularly surprising, because a principal purpose of a bill of rights is to constrain legislation that violates rights. However, what is remarkable about how the Charter is evolving is that these constraints do not generally arise from a judicial ruling that legislative goals are incompatible with the Charter, as the courts have a high tolerance for legislation that restricts rights, whether by intent or effect. Instead of determining whether Parliament should be able to restrict a right in a given situation, the judicial focus is almost entirely on the quality of the means chosen to pursue this rights-restricting objective. But perhaps the most significant change to the parliamentary character of Canadian politics is the extent to which judicial criteria have transformed the policy process. Public and political officials have adopted Charter-screening processes heavily influenced by judicial proportionality criteria, with the intent of insulating legislation from litigation or the prospects of a negative ruling. To appreciate the consequences of this transformation, it is important to bear in mind that only a fraction of the legislation Parliament passes will ever be litigated, and only a portion of this will result in a judicial ruling of unconstitutionality. Reliance by policy and political officials on judicial constitutional norms expands the scope of judicial influence from a handful of specific legislative acts declared unconstitutional to the entire range of a government's legislative agenda.

This legislative emulation of judicial perspectives points to one more important way the Charter is changing the parliamentary character of Canadian politics. The willingness to invoke judicial criteria as a proxy for political decisions about Charter compatibility has contributed to a political culture that increasingly questions the capacity or legitimacy of political actors exercising independent value judgments that implicate rights, particularly when they differ from judicial perspectives. Partisan critics and others dismiss as illegitimate policy positions that are inconsistent with judicial interpretations of the Charter. But if the Charter means only what the judges say it means, and politicians are wary about defending contrary positions out of fear of being labeled intolerant or anti-Charter, it is hardly surprising that the mechanism Charter skeptics counted on to resist judicial hegemony—the notwithstanding clause—is so seldom used. That the Charter would encourage such profound changes to the parliamentary character of Canadian politics in such short order is quite remarkable, particularly for a country with an earlier political and constitutional evolution that was "characterized by continuity and incremental development" (Smiley 1983, 89).

NOTES

1. This assessment is based on interviews that I conducted. In 1999 and 2000, I interviewed officials in the Human Rights Center at the Department of Justice. I also had repeated and candid conversations with John Tait (1994–1995) and George Thomson (1998–1999), who had been deputy ministers of justice, about the influence of constitutional norms on policy evaluation.

REFERENCES

Bender, Paul. 1983. Justification for limiting constitutionally guaranteed rights and freedoms: Some remarks about the proper role of section one of the Canadian Charter. *Manitoba Law Journal* 35: 669–681.

Cairns, Alan C. 1991. *Disruptions*. Toronto: McClelland and Stewart.

———. 1992. *Charter versus Federalism. The Dilemmas of Constitutional Reform*. Montreal: McGill-Queen's University Press.

Campbell, Tom. 2001. Incorporation through interpretation. In *Sceptical Essays on Human Rights*, ed. Tom Campbell, K. D. Ewing, and Adam Tomkins, 79–101. Oxford: Oxford University Press.

Canadian Broadcasting Corporation. 2004. Harper threat to minority rights, Martin says. June 7. http://www.cbc.ca/canada/story/2004/06/07/elxnmartrights1040607.html.

Canadian Broadcasting Corporation. 2006. Martin wraps campaign in constitutional pledge. January 10. http://www.cbc.ca/news/story/2006/01/09/elxn-debates-look.html.

Chaoulli v. Quebec (Attorney General) (2005) 1 S.C.R. 791.

Choudhry, Sujit. 2005. Worse Than Lochner? In *Access to Care, Access to Justice*, ed. Colleen M. Flood, Kent Roach, and Lorne Sossin, 75–100. Toronto: University of Toronto Press.

Clarke, Jeremy. 2006. Beyond the democratic dialogue, and towards a federalist one: Provincial arguments and Supreme Court responses in Charter litigation. *Canadian Journal of Political Science* 39(2): 293–314.

Crosbie, John. 1985. Canada. House of Commons. "Minutes of proceedings and evidence of the Sub-committee on Equality Rights of the Standing Committee on Justice and Legal Affairs." March 27. 1: 33.

Dawson, Mary. 1993. The impact of the Charter on the public policy process and the Department of Justice. In *The Impact of the Charter on the Public Policy Process*, ed. Patrick Monahan and Marie Finkelstein, 51–60. North York: York University Center for Public Law and Public Policy.

Egan v. Canada (1995) 2 S.C.R. 513.

Epp, Charles R. 1998. *The Rights Revolution*. Chicago, Ill.: University of Chicago Press.

Gagnon, Alain-G., and Rafaelle Iacovino. 2007. *Federalism, Citizenship, and Quebec: Debating Multinationalism*. Toronto: University of Toronto Press.

Halpern v. Canada (Attorney General) (2003) 65 O.R. (3d) 161.

Hein, Gregory. 2000. Interest group litigation and Canadian democracy. In *Judicial Power and Canadian Democracy*, ed. Paul Howe and Peter H. Russell, 214–254. Montreal: McGill-Queen's University Press.

Hennigar, Matthew. 2004. Expanding the "dialogue" debate: Canadian federal government responses to lower court Charter decisions. *Canadian Journal of Political Science* 37(1): 3–23.

Hiebert, Janet L. 1996. *Limiting Rights: The Dilemma of Judicial Review*. Montreal: McGill-Queen's University Press.

———. 2002. *Charter Conflicts: What Is Parliament's Role?* Montreal: McGill-Queen's University Press.

———. 2006. Elections, democracy and free speech: More at stake than an unfettered right to advertise. In *Party Funding and Campaign Financing in International Perspective*, ed. Keith Ewing and Samuel Isacharoff, 273–293. London: Hart Publishing.

Hogg, Peter W., and Allison A. Bushell. 1997. The Charter dialogue between courts and legislatures (or perhaps the Charter of Rights isn't such a bad thing after all). *Osgoode Hall Law Journal* 35: 75–124.

Hyde v. Hyde and Woodmansee (1866) L.R. 1 P.&D. 130 at 133.

Kahana, Tsvi. (2001). The notwithstanding mechanism and public discussion: Lessons from the ignored practice of section 33 of the Charter. *Canadian Public Administration* 44: 255.

Kelly, James B. 2005. *Governing with the Charter: Legislative and Judicial Activism and Framers' Intent*. Vancouver: UBC Press.

Knopff, Rainer. 1998. Populism and the politics of rights: The dual attack on representative democracy. *Canadian Journal of Political Science* 31(4): 683–705.

Knopff, Rainer, and F. L. Morton. 1985. Nation-building and the Canadian Charter of Rights and Freedoms. In *Constitutionalism, Citizenship and Society in Canada*, ed. Alan Cairns and Cynthia Williams, 133–182. Toronto: University of Toronto Press.

Laforest, Guy. 1995. *Trudeau and the End of a Canadian Dream.* Montreal: McGill-Queen's
University Press.

———. 2006. One never knows... Sait-on jamais? In *Canada: The State of the Federation
2005, Quebec and Canada in the New Century. New Dynamics, New Opportunities,* ed.
Michael Murphy, 53–81. Queen's University: Institute of Intergovernmental Relations.

LaSelva, Samuel V. 1996. *The Moral Foundations of Canadian Federalism.* Montreal:
McGill-Queen's University Press.

M. v. H. (1999) 2 S.C.R. 3.

MacIvor, Heather. 2004. The Charter of Rights and party politics. *Choices* 10(4): 1–28.

———. 2006. *Canadian Politics and Government in the Charter Era.* Toronto: Thomson-
Nelson.

Manfredi, Christopher P. 2004. *Feminist Activism in the Supreme Court.* Vancouver: UBC
Press.

Miron v. Trudel (1995) 2 S.C.R. 418.

Nanos, Nik. 2007. The Charter values don't equal Canadian values: Strong support for
same-sex and property rights. *Policy Options* 28: 50–55.

Petter, Andrew. 2007. Taking dialogue theory much too seriously (or perhaps Charter
dialogue isn't such a good thing after all). *Osgoode Hall Law Journal* 45(1): 147–167.

Plant, Geoffrey. 2007. "Governing in the shadow of the Charter." Presented at the Canadian
Bar Association Conference, Calgary, June 1, 2007.

R. v. Oakes (1986) 1 S.C.R. 103.

Reference Re Amendment of the Constitution of Canada (nos. 1, 23, and 3) (1981) 1 S.C.R. 753.

Reference re Public Service Employee Relations Act (Alta.) (1987) 1 S.C.R. 313.

Reference re Same-Sex Marriage (2004) SCC 79, (2004) 3 S.C.R. 698.

Romanow, Roy, John Whyte, and Howard Leeson. 1984. *Canada... Notwithstanding: The
Making of the Constitution 1976–1982.* Toronto: Carswell/Methuen.

Rosenberg, Gerald N. 1991. *The Hollow Hope.* Chicago, Ill.: University of Chicago Press.

Russell, Peter H. 1983. Bold statescraft, questionable jurisprudence. In *And No One Cheered,*
ed. Keith Banting and Richard Simeon, 210–238. Toronto: Methuen.

———. 2004. *Constitutional Odyssey. Can Canadians Become a Sovereign People?* 3rd ed.
Toronto: University of Toronto Press.

Sauvé v. Canada (Chief Electoral Officer) (2002) S.C.C. 68, [2002] 3 S.C.R. 519.

Smiley, Donald. 1983. A dangerous deed: The Constitution Act, 1982. In *And No One
Cheered,* ed. Keith Banting and Richard Simeon, 74–95. Toronto: Methuen.

Smith, Miriam. 1999. *Lesbian and Gay Rights in Canada: Social Movements and Equality-
Seeking, 1971–1995.* Toronto: University of Toronto Press.

———. 2008. *Political Institutions and Lesbian and Gay Rights in the United States and
Canada.* New York: Routledge.

Taylor, Charles. 1993. *Reconciling the Solitudes: Essays on Canadian Federalism and
Nationalism.* Montreal: McGill-Queen's University Press.

Trudeau, Pierre. 1987. Canada. "Evidence of the Special Joint Committee of the Senate and
of the House of Commons the 1987 Constitutional Accord." August 27. 14: 139–140, 153.

Vriend v. Alberta (1998) 1 S.C.R. 493.

Whyte, John D. 1990. On not standing for not with standing. *Alberta Law Review* 28(2):
347–357.

PART II

CANADIAN FEDERALISM

CHAPTER 5

CANADA: A DOUBLE FEDERATION

DAVID E. SMITH

A SINGULAR FEDERATION

Along with the United States (1787), Switzerland (1848), and Australia (1901), Canada is one of the early modern federations. Sometimes the adjectives *classical* and *traditional* are used as well. These are inappropriate because, unlike its federal predecessors (which are republics), Canada is a parliamentary monarchy whose sovereign is the sovereign of the United Kingdom. Created in 1867 by an Act of Parliament at Westminster (originally entitled the British North America Act but in 1982 renamed the Constitution Act),[1] Canada is the world's first parliamentary federation. Most significant, at the end of the nineteenth century, when the colonies of Australia contemplated federal union, they favored American over Canadian example. The essential reason for that preference lay, in the words of the then attorney general of Victoria and delegate to the constitutional conventions of the 1890s (Isaac Isaacs), in the belief that "[Canada] is a Federation upon the centralizing principle, just as the United States is a Federation on the decentralization principle, the principle I hope we shall follow" (Australia 1986, 175). For some Australian scholars that principle was realized to such an extent that they see their country now in republican terms (Galligan 1995).

In fact, the Australians were wrong in their assessment of the emerging nature of Canadian federalism. It is true that the division of powers between federal and provincial jurisdictions agreed to by the Fathers of Confederation in the sixth decade of the nineteenth century favored the center over the parts, but by the last decade, and as a result of a series of opinions of the Judicial Committee of the Privy Council (JCPC; the Supreme Court of Canada became the country's final court of appeal only in 1949), that orientation was in the process of being reversed. If the object of the Australian delegates was to design a federal system that would protect the interests of the states, it is ironic that they should have opted to imitate the American over the Canadian constitutional arrangement of power between the center and the units of the federation.

For Canada, the significance of the Australian rejection lay in its making the British North American federal experiment unique among the early federations. All political systems, federal and unitary, have their distinctive characteristics; yet federal, but not unitary, systems are presumed to share common traits (Watts 1999). Arguably, the poverty of analysis of unitary political *systems*, as opposed to unitary *government* leads to the same inference. Federalism is about sameness; that is what makes for comparability.

By contrast, Canada is about difference in language, religion, law, economy, even geography—two of the ten provinces (Prince Edward Island, and Newfoundland and Labrador) are islands, whereas a third (British Columbia) is walled off from the rest of the country by the Rocky Mountains. In this last respect, Canada is markedly different from the United States, where apropos state boundaries Samuel Beer once wondered if "there could have been a United States, if the rectangle had not been invented" (Beer 1978, 16). In its constitutional recognition of language, religion, and law, Canada is unlike the United States and Australia, and rather more like Switzerland, a country to which Canadians paid slight attention until the 1960s, when, in response to the rise of nationalist sentiment in Quebec, countries that were culturally segmented attracted scholarly study (McRae 1974).

There are two explanations for federal states. One is to acknowledge and protect difference through constitutional and institutional means. Here is the reason for the introduction, not always successfully, of federations in Africa, Asia, and the Caribbean after World War II. The other is to permit territorial expansion and to provide for effective administration of the resulting area. Unlike the United States or Switzerland or Australia, each of which may trace its federal origin to one or other of these motivations, the Canadian federation is the product of both. In short, Canada is a double federation—based on peoples and territory.

Since Parliament's passage of the Official Languages Act in 1969, English and French are official languages to be used without prejudice within the reach of federal jurisdiction. The Act's intent is that every part of Canada, linguistically, will be part of a whole. Demographically, the matter is different. Only in Quebec is French the language of the majority, although there are large French-speaking minorities in Ontario and New Brunswick, the latter of which declared itself officially bilingual (also in 1969), and is still the only province to do so. Conversely, English is the predominant language in the other nine provinces, whereas in Quebec there is a significant English-speaking minority. In 2006, 7.7% of the province's population declared English their mother tongue. Thus, the dual-language regime envisioned forty years ago is confined to New Brunswick, in practice to portions of Ontario, and to the provision of federal services, where demanded, across the country.

In the 1860s, the touchstone of cultural dualism was religion rather than language. The heart of that issue was religion and education. The Constitution Act, 1867 perpetuated existing educational rights enjoyed by denominational minorities (that is, by Protestants or Roman Catholics) at the time a province, then or later, became part of the union. Along with its distinctive religious and linguistic majority, the new province of Quebec also stood apart from the rest of the country, where the common law prevailed, by retaining its civil law system. The Constitution Act, 1867 makes criminal law a matter exclusively for Parliament to determine.

The cultural factors of religion, language, and law, which disposed the drafters of the 1867 agreement toward federation, were regionally specific to Lower Canada. In the Maritime colonies of Nova Scotia, New Brunswick, and Prince Edward Island (the first two were original partners in the Confederation; the last joined in 1873), the concern was economic, particularly to increase trade with the colonies of the St. Lawrence River valley. Here was the second reason for federation: expansion. This motivation was seen again, when, in 1869, Canada purchased from the Hudson's Bay Company the immense area of Rupert's Land and the North-Western Territory,[2] in anticipation of the new country's westward expansion to the Pacific Ocean and absorption of the colony of British Columbia.

Taken together, difference and distance created in Canada a federation within a federation. Like the United States, Canada sought and received millions of immigrants, many of whom settled in the West and made the prairie grain economy the principal source of national wealth during the first half of the twentieth century. Farmers' attention was focused on matters like building schools, roads, and grain elevators, subjects that fell within the domain of the provinces, and securing fair and efficient handling of their crops by the railroads and the grain exchanges—responsibilities that fell largely to Parliament. Expansion, breadth, and purpose described this dimension of federalism.

By contrast, the federalism of the Quebec homeland was about autonomy and localism. From 1840 to 1867, Upper and Lower Canada were joined in one political entity: the Province of United Canada. Each section sent an equal number of members to the legislature, which after 1849 was, in its operations, bilingual. As the Protestant English population of the colony came to surpass the Roman Catholic French portion, concern for protection of the latter population grew. Seen from this perspective, federalism was a shield.

The story of Canadian federalism is, to a large extent, an account of the successes and failures at harmonizing the often conflicting objectives of purpose and protection. Nowhere was the difficulty associated with reconciliation more evident than in the series of provincially based conflicts that pitted the (usually) French and Roman Catholic minority against the (inevitably) English and Protestant leaders of the majority (Cook 1965).

The demography and society of modern Canada are more complex than the dualism at the root of Confederation would suggest. Literally so, because mass immigration from continental Europe early in the past century and from Europe, the Caribbean, and Asia in the years after World War II challenged conventional interpretations of Canada, whether in or outside of Quebec. Here is an important explanation for the emergence in 1971 of the federal government's official policy of multiculturalism. Described as falling within a "bilingual framework," the policy arose in response to strong opposition from so-called "other ethnic groups" to the terms of reference of the Royal Commission on Bilingualism and Biculturalism (1963–1969), which spoke of Canada as being composed of "two founding peoples." In Quebec, language controversies beginning in the 1970s, and legislative initiatives by provincial governments of different partisan stripes to promote the use of French, constituted a comparable response to societal change in that province.

Societal change within a province and governmental response to that change are understandable subjects of federal study. Less susceptible to conventional federal analysis is the increasing urbanization of Canada's population: from 54% in 1941 to 80% in 2001. Constitutionally, local government falls under provincial jurisdiction. Cities, such as Toronto, the country's commercial and transportation hub, 45.7% of whose population in 2006 was not born in Canada, depend upon provincial politicians to be their voice.

Similarly, Aboriginal peoples and, particularly, "status Indians" for whom, according to section 91: 24, the Parliament of Canada has jurisdictional responsibility, present a conceptual challenge to Canadian federal theory. Faster than the population in general, the Aboriginal component grew 45% between 1996 and 2006, from 2.8% to 3.8% of the total population (Curry 2008, A8). Like Canadians at large, the Aboriginal population, too, is becoming more urban. But, unlike the larger comparison group, it is divided among First Nations, Metis (those of mixed ancestry), and Inuit (of the far North). Except for the last, who through their predominance in a territory such as Nunavut have a political voice at the center, Aboriginal groups are divided among the provinces. Politically, they depend either upon provincial or federal governments over whom they exert little influence because they have been comparatively passive in electoral politics (Smith 1997), or upon sympathetic bureaucrats at both levels of government. Judicial redress of Aboriginal grievance has proved a more profitable route than partisan politics largely because the Canadian Charter of Rights and Freedoms (section 25) acknowledges "aboriginal, treaty or other rights and freedoms that pertain to the aboriginal people."

There are occasions when the federalism of the Constitution Act, 1867 or of Canadian history books, with its emphasis on English–French relations, seems removed from the urban, ethnic, and immigrant society large numbers of Canadians experience today. Yet, the old dualism continues to reassert itself, for example, in the form of a debate over Quebec being a distinct society, as was set down in the (ultimately) unsuccessful federal–provincial agreement known as the Meech Lake Accord (1987), or in the very close federalist victory in the Quebec referendum on secession (1995), or in the passage by the House of Commons of a resolution recognizing Quebec as a distinct society in a united Canada (2006).

The same could be said of the other, "purposive" federalism, where the provinces see themselves thwarted by Ottawa in its pursuit of growth, particularly in the area of natural resources. Examples are the federal government's National Energy

Policy of 1980 (deemed by Alberta and Saskatchewan to discriminate against them); the offshore oil and gas agreements concluded by Ottawa with Nova Scotia and Newfoundland and Labrador in the 1990s (deemed by the other provinces as prejudicial to them but preferential to the participating provinces); and the continuing controversy over equalization between Ottawa and the so-called have-not provinces that receive grants from the center to provide improved services to their residents despite the fact that the principle of equalization is entrenched in the Charter.

PARLIAMENTARY FEDERALISM

The first paragraph of the preamble to the Constitution Act, 1867 poses a contradiction with which the Canadian political system has wrestled for more than a century. The original provinces, it says, "expressed their desire to be federally united into One Dominion under the Crown of the United Kingdom…with a Constitution similar in Principle to that of the United Kingdom." How, then, to reconcile federation, distinguished by independent and coordinate spheres of jurisdiction and a division of powers, with a Constitution with a hallmark that is a supreme and sovereign Parliament?

The Constitution Act, 1867 and its amendments deal almost exclusively with the structure of the federation and not with parliamentary government. Excluding its attached schedules, the Act has 147 sections. Sections 9 to 16 deal with the executive power; sections 17 to 52, with the legislative power (basically the structure and composition of the Senate and the House of Commons); sections 58 to 87 and 134 to 147, with the provinces, largely Ontario and Quebec, with provincial constitutions that are found within the enactment that founds Canada. Sections 91 to 95 are the best known because they set out the division of powers that have been the prime source of federal–provincial legal wrangling. The remaining sections deal with taxation and revenues, and the composition of the judiciary. Thus, the skeleton of federalism is legislative in character. Although the details of the scheme, beginning with it being a parliamentary federation, are different from the U.S. Constitution adopted eight decades earlier, there is no doubt but that the inspiration for Confederation lay in the federal experiment the founding fathers had launched at Philadelphia.

Government, as that term is used in a Westminster–style system, was another matter. Section 9 of the Act states: "The Executive Government and Authority of and over Canada is hereby declared to continue and be vested in the Queen." The next section refers to, but does not create, the office of governor general; the one after that says that there "shall be…a Queen's Privy Council for Canada." All the rest as it relates to the operation of responsible government in a constitutional monarchy depends upon convention. By the time of Confederation, all the politicians of British North America had had two decades' experience with responsible government, which for them meant the Crown, in the form of the colonial governor, took advice from those members of the legislature who commanded the support of the elected chamber.

Regarding other elements of "unwritten constitution" inherited from the United Kingdom, ranging, for instance, from the role of the opposition parties to the meaning of a "defeat" in the Commons, to interpretation of the prerogative powers of the Crown, everything depended, respectively in these cases, upon evolving understandings between partisan politicians in Ottawa, rulings of the speaker (whose selection and duties, unlike his counterpart at Westminster, are set down in sections 44–49), or interpretations of the Constitution by nineteenth-century authorities like Walter Bagehot (1961). The desire may have been for a constitution similar in principle to that of the United Kingdom; but, without a codified document to imitate, differences were bound to appear, most particularly in respect to Canadian federalism.

With regard to cultural dualism, section 133 of the 1867 Act provides for the equal treatment of the English and French language in all the activities of Parliament, as well as in the legislature of Quebec, and in the courts of Canada established under the Act, or in any court in the province of Quebec. Thus, the dichotomy of language and culture that pressed for constitutional recognition late in the eighteenth century was acknowledged in and through the House of Commons at Confederation. Redistribution of federal electoral districts, which until the 1940s saw Quebec as the basis for calculating the allocation of seats to other provinces, now sees Quebec guaranteed seventy-five seats in the House of Commons regardless of the province's population decline relative to the national total. Through its standing orders and by convention, the House offered a model of bilingualism long before the enactment of the Official Languages Act. Alternation in the speaker's chair of persons fluent in one or other of the two languages, along with appointment of a deputy speaker possessing a full knowledge of the language *not* that of the speaker, testified to the integrative capacity of the lower chamber. In its operation and in its composition, the Commons was tailored less to fit Canadian federalism than it was to promote that polity at the center.

Aside from the Quebec dimension, territoriality is a weak feature of Canada's central legislative institutions. There are no committees of either chamber of Parliament mandated to deal with issues specific to a province or a region like the prairies (which conventionally means Manitoba, Saskatchewan, and Alberta) or the Atlantic provinces—that is, those provinces east of Quebec. Sometimes a matter will arise in Parliament of particular concern to a province or region, but it is treated as exceptional and temporary. Historically, national political parties do not wish to be confined to or identified with one or a few geographically concentrated provinces. Whether a proportional—rather than the current plurality-based—electoral system would nationalize campaigns even more than today, as some proponents believe (or, the reverse, as some others claim), is open to question. The fact remains that party discipline and the need to pull electoral support from more than one or even two provinces moderates the sense of territorialism in representation in the Commons.

It is in the executive, through a practice Canadians call the *federalization of the cabinet*—normally each province has at least one minister but total numbers per province reflect size of population and demographic heterogeneity (Gibson 1970; Smith 1984)—that federalism appears at the center in Canada. Canada's first prime minister, Sir John A. Macdonald, introduced this practice, whose roots lay in the coalition governments of United Canada, 1840–1867, and with it two features of Canadian federal politics that continue to this day. First, Canadian cabinets are necessarily large, because they must encompass personnel from all provinces and the principal linguistic, religious, and racial groups. Second, geography and demographic differences that are geographically identifiable take precedence to political philosophy. Canadian political parties are almost aggressively "atheoretical." Holding the federation together, more commonly referred to as *the quest for national unity*, is the preeminent task of Canadian parties. At one time, long-serving cabinet ministers in complete control of their portfolios and of the party in their provinces provided the bedrock of national politics (Ward and Smith 1990; Whitaker 1977). Changes in the media, technology, and the economy undercut the power of cabinet ministers but increased that of the prime minister's office (Savoie 1999). They (and the Charter of Rights and Freedoms after 1982) also gave interest groups and the general public in the provinces new avenues for the expression and redress of grievances. The national parties have been squeezed from the top and the bottom (Smith 2007).

The upper chamber of Parliament is the Senate of Canada. Its members are appointed (by the governor general on recommendation of the prime minister), originally for life, but after a constitutional amendment in 1965, they must now retire at age seventy-five. Although senators are appointed from within the individual provinces, and in the case of Quebec from constitutionally specified districts (a provision intended to protect the English-speaking and Protestant minority), their number is distributed not by province, as they are by states in the United States and Australia, but by senatorial district, of which there are currently four (Ontario, Quebec, the three Maritime provinces, and the four western provinces). Each district has twenty-four senators, although six additional senators were granted Newfoundland and Labrador on its joining Confederation in 1949. In addition, and from as early as 1887, senators were appointed from the Northwest Territories; today, there is one senator for each of the three northern territories: Yukon, Nunavut, and the Northwest Territories. Thus, the Canadian Senate is unelected, unequal, and, say its critics, ineffective.

Although the desire may have been for a constitution on the British model, it would be a mistake to see the Senate as a British North American House of Lords. Nor, as modern critics lament, is it a copy of the upper houses of the United States or Australia. On the contrary, the Canadian Senate was purposely made to deal with the foundational concerns of the 1867 union—in particular, Quebec's. For if representation-by-population was the rallying cry of Upper Canadians in the lead-up to Confederation, and if a Commons based on that principle may be viewed as Ontario's house, then the Senate, with equal numbers of senators from Ontario and

Quebec, may be seen as the Quebec counterpart. In addition, the guarantee of equal (regional but not provincial) representation with the more populous central provinces was responsible for the entry of the Maritime colonies. More time was spent by the colonial delegates at the Quebec conference in 1864 on the matter of the Senate than on any other question because the stakes were so high: "On no other condition," said George Brown, a prominent advocate of union, "could we have advanced a step" (Canada 1951, 88).

With the paradoxical exception of Quebec, which looks to government both in Ottawa and in Quebec City for recognition and protection of its distinctiveness, it is in the parts of the Canadian federation rather than at its center where difference is expressed. For instance, it was the provinces, because of their jealously guarded natural resources, that experimented with public development strategies (Nelles 1974). Similarly, it was the socialist government formed by the Cooperative Commonwealth Federation in Saskatchewan in 1944 that introduced hospitalization and medicare programs that later became models for comparable federal programs. The diversity that advocates of federalism customarily celebrate may only be experienced if one moves across the federation.

The English-speaking Fathers of Confederation would be surprised at this development, for, like later Australian observers, they, too, thought they had created a federal system based on the centralizing principle. And they had; the central government was granted, among others, unlimited taxing power, sweeping appointment power (senators, lieutenant governors, superior court judges in each province, and, after its creation in 1875, justices of the Supreme Court of Canada), as well as the power to disallow any piece of provincial legislation within one year of its passage, along with the power, exercised by the lieutenant governor, to reserve for the federal government's decision any Act he or she deemed of dubious constitutional or, for that matter, political worth. The letter of the 1867 Act was so clear that, a century later, the twentieth-century's best-known scholar of federal government described the Canadian arrangement as "quasi-federal in law [but] predominantly federal in practice" (Wheare 1953, 21).

The transformation was the work of the JCPC in London. After 1885, and as a result of judicial interpretation of the division of powers set out in sections 91 and 92, the pendulum of power swung from central to provincial jurisdiction (Cairns 1971; Saywell 2002). Section 91 had provided Parliament with a general or residual power to make laws for the "peace, order, and good government of Canada." To illustrate the ambit of that authority, the same section listed twenty-some fields of jurisdiction—for example, currency and coinage. In section 92, sixteen fields of jurisdiction were assigned to the provinces. From the mid 1880s, the JCPC interpreted this distribution in such a way as to limit Parliament, except in times of emergency such as war, to the fields noted in the illustrative list. At the same time, the JCPC interpreted "property and civil rights," which fell to the provinces, in such a broad manner as to create a de facto provincial residual power.

An index of the distinction Canada has attained as a consequence of this inversion of the founding fathers' intent may be seen in the matter of the treaty power.

The only reference to treaties in the Constitution Act, 1867 (section 132) speaks of "[t]reaties between the Empire and…Foreign Countries." As a result of the Statute of Westminster, 1931, by which Westminster acknowledged the legislative autonomy of Canada and the other Dominions, that provision became spent. In an opinion rendered by the JCPC in 1937, and in marked contrast to rulings by high courts in the United States and Australia on the same issue—whether a central government in a federation may (via treaty) acquire legislative authority it lacks under domestic distribution of powers—the treaty power in Canada was bifurcated. In consequence and to the present day, if the subject of a treaty falls within provincial jurisdiction, then the Crown in right of Canada, which is the sole personality recognized internationally to conclude a treaty, may not implement its obligation through federal legislation, but must depend for that effect upon cooperative action of the several provinces. Using this opinion as rationale, Quebec provincial governments have argued for a role in international discussions on the social and cultural subjects found under section 92. Membership and increased participation in *La Francophonie* (a French-speaking counterpart to the Commonwealth) is a federal counterresponse to Quebec's diplomatic ambitions.

It is frequently said that Canada is one of the most decentralized federal systems in the world (Simeon 2006, 1). If true, no event has contributed more to consolidating and centralizing power within the provinces than the emergence of the provincial Crown. In a constitutional monarchy, the Crown is the structuring principle of government—the prerogative exercised on advice of the political executive, the reservoir of power delegated to it by the legislature, its monopoly over appropriation measures, extensive appointment power, and authority over the organization of government—all these, the JCPC confirmed in Liquidators of the Maritime Bank (1892), applied with equal force to the Crown in the provinces as it did to the federal Crown. The implications of that opinion proved substantial, because the provinces' unicameral legislatures posed even fewer constraints on governmental use of Crown power than the bicameral Parliament (Smith 1995). Only five of the provinces ever had upper chambers. With the dates of abolition in parentheses, they were Manitoba (1876), New Brunswick (1891), Prince Edward Island (1893), Nova Scotia (1928), and Quebec (1968).

THE PROVINCES

Canada is an immense country of great diversity, including the size and population of its provinces. Of a total population (2006) of 31.6 million, Ontario has more than twelve million, whereas Quebec with 7.5 million is almost matched by the combined populations of Alberta and British Columbia. All the other provinces have almost static populations and—with the exception of Manitoba, with a population in 2006 that approached almost 1.2 million—have fewer than a million people, with Prince

Edward Island standing at just 135,000. The combined population of the three northern territories is fewer than 100,000. The Maritime provinces apart, the other seven share a common feature—they all have very large, resource-rich, sparsely populated northern hinterlands. Otherwise, most of the population in each is located close to the American border. Because provinces control natural resources, the provincial capital assumes a quasi-imperial role with regard to the exploitation and regulation of resources. For most Canadians, Canada is a horizontal country— from Atlantic to Pacific, bound in the first instance by the routes of the fur trade and, after Confederation, by the bands of steel of the transcontinental railroads. The North still does not figure in the consciousness of most Canadians. Notwithstanding that history, the axis of economic activity in most provinces is vertical, an alignment reinforced and extended by expanded trade with the United States under the Free Trade Agreement of 1989. A complementary feature is that most are identified with one or a few specific economic activities: Ontario, for example, with manufacturing and the financial services industries; Alberta and Saskatchewan with oil and gas; British Columbia with timber and fisheries.

Judicial interpretation of sections 91 and 92, along with geography and economy, work toward a common purpose: to strengthen the provinces. But not in a mathematician's sense. Population and resources are important in accounting for influence, but more important is what might be called the *institutional completeness* of a province. There is a long history of idiosyncratic and, from the perspective of Ottawa, difficult premiers. But it *is* history. Before World War II, men like Mitchell Hepburn of Ontario or William Aberhart were not engaged in province building when they confronted the federal government. Wanting "better terms" or simply more money is not the same thing. After World War II, province building, either by incremental means elsewhere or in Quebec through the Quiet Revolution bent on modernization, was ready to replace old regimes and values (Black and Cairns 1966; Young et al. 1984).

The first province to lead in this innovation and to become a model for the rest, was Saskatchewan. The election in 1944 of the Cooperative Commonwealther Federation (CCF), a socialist party with a platform that embraced economic planning and ambitious social programs, tested the limits of federalism. The CCF—and, in particular, its first premier in Saskatchewan, Tommy Douglas (crowned as the "greatest Canadian," following a television poll in 2004)—are now identified with medicare, the most popular public policy in the country. It is sometimes forgotten that the way medicare came about in Canada was via an indirect route. At the end of the war, the federal government proposed a national health scheme in Canada that resembled the one eventually introduced in Great Britain. Premiers like Duplessis of Quebec and Aberhart of Alberta resisted what they saw as federal "intrusion" into provincial jurisdiction. Douglas saw the matter differently: The goal of a policy was more important than the jurisdiction carrying it out. If health reform could not be achieved as Ottawa intended, then it could arise by another mechanism—Ottawa's sharing the cost of medical services with the provinces. In other words, like-minded politicians at both levels of government, even when of different political parties, could work together, cooperatively, to achieve a common end through fiscal federalism. In the decades after 1944, Saskatchewan pioneered in the delivery of health services to its provincial residents; in the late 1950s and into the mid '60s, under the leadership of sympathetic Progressive Conservative and Liberal governments, Ottawa worked to make these programs available to all Canadians.

Before its policies could be realized, however, Saskatchewan had to be inventive on another front: administration. It was this province, one of the worst hit by drought and depression less than a decade before, that began the bureaucratic revolution that would transform provincial government in Canada. Designing and implementing complex programs within the parliamentary timetable required economic planning, budgetary oversight, and a bureaucracy based on competition and merit. Other provinces followed Saskatchewan's lead, even (on occasion) hiring some of its public servants. Modernizing the state had long-term implications for Saskatchewan and for Canada, because the CCF, later renamed the New Democratic Party (NDP), remained in power in Regina for decades after 1944.

In 1997, when the Supreme Court of Canada heard arguments about whether Quebec might secede unilaterally from the federation, the Saskatchewan NDP attorney general made a convincing argument in opposition to that proposition. Two "principles," he said, underlay Confederation—the "federal principle" and the "nation principle": "Federalism permits the continuation of societies and their core defining institutions, within a national structure." When it came to write its opinion, the Court quoted approvingly from Saskatchewan's factum: "A nation is built when the communities that comprise it make commitments to it, when they forego choices and opportunities on behalf of the nation.... The threads of a thousand acts of accommodation are the fabric of a nation" (Canada 1998, paragraph 96).

The courts and the division of powers, the politicians and federal–provincial relations (the most visible illustration of what is often called *executive federalism*)— these perspectives emphasize conflict more than they do accommodation. Yet it is the latter, whether one is speaking of territorial or cultural federalism, that explains the longevity of Confederation. Federation persists because the relationship between the center and the parts is essentially one of reciprocity, whether measured collectively or individually, concretely or abstractly. The guarantees set down in the Charter (Constitution Act, 1982, part I) as well as the commitment to promote "equal opportunities for the well-being of Canadians" (Constitution Act, 1982, part III) are central to the architecture of modern Canada. It is noteworthy that they are also part of the expanding "written" Constitution. So, too, are guarantees of rights of Aboriginal peoples, official languages, and minority language educational rights. The cliché about challenges versus opportunities appears appropriate in this context, for it is far from clear how the interplay of pan-Canadian values and "provincial rights" will proceed or which order of jurisdiction it will benefit. In this regard, the Charter and rights, more generally, are the frontier of the twenty-first century.

After Confederation, the *frontier*, as that term was used to describe the harnessing of the West for the use of homesteaders and founding a national economy based on grain, strengthened the central government for some decades. It was a tenet of British constitutional practice that natural resources accompanied any conferral of self-government. This happened with Ontario and Quebec, with constitutional origins that lay in the 1867 Act that created Canada. It happened when the other provinces, with constitutional roots that lay in a series of imperial orders-in-council, became self-governing. But it did not happen when Parliament passed the Manitoba Act (1870), or the Saskatchewan and Alberta Acts in 1905. In those instances, Parliament retained the resources of the prairie provinces for "the purposes of the Dominion" (Martin 1973), central to which was the use of land to attract settlers and build railroads. They were not transferred to the respective provinces until 1930, after several Royal Commission inquiries regarding what compensation the affected provinces should receive for being deprived of their resources, and after some decades of provincial government and intraparty pressure brought to bear on the Ottawa government. Nor were they transferred to the provinces with any knowledge regarding the wealth of oil and natural gas waiting to be discovered.

Ottawa's dealings with the frontier seemed perpetually inept and inflammatory, whether seen in the fear Aboriginal peoples at Red River felt in the nineteenth century for their land claims before the tide of the new or, a century later, in the outrage Alberta and Saskatchewan expressed for what in their minds was the federal government's confiscatory and unconstitutional taxation of the petrochemical industry. The problem, as David Mills, a prominent member of Parliament, noted early on was that the Conservatives—although his criticism might apply equally well to later Liberal governments—failed to do what "the theory of their system required" (Canada 1870a, 1178). Unfortunately, Mills failed to divulge the essence of that theory or in what respects the Conservatives had fallen short. Still, the nub of the complaint remained: There was no theory to apply to the West. At almost the same time, a Conservative minister (Christopher Dunkin) described the original members of Confederation—that is, Ontario, Quebec, and the Maritime provinces—as "the three kingdoms" (Canada 1870b, 280). The allusion was to the United Kingdom, which encompassed England, Scotland, and Ireland, along with the principality of Wales, and notwithstanding the diversity of which appeared to the Fathers of Confederation the paradigm of a successful nation.

How did the vast area west of Ontario fit in this, comparatively, tight "three-kingdoms" federation? For the first but not the last time, the creation in 1870 of a new province—the postage stamp–size province of Manitoba with a full complement of Canadian constitutional features (bicultural, bilingual, bicameral)—demonstrated at least one structural flaw with Confederation: Expansion of the federation threatened rather than strengthened the union. Again, early in the last century when the territory west of Manitoba sought provincial status, a proposal to create one new prairie province was rejected by the Liberal federal government of the day because such a massive entity would rival Ontario and Quebec. Rather than create new provinces and therefore upset the status quo, a few years later, a Conservative federal government transferred large portions of the Northwest Territories that embraced Hudson Bay to the existing provinces of Ontario, Quebec, and Manitoba.

One way for the federal government to limit the disruptive capacity of the West on the existing federation was for Ottawa to act like an imperial power and treat the

West as a colony. The retention of the prairie provinces' natural resources may be cited in support of that contention. So, too, were discriminatory freight rates and tariffs that favored manufacturing based in central Canada to the detriment of agriculture, and that formed staple indictments of national policies by western politicians. It was grievances like these that made the West a seed-bed of political protest and stony ground for the cultivation of national political party support.

After World War II, and in response to the winds of prosperity and technological change, it was widely expected by social scientists that Quebec society (dominated by the Roman Catholic Church) and the prairie West (ravaged by drought and depression) would be transformed into close approximations of modern, secular, urban Ontario. Paradoxically, when change did come, movement was toward divergence rather than convergence, and for reasons that may be traced to the double federation that exists at the heart of the Canadian federal system.

REGIONALISM

Aside from the senatorial divisions or regions on which Senate representation is based, there is no formal, constitutional acknowledgment of regions in Canada. All is provinces, even when the discussion turns to the Maritime provinces, which, from the beginning in economic matters, have often been treated as a unit. More than that, politics is a great leveler, so that on many issues a province is a province is a province. Federalism inhabits a world of governments, so much so that relations between the provinces and the center are less likely today to be labeled federal–provincial than they are intergovernmental. This nomenclature lends support to the theory that relations between governments in Canada are "diplomatic" in character (Simeon 1972). All this being said, regionalism as a counterweight to federalism and provincialism appears to be growing, and this in response to actions of federal and provincial governments themselves.

To take one example: Despite their different histories, the three prairie provinces were, for a long time, treated as a unit or region. Common topography, settlement, and constitutional origin would be one explanation, but almost as determining was the instrumental practice by Statistics Canada and its predecessor of collecting and reporting data by "region." Because of the rapid influx of population into the prairies after 1900, the federal government agreed to introduce in 1906 the first (of what was to last a half century) of quinquennial censuses. The prairie provinces became a statistical unit for other than government agencies, as witness reports of polling data from the first half of the last century. Societal and commercial patterns reflected this orientation. This was the era when Winnipeg was the undisputed capital of the region.

All of this changed after the war. The rise of oil and natural gas industries in Saskatchewan and Alberta, and the emergence of the CCF in the former province, with its distinctive social and economic planning philosophy, set the two western-most provinces apart from Manitoba (Richards and Pratt 1979). Indeed, it was possible to say that, over time, those two provinces became a common labor market, with (usually) people from Saskatchewan migrating to Alberta in search of work. Throughout this period, British Columbia was treated as a region unto itself (Resnick 2000). A significant cause for change in this bifocal perspective on the West came as a result of federal government initiative. After the federal general election of 1972, no Liberal was elected west of Manitoba. To fulfill the convention that the cabinet should be federalized with, in this instance, ministers from the three westernmost provinces, the prime minister selected one senator from each of the provinces to sit in cabinet.

Apropos the discussion of regionalism, Trudeau called together a meeting (the Western Economic Opportunities Conference [WEOC]), held at Calgary in 1973, of the four western provincial premiers and himself. That conference, which considered in some detail, and after extensive background preparation, the West's (not just the prairies') economic grievances against the federal government, which was televised and which was attended by NDP premiers from all but Alberta (represented by Progressive Conservative Peter Lougheed), acted as a catalyst for western provincial cooperation that continues to the present: "While the WEOC was a one-time event, the Western Premiers' Conference can trace its origins to that meeting and is now a well-established institution" (Meekison 2004, 183). Further to the matter at hand: "[Cooperation] goes beyond developing a common front for federal–provincial questions and extends as well to matters of interprovincial cooperation, one example being internal trade" (Meekison 2004, 191).

WEOC, like the legendary Royal Commission on Dominion–Provincial Relations of the late 1930s, with whose report modern conceptions of fiscal and jurisdictional federalism in Canada begin, demonstrated a truth about federal government here and doubtless elsewhere: Federalism cannot abide great discrepancies in standards. This is the case whether the issue at hand is health or employment, debt or taxation. Regional disparities are a threat to national unity. As such, they necessitate a response from the center. The reason for this is that, for at least seventy years, the belief has been growing that people matter more than their provincial governments. The Charter has done much to solidify that sentiment and to generalize it to all governments. At the same time, the proliferation of shared cost programs and the increasing sophistication of tax collection and tax-sharing arrangements point in the same direction.

CONCLUSION

There once was a debate about whether Confederation was an act or a pact—that is, whether constitutive power in 1867 lay at Westminster or with colonial politicians. In contrast to the United States and Australia, there was no room for the people. The balance of academic opinion favored act over pact because the colonies lacked legislative autonomy to create a separate order of government. Yet the question, with its binary answer, seems antique in the twenty-first century. In the future, constitutional change that does not involve the people is change that will never happen (Russell 2004).

To the extent that prediction is accurate, then the usual vocabulary associated with federalism, the provinces, and regionalism is seriously incomplete. Conflict of jurisdiction remains a necessary element of that vocabulary, just as are province-building and pan-Canadian initiatives. However, such phrases are no longer sufficient to a full understanding of the subject of Canadian federalism today. They fail to explain the argument, increasingly heard, that premiers are defenders of the federal "principle," and that the lists of legislative powers in sections 91 and 92 are not, together, exhaustive, but rather that both orders of government must, in matters like the environment or culture, work together to produce national policy. Conversely, traditional terminology makes no allowance for a higher law that binds all governments. Last, regionalism today is about much more than political geography: Race, language, gender, urban or rural location, all contribute to a regionalism of the mind far stronger than at any time in the past.

The first and, arguably, still among the most complex of parliamentary federations—bilingual, with an entrenched Charter of Rights and Freedoms—the Canadian Constitution stands apart from that of the United Kingdom its founders sought to imitate. It also stands apart from all others.

NOTES

1. After 1867, a series of amendments to the British North America Act (with the respective year of passage attached to the title) followed. In 1982, all these statutes received new nomenclature and they were brought together in Canada 2001 (*A Consolidation of the Constitution Acts, 1867 to 1982*).

2. "Prior to 1870, 'North-Western Territory' referred to the area outside Rupert's Land but still administered by the Hudson's Bay Company, mostly consisting of the lands that drained into the Arctic Ocean rather than Hudson's Bay. After the 1870 transfer of both regions to Canada, they became (minus the new province of Manitoba) 'the North-West Territory,' a name that has since evolved into 'Northwest Territories'" (Wilson 2007, xviii).

REFERENCES

Australia. [1897] 1986. *Official Report of the National Australasian Convention Debates, Adelaide Session*. Sydney: Legal Books Pty.

Bagehot, Walter. [1867] 1961. *The English Constitution*. New York: Dolphin Doubleday.

Beer, Samuel. 1978. Federalism, nationalism, and democracy in America. *American Political Science Review* 72: 9–21.

Black, Edwin., and Alan C. Cairns. 1966. A different perspective on Canadian federalism. *Canadian Public Administration* 9: 27–44.

Cairns, Alan C. 1971. The judicial committee and its critics. *Canadian Journal of Political Science* 4: 301–345.

Canada. 1870a. Debates of the House of Commons. April 25.

———. 1870b. Debates of the House of Commons. March 8.

———. [1865] 1951. *Parliamentary Debates on Confederation of the British North American Provinces*. Ottawa: King's Printer.

———. *Reference re Secession of Quebec* (1998) 2 S.C.R. 217.

———. 2001. *A Consolidation of the Constitution Acts, 1867 to 1982*. Ottawa: Department of Justice.

Cook, Ramsay. 1965. *Provincial Autonomy, Minority Rights and the Compact Theory, 1867–1921*. Study prepared for the Royal Commission on Bilingualism and Biculturalism. Ottawa: The Queen's Printer.

Curry, Bill. 2008. Rising number of natives creates "time bomb." *Globe and Mail*, January 16, A8.

Galligan, Brian. 1995. *A Federal Republic: Australia's Constitutional System of Government*. Melbourne: Melbourne University Press.

Gibson, Frederick W., ed. 1970. *Cabinet Formation and Bicultural Relations: Seven Case Studies*. Studies of the Royal Commission on Bilingualism and Biculturalism. Ottawa: Information Canada.

Martin, Chester. [1937] 1973. *Dominion Lands Policy*. Toronto: McClelland and Stewart.

McRae, K. 1974. *Consociational Democracy: Political Accommodation in Segmented Societies*. Toronto: McClelland and Stewart.

Meekison, J. Peter. 2004. The Western Premiers' Conference: Intergovernmental cooperation at the regional level. In *Reconsidering the Institutions of Canadian Federalism (Canada: The State of the Federation, 2002)*, ed. J. Peter Meekison, Hamish Telford, and Harvey Lazar, 183–209. Montreal: McGill-Queen's University Press.

Nelles, H. V. 1974. *The Politics of Development: Forests, Mines and Hydro-Electric Power in Ontario, 1849–1921*. Toronto: Macmillan of Canada.

Resnick, Phillip. 2000. *The Politics of Resentment: British Columbia Regionalism and Canadian Unity*. Vancouver: University of British Columbia Press.

Richards, John, and Larry Pratt. 1979. *Prairie Capitalism: Power and Influence in the New West*. Toronto: McClelland and Stewart.

Russell, Peter H. 2004. *Constitutional Odyssey: Can Canadians Become a Sovereign People?* 3rd ed. Toronto: University of Toronto Press.

Savoie, Donald. 1999. *Governing from the Center: The Concentration of Power in Canadian Politics*. Toronto: University of Toronto Press.

Saywell, John T. 2002. *The Lawmakers: Judicial Power and the Shaping of Canadian Federalism*. Toronto: University of Toronto Press.

Simeon, Richard. 1972. *Federal–provincial Diplomacy: The Making of Recent Policy in Canada*. Toronto: University of Toronto Press.

———. 2006. Making federalism work. In *Open Federalism*, 1–5. Kingston, Ont. : Institute of Intergovernmental Relations.

Smith, David E. 1984. The politics of the federal cabinet. In *Canadian Politics in the Eighties*, 2nd ed., ed. G. Williams and M. Whittington, 351–370. Toronto: Methuen.

———. 1995. *The Invisible Crown: The First Principle of Canadian Governmentv*. Toronto: University of Toronto Press.

———. 1997. Saskatchewan perspectives. In *Saskatchewan and Aboriginal Peoples in the 21st Century: Social, Economic and Political Changes and Challenges*, 4–36. Regina: Federation of Saskatchewan Indian Nations.

———. 2007. *The People's House of Commons: Theories of Democracy in Contention*. Toronto: University of Toronto Press.

Ward, Norman, and David Smith. 1990. *Jimmy Gardiner: Relentless Liberal*. Toronto: University of Toronto Press.

Watts, Ronald L. 1999. *Comparing Federal Systems*, 2nd ed. Montreal: McGill-Queen's University Press.

Wheare, K. C. 1953. *Federal Government*, 3rd ed. London: Oxford University Press.

Whitaker, Reginald. 1977. *The Government Party: Organizing and Financing the Liberal Party of Canada, 1930–58*. Toronto: University of Toronto Press.

Wilson, Garrett. 2007. *Farewell Frontier: The 1870s and the End of the Old West*. Regina: Canadian Plains Research Center.

Young, R. A., Philippe Faucher, and André Blais. 1984. The concept of province-building: A critique. *Canadian Journal of Political Science* 17(4): 783–818.

CHAPTER 6

QUEBEC

ALAIN NOËL

For almost twenty years, between the early 1960s and 1981, the provinces and the federal government tried to agree on a new constitution to replace the British North America Act, 1867 (BNA Act). They did not succeed, because of the lack of a consensus on the division of powers, the amending formula, and the status of Quebec in Canada. The Quebec government, in particular, would not approve of a new constitution without a revision of the existing division of powers that would grant it more leverage over social policy.

When a first ministers' constitutional conference began in November 1981, the same disagreements were evident. Eight provinces, including Quebec, stood opposed to the latest federal proposition for a new Constitution. The political context, however, had changed. For one thing, the Supreme Court had ruled at the end of September that a "substantial degree" of provincial consent, not unanimity, was required to change the Constitution. In addition, Prime Minister Pierre Elliott Trudeau had recently returned to power with a majority government. He was determined to obtain constitutional change. The Quebec government of René Lévesque, also just reelected, was still dealing with the aftermath of its 1980 sovereignty referendum defeat. Ottawa was on the offensive, Quebec on the defensive.

On November 4, the relatively united opposition of the provinces collapsed. Overnight, federal officials met with all provincial premiers except Lévesque and reached an agreement on a new constitutional package. All knew this package would be unacceptable to the Quebec government. Not only did the agreement fail to modify the division of powers along the lines long advocated by Quebec, it also made future changes on core aspects of the Constitution subject to unanimous provincial consent. What Saskatchewan premier Allan Blakeney described as "the tyranny of unanimity," noted Peter Russell (1993, 121), was "briefly lifted to put through a change in the amending process very much against Quebec's interests and then reimposed to ensure that the new process would be difficult, if not impossible to change in the future." The Constitution Act, 1982 was designed to last, but it could not have been adopted if the first ministers had respected the very rules they were creating for future generations.

All political parties represented in Quebec's National Assembly denounced this imposition, and subsequent Quebec governments have steadfastly refused to approve the country's main constitutional document. Attempts were made in the 1980s and '90s to bring Quebec in, but they failed. Modern-day Canada remained built over this division, which most politicians have come to see as better left unaddressed.

Quebec thus occupies a unique place in Canada's constitutional and political order, at once present and absent—a province like the others, but also one that stands aside. This peculiar constitutional status cannot but shape everyday politics in the province. Public attitudes toward Canada remain lukewarm and the rate of support for sovereignty rarely goes below 40%. At every general election since 1993, Quebec has sent a majority of sovereigntist members of Parliament to the House of Commons. On a number of policy issues, Quebecers also stand apart. In 1999, for instance, all first ministers except Lucien Bouchard, the Quebec premier (who was supported in his stand by the opposition Liberal Party) agreed on a new Social Union Framework Agreement. Quebec public debates and policy choices tend to be different as well, and contribute to define a distinct social model within Canada.

This unique political situation can be appraised in a number of ways. This chapter focuses on three dimensions: the difficulties and more or less frozen state of Canada–Quebec relationships, the distinct and evolving character of Quebec politics, and the contemporary challenges of governance in a complex, postmodern society. Anchored in constitutional history, the first theme allows us to identify continuities and discontinuities in Canada–Quebec relationships, and to see how the current stalemate basically reflects the preferences of the country's English-speaking majority. The second theme concerns Quebec politics as such. The aim is to show how much Quebec has changed throughout past decades, by developing a new social and political model—one that is distinct in North America, somewhat detached from Canada, but in tune with public attitudes in the province. The last theme looks at future challenges for Quebec, associated with the governance of the federation, but also with globalization, demographic change, and evolving public expectations about democracy and social justice.

THE QUEBEC AND CANADA STALEMATE

Canada is a young country, but an old federation. If we exclude ancient political arrangements that prefigured modern federalism, such as the Iroquois Confederation in North America, only the United States and Switzerland have older federal institutions (Watts 2008, 3). Canada's current federal regime was created in 1867, but the political regime was even older than the BNA Act. The colonies were already evolving toward democracy, as we now understand it, with responsible government and limited manhood suffrage.

When they agreed on the BNA Act, the Canadian founders were less influenced by the American, or contractual, view of constitutionalism than by an ancient, more British, understanding, whereby any new constitutional arrangement must recognize existing laws, institutions, and customs. Aboriginal rights acknowledged in old treaties and laws were incorporated more or less explicitly into the fabric of the constitution (Macklem 2001, 4–5, 136, 286–287), and so were the elements of dualism introduced first with the Quebec Act of 1774 and the Constitutional Act of 1791, and then with the accommodations devised by politicians to make the United Canada legislature work between 1841 and 1867. The country created in 1867 was thus less a new nation than "an irregular and multiform assemblage" that granted some recognition and autonomy to preexisting nations (Tully 1995, 142).

Almost immediately, interpretations diverged on the meaning of the BNA Act. "Within months of Confederation," wrote historian Arthur Silver, a "Canada First Group" was created to promote the idea of a single Canadian nationality "with a common vision and sense of purpose" (Silver 1997, 250). From this perspective, soon dominant in English-language newspapers, French Canadian distinctiveness or, even worst, a special status for Quebec constituted threats that could undermine the country. "Canada needed to become a nation—like the United States, united and strong" (Silver 1997, 221, 251).

By contrast, Quebecers saw the new federation as an arrangement that acknowledged the existence and self-governing capacity of their own nation, "an autonomous French Canadian country under the control of French Canadians." Far from adhering to a new Canadian nation, they sought in Confederation "the greatest possible amount of provincial *sovereignty*....combined with a modicum of federal *association*" (Silver 1997, 218–219 [emphasis in original]).

Quebec nationalist leader Henri Bourassa summed up this perception in 1902, with his theory of a "double pact," according to which Canada was at once a partnership between two peoples, English and French, and an agreement between provincial governments, working together in a decentralized federation. The dualist, binational foundations of the country affirmed both the specific character of Quebec society and the rights of francophone minorities across Canada; the interprovincial pact underscored the legislative and financial autonomy of the provinces in the federation (McRoberts 1997, 19–23; Silver 1997, 250).

The Canadian federation could thus be understood in opposite ways, either as the creation of a new nation or as a partnership between two existing nations now organized in an array of autonomous provinces. All along, tensions were fueled by these opposed visions, sometimes leading to genuine political crises, as with the hanging of Louis Riel in 1885, the adoption of conscription in World War I, or the abolition of bilingual schools in Manitoba in 1916. During the first half of the century, however, Canada remained a rather decentralized federation, resulting in part

from powerful political currents in favor of the provinces and in part from decisions from the Judicial Committee of the Privy Council (see chapter 5, this
volume).

The balance of political forces began to shift during the 1930s. Particularly
severe in Canada, the Great Depression shook provincial governments, especially in
the West, and reinforced the case for a predominant, interventionist federal government. In 1937, Prime Minister William Lyon Mackenzie King appointed a Royal
Commission to reexamine the workings of the federation in light of this experience.
Released three years later, the report of the Rowell-Sirois commission recommended
making unemployment and old-age insurance federal responsibilities, leaving all
personal, corporate, and inheritance taxes to the federal government, and supporting the provinces with federal transfers based on their fiscal needs (Guest 1980,
91–92). Responsibilities over unemployment insurance and old-age insurance were
ceded to the federal government by constitutional amendments in 1940 and 1951
and, during wartime in 1942, the provinces agreed to let Ottawa levy all direct taxes,
presumably on a temporary basis for the duration of the war, but, as time would
show, in effect permanently.

More fundamentally, the Rowell-Sirois commission outlined a new vision for
the country, in which the ancient arrangements of a decentralized federation
appeared less relevant and engaging than the search for efficient and generous programs that would be designed on a "national" basis and supported by countrywide
sharing. This idea of a "national standard for social programs," observed James Rice
and Michael Prince (2000, 59–60), "reverberated through the politics and practices
of Canadian federalism ever since."

Bent on preserving its autonomy, the Quebec government resisted this evolution. In 1953, Premier Maurice Duplessis appointed his own Royal Commission on
constitutional problems to define a concurrent vision. Three years later, the Tremblay
report reaffirmed the paramount importance for Quebec of the federal principle,
and proposed to leave the main financial resources to the provinces, which had clear
constitutional responsibilities for rapidly expanding social programs. The report
also denounced the use of what Ottawa called a "federal spending power"—nowhere
to be found in the BNA Act—regularly invoked to intervene in areas of provincial
competence. For "what would be the good of a careful distribution of legislative
powers, if one of the governments could get around it and, to some extent, annul it
by its taxation methods and its fashion of spending?" (Royal Commission of Inquiry
of Constitutional Problems 1956, 217). Meanwhile, Duplessis had occupied unilaterally part of the income tax field, making Quebec the first and still only province
with its own self-managed personal income tax.

In the 1950s, this emerging Canada–Quebec confrontation was limited by the
conservative orientations of the contending governments. The Duplessis government, in particular, remained reluctant to intervene in social matters, and was
mostly bent on preventing federal interventions in areas of provincial competence.

The election of a reformist Quebec government led by Liberal Jean Lesage in
1960 brought matters to a head. Committed to expanding social programs on its

own, the Lesage government reinterpreted the autonomist message of the Tremblay commission in a progressive fashion. For a while, Ottawa proved accommodating. The Liberal government of Lester B. Pearson allowed Quebec to opt out of a number of federal programs with financial compensation sufficient to create distinct provincial programs. In 1964, notably, Ottawa accepted that Quebec create its own pension program, alongside the Canada Pension Plan. For Pearson, this was possible, indeed necessary, because Quebec was different: "[I]t is more than a province because it is the heartland of a people: in a very real sense it is a nation within a nation" (quoted in McRoberts 1997, 40).

This opening, sensitive to the country's dualism, would not last. Almost immediately, resistance to opting out grew within the federal public service, in the House of Commons, and in public opinion (quoted in McRoberts 1997, 42–45). When Pierre Elliott Trudeau, a Quebec intellectual opposed to any form of special status for his province, entered federal politics in 1965, the tide had turned. He had no difficulty rallying a majority to his avowedly undifferentiated, individualist view of Canada. From then on, the federal government would promote institutional bilingualism and multiculturalism, but refuse the national dualism sought by the Quebec government (Simeon and Robinson 1990, 188–189).

Trudeau was helped in this task by the apparently unending escalation of demands coming from Quebec. A constitutional reform proposal had failed in 1966 because the agreed-upon compromise ended up being insufficient for the Lesage government. Later that year, a new Quebec government led by Daniel Johnson was elected with a call for "equality or independence." At about the same time, former Lesage minister René Lévesque formed a sovereigntist party, the Mouvement Souveraineté Association, which would later be renamed Parti québécois (PQ) to become, by 1970, the province's official opposition.

Options were indeed polarizing, with Trudeau and his monist view of Canadian unity on one side, and Lévesque and his proposal for sovereignty association on the other. Little room was left for accommodation. The defeat of the sovereignty association project in the Quebec referendum of 1980, with a strong 59.5% for the no side, opened the door to Trudeau's own solution—a made-in-Canada Constitution Act with a Charter of Rights and Freedom, adopted without the approval of Quebec's National Assembly in 1981–1982.

A desire for compromise and closure nevertheless remained. In September 1984, the Progressive Conservative Party of Brian Mulroney won a convincing victory with a program of "national reconciliation" meant to improve relations between Ottawa and the provinces, and to bring Quebec to sign the Constitution. At about the same time, a Liberal government led by Robert Bourassa was elected in Quebec, and it put forward specific and modest conditions for a constitutional agreement. By April 1987, the first ministers had reached a consensus, the Meech Lake Accord, which notably recognized Quebec as a "distinct society" and limited the use of the federal spending power. Before all provincial legislatures could approve this Accord, however, opposition mounted in Canada. Many objected, in particular, to the

Accord's reference to Quebec as a distinct society, seeing this recognition as contrary to the idea that all citizens and all provinces should be equal (McRoberts 1997, 198–199). When, by the deadline of June 30, 1990, the Accord failed to receive the approval of all provincial legislatures, political tensions increased across the country and support for sovereignty reached record levels in Quebec. The Charlottetown Accord, a subsequent attempt at constitutional change, also failed, for lack of public support in a 1992 pan-Canadian referendum.

In October 1995, the PQ government of Jacques Parizeau held a referendum on sovereignty, and lost it by barely 54,288 votes. With an extremely high turnout of 93.52%, the no side won with 50.58%, against 49.4% for the yes. Quebec sovereigntists could have rejoiced in this unprecedented result, but they nevertheless were defeated, and the bitter remarks of Parizeau on referendum night made a positive reading of the outcome difficult. In Canada, this "near-death" experience gave additional weight to those who argued for a hard-line approach to Quebec sovereignty. The government of Jean Chrétien sponsored an array of events to advertise Canada in Quebec to little avail. Parliament also adopted a Clarity Act, according to which the Canadian House of Commons has an obligation to declare whether it considers any referendum question announced by a provincial government acceptable, and whether, in the event Ottawa would lose, it accepts the winning majority as sufficient (Clarity Act 2000). Inimical to the federal principle and incoherent with the democratic preference for transparent, preestablished rules about the required winning majority, this Act was introduced in response to a fairly balanced judgment from the Supreme Court, which declared that a clear referendum expression of support for secession would impose an obligation to negotiate on all parties (Supreme Court of Canada 1998, article 88). The purpose of the Act was to circumscribe and downplay this obligation to negotiate introduced by the Court (Rocher and Verrelli 2003, 218).

From a constitutional standpoint, Quebec and Canada have thus reached an impasse. Quebecers remain unhappy with a Constitution adopted without their consent, and the appeal of sovereignty continues to distance many from Canadian politics, even though public support for change does not seem sufficient to warrant another referendum (Mendelsohn et al. 2007). Canadians outside Quebec appear more satisfied with a Constitution that institutionalizes their preference for a monochrome Canada and seem more than happy to move on to other questions, but they must do with a reluctant partner that often prefers to stay on the sidelines (Laforest 1993, 86). Short of a radical political move by Quebecers, this situation is unlikely to change. Significant constitutional change now requires the unanimous approval of Parliament and all provincial legislatures. In some provinces, it must also receive majority approval in a referendum (Taillon 2007).

This stalemate does not mean that Quebec and Canada cannot evolve. Throughout the years, each society has changed significantly. Quebec certainly was transformed by the broader social and political debates that accompanied its quest for a new constitutional status.

Quebec Transformed

Historically, Quebec has been a relatively poor region of North America, and the home of a French Canadian population that was also disadvantaged in its own society. Compared with Ontario, Quebec had lower income per capita and higher unemployment rates and, within the province, French Canadians stood as one of the poorest ethnic groups. In 1961, at the start of the Quiet Revolution, the average income of Quebec francophones was about two thirds (66%) that of the province's anglophones. Francophones tended to occupy low-skilled, low-paying jobs, whereas anglophones predominated in skilled and management positions. The main economic leverages tended to escape francophones. Even within the Quebec government, the minister of finance (earlier the treasurer) was, until 1944, almost always an anglophone (Levine 1997, 55). Language skills alone could not explain this division of labor and these income differences. On average, a bilingual francophone earned less than a bilingual anglophone, and they both had lower incomes than a monolingual anglophone. "Ethnic origin," noted the Royal Commission on Bilingualism and Biculturalism (1969, 21–23) established by the Pearson government, seemed to have "a greater impact on incomes than…linguistic knowledge."

A number of factors explained the relative poverty of the province, notably less favorable initial conditions for agriculture, and an abundance of labor, which depressed wages, encouraged emigration, and favored investments in less productive, low-wage sectors such as textiles and clothing. Combined with the lack of a strong francophone business sector and the existence of a clear ethnic cleavage, this relative poverty gave rise to a dual labor market, where linguistic discrimination became the norm (Noël 1993, 424–428).

Social disparities such as these tend to last. Inequalities anchored in existing categories are ubiquitous in human societies, and they normally endure because they rest on institutionalized practices of social closure and control that are reproduced through time. Men versus women, blacks versus whites, Indians versus non-Indians, Catholics versus Protestants, Flemish versus Walloons, regardless of the dichotomy, powerful social mechanisms emerge that make categorical inequalities durable (Tilly 1998, 7–9). A recent World Bank report uses the term "inequality traps" to explain how social and economic inequalities engender institutions, rules, and power relations that reinforce and perpetuate, rather than attenuate, initial disadvantages (World Bank 2005, 20–23). In Quebec, the linguistic divide created such a trap. Quebec Liberation Front militant Pierre Vallières presented this reality in stark terms when he entitled his 1968 hard-hitting essay *White Niggers of America* (Vallières 1971).

By definition, a social trap is not easily eliminated. For change to occur, argues sociologist Charles Tilly (1998, 227), members of the subordinate category must "not only mobilize broadly but actually gain power." Gaining and exercising power, however, is difficult. Consider the case of Quebec. French-speaking Quebecers certainly had a provincial government of their own, and they controlled a host of municipal and social institutions as well. Yet, they long seemed reluctant to use political power actively to undo their economic and social subordination.

This relative passivity was often attributed to the hold of outdated ideologies or the dominance of traditionalist elites. In his 1956 essay on Quebec's asbestos strike, for instance, Trudeau (1974, 65, 17) blamed "our ideologies, which featured a ready-made suspicion of industrialization, withdrawal into the self, and peasant nostalgia," and prevented state intervention or "any political action likely to result in economic reforms." There were, however, significant reformist currents pushing for change at least since the 1930s, a fact that brought many authors to emphasize less ideas than the lasting power of traditionalist elites (Behiels 1985; Vaillancourt 1988, 64–66). Reformist movements, however, also existed that challenged these elites.

The focus of these conventional explanations on ideologies and elites was not so much wrong as incomplete. Conservative views had a strong hold in Quebec politics because the relative poverty of the province and its linguistic economic cleavage contributed to create a major obstacle to change: a political life marred by distrust and patronage. Politics, in Quebec, was disreputable, and as a consequence state intervention held few promises, even for those who were not wedded to conservative ideologies.

Patronage, of course, was not unique to Quebec. John A. Macdonald relied extensively on partisan favors and appointments to consolidate his party and government, and he considered patronage "the true constitutional principle," without which responsible government would be impossible. Pivotal in the country's formative years and elevated to the status of a constitutional practice by its founders, partisan favoritism became entrenched in Canada, more so than in the United Kingdom or the United States (Simpson 1988; Stewart 1982, 21–22, 29).

The same was true in Quebec, but with more profound consequences. Because the province was relatively poor and because French Canadians had little access to high-level jobs in the private sector, the politics of patronage became particularly intense. Partisan politics generated passions precisely because it worked as an important distributive process. But at the same time it became despised as skewed and corrupt. Quebec's political culture thus sustained both "a climate of strong party loyalties" and "a profound cynicism about politics and politicians, and deep anxiety about the corroding influence of politics on many areas of national life" (Heintzman 1983, 18). To sum up, it was not state intervention as such that Quebecers resisted, presumably out of conservatism, but rather politics itself, because it would vitiate any reform undertaken by the state (Heintzman 1983, 31).

There is a universal dimension to this problem. In countries where citizens have good reasons to have little trust in each other and in public institutions, even well-meaning persons, who would prefer fair rules and reforms, refrain from acting positively or even faithfully because such a behavior would be self-defeating. Why should one respect the law, pay taxes, or promote social justice if nobody does and if tax money is not put to good use? Distrust thus breeds distrust, creating a second type of social trap, wherein few dare invest in much-needed public actions and state interventions. It is relatively easy to contrast low-trust societies, in which corruption is rampant, with high-trust ones, in which law abiding is the norm, but much more difficult to chart the road that may lead from one situation to the other or, to borrow from Swedish political scientist Bo Rothstein, figure out how to go "from Moscow to Stockholm" (2005, 6–7).

Consider, for instance, how Trudeau, who roundly denounced Quebec society's resistance to change, himself declined to promote the very reforms he claimed were necessary. In a 1958 Democratic Manifesto, he wrote:

> [T]his is why I am not otherwise hurried to call for nationalizations and controls in the province of Quebec: incompetence, fraud and oppression already characterize public administration at all levels in our society (provincial, municipal, school boards, parishes) and the population proves unable to bring correctives to this: would we be much better served if by circumstances this same State decided to nationalize and manage everything, placing its venal and mediocre creatures at the head of hospitals, universities, professional corporations, trade unions, public services, and large industries? [author's translation] (quoted in Heintzman 1983, 42)

Trudeau preferred waiting for an eventual transformation of mentalities or else counted only on the federal government. Even after 1960, in the midst of the Quiet Revolution, he remained skeptical, seeing in the debates and reforms of the time little other than verbal agitation and nationalist bravado (Lévesque 1986, 232–233; McRoberts 1997, 59).

To build trust, however, there is no escaping public deliberation and determined state intervention. More precisely, according to Bo Rothstein (2005, 199, 210–211), three ingredients are needed: first, transformative actions undertaken by political leaders and carried on by the state to demonstrate that there is a "new game in town"; second, an open democratic process that allows for dialogue and deliberation to challenge prevailing patterns; and third, institutions that establish universal rules and increase equality, to sustain trust and social capital.

This is precisely what the Quiet Revolution was about. Often presented as a mere process of catching up, modernization, or provincial state building, the period that began with the election of Jean Lesage and the Liberals in 1960 was in fact a moment of profound renovation in Quebec politics (Heintzman 1983, 50–51). Two social traps were effectively undone more or less at once: the low-trust trap of Quebec politics and the French–English inequality trap that marred Quebec society.

First came debates and determined political actions to break the mold of patronage, distrust, and inaction. "The only power at our disposal," said Premier Jean Lesage, "is the state of Quebec.... If we refuse to use our state, we would deprive ourselves of what is perhaps our only means of survival and development in North America" (quoted in Simeon and Robinson 1990, 179). The civil service was reformed and expanded, electoral and campaign finance laws were changed, new departments and Crown corporations were created, and a host of economic and social policies were introduced. The general idea was to make politics reputable again, so that the state could become, in the words of René Lévesque, "one of us, the best of us" [author's translation] (quoted in Levine 1997, 85). At the same time, language, economic, and education policies attacked linguistic inequalities and, in due course, would come to eliminate them thoroughly.

These transformations took time. Major steps were still taken in the late 1970s, when PQ and Lévesque came to power. Two PQ laws, in particular, proved determinative: first, the 1977 law on political party financing, which forbade any contributions by business, trade unions, or groups, and restricted individual donations to $3,000 a year (Godin 2001, 157; Lévesque 1986, 386; Tremblay 2006, 193). This law, which Premier Lévesque saw as his most significant achievement, instituted the strictest party financing rules in the world and made Quebec politics practically scandal free for decades, thus consolidating the cultural turn initiated by the Lesage government. Second, Bill 101, the Charter of the French Language, which required public signs and commercial advertising to be in French, reserved English-language schools for children whose parents had been educated in English in Quebec, and demanded that major companies adopt programs to allow their employees to work in French (McRoberts 1988, 276–277). With the 1977 law on party financing, the new linguistic regime completed the transformation launched during the 1960s.

By the 1980s, the two social traps that plagued Quebec had been undone, and trust and linguistic equality were anchored solidly. During the process, an entire society was transformed. A new political culture emerged that was shaped by two decades of mobilization and state intervention. Compared with other North Americans, Quebecers had become more egalitarian and less authoritarian, more supportive of gender equality, and more favorable to trade unions and state intervention. All in all, Quebec stood out as "the most consistently Liberal" and "most postmodern" society on the continent (Adams 2003, 82; Baer et al. 1993, 28). When asked whether government "should see to it that everyone has a job and a decent standard of living" rather than being left "to get ahead on his [sic] own," 73% of French-speaking Canadians (mostly Quebecers) agreed, compared with 44% of English-speaking Canadians and 24% of Americans (Perlin 1997, 89). In 2002, 68% of Quebecers agreed that "it is the responsibility of the government to reduce the differences in income between people with high incomes and those with low incomes," compared with 42% in the rest of Canada (Mendelsohn et al. 2007, 50). A clear marker of the Left–Right ideological divide, this last question resonates to people practically all over the world (Noël and Thérien 2008, 32–55). Indeed, it conveys at once a person's support or lack of support for equality and her trust or distrust in state intervention. Quebec's recent history was one of reforms meant to build trust in the state and promote equality. Not surprisingly, it left Quebecers well disposed toward an active and egalitarian state.

Well disposed and well organized. Indeed, the mobilization of the 1960s and '70s dotted Quebec with strong collective organizations. Trade unions, for instance, came to negotiate collective agreements for 40.5% of the labor force in 2006, compared with 28.2% in Ontario and 13.1% in the United States (Labrosse 2007, 3). Faced with a strong labor movement, business also organized, which facilitated socioeconomic collaboration and coordination (Haddow and Klassen 2006, 48–49, 124–126). The feminist movement was also shaped by this context, as it grew and developed alongside a strong labor movement and a host of popular and social movements. Peak associations, networking, and collaborative practices multiplied to encompass most activities, groups, sectors, and regions, and to define something like a distinct social model, anchored in participation and egalitarianism (Hamel and Jouve 2006, 7). A comparative study of gender attitudes attributed to these patterns of mobilization the fact that Quebec ended up as "the most progressive social space" in North America (Adams 2003, 87; Clement and Myles 1994, 234).

Public policies reflected these values. For one thing, the Quebec state remained rather interventionist. If we leave aside the smaller Atlantic provinces, Quebec had, in 2006, the highest provincial revenues and expenditures per capita (Observatoire de l'administration publique 2007b, 8; 2007c, 8). Second, social policies acquired a social–democratic character, even though the general context remained that of a Liberal welfare state (Bernard and Saint-Arnaud 2004). Quebec, for instance, spent more per capita than any other province on health and social services (Observatoire de l'administration publique 2007a, 6), and it did so as well on family policy. In the 2000s, these differences became striking. For families, Quebec expenditures as a share of gross domestic product and the type of help and services provided— income support for parents, universal public daycare, a generous parental leave program—moved closer to what could be found in Scandinavia or France than to the typical Canadian situation (Ministère de la Famille, des Aînés et de la Condition féminine 2007, 20; Roy and Bernier 2006, 95). These policies contributed to a rise in the province's birth rate, and they contributed, as well, to give Quebec the lowest level of child poverty in Canada (Ministère de la Famille, des Aînés et de la Condition féminine 2007, 25–29; Ministère de la Santé et des Services sociaux and Institut national de santé publique du Quebec 2007, 67–69). Taxation in Quebec also tended to be more progressive (Boothe and Boothe 2006; Godbout 2005, 22–24). Combined with relatively generous social programs, this tax structure produced a more even distribution of income than anywhere else in Canada (Rigaud et al. 2008, 28).

Nearly fifty years after the beginning of the Quiet Revolution, Quebec had become a different, postmodern society. French speaking and North American, this transformed society placed much value on equality, and organized itself in dense associative networks that were recognized, supported, and consulted by a relatively interventionist and generous welfare state. A Quebec model had emerged. This model, however, never went undisputed. Intense debates accompanied its creation, and, unsurprisingly, they continued in the face of new challenges.

Looking Ahead

Quebec's political landscape is largely defined by the two debates presented so far: the first over recognition and autonomy within Canada, which in effect is a debate about national identity, and the other over economic development and social justice, which basically opposes the Left and the Right. After the 1995 referendum, the first debate appeared muted. Sovereignty was not an option in the short term, and all agreed that the Canadian Constitution was unlikely to be amended. The question of autonomy, however, came back through a conflict on fiscal imbalance between Ottawa and the provinces. In parallel, preoccupation about national identity was rekindled by popular concerns over the institutional accommodations associated with multiculturalism. As for the debate over social and economic development, it first seemed less intense because Quebec politics remained rather consensual over questions of public policy and social justice, but it never vanished. All in all, the Quebec Liberal Party defended more mainstream, market-oriented approaches, and the PQ vied for more distinctive, social–democratic orientations (Haddow and Klassen 2006, 123–130). Given this relatively consensual context, some debates were likely to be defined outside the partisan arena. This is what happened in 2005, when a group organized around former Premier Lucien Bouchard launched a manifesto calling for a more "lucid" adjustment to North American public policy norms.

Consider, first, the autonomy and fiscal imbalance issues. In 1995, the federal government restructured and cut transfers to the provinces to reduce its own deficit. The turn was drastic and the impact severe. Between 1994–1995 and 1997–1998, cash social transfers to the provinces were reduced by a third (33%), and the federal share of social programs' financing went from 18.1% to 11.8% (Commission on Fiscal Imbalance 2002, 81–82). As a result, in just a few years, Canada became the only G7 country able to obtain a budgetary surplus year after year (Courchene 2008, 37). Provincial governments, however, were left with lower federal transfers to meet rising social expenditures, in particular for health care.

Faced with this radical and unannounced federal retrenchment, provincial governments allied together to propose a more structured, more predictable social union process for the country, in which the level and conditions of federal transfers would be negotiated between governments, and in which a province could opt out with compensation if it preferred to run its own program (a perennial Quebec demand). This interprovincial proposal failed to move the federal government, however, and it was replaced by a watered-down version conceived by Ottawa, the 1999 Social Union Framework Agreement, which Quebec refused to sign and which ended up being, for all practical purpose, irrelevant (Noël 2002; Noël et al. 2003, 3–4).

The Quebec government soon reopened the debate by creating a commission to assess the distribution of financial resources between the federal government and the provinces. In its 2002 report, the Séguin commission concluded that there was, indeed, a fiscal imbalance in the federation, because the gap between federal and provincial revenues had become too wide given the responsibilities attributed by the Constitution to each order of government, and because federal transfers did not correct this gap adequately. The report proposed the abolition of existing social transfers, which were to be replaced by a new division of financial resources giving more revenues to the provinces, as well as measures to improve the equalization

program and limit the use of the federal spending power, "a means of intervention…whose constitutionality has not been established" (Commission on Fiscal
Imbalance 2002, 115).

The federal government rejected this proposal, arguing that the provinces
remained free to increase their own revenues, but all provincial governments and
many experts concurred, a consensus facilitated by mounting federal surpluses
(Noël 2005). In its own report on the question, the Council of the Federation reached
similar conclusions. A federal expert panel on equalization and territorial formula
financing also concluded that reforms were needed to restore the equalization program (Noël 2007b). During the federal electoral campaign that took place at the end
of 2005 and beginning of 2006, all parties except the outgoing Liberal Party promised to address the question. Conservative leader Stephen Harper, in particular,
made a commitment to eliminate fiscal imbalance and limit, as well, the use of the
federal spending power, to put an end to an era of "domineering and paternalistic
federalism" (Harper, quoted in Noël 2006a).

In its March 2007 budget, the Harper government followed up on these commitments. Social transfers were improved and made more stable, and the equalization program was reestablished on better foundations. These reforms did not,
however, eliminate the fiscal imbalance between the two orders of government.
Transfers improved but the gap between the revenues collected by Ottawa and by
the provinces remained important, still allowing the federal government to intervene in areas of provincial competence (Noël 2007a, 117–118). Debates over the issue
nevertheless decreased in intensity, with the Quebec government of Jean Charest
appearing somewhat satisfied with enhanced transfers. Disagreements persisted on
the Conservative engagement regarding the federal spending power, but the distance between Ottawa, Quebec, and the other provinces remained so important
that a significant evolution seemed unlikely. Meanwhile, a symbolic breakthrough
was achieved in 2007 with the acceptance by all parties in the House of Commons
of a motion presented by the prime minister to the effect that Quebecers form a
nation within Canada. Some ambiguity remained given the resolution's different
wording in French and in English, but a gesture was nevertheless accomplished,
with an indirect acknowledgment of the country's multinational character.

This relative truce in intergovernmental relations did not make Quebec debates
over nationality and identity any less intense. Indeed, as in many western nations,
public preoccupation developed during the mid 2000s over the accommodation of
cultural and religious differences in a diverse society. In Quebec, these issues are
necessarily tied to the national question, because they concern the fate of a language
and a culture still perceived as precarious in North America (Gagnon and Iacovino
2006). In May 2008, a commission cochaired by historian Gérard Bouchard and
philosopher Charles Taylor concluded that existing tensions had more to do with
perceptions than with actual conflicts. It recommended maintaining Quebec's
approach to integration, understood as "interculturalism" (Bouchard and Taylor
2008). Many disagreed with these conclusions. The two opposition parties in the
National Assembly (Action démocratique [ADQ] and PQ) suggested a broad public

debate on an internal Constitution for Quebec to clarify better the issues of identity and citizenship.

Visually, Quebec debates over the national question and identity could be represented on a vertical axis, with federalists at one end—say, on top—and sovereigntists at the other, at the bottom. The other axis of Quebec politics would then go from left to right, along lines familiar across the world, and divide those who favor efforts to promote equality, on the left, from those who think ensuring an equality of opportunity is by and large sufficient (see Noël and Thérien 2008). Because Quebec's modern history was largely defined by a fight against French–English inequalities, the egalitarian values of the Left gained a strong standing in public attitudes and institutions. These values, however, always remained contested. After 1970, when the PQ became the official opposition, the Quebec Liberal Party clearly became a center Right party and it was supported in its orientations by the main private newspapers and most business associations, which remained federalist and on the Right. Still, as explained earlier, the Quebec model tended to institutionalize center Left orientations.

In October 2005, a small group that included prominent former politicians, notably Lucien Bouchard, business persons, and experts, published a manifesto entitled "For a Clear-Eyed Vision of Quebec" (Bouchard et al. 2005, 5). Worried by population aging and demographic decline, which would undermine economic growth in a context of fierce global competition, the authors portrayed Quebecers as mired in their comfort and illusions, and they denounced "pressure groups of all kinds, including the big unions, which have monopolized the label 'progressive' to better resist any changes imposed by the new order." The authors of this manifesto called for determined actions to reduce Quebec's public debt, as well as for major investments in education that would demand higher tuition fees, a more competitive labor market, lower income taxes, higher electricity tariffs, some form of guaranteed minimum income, and a larger role for the private sector. A leftist defense of existing social programs and of equality was soon released (Aktouf et al. 2005).

Even though Bouchard and his co-authors emphasized the distinctive character of Quebec's predicament, their diagnosis and call to action were very much in line with the center Right arguments that prevail in European public debates (Castles 2004, 1; Noël 2006b). In Quebec, as elsewhere in the world, the Left and the Right are in search of a new equilibrium. In recent years, this search has led to a *rapprochement* between the two sides, with the Left becoming more sensitive to the requirements of competitiveness and fiscal balance, and the Right more open to the need to fight poverty and social exclusion (Noël and Thérien 2008, 166–197). The Quebec election of March 27, 2007, which saw the ADQ win 31% of the votes and become official opposition, behind Jean Charest's Liberals, who obtained only 33% of the vote and forty-eight of the National Assembly's 125 seats, convinced many that Quebec society was moving to the Right. Charest soon discovered, however, that a broad consensus remained on the Quebec model and that he was better to govern near the center, perhaps with lower income taxes and higher tuition fees, but also with measures against poverty and in favor of employment. Contrary to what is often said, Quebec's social model appears well anchored in public opinion. As with the national question and identity, core values endure, even though debates continue on specific policy issues. Closure is never possible on such questions.

CONCLUSION

Canadian politics cannot be understood fully without taking into account the special status of Quebec. In Canadian history, this status has always been recognized, whether it was done proudly and openly, prudently and implicitly, or reluctantly and by default. With the adoption of the 1982 Constitution Act, recognition took the latter form, and this led to a series of conflicts and misunderstandings, from the failure of the Meech Lake Accord to the Social Union Framework Agreement. Provincial autonomy was also challenged, as the federal government obtained mounting budgetary surpluses while the provinces struggled to make ends meet. Over time, positions have hardened and change has become difficult, but it is not impossible, as is indicated by the gestures that gave meaning to Stephen Harper's open federalism, on recognition and fiscal imbalance in particular. A built-in tension nevertheless remains, and it will not be overcome easily. On many issues, Quebec and Canada are moving further apart rather than closer to each other.

In a similar fashion, one could say that Quebec politics is very much Canadian politics. Prior to the Quiet Revolution, Quebec society was largely defined by the fate of French Canadians as a disadvantaged minority within an English-speaking country. Poverty, inequality, and patronage plagued Quebec politics, and a long political fight was necessary to undo two social traps that made progress difficult. Out of this fight was born a nation that no longer defined itself as an ethnic minority, but rather as an inclusive society, built around a liberal and relatively egalitarian vision of citizenship. Some still cling to the French Canadian identity but, by and large, Quebec politics has moved beyond this understanding to define a project fit for a modern, progressive nation, within or with Canada.

Contemporary Quebec politics expresses many of the same dilemmas and controversies that animate politics elsewhere in the world. Quebecers debate with passion the meaning of national autonomy, citizenship, identity, and belonging. They divide just as convincingly over the public debt, economic growth, public intervention, and social justice, and they care as well about wars in the Middle East, hunger in the world, or the evolution of American politics. Quebec, however, remains a small nation with an uncertain political status. When all is said and done, this founding question remains, and it conditions much of the rest.

Acknowledgment. I am grateful to Guy Laforest for helpful comments and suggestions on this chapter.

REFERENCES

Adams, Michael. 2003. *Fire and Ice: The United States, Canada and the Myth of Converging Values*. Toronto: Penguin.

Aktouf, Omar, et al. 2005. Manifeste pour un Quebec solidaire. www.ccmm-csn.qc.ca/ MGACMS-Client/Protected/File/J764Y66955UG45B7Z43BP3G6F9MW88.pdf.

Baer, Douglas, Edward Grabb, and William Johnston. 1993. National character, regional culture, and the values of Canadians and Americans. *Canadian Review of Sociology and Anthropology* 30(1): 13–36.

Behiels, Michael D. 1985. *Prelude to Quebec's Quiet Revolution: Liberalism versus Neo-Nationalism, 1945–1960*. Montreal: McGill-Queen's University Press.

Bernard, Paul, and Sébastien Saint-Arnaud. 2004. Du pareil au même? La position des quatre principales provinces canadiennes dans l'univers des régimes providentiels. *Canadian Journal of Sociology* 29(2): 209–239.

Boothe, Paul, and Katherine Boothe. 2006. Personal income tax and redistribution in the Canadian federation. In *Dilemmas of Solidarity: Rethinking Redistribution in the Canadian Federation*, ed. Sujit Choudhry, Jean-François Gaudreault-Desbiens, and Lorne Sossin, 75–104. Toronto: University of Toronto Press.

Bouchard, Gérard, and Charles Taylor. 2008. *Fonder l'avenir: Le temps de la conciliation; Rapport*. Quebec: Commission de consultation sur les pratiques d'accommodements reliées aux différences culturelles. www.accommodements.qc.ca/documentation/ rapports/rapport-final-integral-fr.pdf.

Bouchard, Lucien, et al. 2005. For a clear-eyed vision of Quebec. October 19. www.pourun-quebeclucide.com/documents/manifesto.pdf.

Castles, Francis G. 2004. *The Future of the Welfare State: Crisis Myths and Crisis Realities*. Oxford: Oxford University Press.

Clarity Act, S.C. 2000, c. 26. www.canlii.org/ca/sta/c-31.8/whole.html.

Clement, Wallace, and John Myles. 1994. *Relations of Ruling: Class and Gender in Postindustrial Societies*. Montreal: McGill-Queen's University Press.

Commission on Fiscal Imbalance. 2002. *A New Division of Canada's Financial Resources: Report*. Quebec: Commission on Fiscal Imbalance. www.desequilibrefiscal.gouv.qc.ca/ en/pdf/rapport_final_en.pdf.

Courchene, Thomas J. 2008. This just in: Surpluses across the board. *Policy Options* 29(4): 37–39.

Gagnon, Alain G., and Raffaele Iacovino. 2006. *Federalism, Citizenship, and Quebec: Debating Multinationalism*. Toronto: University of Toronto Press.

Godbout, Luc. 2005. *Des baisses d'impôt: Pour qui, comment et quand? Douze constats à prendre en considération avant de procéder à de nouvelles baisses d'impôt sur le revenu au Quebec*. Scientific series, June 2005. Montreal: CIRANO. www.cirano.qc.ca/pdf/ publication/2005s-29.pdf.

Godin, Pierre. 2001. *René Lévesque, tome 3: L'espoir et le chagrin 1976–1980*. Montreal: Boréal.

Guest, Dennis. 1980. *The Emergence of Social Security in Canada*. Vancouver: University of British Columbia Press.

Haddow, Rodney, and Thomas Klassen 2006. *Partisanship, Globalization, and Canadian Labour Market Policy*. Toronto: University of Toronto Press.

Hamel, Pierre, and Bernard Jouve. 2006. *Un modèle québécois? Gouvernance et participation dans la gestion publique*. Montreal: Presses de l'Université de Montréal.

Heintzman, Ralph. 1983. The political culture of Quebec, 1840–1960. *Canadian Journal of Political Science* 16(1): 3–59.

Labrosse, Alexis. 2007. *La présence syndicale au Quebec en 2006*. Direction des études et des politiques, July. Quebec: Ministère du Travail. www.travail.gouv.qc.ca/publications/rapports/bilanrt/pres_synd2006.pdf.

Laforest, Guy. 1993. *De la prudence*. Montreal: Boréal.

Laforest, Rachel. 2007. The politics of state/civil society relationships in Quebec. In *Canada: The State of the Federation 2005. Quebec and Canada in the New Century; New Dynamics, New Opportunities*, ed. Michael Murphy, 177–198. Montreal: McGill-Queen's University Press.

Lévesque, René. 1986. *Attendez que je me rappelle ....* Montreal: Québec/Amérique.

Levine, Marc V. 1997. *La reconquête de Montréal*. Montreal: vlb éditeur.

Macklem, Patrick. 2001. *Indigenous Difference and the Constitution of Canada*. Toronto: University of Toronto Press.

McRoberts, Kenneth. 1988. *Quebec: Social Change and Political Crisis*, 3rd ed. Toronto: McClelland and Stewart.

———. 1997. *Misconceiving Canada: The Struggle for National Unity*. Toronto: Oxford University Press.

Mendelsohn, Matthew, Andrew Parkin, and Maurice Pinard. 2007. A new chapter or the same old story? Public opinion in Quebec from 1996–2003. In *Canada: The State of the Federation 2005. Quebec and Canada in the New Century; New Dynamics, New Opportunities*, ed. Michael Murphy, 25–52. Montreal: McGill-Queen's University Press.

Ministère de la Famille, des Aînés et de la Condition feminine. 2007. *Le Québec soutient ses familles: Des politiques généreuses et innovatrices, des résultats significatifs*. Quebec: Gouvernement du Quebec. www.mfa.gouv.qc.ca/publications/pdf/SF_quebec_soutient_familles.pdf.

Ministère de la Santé et des Services sociaux and Institut national de santé publique du Québec. 2007. *Troisième rapport national sur l'état de santé de la population du Québec; Riches de tous nos enfants: La pauvreté et ses répercussions sur la santé des jeunes de moins de 18 ans*. Quebec: Gouvernement du Québec. http://publications.msss.gouv.qc.ca/acrobat/f/documentation/2007/07-228–05.pdf.

Noël, Alain. 1993. Politics in a high-unemployment society. In *Quebec: State and Society*, 2nd ed., ed. Alain-G. Gagnon, 422–449. Scarborough: Nelson Canada.

———. 2002. Without Quebec: Collaborative federalism with a footnote? In *Building the Social Union: Perspectives, Directions and Challenges*, ed. Tom McIntosh, 13–30. Regina: Canadian Plains Research Center and Saskatchewan Institute of Public Policy.

———. 2005. "A report that almost no one has discussed": Early responses to Quebec's Commission on Fiscal Imbalance. In *Canadian Fiscal Arrangements: What Works, What Might Work Better*, ed. Harvey Lazar, 127–151. Montreal: McGill-Queen's University Press.

———. 2006a. Il suffisait de presque rien: Promises and pitfalls of open federalism. In *Open Federalism: Interpretations, Significance*, ed. Keith G. Banting, Roger Gibbins, Peter M. Leslie, Alain Noël, Richard Simeon, and Robert Young, 25–37. Kingston: Institute of Intergovernmental Relations.

———. 2006b. Mythes lucides, enjeux de citoyenneté et pactes sociaux. In *Agir maintenant pour le Québec de demain: Des réflexions pour passer des manifestes aux actes*, ed. Luc Godbout, 161–179. Quebec: Presses de l'Université Laval.

———. 2007a. L'héritage de la Commission Tremblay: Penser l'autonomie dans un cadre fédéral rigide. *Bulletin d'histoire politique* 16(1): 105–122.

————. 2007b. When fiscal imbalance becomes a federal problem. In *The 2006 Federal Budget: Rethinking Fiscal Priorities*, ed. Charles M. Beach, Michael Smart, and Thomas A. Wilson, 127–143. Montreal: McGill-Queen's University Press.

Noël, Alain, France St-Hilaire, and Sarah Fortin. 2003. Learning from the SUFA experience. In *Forging the Canadian Social Union: SUFA and Beyond*, ed. Sarah Fortin, Alain Noël, and France St-Hilaire, 1–29. Montreal: Institute for Research on Public Policy.

Noël, Alain, and Jean-Philippe Thérien. 2008. *Left and Right in Global Politics*. Cambridge: Cambridge University Press.

Observatoire de l'administration publique. 2007a. Structure et taille de l'état: Les dépenses par mission. In *L'État québécois en perspective*. Winter. Quebec: École nationale d'administration publique. www.etatquebecois.enap.ca.

————. 2007b. Structure et taille de l'etat: Les dépenses totales. In *L'État québécois en perspective*. Winter. Quebec: École nationale d'administration publique. www .etatquebecois.enap.ca.

————. 2007c. Structure et taille de l'etat: Les revenus totaux. In *L'État québécois en perspective*. Winter. Quebec: École nationale d'administration publique. www .etatquebecois.enap.ca.

Perlin, George. 1997. The constraints of public opinion: Diverging or converging paths? In *Degrees of Freedom: Canada and the United States in a Changing World*, ed. Keith Banting, George Hoberg, and Richard Simeon, 71–149. Montreal: McGill-Queen's University Press.

Rice, James J., and Michael J. Prince. 2000. *Changing Politics of Canadian Social Policy*. Toronto: University of Toronto Press.

Rigaud, Benoît, with Luc Bernier, Louis Côté, Joseph Facal, and Benoît Lévesque. 2008. La politique économique québécoise entre libéralisme et coordination. In *L'État québécois en perspective*. Spring. Quebec: École nationale d'administration publique. www .etatquebecois.enap.ca.

Rocher, François, and Nadia Verrelli. 2003. Questioning constitutional democracy in Canada: From the Canadian Supreme Court Reference on Quebec Secession to the Clarity Act. In *The Conditions of Diversity in Multinational Democracies*, ed. Alain-G. Gagnon, Montserrat Guibernau, and François Rocher, 207–237. Montreal: Institute for Research on Public Policy.

Rothstein, Bo. 2005. *Social Traps and the Problem of Trust*. Cambridge: Cambridge University Press.

Roy, Laurent, and Jean Bernier. 2006. *La politique familiale, les tendances sociales et la fécondité au Québec: Une expérimentation du modèle nordique?* Quebec: Ministère de la Famille, des Aînés et de la Condition feminine. www.mfa.gouv.qc.ca/famille/.

Royal Commission of Inquiry on Constitutional Problems. 1956. *Report*, vol. II. Quebec: Province of Quebec.

Royal Commission on Bilingualism and Biculturalism. 1969. *Report*, vol. 3A. Ottawa: Queen's Printer.

Russell, Peter H. 1993. *Constitutional Odyssey: Can Canadians Become a Sovereign People?* 2nd ed. Toronto: University of Toronto Press.

Silver, Arthur I. 1997. *The French-Canadian Idea of Confederation, 1864–1900*, 2nd ed. Toronto: University of Toronto Press.

Simeon, Richard, and Ian Robinson. 1990. *State, Society, and the Development of Canadian Federalism*, vol. 71 of the studies commissioned by the Royal Commission on the Economic Union and Development Prospects for Canada. Toronto: University of Toronto Press.

Simpson, Jeffrey. 1988. *Spoils of Power: The Politics of Patronage*. Toronto: Collins.

Stewart, Gordon. 1982. John A. Macdonald's greatest triumph. *Canadian Historical Review* 63(1): 3–33.

Supreme Court of Canada. *Reference re Secession of Quebec* (1998) 2 S.C.R. 217. http://scc .lexum.umontreal.ca/en/1998/1998rcs2-217/1998rcs2-217.html.

Taillon, Patrick. 2007. Les obstacles juridiques à une réforme du fédéralisme. *Cahier de recherche de l'Institut de recherche sur le Québec*. Montreal: Institut de recherche sur le Québec, April. www.irq.qc.ca.

Tilly, Charles. 1998. *Durable Inequality*. Berkeley: University of California Press.

Tremblay, Martine. 2006. *Derrière les portes closes: René Lévesque et l'exercice du pouvoir 1976–1985*. Montreal: Québec/Amérique.

Trudeau, Pierre Elliott. 1974. The province of Quebec at the time of the strike. In *The Asbestos Strike*, ed. Pierre Elliott Trudeau, 1–81. Toronto: James Lewis and Samuel.

Tully, James. 1995. *Strange Multiplicity: Constitutionalism in an Age of Diversity*. Cambridge: Cambridge University Press.

Vaillancourt, Yves. 1988. *L'évolution des politiques sociales au Quebec, 1940–1960*. Montreal: Presses de l'Université de Montréal.

Vallières, Pierre. 1971. *White Niggers of America*. Toronto: McClelland and Stewart.

Watts, Ronald L. 2008. *Comparing Federal Systems*, 3rd ed. Montreal: McGill-Queen's University Press.

World Bank. 2005. *World Development Report 2006: Equity and Development*. Washington, D.C.: World Bank. www.worldbank.org.

....

CHAPTER 7

INTERGOVERNMENTAL FISCAL RELATIONS: WORKHORSE OF THE FEDERATION

....

HARVEY LAZAR

CANADA is a federation of ten provinces and three territories spanning a vast geography and a diversity of peoples and economies. The Constitution Act, 1867 sets out some of the basic parameters for how the federation is to work by specifying the powers of both the general or federal government and provincial governments. Territories are the constitutional responsibility of the federal government, which has in recent decades delegated a growing number of provincial-like powers to territorial governments.

This chapter focuses on the role of intergovernmental fiscal relations. For this purpose, the Constitution is only a starting point. Within its framework there is a constant competition of ideas, interests, and identities concerning its interpretation and application. Almost all the voices at the bargaining table in the run-up to the founding 1867 Constitution remain there today—those favoring strong central authorities, Quebec autonomists and other advocates of classical federalism, equality of the provinces' proponents, Quebec secessionists, and a variety of regional perspectives. Indeed, the number of regional views grew as the federation itself expanded from an original four provinces to ten in 1949. The emergence of a significant Aboriginal voice added to the competition beginning in the late twentieth century. These internal strains influence the daily workings of the federation. At times, they also raise primordial questions. The fact that Quebec is both the homeland of the great majority of Canadian francophones and the only Canadian jurisdiction in which francophones are in a majority has important implications for the way the Canadian federation operates. These competing voices are a *permanent* characteristic of Canadian federalism.

Like other polities, Canadian federalism is also subject to external pressures. These can alter domestic priorities and the relative role of the two orders of government. They often also affect provinces differentially. In a world of porous borders, external pressures can loom significant.

Canadian federalism has few mechanisms for managing its diversity. The process of constitutional amendment is difficult. Regionally powerful federal cabinet ministers are a relic of the past. Canada's appointed upper chamber lacks democratic legitimacy. The political party system is fragmented. The first-past-the-post electoral system amplifies differences among regions in the House of Commons (Meekison et al. 2004, 9–15).

To a considerable extent, the judicial system has refereed the federalism contest. Until 1949, the Judicial Committee of the Privy Council in London was the final arbiter of the Canadian Constitution. Since 1949, the Supreme Court of Canada has played that role, expressing opinions and rendering decisions on such fundamental issues as constitutional patriation, secession, Aboriginal rights, and aspects of federal–provincial fiscal relations.

But Canada's judicial system is not designed to mediate the competition on an ongoing basis. Since the end of World War II, that role has fallen to the executive branches of the federal and provincial governments, a practice characterized as "executive federalism." In recent decades, territorial, Aboriginal, local, and supranational actors have also become more involved in what has become an increasingly complex, multilevel system.

A principal theme of this chapter is that executive federalism, and especially the intergovernmental fiscal arena, bears a large burden, possibly too large, in managing the pressures on Canadian federalism. Canada's federal system might work better if other governing structures shared in this burden more fully or if the Constitution provided legally enforceable rules about how executive federalism is to work in practice. But no new governance structure is on the horizon and the Constitution is silent on intergovernmental fiscal decision rules.

In these circumstances, fiscal relations between federal and provincial governments have evolved organically. *Money* has served as the lubricant that facilitates these relations. It is a contingent asset, however. For money to be an asset, Ottawa must have revenues in "excess" of its own expenditure responsibilities. Under those conditions, it may be able to use its spending leverage to encourage provinces to cooperate in the pursuit of what are often but not always agreed intergovernmental priorities.

The absence of binding decision rules has an upside. This *flexibility* permits governments to innovate in how they relate to one another without the limitations constitutional rules would require. *Ambiguity* is a further asset. There is also the fiscal federalism *tool kit*—the financial leverage available to the federal government (the spending power, defined later), various forms of intergovernmental transfers, asymmetrical arrangements, and revenue-sharing instruments that are on the asset side of the ledger. Arguably, this combination of money, flexibility, ambiguity, and the tool kit is at best a modest set of assets for managing the diversity of the federation.

These concerns about the adequacy of the assets for federation management raise a second theme that has to do with how well Canadians are served by these intergovernmental governance arrangements. Those who favor a strong federal government argue it is efficient to centralize revenues more than expenditures. The intergovernmental transfers (also referred to as *grants* later) that close the resulting fiscal gap can be equitable, efficient, and nation building. Indeed, some voices from poorer provinces see interregional redistribution as an essential right. Conversely, decentralizers oppose the idea of Ottawa purposively raising more money than it needs to pay for its own spending responsibilities to use the "excess" to make transfer payments to the provinces, especially if the transfers are conditional and have the specific purpose of influencing provincial expenditure priorities in areas of exclusive provincial jurisdiction. Indeed, decentralizers may claim that the Constitution does not authorize the federal government to make such payments. The Quebecers in this group often argue that if other provinces wish to accept such a role for Ottawa, the solution rests in asymmetrical arrangements whereas proponents of provincial equality contest the idea that fiscal arrangements can be offered to some provinces and not others. The fiscal conservatives among the decentralizers are more concerned with the adverse incentive effects of federal transfers, arguing, for instance, that the government that spends should also tax. Each of these theories has political legitimacy in the sense that it reflects the position of a substantial proportion of the polity. Thus, in assessing how well the system of intergovernmental fiscal relations functions, we take account of whether and to what extent the intergovernmental arena is open to these different views and the extent to which outcomes reflect a reasonable balance that the competitors can accept.

The next section touches on relevant constitutional provisions. The main body then takes an historical perspective, examining intergovernmental relations over four historical periods since the end of World War II. The conclusions focus on the themes referred to earlier.

Constitutional Provisions

Fiscal federalism is mainly about the assignment of expenditure and revenue responsibilities between the different orders of government and the related role of intergovernmental transfer payments. The Constitution Act, 1867 gives the federal government the power to raise money "by any mode or system of taxation" and provinces the power of "direct taxation within the province." In conjunction with court decisions, these provisions effectively enable both orders of government to levy personal and corporate income tax, sales and value-added taxes, payroll taxes, and user charges. Both orders of government are also free to borrow. There is thus extensive de jure concurrency in the allocation of major revenue bases. Equally important, both orders of government exercise these powers. The Constitution makes no provision, however, for federal and provincial governments to coordinate their taxation measures.

As for other legislative powers, the Constitution assigns a list to the federal government and a second list to provincial governments. Many of Canada's political priorities since the end of World War II relate to social policy and fall mainly under the provincial list. This is significant because social programs absorb a very high proportion of government spending. The areas of explicit concurrency are few. The word *explicit* is emphasized here, because substantial concurrency is achieved in areas of provincial legislative competence by the federal government exercising its "spending power" (see chapter 15, this volume). Based on judicial interpretations, it authorizes Parliament to spend money from the Consolidated Revenue Fund on any object, providing that the legislation authorizing the expenditures does not amount to a regulatory scheme within provincial legislative competence. Although contested, this power has been used extensively since the end of World War II.

A critical part of the 1867 constitutional settlement was Canada's commitment to provide grants and certain other payments to provincial governments. After many years of pressure from the provinces and the first Dominion–Provincial Conference of First Ministers in 1906, a 1907 constitutional amendment increased Dominion grants to all provinces. (In the nomenclature of Canadian federalism, *Dominion* rather than *federal* was the term customarily used to refer to the central government until after World War II.) In 1940, provinces agreed unanimously to a constitutional amendment allowing the Dominion to legislate on unemployment insurance. In 1951 and 1964, further amendments authorized Ottawa to pay old-age pensions and supplementary benefits. In 1957, the federal government introduced a formal program for making equalization payments to less affluent provinces, and the principles underlying this program were entrenched in the Constitution Act, 1982. Although the amendments beginning with unemployment insurance enhance the constitutional authority of the federal government in social policy, provincial governments continue to have the larger share of the legislative power in this broad domain.

BUILDING THE WELFARE STATE, 1945–1972

In the years after Confederation, power gradually shifted from the Dominion to the provinces. Public finances were centralized during World War I, but Ottawa's taxation effort declined after the war and public finances again decentralized. With the state playing a relatively modest role in the economy, intergovernmental fiscal relations were correspondingly limited. Until the Great Depression, the Dominion and provincial governments operated largely independently of one another in the "classical" mode.

The 1930s exposed the shortcomings in Canadian governance. Although efforts were made to better coordinate Dominion and provincial revenue and expenditure responsibilities, the results were haphazard and the outcomes unsatisfactory. During World War II, all provinces agreed to "rent" their personal and corporate income taxes and succession duties to Ottawa at its request. In return, the Dominion made unconditional grants to the provinces.

Memories of the Depression made people fearful that economic hard times would recur when the war was over. Fortunately, there were new ideas from the intellectual community about what could be done to assuage these anxieties. In 1945, Ottawa announced a commitment to "high and stable employment and income, and a greater sense of public responsibility for individual economic security and welfare" (Canada, Dominion–Provincial Conference 1945, 17). It proposed to operate capital investment policy on a countercyclical basis to stabilize employment and to provide financial support against various contingencies. In the latter category were initiatives relating to unemployment insurance and unemployment assistance, old-age pensions, and public health insurance. Some of the new programs were to be paid for by the Dominion, and others cost shared between the Dominion and provinces, with Ottawa incurring the bulk of expenditures. To finance this reconstruction package, the Dominion proposed that the wartime tax agreements be continued. In return, Ottawa would make unconditional general transfer payments to provinces and conditional grants in respect of items like health insurance.

At the Dominion–Provincial Reconstruction Conference, which ran intermittently from August 1945 until May 1946, the reaction of provincial premiers was mixed, reflecting the varying economic interests of provinces, different views about the nature of the federation, and partisan party political considerations. The premiers of Ontario and Quebec led the opposition, supported by Alberta. They held to the classical view of federalism, which required both orders of government to stick to their own legislative powers. Although Prime Minister Mackenzie King argued that his proposals were necessary for meeting the new tasks of the state, Premier George Drew of Ontario stated:

> Any arrangement...which provided for a centralized collection of the greater part
> of the tax requirements of provincial governments and made them mere
> annuitants of the central government would place the provincial governments
> under the control of the central government to an extent that meetings of the
> legislature would become almost meaningless. (Canada, Dominion–Provincial
> Conference [1954] 1946, 11)

Premier Maurice Duplessis of Quebec similarly argued that provinces required financial independence. Foreshadowing strong positions Quebec governments were to take in the years ahead, Duplessis continued: "The exclusive rights of the Provinces in matters of social legislation, education, civil rights, etc., must be safeguarded in their entirety if confederation is to endure" (Canada, Dominion–Provincial Conference [1954] 1946, 235).

Less wealthy provinces were broadly sympathetic to federal objectives. Indeed, one of them, Saskatchewan, North America's first social–democratic government, played a pioneering role in implementing some of the proposed new programs.

With such large differences, the reconstruction Conference ended without agreement. Yet, remarkably, by the early 1970s, almost all the federal proposals, modified through negotiations with the provinces, had been implemented. To explain this outcome, three tightly linked streams of federal–provincial negotiations—on new programs, revenue arrangements, and Quebec autonomy—are discussed separately later in the chapter.

With respect to the transformation in the program landscape, the Dominion–provincial stalemate required that Ottawa's first initiatives be ones that did not require provincial delivery systems. The Dominion was already delivering unemployment insurance and family allowances directly. In 1952, with provincial agreement, Ottawa replaced its first Old Age Pension Act, which was a means-tested provincially administered pension program that it had been cost sharing since 1927, with a universal, federally administered Old Age Security pension to all residents age seventy and older. Between 1953 and 1956, the federal government also signed cost-sharing agreements with all provinces covering a number of categorical social assistance programs.

Regarding health, the federal authorities focused initially on providing grants to provinces to help them improve their capacity to supply health care. The first public hospital insurance scheme was introduced in 1947 by Saskatchewan and, within a few years, Alberta and British Columbia had followed suit. At the urging of these provinces, in 1957 the federal Liberal government of Louis St. Laurent introduced legislation undertaking to pay half the cost of provincial plans for hospital insurance and diagnostic services subject to certain conditions. More significant, to ensure provincial support for Ottawa's use of the spending power, the legislation was only to come into force when six provinces representing at least half of Canada's population had signed agreements with Ottawa. The Liberals were defeated before the legislation became law. Later that year, with a new Progressive Conservative government in power, the legislation was reintroduced and passed *unanimously* by the House of Commons without the six-province requirement. By 1961, all provinces had entered into agreements with the federal government. The cost-sharing provisions proved a powerful incentive for provincial participation.

The other major program initiative of the St. Laurent government was equalization, established in 1957. The legislation provided an unconditional per capita grant to any province with fiscal capacity from personal and corporate income tax and succession duties below the average of the two provinces with the highest fiscal capacity. The formula was subject to review in five years. By the 1970s, equalization had become a fundamental part of the Canadian welfare state.

The decade of the 1960s was marked by a new dynamic in the federation arising from the election of two new governments. In 1960, the Quebec Liberal Party (QLP) won office in Quebec City. The QLP was sympathetic to many of the 1945 federal reconstruction proposals, but considered them within the purview of the provinces, not Ottawa. The Quebec government pressed its case forcefully against a backdrop of growing separatism in the province. In 1966, the QLP was replaced by a Union Nationale administration that flirted even more openly with separation.

The second key election involved the return of the federal Liberals to power in 1962 under the leadership of Lester Pearson. With a strong commitment to act on much of the unfulfilled 1945 policy agenda, Pearson had to engage in a difficult balancing act, weighing these commitments against the need to avoid adding fuel to Quebec separatism while minimizing antagonisms with other provinces.

By the early 1970s, the welfare state in Canada had many new components:

- A Canada–wide contributory pension system, payable at age sixty-five, made up of a Canada Pension Plan (CPP) delivered by the federal government in all provinces except Quebec and a parallel Quebec Pension Plan (QPP) operated by the Quebec government
- In all provinces, a federally delivered Guaranteed Income Supplement to top up Old Age Security, both payable at age sixty-five, for pensioners without private income
- Provincially delivered public medical insurance in all provinces, with the federal government covering half the costs subject to provinces meeting certain conditions
- A Canada Assistance Plan (CAP) under which the federal government covered half the costs of much-expanded provincial programs of social assistance and social services
- A major expansion of provincial postsecondary education systems, with Ottawa covering half of provincial operating costs for provincial institutions
- A much enlarged system of unemployment insurance delivered by the federal government

Parliament and provincial legislatures were minor players in this expansion (Simeon 1972, 62–65, 85–86). Except for unemployment insurance, the intergovernmental arena was where the crucial decisions were taken. The open-ended federal cost sharing for medical care, CAP, and postsecondary education contributed importantly to the major enlargement in provincial services that occurred.

This vast growth of the welfare state brings us to the federal–provincial revenue-sharing negotiations. As noted earlier, in 1945, Ottawa had proposed extending the wartime tax arrangements. Provincial objections to Ottawa's initial position ranged from issues of principle to the amounts on offer. But within a year, all provinces except Ontario and Quebec had signed new five-year renewal agreements in return for enhanced unconditional grants.

The tax rental agreements were extended in 1952 for an additional five years by all the original agreeing provinces and was accepted as well by Newfoundland, which had entered into union with Canada in 1949. This time, Ontario also rented its personal and corporate income taxes.

A critical milestone was the 1954 Quebec decision to levy its own personal income tax. For almost a decade after the war, taxpayers in that province had paid federal income taxes; but, because Quebec had not renewed its tax agreement with Ottawa, no federal grants were paid to Quebec. A new tax rental agreement was reached that provided to provinces inside the new 1957–1962 federal–provincial arrangements a standard rate (share) of the federal personal and corporate tax and succession duties. The federal government offered to abate federal tax by the same standard rates for any province that did not participate. Only Quebec chose that course.

In 1962, over the objections of most provinces that saw little upside in levying their own income taxes when Ottawa was sharing its revenues with them, the government of Canada decided to replace the tax-sharing agreements with new arrangements under which all provinces would be responsible for levying their own income taxes and succession duties. At the request of any province, Ottawa would collect these taxes at no charge, provided that the province levied its tax on the same definition of taxable income as the federal government. There would be no restriction on the level of provincial taxes. The same nine provinces as in the 1952 and 1957 agreements accepted the new approach, thus preserving a large measure of tax harmonization.

In making this decision, the federal government was risking the uniformity of the tax system and its ability to manage the economy. However, tax sharing violated the principle of fiscal responsibility. Quebec considerations were also important. With Quebec levying its own taxes and other provinces not doing so, the gulf between Quebec and other provinces would grow, with potential damage to national unity (Burns 1980, chaps. 8 and 9).

Quebec's unwillingness to rent its taxes during peacetime provides a useful segue into other actions it took to protect its autonomy. Many of the joint federal–provincial programs in the postwar welfare state were in exclusive provincial jurisdiction. Quebec was unwilling to participate in some cases. In 1951, the federal government began to disburse grants to universities. Although Quebec's universities initially accepted their share, the Duplessis government pressured them to stop doing so. After Duplessis' death, his successor Premier Paul Sauvé, demanded financial compensation and, in 1960, the federal government lowered its corporate income tax rate in Quebec, leaving room for the province to raise its rate without an overall increase. The additional provincial revenues could, in principle, be used to offset the amounts Quebec universities were no longer receiving. Similar "opting out" agreements were reached with Quebec in respect of youth allowances and student loans in 1962. On a much greater scale, in 1965, federal legislation provided an opting-out framework for specified federal programs that enabled any province to receive personal income tax abatements in lieu of federal cash. Only Quebec accepted. In the case of hospital insurance, the largest of these programs, the "opt-out" terminology was arguably ambiguous. The arrangement allowed Quebec to enhance its revenue autonomy but, like other provinces, Quebec still had to meet the federal government's conditions for that grant.

The other major negotiation resulted in the CPP and QPP. The 1951 constitutional amendment that empowered the federal government to legislate on old-age pensions also specified that if provincial and federal laws were in conflict, provincial law had precedence. When the Pearson Liberals promised contributory pensions for working people, the QLP quickly indicated it would provide its own plan. Quebec's initial motive may have simply been to keep Ottawa out of its jurisdiction. But once the Quebec government decided to act, it saw other benefits, including the opportunity to use the big fund that would accumulate in the early decades of the program to encourage Quebec development. Quebec officials presented their plan at a federal–provincial meeting, where it proved more attractive to the other nine provinces than the federal proposal. Because Ottawa needed provincial support for a national plan, these provinces successfully used this lever to negotiate two key provisions: that they have the exclusive right to borrow from the pension fund at a subsidized rate of interest and that any plan amendment would require the support of two thirds of the provinces with two thirds of the population. The final result was two separate but virtually identical plans so that all workers, wherever they were in Canada, enjoyed equal benefits and contributed at equal rates. There had been much give and take, with the final plan looking much more like the original Quebec document than the federal one (Simeon 1972, chap. 3).

Thus, in the quarter century after World War II, federal and provincial governments erected a Canada–wide welfare state. Three factors help to explain this achievement. One was democratic politics and the broad political consensus across Canada that the state had a substantial role to play in the provision of social and economic security. A robust postwar period economy was the second. With rapid growth and low interest rates, the public debt accumulated during the war years melted quickly. Well into the 1960s, the federal revenue stream permitted a large expansion in public spending.

A third explanation had to do with the intergovernmental arena and fiscal tool kit. One study reported that there were only seven federal–provincial meetings in 1939 whereas in 1967 some 125 federal–provincial committees met, some more than once (Simeon 1972, 125). Frequent multilateral meetings variously at the level of line ministers, finance ministers, and first ministers and their officials, and ongoing bilateral interactions were integral to developing the new programs. The achievements were also shaped by the tools available: direct spending and conditional and unconditional grants to provinces under the federal spending power, opting out, a variety of revenue-sharing arrangements, and the creative use of ambiguity.

Ambiguity was particularly important in Quebec–Ottawa relations. The federal and Quebec governments were in competition. Although each had a strikingly different vision of what the federation should be, both wished to avoid the kind of political backlash that could spin out of control. The asymmetrical and at times ambiguous outcomes on key files enabled both governments to claim success.

Ottawa achieved national programming, delivered by the provinces in some cases and the federal government in others. Quebec protected its autonomy through the successful exercise of its legislative powers. Most significant, Quebec's gains also pushed the entire federation in a more decentralized direction than would have otherwise occurred.

The federalism of this period is typically referred to as "cooperative." But cooperative federalism does not mean friendly or easy intergovernmental relations. Rather, it suggests that governments recognize a degree of interdependence. On any given issue, relations typically entail conflict and competition and, over time, perhaps compromise and agreement (Meekison et al. 2004, 22).

HARD ECONOMIC TIMES, FISCAL RETRENCHMENT: 1973–1997

From the early 1970s until the late '90s the macroeconomic climate was unfavorable. The federal government incurred budgetary deficits annually for twenty-seven consecutive years and federal debt grew. Provincial finances also fared poorly, but not as poorly as Ottawa's. Federal cash grants to provinces had accounted for less than one tenth of federal expenditures in the late 1950s, but they had grown to one fourth by the early 1970s and were still escalating. Not surprisingly, in the circumstances, the government of Canada concluded that open-ended financial commitments to match provincial expenses in large and fast-expanding provincial programs gave it insufficient control over its own budgetary outlays.

The first pivotal event was the 1976 decision of the Pierre Trudeau Liberal government to amend the federal fiscal arrangements legislation to end matching grants for hospital insurance, medical insurance, and postsecondary education, and replace them with a single Established Programs Financing (EPF) block fund. Under the 1977 EPF, the federal contribution to the provinces was paid for by a combination of tax abatements and cash that was initially of roughly equal value. The cash was legislated to increase with population and economic growth. The EPF was by far the largest federal grant to the provinces, with its value far outstripping the two remaining major transfers: equalization and CAP.

During the 1980s, the governments of Liberal Pierre Trudeau (1968–1984 with one brief interruption) and Progressive Conservative Brian Mulroney (1984–1993) altered their payments commitments to the provinces frequently without any semblance of provincial concurrence:

- Equalization was reformed in 1982 to control program costs resulting from higher Alberta oil and natural gas revenues.
- The legislated rate of increase in EPF and CAP was reduced eight times between 1982 and 1995.

- The 1984 Canada Health Act, unanimously passed by Parliament, authorized the withholding of EPF cash payments to any province that permitted physicians or hospitals to impose user charges, thus sending a message to provinces that their financial difficulties should not be solved by restricting access to health care.

The second pivotal event was the 1995 federal budget. Introduced only months before the second Quebec referendum, it was the centerpiece of the first Jean Chrétien–led Liberal government's efforts to restore federal finances. The budget announced that the EPF and CAP would be integrated into a new single Canada Health and Social Transfer (CHST), the cash component of which would be reduced by $6 billion relative to previously planned levels (a 15% cut in total cash transfers from Ottawa). By the time this last measure kicked in, the economy was beginning to improve. The CHST cut was the last reduction in major transfers during this era (1993–2006) of Liberal government.

In explaining the shift from cooperative to a more unilateral and arbitrary federalism, albeit still within an interdependent framework, three points stand out. The first was that the political consensus around the virtues of the welfare state began, for the first time, to be seriously questioned. The second was the worrisome deterioration in federal finances. The third was linked to the first two. The EPF had increased both federal and provincial autonomy by separating federal contributions for health and education from provincial program costs. Events at the outset of the 1980s reinforced this situation. Because provincial finances were stronger then than Ottawa's, the federal government attempted to engage the provinces in negotiation to reach agreement on reduced transfers. Provinces demurred. It turned out that they preferred to criticize federal transfer cuts than to negotiate the amount. Thus, a different pattern of intergovernmental fiscal relations was established. Governments were operating at a greater distance from one another.

Deficit reduction was slow and acrimonious. Along the way, a price was also paid in the form of a weakened social safety net and a reduction in trust among governments. Perhaps more positively, also along the way, the 1977 tax abatement reduced the vertical fiscal gap and also the taxation gap between Quebec and other provinces. Most significant, governments eventually succeeded. By the early 2000s, Canada's public finances had become effectively restored. This last result was less the outcome of intergovernmental coordination than finance ministries reacting similarly to similar external pressures (Leslie et al. 2004, 246).

GOOD TIMES, TOUGH BARGAINING: 1998–2006

In fiscal year 1997–1998, Ottawa enjoyed its first budgetary surplus since 1969–1970. Surpluses were recorded annually until late in the first decade of the 2000s, when this chapter was completed. Provincial government finances also improved dramatically.

With more robust revenue bases, provinces had the option of reducing their fiscal dependence on Ottawa. In particular, when the federal government announced $100 billion in tax cuts beginning in 2001, this created an opportunity for them to occupy at least some of the tax space Ottawa was vacating. However, provincial governments chose not to do so. Beginning in the late 1990s, premiers ran an aggressive political campaign under the rubric of "vertical fiscal imbalance," demanding restoration of the 1995 transfer cuts and higher equalization payments. In 2003, premiers created a new Council of the Federation to spearhead their political demands and "play a leadership role in revitalizing the Canadian federation and building a more constructive and cooperative federal system" (Council of the Federation 2003, 1). They succeeded in their fiscal demands. Over several budgets beginning in the late 1990s, the federal government increased funding for CHST (and successor programs) and equalization, and committed also to annual increases for up to ten years, thus providing enhanced stability and predictability in provincial finances. Federal grants rose from around 15% of provincial revenues in 1997–1998 to more than 18% in 2006–2007 (Canada 2007, table 31).

The federal government had different priorities. The Liberals were concerned that they were not receiving sufficient political credit for their provincial grants. Ottawa was also concerned that increases in health transfers that provinces were demanding would dissipate in higher remuneration for existing health care professionals without improving access to health services or its quality. Yet the federal government augmented its transfers to provinces and territories from 13% of federal budgetary expenses in 1997–1998 to 19% by 2006–2007 (Canada 2007, tables 7 and 11).

In brief, both orders of government recognized their interdependence. Ottawa needed provincial delivery systems. It also required provincial buy-in if its direct transfers were not to be offset by reductions in provincial spending for similar clients. Most provinces saw the receipt of federal grants as normal in the way the federation worked. This interdependence led, among other things, to a series of federal–provincial–territorial (FPT) first ministers' accords in 2000, 2003, and 2004 that included increased long-term federal health care funding, the splitting of the CHST into a separate Canada Health Transfer (CHT) and a Canada Social Transfer (CST) to enhance transparency, the earmarking of much of the new federal money, and provincial commitments to new accountability measures that focused on performance.

The Paul Martin Liberals also replaced the traditional formula-driven equalization program with a controversial fixed-ceiling approach that was to be escalated at a fixed rate. More money was included and a panel was to advise on provincial allocations. To the dismay of several provinces, the Martin government also controversially extended and strengthened existing federal offshore accords with Newfoundland and Labrador, and Nova Scotia to compensate those provinces for any reductions in equalization arising from increased resource revenue from offshore development.

Reflecting new priorities, after eighteen months of consultation with Aboriginal leaders, culminating in a first ministers' meeting in Kelowna in November 2005, the government also committed $5 billion over ten years to improve the quality of life of Aboriginal people—an indication of their growing voice.

The FPT negotiations on equalization and, especially, health were "high politics," involving as they did huge sums and the iconic status of "medicare" as a unifying force in the federation. But intergovernmental relations operate at several levels, and the tension and high-stakes bargaining on health were not representative of all intergovernmental fiscal relationships. In the vast majority of program areas, intergovernmental relations were professional and nonconfrontational (Lazar 2006). Two major illustrations of this approach were the federal–provincial agreements on a much improved system of child benefits in 1998 and crucial 1998 amendments to the CPP (requiring provincial support) and QPP to ensure that these programs remained affordable and sustainable, and continued to parallel one another.

While the provinces were pressing the federal government to restore major transfers, they were also arguing for new rules to prevent a repetition of the unilateral and arbitrary exercise of the federal spending power that had marked the era of deficit politics. The federal government had its own agenda and the outcome was the 1999 nonlegally binding Social Union Framework Agreement (SUFA). It acknowledged the legitimacy of the federal spending power and placed modest limits on its use. New shared cost programs in areas of provincial/territorial responsibility would require the consent of a majority of the provinces. Provinces/territories that, because of existing programming did not require the total transfer to fulfill agreed objectives, would be able to reinvest any funds not required in the same or a related priority area. SUFA was accepted by all FPT governments except Quebec. Although some observers are skeptical that SUFA has altered government behavior, there are no independent studies to corroborate this view.

Quebec again pursued a distinctive policy. Quebec participated in the development of the initial provincial negotiating position on SUFA, but dropped out when the opting-out provisions did not meet its requirements (Noël 2000, 22–23). Quebec proposed that the CHST be eliminated with an offsetting transfer of tax room, a proposal that found little favor with other governments. Quebec insisted that its acceptance of the 2004 FPT Health Accord be interpreted in a way that reflected its specificity, and released an accompanying document jointly with the federal government to that effect (Canada and Quebec 2004).

Money made a huge difference. The federal government used its swollen coffers and spending power to strengthen Canada–wide programs, through both direct and intergovernmental transfers. Although conditionality in federal transfers remained light by the standards of other federations, there was a trend toward more conditions to enhance accountability and increase federal visibility (Lazar 2008). On the provincial side, the overriding aim was to secure more money while minimizing federal strings. There was no overarching national vision. Agreements were "one-off" deals. Political pragmatism, rather than lofty goals, characterized these years.

OPEN FEDERALISM, 2006–2008

In 2006, the federal Conservative Party defeated the Liberals, forming a minority government. In its election platform the Stephen Harper–led Conservatives committed to strengthening national unity through "open federalism" and to "work with the provinces in order to achieve a long-term agreement which would address the issue of fiscal imbalance in a permanent fashion" (Conservative Party of Canada 2006, 42–43).

In its inaugural 2006 budget, the government articulated a set of principles to guide its approach to intergovernmental fiscal relations, including fiscal responsibility and predictable, long-term fiscal arrangements. Ottawa also committed to using excess federal revenues for tax cuts rather than new programs in areas of clear provincial jurisdiction. It stated that "an appropriate matching of revenues to expenditure responsibilities for both orders of government enables Canadians to better hold their governments to account" (Canada 2006, chap. 6).

On big issues, the government's 2006, 2007, and 2008 budgets showed considerable continuity with the policies of previous governments:

- The federal government proclaimed its adherence to SUFA rules.
- It identified health care, postsecondary education and training, and infrastructure as "shared priorities."
- It endorsed the 2004 FPT Health Accord, which runs to 2013–2014.
- The CST was extended to 2013–2014.
- Equalization and territorial formula financing were put on the same timetable as the Liberals had them, with extensions to 2013–2014.
- The special offshore deals with Newfoundland and Labrador, and Nova Scotia were arguably respected.
- The Gas Tax Fund to help finance municipal infrastructure was made permanent.

There were differences. The Harper government enriched equalization (discussed later in the chapter) and CST significantly, in the latter case also altering the provincial allocation in a way that benefited the nonequalization receiving provinces. It canceled Liberal initiatives on child care and Aboriginal programming, and replaced both with programs or plans that fit better with its conservative philosophy. Yet it also intruded into provincial jurisdiction with its "patient wait time guarantee" priority.

Given its extensive commitments, the government understandably declared that it had satisfied its fiscal balance election promise. More surprisingly the federal finance minister announced his expectation that this restoration of fiscal balance would end disputes with provinces. Given the competing interests of the provinces, such an outcome was impossible. The Ontario government, for example, argued it was being treated unfairly across a range of programs, ranging from the CHT to employment insurance, and that given the relative decline of the Ontario economy its taxpayers should not be "subsidizing" other provinces to the extent that federal policies required. The federal Conservatives responded by strongly attacking the tax policies of the Ontario Liberal government during the winter and spring of 2007–2008 in what was a partisan political disagreement.

Another example arose in reaction to the amended equalization program. In its 2007 budget, the federal government, acting on the advice of the expert panel that the Martin government had appointed, made two key changes in the equalization standard (Canada, Expert Panel on Equalization and Territorial Formula Financing 2006). The government included the fiscal capacity of all ten provinces in the standard whereas it had previously included five provinces only, and Alberta—by far the largest hydrocarbon-producing province—was not one of them. The government also reduced the rate of resource revenue inclusion from 100% to 50%. The effect of including half of Alberta's resource revenues in the standard more than offset the effect of lowering the resource inclusion rate. The result enriched the equalization standard significantly. A fiscal capacity cap was implemented to ensure that equalization payments did not bring the overall fiscal capacity of any equalization-receiving province to a higher level than that of the nonequalization-receiving province with the lowest fiscal capacity (Ontario in 2008). As for the special arrangements with Newfoundland and Labrador, and Nova Scotia, Ottawa offered those provinces two options. They could continue under the equalization formula agreed to when the 2005 accords were signed, enabling both to receive the same benefits as before budget 2007, with no fiscal capacity cap on either equalization or the offshore accord payments, or each province could accept the new strengthened equalization formula and continue receiving payments under the offshore accords subject to the cap (Canada, Budget 2007).

The two provinces demanded the new rules with the old deals and they attacked Ottawa forcefully. The Saskatchewan government also joined the fray, claiming that if offshore resource revenues could be sheltered, so, too, should onshore resource revenues.

Although it is clear that the federal government has designed its fiscal transfers to afford provinces stability and predictability, external pressures may test Ottawa's steadfastness. In the early 2000s, high commodity prices, especially oil prices, began exerting upward pressure on the external value of the Canadian dollar, making central Canada's manufacturing industries less competitive. As large net importers of commodities, central Canadian industry and especially Ontario's were also directly disadvantaged by high commodity prices. Continuing a trend that had been present for some time, in 2007 Ontario's per capita gross domestic product dipped below the national average, and forecasts suggested this downward trend would continue. Forecasts also indicated Ontario's relative fiscal capacity under the equalization formula could fall below the national average in 2010–2011, thus qualifying the province for equalization payments. In that event, the fiscal capacity of the nonequalization-receiving province with the lowest fiscal capacity, probably British Columbia, would determine the fiscal cap. Because British Columbia has a substantially higher fiscal capacity than Ontario, this would trigger large increases in program costs and would affect provincial allocations (TD Economics 2008). The decision-making dynamics around such an event could create pressure on the stable framework the federal government has sought to achieve.

Any equalization formula creates winners and losers. What has made this issue so divisive in the late 2000s is the high world price for oil and the uneven resource endowments of the provinces. In these circumstances, with billions of dollars at issue, intergovernmental disputes are to be expected.

In a related sphere, the challenge of greenhouse gas emissions will require a major public debate on a national carbon tax, probably sooner than later, that will inevitably pit hydrocarbon-rich and hydrocarbon-poor provinces against one another. Although the intergovernmental fiscal arena cannot prevent this, it can ensure that the competing voices receive a fair hearing as governments work toward a result that most can hopefully can live with.

CONCLUSION

During World War II, the Dominion developed plans to meet the public's strong expectations that the state would play a much greater role in the provision of social and economic security when peace had returned. Because many of Ottawa's proposals were within provincial jurisdiction, Dominion–provincial cooperation was essential. Thus, "executive federalism" was born as an instrumental response to the democratic will of the people.

The federal–provincial arena brought together the federal spending power, provincial jurisdiction, and new program ideas. This arena was also where revenue sharing and tax harmonization deals were negotiated, and Quebec's autonomy demands mediated. By the time Parliament and the provincial legislatures became engaged, the deals had been struck and they had little scope for influencing the results. Legislators knew that the welfare state actions reflected the public will, and the executives generally enjoyed majority support in their legislatures.

Although the postwar agenda was initially driven mainly by Ottawa, what emerged was not a centralized federation but one that blended pan-Canadian and provincial dimensions. The new programs created social rights of citizenship—broadly similar benefits and services in all provinces. Yet the provinces designed and delivered most of the new service programs. The success of the new policy ideas carried the seeds of fiscal decentralization.

Deprived of money during the 1980s through the mid '90s, the incentive for governments to work together weakened. Although still operating within a framework of broad interdependence, they became more autonomous. Provinces declined to negotiate lower transfers, and the federal government consequently acted unilaterally, at times arbitrarily, in its adjustments to fiscal arrangements. The political incentives that facilitate intergovernmental cooperation when money is plentiful had not been invented (and still have not) for periods when it is in short supply. When, in the late 1990s, the tide came in again and public finances improved, the intergovernmental forum once again became the place where critical political priorities, in this case health care, were negotiated.

The 1867 Constitution provided larger per capita Dominion payments to the less affluent provinces than the more affluent. Through subsequent political and constitutional decisions, a consensus emerged that this horizontal redistributive role was an appropriate one for Ottawa. This remains the case today.

Because provinces surrendered their principal revenue sources in 1867, the Constitution required the Dominion to make transfer payments to them. One result was that the 1867 Constitution also created the precedent for the idea that a vertical gap is appropriate for the finances of the federation. As the state expanded in the twentieth century, provinces came to raise more of their own revenue, but time and again when provincial governments had a choice, they opted to receive a significant portion of their revenues from Ottawa. Sometimes their decisions were in response to federal cost-sharing incentives and in other cases they were not. This behavioral pattern is ingrained in the dynamics of the federation.

For the federal government, the opposite is true. Ottawa has purposively collected revenues in excess of the amounts required to fund its own programs to have the financial wherewithal to use its spending power to meet national equity and efficiency goals, and for nation building.

The magnitude of the federal government's specific-purpose vertical grants to the provinces is the measure of the vertical fiscal gap. Debating the size of the gap is a technical way of debating the merits of the competing voices in the federation. Since the expansion of the welfare state in the 1960s, the vertical gap has typically been broadly in the order of 10% to 20% of provincial revenues. These grants are, on the whole, relatively unconditional. Adding equalization, which is unconditional, increases overall provincial reliance on federal grants to the 15% to 25% range. (Provincial dependence on federal transfers varies sharply. In recent years, it has been less than 10% for Alberta, the highest income province, and around 40% for the lowest income provinces [Canada 2007, tables 17–31].)

In almost all other federations, constituent units rely more heavily on federal transfers than is the case in Canada, and typically those grants are more conditional (Watts 2005). These facts suggest that the voices of decentralization in the federation must be enjoying a reasonable hearing in the intergovernmental fiscal arena. Yet most benefits and services are broadly similar across the federation, suggesting that those favoring national programs have not been excluded from decision making.

The intergovernmental fiscal arena remains remarkably informal and under institutionalized given the huge amount of business it handles. There are no rules on whether and when first ministers are to meet, and yet they oversee the vast interdependence among FPT governments. Finance ministers engaged in extensive fiscal and budgetary coordination in the 1960s and '70s, but their relationship since then has been neither as close nor as intense. The absence of rules, or at least rules of thumb, for managing fiscal relations during tough fiscal times is especially troubling. Among line ministries there is great variability in FPT institutionalization, and the limited evidence does not suggest more institutionalization necessarily leads to better policy outcomes. In any case there is no discernible trend for the arena to become more institutionalized (Simmons 2004). If anything, the trend is in the other direction. This is partly because there is no overarching galvanizing national project as there was during the postwar era, but it is also the case that governments see a more structured intergovernmental arena as a threat to their sovereignty.

The intergovernmental arena plays a dual role. In implementing Canadian priorities, the welfare state from 1945 to the early 1970s, and health care in recent years, it has been *instrumental*. During the period of fiscal retrenchment it was less effective; but, as it turned out, the more autonomous relations of those years did not stand in the way of restoring public finances. Whether this could have been achieved in a more cooperative way remains a question.

The government of Canada has nation-building responsibilities. When it has pursued these *symbolic* purposes through spending power, it has often collided with Quebec governments focused on building the Quebec nation. To the extent that the Canada–Quebec contest has been mediated in the intergovernmental fiscal arena, the flexibility and scope for ambiguity inherent in the fiscal tools have allowed for results that were less emotionally charged and divisive than perhaps would have been the case had they been mediated in the constitutional forum.

In defending its constitutional space, Quebec has influenced the entire realm of fiscal federalism. In deciding to raise its own personal income tax in 1954, it contributed fundamentally to the federal decision that required other provinces to raise theirs. Through its QPP initiative, it helped shape the unique powers other provinces enjoy in relation to CPP amendment. The opting-out concept was invented to accommodate Quebec, but was made available to all provinces, creating choices for them that would not have otherwise existed. As Simeon (2009, 49) noted: "Quebec's consistent assertion of provincial autonomy has also helped promote strong provincialist strategies in other provinces, especially in wealthy provinces, such as Alberta. The causal arrow runs both ways: a decentralized Canada helps accommodate Quebec; the presence of Quebec ensures that Canada's federalism will be highly decentralized."

There are shortcomings in the way the intergovernmental arena operates. It lacks transparency. Meetings of FPT finance ministers are especially private. Equally important, Parliament and the provincial legislatures do a remarkably poor job of overseeing these relationships. It is difficult for them to influence the intergovernmental negotiation process, but they rarely even become involved in after-the-fact assessments.

In facing strong external and internal change pressures, the Canadian federation is by no means unique. What is different about Canada is the narrow range of institutions, with few resources or decision rules to support them, that are called upon to mediate these pressures. The Supreme Court's important role is exceptional and episodic. For the rest, the task falls to executive federalism, the workhorse of the federation.

REFERENCES

Burns, R. M. 1980. *The Acceptable Mean: The Tax Rental Agreements, 1941–1962.* Toronto: Canadian Tax Foundation.

Canada. 2006. *Restoring Fiscal Balance in Canada.* Ottawa: Department of Finance Budget 2006. http://www.fin.gc.ca/budget06/fp/fptoce.htm.

———. 2007. *Fiscal reference tables.* Ottawa: Department of Finance. http://www.fin.gc.ca/toce/2007/frt07_e.html.

Canada, Budget. 2007. Restoring fiscal balance for a stronger federation. *The Budget Plan.* Ottawa: Department of Finance, chap. 4. http://www.budget.gc.ca/2007/bp/bptoce.html.

Canada, Dominion–Provincial Conference. 1945. *Proposals of the Government of Canada.* Ottawa: King's Printer.

Canada, Dominion–Provincial Conference (1945). 1946. *Dominion and Provincial Submissions and Plenary Conference Discussions.* Ottawa: King's Printer.

Canada, Expert Panel on Equalization and Territorial Formula Financing. 2006. *Achieving a National Purpose: Putting Equalization Back on Track.* Ottawa: Department of Finance.

Canada and Quebec. 2004. *Asymmetrical Federalism that Respects Quebec's Jurisdiction.* Ottawa. http://www.scics.gc.ca/cinfo04/800042012_e.pdf.

Conservative Party of Canada. 2006. *Stand Up for Canada.* Federal Election Platform 2006.

Council of the Federation. 2003. Founding Agreement. http://www.councilofthefederation.ca/pdfs/850095003_e.pdf.

Lazar, Harvey. 2006. The intergovernmental dimensions of the social union: A sectoral analysis. *Canadian Public Administration* 49(1): 23–45.

———. 2008. *Displacement in federal transfer payments: Exploring concept and practice with special reference to the Canada Millennium Scholarship Foundation.* Montreal: The Canada Millennium Scholarship Foundation. http://www.millenniumscholarships.ca/images/Publications/Displacement_Fed_FEB08_EN.pdf.

Leslie, Peter, Ronald H. Neumann, and Russ Robinson. 2004. Managing Canadian fiscal federalism. In *Reconsidering the Institutions of Canadian Federalism,* ed. J. Peter Meekison, Hamish Telford, and Harvey Lazar, 213–248. Montreal: McGill-Queen's University Press.

Meekison, J. Peter, Hamish Telford, and Harvey Lazar. 2004. The institutions of executive federalism: Myths and realities. In *Reconsidering the Institutions of Canadian Federalism,* ed. J. Peter Meekison, Hamish Telford, and Harvey Lazar, 3–31. Montreal: McGill-Queen's University Press.

Noël, Alain. 2000. General study of the framework agreement. In *The Canadian Social Union without Quebec,* ed. Alain-G. Gagnon and Hugh Segal, 9–35. Montreal: Institute for Research on Public Policy.

Simeon, Richard. 1972. *Federal–Provincial Diplomacy: The Making of Recent Policy in Canada.* Toronto: University of Toronto Press.

————. 2009. Debating secession peacefully and democratically: the case of Canada. In *Democracies in Danger*, ed. Alfred Stepan, 41–58. Baltimore, Md.: Johns Hopkins University Press.

Simmons, Julie. 2004. Securing the threads of cooperation. In *Reconsidering the Institutions of Canadian Federalism*, ed. J. Peter Meekison, Hamish Telford, and Harvey Lazar, 285–311. Montreal: McGill-Queen's University Press.

TD Economics. 2008. *Ontario Poised to Collect Equalization in 2010–2011*. Toronto: TD Bank Financial Group. http://www.td.com/economics/special/db0408_equal.jsp.

Watts, Ronald L. 2005. *Autonomy or Dependence: Intergovernmental Financial Relations in Eleven Countries*. Kingston: Institute of Intergovernmental Working Papers. http://www.queensu.ca/iigr/working/archive/pubwork2005.html.

CHAPTER 8

....

LOCAL GOVERNMENT

....

ANDREW SANCTON

WHAT IS LOCAL GOVERNMENT?

....

The term *local government* does not appear in the Constitution Act, 1867. The closest reference is found in section 92 (8), where the authority to make laws relating to "Municipal Institutions in the Province" is placed under the exclusive jurisdiction of provincial legislatures. Municipalities had existed in one form or another in British North America since 1785, when the City of Saint John, New Brunswick, was incorporated by royal charter. All Canadian provinces have enacted laws that provide for the existence of municipalities (in other words, corporate entities with defined territories and delegated legal authority to enact bylaws relating to a range of government functions generally considered to be local in nature). Such entities are generally designated as cities, towns, villages, counties, or townships.

In its Financial Management System, Statistics Canada (2004, 131) defines "local governments" as including both municipalities and their associated "autonomous boards, commissions and funds," and "school boards." Although commonly accepted (Magnusson 1985), such a definition is far from precise. For example, Statistics Canada (2004, 32) categorizes "autonomous public health boards that are responsible for delivering health services within a specific geographic area" as "provincial and territorial" rather than local. Given that members of some such health boards attain office as the result of local elections and that some locally elected school boards no longer have the authority to raise any portion of their own revenues by local taxation, it is not at all obvious that school boards are still a distinct form of local government and that health boards are not. In any event, for the purposes of this chapter, neither health boards nor school boards will be included.

Because of definitional inconsistencies across ten provinces and three territories, it is pointless to attempt to count the number of "autonomous boards, commissions, and funds" associated with municipalities. The best that can be done is to point to examples. In various provinces there are separate local commissions or boards for parks, police, utilities, public transit, libraries, and watershed conservation, not to mention hundreds of boards and commissions established by contiguous munici- palities to administer different services (especially recreational facilities such as hockey arenas) that they choose to deliver jointly.

Counting the municipalities themselves is less problematic, although even here there are difficulties. For example, New Brunswick contains 269 "local service dis- tricts" that provide municipal services to 37% of the province's population (Infrastructure Canada 2006), but these districts are not counted as municipalities because they are not subject to the province's Municipalities Act. British Columbia does not have a Municipalities Act. Its Local Government Act (section 5) defines "local government" as comprising the province's 155 "municipalities" and twenty- seven "regional districts." For our purposes, regional districts are considered munic- ipal governments. They act as municipal governments in (unincorporated) areas of the province that otherwise do not have municipalities and they provide intermu- nicipal services and regional planning in areas that do. Quebec's eighty-six "munici- pal regional counties" act in the same way and are clearly municipalities because they are governed by the Municipal Code of Quebec. Ontario's thirty regional gov- ernments and counties are likewise governed by the Ontario Municipal Act, but

Table 8.1 Municipal Governments in Canada, January 2006

Province/Territory	Local Governments (including single tier)	Regional Governments (upper tier)	Supraregional Governments
Alberta	353	n/a	n/a
British Columbia	155	27	n/a
Manitoba	203	n/a	n/a
New Brunswick	103	n/a	n/a
Newfoundland and Labrador	282	n/a	n/a
Nova Scotia	55	n/a	n/a
Northwest Territories	16	n/a	n/a
Nunavut	25	n/a	n/a
Ontario	415	30	n/a
Prince Edward Island	75	n/a	n/a
Quebec	1,141	86	2
Saskatchewan	807	n/a	n/a
Yukon	8	n/a	n/a
Total	3,638	143	2

n/a, not applicable.
Source: Infrastructure Canada. 2006. *Canada Profile: Commonwealth Local Government Forum*. Ottawa: Government of Canada.

their territories are made up exclusively of areas that are also covered by lower tier municipalities. In small towns and rural areas near Montreal and Quebec City, there are three separate levels of incorporated municipal government: the local municipality, the municipal regional county, and the metropolitan community, labeled in Table 8.1 as "supraregional governments."

Outside Ontario, Quebec, and British Columbia, residents either have no municipal government at all (unincorporated areas) or only one level of municipal government. Even in Ontario and Quebec, many residents live in areas with only one level of municipal government, the most notable examples being the 2.5 million people in the city of Toronto, a new municipality created in 1998 by a provincial law that amalgamated the upper tier municipality of metropolitan Toronto and its six constituent lower tier municipalities.

FUNCTIONS OF LOCAL GOVERNMENT

It is impossible to determine municipal functions simply by reviewing provincial legislation for municipalities.[1] Different provinces delegate authority in different ways, and many important local functions derive from legislation that appears other than explicitly municipal. It might seem safe to assume that garbage collection is always delegated to local government, but in Prince Edward Island it is a provincial responsibility. Generally, however, we can expect local governments everywhere to regulate the built environment and to provide services to real property, including the provision of local roads and sidewalks. Local governments also provide recreational and cultural facilities such as parks, community halls, and public libraries. In more urban areas, local governments provide public transit, regulate taxis, purify and distribute piped water, and provide for sewage collection and treatment.

Except in Newfoundland and Labrador, where urban policing is a responsibility of the Royal Newfoundland Constabulary, urban municipalities generally have a responsibility for policing, although there are varying mechanisms in different provinces to insulate police from the direct control of municipal councils. Some urban municipalities obtain their policing through contracts with the Royal Canadian Mounted Police (RCMP) or with provincial police forces (Ontario and Quebec). The RCMP or provincial police forces generally provide policing in rural areas. Arrangements vary from province to province concerning the extent to which rural municipalities contribute to the cost. In Ontario, rural municipalities have paid the full cost since 1998.

Ontario is the only province in which municipalities have the statutory responsibility to provide certain social services (including income security payments) and to contribute to their funding. In Alberta, the Family and Community Support Services Act allows the provincial government to fund 80% of the costs of approved municipal preventative social service programs. In British Columbia, larger urban municipalities (especially the city of Vancouver) are engaged in social-planning functions mainly aimed at attracting funding from other levels of government, coordinating the work of nonprofit agencies, and providing modest municipal subsidies to various kinds of social service organizations, including community centers and nonprofit child care centers. In other provinces, there is even less municipal involvement in social services, ranging from none at all to minor expenditures for nonrecreational social service programs in community centers and to the staffing of social-planning groups. Quebec and Ontario are the only provinces that delegate any financial responsibility for social housing.

Municipalities in Alberta and Ontario are responsible for providing land ambulance services. The city of Winnipeg has a contractual arrangement with the regional health authority to provide ambulance services within its territory, but this is not a municipal responsibility elsewhere in the province.

The regulation of air quality is a local (regional district) responsibility in British Columbia. Only in Ontario is public health explicitly a local responsibility, often carried out through regional or county public health units. In Manitoba, municipalities have responsibility for the inspection of food service establishments and for insect control.

Public utilities (other than water supply) are difficult to categorize. For example, electrical distribution in Ontario's urban areas is the responsibility of business corporations, most of which are still owned by municipalities. Some small Ontario municipalities own local telephone companies, and the city of Kitchener owns the local natural gas distribution system. In Quebec, the city of Westmount still operates the local electricity distribution system. Two of Canada's major publicly traded utilities corporations, EPCOR and Telus, can trace their origins to being line departments of the city of Edmonton. Not surprisingly, they are still heavily involved in providing electricity, natural gas, and telecommunications infrastructure within the Edmonton region.

PROVINCIAL CONTROLS OVER LOCAL GOVERNMENT

Provinces do not have written constitutions analogous to the Constitution Act, 1867.[2] This means that it is impossible for Canadian municipalities to have what is known in the United States as "home rule," a set of provisions in state constitutions that generally prevents the state legislature from interfering with local control over municipal structures and boundaries (Cameron 1980). Provincial legislatures can do whatever they want with local governments, including abolishing all of them all at once. This possibility applies even to municipalities that predate the provinces in which they are located.

There is in every province at least one general law that establishes the basic rules and structures of municipal government. Such laws are frequently amended as a result of particular issues and problems, many of which were unforeseen when the legislation was originally approved. In principle, municipalities favor broad and general grants of functional authority together with considerable autonomy regarding how to structure themselves and regulate their own behavior. In practice, their actions are more easily defended in courts of law against aggrieved residents and businesses if the legislative authority under which they are acting is clear and explicit.

Some major Canadian cities—Toronto, Montreal, Winnipeg, and Vancouver, for example—are governed by provincial laws specifically tailored for their own purposes. Such laws, often called *charters*, give no more protection to cities against arbitrary provincial legislation than is available under general municipal legislation, but they usually provide for more functional authority than is generally found in smaller places so that these cities can potentially act more effectively in relation to complex urban issues.

Not to be confused with special laws for major cities are laws that are routinely passed by provincial legislatures with special provisions for particular municipalities. Sometimes such legislation is so detailed and particular that it is classified as "private legislation," meaning, among other things, that the law is not published alongside the more important "public legislation." At the other end of the scale are general provincial laws that apply to municipalities because they apply to all landowners in the province, or to all employers. For example, provincial labor relations law applies to municipalities, meaning that municipalities have no control over the regulation of their own collective bargaining. It is therefore no easy task to list exactly which provincial laws apply to which municipalities. All provinces except British Columbia have established quasi-judicial administrative tribunals to which various types of municipal decisions, usually relating to land use, can be appealed. The scope of such appeals, the procedures under which they are heard, and the extent to which such tribunals can be overruled by ministers vary greatly from province to province. By far the best known and most powerful of these tribunals is the Ontario Municipal Board (OMB) (Chipman 2002). In addition to hearing appeals relating to municipal structures and various financial matters, the OMB has more control over land-use planning than any other such provincial tribunal in the country. Almost every municipal land-use planning decision is subject to an OMB appeal. On controversial decisions in major cities, such appeals are routine, meaning that the local politics of land-use planning is quite different in Ontario than in any other jurisdiction in North America. Municipal councilors know that their decision is but a stage in the process leading to final determination by the OMB.

Provincial governments also control municipalities through the power of the purse. The most direct form of financial control is through grants allocated to municipalities for particular purposes; but, by legislation and regulation, provincial governments also control the methods by which municipalities raise their own revenues, especially from the tax on real property. To a lesser extent, even the federal government influences municipalities through the conditions it attaches to the relatively limited funds that flow from it to the nation's municipalities. Municipal sources of revenue will be explored in more detail later in this chapter.

Because municipalities are so dependent on policies adopted by other levels of government, they have formed various organizations to protect and advance their interests. At the federal level, there is the Federation of Canadian Municipalities, which has been especially prominent in recent years because of its successful campaigns to convince the federal government to eliminate the goods and services tax for municipalities and to share its tax revenues from gasoline with municipalities (Stevenson and Gilbert 2005). But, because the day-to-day intergovernmental issues of most relevance to municipalities remain at the provincial level, it is the provincial associations of municipalities that are generally the most important. In some provinces there are different organizations for different types of municipalities; in others, there is just one common association. However they are organized, municipalities have difficulty speaking with one voice because the interests of a major city are inevitably going to be different from those of a small rural township. This explains why the cities of Toronto and Montreal are no longer members of their respective provincial associations.

Special-Purpose Bodies

One of the long-standing objectives of most municipal organizations has been to insist that all local public services funded by local taxes be under the direct control of municipal councils.[3] This is why municipalities have usually supported provincial policies aimed at reducing or eliminating the authority of school boards to levy their own property taxes. To the extent that other boards can draw directly on municipal financial resources without council approval (for example, police boards in some provinces), municipal organizations generally tend to oppose such arrangements. By contrast, these arrangements are usually favored by the employees of such boards and by those especially interested in the services that they provide, the argument being that some services are too important or too sensitive to be subject to financial interference by municipal councils.

Some special-purpose bodies are partially or completely self-financing. The most common examples are local commissions for public transit and for utilities of one kind or another. The idea is that the existence of a distinct governance structure encourages them to be "run like a business." As long as a municipal council has control over the level of subsidies, if any, to its associated special-purpose bodies, then it is unlikely to object to their existence, even if they are established by provincial legislation.

Many special-purpose bodies result from intermunicipal agreements. If two or more municipalities agree to deliver a service jointly, they might establish a separate entity with a governing body that comprises representatives of the municipalities concerned. An example is the Buffalo Pound Water Administration Board, which for more than fifty years has been supplying water to the cities of Regina and Moose Jaw and various municipalities in between (Sancton et al. 2000, 53–54). Not all local special-purpose bodies are linked to municipal governments. For example, the federal government establishes local boards to operate federal airports and ports. These governing bodies contain municipal representatives, but remain agencies of the federal government.

INCORPORATIONS AND ANNEXATIONS: FROM RURAL TO URBAN

Legislation in most provinces provides for a mechanism whereby property owners may petition the provincial government to be incorporated as villages, towns, or cities depending on the number of residents involved. Such locally generated incorporations were commonplace in the nineteenth and early twentieth centuries, but the practice has fallen into disuse because ministers of municipal affairs today generally wish to reduce the number of municipalities rather than facilitate their increase. The only exception is British Columbia, where between 1987 and 2005 eleven new incorporated municipalities were established. On its website, the government of British Columbia provides detailed instructions regarding how the locally initiated process of municipal incorporation is expected to happen.

The boundaries of newly incorporated urban municipalities usually included a small amount of peripheral urban land to allow for future development. After land was developed, the urban municipality might have been granted the authority to annex land for development from its rural neighbor. If annexation is to be allowed at all, provincial governments must provide a procedure for it. Such a procedure usually involves some form of local negotiation and agreement.

An alternative to local agreement is for the provincial government to provide that annexation issues be settled by some form of administrative or quasi-judicial tribunal, such as the OMB. The problems here are predictable. Such a process can be very expensive, especially when highly paid lawyers and experts become involved in public hearings. Because municipalities are not constitutionally protected against changes in their boundaries without their consent, provincial governments can always use their legislative authority to sort out boundary disputes.

The best Canadian example of a city that has continually expanded its territory through annexation is Calgary. Annexations from contiguous rural municipalities are almost always on the agenda and are eventually determined by the Alberta Municipal Government Board. Despite the city of Calgary's explosive growth in recent years, annexation has enabled it to include within its borders 91.6% of the 2006 population of what Statistics Canada defines as the Calgary census metropolitan area.

Two-Tier Systems of Urban Government

Continual annexation is often politically difficult, especially when the boundaries of two established urban communities approach each other or when a provincial government wants to maintain the existence of established suburban and rural municipalities that are coveted by central cities. Provincial governments in Manitoba, Ontario, British Columbia, and Quebec have, at various times, instead established two-tier systems of urban government in which an upper tier metropolitan or regional authority encompasses the central city and the urbanizing municipalities around it (Sancton 2002). The main functional purposes of the upper tier have been to regulate and shape outward expansion while also providing the necessary physical infrastructure, especially roads, sewers, and water supply systems.

The first Canadian urban two-tier system was the municipality of metropolitan Toronto (1954–1997), otherwise known as *Metro*. It became known throughout the world for its success in the 1950s and '60s in planning and financing the rapid outward expansion of Toronto into the rural townships of Etobicoke, North York, and Scarborough. By the 1970s, its problems were mounting, especially when the Ontario government decided that its boundaries would not be extended outward such that it would continue to encompass most of the Toronto city region. Instead, the province created the two-tier "regional municipalities" of Halton, Peel, York, and Durham. During the same period, the province also created new two-tier systems in Ottawa-Carleton, Niagara, Waterloo, Sudbury, and Hamilton.

Between 1960 and 1971, the corporation of greater Winnipeg covered the territory of the city of Winnipeg and eleven suburban municipalities, and performed similar functions as Metro did in Toronto. Its ten councilors were elected from ten wards deliberately constructed to cross municipal boundaries and to take in both suburban and central city areas. Innovative as such an arrangement was, it served to intensify conflict between the corporation and its constituent municipalities.

In the mid 1960s, the government of British Columbia established "regional districts" throughout the province to provide municipal services in unincorporated areas and to facilitate regional planning and joint service provision among municipalities within the same region. It is through the regional districts that a light and flexible form of two-tier urban government was established for Vancouver (Greater Vancouver Regional District, now Metro Vancouver) and Victoria (Capital Regional District). British Columbia's regional districts have existed for more than forty years, making them the most durable of all the Canadian regional reforms of the postwar period.

In 1969, the Quebec National Assembly approved laws creating "urban communities" in Montreal and Quebec City and a "regional community" for the Outaouais area. Each of these three new institutions (1970–2001) was effectively a form of upper tier metropolitan government. More recently, in 2001, the province established new supraregional "metropolitan communities" for much larger areas around Montreal and Quebec City. What these new institutions gained in territory, they lost in functional authority. Although they are supposed to provide a form of strategic direction to their respective territories, they do not provide any actual services to their inhabitants.

MUNICIPAL AMALGAMATIONS
AND DEAMALGAMATIONS

Many two-tier urban systems established in the postwar period have been replaced by amalgamated municipalities (Sancton 2000). The first such amalgamation was sponsored in Winnipeg in 1971 by a New Democratic Party government. Known as "unicity," the Winnipeg amalgamation was designed to promote equity in taxation and service levels and to provide new opportunities for citizen participation. There were fifty small wards with councilors who were grouped into territorially based community committees and assisted by residents' advisory groups elected in open community meetings. Throughout the years, most of the new participatory mechanisms built into the unicity structures have atrophied. For example, the size of the council has been reduced from fifty to fifteen. Even the territory has been reduced. In 1991, a Progressive Conservative government allowed voters in the rural area of Headingley to hold a referendum on secession. When 86.7% of voters chose to leave, legislation was approved in 1992 to allow them to do so.

The best-known and most extensive program of municipal amalgamations was implemented by the Progressive Conservative government in Ontario in the 1990s. Amalgamations in Ontario were brought about by three separate laws. The first, part of the Savings and Restructuring Act, 1997, provided a mechanism for the minister of municipal affairs, if asked by a single municipality, to appoint a commissioner with the authority to order municipal restructuring if local municipalities could not agree. Although the use of commissioners was limited, their potential appointment prompted hundreds of "voluntary" amalgamations. The second, the City of Toronto Act, 1997, amalgamated the constituent parts of the municipality of metropolitan Toronto. The third, the Fewer Municipal Politicians Act, 1999, amalgamated the constituent units of the regional municipalities of Ottawa-Carleton, Hamilton-Wentworth, and Sudbury. The Conservative government justified the municipal amalgamations primarily on the grounds that they would save money, reduce "overlap and duplication," and eliminate the positions of hundreds of municipal politicians.

The Parti québécois government in Quebec introduced its program for municipal amalgamations in April 2000. Two pieces of legislation followed: one authorizing the minister of municipal affairs to order amalgamations in smaller cities, towns, and villages. and another specifying the details of amalgamations in the territories covered by the Montreal and Quebec urban communities and the Outaouais regional community. The Outaouais amalgamation created the new city of Gatineau. These amalgamations came into effect in 2002. Like the Winnipeg unicity amalgamation thirty years before, the Quebec ones were aimed primarily at eliminating differences in levels of municipal taxation and services within the territories that were amalgamated.

The Liberal opposition leader in Quebec, Jean Charest, committed himself, if elected, to legislate a mechanism for deamalgamation. The issue became a dominant one in the 2003 provincial election, and the Liberals were elected. They then went on to do roughly what they had promised. Deamalgamation referendums were held in eighty-seven former municipalities on June 20, 2004, within parts of twenty-nine amalgamated municipalities in which 10% of eligible voters had petitioned for such a referendum. For a deamalgamation to be approved, 50% of the votes cast representing 35% of the total eligible voters had to be affirmative. This threshold was met in thirty-one former municipalities that were part of twelve different amalgamated municipalities. Fifteen of the affirmative decisions for demerger were within the amalgamated city of Montreal. Consequently, difficulties with implementing deamalgamation were more intense there than anywhere else in Quebec.

The result is that Montreal now has an incredibly complex set of relationships between the amalgamated city and the fifteen municipalities that regained their incorporated status in 2005. The system is made even more complex by the fact that, as part of its strategy to prevent deamalgamation, the city of Montreal went to great lengths to decentralize authority to the "boroughs" that were created at the time of amalgamation. After deamalgamation, Montreal has nineteen boroughs, each with its own directly elected mayor, who sits on the Montreal city council as well as the borough council. On the island of Montreal (the territory of the former Montreal Island Community), there are now thirty-five directly elected mayors.

From the mid 1990s until the mid 2000s, municipal amalgamations were on the political agendas of almost every provincial government. In some, such as Newfoundland and Labrador, Prince Edward Island, and New Brunswick, plans for amalgamation were modest, and achievements even more so. In Saskatchewan, a provincial commission recommended extensive amalgamation in rural areas, but a cautious government decided against implementing a plan that had generated a great deal of local opposition. In 2000 in Alberta, a similar commission explicitly rejected amalgamation for the Edmonton region (Garcea and LeSage 2005). Only in British Columbia does the provincial government specifically eschew a policy of forced municipal amalgamation. But on January 1, 1995, the British Columbia municipalities of Abbotsford and Matsqui were amalgamated after a majority of voters in both communities approved by way of referendums the creation of a new city of Abbotsford (Sancton et al. 2000, 49).

MUNICIPAL ELECTIONS

In major Canadian cities prior to the late nineteenth century, party organizations generally controlled municipal elections, even though they were not conducted on an explicitly partisan basis (Underhill 1974, 333).[4] But since then, support for nonpartisanship at the municipal level has generally taken hold, even if everyone understands that political parties are often at work behind the scenes. Support for nonpartisan elections can be traced back to the North American urban reform movement that reached its apogee around the turn of the twentieth century. It was aimed at eliminating the municipal corruption associated with party-based urban political machines and introducing professional management to city governments (Weaver 1977). The influence of this movement appears to have been strong everywhere in Canada, because none of the occasional attempts to introduce political parties to municipal politics has been successful. In most places even attempts to elect local slates of like-minded candidates have failed miserably, although in some prairie cities (especially Winnipeg), formal slates of probusiness candidates have dominated municipal elections in the past.

British Columbia and Quebec are the two provinces in which local political parties have been most successful. At-large municipal elections in British Columbia have encouraged slate building. For example, voters in the city of Vancouver would have trouble keeping track of ten independent at-large councilors and a mayor. Instead, they have been able to vote since 1937 for a slate presented by the right-wing Non-Partisan Association or for various slates offered by the center and the Left, most recently Vision Vancouver and the Coalition of Progressive Electors, respectively. Quebec's local political parties trace their origins back to Montreal's Civic Action League, whose candidate for mayor, Jean Drapeau, won a surprise victory in 1954. From 1960 until 1986, Drapeau and his Civic party completely dominated Montreal city politics. Local political parties remain in Montreal, and in other large Quebec cities, but new ones now emerge and disappear with considerable regularity.

The terms of office for municipal councilors have been extended in recent years, the justification being that municipal councils need longer periods of time between elections to make strategic and long-term decisions and to be more like governments at other levels. The terms are either three or four years (four in the two largest provinces of Ontario and Quebec), except in rural Saskatchewan, where the terms are for two years. Vacancies are filled either by council appointment or by by-election, depending on the province and the circumstances. Council membership ranges in size from sixty-five and forty-five in Montreal and Toronto, respectively, to as few as four in some rural municipalities.

Representation on municipal councils can be quite complicated. Except in some small municipalities in Newfoundland and Labrador, all mayors are directly elected by all voters in the municipality. In the 2006 Toronto election, 333,000 people cast a ballot in favor of David Miller when he was reelected as mayor of Toronto. In many municipalities, especially smaller ones, each member of council is also elected by the entire municipal electorate; each voter has as many votes for council as there are council members. "At-large" systems are favored in larger places by those who want all council members to focus on the well-being of the municipality as a whole rather than just on the interests of a particular ward. The largest municipality in the country with an at-large electoral system is the city of Vancouver. In a plebiscite in 2004, 56% of Vancouver voters supported the existing system instead of converting to a ward system. In the 2005 election, the average voter cast 8.2 votes for councilors out of a maximum of ten. As indicated, they were greatly aided by the fact that there were municipal political parties and the party names (or acronyms) were on the ballot. Many municipalities (for example, London, Ontario; and St. John's, Newfoundland) elect some members of the municipal council at-large and others by ward. In many Ontario municipalities that are part of two-tier systems, some councilors are directly elected at the same election to serve at both levels ("double direct" election). The city of Edmonton has a ward system, but two members are elected from each of six wards.

Mechanisms for drawing ward boundaries vary from province to province. In Quebec, the job is done by the same provincial agency that manages provincial elections. Unlike the United States (Briffaut 1993), there is no jurisprudence requiring absolute (or even relative) equality of ward populations in the same municipality. In the 2006 elections in the city of Ottawa, there were 17,436 voters in the suburban ward of Orleans and only 8,990 in the rural one of Osgoode. The OMB has explicitly endorsed such disparities for Ottawa by pointing out that "[t]he Supreme Court of Canada in the *Carter* Case reviewed the extent to which variance from strict representation by population was permissible. The decision establishes that 'effective representation' not representation by population, is the common law standard for electoral boundaries in Canada" (Ontario Municipal Board 2003). The Supreme Court, however, has never ruled on any cases relating to representation by population in municipal institutions. In fact, it has explicitly noted that the wording of section 3 of the Charter "is quite narrow, guaranteeing only the right to vote in elections of representatives of the federal and the provincial legislative assemblies. As Professor Peter Hogg notes in *Constitutional Law of Canada*...the right does not extend to municipal elections or referenda." (*Haig v. Canada [Chief Electoral Officer]* 1993).

The general absence of political parties in municipal elections and the fact that data relating to such elections (outside Quebec at least) are held almost exclusively by each individual municipality mean that research on Canadian municipal elections is difficult and sparse. What we do know is that turnout rates are generally lower for municipal elections than for federal and provincial, and that incumbency is a huge advantage. The best data and analysis that we have comes from Ontario (Kushner et al. 1997), especially Toronto (Hicks 2006).

Mayors and Local Political Leadership

The political heads of Canadian urban municipalities are generally known as mayors and are directly elected by all the eligible voters in a municipality. They are symbolically important in their respective communities and are often considered local leaders and spokespeople, even in relation to subjects over which their municipality might have little or no functional responsibility. In most municipalities in Canada, mayors have very limited governmental authority. Their one vote on the municipal council has the same weight as the one vote of each of their council colleagues and they usually have few, if any, ways in which they can use their mayoral office to influence such votes. Although they have general responsibilities to oversee the work of municipal staff, it is the council as a whole to whom the staff is formally responsible.

It appears, however, that in many of Canada's smaller municipalities, mayors wield a great deal of political power, especially if they are experienced in municipal affairs and are well respected in their communities. Even in larger municipalities, mayors sometimes are able to exert far more political power than the formal attributes of their position suggest. Long-serving popular mayors such as Steven Juba in Winnipeg (1957–1977), Jean Drapeau in Montreal (1954–1957 and 1960–1986), and Hazel McCallion in Mississauga (1978–) completely dominated their respective municipal councils and came to personify the cities that they led (Levine 1989). In these environments, it does not matter how limited the authority that is granted the mayor by the relevant provincial statute.

But most of the time, the legal authority of the mayor in larger cities is still very important. In Montreal, Winnipeg, and Toronto, the mayor no longer presides over the municipal council, the theory being that he or she is better able to provide political leadership for the council without having the obligation to act as a neutral chairperson at the same time. Instead, council members choose another councilor to act as "speaker." In each of these three cases, the mayor appoints most or all of the members of an executive committee. Sometimes these executive committees are thought of as municipal "cabinets," but only in Montreal does the committee comprise members of the same party. It meets behind closed doors and has the authority to make certain final decisions without council approval. In short, only in Montreal is the executive committee really like a cabinet in a parliamentary system.

Elsewhere, the challenge in providing mayoral leadership is difficult. Mayors of large cities—at least those who are in central cities rather than in suburbs—are exceptionally visible in the local media, but, unlike prime ministers and premiers, they have very few resources that they can use to impose their will. The skilled mayor cajoles and persuades fellow council members, but rarely has the opportunity personally to decide on the adoption of a new policy.

DEVELOPERS, COUNCILORS, AND CITIZENS

Politics in Canadian municipalities is primarily about the built environment. Local issues relating to schools, hospitals, social services, and, to a lesser extent, even the police are generally not on the municipal political agenda, because they are handled directly by the province and/or by special-purpose agencies of one kind or another. However, all municipal councils set policy for local land use and infrastructure, with varying degrees of supervision from their respective provincial governments.

This means that the people with the greatest financial stakes in local politics are the people who make their living from building. Although there is a common perception that builders and developers usually get their way in municipal politics, it is equally true that for many projects they often meet serious challenges from environmentalists, neighborhood activists, or people who simply say "Not In My Back Yard." At its core, Canadian municipal politics often seems little more than a constant battle between these two sides, sometimes with developers in the ascendancy (usually when people are worried about employment and economic growth) and sometimes with citizens groups apparently able to veto almost any project that is physically near to mobilized residents.

Because municipalities are the level of government physically closest to most citizens, it is often assumed that citizens identify more with the local level than with the provincial and federal. There is considerable evidence, however, that this is not the case, with statistics for voter turnout being the most obvious example (Treisman 2007). The harsh reality is that Canadian nonpartisan municipal government is often difficult to understand, technical in its functional scope, and generally not covered well by the media. It often seems especially distant from those who do not own their own homes: the young, the poor, the transient. Municipalities frequently launch programs of one kind or another to "engage" citizens in land-use planning, budgetary choices, or the determination of future municipal "strategy" (Graham and Phillips 1998), but there is little evidence that such programs attract large numbers of ordinary citizens.

Instead, municipal politics is characterized by large-scale eruptions of citizen involvement over particular issues. These were especially important and especially well documented during the late 1960s and '70s, when citizens' groups successfully challenged the then-orthodox view that decisions about municipal development were best made by the "professionals," especially engineers, land-use planners, and social workers. The victory of the "Stop Spadina, Save Our City" group in Toronto in 1971, when the Ontario government decided to cancel its support for the inner city portion of the Spadina expressway, was the apogee of citizen–group success (Magnusson 1983). The combination of nonpartisan politics and generally low voter interest means that highly motivated groups of mobilized citizens have considerable power to influence municipal councils. Isolated individuals might not be able "to fight city hall," but groups of angry voters can.

SENIOR MUNICIPAL MANAGEMENT

Employees of municipal governments are not civil servants. This is because municipalities are corporations that are legally separate from provincial governments, with employees that do serve the Crown and hence are its "servants." However, this legalistic and symbolic distinction pales in significance to the other differences between

soldiers. In the 1930s, both the federal government and provincial governments stepped in when municipalities proved manifestly incapable of supporting millions of unemployed and indigent citizens. There was another urban housing crisis after World War II, and once again the federal government, mainly through the Central (now Canada) Mortgage and Housing Corporation, became a key force in Canadian urban development. In the late 1960s, as inner cities in many parts of the United States were being destroyed by rioting and the retreat to the suburbs, the federal government tried to ensure that Canadian cities did not suffer the same fate. The establishment in 1971 of the Ministry of State for Urban Affairs was its most significant initiative, but the ministry was abolished, apparently as a cost-cutting measure, in 1979. There were more federal urban initiatives in the early 2000s (Sancton 2008). Meanwhile, the involvement of provincial governments in urban affairs became so ubiquitous that it scarcely drew anyone's notice.

Municipal governments are probably less crucial now to the overall well-being of their respective urban areas than they were a hundred years ago. This is not to suggest that municipal governments are not important. It is only to suggest that urban areas have become so economically dominant and so populous that Canadian federal and provincial governments must be just as concerned with the well-being of cities as urban municipalities are. Municipalities continue to shape the fine-grained features of the development and redevelopment of our urban built environment and they continue to finance such crucial services as policing and firefighting. The importance of local government derives from the inherent importance of these traditional functions, not from its alleged potential to displace other levels of government in the eyes of Canada's urban population.

NOTES

1. Much of the information in this section derives from my synthesis of "provincial overview" papers prepared for the Social Sciences and Humanities Research Council of Canada (SSHRCC)-funded Public Policy in Municipalities project based at The University of Western Ontario and directed by my colleague, Robert Young.

2. For a comprehensive account of recent "reforms" in each province, see Garcea and LeSage (2005).

3. For an important collection of essays on this subject, see Richmond and Siegel (1994).

4. Unless otherwise noted, material in this section derives from the "provincial overviews" referred to in note 1.

5. Kitchen (2002) and McMillan (2006) are important sources for municipal financial data, but their analysis and presentation of the data in the Statistics Canada Financial Management System are slightly different from what is presented here. Numbers in this paragraph are calculated from data series contained in tables 3850002 and 3850004 of CANSIM II. The calculation relating to GDP also derives from CANSIM II data and was made by Ajay Sharma, a research assistant for the SSHRC-funded project on Public Policy in Municipalities. Percentages in the rest of this section also derive from Sharma's work for this project.

REFERENCES

Briffaut, Richard. 1993. Who rules at home? One person/one vote and local governments. *University of Chicago Law Review* 60: 339–424.

Cameron, David M. 1980. Provincial responsibilities for municipal government. *Canadian Public Administration* 23: 222–235.

Chipman, John G. 2002. *A Law unto Itself: How the Ontario Municipal Board Has Developed and Applied Land-Use Planning Policy*. Toronto: University of Toronto Press.

Crawford, Kenneth G. 1954. *Canadian Municipal Government*. Toronto: University of Toronto Press.

Garcea, Joseph, and Edward C. LeSage, Jr., eds. 2005. *Municipal Reform in Canada: Reconfiguration, Re-empowerment, and Rebalancing*. Toronto: Oxford University Press.

Graham, Katherine A., and Susan D. Phillips, eds. 1998. *Citizen Engagement: Lessons in Participation from Local Government*. Toronto: Institute of Public Administration of Canada.

Haig v. Canada (Chief Electoral Officer), (1993) 2 S.C.R. 995.

Hicks, Bruce M. 2006. *Are Marginalized Communities Disenfranchised? Voter Turnout and Representation in Post-Merger Toronto*. IRPP working paper series no. 2006–03. Montreal: Institute for Research on Public Policy.

Infrastructure Canada. 2006. *Canada Profile: Commonwealth Local Government Forum*. Ottawa: Infrastructure Canada.

Kitchen, Harry. 2002. *Municipal Revenue and Expenditure Issues in Canada*. Toronto: Canadian Tax Foundation.

Kushner, Joseph, David Siegel, and Hannah Stanwick. 1997. Ontario municipal elections: Voting trends and determinants of electoral success in a Canadian province. *Canadian Journal of Political Science* 39: 539–553.

Levine, Allan, ed. 1989. *Your Worship: The Lives of Eight of Canada's Most Unforgettable Mayors*. Toronto: James Lorimer.

Magnusson, Warren. 1983. Toronto. In *City Politics in Canada*, ed. Warren Magnusson and Andrew Sancton, 94–139. Toronto: University of Toronto Press.

———. 1985. The local state in Canada: Theoretical perspectives. *Canadian Public Administration* 28(4): 575–599.

McMillan, Melville H. 2006. Municipal relations with the federal and provincial governments: A fiscal perspective. In *Municipal–Federal–Provincial Relations in Canada*, ed. Robert Young and Christian Leuprecht, 48–81. Montreal: McGill-Queen's University Press.

Ontario Municipal Board. 2003. Decision/order no. 0605. May 8.

Osborne, David, and Ted Gaebler. 1992. *Reinventing Government: How the Entrepreneurial Spirit Is Transforming the Public Sector*. Reading, Mass: Addison-Wesley.

Richmond, Dale, and David Siegel, eds. 1994. *Agencies, Boards and Commissions in Canadian Local Government*. Toronto: Institute of Public Administration of Canada.

Sancton, Andrew. 2000. *Merger Mania: The Assault on Local Government*. Montreal: McGill-Queen's University Press.

———. 2002. Signs of life: The transformation of two-tier metropolitan government. In *Urban Affairs: Back on the Policy Agenda*, ed. Caroline Andrew, Katherine A. Graham, and Susan D. Phillips, 179–198. Montreal: McGill-Queen's University Press.

———. 2008. The urban agenda. In *Canadian Federalism: Performance, Effectiveness, Legitimacy*, 2nd ed., ed. Herman Bakvis and Grace Skogstad, 114–133. Toronto: Oxford University Press.

Sancton, Andrew, Rebecca James, and Rick Ramsay. 2000. *Amalgamation vs. Inter-Municipal Cooperation: Financing Local and Infrastructure Services*. Toronto: Intergovernmental Committee on Urban and Regional Research.

Siegel, David. 1994. Politics, politicians, and public servants in non-partisan local governments. *Canadian Public Administration* 37: 7–30.

Statistics Canada. 2004. *Financial Management System*. Ottawa: Statistics Canada.

Stevenson, Don, and Richard Gilbert. 2005. Coping with Canadian federalism. *Canadian Public Administration* 48: 528–551.

Treisman, Daniel. 2007. *The Architecture of Government: Rethinking Political Decentralization*. Cambridge: Cambridge University Press.

Underhill, F. H. [1910–1911] 1974. Commission government in cities. In *Saving the Canadian City, the First Phase, 1880–1920*, ed. Paul Rutherford, 325–334. Toronto: University of Toronto Press.

Weaver, John C. 1977. *Shaping the Canadian City: Essays on Urban Politics and Policy, 1880–1920*. Toronto: Institute of Public Administration of Canada.

PART III

GOVERNING INSTITUTIONS

CHAPTER 9

PARLIAMENT AND LEGISLATURES: CENTRAL TO CANADIAN DEMOCRACY?

PAUL G. THOMAS

CONSTITUTIONAL theories of representative and responsible government put legislatures at the center of Canadian democracy. Yet for many decades there has been much talk about the decline of legislatures and the need to reform them to protect democratic principles and practices. Historical developments, contemporary events, and anticipated future trends all present challenges to the relevance and effectiveness of legislatures in terms of their role in the policy process, their capacity to hold the political executive accountable, and their contribution to the health of Canadian democracy.

Opinion surveys suggest that public respect and support for legislatures has reached an all-time low. During the 1970s and '80s, there was much talk about the need to modernize and to revitalize the institution, but more recently the focus of public debate has shifted from "parliamentary reform" to the broader topic of "democratic reform." This shift might suggest that the public regards parliamentary reform as futile or of marginal value and wants to see new forms of direct democracy replace traditional mechanisms of representative democracy. This chapter asks the fundamental question: Are we witnessing the gradual eclipse of legislatures as a central institution of Canadian democracy?

The answer to be given here is that legislatures are not as powerless and irrelevant as the prevailing negative stereotype suggests. Clearly they face serious challenges in performing their traditional functions effectively. In relative terms, they have lost influence to other institutions in the policy process. However, legislatures remain a vital link between citizens and their governments, as a source of both support and legitimacy for government actions. Their influence in the governing process is not easily measured, because it usually occurs in conjunction with outside events, behind the formalities of the parliamentary process and indirectly over time. Looking to the future, even if more direct forms of democracy are adopted, legislatures will still matter as forums for public discussion and as a source of democratic accountability. The premise for this chapter is that strengthening legislatures would benefit governments that today face a deficit in terms of the trust and confidence of citizens.

The remainder of this chapter consists of four main sections. First, there is a discussion of the explicit and implicit functions attributed to legislatures in the political science literature and how these relate to the main formal roles of legislatures within the Canadian political system. Second, the issue of the alleged decline of legislatures will be examined. Third, there will be an examination of the organizational arrangements, procedures, and activities through which legislatures fulfill their formal constitutional responsibilities and perform a number of informal functions within the Canadian political system. The final section of the chapter speculates on the potential for reforms that will enable legislatures to cope with the challenges they face today and may face in the future.

THE ROLES AND FUNCTIONS OF LEGISLATURES

Scholars studying the legislative process in different countries have found it helpful to distinguish between the formal constitutional roles of legislatures and the informal functions they serve within the political system. In Canada's cabinet—parliamentary system, legislatures have four main constitutional roles: (1) to review and approve legislation, including that related to taxing and spending; (2) to conduct scrutiny of the ongoing policies and the administration of programs; (3) to protect the rights of individual citizens and to provide redress of grievances for actions or inactions by public officials; and (4) to serve as the primary political forum for the discussion of the overall performance of governments as a basis for promoting ultimate democratic accountability to the electorate. In practice, these roles overlap in terms of the actual activities and impacts of legislatures.

During the twentieth century, political scientists became increasingly dissatisfied with using formal constitutional descriptions as the starting point for their investigations of the roles of legislatures (Suleiman 1986). In general, they noted the gap that existed between constitutional theory that placed legislatures at the center of political life and the growing perception that legislatures were losing authority, influence, and relevance to other parts of the political system. By the late 1960s, more empirically oriented studies of the actual functioning of legislatures first made their appearance in Canada. By adopting a wider systems perspective, and borrowing research techniques from fields such as sociology, legislative scholars sought to identify less obvious contributions of legislatures to the overall health and performance of the political system beyond what was attributed to them by constitutional theory. At a time when everyone was claiming that "the real action" had shifted to the cabinet and the bureaucracy, the adoption of the systems approach represented a way for legislative scholars to defend the importance of their field of inquiry.

Based upon a systems perspective, a number of functions performed by legislatures were identified. Simply put, a function represents the contribution to and the effect upon the political system arising from the activities of legislatures. Table 9.1 sets forth a list of functions commonly attributed to legislatures. A list of more concrete activities that contribute to the performance of these functions is also shown in table 9.1. Some functions are formally recognized or explicit, whereas others are implicit or latent in the activities of legislatures. The functions overlap in practice, with one type of activity contributing to more than one function. Demonstrating the linkages between concrete legislative activities and the broader representational and systems maintenance functions of legislatures involves conceptual and analytical challenges too numerous to be reviewed in the space available here.

Talk of decline presumes that there are identifiable and agreed-upon measures of the effectiveness of legislatures. However, there are both normative and empirical debates regarding whether legislatures are effective (Arter 2006a; 2006b). Concepts such as the independence of legislatures, their deliberative capabilities, efficiency, organizational capacities, professionalism, and performance within the wider policy process are conceptualized and studied in different ways in various countries. Often the U.S. Congress, which is seen as exceptional among legislatures for the real power it wields, is used as the starting point for comparing legislatures around the world. Nelson Polsby (1975) identified four categories of legislatures, as displayed in table 9.2. Canadian legislatures appear to fit most fully into the category of "arena" legislatures. Such legislatures are a place where societal differences and disagreements

Table 9.1 Functions of Legislatures

Policy-Making Functions	■ Making laws ■ Controlling taxing and spending ■ Scrutinizing the government and the bureaucracy
Representational Functions	■ Recruiting and identifying leaders ■ Dealing with the bureaucracy on behalf of constituents ■ Clarifying policy choices for the electorate (an education function)
Systems/Maintenance Functions	■ Creating governments ■ Making the actions of governments legitimate ■ Mobilizing public support for the outcomes of the policy process ■ Managing conflict within the political system ■ Contributing to integration within the political system

Table 9.2 Types of Legislatures

Type of Parliament	Internal Structure	Example
Transformative	Highly complex	U.S. Congress
Arena	Complex	Canadian Parliament
Emerging	Evolving	Bolivian Congress
Rubber stamp	Little internal structure	Old U.S.S.R.

Source: Polsby, Nelson W. 1975. Legislatures. In *Handbook of Political Science: Governmental Institutions and Processes*, vol. 5, ed. Fred Greenstein and Nelson Polsby, 49. Reading, Mass: Addison-Wesley.

are represented, articulated, and accommodated into public policy. However, most of the initiative in terms of legislation, spending, and administrative action is controlled by ministers and the bureaucracy, usually with input from actors outside government.

The slogan "government proposes, Parliament disposes" seems to capture accurately the place of Canadian legislatures in the policy process most of the time. However, measuring the influence and effects of legislatures is far from straightforward. Measures can be quantitative or qualitative. For example, the number of executive initiatives (government bills and spending proposals) that are passed in a legislative session is a quantitative measure that emphasizes the efficiency of the legislature. The number of bills rejected, modified, withdrawn, or seriously delayed could serve as an indicator of the capacity of the legislature to challenge the executive. The number of bills introduced by private members that make it into law might be a measure of the influence of individual legislators. A more qualitative measure would involve an estimate of legislative influence on the agendas of governments. Such influence is difficult to measure, because there are usually other sources of pressure, the influence of legislators often occurs through hidden processes like private caucus meetings, and legislative influence often takes place over several years, with the legislature serving as a kind of incubator of fledgling policy ideas struggling to be born.

To this point, the discussion has implied that the legislature represents a unified institution with a set of collective roles or functions with which all or most of its members identify. In reality, however, competitive, disciplined political parties are the dominating presence in terms of the organization and dynamics of most Canadian legislatures. The exceptions are the nonpartisan, consensus-based legislatures in the northern territories of the Yukon and Nunavut.

At the national and the provincial levels, cabinet—parliamentary government has evolved over time to become "party government." The implicit, ideal model involves competitive disciplined political parties presenting ideas to voters and obtaining a mandate to implement their election platforms should they win office. It is on the basis of such appeals by parties and their leaders that most electors vote. The party, normally the one with the largest number of members in the legislature, is expected to provide leadership and direction to government, including the formulation of nearly all the legislation and spending approved by the legislature. Because governing parties see themselves as required to deliver on their election promises, it is not their job to compromise with the opposition. To do so would make them less responsive and accountable to the voters who elected them.

The value of opposition is recognized as a check on the use of executive power, as an outlet for alternative perspectives, and as a means for ensuring peaceful alternation in office. For these reasons, public law recognizes the role of "Her Majesty's Loyal Opposition" (loyal to the principles of the political system), whereas support (funding, staffing, space, procedural rights, and so forth) is provided to enable the opposition to mount more effective challenges to the government. All of this sounds familiar, basic, and somewhat idealistic, but bears repeating to reinforce the point that competitive political parties are today seen as central to the achievement of both parliamentary and democratic accountability.

Political parties provide the main basis for the organization of legislatures and they provide much of the energy that fuels the institution (Thomas 1994). Elected on the basis mainly of a party label, individual legislators see themselves as being part of an organized, disciplined team. Mechanisms like secret caucus meetings and party discipline further promote the unity of parties within the parliamentary arena. Nearly every vote on bills and spending proposals in Canadian legislatures occurs along party lines. In short, individuals with political ambitions get ahead by obtaining a party nomination; securing election on the basis of the party's history, platform, and leader; supporting the party and its leadership on crucial votes in the legislature; and often anticipating that party loyalty will help them to move up the career ladder to become a cabinet minister or even first minister.

With political parties and partisanship dominating the internal operations of legislatures, several sets of relationships emerge. The most obvious is the ongoing competition between the leadership of the governing party and the leadership of the opposition parties for media attention and for public support. Beyond this adversarial government-versus-opposition dynamic, there are also fluctuating intraparty relationships between the leaders of each party and their backbench followers. Finally, there are relationships among backbenchers within and across parties, including within the caucus and caucus committees for each party, and parliamentary committees where all parties are represented. The partisan battles among the parties in the legislative "arena"(to use Polsby's term) gain almost all the media attention, with the result that the public's image of legislatures is mainly one of conflict and negative theatrics. Less noticeable is a more constructive, consensus-oriented component of legislative life, which is difficult to document because the activities usually take place in private. All these different modes of interaction within legislatures add to the complexity of assessing whether legislatures have been losing authority and influence to other institutions and actors.

QUESTIONING THE "DECLINE THESIS"

The notion of decline implies that there was an earlier historical period when legislatures played a more influential role in the policy process and in holding the executive accountable. However, the available evidence suggests that executive dominance within Canadian legislatures has been the long-standing pattern. What seems to have changed over time is the basis for that dominance. Legislatures have faced both long-term forces and short-term developments in their external and internal environments that have made the performance of their roles more difficult. For a variety of reasons discussed later, legislatures were slow to adapt their structures, procedures, and capacities to meet these new challenges. In contrast, cabinets, but even more so public bureaucracies and interest groups outside the government, adapted more quickly to the complex and congested policy environments that emerged during the twentieth century.

In the space available here, challenges confronting legislatures can only be presented as brief statements without much elaboration:

- The expanding scope and complexity of government activity
- The expansion of public bureaucracies as repositories of expert policy knowledge
- The need to involve the bureaucracy in the formulation of policy and to grant it extensive delegated authority to implement policies
- The proliferation of organized pressure groups as an alternative channel of representation
- The professionalization of party organizations and the use of polling and focus groups to capture public opinion
- The growing concentration of power in the hands of the first minister, his or her office, and in the other central agencies that serve cabinets
- The development of "executive federalism" in which first ministers, other cabinet ministers, and intergovernmental officials negotiate policy, program, and financial deals with little or no input from legislatures and legislators
- The adoption in 1982 of the Canadian Charter of Rights and Freedoms, putting limits on the use of legislative authority
- The rise of international terrorism and the need to provide national security agencies with additional powers that challenged the capacity of legislatures to protect the rights of citizens
- The development of aggressive media that focus more on governments than on legislatures, and the response by governments that adopt the art of "spin" in their communications
- The decline in public trust and confidence in all political institutions, including legislatures, leading to reduced attention to and involvement with the traditional political process
- The rise of "new public management" within bureaucracies that has contributed to "depoliticization" by promoting a "managerial" approach to issues

- The tightening of procedural control within legislatures by the governing party through changes in the rules

In combination, these trends have challenged legislatures, but before labeling the outcome a decline, several qualifications are in order.

The statement that legislatures have lost influence must first be qualified by the observation that first ministers and cabinets are part of the legislature and clearly they have gained power. Therefore, the "real losers" in terms of executive—legislative relations are the opposition parties and the backbenchers from all parties.

The perception that backbenchers have completely lost any meaningful role also has to be qualified. In both Ottawa and some provincial capitals, parliamentary parties have increased caucus democracy to allow more input into policies and strategies being followed by party leaders. It is easier for caucuses to block, delay, or modify the stances being taken by their leaders than it is to initiate. In the case of the governing party, there is some evidence that ministers anticipate caucus reactions when developing legislation and spending (Thomas 1994). Caucus influence usually depends on outside pressures and requires backbenchers to develop a "collective voice" on an issue. After a caucus is granted influence in private, there is more of an onus on backbenchers to follow the party line in other parts of the parliamentary process.

Attempts by individual backbenchers to contribute directly to public policy remain largely an exercise in futility. The House of Commons and several provincial legislatures have made rule changes allowing more time to debate private members' bills (those introduced by noncabinet members) and resolutions that provide greater opportunity for backbenchers to publicize their policy ideas with the hope of seeing them eventually become the basis for government policy. However, the fact that private members' bills cannot involve the expenditure of public money is a fundamental constraint and most backbenchers choose to introduce resolutions that simply exhort governments to take some action. Time for private members' business is scarce—an average of four hours per week when provincial legislatures meet—so very few private members' bills become law (White 2006, 257).

A further qualification of the decline thesis is that it focuses mainly on lawmaking and control of spending. Decline with respect to these traditional roles might be offset to some degree by growth in importance and effectiveness of such informal functions as the representation of public opinion and the mobilization of public support for actions by governments. Legislatures have sought to equip themselves better to perform these communications functions by adding staff, constituency offices, and various new information technologies, such as websites and online consultations. By debating and publicizing the actions of governments, legislatures can help to shape the policy agenda and parameters of policy. Legislatures are not the only institutions that perform these functions—for example, interest groups and the media are also involved. Demonstrating the separate contribution of the legislatures at different stages in the overall policy cycle is a difficult analytical and empirical challenge, which really has not been attempted in the academic literature.

Finally, before lapsing into easy generalizations about the decline of Canadian legislatures, we need to recognize the different political contexts in which they operate. The most important contextual factor is the nature of the party system—for example, whether it is highly competitive or one-party dominant. Long periods of one-party rule can weaken legislative democracy. Whether governments are in a majority or minority position in the legislature is related to the level of party competition. The decline thesis presumes the tight control and predictability of majority governments. Minority situations are not uncommon, however, and in such circumstances there can be both intraparty and interparty negotiations over whether a government survives, whether its bills pass, whether amendments are accepted, and how the legislature will operate on a day-to-day basis (Thomas 2007). When there is a minority government, the opinions and the votes of individual backbenchers actually matter.

The size and organizational capacity of Canadian legislatures vary significantly. During the 1990s, five provincial legislatures were reduced in size, mainly as an economy measure to impress the public. Compared with the House of Commons, provincial legislatures are relatively small (most have fewer than a hundred members) and the cabinet forms a high proportion of the membership, which usually means less criticism of government performance. In addition to being small, the three territorial legislatures are less mature and professional in organizational terms. Small legislatures typically have short sessions, limited committee systems, and few professional staff. On the other hand, they tend to have stable memberships, thus allowing provincial legislators more opportunity than members of Parliament, whose turnover is high, to learn how government works, as well as more face-to-face dealings with ministers and public servants.

In summary, rather than absolute decline, Canadian legislatures have faced institutional adaptation challenges. For the most part, they have been slow to modify their structures, procedures, and internal cultures to cope more effectively with the new demands and pressures they face. Reform to legislatures has been a slow process in part because there are philosophical and practical disagreements over what are the most *desirable* and *feasible* roles for legislatures to play in the wider policy process. Legislatures are given the dual role of supporting strong and responsive government by enabling the efficient passage of government business, yet at the same time they are expected to hold the first minister and the cabinet accountable. There is an inevitable tension between these two roles.

Typically, governments regard the legislature mainly as a nuisance to be tolerated or an obstacle to be surmounted, and less as an institution capable of improving legislation and/or helping to hold the bureaucracy accountable. Opposition parties are often supportive of a stronger role for the legislature when out of office, but their enthusiasm for legislative reform typically wanes when they become the government. Competitive political parties are deeply embedded into the structures, procedures, and cultures of Canadian legislatures. As a result, legislatures do not have a strong sense of collective identity and unified purpose that might support institutional adaptation to changing circumstances. Having identified the wider, changing contexts that influence the role of legislatures, it is possible to examine in more concrete terms how legislatures perform their formal roles and informal functions.

THE LAWMAKING PROCESS

Passing laws is what most people have in mind when they think of legislatures. Legislatures are supposed to be supreme. Apart from respecting the division of powers in the federal system, the provisions of the Canadian Charter of Rights and Freedom and certain prerogatives reserved to the Crown and the political executive, legislatures are theoretically free to pass laws on any subject (Forcese and Freeman 2005, chap. 5). The actual formulation of laws, however, is done under the direction of ministers and cabinets, on advice from the public service, and often based on demands from groups outside of government. Individual legislators, especially those in opposition, are usually the last to know either that legislation is coming or the content of proposed bills.

Typically, bills are drafted by the bureaucracy in very general terms, with the details to be filled in later through regulations and the exercise of administrative discretion. After review and approval by ministers, they are tabled in the legislature. By this point, there is considerable momentum for adoption. The volume and complexity of legislation has increased. Most legislation does not represent completely new policy—more often it involves amendments to existing statutes based on experience in applying the existing policies. Most bills are highly technical and narrow in their impact, and they are passed expeditiously. In contrast, a small number of bills are broad and controversial, and they take up a disproportionate amount of time in legislative sessions. In short, the legislative process can be variable, but most bills pass without major amendments.

All bills are dealt with by the same procedures, which vary only slightly among Canadian legislatures. Bills undergo three "readings," or opportunities for debate. First reading introduces the bill and debate rarely takes place. Second reading involves the main debates on bills and constitutes approval in principle. Substantive amendments have to be introduced at this point or risk being ruled out of order later. Some legislatures—such as the House of Commons and the Ontario legislature—have experimented with the referral of bills to committees after first reading to allow more room for amendments.

Clause-by-clause examination of bills occurs at the committee stage after second reading. This can take place on the floor of the legislature or in a separate standing, legislative, or special committee. Legislatures in Manitoba, Ontario, Quebec, the Northwest Territories, and the House of Commons in Ottawa routinely seek public input at the committee stage. After bills have completed the committee stage, they are reported back with or without amendments, and debate takes place at third reading. In the national Parliament, bills must undergo a similar process in the appointed Senate (discussed briefly later). The final steps to bills becoming laws are royal assent and proclamation.

The ability of governments to gain approval for their legislative program is usually seen as a matter of confidence, a topic around which controversy swirls (Heard 2007). The legislative program is announced in the Speech from the Throne, which is followed by a number of days of highly partisan debate and culminates in a vote that decides whether the government stays in office. A vote after the debate of a government's budgetary plans is another confidence occasion. Whether the passage of individual bills is a confidence matter is somewhat unclear, but the consensus among authorities is that only governments can declare whether the defeat of a particular bill requires resignation and a possible election. In a majority government situation, the process is controlled and predictable. There is more uncertainty and opportunity for input from legislatures when there is a minority government in place.

In summary, legislatures generally have limited, but still important, influence with respect to the approval of legislation. Debates and other opportunities for public input can uncover problems with proposed legislation leading, possibly, to amendments. The entire process can add to understanding of, support for, and the legitimacy of the laws that are eventually passed. At the heart of the process is a tension between the government's need to have legislation passed in a reasonable period of time and the right of elected representatives to understand, discuss, and attempt to change proposed laws.

Scrutiny and Redress of Grievances

In principle, legislatures have a role to play in monitoring the impact of legislation to determine whether it is having the desired impact. In part, this involves reviewing the exercise of delegated legislative authority to determine whether regulations and their application have gone beyond the parameters of the authorizing legislation. More generally, upholding the rights of individual citizens in relation to the use of public power has traditionally been seen as a fundamental role of legislatures (Thomas 2007).

The potential scope of the scrutiny task is vast. Also, the work is difficult, time-consuming, and, for the most part, politically unrewarding. Most of the scrutiny is conducted by opposition members whose primary purpose is to embarrass the government. Members of the governing party are not encouraged to identify problems that could embarrass ministers.

Historically, the scrutiny function derived from the requirement that legislatures approve all taxing and spending. Financial measures are usually considered confidence matters, and a defeat on a supply (expenditure) or a tax bill could force the resignation of a government. Therefore, governments exercise exceedingly tight control over all aspects of the budgetary process. The processes for dealing with financial measures are too detailed to be reviewed fully here.

Government financial matters are enormously complicated and only a tiny minority of legislators carefully study and master documents like taxation changes and spending forecasts. Changes to the formats for estimates of future spending and the production of performance reports on past spending have been introduced in the House of Commons and in a few provinces. Unfortunately, little actual use appears to have been made of the new documents (Good 2007, chap. 9). In short, constitutional theory might imply that legislatures control taxing and spending, but in fact these are largely executive functions. At best, debates and votes on financial matters provide legislators with a chance to express their views on policy and administrative matters, with the faint hope that over time they might have some limited, indirect influence over the direction of taxing and spending.

Beginning in the 1960s, legislatures began to recognize that they could not perform the broader scrutiny and accountability functions that flowed out of their financial duties without some help. This has led to the creation of various parliamentary agencies or "officers of Parliament" to assist with the scrutiny function (Thomas 2003). The roster of parliamentary agencies varies at the national and the provincial levels. It includes auditors general (OAG; the longest established), ombudsmen, information and privacy commissioners, electoral officers, language commissioners, ethics commissions, public-sector integrity commissioners, and human rights commissions. Most such agencies investigate problems of fairness between citizens and government bodies and resolve them through mediation and publicity. A few have the authority to make binding decisions. Agencies report annually, but there is little follow-up in the legislature or its committees, which lessens the effectiveness of the agencies and raises the issue of whether they are themselves sufficiently accountable.

The financial duty of legislatures to provide retrospective scrutiny of spending is based on the publication of the annual public accounts. These documents are voluminous and detailed. To help interpret them, legislatures have the support of OAGs, who examine the legality, accuracy, and efficiency of departmental and non-departmental spending and file reports with the legislatures. Parliament and all provincial/territorial legislatures operate standing committees on public accounts (PACs), which are usually chaired by a member of an opposition party. The PACs consider the OAGs' reports and present their recommendations to the legislature for consideration by the government. Beginning in the late 1970s, OAGs adopted "value-for-money" auditing, which, according to the critics, took them into the more subjective and controversial area of assessing the worth of programs. The same critics also complain that OAGs dictate the agendas of PACs through the selection of topics for investigation and reporting. In defense of legislative auditors, it is not their fault that only a small minority of legislators exhibit a sustained interest in financial and managerial issues. Arguably, without their participation, the legislative scrutiny of financial matters would be considerably weaker.

Public service reform (PSR) initiatives have been underway to a greater or lesser extent in all Canadian jurisdictions since the early 1990s (Thomas 2001). The implications of PSR for the future of parliamentary democracy have not been widely discussed. Only three of the PSR initiatives and their potential impacts on parliamentary scrutiny and accountability can be mentioned briefly in the space available here. First, there is an emerging acceptance of the notion that deputy ministers should be held directly accountable before the legislature for the management of departments. This so-called "accounting officer" arrangement is meant to modify somewhat the concept of ministerial responsibility, which is seen by reformers to provide an inadequate basis for bureaucratic accountability. At the national level, the concept was part of the Federal Accountability Act passed by Parliament in December 2006. Other jurisdictions will be watching to see if the accounting officer arrangement leads, as intended, to clearer and stronger accountability to Parliament or whether it blurs accountability and leads to "buck passing" between ministers and deputy ministers when something goes wrong.

Second, under the slogan of "steering versus rowing," governments across Canada have moved to devolved decision making of various kinds, including the use of third parties to deliver public programs. The adoption of special operating agencies, the privatization of Crown corporations, contracting out the delivery of services to commercial firms and nonprofit organizations, the use of public—private partnerships, and other networking arrangements are all examples of this type of thinking. There are two major implications for parliamentary accountability from these new approaches. First, many important matters related to public policy no longer fall clearly and fully within the scope of ministerial responsibility as traditionally understood. Second, legislatures have largely failed to develop the mechanisms to ensure that accountability for results is enforced.

Performance measurement and reporting is a third prominent feature of PSR. The broad aim of such initiatives is to shift from a process-based to results-based model of accountability to demonstrate that value for money is being achieved. At the national level and in the larger provincial jurisdictions, hundreds of documents on plans and performance are being tabled in the legislatures. This activity is still relatively new. Use of performance reports by legislatures appears to be limited, haphazard, fitful, and inconsequential in terms of requiring ministers and public servants to explain and defend the performance of departments and programs.

Various explanations can be offered for the nonuse of performance reports. Too much information, most of which is not relevant to the preoccupation of legislators, is seen to be part of the problem. The new documents deal mainly with inputs (spending and activities) and outputs (taxes and volumes of services delivered), but do not usually cover outcomes (impacts in the real world). It has been difficult for legislators to drop their usual partisan orientation to the use of information. Generally, legislatures are negative, partisan, short range, and shifting in their approach, whereas the performance model of governing presumes they can become constructive, objective, systematic, and future oriented in their approach.

COMMITTEES: THE BEST HOPE FOR REFORM?

Committees of various kinds have become the main working units of Canadian legislatures in terms of the review of legislation, the discussion of spending, and the scrutiny of administration. More autonomy and influence for committees is usually seen as the best avenue of reform if the intention is to increase the influence of legislatures in the wider policy process, give backbenchers more meaningful roles, and increase the parliamentary accountability of ministers and public servants. Generalizing about committees within the legislative process, however, is difficult.

Committees in Canadian legislatures have a superficial similarity in terms of how they are described (standing, special, joint, and so on), the formal roles they are assigned, and their basic structures (for example, membership is divided among the parties based on their representation in the full chamber). Reflecting their differences in size, legislatures in Canada have anywhere from four to twenty committees. In smaller legislatures there are fewer backbenchers to serve on committees, and often committees also contain government ministers, which may weaken their independence. Committees require time to meet, and provincial legislatures typically meet only for fifty to seventy days in a year. Some legislatures allow committees to meet between sessions when they do not compete with the full chamber for the attention of members.

The procedures for handling bills, the approval of spending, and the conduct of inquiries are other factors that affect the strength of the committee system. As White (2006) points out, larger provincial legislatures are more likely to refer bills and estimates of spending to more extensive and more active committee systems. A 2005 survey (Docherty 2005, 149) found that five provincial legislatures—Manitoba, Nova Scotia, Ontario, Quebec, and Saskatchewan—routinely sent bills to standing committees after second reading to allow for witnesses to testify. In Ottawa, under the short-lived Liberal government of Paul Martin (2003–2006), bills were to be sent after first reading to the appropriate standing committee to allow more opportunity for substantive amendments.

Numerous other procedural matters can contribute to the effectiveness of the committee systems, such as

- Whether members select their committees or are assigned
- The number of committees on which members serve
- The freedom of committees to select their own topics and set their own schedules
- Whether chairs of committees are selected by the committee members or chosen by the government
- Whether the committees have professional staff beyond the clerk who advises on procedure
- Whether there is a requirement for governments to respond to committee reports

Changes to the organization and procedures are the most popular way to strengthen committees, but the power of the government and strong partisanship mean only a marginal increase in committee influence.

Reports from committees have four potential audiences: other members of the legislature; the government, including the public service; organizations outside of government; and the media, who cover committees only when something sensational is happening. Committee reports have to compete to capture the attention of these audiences. This means they must deal with important, timely topics, be well informed and credible, and be written in an engaging format that is usable by the media. Too often, committee reports do not meet these requirements. However, many factors beyond timing, content, and format will affect the fate of committee reports, particularly whether the government is open to advice. Few reports are adopted fully and immediately. This does not mean that the processes of committee hearings and report writing are a complete waste. Reports may help to shape, over time, a climate of opinion around various policy issues. Moreover, the processes of committee work constitute a type of discursive accountability in which both ministers and public servants have to answer for the use of public authority and public money. Despite their limits, committees still represent the greatest opportunity for backbenchers to participate in policy debates and to enforce accountability.

THE SENATE AND BYGONE BICAMERALISM AT THE PROVINCIAL LEVEL

The existence of a second chamber or upper house is sometimes seen as a potential check on executive dominance, especially if it is elected on a different basis and represents a different partisan composition to the lower house, where the confidence convention applies. Only the Senate at the national level survives as an appointed upper chamber. Historically, half the provinces had upper houses, usually called *legislative councils,* but gradually during the late nineteenth and early twentieth century they were abolished. The province of Quebec was a holdout, not abolishing its legislative council until 1968. The idea of reestablishing second chambers to lessen executive control in provincial legislatures is never discussed today, possibly because the public wants fewer rather than more politicians on the government payroll, and the governing party would face a less predictable legislative process were an upper house to be controlled by another party.

At the national level, the appointed Senate has existed since Confederation and, almost since the founding of the country, there have been calls for Senate reform. As an appointed body, the Senate is regarded as an anachronism by many people. Yet all past attempts to reform the institution in a fundamental way have failed. In 2007–2008 there was a proposal from the minority Conservative government to move gradually toward an elected Senate. This is not the place to debate Senate reform. However, dismissal of the current Senate as a completely useless institution can be shown to be inaccurate.

Many Canadians see the Senate as an ineffective institution with members who are underworked and overpaid, and can be counted upon to bow to the demands of the prime minister who appointed them. This image is wrong in some specifics and exaggerated in general. A more balanced assessment suggests that the Senate can, at times, play a useful, complementary role to the House of Commons. As David Smith (2003) has argued, contemporary criticisms of the Senate reflect changing conceptions of democracy, representation, legitimacy, and accountability, whereas disagreements over these fundamental values make it difficult to find agreement on possible reforms.

Originally the Senate was intended to represent regional interests and to provide a check on potentially rash actions by the popularly elected Commons. It would perform these two functions mainly through the review of legislation. Gradually during the twentieth century, the Senate added two somewhat distinctive functions. The first is to provide, albeit to a limited extent, representation and protection for minorities and other special interests. Second, particularly since the 1960s, the Senate has developed an explicit oversight role that involves a significant amount of time spent in committees conducting investigations of public policy and its administration.

There are numerous criticisms of how the Senate performs these four functions. With its members selected on the basis of party patronage, the Senate is seen as a tame institution that does little to lessen executive dominance. The expression of regional concerns is said to be overridden by party loyalty. Senators from the governing party are seldom willing to challenge the prime minister and the cabinet on legislation, spending, and executive actions. Although Senate committees have conducted some useful investigations throughout the years, critics suggest such studies could be done more expertly and independently by outside bodies such as royal commissions and think tanks. The fact that many senators have corporate connections, in combination with a perceived light workload and generous compensation until they reach the mandatory retirement age of seventy-five, makes them easy targets for criticism.

This unflattering portrait of the Senate involves some serious inaccuracies, omissions, and exaggerations. The Senate does more useful work than is popularly imagined. Its membership includes many talented, often politically experienced, hard-working individuals who earn their pay. It is not a total failure as a voice for regional concerns. Most senators perform as regional representatives in the privacy of caucus, in interactions with ministers and the bureaucracy, and in committee hearings that attract little media attention, so these efforts go unnoticed. Because of improved drafting in the bureaucracy (including "Charter proofing" of bills to protect rights), the legislative review function of the Senate has declined in importance, but some senators continue to demonstrate the capacity for detailed legislative work. The Senate could add more value to the legislative process if governments did not send bills over from the Commons just before parliamentary breaks and insist on speedy passage without major changes.

Under favorable circumstances, the Senate has in the past had modest, but still important, influence within the national policy process. Through its system of standing and special committees, the Senate undertakes reviews of existing policies and programs and, unlike members of outside bodies, senators stay around to "lobby" government for the adoption of their recommendations. Appointment to the age of seventy-five and the lack of reelection pressures means that the institution (particularly its committees) operates on a less adversarial, more informal, slower, and more stable basis than the Commons. This means that institutional knowledge of government and its operations can develop over time. Even though most senators have a party background, their secure tenure and the limited opportunities to be in cabinet contribute to an independence of mind not found in the Commons.

There have been numerous attempts at comprehensive reform to the Senate, but they have all failed. The reasons are too numerous and complicated to be discussed fully here. One of the contributing factors has been shifts in the aims of the proposed reforms. Before the 1960s, the aim was to change the image of the Senate as a pure patronage body and to increase its productivity. Beginning in the 1960s, the focus shifted to improving the Senate as a forum for the expression and mediation of regional interests. During the 1980s and '90s, Senate reform became entangled in the process of wider constitutional reforms. Only recently has Senate reform been presented as a potential means to curb prime ministerial power and as one of a number initiatives intended to deal with the so-called "democratic deficit." These different emphases are not, of course, mutually exclusive, as is illustrated in the case made by the Harper government since 2006 for the eventual creation of a "triple E" Senate which is elected, equal, and effective.

Conclusion: "Parliamentary" Reform or "Democratic" Reform

Canadians disagree over what kind of democracy they want in the twenty-first century (Smith 2007). They are seriously dissatisfied with the performance of existing political institutions, including political parties and legislatures. This has led to talk of a so-called democratic deficit. Many citizens appear to favor more direct forms of democracy. However, these opinions are based on limited knowledge of the main institutions of government and how they work in practice.

Proposals for "parliamentary" reform intended to make the role of the individual legislator more effective address only indirectly the so-called democratic deficit (Aucoin and Turnbull 2004; Rowbotham 2005). Reducing party discipline, through reforms such as more "free" votes and greater autonomy for committees, might allow legislators more freedom, but they may not necessarily act on the wishes of their constituents. With attention to politics limited, and confidence in political institutions low, parliamentary reforms may well fail to impress or simply go unnoticed by most citizens.

Canadian legislatures represent a form of governing based upon discussion. It is not the role of legislatures actually to govern; mostly, they react to and debate public policies and actions of the executive. By watching and discussing, legislatures "control" the actions of governments but only in the limited sense of helping to set the parameters of acceptable behavior and by requiring public office holders to explain and defend their actions before a skeptical opposition as a condition for retaining public support. It is better to recognize what legislatures are really like than to chase illusions about what they might be.

Calls for legislatures to make themselves more effective fail to recognize that, because they are dominated by competitive parties, they have little collective identity. For legislatures to gain real power would require fundamental constitutional changes. Separating the executive from the legislature more formally and fully, as in the U.S. political system, would mean a larger role for legislatures, but it would also mean more dispersed power and the blurring of accountability.

The pressures for "democratic" reform may lead to changes that might benefit legislatures. For example, the Parliament of Canada, six provincial legislatures, and one territorial legislature have passed statutes providing for fixed dates for elections. The other four provinces and two territories were (as of May 2008) sticking with constitutional convention, which leaves the prerogative over election timing with the first minister. The threat of calling a snap election has often been seen as a way to control rebellious backbenchers in the governing party. More often, however, the threat seems to have been used as a tactical weapon in relation to the opposition parties rather than as a tool of discipline within the governing party, but there are not careful studies on this topic.

Electoral reform has also become an active topic at the national level and in several provinces as a way to deal with voter disengagement. The replacement of the simple plurality electoral system with some modified system of proportional representation (mostly likely a mixed-member system) would have a number of consequences for legislatures. Predicting the direct and indirect consequences of such changes involves uncertainty and controversy, even among well-informed commentators. New electoral systems would interact with the historical traditions, the prevailing patterns of party competition, and the contemporary controversies within each jurisdiction to produce, potentially, new partisan alignments within legislatures across the country. Minority government situations could become more common. Formal or informal coalitions could develop. At the very least, more extensive negotiations over policy would take place both among and within parties represented in the legislature. Scrutiny of the executive could increase, but accountability could be blurred as a result of more parties playing a role in decisions.

The central theme of this chapter has been the failure of legislatures to adapt to changing circumstances. This failure has allowed other institutions, like bureaucracies and pressure groups, to assume all or part of the functions usually attributed to legislatures. Once lost, such functions are not easily retrieved. A number of obstacles to institutional adaptation have been identified in this chapter: the dominance of parties, the unwillingness of executives to grant legislatures more influence, the small size of legislatures, inadequately prepared legislators whose overriding loyalty is to their parties, nonexistent or weak identification with the institution on the part of members, a shortage of professional staff and inadequate information, and a public mood of indifference and suspicion.

The information and communications revolution is currently posing another challenge to legislatures, with some commentators predicting the displacement of representative institutions by more direct forms of online democracy (Matsusaka 2005). More likely is the emergence of some form of hybrid democracy in which traditional processes of representative and responsible government operate in conjunction with newer forms of direct democracy (Thomas 2001).

Legislatures remain our central representative institutions. Whatever other channels exist to represent opinion, to debate issues, and to enforce accountabilities, legislatures sit at the apex of the formal structures of government. They are part of the discussion model of governing outlined earlier in this chapter. Other institutions represent forums for public policy debates, but only legislatures can represent the opinions of citizens in all their diversity. Transparent debate by the public's elected representatives will remain critical for the preservation of the legitimacy of the political system.

REFERENCES

Arter, David. 2006a. Conclusion: Questioning the "Mezey Question": An interrogatory framework for the comparative study of legislatures. *The Journal of Legislative Studies* 12(3–4): 462–482.

———. 2006b. Introduction: Comparing the legislative performance of legislatures. *The Journal of Legislative Studies* 12(3–4): 245–257.

Aucoin, Peter, and Lori Turnbull. 2003. The democratic deficit: Paul Martin and parliamentary reform. *Canadian Public Administration* 46(4): 427–449.

Forcese, Craig, and Aaron Freeman. 2005. *The Laws of Government: The Legal Foundations of Canadian Democracy.* Toronto: Irwin Law.

Good, David A. 2007. *The Politics of Public Money: Spenders, Guardians, Priority Setters and Financial Watchdogs inside the Canadian Government.* Toronto: University of Toronto Press.

Heard, Andrew. 2007. Just what is a vote of confidence? The curious case of May 10, 2005. *Canadian Journal of Political Science* 40(2): 395–416.

Matsusaka, John G. 2005. The eclipse of legislatures: Direct democracy in the 21st century. *Public Choice* 124(1 and 2): 157–177.

Polsby, Nelson W. 1975. Legislatures. In *Handbook of Political Science: Governmental Institutions and Processes*, vol. 5, ed. Fred Greenstein and Nelson Polsby, 275–319. Reading, Mass.: Addison-Wesley.

Rowbotham, Cloë. 2005. *Is Parliamentary Reform Democratic Renewal?* Ottawa: Institute on Governance.

Smith, David E. 2003. *The Canadian Senate in a Bicameral Perspective*. Toronto: University of Toronto Press.

———. 2007. *The People's House of Commons: Theories of Democracy in Contention*. Toronto: University of Toronto Press.

Suleiman, Ezra N. 1986. *Parliaments and Parliamentarians in Democratic Politics*. New York: Holmes and Meier.

Thomas, Paul G. 1994. Parties and Parliament: The role of party caucuses. In *Canadian Parties in Transition*, ed. Alain-G. Gagnon and A. Brian Tanguay, 39–48. Toronto: Nelson.

———. 2001. Parliament and the public service. In *The Handbook of Canadian Public Administration*, ed. Christopher Dunn, 341–368. Toronto: Oxford.

———. 2003. The past, present and future of officers of parliament. *Canadian Public Administration* 46(3): 287–314.

Thomas, Paul E. J. 2007. Measuring the effectiveness of a minority parliament. *Canadian Parliamentary Review* 30(1): 22–31.

White, Graham. 2006. Evaluating provincial and territorial legislatures. In *Provinces: Canadian Provincial Politics*, 2nd ed., ed. Christopher Dunn, 255–278. Toronto: Broadview Press.

CHAPTER 10

··

FIRST MINISTERS, CABINET, AND THE PUBLIC SERVICE

··

DONALD J. SAVOIE

THE roles and responsibilities of first ministers, cabinet, and the public service in a parliamentary system based on the Westminster model should be fairly straightforward. The prime minister leads the government, the cabinet establishes policies and directs the work of government, and the public service implements policies, delivers public services, and provides policy advice to ministers. The public service serves the government in a nonpartisan fashion and is expected to "speak truth to power" to their political masters without fear or favor. All of this is based on unwritten constitutional conventions rather than on law. It is a matter of convention, not law, that the prime minister is a member of the House of Commons, that the cabinet exists, and that its deliberations are held in secrecy. The public service, meanwhile, has been told time and again that it has no constitutional personality distinct from the government of the day.

Accordingly, relations among the prime minister, the cabinet, and public servants, inspired by British experience, have developed without and even despite the law rather than within the framework of the law (Tomkins 2003, 85). This is not to suggest for a moment that constitutional conventions hold no advantages. They do and they matter. Wheare (1951, 179), in his much acclaimed *Modern Constitutions*, explains that a constitutional convention is "a binding rule, a rule of behavior accepted as obligatory by those concerned in the working of the constitution." Thus, conventions matter because of the political problems that would be created if they were not respected (Jennings 1959, 134). Still, constitutional conventions are not legally binding and, as a result, they have a capacity to adjust to changing circumstances. This flexibility has allowed a number of major developments in the operations of Canada's political and administrative institutions in recent years. It has allowed the prime minister to reshape relationships in government almost at will—as, for example, turning cabinet into little more than a focus group for his benefit and the benefit of his advisors.

The purpose of this chapter is to explore how the relationship among the prime minister, cabinet, and the public service has evolved in recent years and to identify the underlying forces that have shaped it. It begins by looking at the growing power of the prime minister and central agencies—notably, the Prime Minister's Office (PMO)—in relation to others in government. We then review how cabinet has been transformed into little more than a focus group and why it no longer directs the work of government. Many observers, including a good number of practitioners, have recently made the case that Parliament no longer performs the role it once did, whereas a spate of public opinion surveys reveal that political institutions, politicians, and public servants have all fallen sharply in public esteem. The implications for the public service are far reaching. There have also been other recent developments that have transformed the role of the public service, ranging from access to information legislation to sustained attempts to introduce private-sector management practices to government operations. All of these suggest that Canada's key political and administrative institutions have been knocked off their moorings and that the internal logic of appropriateness that guides their work has been altered.

The Prime Minister: He's the Boss

While serving in the Trudeau cabinet, Jean Chrétien invariably referred to Pierre Trudeau as "le boss." When he became prime minister, Chrétien left no doubt in his cabinet that he was now "the boss" (Savoie 1999a, 71). Various forces that in the past served as a check against the prime minister's political power are no longer as effective. In Canada today, federal political parties are little more than partisan political machines providing some fund-raising capacity and poll workers needed to fight an election campaign. They are hardly effective vehicles for generating public policy debates, for staking out policy positions, or for providing a capacity to ensure their own competence once in office. Tom Axworthy, one-time chief of staff to Pierre Trudeau, maintains that in Canada, in the 1960s, if one were interested in policy, the place to be was on the floor of a party convention. That, he insists, is simply not a recognizable model today (Bryden 2006).

It is also argued that the omnipresent regional factor in Canadian politics is an important reason why national political parties are not good vehicles to debate and formulate policy positions. One observer of Canadian politics writes: "We do not have party government in the national institutions because of the lack of capacity of parties to reconcile inside themselves regional interests from across the whole country" (Sutherland 1996, 11). Regional cleavages dominate the national public policy agenda in Canada, and national political parties shy away from attacking regional issues head on for fear that they would split the party along regional lines and hurt its chances at election time. The thinking goes, at least in the parties that have held power in Ottawa, that regional issues are so sensitive and politically explosive that they are better left in the hands of party leaders and a handful of advisors. In the two main political parties that have held power in Ottawa, the terms of the truce between the various factions are now established by party leaders and some of their most trusted advisors.

Prime ministers no longer have to rely on ministers—notably, regional ministers—to gain a sense of where voters stand on any issue. Public opinion surveys are more reliable, more objective, more to the point, and easier to deal with than ministers. They can also be used to address any public policy issue. All prime ministers in Canada since the 1970s have had their own pollsters to interpret events and provide advice. Surveys can enable prime ministers and their advisors to challenge the views of ministers. After all, how can even the most senior ministers dispute what the polls say? If, say, the minister responsible for Nova Scotia claims that government spending cuts are hurting the party in that province, PMO staffers can point to a public opinion survey suggesting that the majority of Nova Scotians support the government's efforts to deal with the deficit and debt problems. There are now public opinion surveys documenting the views of Canadians on virtually every public policy issue.

Pollsters, better than ministers, can assist a prime minister in deciding what is important and what is not, what is politically sensible and what is not. A pollster, always at the ready with data, can be particularly helpful in dealing with the problem of political overload, a pervasive sense of urgency generated by a media now able to secure inside information and an accompanying feeling of being overwhelmed both by events and by the number of matters needing attention. A pollster can also advise prime ministers on "hot button" issues, a role once left to cabinet ministers.

The PMO has grown substantially over the past forty years and now plays an important role in shaping new policy initiatives. Prime ministers since Pierre Trudeau, have employed anywhere between eighty to 120 staff members in their own offices. Trudeau was the architect of the modern PMO. He felt that the Pearson years (1963–1968) lacked a proper planning capacity at the center and, as a result, were marked by confusion and chaos. He resolved that things would be different in his government: "One of the reasons why I wanted this job, when I was told that it might be there, is because I felt it very important to have a strong central government, build up the executive, build up the Prime Minister's Office" (Radwanski 1978, 146). Tom Kent, principal secretary to Prime Minister Pearson, describes the PMO before Trudeau. He writes: "The PMO was [up to the end of the Pearson years] utterly different from what it became in the Trudeau era and has since remained. There was no bevy of deputies and assistants and principals this-and-that, with crowds of support staff" (Kent 1988, 225). When Chrétien became prime minister, one of the first decisions he made was to abolish the chief of staff position in ministerial offices, a position that his predecessor, Brian Mulroney, had established. However, Chrétien decided to retain a chief of staff for his own office.

Prime ministers can also turn to the clerk and secretary to the cabinet, and to the Privy Council Office (PCO) for help. The prime minister and the clerk enjoy a unique relationship, one that is not found anywhere else in government. For one thing, the prime minister is completely free to appoint whomever he or she wishes to the position. No other minister enjoys the same prerogative with respect to his or her deputy minister. For another, the clerk of the PCO is not only head of the public service, but is also dean of the community of deputy ministers. As the prime minister's closest advisor, the clerk has a direct hand in deciding who should become a deputy minister and who should not. As anyone who has worked in government can attest, no one should underestimate the power of appointment that is in the hands of both the prime minister and the clerk. The ones who wield this power decide who, at the highest levels in the public service, wins and who doesn't, who is ascendant and who is not (Savoie 1999a, 111).

Paul Tellier, clerk of the PCO from 1985 to 1992, time and again reminded deputy ministers, assistant deputy ministers, and others that he was wearing not one but two hats—one as the prime minister's deputy minister and the other as secretary to the cabinet. In 1992, he added yet another hat, that of head of the public service (Canada 1997, 7). The last position was formally recognized through special legislation enacted to implement the Public Service 2000 initiative, which was introduced to modernize government operations. The first hat, deputy minister to the prime minister, is the one that has come to matter the most to the clerk in recent years at the expense of responsibilities to cabinet and to the public service.

The PCO has also grown throughout the years. Today, it houses an elaborate network of policy advisors and coordinators. Privy Council Office officials enjoy a higher classification and better pay than their counterparts in line departments. Indeed, the PCO is now home to several deputy minister-level positions. It is also home to some twenty-four policy secretariats that parallel the work of policy shops in line departments, including federal–provincial relations. The PMO and PCO have about 800 officials working on virtually every policy sector and they are able to "permeate and dominate" any policy issue (Savoie 1999a, 153).

The prime minister, with the support of the PMO-PCO, also makes all major announcements from foreign affairs to new spending for the environment, economic development, and the like. Departments understand this and have adjusted their spending proposals accordingly. New spending plans are now pitched to prime ministers and their advisors, rather than to the regular policy process managed by cabinet and its committees, which is slow, cumbersome, and, more important, holds little chance of success. When the Canadian military wanted new tanks, military officials turned to the prime minister for the decision. Lieutenant-General Leslie told the *Globe and Mail* that he hoped that "Stephen Harper will replace the old tanks," adding that he expected "the Prime Minister's decision within about a week" (Smith 2007, A1). There was a time when cabinet, on the recommendation of the minister of national defense, was responsible for such decisions.

From Cabinet Government to Court Government

Some students of parliamentary government argue that the shifts that have taken place are in the direction of a presidential form of government. They claim that it is increasingly difficult to write about collective ministerial responsibility or prime ministers as leaders of teams because prime ministers are fast becoming—like presidents—individuals at the top of the pile. Patrick Weller (1985, 8), for one, argues that "[prime ministers'] control over government activities is regarded as excessive, and their accountability as far too limited. Observers complain that the system has changed from Cabinet government to prime ministerial government or that the office of the prime minister has been presidentialized." John Mackintosh (1968, 51), a Labor member of Parliament from 1966 to 1974, was the first to express concern over the growing influence of the prime minister in his study of the British cabinet in 1968. He was later joined by others expressing the same viewpoint, including the much-quoted cabinet minister, Richard Crossman (1975; 1976; 1977). Mackintosh answered his critics in the early and mid 1970s, but by the late '70s he felt it was no longer necessary. He simply made the point that "events since 1968 have done so much to confirm the general case argued in this book" that he felt it unnecessary to make the case (Weller 1985, 4). The debate is hardly limited to Britain (Savoie 1999a).

The first sign that prime ministers have the upper hand is now evident even before they and their party assume power. Transition planning has become an important event designed to prepare a new government to assume power. Two former senior government of Canada officials write that "the first modern effort at transition planning in the public service...occurred for the June 1968 general election" (Manion and Williams 1993, 100). They add that transition planning has grown to become an elaborate planning process and now includes "the entire deputy minister community" (Manion and Williams 1993, 108). The focus of the exercise is the prime minister, if only because the exercise is well on its way by the time cabinet ministers are appointed.

Few observers in Canada believe that the prime minister is still primus inter pares. The only time when the Canadian prime minister is still primus inter pares is when he chairs a first ministers' conference. Provincial premiers are not his political equals, but they shape the discussions at the conference and advance whatever position they wish, even when it is in sharp opposition to the prime minister's position. First ministers meet from time to time and their meetings cover a wide array of topics. The prime minister will consult with the chair of the annual premiers' conference in preparing the agenda. Premiers have held an annual get-together for the past forty-four years at which they reviewed current economic circumstances and their relations with Ottawa.

Within the federal government, Cabinet ministers have become much more the prime minister's subordinates than his "pares." John Crosbie, a senior minister in the Mulroney Progressive Conservative government, summed up the situation well

when he explained why Brian Tobin, a senior minister in the Chrétien Liberal government, left the federal cabinet to become leader of the Liberal Party in
Newfoundland and Labrador. He wrote:

> [I]n politics, never underestimate the importance of being number one. It is
> inevitably frustrating to work as a member of a government led by someone else. No
> matter how much power and authority leaders delegate to you or how well they treat
> you, they are still number one, and, when they choose to exercise their authority, they
> naturally have their way. If my leader became trapped by some political circumstances
> and blurted out a policy pronouncement in my area of responsibility—even if he
> didn't know much about the subject—I had to live with it. Even if he was completely
> wrong, I couldn't correct what he had done. (Crosbie 1997, 476)

Prime ministers do not always bypass their cabinets or only consult them after the
fact on the great majority of issues. They will pick and choose issues they will want to
direct. Indeed, in some circumstances and on certain issues a prime minister may well
decide not to exert his or her authority and let the cabinet's collective decision-making
process runs its course. He or she may also even let government caucus have its day from
time to time and accept that a government proposal or legislation should be pulled back
and reworked to accommodate the views of caucus members. There are issues on which
a prime minister and his or her senior advisors may hold no firm view, and a detached
assessment of the costs and benefits of getting involved could suggest that it is best to
keep one's political capital in reserve for another day and for another issue.

Prime ministers have also come to dominate government at a time when the
policy process has become increasingly complex and cross cutting, and when government is not only larger but also far more open to outside scrutiny than was the case
forty years ago. This may well be an important reason why prime ministers now feel
the need to govern from the center or the PMO and the PCO. The Glassco Commission
calculated in the early 1960s that there were 216,000 employees in the Canadian public
service employed in eighty federal government departments and agencies (Cole
1966, 2). During the Trudeau years alone, 117 new departments, agencies, or Crown
corporations were established (Osbaldeston 1989, 120). Today, there are about 450,000
public servants employed in 150 federal government organizations covered by the
Financial Administration Act (FAA), including forty-three parent Crown corporations; another 140 organizations that fall outside of the FAA; seventeen special operating agencies as well as about 200 semi-autonomous organizations housed within
federal departments and agencies; 143 mixed, joined, or shared governance entities;
and twenty-six foundations (Canada 2004). In 1967, Lester Pearson spent a considerable amount of time reading his correspondence and would often play a direct role in
responding to it. Today, the Canadian prime minister receives more than two million
pieces of correspondence every year, which go through an elaborate triage with only a
very small number actually placed before the prime minister. The bulk of the correspondence is now handled by a special unit in the PCO (Stewart 2006).

Access to information legislation, the need to respond quickly to emerging issues
and to be seen to be doing so, the government overload problem, the need to establish priorities quickly, and the rise of the new media have all combined to shift

political power away from cabinet to the prime minister and carefully selected advisors. These forces have also pushed the government to move away from formal processes and hierarchy and to embrace informal relations and flattened hierarchies. Jean Chrétien (1985, 85) explained the workings of cabinet government in this fashion: "Within Cabinet a minister is merely part of a collectivity, just another advisor to the prime minister. He can be told what to do and on important matters his only choice is to do or resign." Resignations on matters of policy or principle are now rare occurrences in Canada. Ministers are more likely to resign to accept an appointment from the prime minister than quit over a policy issue (Sutherland 1991, 101–103).

Prime ministers and their advisors will also look to any number of sources for new policy initiatives, among them the campaign platform, matters that are of strong interest to the prime minister, issues that surface when heads of government meet, and issues identified by think tanks and even by the public service. Shaping new policies, however, hardly takes up all or even most of a prime minister's agenda. Prime ministers lead busy lives. There are many more demands on a prime minister's time that can possibly be accommodated. Prime ministers must attend to cabinet, caucus, House duties, international obligations, and federal–provincial relations. They should be available to meet disgruntled ministers or ministers who have a particular project to promote. They must increasingly pay attention to the media. They are leaders of political parties, a responsibility that requires time and energy. They must manage their own expanded offices and oversee an elaborate appointment process. They must also manage their ministers and caucus members. A prime minister's focus, even on a handful of priorities, can never be taken for granted. It only takes a crisis to shift his or her attention elsewhere. One can imagine what it was like in Harper's PMO after the media took his government to task in summer 2006, when Canadian citizens were left stranded in war-torn Beirut while citizens of other countries were being evacuated.

Access to the prime minister is a key measure of influence. As the number and status of political advisors to Canadian prime ministers has grown in recent years, it has become more difficult even for senior public servants to have time with the prime minister. Accordingly, it is also now far more difficult than it was forty years ago for senior public servants to know the prime minister and his or her policy preferences, as well as partisan advisors and assistants do (Foster 2005, 161). This is also true for ministers.

This is not to suggest that ministers have no influence. Although they have less than in years past in relation to the prime minister, they still have some. Their influence depends on a number of factors, but their relationship with the prime minister is at the top of the list. There are other factors—their standing in the party and in the media, and their ability to sell their ideas to the prime minister and his advisors and to navigate the government system are all important. Ministers need to be close advisors to the prime minister, so to speak, to have an impact in shaping policies. All prime ministers will have several such ministers. The minister of finance invariably falls into this category, as do a handful of the prime minister's closest supporters from the party's leadership race.

Mitchell Sharp, a former deputy minister in the 1950s and later a minister in the 1960s and early '70s, compares policy making before and after Trudeau. He explained that

> in the St. Laurent and Pearson governments, deputy ministers were clearly responsible for policy and for working with the minister to define policy in your area of responsibility. Your minister would of course challenge your ideas, but then he would agree on a position with you and take the ideas to Cabinet and have it out with his colleagues. Things did not work quite like that under Trudeau. It was different.... You have to understand that the art of governing was different then. Ministers had a strong base and had strong personalities. They would go to Cabinet and take on even the prime minister. Some ministers would threaten to resign over policy, and some actually did. So it was different then for a deputy minister working with a minister. I am not sure that we bothered too much with central agencies like the Prime Minister's Office and the Privy Council Office. They didn't much bother you. (Savoie 1999b, 661)

No one would even think of making such a claim today in Ottawa.

Ministers must now learn to work with the center of government and with partisan advisors and senior public servants operating at the center to have any chance of success or, in many instances, survival. Ministers now have to learn to work with the PMO more so than they have to learn to work with cabinet and cabinet colleagues. Harper's PMO went so far as to ask exempt staff working for cabinet ministers to "secretly provide" an assessment of their bosses' communication skills (Galloway 2006, A4). Ministers no longer run their own offices as they once did, let alone their departments. Ministers are no longer free to appoint their chiefs of staff without running potential candidates by the PMO. Meanwhile, public servants, notably the ambitious ones, must in turn spend a great deal of time assessing who has influence around the prime minister and how to access them to move their files forward.

Brian Mulroney was very fond of the old saying "you dance with the one who brung you." Those who give of their time and resources to help secure the party leadership for the prime minister and who play an important role in the general election campaign will be rewarded either by being offered a position in government or by having access to its most senior levels. Loyalty is a much valued asset in partisan politics. Modern election campaigns depend less on foot soldiers than in years past and more on money, expertise in developing political and policy strategies, and on a strong capacity to deal with the media.

Public Servants: Now Busy Serving the Prime Minister

Government today calls for a different relationship at the top, and prime ministers and their advisors now look for senior public servants with different skills than in the past. Having an intimate knowledge of a sector or a government department is less important than it once was. Policy work is different from, say, forty years ago.

Networking in support of horizontal or governmentwide objectives, such as climate change, has become an important policy skill. In addition, elected politicians, starting with the prime minister, are demanding that public servants be much more responsive to their policy agenda, to assist in managing political crises, and to assist in dealing with the media. When a senior government of Canada official retired from the federal public service in November 2006, he was asked to reflect on the most important change during his time in government. He responded that

> there was a time when the most senior public servants would not only pursue
> what the Prime Minister wanted, but also told him what he should want, not just
> what he wanted to hear, but what he should hear, not just respond to a short-term
> political agenda, but also present a much longer term perspective for him to
> reflect. All of this has changed. (Consultations with a former senior government
> of Canada official, Moncton, New Brunswick, November 21, 2006)

This has come at a price. As Christopher Hood argues, demand-led policy work (in other words, responding to the policy biases of ministers) has led to impoverished policy expertise (Hood et al. 2002, 30; Savoie 1994, 340).

The policy role of public servants is less about securing an intimate knowledge of the relevant sector and offering policy options and more about finding empirical justification for what the elected politicians have decided to do (Travers 2006). In brief, the ability to know when to proceed, to delay, to be bold, to be prudent, to sense a looming political crisis, to navigate through a multitude of horizontal processes and networks, and then to develop a capacity to justify what elected politicians have decided have come to matter a great deal (Axworthy 1988, 252).

These skills are more akin to the political world than that found in Weber's classic bureaucratic model. Indeed, Weber (1946, 215–216) insisted that political skills should be vastly different from, if not opposite to, bureaucratic skills, for the relationship to work. This is no longer the case. Political skills, albeit not necessarily in a partisan sense, are in high demand. This may explain, in part, why deputy ministers are rotated more often than in years past.

Many forces have reshaped the relationship between politicians and public servants, a relationship that has grown increasingly complex in recent years. Gone are the days when public servants rose through the ranks of their departments to become deputy ministers. Gone, too, are the days when deputy ministers would work policy proposals with their ministers and see the ministers "have it out with colleagues."

There are now essentially two policy-making processes in the federal government, and public servants have had to adjust. As we have seen, the policy process that dominates is led by the prime minister and his advisors. Ambitious senior public servants will want to be visible to prime ministers and their advisors. To become visible, one has to be responsive to the wishes of prime ministers and their closest advisors. Prime ministers—like monarchs of past years—will always value and reward responsive loyalty. They do not appreciate inconvenient counsel, particularly when it comes to their pet projects or policy preferences.

The second policy-making process is porous and includes a multitude of policy actors from federal government departments, other levels of government, lobbyists, interest groups, think tanks, consultants, and policy networks. Here, the process is guided by many hands operating both inside and outside government. The role of public servants is to network, to find common ground, and to strike partnership arrangements. Having an intimate knowledge of a sector or a department and its program history has come to matter less here, as well. The process today requires patience, negotiating skills, and an ability to network. It holds little appeal for those who would like to embrace bold initiatives and who have a strong sense of ownership of their work. It also calls on public servants to become policy actors in their own right, able to present and defend policy positions outside of government circles, although they are constantly reminded that they serve in an institution that does not have a personality distinct from the government of the day. This explains why we have witnessed a convergence of skills between elected politicians and senior public servants. It may also explain why, according to Graham Wilson and Anthony Barker (2003, 370), senior public servants have lost some of their self-confidence and their willingness to argue against policies they think unwise (see also Peters and Pierre 2004, 40).

One only has to read the testimonies of recently retired public servants before parliamentary committees and public inquiries to appreciate the extent to which the balance has shifted. Paul Tellier, former clerk of the PCO and secretary to the cabinet, accepted in November 2006 an invitation by Prime Minister Harper to co-chair an advisory committee on the renewal and future development of the public service (Canada 2006). He told the media that senior public servants need to rediscover the capacity to "say no to ministers when required." He added, "A deputy minister has to be able to put his foot down and say—I don't think the government should do this." He went on to say:

> It's a question of leadership—and the first challenge is to protect integrity and
> promote ethics, which is leadership. The sponsorship scandal (which saw
> advertising firms friendly to Chrétien's Liberal party receive untendered
> contracts) should never have happened and I think that public servants have to
> carry some blame for this. (May 2006b)

Tellier's desire to strengthen the capacity of senior public servants may well have to do with the location of political power and its use. It is one thing to say no to a minister when required, but it is quite another matter to say no to the prime minister. Ministers do not appoint deputy ministers, the prime minister does. Deputy ministers have an accountability relationship with the prime minister stronger than they have with their minister. One will pay particularly strong attention to the wishes of the one who has the power to appoint, dismiss, or promote. Deputy ministers know full well that if they have a major disagreement with their ministers, they can appeal to the secretary to the cabinet. The PCO instructs deputy ministers to consult the PCO with a directive that reads:

> Ultimately, a matter which results in an apparently irreconcilable difference
> becomes a matter for resolution by the Prime Minister, with advice from the
> Clerk. Deputy Ministers should also consult the Clerk in cases where problems
> have occurred in the management of the department or the Minister's portfolio,

and which may have an impact on the Ministry's ability as a collectivity to maintain the confidence of the House of Commons and move forward its legislative and policy agenda. (Canada 2003, 13)

Ministers, better than anyone, know that their deputy ministers work "with" them, not "for" them. There is a story that has made the rounds for years in Ottawa that a minister went to see Trudeau with a request to have his deputy minister sacked or transferred elsewhere. Trudeau replied that he knew the deputy minister well and he had more confidence in the deputy than in the minister. The minister swallowed his pride, went back to the department, and carried on.

There is evidence to suggest that senior public servants have, of late, become more responsive to the prime ministers and their advisors. Lawrence Martin writes in the *Globe and Mail* that, in Ottawa, bureaucrats now either "fall in line or fall out of favor." He quotes a deputy minister: "When you live in a world where options aren't necessary, I suppose you don't need much of a bureaucracy" and makes the point that the "government does not want high-level bureaucrats to exercise the challenge function" (Martin 2006, A1, A6). Jim Travers (2007, A17) writes in the *Toronto Star* that the view among senior bureaucrats in Ottawa is that "instead of sous-chefs helping the government prepare the national menu, bureaucrats complain that they are being used as short-order cooks."

The central message, at least from recently retired public servants and independent observers, is that senior public servants have been overly responsive to the wishes of elected politicians in more recent years. Even some ministers who appeared before Justice Gomery felt that things have gone too far. (The Gomery Commission was established by Paul Martin to inquire into some of the advertising activities of the Chrétien government.) Former Treasury Board President Lucienne Robillard expressed her astonishment before the Commission that a government document had been submitted to ministers, which reported that "ministers should recommend strengthening the Liberal party organization in Quebec. This means hiring organizers, finding candidates, identifying ridings where the party can win" (Canada 2005, 11256). She said it was "unusual" for such a document to be submitted by public servants to Jean Chrétien, as prime minister, rather than by party organizers to Chrétien as party leader. The fact that the majority of cabinet documents in Canada are now produced by consultants rather than by career public servants may explain the content of this and other government documents (Savoie 2003, 119).

The views of other ministers and senior political staff before Justice Gomery also reveal that they now exert considerable influence even over the administrative responsibilities of public servants. Prime Minister Jean Chrétien acknowledged that he interviewed one career official, Roger Collet, before he was appointed to a public service position, although he insisted that he was not a "micromanager" (Canada 2005, 12563, 12567). He claimed that he simply wanted to make sure that Collet understood the challenge at hand and that he was up to the job. This suggests that Chrétien felt that he was in a better position to apply the merit principle than senior public servants.

Chrétien's chief of staff, Jean Pelletier, told the Gomery inquiry that public servants were not happy with his involvement in the sponsorship program. But, he explained that

> this is part of a system that public servants jealously guard as their prerogative and when they do not decide everything, they are not happy. There was one Deputy Minister or one Assistant Deputy Minister who wanted to control the program by himself. I think that the Clerk did not agree with this and even more obviously the Prime Minister did not agree. (Canada 2005, 12456)

He added, "I recall very well that officials in the Privy Council Office wanted to decide everything on the 'use' of the fund under the sponsorship program and they were not happy that they were not taking the final decision but rather the Prime Minister. That I remember very well" (Canada 2005, 12415). This did not deter Pelletier from having a hand in the management of the sponsorship program. Pelletier also acknowledged that he had sent a letter to all ministers that he had designated a partisan official from the PMO, rather than a public servant, as the individual responsible for overseeing the application of a new policy on advertising (Canada 2005, 12339).

One Chrétien minister, Stéphane Dion, claimed with pride before Gomery that he had a particularly strong working relationship with the prime minister. He believed that "few ministers had that kind of direct relationship with him" (Canada 2005, 10906). Denis Coderre, another former Chrétien minister, acknowledged that he had made the case "against the hiring of additional public servants to deliver the Sponsorship Program" (Canada 2005, 11045). He explained that hiring public servants does not mean that it is less costly to deliver government programs and services or sponsorship initiatives than through an external agency. The bulk of the sponsorship program was delivered by outside consultants, not public servants. Coderre's message was not lost on public servants: If they were not sufficiently responsive, they can be replaced in both policy and administrative matters by outside consultants. This option gives, among other things, elected politicians the ability to pick and choose a delivery mechanism that best suits their partisan political interest.

But what about deputy ministers? Where do they come from? Efforts by the Mulroney, Chrétien, Martin, and Harper governments to recruit deputy ministers from outside government have met with little success. Almost all deputy ministers appointed since 1997 held a senior management position in the PCO before their appointment. This speaks to the "rising star" approach to staffing senior levels in government when someone is identified early in his or her career as having the qualities to assume senior positions (Bourgault 2005, 11). It also speaks to the importance of the PCO in the government.

The loyalty of deputy ministers, as Jacques Bourgault (2005, 12) argues in his study of deputy ministers prepared for a government of Canada agency, is to the center "rather than departmental." Former agriculture minister Eugene Whelan said, at a Senate committee meeting in 2006, that deputy ministers of agriculture can no longer tell "a sow from the cow" and that he longed for the glory days of the public service when the deputy minister of agriculture lived and breathed farming and stayed in the job for 20 years. They would rather quit than be shuffled somewhere else. Some think that all you need now is a good education and you can run anything. (May 2006c, B4)

Deputy ministers in the past often stayed with the same department throughout their careers. Now they have a "multiplicity" of assignments at the deputy minister level before retirement. Indeed, some deputy ministers can have up to five assignments at the deputy minister level before leaving government. Gordon Osbaldeston (1989), in his study of accountability in government, was highly critical of the short stay of deputy ministers in line departments, insisting, among other things, that it made accountability more difficult. The length of time a deputy minister stayed in one department between 1867 and 1967 was, on average, twelve years; it fell to three years between 1977 and 1987 (Bourgault 2005, 14). Ned Franks examined the length of stay of deputy ministers between 1996 and 2005 and concluded that the stay during this period dropped still further, to 2.9 years. He reports that on December 21, 2005 (after twelve years of uninterrupted Liberal rule), eleven of the twenty-two serving deputy ministers had held office for less than two years and only two had been in office for more than three years (Franks 2006, 7). Jodi White, the head of Canada's Public Policy Forum, asked how could proper management leadership be exercised or how could a deputy minister represent a department properly in a department like Industry Canada, which has had "thirteen deputy ministers in twenty years?" (May 2006d). She could have added that between 1984 and 2002, the Canadian government had six clerks of the PCO, seven secretaries to the treasury board, and seven deputy ministers of finance (May 2006c).

The desire to have senior public servants embrace a political agenda with enthusiasm may well explain why the Harper government included a clause in its accountability bill to appoint "special advisors" to deputy ministers through an order-in-council or place authority in the hands of the government of the day rather than through the Public Service Commission. Maria Barrados, President of the Public Service Commission, estimates that there are about 200 such advisors in government, and calls the move unacceptable. She maintains that it gives the government "access to the bureaucracy that is inappropriate to me and violates the spirit and core of what the Public Service Commission is all about and supposed to do." She feared the further politicization of the public service not in a politically partisan sense, but "in the sense of public servants being too accommodating to their political masters" (May 2006a).

LOOKING BACK

Most of the limits placed on the exercise of political power in a parliamentary system based on the Westminster model have traditionally arisen by way of convention rather than having been imposed by statute law (Nolan and Sedley 1977, 33; Tomkins

2003, 42). The PCO has long urged that the public service has no separate account-ability or constitutional status of its own, and cabinet has been turned into a focus group for the prime minister. The prime minister and his or her advisors have become the focal point for all important political, policy, and even many program decisions.

The traditional bargain guiding the relationship between elected politicians and public servants has collapsed. Prime ministers and their political advisors sit at the apex of political power from which they can survey developments, and pick and choose issues to pursue. The changing role of the media and access to information legislation have served to centralize further decisions at the center of government as prime ministers and their advisors continually search for ways to place the govern-ment on a solid political footing. Issues that matter less to prime ministers and their advisors are turned over to networks of policy specialists. This process is slow, cum-bersome, and complex, and not easily accessible to nonspecialists, including ministers.

Public servants have had to adjust to this new world all the while trying to cling to requirements of the traditional bargain (Savoie 2003). Meanwhile, public pres-sure for public servants to be accountable has never been stronger. Public servants have successfully resisted such a development, insisting that ministers should be responsible or answerable for all things in government.[1]

In government, senior public servants have seen their accountability to the prime minister grow stronger as those to their ministers have weakened. It has become increasingly difficult for senior officials to speak to the traditions and long-standing policy positions of their departments as prime ministers search for respon-sive senior public servants to pursue their policy agenda. Deputy ministers, much like their ministers, have become birds of passage in departments. They do not pos-sess the kind of intimate knowledge of the relevant sector and their departmental history that their predecessors did.

NOTES

1. Stephen Harper had a significant change of heart in his decision to introduce Britain's accounting officer concept to Canada. While in opposition, he argued that deputy ministers as accounting officers should be directly accountable to Parliament. Once in power, he decided essentially to embrace the status quo (Savoie 2008).

REFERENCES

Axworthy, Thomas. 1988. Of secretaries to princes. *Canadian Public Administration* 31: 247–264.

Bourgault, Jacques. 2005. *Profile of Deputy Minister in the Government of Canada*. Ottawa: Canada School of Public Service.

Bryden, Joan. 2006. Volpe should quit Liberal race. September 26. www.thestar.com.

Canada. 1997. *Privy Council 1997–98 Estimates. Part III: Expenditure Plan* Ottawa: Government of Canada.

———. 2003. *Guidance for Deputy Ministers*. Ottawa: Privy Council Office.

———. 2004. *Federal Institutional Governance Universe*. Ottawa: Treasury Board Secretariat.

———. 2005. Commission of inquiry into the sponsorship program and advertising activities. Ottawa: Public Works and Government Services.

———. 2006. *Prime Minister Harper Establishes Advisory Committee on the Public Service*. Ottawa: Office of the Prime Minister.

Chrétien, Jean. 1985. *Straight from the Heart*. Toronto: Key Porter Books.

Cole, Taylor. 1966. *The Canadian Bureaucracy and Federalism*. Denver, Colo.: University of Denver Press.

Crosbie, John. 1997. *No Holds Barred: My Life in Politics*. Toronto: McClelland and Stewart.

Crossman, Richard. 1975, 1976, 1977. *The Diaries of a Cabinet Minister*, vols. 1–3. London: Hamish Hamilton and Jonathan Cape.

Foster, Christopher. 2005. *British Government in Crisis*. Oxford: Hart Publishing.

Franks, Ned. 2006. "Tenure of Canadian deputy ministers, 1996–2005: Notes and Comments." Kingston, Ont., unpublished paper.

Galloway, Gloria. 2006. Harper's PR aide secretly asks cabinet staff to critique bosses. *Globe and Mail*. November 17, A4.

Hood, Christopher, Martin Lodge, and Christopher Clifford. 2002. *Civil Service Policy-Making Competencies in the German BMWi and British DTI: A Comparative Analysis Based on Six Case Studies*. London: Smith Institute.

Jennings, Ivor. 1959. *The Law and the Constitution*. London: University of London Press.

Kent, Tom. 1988. *A Public Purpose: An Experience of Liberal Opposition and Canadian Government*. Montreal: McGill-Queen's University Press.

Mackintosh, John. 1968. *The British Cabinet*. London: Methuen.

Manion, John L., and Cynthia Williams. 1993. Transition planning at the federal level in Canada. In *Taking Power: Managing Government Transitions*, ed. Donald J. Savoie, 99–144. Toronto: Institute of Public Administration of Canada.

Martin, Lawrence. 2006. The unwritten bylaw of Bytown: Fall in line or fall out of favour. *Globe and Mail*, August 9, A1, A6.

May, Kathryn. 2006a. Accountability bill will saddle PS with political cronies. *Ottawa Citizen*, October 10, A1.

———. 2006b. Mulroney's old top guns to fix PS for Harper. *Ottawa Citizen*, November 22, A1.

———. 2006c. The hole in accountability. *Ottawa Citizen*, November 18, B1, B4.

———. 2006d. We're not very good leaders and we can't make decisions, insecure bureaucrats say. *Ottawa Citizen*, October 3, A1.

Nolan, Lord, and Sir Stephen Sedley. 1977. *The Making and Remaking of the British Constitution*. London: Blackstone Press.

Osbaldeston, Gordon. 1989. *Keeping Deputy Ministers Accountable*. Toronto: McGraw-Hill Ryerson Canada.

PCO. 2007. PCO Secretariats. http://pco-bcp.gc.ca/docs/org-march2007.

Peters, B. Guy, and Jon Pierre, eds. 2004. *Politicization of the Public Service in Comparative Perspective*. London: Routledge.

Radwanski, George. 1978. *Trudeau.* Toronto: Macmillan.

Savoie, Donald J. 1994. *Thatcher, Reagan, Mulroney: In Search of a New Bureaucracy.* Pittsburgh, Pa.: University of Pittsburgh Press.

———. 1999a. *Governing from the Centre: The Concentration of Power in Canadian Politics.* Toronto: University of Toronto Press.

———. 1999b. The rise of court government. *Canadian Journal of Political Science* 32: 635–664.

———. 2003. *Breaking the Bargain: Public Servants, Ministers, and Parliament.* Toronto: University of Toronto Press.

———. 2008. *Court Government and the Collapse of Accountability in Canada and the United Kingdom.* Toronto: University of Toronto Press.

Smith, Graeme. 2007. All LAV IIIs to be replaced within the year. *Globe and Mail,* April 3, A1.

Stewart, J. D. M. 2006. The Machine sends its thanks. *The Star,* September 24. www.thestar.com.

Sutherland, Sharon. 1991. Responsible government and ministerial responsibility: Every reform is its own problem. *Canadian Journal of Political Science* XXIV: 91–120.

———. 1996. *Does Westminster Government Have a Future?* Occasional paper series. Ottawa: Institute of Governance.

Tomkins, Adam. 2003. *Public Law.* Oxford: Oxford University Press.

Travers, Jim. 2006. Mandarins learning to like Harper. *The Star,* August 22, A17.

———. 2007. Branding Team Harper. *The Star,* February 6, A17.

Weber, Max. 1946. Bureaucracy. In *Max Weber: Essays in Sociology,* ed. Hans Heinrich Gerth and C. Wright Mills, 51–54. New York: Oxford University Press.

Weller, Patrick. 1985. *First among Equals: Prime Ministers in Westminster Systems.* London: George Allen and Unwin.

Wheare, Kenneth. 1951. *Modern Constitutions.* Oxford: Oxford University Press.

Wilson, Graham K., and Anthony Barker. 2003. Bureaucrats and politicians in Britain. *Governance* 16: 349–372.

PART IV

POLITICAL
PROCESSES

CHAPTER 11

··

POLITICAL PARTIES AND
THE PRACTICE OF
BROKERAGE POLITICS

··

R. KENNETH CARTY

WILLIAM CROSS

POLITICAL parties are central to the Canadian political experience. Indeed, they are more central to the very nature and working of the country than they are in most other established liberal democracies. Canada was initially created by party politicians anxious for an institutional framework that would allow them to break existing stalemates. It was subsequently expanded and restructured, often on partisan terms, and then later constitutionally reengineered, by party leaders. And, after 125 years of electoral competition, one of the major parties in the federal Parliament is dedicated to the breakup of the country.

Despite their part in defining Canadian political life, or the importance they play in shaping and energizing the country's democratic processes, Canadian political parties are, by comparative standards, among the most organizationally weak and decentralized of parties in established democratic party systems. Under-institutionalized and thinly regulated, they persist remarkably unchanged from the basic cadre-style structures of the mid nineteenth century that gave them birth. The parliamentary and electoral system within which they work has changed little, but, as organizations positioned to mediate between the wider society and its governing institutions, the parties have not been immune to the enormous social, economic, and demographic changes that have continually reshaped Canadian society. This has forced them to reinvent themselves more than once, and it is possible to identify several distinct periods during which the old parties successfully reemerged in new guise (Carty et al. 2000). Those reorderings of the party system have flowed from significant institutional alterations in Canadian governance and marked realignments of the electorate. Despite these changes, much of the essence of Canadian parties would be recognizable to André Siegfried, whose 1906 descriptions still ring true.

This chapter begins by providing an account of the distinctive character of brokerage party politics practiced by Canadian parties and the organizational structures they have, of necessity, developed in response to its demands. In the second half we turn to an account of the internal life of the parties and assess their ability to perform the basic functions demanded of them as principal institutions of democratic linkage.

The Distinctive Character
of Canadian Parties

Accounts of the parties traditionally divide them into two simple groups: the two major parties and then all the others. The major parties, the Liberals and the Conservatives,[1] are the only parties ever to have formed a national government. These two parties have persisted throughout the life of the system, adapting as necessary, but seeking to maintain a nationwide constituency and practicing system-tending politics. For most of the twentieth century, the Liberals have dominated as the centerpiece in a system of polarized pluralism (Johnston 2008). Other parties, variously referred to as *minor parties, third parties*, or *protest parties*, have sought unsuccessfully to break up the cozy duopoly that has long governed electoral competition. But operating from a smaller base, and protesting existing political practice, the nature and structure of the political system, the character of the socioeconomic order, or sometimes all of these, they have typically had a limited life. Parties with a distinctive geographical base have sometimes managed to persist for decades, but their very character as regionally defined parties ultimately inhibited them from displacing either of the two large national parties.

These differences have been aggravated and exaggerated by the electoral system, which has systematically overrewarded (with a greater seat share than vote share) the largest party and made survival difficult for small parties. One consequence has been to solidify the organizational structures and practices of the large parties as the norm to which successful parties should conform. This impact of the major parties' example and experience has been particularly important in the absence of any significant legal or regulatory framework governing most aspects of party life.

Heavily influenced by the Lipset and Rokkan (1967) paradigm, most accounts of democratic party systems begin with an analysis of the social cleavages that underlie partisan divisions and define the social bases of the individual parties.

Canadian parties have long been described as one of the great exceptions to this paradigm (Alford 1963; Rose 1974). And by comparative standards, there is some truth to that interpretation. However, for all their heterogeneous character, the two large national parties are neither identical nor completely disconnected from the country's social structure. For decades, the Liberals depended on heavy support from French-speaking Catholic Quebec, but when displaced from their privileged place they quickly adapted and found an alternate base on which to construct a winning coalition. Blais (2005) has demonstrated that there remains a marked religious cleavage leading (English-speaking) Roman Catholics disproportionately to support the Liberals, and his argument suggests that support has been critical to Liberal predominance. If less powerful than in many European systems, class has also played some part in structuring partisanship, especially in providing a base and organizational dynamic for the social democratic New Democratic Party.

Nevertheless, the relative weakness of social divisions in structuring partisan conflict, and thus defining individual parties, has led scholars to recognize that the major Canadian parties are significantly different from their counterparts in most other democracies. The principal functions of the country's major parties are not those of mobilizing distinctive communities and articulating conflicting claims rooted in their interests. Canadian parties are organized to do just the opposite. In the name of accommodating the potentially destructive internal tensions of a weakly integrated national community, they work to obscure differences and muffle conflicting interests. This is the brokerage politics model of democracy. In it, *brokerage parties* are organized and operate in a way that positions them to act as principal instruments of national accommodation rather than democratic division (Carty 1995; Meisel 1963).

Thus, Canada's brokerage parties operate by denying that they should be representative of particular social groups in the national community. Their implicit position is that representative politics of that kind is an inappropriate underpinning for Canadian political life. This is not to say that the parties practice what they preach, for both the Liberals and the Conservatives have at times been quick to recognize and appeal to the interests of distinctive regional or social groups in the electorate. However, they do so claiming that national unity requires a party that can rise above such divisions and argue that only they can do so. This leaves the brokerage party as a distinctive type of party characterized by a unique mix of features.

At the core of a brokerage party's approach to democratic politics is a fierce *electoral pragmatism*. These are organizations consumed with winning and holding office, and they combine an organizational ruthlessness marked by a propensity to abandon losing leaders, with an ideological catholicity that engenders great policy flexibility. Over time, Conservatives and Liberals have shifted sides on major defining issues as well as being prepared to adopt programs only recently denounced and campaigned against. Part of the Liberal's electoral success as the party of the center appears to rest on its practice of campaigning to the Left but governing to the Right. Although the Conservatives are conventionally portrayed as on the Right, there have been periods when they have found themselves to the Liberals' Left. For both, the primary consideration is to find the place that will give them a majority government at that moment.

Brokerage parties' commitment to the broadest possible support base increases their internal diversity and fragility. In response, they are forced to magnify the importance of partisan boundary maintenance as a tool of interparty differentiation. When combined with a fixation on government seeking for its own sake, and reinforced by a self-justifying rhetoric as nation builders, the result is a deep *antipathy to coalition politics*. When the electoral system does not produce a majority (the electorate rarely provides one; it has done so just twice in the past fifty years), the parties prefer to govern alone with a parliamentary minority. In fully half (nine of eighteen) of the general elections of the past half century, the party with the largest parliamentary presence did not have a majority, but in not a single instance was an interparty coalition government formed. In those situations, the parties' basic instinct is to amplify and sharpen partisanship in the hope that the next election will return the system to "normal." This syndrome is rooted in the working of the first-past-the-post electoral system, which helps account for these parties' opposition to fundamental electoral reform.

As organizations with such comparatively ill-defined bounds, brokerage parties make unquestioning *party allegiance*, rather than some ideological test or personal loyalty, the supreme political virtue. André Siegfried (1966) noted this one hundred years ago when he described the parties as almost "sacred institutions" to which individuals owe "absolute loyalty" and could oppose "even in the smallest matters" only at the cost of their reputation and career. This inhibits easy partisan change and, thus, considerably increases the sense of turmoil in periods of party system reorganization that stimulate episodes of parliamentary floor crossing.

Party loyalty reinforces another key characteristic of Canada's brokerage parties—the preeminence of and *domination by the leader*. As chief broker, the leader is responsible for assembling and maintaining a winning coalition. To do this, leaders are given enormous personal latitude to determine and articulate policy, to craft and organize their party's electoral appeals and campaigns, and to manage the careers of even senior party personnel. So important is the position, that for most of a century now, leadership selection has been stripped from the parliamentary caucus and made the prerogative of the wider party meeting in convention. This makes for an extraordinarily strong leadership but also for a fragile one. The parties' only evaluative criteria for leaders is electoral success, and failure can lead to challenges from anywhere in the organization. The leadership is such an important prize that even electorally successful leaders who have overstayed, and so thwarted the ambitions of would-be successors, can be deposed by an internal party uprising.

Flexible brokerage parties that are politically pragmatic, office focused, and leader-centric have an enormous capacity to respond to a changing environment and shifting electoral imperatives. But, this portrait of Canadian brokerage parties raises the question as to whether they are just a North American version of Kirchheimer's (1966; see also Krouwel 2006) catch-all party. Certainly the two appear to share similar approaches to governing, to the central importance they give to leadership selection, and to the role of candidate nomination in establishing their legitimacy. But, that noted, brokerage parties differ from European catch-all parties in important ways that reflect their characteristic approach to electoral dynamics and the management of the country's political life. These differences establish them as a distinct and unique type of political party.

Catch-all parties grow out of a system of social cleavage politicization and recognize that this underlying structural reality means that, whatever their efforts to expand their base, they cannot actually hope to catch all voters. Brokerage parties reject the notion that socioeconomic dimensions of the society close off some voters to them and deny a vision of politics in which that is a determining constraint. In practice, this difference means that catch-all parties deliberately restrain their natural "expressive function" in an attempt to attract voters across existing structural divides whereas brokerage parties have the expressive function—in the Canadian case, a claim to nation building—central to their *raison d'être* and so make it a principal tool of political mobilization.

Party loyalty is understood differently in these two kinds of parties. It is a defining virtue of the brokerage party, given its importance in maintaining support, whereas the catch-all party's ambition to attract support from other parties leads it to accept the attenuation of strong partisanship as the price of success. In both, the party leader plays a central role, particularly as a focus of electoral campaigns. In the catch-all party, the leader carries the message, personifying the appeal; but, in the brokerage party, the leader has a more powerful policy-defining role as the key actor in the brokerage, generating activity that defines the party and its appeal.

One further critical feature distinguishes these parties from one another. Catch-all parties can coexist relatively easily with others of their kind in a single-party system. Indeed, Kirchheimer (1966) argues that catch-all parties emerge as a competitive response to the success of their opponents and points to cases like Great Britain and postwar West Germany as classic examples of systems with two large opposing catch-all organizations. However, the very defining characteristic of the brokerage party—its claim to encompass the entire political community—suggests that there is likely to be only one successful brokerage party in a system at a time. In the Canadian case, this has generally been the Liberals, who emerged as the country's "natural governing party" early in the twentieth century and have rarely relinquished the position. More often than not, this has left the Conservatives at a significant competitive disadvantage, playing the role of would-be national brokers. Thus, the inherent propensity of the successful brokerage party is to become a dominant party rather than just one element in a system of balanced electoral competition.

Major parties may adopt the brokerage model as the standard for national politics, but that option is not available to small parties. Since the introduction of universal suffrage after World War I, almost every Canadian Parliament has had some members from parties that explicitly reject the very premises that define brokerage politics. For the most part, those parties have represented identifiable constituencies—particularly, regional ones, given the biases of a geographically organized electoral system. Some have sought to build a mass-style organization, but most soon drifted into adopting many of the organizational norms and forms of the larger parties. But in doing so, they opened themselves and made it possible for the brokerage parties to soak up their supporters and drive them from the field. Such were the successive fates of the Progressives in the 1920s, Reconstruction in the 1930s, the Bloc Populaire in the 1940s, Social Credit and the Ralliement des Créditistes in the 1960s, and Reform in the 1990s. The social–democratic Cooperative Commonwealth Federation only avoided that fate in the early 1960s by constructing an organizational partnership with the trade unions that allowed it to transform itself into the New Democratic Party.

"Stratarchical" Party Organization

Katz and Mair (1993) suggest that there are three organizational faces to political parties, and an analysis of the interrelationships among them exposes the dynamics governing their internal working. And they argue that an analysis of the evolution of the relationships between the "party in public office" (the parliamentary caucus), the "party on the ground" (local membership units), and the "party in central office" (the bureaucratic apparatus) can provide an account of the transformation of party types over time (Katz and Mair 2002). Although this has proved a powerful framework for examining party structure and organization in most western parliamentary democracies, it can be misleading in the Canadian case.

As the direct descendants of nineteenth-century cadre-style political machines, Canadian parties still bear many of the marks of their origins. Rooted in loosely connected constituency-level organizations, they did not develop a coherent single national organization with a corresponding effective party in central office. Never empowered, that face of the party was excluded from the primary business of organizing and managing election campaigns. Thus, from the beginning, Canadian parties have had an essentially dyadic structure. On the one hand, there is the party on the ground organized in a set of local constituency-focused associations; on the other, the party in central office consisting of its leader-focused parliamentary caucus. The enduring organizational challenge of Canadian parties has been to accommodate and balance these two parts with their competing and often divergent interests.

At the heart of Canadian parties' organization structure is a *stratarchical* arrangement that establishes the relationships between these two faces of the parties (on party stratarchy, see Mair 1994, 17). The core organizational bargain leaves the parliamentary party free to determine and articulate party policy whereas the locally organized membership chooses the party's key personnel—candidates and leaders. In effect, disciplined support for the party in public office is exchanged for local autonomy in the management of the party on the ground's affairs. This internal division of labor is guaranteed by a norm of mutually autonomous coexistence. But of course, if this principle is clear and simple in theory, it is inevitably less so in practice. There is an ongoing pattern of intraparty tension and rivalry as each side seeks to expand its influence over the other. The leadership would like more control over personnel recruitment and advancement; the members would like more authoritative say in party policy making (Carty and Cross 2006).

Institutionalizing this pattern of political relationships has led Canadian parties to develop a *franchise* style of organization (Carty 2002). The party center, largely dominated by the leader, determines policy, articulates strategy, and manages party communication (in franchise terms, this amounts to creating and advertising a product). In each of the hundreds of local electoral districts, individual party members come together to find candidates and to organize and manage the constituency campaigns that harvest electoral support (in franchise terms, this is about finding and delivering customers). Highly decentralized, this form allows brokerage parties to establish a presence in each of the many enormously varied constituencies that make up the country's electoral map (Carty and Eagles 2005). The loose connections between individual local associations leaves them shaped by the interests of the particular group of supporters who control them, their extraordinary permeability means that their composition may change dramatically between successive elections, and their considerable autonomy can produce neighboring associations in the same party with quite different political or social complexions.

Levitsky (2003) argues that populist parties survive best when weakly institutionalized, and much the same logic appears to hold for these franchise-style brokerage parties. Their thinly institutionalized character allows them to penetrate distinctive and divergent elements of the community, supports mechanisms of accommodation among competing values and interests, and provides a frame that facilitates their reorientation in the face of significant realignments in the electorate.

Multilevel Parties

Federalism ensures that political parties will exist and compete in provincial as well as national arenas. In the early decades of the federation, parties were tightly integrated across the two levels by the judicious use of governmental patronage. However, this changed with the twentieth-century professionalism of the public services and the increased importance of provincial governments in the widespread provision of social services. As the political agenda of individual provinces began to vary, and differ from that of national government, their patterns of electoral competition began to diverge. And with that came a growing separation of national and provincially oriented party organizations as they responded to different competitive incentives and realities. The result is a pattern of party life quite different from most other multilevel political systems.

Parties of the same name now have distinct and autonomous organizations within an individual province so that, for instance, in Ontario there is both a Liberal Party of Canada (Ontario) and an Ontario Liberal Party operating as quite independent political entities. This formal organizational separation suits the imperatives of the respective leaderships and the parties in public office, but it also obscures the extent to which partisans at the grassroots actually separate their working party organizations and activity. Research on the most ubiquitous of the parties—the Liberals—now suggests that there is considerable variation in the strength and character of interlevel organizational activity across the country (Koop 2008).

This bifurcation of party organizations produces a number of distinctive patterns. First, not all parties exist at both levels all across the country. Only the Liberals have generally had even a nominal presence in each of the eleven (ten provincial and one national) party systems. And there have often been parties operating at one level only—the Saskatchewan Party contests provincial but not national elections. Second, even when a party exists at both levels, the disaggregation of federal and provincial politics can leave parties of the same name with very different support levels: British Columbia's Liberals easily dominate provincial politics, but find themselves competing for second or third place in national-level contests in the province. A third characteristic of this fragmented party politics is a set of competitive alignments across the country that leaves individual parties in very different positions. In British Columbia, the Liberals define the right end of the provincial spectrum; in Manitoba they constitute its center; in New Brunswick, the left end. In Quebec, the party is on the federalist side of a federalist—separatist divide. This makes it difficult for Liberal partisans in these provinces to discern common interests, and it makes it difficult for their parties to occupy common political ground. Finally, the separation of party organizations appears to inhibit the development of partisan career ladders, common in other federal systems, which reach across levels and contribute to political integration.

Taken together, these features contribute to patterns of party politics in the provinces that are quite different from those of the nation as a whole. With less diverse electorates, the provinces have smaller and more polarized party systems (Stewart and Carty 2006). Provincial parties look and behave more like conventional parties that articulate and mobilize distinctive local interests. Inevitably, the most successful of them are catch-all organizations, and so their dynamics differ from those of the great national brokerage parties despite the fact that all utilize a version of the same franchise model to structure and organize their activity.

Finally, one of the distinctive features of Canadian political life is the absence of national and provincial parties from local government. In many cities, idiosyncratic local municipal party structures exist, with varying capacity to persist over time. In some instances, informal ties and political sympathies link municipal political organizations to local provincial or national party associations. However, the provincial and national parties have no well-developed roots in local government, which deprives them of an important local base of activity and recruitment, as well as depriving partisans of the opportunity to integrate their local political participation with their involvement in provincial or national political life.

The Internal Life of the Parties

Parties operate as the primary agents of linkage between citizens and the state in a system of representative government. Implicit in this linkage function are the notions of both representation and participation. Not only do parties serve to represent the interests of their supporters, but through their personnel recruitment function they play a key role in determining which societal groups are represented in the governing class. Given their privileged place in national politics, democratic parties are also expected to be participatory organizations, offering citizens opportunities to engage in their key decision making (Katz 2001, 278). For Canadian parties, these include both personnel and policy questions. Before assessing how well the parties perform these functions, we start by considering who chooses to participate as party members.

Party Membership

Canada's parties are membership organizations. Individuals, eligible electors or not, are welcome to join the parties, and voice in many party decisions is restricted to members. Parties regularly recruit new members and trumpet any sizeable increases in membership numbers as evidence of growing voter support. Nevertheless, relatively few Canadians belong to a political party on an ongoing basis, and very few seem to choose parties as their principal vehicle for participation in public affairs. Assessing any party's actual size is difficult, given the transient nature of many members' involvement in the party. It is clear that many voters join parties solely to participate in a single event, such as a local nomination meeting or a leadership vote, and then simply let their membership lapse. The result is that party membership numbers resemble a calm, flat sea for long periods only to be punctuated by periodic large waves of members flooding into the parties, typically attracted by personnel recruitment contests (Carty 2008). Although the parties do not routinely release their membership numbers, the best estimates are that between 1% and 2% of Canadians belong to parties on an ongoing basis. This places Canada near the bottom of comparative league tables of party membership numbers in western democracies.

Not only do few Canadians belong to political parties, but those who do are not very active. Surveys of party members indicate that, in an average month, about half of them spend no time at all on party activity whereas only about one in five spends three or more hours on party activity (Cross and Young 2004). These modest patterns characterize the membership activity of the most committed partisans—those who maintain their memberships between elections—and do not include the far more limited participation of individuals who may be simply mobilized to attend a single candidate selection meeting in their local community. However, even those most committed members are significantly more likely to engage in low-intensity activity, such as contributing funds or displaying an election sign, than they are to volunteer in an election campaign or serve on a local party committee.

Party members are not a very representative group—of their party's own voters, let alone the electorate or the general population. Members tend to be disproportionately male (approximately six in ten are men), well educated (more than half are university educated), Canadian born (nine in ten are native born), and older (the average age is almost sixty, and only one in twenty party members is younger than thirty). In short, the portrait of political party members looks nothing like the Canadian mosaic.

Young voters define the parties' most obvious participation deficit. Comparative studies suggest that younger, postmaterialist voters are rejecting traditional, hierarchical forms of political participation in favor of more direct, egalitarian methods (Inglehart 1990; Nevitte 1996). Commenting on the decline in party memberships among European youth, Whiteley (2007, 2) observes "young cohorts of political activists prefer to get involved in single interest pressure groups and in other types of voluntary organizations, rather than in parties." Writing about the Canadian case, O'Neill (2001, 8) argued that "younger generations are more likely to engage in 'new politics'...and to be involved with nontraditional institutions and processes such as grassroots social movements and protest behaviour." Available evidence supports this contention. Young and Everitt (2004) and O'Neill (2001) have both found that young Canadians are significantly more likely to belong to an interest group than to a political party. Cross and Young (2008) suggest that there are two primary reasons why young activists are rejecting parties, both relating to questions of efficacy. On the one hand, young activists are skeptical of ordinary members' ability to influence party decision making; on the other, they doubt parties' capacity to influence public policy. They believe parties to be elite dominated, generally out of touch with the public, and ineffectual at advancing their policy agendas.

The weakness of Canada's parties in recruiting and holding significant numbers of younger members raises questions about their long-term viability as membership-driven organizations. With more Canadians being attracted to advocacy organizations, the ability of parties to link the impulses of civil society to the institutions of the state will be jeopardized. This is troubling for a political system that has traditionally relied on brokerage parties to foster accommodation across its deeply ingrained regional and linguistic cleavages. Advocacy groups, focused on a narrower set of issues, rarely share the nation-building impulses that have long characterized the country's leading parties.

Personnel Recruitment

Leadership Selection

Among parliamentary democracies, Canada's parties have been at the forefront in terms of expanding voice in party leadership selection beyond the parliamentary caucus. Although the major parties in countries such as New Zealand, Australia, and Ireland continue to restrict the franchise in those contests to their elected parliamentarians, for almost a century now Canada's parties have included rank-and-file members in their process of leadership choice. These processes changed over time as the parties responded to pressures to increase responsiveness and enhance their members' participation (Carty 2007; Courtney 1995).

Choosing its leader remained the prerogative of the party in public office until after World War I. The Liberals had divided during the war and recognized that their parliamentary caucus was both geographically and linguistically unrepresentative of their historical base, and so determined to use a convention of delegates from every electoral district to choose their new leader. During a period when the franchise was being expanded and populist impulses were driving new political movements, involving activists was seen both as a more democratic process and one more likely to result in the selection of a leader with appeal in the party's areas of electoral weakness. The Conservatives responded by adopting a similar convention method in 1927, and no major national party has resorted to selection of its leader by the parliamentary caucus since.

For the following half century, leadership selection conventions were largely populated by the parties' local, regional, and national elites. Ordinary rank-and-file party members did not play any meaningful role in the process. The "contests" were either carefully managed, and thus the result preordained, by the outgoing leadership or they were the outcome of competitive dynamics that unfolded in the convention itself, allowing no opportunity for the grassroots membership to influence the choice. This changed dramatically with an increase in the number of delegates accredited to the conventions and a corresponding penetration of local associations by the campaigns of leadership contestants. In an attempt to pack the convention with supportive delegates, campaigns mobilized personal supporters to become instant party members and participate in delegate selection meetings. This launched an era of "trench warfare" that nationalized the selection process and gave party members a more meaningful opportunity to influence the outcome through their selection of pledged delegates (Carty 2007).

The process changed once again in the 1990s, when the parties began to adopt universal membership votes to select their leader (Carty and Blake 1999; Cross 1996; LeDuc 2001). Although the individual mechanics vary, their essential characteristic is that party members cast a ballot directly for their preferred leadership candidate, rather than a convention delegate who cannot be bound or held accountable. The populist Alliance Party was among the first to use a direct vote, with the winner being the candidate with a simple majority of the membership. For their part, the brokerage parties have rejected processes that provide for unmediated direct votes in the interest of geographically weighting members' preferences in a way that mirrors the electoral system and thus is more representative of the political imperatives of national politics.

Although the trend has been toward more inclusive methods of party leadership selection, with grassroots members having a more consequential role in the choice, relatively few voters have participated in these contests. This reflects the reality that party leadership contests are seen as private, internal matters, not public elections, even when the winner becomes the country's prime minister. Participation is limited by the small membership numbers, the cost of local association fees,[2] and cutoff dates, as well as the difficulty many may have in attending a party's single polling location in a large electoral district. Thus, when the Liberals came to choose a new leader (and prime minister) in 2003, about 133,000 participated across the country, representing only about one in forty of the party's voters. Turnout in that leadership contest was typical of Canadian party practice in which only about 2% or 3% of a party's supporters participate in the choice (Cross 2004). This contrasts sharply with the experience of American parties, from whom leadership conventions were initially borrowed, where leadership selection processes are governed by state laws and participation rates often exceed 25%.

One Canadian party has come close to adopting American—style primaries: the Alberta provincial Conservative Party. In both 1992 and 2007, it held open votes, which essentially allowed any interested Albertan to vote. In both cases, the participation rates of party supporters—21% and 35%, respectively—far exceeded anything experienced by a national party (Stewart and Archer 2000). The Alberta Conservative case provides a measure of Canadians' willingness to participate in leadership selection processes when parties adopt accessible procedures and open the choice to all interested voters.

Candidate Selection

Choosing candidates to contest elections is one of a political party's principal functions, differentiating it from other politically active organizations such as interest groups. In Canada it is extremely rare for a member of Parliament to be elected without first winning the endorsement of a political party. The nomination process, by serving as gatekeeper to the party in public office, provides for "nothing less than control of the core of what the party stands for and does" (Ranney 1981, 103). Given the franchise bargain governing Canadian party organizations, it is in the candidate nomination process that the membership has its greatest influence and where critical intraparty power struggles between center and periphery are fought. For brokerage parties, the candidate selection process constitutes the critical mechanism that allows the party to penetrate and establish a presence across the country's diverse electoral districts. This reinforces the decentralizing imperatives of the franchise bargain, but leaves the party subject to the impulses and interests of whatever local groups capture their constituency associations.

Although the candidate nomination process has traditionally allowed local activists broad discretion in the selection of their candidates, the importance of the process for defining the image of the national party is challenging the norm of local autonomy. In both major parties, central elites (including the leaders themselves) are seeking to exercise increasing control over local nomination decisions, sometimes to promote the candidacy of a specific individual, other times to deny a nomination to an undesirable candidate. The Liberal Party's constitution now explicitly provides its leader with this authority whereas other parties exploit the provision of the Canada Elections Act, requiring the leader to endorse local candidates who carry the party label to accomplish essentially the same ends. More often than not, the leadership will seek to persuade local activists, but they also intervene to rig selection rules and, in some cases, make direct appointments to achieve their ends. Local party associations have traditionally required incumbents to face a reselection meeting before each election. Although most are easily renominated, every election sees a few defeated, reasserting the power of the party on the ground to shape the parliamentary caucus. This imbalance can be completely overturned by a leader who guarantees the reselection of all sitting members of Parliament, as occurred in both Liberal and Conservative cases during the minority Parliament preceding the 2006 general election. The result was that partisans in the districts that their party was most likely to win had no say over who their candidate was to be that year (Cross 2006, 76–77).

The nomination process is structured in much the same way as leadership contests. They are organized as private events run by volunteers with little recourse to impartial oversight or regulation. Participation is restricted to dues-paying party members, voting is typically limited to one place in each electoral constituency, polls normally are open for only an hour or two, and membership cutoff dates are imposed. The central dynamic of most nomination contests is the personal ambition of the candidates involved and their capacity to find the resources necessary to conduct a campaign. Although every election includes several vigorously contested contests in which a large number of instant members are mobilized to come to the selection meeting, these are exceptional cases. Despite the relative openness of the process, most nominations, and particularly those in districts where a party's electoral prospects are slim, are acclaimed. When contests do take place, the number of activists voting is rarely more than a few hundred, evidence that the parties are not able to attract many of their own supporters to participate.

Their highly decentralized and fragmented nomination processes have made it difficult for the parties, as national institutions, to select a socially representative slate of candidates. Individuals from traditionally underrepresented groups can not easily displace sitting incumbents deeply ensconced in their districts; they are more likely to be nominated in constituencies where their electoral prospects are modest. As a result, the parties have returned disproportionately small numbers of women and "visible minorities" to the House of Commons, where they make up about 20% and 7.5%, respectively.

Policy Formulation

Political parties dominate Canada's public policy agenda. During election periods, election expense laws ensure that their messages dominate the public's political agenda. Between elections, the parties' leaderships control the flow of policy debate in Parliament, with limited opportunity for other groups to influence it. However, although rank-and-file party members are interested in shaping and driving their party's policy agendas, they feel disenfranchised. Survey evidence indicates three quarters of them believe they should have more influence in this area of party decision making (Cross 2004). In contrast to the role played by partisans in the policy units of many European parties, policy making in Canadian franchise parties has long been understood to be the preserve of the parliamentary leadership. Members of the party on the ground are to concern themselves with personnel decisions and the management of the local ground wars of election campaigns.

This somewhat artificial divorce between personnel and policy, which is at the heart of the stratarchical division of power in Canadian parties, is designed to serve the electoral imperatives of brokerage politics. It supports the capacity of the party leader to act as a party's chief broker in the continuing efforts to built national accommodations that will appeal to the broadest possible electorate. Because these two dimensions come together in the leadership, they inevitably strengthen the position of party leader. At the same time, internal policy conflicts, however defined, are ultimately focused on a leader whose very openness to the membership renders it potentially quite fragile.

This brokerage imperative is strongest when a party is in power and the leader has the advantage of controlling the levers of the state. In opposition, the weakness of the model is exposed and parties in that position respond by extending a greater policy role to their members, only to again retract it after they return to power. This cycle, in which the policy role of members significantly changes—increasing when the party can do little to implement its decisions and contracting when it could—is destabilizing, and likely to produce an alienated membership (Clarkson 1979; Wearing 1981), internal leadership conflict (Perlin 1980), or both. In the smaller parties, the grassroots membership regularly plays a more significant role in determining policy. Given that those parties have never come to office, their members' impact is limited to the party's capacity to alter or influence the public agenda.

PARTY POLITICS IN CANADA

Canadian parties have evolved their franchise organizations to practice an elitist brokerage politics in response to the challenge of linking the country's society to its governing institutions. This is no easy task, for the two are not easily balanced. Canada's social order reflects its new world character. A plural, heterogeneous population characterized by continual growth and change provides for no settled political equilibrium. By contrast, the nation's core democratic institutions are rooted in the constitutional accommodations structured by its nineteenth-century political inheritance. Simply put, national political parties are squeezed between the impulses of an open, dynamic North American immigrant society and the practices of its closed, hierarchical European institutions. As the political system's shock absorbers, the parties have had to continually adapt to survive. On three occasions in the twentieth century, electoral realignments reflecting major social changes and institutional adaptation in response to a federalizing state stimulated a reorganization of the party system and the reconstruction of its basic units in the aftermath of the 1921, 1958, and 1993 general elections (Carty et al. 2000). Each time, the country's national parties—condemned to constant electoral nation building—have remerged with a renewed version of the same simple organizational formula: a stratarchical structure to centralize authority over policy and decentralize power in the service of brokerage politics.

NOTES

1. The Conservatives have operated under different names over time—Liberal Conservatives in the early years of the federation, Progressive Conservatives in the second half of the twentieth century—but have been essentially the same party. The current name is the Conservative Party of Canada.

2. Membership fees for most local associations are typically in the $10 to $20 range. For individuals being asked to come to a single meeting, this can seem like a substantial admission fee or even a "poll tax." In many cases, the reluctance of individuals to pay forces candidates to absorb the cost (despite party rules to the contrary) in their limited budgets.

REFERENCES

Alford, Robert R. 1963. *Party and Society: The Anglo-American Democracies*. Chicago, Ill.: Rand McNally.

Blais, André. 2005. Accounting for the success of the Liberal Party in Canada. *Canadian Journal of Political Science* 38(4): 821–840.

Carty, R. Kenneth. 1995. "On the road again": The stalled omnibus in Canada. In *Canada's Century: Governance in a Maturing Society. Essays in Honour of John Meisel*, ed. C. E. S. Franks, J. E. Hodgetts, O. P. Dwivedi, Doug Williams, and Seymour Wilson, 187–202. Montreal: McGill Queens University Press.

———. 2002. The politics of Tecumseh Corners: Canadian political parties as franchise organizations. *Canadian Journal of Political Science* 35(4): 723–745.

———. 2007. Leadership politics and the transformation of Canadian parties. In *Political Leadership and Representation in Canada: Essays in Honour of John C. Courtney*, ed.

H. J. Michelmann, Donald C. Story, and Jeffrey S. Steeves, 16–38. Toronto: University of Toronto Press.

———. 2008. Brokerage politics, stratarchical organization and party members: The Liberal Party of Canada. In *Partier og partisystemer i forandring:* [Changing parties and party systems] *Festskrift til Lars Bille,* ed. Karina Kosiara-Pedersen and Peter Kurrild-Klitgaard, 301–313. Odense: University of Southern Denmark Press.

Carty, R. Kenneth, and Donald Blake. 1999. The adoption of membership votes for choosing party leaders: The experience of Canadian parties. *Party Politics* 5(2): 211–224.

Carty, R. Kenneth, and William Cross. 2006. Can stratarchically organized parties be democratic? The Canadian case. *Journal of Elections, Public Opinion and Parties* 16(2): 93–114.

Carty, R. Kenneth, William Cross, and Lisa Young. 2000. *Rebuilding Canadian Party Politics.* Vancouver: UBC Press.

Carty, R. Kenneth, and Munroe Eagles. 2005. *Politics Is Local: National Politics at the Grassroots.* Oxford: Oxford University Press.

Clarkson, Stephen. 1979. Democracy in the Liberal Party: The experiment with citizen participation under Pierre Trudeau. In *Party Politics in Canada,* 4th ed., ed. Hugh G. Thorburn, 154–160. Scarborough, Ont.: Prentice-Hall.

Courtney, John C. 1995. *Do Conventions Matter? Choosing National Party Leaders in Canada.* Montreal: McGill-Queen's University Press.

Cross, William. 1996. Direct election of provincial party leaders in Canada, 1985–95: The end of the leadership convention? *Canadian Journal of Political Science* 29(2): 295–315.

———. 2004. *Political Parties.* Vancouver: UBC Press.

———. 2006. Candidate nomination in Canada's political parties. In *The Canadian Federal Election of 2006,* ed. Jon H. Pammett and Christopher Dornan, 171–195. Toronto: Dundurn.

Cross, William, and Lisa Young. 2004. The contours of political party membership in Canada. *Party Politics* 10(4): 427–444.

———. 2008. Factors influencing the decision of the young politically engaged to join a political party: An investigation of the Canadian case. *Party Politics* 14(3): 345–369.

Inglehart, Ronald. 1990. *Culture Shift in Advanced Industrial Society.* Princeton, N.J.: Princeton University Press.

Johnston, Richard. 2008. Polarized pluralism in the Canadian party system. *Canadian Journal of Political Science* 41(4): 815–834.

Katz, Richard S. 2001. The problem of candidate selection and models of party democracy. *Party Politics* 7(3): 277–296.

Katz, Richard S., and Peter Mair. 1993. The evolution of party organization in Europe: The three faces of party organization. *The American Review of Politics* 14(4): 593–617.

———. 2002. The ascendancy of the party in public office: Party organization change in twentieth-century democracies. In *Political Parties: Old Concepts and New Challenges,* ed. R. Gunther, J. R. Montero, and J. Linz, 113–135. Oxford: Oxford University Press.

Kirchheimer, Otto. 1966. The transformation of the western European party systems. In *Political Parties and Political Development,* ed. Joseph LaPalombara and Martin Weiner, 177–200. Princeton, N.J.: Princeton University Press.

Koop, Royce. 2008. *Multi-Level Party Politics: The Liberal Party from the Ground Up.* PhD diss., unpublished, University of British Columbia.

Krouwel, A. 2006. Party models. In *Handbook of Party Politics,* ed. Richard S. Katz and W. Crotty, 249–269. London: Sage Publications.

LeDuc, Lawrence. 2001. Democratizing party leadership selection. *Party Politics* 7(3): 323–341.

Levitsky, Steven. 2003. *Transforming Labor-Based Parties in Latin America: Argentine Peronism in Comparative Perspective*. Cambridge: Cambridge University Press.

Lipset, Seymour M., and Stein Rokkan. 1967. Cleavage structures, party systems, and voter alignments: An introduction. In *Party Systems and Voter Alignments*, ed. Seymour M. Lipset and Stein Rokkan, 1–64. New York: Free Press.

Mair, Peter. 1994. Party organizations: From civil society to the state. In *How Parties Organize: Change and Adaptation in Party Organization in Western Democracies*, ed. Richard S. Katz and Peter Mair, 1–22. London: Sage Publications.

Meisel, John. 1963. The stalled omnibus: Canadian parties in the 1960s. *Social Research* 30(3): 367–390.

Nevitte, Neil. 1996. *The Decline of Deference: Canadian Value Change in Cross-National Perspective*. Peterborough, Ont. : Broadview.

O'Neill, Brenda. 2001. Generational patterns in the political opinions and behaviour of Canadians. *Policy Matters* 2(5): 1–48.

Perlin, George C. 1980. *The Tory Syndrome: Leadership Politics in the Progressive Conservative Party*. Montreal: McGill-Queen's University Press.

Ranney, Austin. 1981. Candidate selection. In *Democracy at the Polls*, ed. David Butler, Howard Penniman, and Austin Ranney, 70–106. Washington, D.C.: American Enterprise Institute.

Rose, Richard. 1974. *Electoral Behavior*. New York: Free Press.

Siegfried, André. [1906] 1966. *The Race Question in Canada*. Toronto: McLelland and Stewart.

Stewart, David K., and Keith Archer. 2000. *Quasi-Democracy? Parties and Leadership Selection in Alberta*. Vancouver: UBC Press.

Stewart, David, and R. Kenneth Carty. 2006. Many political worlds? Provincial parties and party systems. In *The Canadian Provinces*, 2nd ed., ed. C. Dunn, 97–113. Peterborough: Broadview Press.

Wearing, Joseph. 1981. *The L-Shaped Party: Organizing and Financing the Liberal Party of Canada, 1930–58*. Toronto: McGraw-Hill Ryerson.

Whiteley, Paul. 2007. "Are groups replacing parties? A multi-level analysis of party and group membership in the European democracies." Presented at the European Consortium for Political Research workshop on Partisanship in Europe: Members, Activists and Identifiers. Helsinki, May 7–12.

Young, Lisa, and Joanna Everitt. 2004. *Advocacy Groups*. Vancouver: UBC Press.

....

CHAPTER 12

POLITICAL PARTIES AND THE ELECTORAL SYSTEM

....

RICHARD JOHNSTON

AMONG Westminster systems, Canada is the deviant case. Long-lived governments coexist with volatile outcomes. Canada was the first Westminster system to exhibit multiparty competition as a chronic feature. The social foundations of the party system are peculiarly cultural. For decades, policy differences between the major parties were, by comparative standards, weak. Within Canadian provinces, differences between closely spaced federal and provincial outcomes are wide, sometimes shockingly so.

This chapter introduces the literature that makes these points and outlines its controversies. For the most part the review stays at the level of the party *system*. The focus is not on, or does not start with, attributes of individual party organizations. Nor is voter psychology the central preoccupation. From the systemic perspective, the existing literature does not add up to a satisfactory interpretation. Theory and evidence from the comparative study of elections intrudes too rarely. By the same token, the Canadian case rarely enters the consciousness of scholars outside Canada. The Canadian literature struggles to keep up with change in the system, much less with the continuity that lurks beneath the change. Accordingly, the chapter also proposes a conceptual departure and outlines a program for future research.

LOCATING THE CANADIAN CASE

....

Predominance of One Party

The Liberal Party of Canada has tended to enjoy power for long stretches and to be out of power for only short ones. In the twentieth century, the Liberals enjoyed more years in government than any of their obvious comparators on the Westminster scene, the British Conservatives, the Australian Liberals, and the pre-1996 New Zealand National Party. Indeed, the real points of comparison, according to Blais (2005), are the Swedish Social Democrats, the Japanese Liberal Democrats, and Ireland's Fianna Fáil, each the dominant player in what Sartori (1976) calls a "predominant" party system. (Interestingly, Sartori does not class Canada as such a system.) And one-party dominance has long been a theme in the study of Canadian elections (Pinard 1966; Pinard 1967; Smiley 1958).

Volatility

It is equally true, however, that the Canadian system exhibits more volatility than its comparators. Lovink (1973) and Blake (1991) show that turnover of individual members of Parliament is high by comparative standards. Some of the volatility is episodic, as several elections mark sharp departures with their immediate predecessors. In themselves, sharp discontinuities are not that unusual. But in other systems, most great electoral breaks occurred before the middle of the twentieth century and accompanied the shift toward class politics (Bartolini and Mair 1990). In Canada, as figure 12.1 shows, such breaks keep recurring. The figure plots an index of volatility (Pedersen 1979) with values that are the minimum percentage of the electorate that would have to shift parties to convert a given year's distribution of national vote shares into the distribution for the immediately preceding election. High-volatility elections are circled. The first outstanding reading is for 1921, the year in which the progressive movement broke through to national politics, mostly at the expense of the Conservatives (Morton 1950). This election and the one in 1935 have much in common with the early twentieth-century disruptions observed elsewhere. But no other Canadian breakpoint fits this description. For example, an election that rivals 1921 for volatility is the next one, in 1925. This outcome simply reversed much of the 1921 shift. Another high point actually comprises three elections: 1957, 1958, and 1962. The 1957 election brought twenty-two years of Liberal rule to an end, and the 1958 election produced a Conservative landslide. Together, the 1957 and 1958 shifts cumulated to a change as dramatic as those in 1921 and 1935. But, the 1962 shift repeated the task of 1925: to move the system back toward the status quo ante.[1] The 1984 election represented a sharp departure from 1980; this was like the 1957–1958 sequence in that it removed a long-standing Liberal government and produced a Conservative landslide. But the highest volatility election of all, in 1993, took those same Conservatives to a virtual nullity. The 1990s continued to be unsettled and then the 2004 election restored the Conservatives as a credible opposition. In sum, the Canadian pattern has four distinctive features: the number of elections representing severe *dis*continuity is high, discontinuous elections occurred as often after 1950 as before, discontinuity often represents a return to an older pattern of competition, and discontinuity tends to be visited disproportionately on the Conservative Party.

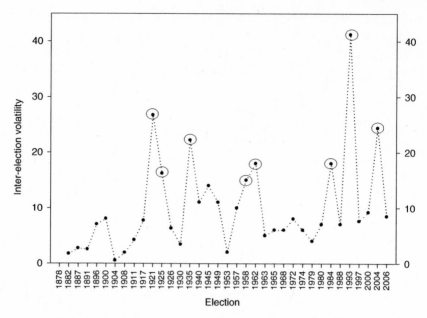

Figure 12.1. Volatility in Canadian elections. Entries are index values for "total volatility" (Pedersen 1979) between the indicated election and the immediately preceding one.

Policy Differences

Some argue that this volatility is the natural product of weak policy differences among the parties. LeDuc (1985) and Bakvis (1988) make this connection. It is the central theme in Clarke and Kornberg (1992) and—most influentially—in Clarke et al. (1996). The verdict from actual studies of the opinion–vote relation is mixed, however. Pétry (1995) finds that Liberal governments are willing to enact popular elements in rival parties' programs. Sometimes this means tacking to the Right, sometimes it means moving Left. Pétry (1999) also finds that both governing parties are responsive to opinion on high-profile issues. So far, then, Canadian parties may be said to blow with the wind, and *not* to conform to the platform policy model proposed by, among others, Budge et al. (2001). But Pétry and Mendelsohn (2004) show that the Liberal/Conservative difference reflects substantive policy preferences: Liberal Party preferences lie to the Left of mass opinion, and, in government, the Liberal Party resists rightward pressure. Cross and Young (2002) offer complementary evidence from surveys of Conservative and Liberal Party elites. Nadeau and Blais (1990) and Bélanger (2003) show that voters see differences among the parties in issue ownership, mainly to the advantage of the Liberals. Differences among authors may reflect evolution in the system. Comparative Manifestos Project data (Budge et al. 2001; Klingemann et al. 2006) show that before the mid 1970s, the Liberal and Conservative parties were indeed very similar on the classic left–right dimension of policy. In the 1970s, however, the Conservatives pulled to the Right. The New Democratic Party (NDP) stayed pretty much in place on the Left, but became progressively more important as an electoral force. By the late 1980s, the system exhibited considerable ideological range, and the disruptions of the 1990s increased the range still further—by pushing the right flank further Right.

Social Foundations

Weak policy differences might imply weak social foundations. Rose (1974) found that in only three systems was less variance explained by group affiliation than in Canada. Rose's finding has had a long shelf-life as a stylized fact. But rarely, if ever, mentioned are the identities of the three ostensibly weaker systems: Ireland, the United States, and Great Britain. Few would present the British system, in particular, as an example of weak social roots, so the blinkered invocation of Rose's finding (Rose 1974) seems singularly inapt. The problem lies with a basic misapprehension of multivariate estimation. Classic indicators of "explained variation," such as the coefficient of determination (R^2), yield small values for consolidated party systems (Johnston forthcoming).[2]

Archaic Divisions

The foundations of Canada's system do seem archaic, however. Laponce (1972) showed with national data that the best single predictor of major-party preference was Catholic religion. The finding was anticipated by local studies, notably Meisel (1967), and goes all the way back to Siegfried (1907). Although Wearing (1996) argues that the importance of religion is not exceptional, Canada is the only Westminster system for which this was still true in the late twentieth century. Moreover, by the 1970s, it was hard to see much connection between the system's religious base and its secular issue superstructure. Mendelsohn and Nadeau (1997) and Bittner (2007) confirm the disconnection by showing that the cleavage persists mainly among voters out of the communication mainstream. In a sense, this disconnection reinforces the standard emphasis on the major parties' weak issue differentiation. Consistent with this disconnect, Irvine (1974) and Irvine and Gold (1980) argued that perpetuation of the system's archaic basis rests on mere prepolitical socialization within families. Johnston (1985) demonstrated the inadequacy of this account but offered no substantive alternative. Brodie and Jenson (1988; 1996) argued that the key lies in control of the agenda by the major parties. The parties' strategic interest lies in keeping matters of current policy substance out of electoral discourse, and they do so by priming cultural issues. The analysis by Brodie and Jenson (1988) begs the question of why, in most other countries, center right parties have signally failed to control the agenda in this way. Also, their analysis seems more appropriate to explaining a language gap; part of the puzzle of the denominational gap is that it cannot be resolved into a language one. In any case, under first past the post (FPP), class politics actually favors parties of the Right (Iversen and Soskice 2006). Besides, part of the mystery of the Catholic–Liberal connection was the Liberal Party's own reluctance to prime religious issues. The importance of religion remains a puzzle (Blais 2005).

Weak Class Basis

The cleavage that dominates most polities, especially in the Westminster world, is class. But in Canada, class differences in the vote are strikingly weak. Alford (1963) was the first to observe this with survey data, and his formulation also laid the basis for a generation of comparative accounts. One reaction to Alford was denial. For starters, there is the very existence of the Cooperative Commonwealth Federation/New Democratic Party (CCF/NDP), in contrast to the outright failure of socialist and social democratic parties in the United States (Horowitz 1966; Lipset 1968). Also contested is Alford's classification of Canadian parties: Liberals on the Left and Social Credit on the Right (Alford 1963). Contrasting the Liberals and Conservatives, on one hand, with both minor parties, on the other, produces a sharper class cleavage (Ogmundson 1975). Myles (1979) extended the argument from classification of parties to indicators of class difference. In particular, he advocated use of odds ratios rather than regression coefficients, and concluded that Canadian and American class effects were substantively identical. Hunter (1982) further extended the argument by moving away from a dichotomous representation of class. But the denial seems hollow. It requires that one take the now-defunct Social Credit seriously as a representative of working-class interests. It also finesses the comparative weakness of the NDP. Some authors looked for anticipatory signs of NDP strength (Ornstein et al. 1980; Wilson 1968; Wilson 1974): Where the NDP flourishes, its electoral base conforms to the Anglo-Australasian social–democratic model. In the most recent systematic comparative study (Evans 1999), however, the outstanding fact about the Canadian system is still its weak class basis.

Appropriately, some of the literature addresses this history of futility. Horowitz (1966) anatomized the structural barriers to union affiliation with the CCF, especially before the rival federations merged in 1956 as the Canadian Labor Congress (CLC). Archer (1985) argued that the union–party link has nonetheless been a misfire. Jenson (1990) is similarly pessimistic in emphasizing the peculiar history of Canadian labor relations. Brodie and Jenson (1988; 1996) argued that the roots of failure lie in the party system itself: The Liberal and Conservative parties engage in obfuscation and the NDP is too timid. Gidengil (1989) argues that, objectively speaking, class interests do not always align the same way in each region, so the basis for a nationwide class division is intrinsically weak. Johnston (1991) tries to link the weakness of the class divide to the strength of the religious one, by exploring the geographical contingencies of Catholics' local preponderance.

Geography

This brings us to geography, a commonplace in Canadian political commentary (Lipset 1968; Macpherson 1953; Schwartz 1974). Pieces by Blake (1972) and Irvine (1971) are both essays in how to represent geography in a multivariate framework; neither seeks to uncover the causal mechanisms in play. The same is true of Elkins and Simeon (1974), Johnston (1980), and Gidengil et al. (1997). To the extent that these contributions embraced theory, it was to confront it: The governing expectation in the 1960s and '70s was that the passage of time would efface mere geography. Stokes (1967) identified such a pattern in the United States and implied that the operative mechanism lay in the communications stream. Lipset and Rokkan (1967) argued that nationalization of electoral forces would occur as cleavages based on territory yield to ones based on function. This is not to say that regional differences would necessarily disappear, just that, after economic and social modernization picked up steam, geographical variance would shrink. Where Caramani (2004) shows that the nationalization of electoral forces has indeed been the European norm, and that the trend dates from the very onset of party competition, Blake (1972) and Johnston (1980) controvert the expectation for Canada. Still, region in these Canadian analyses was mainly a container. Gidengil (1989) seems to have been the first electoral empiricist since Schwartz (1974) to replace container with contents. Her dependency theory analysis hearkens back to the earliest work, in which region is more than the alternative to class and, indeed, is a condition for the operation of class claims and is an index in its own right of interests in the national political economy.

One place where geography consistently has theoretical content is in its interaction with the electoral system. The touchstone for Canadians has been Cairns (1968), who argued that parties actively exacerbate regionalism precisely because the electoral system encourages them to do so. Lovink (1970), Johnston and Ballantyne (1977), and Johnston (2005) take issue with Cairns, but his original paper enjoys totemic status. Accounts in a political economy tradition, such as Schwartz (1974) and Brodie (1990), also emphasize the political origins of regionalism, although with more weight on federalism than on the electoral system.

Multipartism

Cairns' general point (Cairns 1968), that electoral systems embody strategic incentives, is now a commonplace in the comparative study of party systems. There the critical datum is the system's fractionalization—the number and relative size of its constituent parties. First past the post with single-member districts is the quintessential "strong" electoral system, a system that punishes coordination failure among kindred parties and so should encourage consolidation (Duverger 1963). Duverger (1963) identified a "mechanical" effect whereby FPP strips parties from the system as votes are translated into seats. This can sharpen electoral competition among the advantaged parties, but in doing so may hand victory to a party that could not beat others in a straight fight. Duverger (1963) also identified a second "psychological" effect, in which actors move strategically to minimize this problem by focusing competition on the feasible alternatives. Voters might recognize that certain votes are "wasted" and move to an advantaged party. More likely, according to Cox (1997), elites will engineer selective entry or nonentry of candidates. Multipartism, on this view, should occur only under a proportional formula with a large district magnitude, and not necessarily even there (Cox 1997). Indeed, as Ordeshook and Shvetsova (1994) argue, FPP overrides social heterogeneity: Countries with FPP—Canada prominently among them—are ethnically more heterogeneous than countries with Proportional Representation (PR). But all these arguments fail to cover the multiparty facts of the Canadian case, facts that exercised Cairns (1968) and stood out in Rae (1971).

Given the comparative background, many analysts understandably took Canadian third-party voting as a deviation to be explained. One obvious avenue of explanation emphasizes antipathy to party politics as such. This is a venerable theme, dating back to accounts of Social Credit and its antecedents (Macpherson 1953; Morton 1950), and it remains an influential theme (Conway 1978; Laycock 1990; 2002). Antipathy to the party system overlaps economic or other forms of distress (Bélanger 2004a; Bowler and Lanoue 1992; Gidengil et al. 2001) and general distrust in the political class (Bélanger and Nadeau 2005). However, distress does not always lead to third-party voting. More often, it yields dividends to the major party currently out of office. The redirection of discontent toward a third party arguably also requires an additional structural ingredient—for example, a mainstream opposition party lacking electoral credibility (Pinard 1966; 1967; 1971). Pinard developed this model to account for the abrupt rise of Social Credit in Quebec in 1962. The model has not traveled well, however, particularly as the notion of opposition credibility is underdeveloped (Blais 1973). It seems better adapted to protest parties than to parties with a substantive program, such as the NDP or the first generation of agrarian parties (Pinard 1973; White 1973). Bélanger (2004b) has moved the analysis some distance in clarifying the idea of opposition weakness and in distinguishing new parties by the substance of their appeal. He profited from the nearly simultaneous appearance on the federal scene in the early 1990s of Reform and the Bloc québécois (although he arguably overstates the programmatic content of the Bloc and understates it for Reform).

Arguments from strain and structural conduciveness focus on the moment of third-party insurgency. What is striking in Rae (1971) and Cairns (1968), however, is that Canadian multipartism is chronic. Although the Duvergerian focus on pressures toward bipartism allows for the occasional third-party breakthrough, it does not predict the indefinite perpetuation of fractionalization. Either an insurgent party will be beaten back or one of the older parties will yield. The only way Duverger's Law can be saved in the face of multipartism is through *cross-district* coordination failure. As Duverger is now commonly read (Cox 1997), his Law applies at the constituency level only. Creating a two-party system in the nation as a whole requires a separate logic and practice. Failure by political actors to transcend the locale makes it possible for bipartism to prevail at one level even as the system as a whole is multiparty. This is the gist of Rae's (1971) interpretation of the Canadian case: Localized third-party support makes Canada the exception that proves the general rule. The same view was held by Riker (1976), was reaffirmed by Cox (1997), and was extended by Chhibber and Kollman (2004). Chhibber and Kollman (2004) built on Cox's (1987) analysis of the rise of party-focused competition in the United Kingdom. There, two-party competition emerged as a consequence of the nationalization of the policy agenda. In Canada, Chhibber and Kollman (2004) claim, the agenda has *de*nationalized. As this occurs, the imperative to build pan-Canadian coalitions wanes. One leg of this argument is clearly wobbly: As Gaines (1997; 1999) shows, multiparty competition is ubiquitous at the *riding* level.

Federal–Provincial Gaps

Discontinuity between federal and provincial elections, most startlingly within certain provinces, was noticed early on. Underhill (1955) and Wrong (1957) conjectured that the process was akin to what has come to be called *balancing* (Alesina and Rosenthal 1995; Fiorina 1992), or self-conscious movement away from the party in power at one level to restrain ideological extremism or arrogance at the other. Dawson (1947) and Scarrow (1960) saw a simpler pattern. Provincial elections anticipate the breakup of senescent federal electoral coalitions, and differences widen up to the moment of federal rupture. Sometimes federal outcomes in a province do the same for a decrepit or discredited provincial regime. Tests for these claims are sparse and inconclusive. Wilson and Hoffman (1970) and Perlin and Peppin (1971) went looking for balancing, and Johnston (1980) found hints of electoral anticipation. But all of these accounts are inadequate in face of the sheer scale of divergence.[3]

TOWARD AN INTERPRETATION OF THE CASE

The central peculiarity of the Canadian system, I would argue, is its domination by a party of the center, the Liberal Party. According to Powell (2000), Canada is the only majoritarian system in which the governing party typically covers the policy median. Although such coverage is normal under proportional representation, in majoritarian systems the governing party always sits on one side of the median, usually on the Right (Iversen and Soskice 2006), but never straddles it. Canada converges on the other majoritarian systems only when the Liberals lose. Thus, accounting for Liberal strength is itself a major task for any adequate theory.

However, control of the center by a strong party presupposes at least three nontrivial parties: the center party plus one on each flank. That is, we must also account for the presence of the Conservatives and the NDP and for the twentieth-century shift from bipartism to multipartism. In other consolidated party systems, the two dominant parties control poles on a left–right policy dimension; parties of the center may persist but they do not flourish. Typically, the left pole is controlled by a social–democratic party. In this, Canada is typical, and the exceptional case is the United States. But the United States is like the others in that its leftmost party is one of the major players. In Canada, the leftmost party is the *weakest* mainstream player. And in every other majoritarian system where a socialist party exists, only one major nonsocialist party survives.

The party to disappear could have been the Conservatives, and Granatstein (1967) makes clear that in the 1940s, the party's survival was very much in doubt. He suggests that the party saved itself by coming to terms with the welfare state. In the 1950s and '60s, according to Budge et al. (2001), the party kept pace ideologically with the Liberals. Be that as it may, the example of other countries suggests that, in the long run, the Conservative Party's success may have required staking out the right side of the spectrum, and this is exactly what it did in the mid 1970s. To the extent that the Conservatives moved Right, they gave the Liberals breathing room. Why, then, did the left pole come to be controlled not by the Liberals but by the NDP? Part of the answer lies in the union movement (*pace* Archer 1985), which has never found the Liberals to be a satisfactory agent. Later, I argue that this is the central fact about the rise of the NDP; but, to the extent that it is true, it begs two further questions: Why did a social–democratic party take so long to become a serious player? Why, after the NDP became serious, was it unable to break through to major-party status?

Put another way, why did the Liberal Party not sink when the NDP broke through? Before 1960, Liberal survival reflected the fact that the two old parties diverged on a dominant, *non*economic dimension. On this dimension, the Liberals controlled the pole generally acceptable to Catholics, including French Canadians. If the Liberal position was not itself intrinsically extreme, a more extreme position was not yet feasible in federal politics. The social basis of the difference was religious, but the issue content was about Canada as a British nationality. Although questions of faith, morals, schooling, and ecclesiology divided Catholics from Protestants, such questions sowed division more within traditional parties than between them (Crunican 1975; Miller 1979). Only on the British connection, especially on external relations, were religion and party aligned (Stacey 1977; 1981).

After 1960, a left–right dimension akin to that in other countries emerged, with the Liberals clearly at the center. Because the center is normally ill-fated, the party could survive only if it could control a pole on some other dimension. This it did, but in a very peculiar way. The other dimension is still cultural, although now mainly inward looking. If the cultural complex continued to include the residual Britishness of symbols and the accommodation of new ethnic groups, the strategically critical focus became French–English and—more to the point—Quebec–Canada relations. The electoral system has usually ensured that Quebec will be critical one way or another to electoral success or failure (Bakvis and Macpherson 1995; Johnston et al. 1992). And to the extent the dimension focused on Quebec, it stretched to include a more aggressive posture of Quebec vis-à-vis the Canadian whole. Positions that were unfeasible before 1960 now became imaginable, although, before the 1990s, the extreme position was confined to provincial politics. On this dimension, the Liberals built on their earlier experience—for example, in continuing to recruit francophones and sympathetic anglophones. To the extent that their special claim lay in *managing* the relationship, they found themselves clearly controlling the center. But, critically, the electorate was more segmented than ever between Quebec and the rest. Thanks to this segmentation, the Liberal Party can be culturally centrist for the electorate as a whole precisely because it is off center *within each segment*: the pro-Quebec party outside Quebec and the pro-Canada one inside Quebec. This also makes it possible for the Liberals to benefit from, rather than be harmed by, their centrism on the left–right dimension.

On each dimension, then, the system exhibits what Sartori (1976) calls "polarized pluralism." (To give credit where credit is due, the first recognition that this pattern applies to Canada seems to be in Dobell [1986].) The combination of Liberal policy centrism and electoral strength makes it very difficult for rival interests to coordinate against that party. And polarized pluralism accounts, at least in part, for many of the system's other peculiarities.

The Fractionalization of the Electorate

To the extent that this fractionalization is local, it reflects the implausibility of coordination between the Liberals' chief rivals outside Quebec, the Conservatives, and the NDP. To the extent that choice is dominated by a left–right policy axis, it is simply implausible that NDP supporters would coalesce with ideologically distant Conservative ones to defeat the Liberals, and vice versa. Such coalescence occurs only when the cultural dimension dominates electoral choice.

Conservative Boom and Bust

On the cultural dimension, polarized pluralism has, if anything, deepened with time. The cultural story is also inherently more complex than the left–right one. It has two sides: one for Quebec and one for the West. The central point is that Liberal strength in Quebec has blocked Conservative access to power. The only way for Conservatives to make serious inroads in Quebec is to outflank the Liberals. The result, however, is a radically incoherent ends-against-the-middle electoral coalition, a marriage of francophones and francophobes (Johnston et al. 1992). Each Conservative majority in the twentieth century involved such a move, and moves later in the century were even more successful initially than earlier ones. But such coalitions are unsustainable, and each move toward power is also followed by a serious reverse, usually leaving the party significantly worse off for its moment in power.

Western electorates' movements toward or away from the Conservatives were not always related to Conservative action in Quebec, to be sure. In 1921 and 1935, third-party gains at Conservative expense were driven by economic distress, not by cultural *ressentiment*. In 1935, the Conservative share dropped in both Quebec and the West, but the party had not been very strong in either region, and to link the parallel shifts to the "National Question" would be anachronistic. In 1962, the Conservative share in Quebec dropped to new lows, but the party's share in the West actually grew. The 1993 election, in contrast, witnessed the simultaneous collapse of Conservative support in both Quebec and the West, for opposed yet intimately linked reasons.

The Historic Weakness of the CCF/NDP and of Class Politics

Many features of NDP weakness conform closely to patterns elsewhere. Clearly, labor mobilization is a critical impetus to the rise of left parties (Bartolini 2000), and by cross-national standards, union density in Canada was very small before 1940 (Kumar 1986). Although union density grew rapidly over the following three decades, it has never been high by cross-national standards (Stephens 1979). The growth of organized labor and its consolidation in the CLC did help the cause, however (Horowitz 1968), and the transformation of the CCF into the NDP in 1961 was not cosmetic. It positioned the party to advance everywhere in Canada, even for a while in Quebec. This, in turn, created the ubiquitous local three-party competition observed by Gaines (1997; 1999).

But this is a two-sided story: On one hand, the NDP has grown enough to fractionalize the local vote; on the other, it has not grown enough in most places to displace one of its rivals. The strength of the Liberal Party, although predicated on nonclass considerations, is a particular barrier to NDP advancement. This claim is about the NDP outside Quebec. As such, the claim is distinct from an account of the party's historic weakness inside that province. In Quebec, the party is blocked by the nationalism of the union movement. As a knock-on, the limited appeal of the NDP to Quebecers may depress *non*-Quebecers' willingness to support the party. Conversely, when the NDP aligns itself with Quebec nationalist tendencies, as it does from time to time, it takes on the same sort of incoherence— with the attendant risks to the maintenance of its non-Quebec base—that periodically appears in the Conservative coalition. As is always the case with the cultural component of a country's partisan cleavages, most features of the story are peculiar to time and place (Lipset and Rokkan 1967), but they add up to a pattern that is perfectly consistent with the European evidence: Social–democratic parties tend to be smaller when the electorate includes significant ethnoreligious minorities (Bartolini 2000).

Federal–Provincial Divergence within Provinces

Although Duvergerian pressures for concentration of votes into two broad-gauged alternatives seem blocked in federal elections, they work powerfully in most provincial ones. This is an important factor in the long-run increase in federal–provincial divergence. Although both levels have experienced fractionalization pressures and, early in the twentieth century, provincial outcomes were often more fractionalized than federal ones, federal electorates became steadily more fragmented later in the century where provincial ones did not.

One dynamic factor has been the episodic insurgency already discussed in the federal context. Just as region- or province-specific parties have emerged in federal elections, so on a similar logic have they appeared in provincial elections. Although insurgency is sometimes specific to a province but common to both its provincial and its federal arenas, more often insurgency has been specific to only one arena. As a by-product of Duvergerian pressures, a provincial arena insurgent can quickly become a pole of electoral coordination, such that it is catapulted to local major-party status at the expense of a traditional party. To the extent that the federal arena remains less consolidated, coordination on the provincial arena insurgent only magnifies the federal–provincial discrepancy.

A second driver of federal–provincial dissimilarity has been growth of the NDP. Where the NDP is strong in provincial politics, is it also strong federally. This has been true for some time in the West, where groups with an investment in cultural differentiation (Catholics and francophones, mainly) are relatively weak. Even in the West, however, such groups remain important federally because of the broader gauged national electorate. This helps sustain both the Liberal Party and its chief rival in cultural politics, usually the Conservatives (but Reform/Alliance in the 1990s). Cultural politics exerts less purchase in the region's provincial arenas. This makes the CCF/NDP threat more imminent at that level, so blocking the party is all the more imperative. For the same reasons, blocking it is also easier. Using this logic, when the NDP approaches a certain threshold, only one provincial center right party can survive, and the other will descend into a rapid tailspin. This functionalist logic does not specify the identity of the surviving or disappearing parties, just that only one can survive. If one nonsocialist party happens to be an insurgent, then the federal–provincial discrepancy can be further expanded. If the insurgent is strong in the provincial arena, then both traditional parties will be weak or nonexistent. If the insurgent is a solely federal party, its presence will fractionalize the federal vote even further than is typical of other provinces. When, conversely, circumstances are intrinsically unfavorable to the NDP, consolidation pressures in provincial politics can weaken that party still further. This has traditionally been the case where Catholics are numerous, as in Atlantic Canada. There, the NDP can be stronger federally than provincially, in contrast to the western case. The provincial system remains consolidated, but with the dominant players being the old parties.

CONCLUSION

Like Leacock's knight, the existing literature on the Canadian electoral and party systems rides off in every direction at once. Scholarly contributions tend to be on individual components of the system and usually ignore possible contingencies among components. Analysis comes in waves, as a reflection of current interests and fads. For instance, class differences receive little current attention, yet surely are as pertinent as ever. Some contributions are deemed to be the last word and continue to dominate subsequent commentary even when the electoral framework they describe no longer exists. To say this is not to fault individual contributions. Analysts work with what is available and cannot be held accountable for the future. Besides, the pattern in Canadian scholarship is remarkably parallel to that in the rest of the world:

> [I]t is quite remarkable to note how little progress has been made in our understanding of the systemic element in the past 20 or 30 years. Indeed, despite numerous studies focused mainly on party system change, theoretical interest in party systems has proved limited, with almost no substantial innovation since the publication of Sartori's classic work of 1976. (Bardi and Mair 2008, 148)

But the Canadian literature is now old enough to entertain a plea for unification. And if the field demands unification, it is also ripe for it. Official returns for elections with links to census and other data are more accessible than ever. Recent elections cast a particularly revealing light on earlier ones, as they have unmasked latencies in the older systems. Canadian election studies are just now acquiring their full power in enabling analysis of cumulative individual-level survey files spanning four decades and are often linked to aggregate data. Machine-readable versions of Canadian Gallup data enable individual-level analyses dating back to the 1940s. Also to hand is an increasingly rich inventory of conceptual tools from comparative electoral studies and from game–theoretical models of electoral systems. The interpretive passages in the second half of this chapter exemplify what is possible. Those passages are not a report from the field, however. They are an agenda.

NOTES

1. Note, however, that the national shifts around 1960 mask a profound realignment of the system's regional basis.

2. The older, undifferentiated system also had implications for Canadians' psychological attachment to parties, and controversy has raged over whether Canadians identify with parties in the same way that Americans allegedly do. That controversy is not central to this chapter, however.

3. Discontinuities on this scale naturally raise the question of their implications for voters' psychological commitment to parties within each arena, and here, too, controversy rages. Again, this is a matter for another chapter.

REFERENCES

Alesina, Albert, and Howard Rosenthal. 1995. *Partisan Politics, Divided Government, and the Economy*. New York: Cambridge University Press.

Alford, Robert R. 1963. *Party and Society: The Anglo-American Democracies*. Chicago, Ill.: Rand McNally.

Archer, Keith. 1985. The failure of the New Democratic Party: Unions, unionists, and politics in Canada. *Canadian Journal of Political Science* 18(2): 353–366.

Bakvis, Herman. 1988. The Canadian paradox: Party system stability in the face of a weakly aligned electorate. In *Parties and Party Systems in Liberal Democracies*, ed. Steven B. Wolinetz, 245–268. London: Routledge.

Bakvis, Herman, and Laura G. Macpherson. 1995. Quebec block voting and the Canadian electoral system. *Canadian Journal of Political Science/Revue canadienne de science politique* 28(4): 659–692.

Bardi, Luciano, and Peter Mair. 2008. The parameters of party systems. *Party Politics* 14(2): 147–166.

Bartolini, Stefano. 2000. *The Political Mobilization of the European Left, 1860–1980*. Cambridge, U.K.: Cambridge University Press.

Bartolini, Stefano, and Peter Mair. 1990. *Identity, Competition, and Electoral Availability: The Stabilisation of European Electorates, 1885–1985*. Cambridge: Cambridge University Press.

Bélanger, Éric. 2003. Issue Ownership by Canadian Political Parties 1953–2001. *Canadian Journal of Political Science* 36(3): 539–558.

———. 2004a. Antipartyism and third-party vote choice: A comparison of Canada, Britain, and Australia. *Comparative Political Studies* 37(9): 1054–1078.

———. 2004b. The rise of third parties in the 1993 Canadian federal election: Pinard revisited. *Canadian Journal of Political Science* 37(3): 581–594.

Bélanger, Éric, and Richard Nadeau. 2005. Political trust and the vote in multiparty elections. *European Journal of Political Research* 44(1): 121–146.

Bittner, Amanda. 2007. The effects of information and social cleavages: Explaining issue attitudes and vote choice in Canada. *Canadian Journal of Political Science* 40(4): 935–968.

Blais, André. 1973. Third parties in Canadian provincial politics. *Canadian Journal of Political Science* 6(3): 422–438.

———. 2005. Accounting for the electoral success of the Liberal Party in Canada. *Canadian Journal of Political Science* 38(4): 821–840.

Blake, Donald E. 1972. The measurement of regionalism in Canadian voting patterns. *Canadian Journal of Political Science* 5(1): 55–81.

———. 1991. Party competition and electoral volatility: Canada in comparative perspective. In *Representation, Integration and Political Parties in Canada*, ed. Herman Bakvis, 253–273. Toronto: Dundurn Press, for the Royal Commission on Electoral Reform and Party Financing, Research Studies Vol. 14.

Bowler, Shaun, and David J. Lanoue. 1992. Strategic and protest voting for third parties: The case of the Canadian NDP. *Western Political Quarterly* 45(2): 485–499.

Brodie, Janine. 1990. *The Political Economy of Canadian Regionalism*. Toronto: Harcourt Brace Jovanovich.

Brodie, Janine, and Jane Jenson. 1988. *Crisis, Challenge and Change: Party and Class in Canada Revisited*. Ottawa: Carleton University Press.

————. 1996. Piercing the smokescreen: Stability and change in brokerage politics. In *Canadian Parties in Transition*, ed. Brian Tanguay and Alain Gagnon, 52–72. Toronto: Nelson.

Budge, Ian, Hans-Dieter Klingemann, Andrea Volkens, Judith Bara, and Eric Tanenbaum. 2001. *Mapping Policy Preferences: Estimates for Parties, Electors, and Governments, 1945–1998*. Oxford, U.K.: Oxford University Press.

Cairns, Alan C. 1968. The electoral system and the party system in Canada, 1921–1965. *Canadian Journal of Political Science* 1(1): 55–80.

Caramani, Daniele. 2004. *The Nationalization of Politics: The Formation of National Electorates and Party Systems in Western Europe*. Cambridge: Cambridge University Press.

Chhibber, Pradeep K., and Ken Kollman. 2004. *The Formation of National Party Systems: Federalism and Party Competition in Canada, Great Britain, India, and the United States*. Princeton, N.J.: Princeton University Press.

Clarke, Harold, Jane Jenson, Lawrence LeDuc, and Jon H. Pammett. 1996. *Absent Mandate: Canadian Electoral Politics in an Era of Restructuring*. Toronto: Gage.

Clarke, Harold, and Allan Kornberg. 1992. Risky business: Partisan volatility and electoral choice in Canada, 1988. *Electoral Studies* 11: 138–156.

Conway, J. F. 1978. Populism in the United States, Russia, and Canada: Explaining the roots of Canada's third parties. *Canadian Journal of Political Science* 11(1): 99–124.

Cox, Gary W. 1987. *The Efficient Secret: The Cabinet and the Development of Political Parties in Victorian England*. Cambridge: Cambridge University Press.

————. 1997. *Making Votes Count: Strategic Coordination in the World's Electoral Systems*. Cambridge, U.K.: Cambridge University Press.

Cross, William, and Lisa Young. 2002. Policy attitudes of party members in Canada: Evidence of ideological politics. *Canadian Journal of Political Science* 35(4): 859–880.

Crunican, Paul. 1975. *Priests and Politicians*. Toronto: University of Toronto Press.

Dawson, R. MacGregor. 1947. *The Government of Canada*. Toronto: University of Toronto Press.

Dobell, W. M. 1986. Updating Duverger's Law. *Canadian Journal of Political Science* 19(3): 585–595.

Duverger, Maurice. 1963. *Political Parties: Their Organization and Activity in the Modern State*, trans. Barbara North and Robert North. New York: Wiley.

Elkins, David J., and Richard Simeon. 1974. Regional political cultures in Canada. *Canadian Journal of Political Science* 7(3): 397–437.

Evans, Geoffrey, ed. 1999. *The End of Class Politics? Class Voting in Comparative Context*. Oxford: Oxford University Press.

Fiorina, Morris P. 1992. *Divided Government*. New York: Macmillan.

Gaines, Brian J. 1997. Where to count parties. *Electoral Studies* 16(1): 49–58.

————. 1999. Duverger's Law and the meaning of Canadian exceptionalism. *Comparative Political Studies* 32(7): 835–861.

Gidengil, Elisabeth. 1989. Class and region in Canadian voting: A dependency interpretation. *Canadian Journal of Political Science* 22(3): 563–587.

Gidengil, Elisabeth, André Blais, Richard Nadeau, and Neil Nevitte. 1997. Making sense of regional voting in the 1997 Canadian federal election: Liberal and Reform support outside Quebec. *Canadian Journal of Political Science* 32(2): 247–272.

Gidengil, Elisabeth, André Blais, Neil Nevitte, and Richard Nadeau. 2001. The correlates and consequences of anti-partyism in the 1997 Canadian election. *Party Politics* 7(4): 491–513.

Granatstein, J. L. 1967. *The Politics of Survival: The Conservative Party of Canada, 1939–1945.* Toronto: University of Toronto Press.

Horowitz, Gad. 1966. Conservatism, liberalism, and socialism in Canada: An interpretation. *Canadian Journal of Economics and Political Science* 32(2): 143–171.

———. 1968. *Canadian Labour in Politics.* Toronto: University of Toronto Press.

Hunter, Alfred A. 1982. On class, status, and voting in Canada. *Canadian Journal of Sociology* 7(1): 19–39.

Irvine, William P. 1971. Assessing regional effects in data analysis. *Canadian Journal of Political Science* 4(1): 21–24.

———. 1974. Explaining the religious basis of the Canadian partisan identity: Success on the third try. *Canadian Journal of Political Science* 7(3): 560–563.

Irvine, William P., and H. Gold. 1980. Do frozen cleavages ever go stale? The bases of the Canadian and Australian party systems. *British Journal of Political Science* 10(2): 187–218.

Iversen, Torben, and David Soskice. 2006. Electoral institutions and the politics of coalitions: Why some democracies redistribute more than others. *American Political Science Review* 100(2): 165–181.

Jenson, Jane. 1990. Representations in crisis: The roots of Canada's permeable fordism. *Canadian Journal of Political Science* 23(4): 653–683.

Johnston, Richard. 1980. Federal and provincial voting: Contemporary patterns and historical evolution. In *Small Worlds: Provinces and Parties in Canadian Political Life*, ed. David J. Elkins and Richard Simeon, 131–178. Toronto: Methuen.

———. 1985. The reproduction of the religious cleavage in Canadian elections. *Canadian Journal of Political Science* 18(1): 99–113.

———. 1991. The geography of class and religion in Canadian elections. In *Voting in Canada*, ed. Joseph Wearing, 108–135. Toronto: Copp Clark Pitman.

———. 2005. The electoral system and the party system revisited. In *Insiders and Outsiders: Alan Cairns and the Reshaping of Canadian Citizenship*, ed. Gerald Kernerman and Philip Resnick, 51–64. Vancouver: University of British Columbia Press.

———. Forthcoming. Structural bases of Canadian party preference: Evolution and cross-national comparison. In *Four Decades of Canadian Election Studies: Learning from the Past and Planning for the Future*, ed. Mebs Kanji, Antoine Bilodeau, and Thomas Scotto. Vancouver: University of British Columbia Press.

Johnston, Richard, and Janet Ballantyne. 1977. Geography and the electoral system. *Canadian Journal of Political Science* 10(4): 857–866.

Johnston, Richard, André Blais, Henry E. Brady, and Jean Crête. 1992. *Letting the People Decide: Dynamics of a Canadian Election.* Montreal: McGill-Queen's University Press.

Klingemann, Hans-Dieter, Andrea Volkens, Judith Bara, Ian Budge, and Michael McDonald. 2006. *Mapping Policy Preferences II: Estimates for Parties, Electors, and Governments in Eastern Europe, European Union and OECD 1990–2003.* Oxford: Oxford University Press.

Kumar, Pradeep. 1986. Union growth in Canada: Retrospect and prospect. In *Canadian Labour Relations*, ed. W. Craig Riddell, 95–160. Toronto: University of Toronto Press. Vol. 16 of the Royal Commission on the Economic Union and Development Prospects for Canada.

Laponce, Jean A. 1972. Post-dicting electoral cleavages in Canadian federal elections, 1949–68: Material for a footnote. *Canadian Journal of Political Science* 5(2): 270–286.

Laycock, David. 1990. *Populism and Democratic Thought in the Canadian Prairies, 1910 to 1945.* Toronto: University of Toronto Press.

————. 2002. *The New Right and Democracy in Canada*. Toronto: Oxford University Press.

LeDuc, Lawrence. 1985. Canada. In *Electoral Change in Western Democracies: Patterns and Sources of Electoral Volatility*, ed. Ivor Crewe and David Denver, 75–99. London: Croom Helm.

Lipset, Seymour Martin. [1950] 1968. *Agrarian Socialism: The Cooperative Commonwealth in Saskatchewan. A Study in Political Sociology*. New York: Doubleday.

Lipset, Seymour Martin, and Stein Rokkan. 1967. Cleavage structures, party systems and voter alignments: An introduction. In *Party Systems and Voter Alignments*, ed. Seymour Martin Lipset and Stein Rokkan, 1–64. New York: Free Press.

Lovink, J. A. A. 1970. On analysing the impact of the electoral system on the party system in Canada. *Canadian Journal of Political Science* 3(4): 497–516.

————. 1973. Is Canadian politics too competitive? *Canadian Journal of Political Science* 6(3): 342–379.

Macpherson, C. B. 1953. *Democracy in Alberta: Social Credit and the Party System*. Toronto: University of Toronto Press.

Meisel, John. 1967. Religious affiliation and electoral behaviour: A case study. In *Voting in Canada*, ed. John Courtney, 144–146. Toronto: Prentice-Hall.

Mendelsohn, Matthew, and Richard Nadeau. 1997. The religious cleavage and the media in Canada. *Canadian Journal of Political Science* 30(1): 129–146.

Miller, J. R. 1979. *Equal Rights: The Jesuits' Estates Act Controversy*. Montreal: McGill-Queen's University Press.

Morton, W. L. 1950. *The Progressive Party in Canada*. Toronto: University of Toronto Press.

Myles, John F. 1979. Differences in the Canadian and American class vote: Fact or pseudofact? *American Journal of Sociology* 84(5): 1232–1237.

Nadeau, Richard, and André Blais. 1990. Do Canadians distinguish between parties? Perceptions of party competence. *Canadian Journal of Political Science* 23(2): 317–333.

Ogmundson, Rick. 1975. Party class images and the class vote in Canada. *American Sociological Review* 40(4): 506–512.

Ordeshook, Peter C., and Olga Shvetsova. 1994. Ethnic heterogeneity, district magnitude, and the number of parties. *American Journal of Political Science* 38(1): 100–123.

Ornstein, Michael D., H. Michael Stevenson, and A. Paul Williams. 1980. Region, class and political culture in Canada. *Canadian Journal of Political Science* 13(2): 227–271.

Pedersen, Mogens. 1979. The dynamics of European party systems: Changing patterns of electoral volatility. *European Journal of Political Research* 7: 1–26.

Perlin, George, and Patti Peppin. 1971. Variations in party support in federal and provincial elections. *Canadian Journal of Political Science* 4(2): 280–286.

Pétry, François. 1995. The party agenda model: Election programmes and government spending in Canada. *Canadian Journal of Political Science* 28(1): 51–84.

————. 1999. The opinion–policy relationship in Canada. *Journal of Politics* 61(2): 540–550.

Pétry, François, and Matthew Mendelsohn. 2004. Public opinion and policy making in Canada 1994–2001. *Canadian Journal of Political Science* 37(3): 505–529.

Pinard, Maurice. 1966. La faiblesse des Conservateurs et la montée du Crédit social en 1962. *Recherches Sociographiques* 7(3): 360–363.

————. 1967. One-party dominance and third parties. *Canadian Journal of Economics and Political Science* 33(3): 358–373.

————. 1971. *The Rise of a Third Party: A Study in Crisis Politics*. Montreal: McGill-Queen's University Press.

————. 1973. Third parties in Canada revisited: A rejoinder and elaboration of the theory of one-party dominance. *Canadian Journal of Political Science* 6(3): 439–460.

Powell, G. Bingham. 2000. *Elections as Instruments of Democracy: Majoritarian and Proportional Visions*. New Haven, Conn.: Yale University Press.

Rae, Douglas W. 1971. *The Political Consequences of Electoral Laws*, 2nd ed. New Haven, Conn.: Yale University Press.

Riker, William H. 1976. The number of political parties: A re-examination of Duverger's Law. *Comparative Politics* 9(1): 93–106.

Rose, Richard. 1974. Comparability in electoral studies. In *Electoral Behavior: A Comparative Handbook*, ed. Richard Rose, 3–25. New York: Free Press.

Sartori, Giovanni. 1976. *Parties and Party Systems: A Framework for Analysis*. Cambridge, U.K.: Cambridge University Press.

Scarrow, Howard A. 1960. Federal–provincial voting patterns in Canada. *Canadian Journal of Economics and Political Science* 26(2): 289–298.

Schwartz, Mildred. 1974. *Politics and Territory: The Sociology of Regional Persistence in Canada*. Montreal: McGill-Queen's University Press.

Siegfried, André. 1907. *The Race Question in Canada*. New York: Appleton.

Smiley, Donald V. 1958. The two-party system and one-party dominance in the Liberal democratic state.*Canadian Journal of Economics and Political Science* 24(3): 312–322.

Stacey, C. P. 1977. *Canada and the Age of Conflict*, vol. 1. Toronto: University of Toronto Press.

———. 1981. *Canada and the Age of Conflict*, vol. 2. Toronto: University of Toronto Press.

Stephens, John D. 1979. *The Transition from Capitalism to Socialism*. London: Macmillan.

Stokes, Donald E. 1967. Parties and the nationalization of electoral forces. In *The American Party System*, ed. William N. Chambers and Walter Dean Burnham, 182–202. New York: Oxford University Press.

Tanguay, A. Brian, and Alain-G. Gagnon, eds. 1996. *Canadian Parties in Transition*. Toronto: Nelson.

Underhill, Frank H. 1955. Canadian liberal democracy in 1955. In *Press and Party in Canada*, ed. G. F. Ferguson and Frank H. Underhill, 27–46. Toronto: Ryerson.

Wearing, Joseph. 1996. Finding our parties' roots. In *Canadian Parties in Transition*, ed. A. Brian Tanguayand Alain-G. Gagnon, 14–31. Toronto: Nelson.

White, Graham. 1973. One-party dominance and third parties: The Pinard theory reconsidered. *Canadian Journal of Political Science* 6(3): 399–421.

Wilson, John. 1968. Politics and social class in Canada: The case of Waterloo South.*Canadian Journal of Political Science* 1(3): 288–309.

———. 1974. The Canadian political cultures: Towards a redefinition of the nature of the Canadian political system. *Canadian Journal of Political Science* 7(3): 438–483.

Wilson, John, and David Hoffman. 1970. The Liberal Party in contemporary Ontario politics. *Canadian Journal of Political Science* 3(2): 177–204.

Wrong, Dennis. 1957. The pattern of party voting in Canada. *Public Opinion Quarterly* 21(2): 252–264.

CHAPTER 13

CHALLENGE AND CHANGE: ELECTIONS AND VOTING

ELISABETH GIDENGIL

A vast territory, deep regional and linguistic cleavages, and an increasingly diverse population pose challenges to the administration of elections and the study of voting behavior alike. A keynote of election management in recent years has been change. Campaign financing is more strictly controlled than ever, advanced voting and same-day registration have made it easier for citizens to vote, and Canada now has fixed-term elections. At times, though, efforts to enhance the equity and fairness of the electoral process have come into conflict with the right to freedom of expression guaranteed by the Canadian Charter of Rights and Freedoms.

The study of voting behavior has also been marked by change. Innovations in survey design have cast new light on the importance of campaigns and the impact of media coverage. At the same time, decentralized federalism and a single-member plurality electoral system have enabled students of Canadian voting to contribute to debates about the impact of institutional arrangements. However, Canadian voting behavior continues to offer "a cornucopia of intriguing anomalies" (Meisel 1975, 253).

THE RULES OF THE GAME

Managing Elections

Since 1920, the conduct of federal elections has been the responsibility of Elections Canada, an independent, nonpartisan agency that reports directly to Parliament.

The chief electoral officer (CEO) is appointed by a resolution of the House of Commons and serves until age sixty-five. The CEO can only be removed "for cause" following a majority vote of the Commons and the Senate. The commissioner of Canada elections ensures that the provisions of the Canada Elections Act are enforced, and the broadcasting arbitrator is responsible for the application of the provisions regarding broadcasting (described later in the chapter). Returning officers (one for each electoral district) serve as the CEO's representatives at the constituency level and are responsible for ensuring that the terms of the Canada Elections Act are applied. The transparency of the electoral process was enhanced when the 2006 Federal Accountability Act transferred the authority to appoint and dismiss returning officers (previously the prerogative of the federal cabinet) to the CEO.

The Franchise

Every Canadian citizen eighteen years of age or older has the right to vote (save for the CEO and deputy CEO). This includes prison inmates, regardless of the length of their sentence. In 2002, the Supreme Court ruled that denying the franchise to inmates serving a sentence of two years or more violated section 3 (democratic rights) of the Charter. The contentious nature of the issue is evident in the fact that the Court split five to four. Earlier Charter-based court challenges in 1988 had extended the franchise to federal judges and to persons with mental disabilities.

Voter Registration

To cast their ballot, eligible voters have to be registered. In 1996, Canada switched to a new system of voter registration. Under the previous system, a new voters' list was compiled for each election by enumerators who visited every household in the early stages of the campaign to obtain the names of eligible voters. However, frequent elections, population growth, and increased ethnolinguistic diversity, combined with difficulty in recruiting enumerators, put pressure on the system. These pressures and, perhaps more important, the desire for shorter campaigns and cost savings motivated the change to a permanent voters' list (Black 2003; Courtney 2004). The list is updated automatically through electronic sharing of information among Elections Canada and various federal and provincial government agencies. Names of deceased electors are removed, and "double counting" of electors is (as least theoretically) avoided by cross-checking names and addresses from various government data bases. Otherwise, once on the list, an elector's name stays there unless the person requests it be removed. Voters whose names are not on the permanent list can register during the election campaign or on election day itself.

The change has attracted criticism (Black 2003; Courtney 2004). First, the permanent voters' list is slightly less accurate (Courtney 2004, 92–98). The onus is now on voters to get their names on the Register of Electors, whereas previously, the

onus was on the state to ensure that eligible voters were registered. The completeness and accuracy of door-to-door enumerations were maximized by paying enumerators on a per-elector basis.

Second, door-to-door enumeration encouraged participation. Voters were
reminded that an election would be held in the coming weeks and that they were
eligible to vote in it. In effect, they were given a subtle reminder of their civic duty
to take part (Courtney and Smith 1991). Door-to-door enumeration also contributed to the health of local party organizations by providing a small financial reward
to local party volunteers who served as enumerators (Courtney 2004).

The dramatic fifteen-point decline in voter turnout between 1988 and 2004 has
been attributed by some to the switch to the permanent voters' list. However, it can
bear only part of the blame. The 2000 election was the first conducted on the basis
of the list, but turnout had already dropped significantly in the two preceding elections. Moreover, when people were asked why they did not vote, difficulties with
voter registration were not the main reason.

The most troubling implication of the change relates to participation disparities (Black 2003). Some groups of voters may be particularly affected by inaccuracies in the list. Even before the switch, younger Canadians, the poor, and those with
less formal schooling were less likely to vote, in large part because they tend to be
less psychologically involved in politics (Gidengil et al. 2004). These same groups
are the most disadvantaged by the new system. They are more likely to be tenants,
and frequent moves mean that tenants are less likely to be registered correctly in the
riding where they live. Consequently, they are less likely to receive a voter information card telling them where to vote. They may also find it harder to deal with the
challenges of getting on the list.

Apportioning Seats and Designing Districts

The distribution of seats within and among provinces has also come under fire for
departing significantly from the one person/one vote principle (Courtney 2004).
The allocation of seats is subject to the 1915 "senatorial floor" clause, which stipulates that no province can have fewer members of Parliament than it has senators,
and the 1985 "grandfather clause," which ensures that a province will have at least
as many seats as it had in 1976 or in the 1984–1988 Parliament (whichever was
fewer). As a result, the least urbanized provinces—with their static or declining
populations—receive more seats than their share of the total Canadian population
warrants.

Constituency boundaries within provinces are redefined (following the decen-
nial redistribution of seats among the provinces) by independent electoral boundary commissions (Courtney 2004). The population of a constituency may vary by
as much as 25% above or below the provincial electoral quotient,[1] or more if there
are "exceptional circumstances." One of the main reasons for permitting so much
variation is Canada's sheer geographical size. If seats were allocated strictly based on

population, ridings in sparsely populated rural regions would cover vast distances. According to the governing statute, district boundaries also have to be set in ways that ensure representation of "communities of interest."

The systematic underrepresentation of city dwellers may hamper women's representation because women are more likely to be candidates and to get elected in urban areas (see chapter 18, this volume). It may also result in the dilution of visible minority votes (Pal and Choudhry 2007). The three fastest growing provinces—Alberta, British Columbia, and Ontario—deviate the most from the one person/one vote principle, and all three have large visible minority populations.

Campaign Financing

Campaign financing in Canada is very strictly controlled. As a result of changes to the Canada Elections Act, introduced via the Federal Accountability Act, corporations and trade unions are no longer permitted to make political donations. Only citizens and permanent residents may contribute, and the current annual maximum donation is $1,100 (indexed for inflation) for each political party, district association, candidate, nomination contestant, and leadership contestant. Cash contributions cannot exceed $20. Contributions exceeding $200 must be reported to Elections Canada by the recipient, and the identity of each such contributor and the amount of his or her contribution become matters of public record. Nomination contestants or candidates of a registered party may contribute an additional $1,000 (not indexed) from their own funds, divided between their nomination and election campaigns as they see fit. Independent candidates can contribute up to $1,000 from their own funds. There is a tax credit for donations to parties and candidates.

There is also public funding. Candidates who get at least 10% of the vote in their constituency and parties that spend at least 10% of the maximum allowed are eligible for public reimbursement of up to 50% of their expenses. Registered political parties also receive an annual allowance of $1.75 (indexed to inflation) for each vote they won in the most recent general election. To qualify for reimbursement and for the annual allowance, parties must have received at least 2% of the national vote or 5% in each of the constituencies contested. There are limits on the amounts that parties and candidates can spend campaigning.

The Broadcast Media

Canada's broadcasting industry is regulated by the Canadian Radio-television and Telecommunications Commission. It requires broadcasters to provide equitable treatment of issues, candidates and parties. "Equitable" is taken to mean fair and just, not necessarily equal, which is one reason why coverage tends to be more or less proportional to parties' seat shares in the previous election (Blais et al. 2002).

This same principle is evident in the application of the Canada Elections Act provisions requiring broadcasters to make a certain amount of prime-time airspace available during federal election campaigns for purchase by recognized political parties. The Canadian broadcasting arbitrator allocates the broadcasting time among the parties. One third is divided equally whereas the remaining two thirds is allocated based on seat and vote shares in the previous election. The broadcasting arbitrator also determines the formula for allocating the free time that certain television and radio networks are required to provide. After a 1995 court challenge, the amount of extra time that broadcasters may sell to a political party is no longer capped, provided they do not refuse to sell it to others. Political advertising is not permitted on election day.

Restrictions on so-called third-party advertising have proved more contentious. A provision of the 1974 Election Expenses Act prohibited any individual or group other than a candidate or a registered political party from spending money to promote or oppose the election of any party or candidate. However, it was struck down by the courts in 1984 for violating the right to freedom of expression. The role of business interests in the 1988 election led the 1992 Royal Commission on Electoral Reform and Party Financing to recommend limits on third-party spending. However, the $1,000 limit did not survive a court challenge. The 2000 Canada Elections Act limited third-party spending on election advertising to $150,000 in the country as a whole and to $3,000 in any one electoral district (subject to inflation). The constitutionality of these restrictions was also challenged, but the Supreme Court of Canada overturned the decision of the lower court on appeal in 2004 and they remain in force.

Under the Canada Elections Act, the names of the polling organization and the survey's sponsor, timing of the fieldwork, population sampled, number of people contacted, and margin of error must be provided during the twenty-four hours when polling results are first transmitted to the public. However, an analysis of reports in eighteen newspapers during the 2004 election found that none of the reporting requirements achieved more than a 60% level of compliance except for the name of the polling firm (Ferguson and de Clercy 2005; but see Durand 2002). Barely half provided the margin of error and only 20% provided question wording.

The publication of opinion polls on election day is banned under the provisions of the Canada Elections Act prohibiting the premature transmission of election results. These provisions reflect the difficulties inherent in administering elections across a vast territory spanning six time zones. Before the enactment of the prohibition on broadcasting election results, the election results in eastern Canada could be known before the polls closed in the western provinces. However, the provisions are controversial. The prosecution of a British Columbian who posted real-time results on his website on the night of the 2000 election initiated a series of court cases to determine the ban's constitutionality. In a five-to-four decision, the Supreme Court eventually judged the ban to be a reasonable limit on freedom of expression. However, enforceability remains an issue, given the ability of nonresidents to post results online with impunity. The multiple-time zone problem has since been resolved in part by staggering the hours of voting so that the majority of results are available at about the same time across the country.

Voting Behavior

Campaigns Matter

Perhaps the most important contribution of Canadian voting research lies in the study of campaign dynamics and the impact of the media. Since 1988, Canadian election studies (CES) have combined a rolling cross-section campaign survey with a postelection panel. The sample is broken down into daily replicates. All that distinguishes these replicates (apart from random sampling variation) is the date of interview (Johnston and Brady 2002). Combining rolling cross-section data with daily media tracking has enabled researchers to analyze the dynamic interaction between media coverage and voters' reactions, and to challenge the conventional scholarly wisdom that election campaigns have minimal effects.

Campaign Dynamics

Time of decision provides some of the most telling evidence. Typically, half of Canadian voters only decide how they will vote after the election campaign is underway. The validity of American voters' recall has been questioned (Plumb 1986), but Canadians' postelection recall of their time-of-voting decision is highly reliable (Fournier et al. 2001), perhaps because the electoral time frame is shorter.

Time-of-voting decision is a key mediating variable for campaign effects. Voters who decide long before the election is called are not very susceptible to persuasion. Others are strongly predisposed to support a particular party, and the campaign simply serves to reactivate that predisposition. To be influenced by campaign messages, voters have to be both reachable and persuadable. Campaign deciders fulfill both conditions; they are attentive enough to receive campaign messages and they are more receptive to those messages because they lack strong partisan predispositions. Their vote intentions are much more strongly affected by campaign events and media coverage (Fournier et al. 2004).

The impact of these events should not be overstated. In 1997, the televised leaders' debates had a substantial short-term impact on vote intentions, but the impact had almost completely dissipated by the campaign's close (Blais et al. 1999). Even when their impact is lasting, debates do not necessarily determine the outcome. The 1988 debates boosted the opposition Liberals' share of vote intentions by about five points, but the gains were not enough for the Liberals to defeat the incumbent Progressive Conservatives (PCs) (Blais and Boyer 1996). This does not mean that debates are inconsequential: In 2000, a four-point debate boost was enough to save the PCs from electoral annihilation (Blais et al. 2003b).

Campaign advertising does not seem to have much independent impact on vote choice. In 1988, PC ads affected opinion about the Canada–U.S. Free Trade Agreement and about the Liberal leader, but not the vote (Johnston et al. 1992).

Reform did gain about seven points in the first few days after airing a controversial ad during the 1997 campaign, but the effect had almost completely decayed by election day (Blais et al. 1999). Opinion polls, on the other hand, can have a lasting effect. In 1988, for example, polls affected strategic voting by influencing voters' assessments of the parties' chances of winning the election (Blais et al. 2006).

The Impact of the Media

According to conventional wisdom, the effects of the media are mostly indirect. In other words, the media's power lies not in telling people what to think but in telling them what to think *about* (Cohen 1963; Shaw and McCombs 1977). One of the most important indirect effects occurs when extensive media coverage of some aspect of the campaign induces voters to attach more weight to that aspect when deciding how to vote. Several studies have demonstrated priming effects in Canadian campaigns. Voters who were more exposed to media coverage of the 1988 campaign were more likely to base their vote on perceptions of the leaders' trustworthiness than on their opinion about the free trade agreement or their party identification. This priming effect became progressively stronger as the campaign progressed (Mendelsohn 1994; 1996). The leader-centered focus of campaign coverage and an issue agenda that typically features issues that are already salient to voters, like health and unemployment, mean that the priming of leadership is the typical effect. Issue priming can occur, though, when a new and dramatic issue dominates the campaign (Gidengil et al. 2002).

Another important indirect persuasive effect is media-induced learning. This played a critical role in Reform's 1993 electoral breakthrough (Jenkins 2002a; 2002b). With the PCs slumping in the polls, media coverage of the Reform Party increased dramatically. As awareness of the party's commitment to cutting the budget deficit spread, Reform vote intentions surged. As John Zaller's (1992) reception and acceptance axioms would predict, the impact was greatest on those who were both attentive to the media and predisposed to approve of Reform's position. Over a two-week period, the percentage intending to vote Reform increased twenty-five points among those who met both criteria.

The most important contribution of Canadian research on media coverage and vote choice lies in challenging conventional wisdom and demonstrating that the media can have a *direct* effect on vote choice. The rolling cross-section data demonstrated a clear link between news exposure and PC support during the 1988 campaign (Johnston et al. 1992). In 1993, there was a significant relationship between PC vote intentions and the daily balance of positive and negative mentions of PC leader Kim Campbell in the nightly news (Mendelsohn and Nadeau 1999). Campbell had been party leader for only a few months. In a pattern reminiscent of coverage of Ross Perot in the 1992 U.S. presidential election (Zaller and Hunt 1994), coverage of Campbell was initially very favorable, but once the election got under way, the tone of coverage changed dramatically and the PC vote collapsed. In 1997, media coverage had a significant effect on the vote intentions of people who followed the news *and* had not made up their minds before the campaign began. Systematically positive coverage boosted vote intentions for a party whereas negative coverage did the opposite (Dobrzynska et al. 2003). These effects, though, proved to be temporary. Attention to election news made no difference to how people eventually voted.

Social Cleavages: Anomalies and Anachronisms?

Mark Franklin (1992, 390) suggests that Canada was "at the forefront of a develop-ment that appears to be ubiquitous." Like the United States, Canada during the mid 1980s qualified as a "historical decline" country, where social cleavages had effec-tively ceased to structure vote choice. Yet, evidence has since emerged that social cleavages *do* matter in Canada. Recent election outcomes would be impossible to understand without considering the role of social background characteristics (Blais et al. 2002; Gidengil et al. 2006; Nevitte et al. 2000).

The striking exception is the almost complete lack of a class cleavage in voting, an anomaly first observed by Robert Alford (1963) when he found that Canada ranked even lower than the United States on his class voting index. Alford's basic finding (Alford 1963) remains intact; no matter how social class is measured, how political parties are classified along a left–right scale, or how class voting is mea-sured, repeated efforts have failed to establish an association between social class and vote choice in Canada (see Gidengil 2002). Regional and religious cleavages continue to "supersede class almost entirely as factors differentiating the support for national parties" in Canada (Alford 1963, xi).

The strong religious cleavage in voting has been likened to "a moderately inter-esting, but strikingly peculiar, houseguest who has overstayed his welcome" (Irvine 1974, 570). Its persistence seems anachronistic. The federal political parties have not divided over any religious issues in living memory, and Canadian society has become much more secular. Anachronistic it may be, but the fact that Catholics have typi-cally been much more likely than Protestants to vote Liberal has been a critical ingredient in the Liberal Party's record as "one of the four most successful parties in contemporary democracies" (Blais 2005, 821).

French-speaking Canadians are overwhelmingly Catholic, but this does not explain the religious cleavage. Nor do other social background characteristics that are associated with being Catholic. Focusing on childhood socialization seemed more promising. Children inherit both their parents' religious affiliation and their party preference without making any conscious connection between the two, which would explain why people do not mention religion when asked to explain their vote (Irvine 1974). Ingenious as it was, this explanation had a fatal flaw. Group differ-ences in party vote shares can only persist across generations if the rate of intergen-erational transmission of party loyalties differs across groups (Johnston 1985). This implies that influences outside the family play an important role in perpetuating the religious cleavage: "Liberal [parents] are more successful at transmitting their party loyalty not because they are peculiarly dominant models but because they are more likely to have their influence reinforced by factors outside the home" (Johnston 1985, 107). It turns out that the salience of the religious cleavage varies according to the composition of the province. Voters in heavily Catholic provinces are much more likely to divide along religious lines (Johnston 1991). Without a strong Catholic presence, union membership becomes more salient, at least in voting New Democratic Party.

Johnston (1991) attributed this to strategic voting. However, a recent study using multilevel modeling at the individual, constituency, and provincial levels concluded that "religion appears to trump class as a determinant of vote choice, regardless of the religious composition of the voter's context" (Bélanger and Eagles 2006, 607). At the same time, though, the findings confirm the importance of social context in perpetuating the religious cleavage. The individual-level relationship between being Catholic and voting Liberal is strongest in constituencies where Catholics are numerous.

Matthew Mendelsohn and Richard Nadeau (1997) highlight the importance of the Catholic leadership in shaping the attitudes of rank-and-file Catholics, encouraging a more conservative stance on social questions like abortion and divorce, and more liberal positions on military spending, defense policy, and issues of social justice. They argue that the influence of this Catholic ethos is attenuated by media exposure. The Canadian media offer few religious cues to voters, focusing instead on secular concerns and regional and linguistic conflicts.[2] Catholics, especially if they are nonpracticing, who pay a lot of attention to the media are less likely to base their vote choice on religious considerations.

Regional cleavages run deep in Canada, but have received less attention than class and religion in recent years. This was not always the case. One of the pioneering survey-based studies of voting in Canada was devoted to the territorial dimension (Schwartz 1974), and the 1974 CES focused particular attention on regional and provincial differences in voting behavior. However, when residents were asked to define their region, there was a notable lack of consensus in every province (Clarke et al. 1979). It seemed that regions lacked any real meaning to their inhabitants, and "much of what lies behind apparent regional variation in party support consists of relatively more theoretically tractable environmental factors" (Blake 1978, 293), like voter turnout, competitiveness, and ethnoreligious and occupational composition.

Reform's stunning electoral breakthrough rekindled interest in the regional dimension of voting. To win the fight for the Right, Reform had to break out of its western heartland and win seats in Ontario. However, it failed to win a single Ontario seat in 1997, trailing the Liberals in that province by 30% of the popular vote. The regionalization of the vote demanded an explanation. If the regional differences simply reflected differences in the social makeup of the population, people sharing similar social background characteristics would vote similarly, regardless of their region of residence. There turned out to be little support for this region-as-artifact thesis. People belonging to the same social categories voted differently from one region to another. Voters' priorities differed. Ontario voters were preoccupied with the government's role in job creation whereas western voters were more concerned about fiscal issues (Gidengil et al. 1999).

Party Identification: As Volatile as the Vote?

The concept of party identification has been highly contested in Canada (Gidengil 1992). Research based on the first two CESs led to the conclusion that a Michigan—style conception of party identification as an enduring psychological attachment was "almost inapplicable in Canada" (Meisel 1975, 67). Clarke et al. (1984) offered a more tempered assessment, recognizing the existence of a core of "durable partisans."[3] Still, they concluded, "the keynote of partisanship in Canada was its flexibility" (Clarke et al. 1984, 56). Subsequent panel analyses, using the 1974–1979–1980 CES seemed to confirm the instability of Canadians' party attachments (LeDuc et al. 1984).

This apparent instability has been linked to Canada's decentralized federal system, which encourages voters to develop different party identifications at the federal and provincial levels. Marianne Stewart and Harold Clarke (1998) find that inconsistency across levels is strongly correlated with partisan instability at both levels. They explain this in terms of an evaluative theory of party identification. People update their party identification at a given level in light of new information on the actual or anticipated performance of parties at both levels. Eric Uslaner (1990) suggests that historical and cultural factors are more important. He focused on people's ideological proximity to the federal party with which they identify, their pro-Canada sentiments, and the relative strengths of the (then) two major federal parties at the federal and provincial levels in their province.

Subsequent research suggests that some of the apparent instability in party identification may have stemmed from the lack of an explicit option in the party identification question of not identifying with *any* political party (Johnston 1992). This may have encouraged some people to name the party they were voting for even though they lacked any meaningful attachment to that party, which may in turn be why party identification appeared to be "as volatile in Canada as the vote itself" (Meisel 1975, 67). In 1988, the phrase "none of these" was added to the question, and the proportion of nonidentifiers increased. Doubts have also been raised about whether weak identifiers truly have a long-term psychological attachment (Blais et al. 2001a). Analyses using the revised question and excluding weak identifiers suggest that we cannot make sense of recent elections without taking account of Canadians' party attachments (Blais et al. 2002; Nevitte et al. 2000). However, the stability of those attachments remains to be determined.

Economic and Issue Voting: Judgment Day

Economic voting research began with a simple reward-and-punish model. Voters consult their pocketbooks and decide whether they are satisfied with the incumbent's economic performance. It turns out that in Canada, as elsewhere, the connection between economic conditions and vote choice is anything but straightforward.

First, there is the question of the relative importance of egocentric versus sociotropic evaluations. Do people vote based on their own financial circumstances or based on their perception of how the economy is doing? Research on economic voting in Canada has added an important qualifier to the conclusion that people's perceptions of the state of the country's economy typically matter more to their choice of party than do evaluations of their own financial situation. It turns out that the impact of pocketbook considerations may have been underestimated. Egocentric evaluations can affect vote choice indirectly by affecting voters' assessments of national economic conditions (Clarke and Stewart 1996). For many Canadians, it seems, personal economic circumstances provide a "rough-and-ready" cost-effective indication of national trends.

Canadian research has also highlighted the extent to which economic voting is contingent on voters' attribution of responsibility to the government (Clarke and Kornberg 1992). These attributions are not symmetrical. Canadians are much readier to blame the government for bad economic times than they are to give it credit for good times. As a result, the governing party pays the price for poor economic performance, but does not necessarily reap the electoral rewards when the economy has been doing well. Moreover, voters are less likely to assign either credit or blame when the incumbent prime minister has only recently taken over the helm (Gidengil et al. 2006; Nadeau and Blais 1993).

The decentralized nature of Canada's federal system makes Canada a particularly useful case for examining the impact of multilevel government on attributions of responsibility. Aggregate-level economic voting models covering every federal and provincial election held between 1953 and 2001 suggest that voters do not hold the federal incumbent responsible for the state of the provincial economy. Provincial economic conditions had only a modest independent impact on federal election outcomes over the fifty-year time span (Gélineau and Bélanger 2005). Counterintuitively, voters do not seem to hold provincial incumbents responsible for provincial economic conditions, but do hold them accountable for the state of the country's economy, at least if they are of the same partisan stripe as the party in power federally. The study concludes that "subnational economic voting in Canada seems to function as a referendum on the federal government" (Gélineau and Bélanger 2005, 423). An analysis of popularity rather than vote shares in six provinces in the 1980s and 1990 reports a similar finding. The popularity of provincial governments reflected the federal government's popularity, especially when the same party was in power federally and provincially (Tellier 2006). This same study, though, did find a link between economic conditions and support for provincial incumbents. Voters' attributions of responsibility to their provincial government vary depending on the ideological stripe of the party in power. Governments of the center and the Right are held accountable for budget deficits whereas governments of the Left are expected to deal with unemployment.

Economic voting in Canada is also complicated by the presence of strong regional parties and the regionalized nature of the economy (Godbout and Bélanger 2002). In Quebec, economic voting in federal elections is diluted by the presence of a strong, regionally based opposition party (the Bloc québécois) that mobilizes voters on the basis of nationalist grievances. However, in the rest of the country, regional economic disparities seem to be more consequential than the presence of a strong, regionally based party. Residents of poorer provinces tend to be more concerned about their own financial circumstances and readier to blame the government for their plight. Thus, Atlantic Canadians have been more apt to vote their pocketbooks than voters in Ontario and the West, where voting on the basis of national economic conditions is more typical.

Unemployment is the critical economic consideration. An aggregate-level economic voting model based on federal election outcomes between 1953 and 1988 suggests that neither real disposable income nor inflation mattered, but an increase of one point in the unemployment rate reduced the incumbent's vote by around two points. This paled in comparison with the five- or six-point boost to its national vote share if the party's leader was from Quebec (Nadeau and Blais 1993). According to the model, the Liberals should have been rewarded in 1997 for a drop in unemployment. The mediating role of subjective perceptions explains why they did not reap the benefit (Nadeau et al. 2000). More than 80% of voters failed to recognize that unemployment had gone down; 40% thought that it had gone up. The misperceptions were largely attributable to partisan bias and to regional variations in the unemployment rate.

Economic voting models typically focus on short-term economic change to explain why incumbents do—or do not—get reelected. How voters who are dissatisfied with the incumbent's performance decide among the available alternatives is rarely addressed. It appears, though, that long-term economic decline boosts the vote shares of nonmainstream parties. Support for the incumbent party reflects short-term change in the unemployment rate, whereas support for nonmainstream parties (that is, parties other than the Liberals or the Conservatives) is tied to long-term changes in labor force participation (Perrella 2005).

Most studies of economic voting also assume that economic conditions—or perceptions of those conditions—affect the vote directly. However, perceptions of economic conditions also affect the vote indirectly by influencing people's views on economic issues (Clarke and Kornberg 1992). Between 1988 and 1993, voters' views about the free trade agreement became increasingly negative because of growing skepticism of the government's ability to manage the economy, and pessimism about the state of the economy and their own financial circumstances. Moreover, economic evaluations had more impact on support for the incumbent PCs than did issue attitudes.

According to Michael Alvarez et al. (2000), issue attitudes dominated in the 1993 election, but the economy trumped the issues in the 1988 election, which seems counterintuitive given the centrality of free trade in 1988. This may reflect the fact that their focus was on explaining overall vote shifts between elections, not the vote in a given election. The conclusion changes when the latter approach is adopted. A study simulating how many voters would have voted differently and how party vote shares would have changed if either the economy or the issues had had no effect in eleven Canadian, British, and American elections between 1987 and 2001 found that, for all three countries, the economy mattered, but issues typically mattered more for vote choice and party fortunes alike (Blais et al. 2004).

The most important debate regarding issue voting concerns the proximity-versus-directional models. Do voters vote for the party that is closest to their own position or for the party that takes the strongest stand on their side of the issue? One criticism of the proximity model is well taken. Voters' perceptions of a party's position tend to be biased by their feelings about the party. Voters will assume—correctly or not—that a party they like is close to them on the issues, and this projection effect favors the proximity model. However, even when the test is biased in favor of the directional model (by fixing perceived party locations at the mean value), the proximity model still fares better than the directional model (Johnston et al. 2000; see also Blais et al. 2001c).

Finally, research on issue voting in Canada has highlighted the mediating role of issue importance (Fournier et al. 2003). Evaluations of the incumbent's performance in handling an issue have a greater impact on vote choice among voters who consider the issue to be important. These performance evaluations vary from issue to issue and are not simply a reflection of voters' partisanship.

Party Leaders and Local Candidates: Superstars and Bit Players?

Party leaders take center stage in Canadian elections. Their role as the "superstars of Canadian politics" (Clarke et al. 1991, 89) is ensured by the leader-centered focus of campaign coverage, the lack of strongly defined ideological appeals, and the extraparliamentary mode of selection. However, "personality is *not* the mainspring of Canadian electoral choice" (Johnston 2002, 173 [emphasis in the original]) when it comes to determining election outcomes. Leader evaluations do have a significant independent impact on individual vote choice, but their average net impact on party vote shares was only about three percentage points in eight federal elections held between 1968 and 2000 (Gidengil and Blais 2007; see also Johnston 2002). How do we explain these seemingly contradictory findings? For leader evaluations to affect the outcome, one leader has to be markedly more popular—or unpopular—than the others; otherwise, the effects will be largely offsetting (Blais et al. 2002; Johnston 2002). Contrary to the "presidentialization" thesis (Mughan 1993), party leaders have not become more important to either vote choice or party vote shares in Canada (Gidengil and Blais 2007).

According to conventional wisdom, local candidates are of little importance to the outcome of Canadian elections. Yet, despite the importance of party leaders and party labels, there is evidence of a "personal vote" (Cain et al. 1987) in Canada. Liking the local candidate has an independent effect on vote choice, even controlling for feelings about the party and its leader (Blais et al. 2003a). In fact, in 2000, the local candidate proved to be the decisive factor for 5% of Canadian voters. Had the local candidate not mattered, they would have voted differently. The effect was weaker in Quebec, probably because sovereignty trumps other considerations.

Strategic Voting

The local race also matters when it comes to strategic voting. Expectations about the local outcome had an independent impact on vote choice in 1997, even after taking account of preferences. The further behind a party was perceived to be, the less likely people were to vote for the party's candidate (Blais et al. 2001b). However, expectations regarding which party would win the most seats and which party would form the official opposition had no effect at all. To establish whether this reflected strategic voting, it is necessary to ask how many voters would have voted differently if they had not taken expectations about the local race into account. According to this criterion, only about 3% of voters qualified as strategic voters in 1997. An alternative strategy based on an expected utility model similarly detected a surprisingly low level of strategic voting (Merolla and Stephenson 2007). Even among those with an incentive to vote strategically because their preferred party was perceived to have no chance of winning, only 9% of the 1993–2000 pooled sample followed the logic of the expected utility model. These voters made up only slightly more than 2% of the total sample. Predictably, sophisticated voters appeared to be the most likely to vote strategically.

The strategic voting studies help to explain why Canada is an exception to Duverger's Law (see chapter 12, this volume). The strength of third-party supporters' preference for their own party and their propensity to overestimate their party's chances of winning both contribute to the low incidence of strategic voting, despite the incentives provided by Canada's first-past-the-post plurality system (Blais 2002).

CONCLUSION

There can be little doubt that the fairness and transparency of the electoral process have been enhanced by recent changes in Canada's electoral legislation. However, challenges remain. As Canada's cities continue to grow and the population becomes more diverse, inequities in the distribution of seats within and among provinces will demand redress. Low turnout continues to be a concern, and the implications of the permanent voters' list for those who are least likely to vote remain troubling.

The rolling cross-section design has opened up new possibilities for understanding voting behavior, but the study of campaign and media effects remains in its infancy. Now that data are available for multiple campaigns, the challenge is to develop theoretical insights into the conditionality of these effects and to understand which attitudes are most responsive to campaigns and why. Equally important, Canadian voting research needs to take account of rapid demographic change and devote more attention to the effects of generational and ethnocultural diversity.

NOTES

1. The electoral quotient is the province's population divided by its number of seats.

2. A notable exception occurred during the 2000 campaign when the Canadian Broadcasting Corporation aired a program highlighting the fundamentalist Christian views of Alliance leader Stockwell Day, including his belief in creationism. Interestingly, despite the controversy, "Fundamental Day" had little lasting impact on voters' evaluations of Day or on Alliance vote intentions (Blais et al. 2003b).

3. "Durable partisans" identify very strongly or fairly strongly with their party, report that they have identified with the same party across time, and identify with the same party at both the federal and provincial levels. People who fail to meet all three criteria—intensity, stability, and consistency—are classified as "flexible partisans." This category includes those who do not identify with any party on the assumption that they are in transition from one party to another.

REFERENCES

Alford, Robert R. 1963. *Party and Society: The Anglo-American Democracies*. Chicago, Ill.: Rand McNally.

Alvarez, R. Michael, Jonathan Nagler, and Jennifer R. Willette. 2000. Measuring the relative impact of issues and the economy in democratic elections. *Electoral Studies* 19(2–3): 237–253.

Bélanger, Paul, and Munroe Eagles. 2006. The geography of class and religion in Canadian elections revisited. *Canadian Journal of Political Science* 39(3): 591–609.

Black, Jerome H. 2003. From enumeration to the National Register of Electors: An account and an evaluation. *IRPP Choices* 9(7): 1–22.

Blais, André. 2002. Why is there so little strategic voting in Canadian plurality rule elections? *Political Studies* 50(3): 445–454.

———. 2005. Accounting for the electoral success of the Liberal Party in Canada. *Canadian Journal of Political Science* 38(4): 821–840.

Blais, André, and Martin M. Boyer. 1996. Assessing the impact of televised debates: The case of the 1988 Canadian election. *British Journal of Political Science* 26(2): 143–164.

Blais, André, Elisabeth Gidengil, Agnieszka Dobrzynska, Neil Nevitte, and Richard Nadeau. 2003a. Does the local candidate matter? *Canadian Journal of Political Science* 36(3): 657–664.

Blais, André, Elisabeth Gidengil, Richard Nadeau, and Neil Nevitte. 2001a. Measuring party identification: Canada, Britain, and the United States. *Political Behavior* 23(1): 5–22.

———. 2002. *Anatomy of Liberal Victory: Making Sense of the Vote in the 2000 Canadian Election*. Peterborough, Ont.: Broadview Press.

———. 2003b. Campaign dynamics in the 2000 Canadian election: How the leader debates salvaged the Conservative Party. *Political Science and Politics* 36(1): 45–50.

Blais, André, Elisabeth Gidengil, and Neil Nevitte. 2006. Do polls influence the vote? In *Capturing Campaign Effects*, ed. Henry E. Brady and Richard Johnston, 263–279. Ann Arbor: University of Michigan Press.

Blais, André, Richard Nadeau, Elisabeth Gidengil, and Neil Nevitte. 1999. Campaign dynamics in the 1997 Canadian election. *Canadian Public Policy* 25(2): 197–203.

————. 2001b. Measuring strategic voting in multiparty plurality elections. *Electoral Studies* 20(3): 343–352.

————. 2001c. The formation of party preferences: Testing the proximity and directional models. *European Journal of Political Research* 40(1): 81–91.

Blais, André, Mathieu Turgeon, Elisabeth Gidengil, Richard Nadeau, and Neil Nevitte. 2004. Which matters most? Comparing the impact of issues and the economy in American, British, and Canadian elections. *British Journal of Political Science* 34(3): 555–563.

Blake, Donald E. 1978. Constituency context and Canadian elections: An exploratory study. *Canadian Journal of Political Science* 11(2): 279–305.

Cain, Bruce, John Ferejohn, and Morris Fiorina. 1987. *The Personal Vote: Constituency Service and Electoral Independence.* Cambridge, Mass.: Harvard University Press.

Clarke, Harold D., Jane Jenson, Lawrence LeDuc, and Jon H. Pammett. 1984. *Absent Mandate: The Politics of Discontent in Canada.* Toronto: Gage.

————. 1991. *Absent Mandate: Interpreting Change in Canadian Elections,* 2nd ed. Toronto: Gage.

Clarke, Harold D., and Allan Kornberg. 1992. Support for the Canadian federal Progressive Conservative Party since 1988: The impact of economic evaluations and economic issues. *Canadian Journal of Political Science* 25(1): 29–53.

Clarke, Harold D., Lawrence LeDuc, Jane Jenson, and Jon H. Pammett. 1979. *Political Choice in Canada.* Toronto: McGraw-Hill Ryerson.

Clarke, Harold D., and Marianne Stewart. 1996. Economists and electorates: The subjective economy of governing party support in Canada. *European Journal of Political Research* 29(2): 191–214.

Cohen, Bernard C. 1963. *The Press and Foreign Policy.* Princeton, N.J.: Princeton University Press.

Courtney, John C. 2004. *Elections.* Vancouver: UBC Press.

Courtney, John C., and David E. Smith. 1991. Registering voters: Canada in a comparative context. In *Democratic Rights and Electoral Reform in Canada*, ed. Michael Cassidy, 343–461. Toronto: Dundurn Press.

Dobrzynska, Agnieska, André Blais, and Richard Nadeau. 2003. Do the media have a direct impact on the vote? The case of the 1997 Canadian election. *International Journal of Public Opinion Research* 15(1): 27–43.

Durand, Claire. 2002. The 2000 Canadian election and poll reporting under the new elections act. *Canadian Public Policy* 28(4): 539–545.

Ferguson, Peter A., and Christine de Clercy. 2005. Regulatory compliance in opinion poll reporting during the 2004 Canadian election. *Canadian Public Policy* 31(3): 243–258.

Fournier, Patrick, André Blais, Richard Nadeau, Elisabeth Gidengil, and Neil Nevitte. 2003. Issue importance and performance voting. *Political Behavior* 25(1): 51–67.

————. 2004. Time-of-voting decision and susceptibility to campaign effects. *Electoral Studies* 23(4): 661–681.

Fournier, Patrick, Richard Nadeau, André Blais, Elisabeth Gidengil, and Neil Nevitte. 2001. Validation of time of voting decision recall. *Public Opinion Quarterly* 65(1): 95–107.

Franklin, Mark N. 1992. The decline of cleavage politics. In *Electoral Change: Responses to Evolving Social and Attitudinal Structures in Western Countries*, ed. Mark N. Franklin, Tom Mackie, Henry Valen with Clive Bean et al., 383–405. Cambridge: Cambridge University Press.

Gélineau, François, and Éric Bélanger. 2005. Electoral accountability in a federal system: National and provincial economic voting in Canada. *Publius* 35(3): 407–424.

Gidengil, Elisabeth. 1992. Canada votes: A quarter century of Canadian national election
    studies. *Canadian Journal of Political Science* 25(2): 219–248.
———. 2002. The class voting conundrum. In *Political Sociology: Canadian Perspectives*,
    ed. Douglas Baer, 274–287. Don Mills: Oxford University Press.
Gidengil, Elisabeth, and André Blais. 2007. Are leaders becoming more important to vote
    choice? In *Political Leadership and Representation in Canada: Essays in Honour of John
    Courtney*, ed. Hans Michelmann, Donald Story, and Jeffrey Steeves, 39–59. Toronto:
    University of Toronto Press.
Gidengil, Elisabeth, André Blais, Joanna Everitt, Patrick Fournier, and Neil Nevitte. 2006.
    Back to the future? Making sense of the 2004 Canadian election outside Quebec.
    Canadian Journal of Political Science 39(1): 1–25.
Gidengil, Elisabeth, André Blais, Richard Nadeau, and Neil Nevitte. 1999. Making sense of
    regional voting in the 1997 Canadian federal election: Liberal and Reform support
    outside Quebec. *Canadian Journal of Political Science* 32(2): 247–272.
———. 2002. Priming and campaign context: Evidence from recent Canadian elections. In
    Do Political Campaigns Matter? Campaign Effects in Elections and Referendums, ed.
    David Farrell and Rüdiger Schmitt-Beck, 76–91. London: Routledge.
Gidengil, Elisabeth, André Blais, Neil Nevitte, and Richard Nadeau. 2004. *Citizens*.
    Vancouver: UBC Press.
Godbout, Jean-François, and Éric Bélanger. 2002. La dimension régionale du vote
    économique canadien aux élections fédérales de 1988 à 2000. *Canadian Journal of
    Political Science* 35(3): 567–588.
Irvine, William P. 1974. Explaining the religious basis of the Canadian partisan identity:
    Success on the third try. *Canadian Journal of Political Science* 7(3): 560–563.
Jenkins, Richard W. 2002a. How campaigns matter in Canada: Priming and learning as
    explanations for the Reform Party's 1993 campaign success. *Canadian Journal of
    Political Science* 35(2): 383–408.
———. 2002b. The media, voters, and election campaigns: The Reform Party and the
    1993 election. In *Citizen Politics: Research and Theory in Canadian Political
    Behaviour*, ed. Joanna Everitt and Brenda O'Neill, 215–230. Don Mills, Ont.: Oxford
    University Press.
Johnston, Richard. 1985. The reproduction of the religious cleavage in Canadian elections.
    Canadian Journal of Political Science 18(1): 99–113.
———. 1991. The geography of class and religion in Canadian elections. In *The Ballot and
    Its Message*, ed. Joseph Wearing, 108–135. Toronto: Copp-Clark Pitman.
———. 1992. Party identification measures in the Anglo-American democracies: A
    national survey experiment. *American Journal of Political Science* 36(2): 542–559.
———. 2002. Prime ministerial contenders in Canada. In *Leaders' Personalities and the
    Outcomes of Democratic Elections*, ed. Anthony King, 158–183. Oxford: Oxford
    University Press.
Johnston, Richard, André Blais, Henry E. Brady, and Jean Crête. 1992. *Letting the People
    Decide*. Montreal: McGill-Queen's University Press.
Johnston, Richard, and Henry E. Brady. 2002. The rolling cross-section design. *Electoral
    Studies* 21(2): 283–295.
Johnston, Richard, Patrick Fournier, and Richard Jenkins. 2000. Party location and party
    support: Unpacking competing models. *The Journal of Politics* 62(4): 1145–1160.
LeDuc, Lawrence, Harold D. Clarke, Jane Jenson, and Jon H. Pammett. 1984. Partisan
    instability in Canada: Evidence from a new panel study. *American Political Science
    Review* 78(2): 470–484.

Meisel, John, ed. 1975. *Working Papers on Canadian Politics*, 2nd enl. ed. Montreal: McGill-Queen's University Press.

Mendelsohn, Matthew. 1994. The media's persuasive effects: The priming of leadership in the 1988 Canadian election. *Canadian Journal of Political Science* 27(1): 81–97.

———. 1996. The media and interpersonal communications: The priming of issues, leaders, and party identification. *The Journal of Politics* 58(1): 112–125.

Mendelsohn, Matthew, and Richard Nadeau. 1997. The religious cleavage and the media in Canada. *Canadian Journal of Political Science* 30(1): 129–146.

———. 1999. The rise and fall of candidates in Canadian election campaigns. *Harvard International Journal of Press/Politics* 4(2): 63–76.

Merolla, Jennifer L., and Laura B. Stephenson. 2007. Strategic voting in Canada: A cross-time analysis. *Electoral Studies* 26(2): 235–246.

Mughan, Anthony. 1993. Party leaders and presidentialism in the 1992 British election: A postwar perspective. In *British Elections and Parties Yearbook, 1993*, ed. David Denver, Pippa Norris, David Broughton, and Colin Rallings, 193–204. London: Harvester Wheatsheaf.

Nadeau, Richard, and André Blais. 1993. Explaining election outcomes in Canada: Economy and politics. *Canadian Journal of Political Science* 26(4): 775–790.

Nadeau, Richard, André Blais, Neil Nevitte, and Elisabeth Gidengil. 2000. It's unemployment, stupid! Why perceptions about the job situation hurt the Liberals in the 1997 election. *Canadian Public Policy* 26(1): 77–94.

Nevitte, Neil, André Blais, Elisabeth Gidengil, and Richard Nadeau. 2000. *Unsteady State: The 1997 Canadian Federal Election*. Toronto: Oxford University Press.

Pal, Michael, and Sujit Choudhry. 2007. Is every ballot equal? Visible-minority vote dilution in Canada. *IRPP Choices* 13(1): 1–30.

Perrella, Andrea M. L. 2005. Long-term economic hardship and non-mainstream voting in Canada. *Canadian Journal of Political Science* 38(2): 335–357.

Plumb, Elizabeth. 1986. Validation of voter recall: Time of electoral decision making. *Political Behavior* 8(4): 301–312.

Schwartz, Mildred A. 1974. *Politics and Territory: The Sociology of Regional Persistence in Canada*. Montreal: McGill-Queen's University Press.

Shaw, Donald L., and Maxwell E. McCombs, eds. 1977. *The Emergence of American Political Issues: The Agenda-Setting Function of the Press*. St. Paul, Minn.: West Publishing.

Stewart, Marianne C., and Harold D. Clarke. 1998. The dynamics of party identification in federal systems: The Canadian case. *American Journal of Political Science* 42(1): 97–116.

Tellier, Geneviève. 2006. Effect of economic conditions on government popularity: The Canadian provincial case. *Canadian Journal of Political Science* 39(1): 27–51.

Uslaner, Eric M. 1990. Splitting image: Partisan affiliations in Canada's "two political worlds." *American Journal of Political Science* 34(4): 961–981.

Zaller, John. 1992. *The Nature and Origins of Mass Opinion*. Cambridge: Cambridge University Press.

Zaller, John, and Mark Hunt. 1994. The rise and fall of candidate Perot: Unmediated versus mediated politics—part I. *Political Communication* 11(4): 357–390.

CHAPTER 14

THE DELIBERATIVE AND ADVERSARIAL ATTITUDES OF INTEREST GROUPS

ÉRIC MONTPETIT

INTEREST groups have a bad reputation in modern democracies. Political commentators often depict them as "special interests" capable of obtaining undeserved benefits from governments. They view the action of interest groups as distorting the normal functioning of democratic systems. In a democracy, elected officials represent citizens, and therefore policy decisions should be made on their behalf only. When groups pressure governments to account for their interest in policy decisions, the reasoning goes, they interfere in the normal functioning of democracy; they create a distortion in the line of responsiveness that connects elected officials to citizens. In short, contemporary political commentators rarely credit interest groups for any legitimate role in democracy.

Interestingly, such negative outlooks on interest groups are supported by a number of theories in political science. The most famous among these theories was elaborated by Mancur Olson (1965), who argues that groups with a narrow focus, such as industry, are more successful than more encompassing groups. Individuals, Olson (1965) reasons, are naturally inclined to avoid contributing to collective action. Knowing that the train will depart regardless of whether a ticket is paid, a passenger's natural inclination will be to ride free, unless coercively obliged to pay. Applied to interest groups, this logic suggests that mobilizing individuals into a group in view of seeking a benefit on behalf of a wide collectivity is a challenging task. Individuals should refuse contributing to environmental groups, for example, knowing they will benefit from a cleaner environment regardless of whether they contribute. The rational choice is to free ride. In the absence of any coercive obligation, contribution would

be rational only when one's free riding puts the collective benefit at risk. The formation of an environmental group would thus face higher obstacles than the creation of
an industry association devoted to opposing an environmental policy. Assuming
interests in opposing an environmental policy are concentrated among a few industrial firms, successful opposition likely depends on the contribution of every single
firm to collective action. In short, Olson's theory suggests that mobilization into interest groups should be weaker over issues preoccupying large numbers of citizens and
stronger when small numbers of citizens are concerned (Olson 1965). Consequently,
power distribution among groups would be unfairly distributed, advantaging groups
who represent narrow interests, such as industry. These latter groups should be able to
obtain undeserved benefits or rents from governments. Such negative representations
of interest groups currently dominate political science.

Alternative perspectives, however, are beginning to emerge and they shed a
brighter light on interest groups in democratic countries. Although negative representations of groups assume adversarial political systems, these alternative perspectives insist on a view of political systems as sites of cooperation in search of the
common interest (Schneider and Ingram 2007). These alternative perspectives do
not confine groups to the role of rent seekers, insisting instead on their contribution
to policy debates and deliberations. Groups, proponents of these perspectives
believe, can improve the quality of deliberations over collective problems and solutions, thereby improving policy choices, irrespective of whether they represent a
large or a small faction of society. From such perspectives, interest groups can claim
a legitimate role in democratic policy-making systems.

This chapter begins with a comparison between adversarial and deliberative
perspectives on interest groups and underlines the legitimate attitudes expected of
interest groups in a democracy in each of the two perspectives. Relying on a survey
of actors involved in the development of biotechnology policy, including interest
groups, I examine the extent to which these attitudes prevail in reality. I show that
both perspectives resonate with the reality of interest groups, albeit in different proportions depending on group types and on the policy issue at stake. I also show that
the bad reputation of interest groups is unwarranted.

ADVERSARIAL AND DELIBERATIVE
PERSPECTIVES ON INTEREST GROUPS

Jane Mansbridge (1992) argues convincingly that most theoretical perspectives on
interest groups developed in the past fifty years, including that of Olson (1965),
assume an adversarial political system. Adversarial political systems have two main
characteristics. First, all actors, including interest groups, have a clear understanding of their interests and ensuing policy preferences. In fact, the promotion of their

interests through the realization of their preferences constitutes actors' prime motivation for involvement in politics. Second, policy choices in the adversarial perspective make for winners and losers, and distribute the benefits and costs of policy
choices in a zero-sum manner. A benefit to a particular group can only be a loss to
another one. Naturally, the goal of interest groups is to stay on the winning side.
And achieving this goal will often involve the formation of coalitions among actors
with similar interests, as well as conflicts with those who have different interests.

As an illustration of this adversarial perspective, one could argue that capitalist
industrial firms are interested in profits more than they are interested in a clean
environment. Therefore, industrial firms should prefer an environmental policy
that has positive or no incidence on their capacity to make profits over one that
would have a greater environmental impact, but which would also reduce firms'
productivity. If policy makers decide to adopt an intrusive environmental policy,
the industry loses. To prevent this situation, industrial firms should mobilize within
an interest group, and the group itself should seek to participate in coalitions of
groups with similar environmental policy preferences. Such alliances increase the
chance that they will prevail in their conflict with proponents of a stringent environmental policy.

If most contemporary theoretical perspectives on interest groups, like Olson's
(1965), assume an adversarial political system, not all suggest that the participation
of interest groups in policy making causes a legitimacy deficit. In fact, pluralism
(dominant in political science in the postwar period) considered groups as a greater
source of democratic legitimacy than political parties. Pluralists argue that the bun-
dle of policy proposals assembled in the platforms of political parties poorly reflect
the genuine concerns of citizens. When a citizen votes for a party, he or she endorses
a platform containing policy proposals he or she would like to see implemented.
The platform, however, will likely also contain a number of policy proposals with
which he or she disagrees. In contrast, interest groups compete for the support of
citizens within specialized policy areas. Therefore, citizens can choose to support
groups advancing policy proposals entirely consistent with their preferences across
policy areas. Accordingly, fair competition among a plurality of interest groups provides policy makers with better information on the genuine policy preferences of
citizens than electoral competition during elections. In other words, competition
over the mobilization of citizens between industry and environmental groups
should be policy makers' best source of information on citizens' environmental
policy preferences.

Olson's rational choice theory of interest groups had a devastating effect on the
theory of pluralism (Baumgartner and Leech 1998, 58). Olson's reasoning basically
eliminated the possibility of a fair competition among interest groups. According to
Olson (1965), groups representing diffuse interests will always suffer a disadvantage
over groups representing concentrated interests. This criticism of pluralism echoed
earlier work, notably by Schattschneider (1960) on the mobilization of bias, and by
Bachrach and Baratz (1962) on the unequal capacity of groups to keep issues off the
decision agenda. The criticism was also echoed in work to come, most notably that

by Lindblom (1977) on the privileged access of business to policy makers. By the end of the 1970s, it had become clear for most political scientists that interest group competition was an unfair source of information for policy makers about the genuine concerns of citizens. These criticisms of pluralism fed into the belief that policy makers taking their policy cues from group competition are at the mercy of special interests.

The idea of an unequal distribution of power among interest groups remains largely uncontested today (Baumgartner et al. 2009; Walzer 2004). Mansbridge (1992, 34), however, argues that severe judgments on the extent to which this unequal distribution constitutes a problem rest on a particular understanding of legitimacy, that embedded in the adversarial perspective on democracy. To the extent one assumes conflicts among citizens with fixed preferences during policy making, the outcome can be viewed as legitimate only if citizens are equally represented in the process. This understanding of legitimacy is consistent with a key adversarial principle: one citizen/one vote (Walzer 2004, 22).

Voting is, in fact, the preferred method of conflict resolution in the adversarial perspective. When citizens have fixed preferences, conflicts can be resolved authoritatively, without delays, and in a legitimate manner, if the method is a vote in which every citizen counts as one. Pluralists who expected interest groups to act as efficient mechanisms to aggregate the preferences of citizens viewed them as promoting, indirectly, the principle of one person, one vote. Through their support of interest groups, all citizens have the opportunity to voice their preferences, issue by issue. Therefore, proponents of the adversarial perspective consider it illegitimate that a given group has systematically more power in policy processes than similarly representative groups. In other words, political scientists who were convinced by Olson's explanation of difficulties to mobilize diffused interests automatically saw a breach in the one person/one vote principle. Those who adhere to the adversarial perspective on politics should pose a severe judgment on interest groups if they are convinced that industry mobilizes members far more easily than environmental groups. Interest groups, the adversarial reasoning goes, should create no distortion in the equal representation of citizens.

According to Mansbridge (1992, 37), the adversarial perspective on interest groups is more than a political science theory. It has developed into a political culture, a lens through which several citizens understand their political systems and a source of norms shaping the attitudes of political actors. Immersed in this culture, interest groups should accept authoritative decisions, even when they are on the losing side, to the extent the decisions do not breach the principle of citizens' political equality. The adversarial culture, Mansbridge (1992) further contends, would be particularly prevalent in the United States.

It could be argued that it has a significant importance in Canada as well. A fair share of the research on interest groups in Canada espouses this perspective. For example, Stanbury's (1993) work aims at showing that the public interest rhetoric of some groups hides *conflicts* arising from rent-seeking behavior inherent to all groups. Amara et al. (1999) surveyed Canadian interest groups to better understand lobbying efforts. They argue that the intensity of the competition among groups to stay on the *winning side* of policy decisions has more impact on lobbying efforts than the financial resources of groups. Pross' (1986) concept of a policy community was to study *access* by groups to policy makers. His work inspired Coleman's (1988) study of business groups in Canada, which confirmed Lindblom's (1977) argument suggesting that business enjoys a *privileged access* to policy makers. Two Canadian political scientists, Lisa Young and Joanna Everitt (2004), recently conducted an audit of the contribution of interest groups to Canadian democracy. Their audit rests on criteria that are perfectly consistent with the adversarial perspective on politics—the mobilization capacity of groups, the responsiveness of group leadership to members, and the equality of access to policy makers among groups. Although they acknowledge several shortcomings, notably in equality of access, the two scholars pose a relatively positive judgment on the contribution of interest groups to Canadian democracy.

Mansbridge (1992) argues that the adversarial perspective should not be the only source of norms through which citizens judge interest groups and through which interest groups behave in democratic systems. To the adversarial perspective, she opposes a deliberative understanding of democracy. This latter perspective embeds a different conception of legitimacy, which warrants a different outlook on interest groups and creates different expectations regarding their attitudes in policy processes.

First, the deliberative perspective challenges the idea that the sole motivation of groups' involvement in policy making is the realization of their interest. Rather, groups may be interested in policy involvement for the sake of contributing to the development of better policies or policies that serve the public interest. Group leaders may believe that they possess unique information or expertise worth sharing with policy makers. Consequently, they may want to be part of policy making, irrespective of the particular interest of the members they represent. This is not to espouse the naive view that group leaders can easily put their interest on the back burner to focus their entire attention on pubic interest during policy deliberations (on this particular point, see Mutz [2006, 4]). It simply acknowledges the possibility that group leaders might not be perfectly certain about their policy preferences and those of their members on every single policy issue. And even if they think that they are certain, they might also know that a deliberation with actors who have different interests, as well as different information and expertise, can convince them that a policy option they had not envisioned at the outset can serve their interest and that of their members.

Thus, industry representatives' participation in environmental policy making might not always be to block stringent measures, which they might nevertheless view as costly to industrial firms at the outset. They might want to participate to get firsthand information from civil servants on forthcoming international environmental treaties and their consequences for export markets. From other groups, they might want to know the extent to which a stringent regulation would encourage the growth of green industrial sectors and the advantage these sectors could gain on foreign competition from such a regulation. They might want to participate in order to gain information that they could not expect at the outset, knowing it could be useful to reflect on their policy preferences. Out of the deliberation, industry group leaders might come to the view that a stringent environmental policy would be in the interest of the firms they represent. They might be persuaded that an intrusive domestic environmental policy would contribute to the development of green technologies, with high growth potentials. They might be persuaded that the adoption of a serious environmental policy is necessary to prevent the adoption of trade barriers by countries with better environmental records. Or, more simply, they might be persuaded that protecting the environment is in the public interest. Consequently, they might come to accept that blocking an environmental policy to maximize profit is an unacceptable social attitude.

Second, the deliberative perspective challenges the idea that policy making is a zero-sum game that always engenders conflicts. In the adversarial perspective, policy choices always divide groups. Conflict ends only when a decision is made, and decision legitimacy rests on the principle of one person/one vote. As should be obvious from the preceding paragraph, groups in the deliberative perspective might not have fixed preferences derived automatically from interests; and even if group leaders think they do, they can nevertheless be persuaded to change these preferences. In turn, persuasion opens up the possibility of view convergence among actors, logically reducing the importance of voting as a means to end conflict over a policy choice. Deciding promptly through a vote, or through an authoritative decision consistent with the principle of citizen equality, makes no sense if deliberation can reduce conflict by rallying interest groups and other actors around an appealing policy alternative. Deliberations are not always crystallized around the distribution of policy benefits and costs. Rather, they sometimes enable the emergence of policy alternatives that reduce considerably the number of losers and increase the number of winners.

The deliberative perspective suggests that out of substantive policy discussions among actors with different ideas, information, or expertise, better policy alternatives can emerge. According to Mansbridge (1992, 37), "deliberation often makes possible solutions that were impossible before the process began." Fritz Scharpf (1997) puts it differently, arguing that several policy-making situations are akin to distributive games. He adds, however, that policy-making situations occasionally take the form of "problem solving." Inspired by Habermas's (1987) communicative ethics, the idea of problem solving involves actors engaged in truth seeking. Their prime motivation is the search of the best argument, not power. The function of problem solving is productive, rather than distributive. Problem solving encourages the development of innovative policy solutions that earn the approval of a wide range of actors and interest groups.

The legitimacy of interest groups in the deliberative perspective thus requires different attitudes than in the adversarial perspective. As a reminder, groups are legitimate in the adversarial perspective to the extent that they promote the principle of equality among citizens. The deliberative perspective is far less preoccupied with citizens' representation than it is concerned about the quality of deliberations.

Therefore, in the deliberative perspective, the legitimacy of groups' participation in policy making is not a function of groups' representativeness, but rests on their capacity to contribute something to the deliberation through advocacy. In the deliberative perspective, it is perfectly acceptable that groups that do not represent an important faction of society exercise considerable influence on policy, to the extent that they bring to the deliberation original information, expertise, or ideas. Halpin (2006) makes the argument that representation, as conceived in the adversarial perspective, is unfair. Not only can some citizens not be adequately represented (for example, children or the mentally ill), nature and nonhuman beings affected by policies are excluded. Therefore, Halpin argues, interest groups possessing special knowledge or having solidarity experiences with citizens or entities unable to voice their own concerns should be acknowledged a legitimate role in policy making. The legitimacy of their role would rest on the contribution their knowledge can make during policy deliberations.

It has been argued, notably by industry, that environmental groups without constituent members have undue influence in the development of environmental policy. Some scholars worry also about the rise of so-called checkbook groups (Young and Everitt 2004, 144). Advocacy groups, such as Greenpeace, have little internal democratic structures whereby leaders could be held accountable to members. Members are confined to the role of making a financial contribution. From the adversarial perspective, the policy influence of such advocacy groups is problematic because they provide no guarantee that leaders represent the genuine concerns of their members rather than their own. When suspected of expressing their own concerns, checkbook group leaders are accused of having excessive policy influence, in breach of the principle one citizen/one vote. The legitimacy of checkbook groups, however, appears higher if one thinks of them from the deliberative perspective. Environmental groups should be conceived not so much as representing citizens, as speaking on behalf of nature. To the extent that environmental group leaders have knowledge likely to contribute something original to policy deliberations, their advocacy and policy influence can be understood as no less legitimate than that of industry.

In fact, the legitimacy of policy decisions in the deliberative perspective depends on the extent to which policy processes allow sufficient time for groups with different policy preferences to present and explain their ideas. If the deliberative perspective does not insist on the equality of citizens in policy processes, it values voice inclusion and equality (Mansbridge 1992, 48). Groups representing as wide a range of policy preferences as possible should be given the chance to persuade and be persuaded by the other actors. Again, environmental groups are likely to have original views on environmental policy, which deserve a hearing irrespective of the nature of their membership. Of course, processes of persuasion take time, even more so when groups are far apart at the outset (Montpetit 2008). In other words, the expediency of rapid vote-based decisions in the adversarial perspective, justified by the fixed situations of policy preferences, is unwarranted in the deliberative perspective.

The legitimacy of policy decisions in the deliberative perspective also depends on the equality of interest groups in the face of persuasion. That is, groups should equally expect to be persuaded in the face of compelling arguments or evidence. Group leaders should be equally predisposed to changing their views. If industry is systematically persuasive and environmental groups systematically persuaded in the development of environmental policy, one can legitimately question the inclination of industry to let itself be persuaded. When persuasion is one way, the public interest rhetoric of groups may be a strategy to hide narrow self-interest, as suspected by Stanbury (1993). In the deliberative perspective, all groups are expected to adopt an attitude of openness toward persuasion.

In sum, when politics is understood in adversarial terms, interest groups should accept authoritative policy decisions consistent with the principle of one citizen/ one vote. In contrast, when politics is understood in deliberative terms, interest groups should accept decisions consistent with the principle of one useful policy idea/one chance to persuade. A real chance to persuade involves attitudes of reciprocity whereby groups are equally inclined to changing their policy preferences occasionally. In turn, deliberative processes should encourage view convergence and therefore a reduction in the intensity of policy conflicts.

I suggested earlier that the adversarial culture appears to prevail in Canada, as much as in the United States, at least in scholarly publications. It is true that few Canadian scholars write on interest groups from the deliberative perspective. Susan Phillips is one exception (Phillips et al. 1992). In her reply to Stanbury's (1993) claim that interest groups never look beyond their self-interest, Phillips (1993) argues that such a generalization is abusive. It is more reasonable, she claims, to hypothesize that some groups have genuine concerns about the public interest, seeking policy benefits they cannot appropriate as their own, whereas others do not. Consistent with the deliberative perspective, Phillips' argument acknowledges that searching for the public interest requires policy debates and alteration of thoughts on the part of groups (see also Graham and Phillips 1997). The extent to which groups act in the public interest, she argues, is a matter of empirical research more than theoretical beliefs.

The remainder of this chapter explores the extent to which the deliberative and the adversarial perspectives have some resonance with reality. As Mansbridge (1992) suggests, these are more than theoretical perspectives; they are cultures that can be related to the concrete attitudes of interest groups and other policy actors. These cultures might manifest themselves with different intensity in different countries and among different actor categories. The goal in the next section is to measure the respective relevance of the two perspectives for interest groups and other actors involved in real policy-making situations in North America and Europe.

INTEREST GROUPS AND BIOTECHNOLOGY POLICY

The following empirical analysis rests on a 2006 survey of actors involved in biotechnology policy making in Canada, the United States, the United Kingdom, and

France. The survey includes questions about perceptions of authoritative decisions and policy debates, and is useful in assessing the prevalence of deliberative and adversarial attitudes. The survey also includes questions on opinion change regarding policy issues relevant to the biotechnology sector. Moreover, the survey allows comparisons between interest groups and other actor categories, between industry and advocacy groups, and among Canada, the United States, and Europe. Before moving to the analysis of results, a few words on the survey are useful.

The Biotechnology Actor Survey

The survey was not aimed at the general public, but at individuals who have some form of involvement in the development of biotechnology policy for agrifood and human genetics applications in their respective country. Biotechnology policy is particularly well suited to measure the influence of deliberative norms among actors and interest groups. Indeed, judging by the media coverage, this sector appears particularly adversarial. For some interest groups, biotechnology applications are promising in a diversity of areas, including fights against hunger, against environmental degradation, or against diseases such as Parkinson's. The hopes created by stem cell research in particular gained credibility with the public support of Michael J. Fox and Christopher Reeve. For other groups, biotechnology applications pose unprecedented environmental risks and moral hazards. For some of these groups, genetic engineering is the most powerful instruments humans have had to destroy biodiversity, whereas others claim that biotechnology applications involving embryos, such as several stem cell applications, are akin to playing God. As in the example of environmental policy provided earlier, industry appears to have significant interests in the biotechnology sector, and advocacy groups are numerous. In other words, this sector is one in which conflict among actors appears to prevail and in which deliberations among interest groups seems unlikely. Therefore, traces of deliberation in this particularly adversarial sector can only mean that deliberative attitudes are even more prevalent in the relatively numerous less adversarial sectors.

Potential respondents were first identified though media, parliamentary hearing, and official document searches. Following the snowball method, this first group of individuals was asked to provide additional names. Overall, 1,967 individuals involved in biotechnology were invited by e-mail to fill out the web survey and, by December 2006, 270 individuals had filled it out, at least in part. Among the respondents, seventy-six were interest group representatives, seventy-eight were public servants, and 107 were independent experts. (Nine belonged to other categories). Of these, seventy-three were from Europe, fifty-four were from the United States, and 143 were from Canada. Surveys of a similarly wide range of policy actors across several countries are rare. I am aware of only one similar survey, which has a comparable number and distribution of respondents (Aerni and Bernauer 2005).

Authoritative Decisions and Political Debates

Actors whose attitudes are shaped by the adversarial culture should value decision making, even when divergence of opinion continues dividing actors. For these actors, preferences are fixed and consequently there is no point in the continuation of policy debates. Policy makers should do their job and make decisions, in as consistent a manner as possible, with the principle of one person/one vote. In the biotechnology sector, the adversarial culture should translate into industry demanding policy makers to authorize several applications promptly, having no hope to convince advocacy groups that these applications are safe. Advocacy groups should request bans on several applications, with the same intensity that industry desires authorizations. To the extent that they view politics in adversarial terms, both types of groups should prefer rapid decisions on the part of elected officials over pointless debates.

Conversely, actors whose attitudes are shaped by the deliberative culture should view debates as a means through which differences of views can be bridged. These actors believe in persuasion and they are likely to have a negative opinion of decisions, which simply seek to put an end to policy controversies. This deliberative culture should encourage industry to try to persuade advocacy groups of the benefits of biotechnology applications whereas advocacy groups should attempt persuading industry about their risks. The hope of both—advocacy groups and industry—should be that the other comes to its point of view, at least on a few issues. In fact, agreement among actors holding different views provides the best guarantee that public interest is well served by policy.

Answers to at least two of the survey questions denote an adversarial attitude on the part of respondents. First, respondents were asked whether they agree that the biotechnology policy controversy is a sign that it is urgent to make decisions in view of clarifying the situation. Second, respondents were asked whether they agreed with a statement saying that divergence of opinions over biotechnology is an insufficient reason to delay policy decisions. Those who answered these two questions positively are likely to understand politics principally through the adversarial rather than the deliberative perspective. The questionnaire included a number of questions indicative of a deliberative attitude. For example, one question asked respondents whether they agreed that biotechnology controversy was a positive sign of democratic debate. Agreement is consistent with a deliberative attitude. Another question queried respondents' beliefs about the breadth of views heard during policy debates. Actors who indicated worrying about the exclusions of some opinions during policy debates more likely adhere to deliberative norms. Figure 14.1 presents deliberative and adversarial inclinations among groups and continents/countries. The adversarial and the deliberative attitudes were measured, respectively, using the questions about opinion divergence as a justification of decision delays and about the breadth of views heard during policy debates.

In figure 14.1, the bars are generally higher for the adversarial attitude than for the deliberative one. In fact, 55.2% of the respondents agree or totally agree that divergence

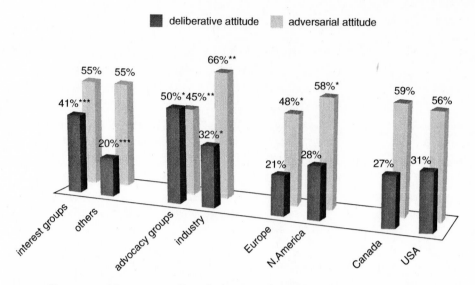

Figure 14.1. Mean comparisons by category for deliberative and adversarial attitudes. ***$P < .01$, **$P < .05$, *$P < .1$ in hypothesis test of means difference between categories. Ho = 0.

of opinion should not be an obstacle to decision making, whereas only 25.9% of the respondents indicated worrying that all points of views had been heard. However, figure 14.1 should be interpreted with care and does not indicate in a straightforward manner that the adversarial attitude prevails over the deliberative attitude. In fact, answers to the other questions indicative of adversarial and deliberative attitudes yield different results. For example, 41.5% of the respondents said that they viewed controversy as a positive sign of democratic debate, whereas 22.6% claimed that controversy justified a decision to clarify the situation. Overall, the answers suggest a fair share of both—deliberative and adversarial attitudes. In other words, reality is characterized by a good mix of adversarial and deliberative attitudes among actors. Neither of the two types of attitude clearly dominates the other. As a reminder, most scholarly work on interest groups assumes adversarial attitudes only.

More interesting are the group and geographical differences presented in figure 14.1. Deliberative attitudes are more prevalent among interest group representatives than they are among independent experts and civil servants. Together, civil servants and independent experts worry about the breadth of views represented during policy debates, on average, 20% of the time versus 41% for interest groups. This difference is significant, meaning that it does not only exist among the 270 respondents, but is also likely to exist among the entire biotechnology policy-making population. Moreover, the difference holds when other factors are held constant in a logistic regression, which includes continent and gender as control variables. In other words, in all likelihood, the deliberative attitude is related to the affiliation of respondents with interest groups. If groups appreciate wide debates more than the other actors, however, they believe in the same proportion as the other actors (55%) that opinion divergence should not prevent policy makers from making decisions.

Breaking down the interest group category between industry and advocacy reveals a greater inclination of the former toward adversarial attitudes and a greater inclination of the latter toward deliberative attitudes. On average, advocacy groups display deliberative attitudes 50% of the time versus 32% for industry. Conversely, industry has an adversarial attitude 66% of the time versus 45% for advocacy groups. These differences are statistically significant in tests of mean differences. Differences regarding deliberative attitudes remain significant when placed in logistic regressions, but not those regarding adversarial attitudes. In other words, the observed differences in adversarial attitudes might be better explained by other factors than the affiliation of the respondent with industry. Likewise, the difference in adversarial attitudes between North America and Europe, significant in a difference means test, loses its significance in a logistic regression. As expected, the last set of bars in figure 14.1 shows that Canada is no less and no more adversarial or deliberative than the United States.

In sum, survey respondents display a mix of adversarial and deliberative attitudes. Interest groups do not believe that difference of views should prevent decisions, as the adversarial perspective would want it, anymore than other policy-making actors. However, they want policy debates to include all views far more than the other actors—a concern consistent with a deliberative attitude. Among interest groups, advocacy groups adopt a deliberative attitude more frequently than industry, although industry does not have a clearly more adversarial attitude than advocacy groups. Likewise, it is not entirely clear that North America is more adversarial than Europe. In short, the analysis reveals so far that adversarial and deliberative attitudes are not as mutually exclusive as we instinctively think.

Fixed Preferences and View Changes

It may be harder for individuals to admit that they prefer authoritative decisions over policy debates than it is to claim that controversy is within the normal course of democracy. Likewise, it may be natural that marginal groups worry about the inclusion of all opinions in policy debates and that mainstream groups worry about prompt decisions. Such inclinations might explain some of the differences displayed in figure 14.1. However, those who have genuine deliberative attitudes should not only admit that they have such attitudes, they should also be inclined to change their policy-relevant preferences. The biotechnology actor survey contains a section in which actors are asked to indicate how their opinion had changed in the past year toward sixteen policy-relevant issues: eight in the agrifood area and eight in the human genetics area. Specifically, actors could answer for each of the sixteen issues that they have become more favorable, less favorable, or that their opinion had remained unchanged. This section of the survey has been used to construct a measure of opinion change intensity. Opinion change intensity is the percentage of issues on which a respondent claims having become either more or less favorable. In other words, a respondent indicating not having changed his or her mind on single issue obtains 0%; one indicating having changed his or her mind on all issues obtains 100%, with the latter suggesting a very high opinion change intensity.

Overall, 33.9% of the respondents claim not to have changed opinion on a single of the sixteen biotechnology issues during the past year, whereas 25.1% of the respondents indicate having changed their mind on 50% or more of the sixteen issues. The mean is 28.3%. Table 14.1 presents the results of two similar regression analyses, measuring the extent to which opinion change intensity varies between continent, categories of actors, and attitudes (gender is used as a control variable). The first regression provides Tobit estimates, which are more appropriate technically because opinion change intensity is not distributed normally, with 33.9% of the observations at zero. The second regression, which provides ordinarily least square (OLS) estimations, is not quite as technically appropriate as the first regression, but it is far more convenient for the interpretation of the results. As table 14.1 indicates, the results of the two regressions are similar, and therefore the OLS estimates will be used in this discussion.

Opinion change intensity among respondents who belong to interest groups is 9.76 percentage points higher than opinion change intensity among independent experts, which serve as the reference category. In other words, out of sixteen biotechnology issues, respondents who belong to interest groups change their mind on an extra 1.6 issues, in comparison with independent experts. Interest group representatives also change their opinion with greater intensity than governmental actors, who are not statistically different from independent experts in terms of opinion change intensity. A similar regression on the interest group subset estimates the difference between advocacy groups and industry, and finds no statistically significant difference in opinion change intensity between the two subsets of interest groups.

Although the regression fails to provide evidence of differences in opinion change intensity between North America and Europe, it does show significant

Table 14.1 Opinion Change Intensity by Category of Actors and Attitudes

Independent Variables	Tobit (opinion change intensity)	Ordinarily Least Square (opinion change intensity)
Gender	−11.46** (5.41)	−8.82** (3.78)
Continent	3.89 (6.17)	2.12 (4.30)
Governmental actors	−0.79 (6.64)	1.61 (4.60)
Interest groups	13.45** (6.51)	9.76** (4.61)
Adversarial attitudes	−14.46*** (5.44)	−10.13*** (3.82)
Deliberative attitudes	11.26* (6.25)	10.88** (4.40)
Constant	24.64*** (6.59)	31.07*** (4.65)
N	236	236
Pseudo R^2	.01	.08

***$P \leq$ .01, ** $P \leq$ .05, * $P \leq$ .1. Standard errors are in parentheses.

difference between actors disclosing adversarial and deliberative attitudes. The measure of adversarial and deliberative attitudes is the same as that used in figure 14.1. Actors who believe in authoritative decisions despite opinion divergence change their mind on 10.1 percentage points fewer issues than the other actors. Conversely, those who believe that more opinions should be included in policy debates change their mind on an extra 10.9 percentage points of the issues.

In sum, the regression analyses reveal that actors who indicated in the survey valuing inclusive policy debates do not only claim having a deliberative attitude, they also act in a manner consistent with this attitude by changing their policy-relevant preferences. Likewise, respondents who answered questions in a manner consistent with an adversarial attitude act accordingly, having more stable policy preferences. As argued in the previous section, of all actor categories, interest groups are those most likely to have deliberative attitudes. Not surprisingly then, they change their minds more frequently than the other actors. Perhaps more surprisingly, actors from interest groups change their opinion with the same intensity, regardless of whether they are of the advocacy or industry types.

Opinion Divergence and Convergence

If actors with a deliberative attitude prefer pursuing debate over ending it with an authoritative decision, it is not only because they believe that actors can be persuaded to change their minds, it is also because they think that opinion change can encourage convergence of opinions. Were opinions to change in all possible directions in the course of policy debates, deliberation would be a rather inefficient means to resolve policy disputes. In other words, if opinion change were to feed into opinion divergence among policy-making actors, deliberation would not make any more sense than it does to those who assume fixed preferences and continued policy conflict. The goal of this last section is to verify the extent to which actors whom we know are capable of changing their minds do so in a manner that encourages opinion convergence or divergence.

Opinion convergence and divergence among the actors was examined over sixteen policy-relevant issues in the biotechnology sector—that is, the same issues as those used previously to construct a measure of opinion change intensity. In contrast with opinion change intensity, however, –1 was assigned to someone who answered "less favorable" and 1 was assigned to someone who answered "more favorable." Those who did not change their mind were given 0. This way of coding the answers for each of the sixteen issues provides information about the direction of opinion change. If industry representatives have become, overall, more favorable to a given issue, the average for this group should be more than 0. Conversely, if advocacy groups have become, overall, less favorable to the issue, the average for this group should be less than 0. For the sake of presentation, figure 14.2 displays opinion swings for the eight agrifood biotechnology issues only. The patterns for the eight human genetics issues are very similar.

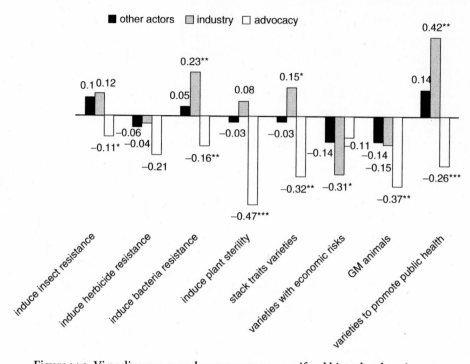

Figure 14.2 View divergence and convergence on agrifood biotechnology issues.
*** $P < .01$, **$P < .05$, *$P < .1$ in hypothesis test of means differences between industry
and other actors and between advocacy and other actors. Ho = o.

Figure 14.2 distinguishes between advocacy groups, industry, and the other
actors. A convergence of views among these categories of actors can be observed
when the three swings are on the same side of the horizontal axis. On three of the
issues, such a convergence exists—on genetic modifications that induce herbicide
and pesticide resistance, on genetically modified varieties that put export markets at
risk (economic risks), and on genetically modified animals. On these three issues,
the opinion of actors is becoming less favorable. On three other issues, the other
actors and industry groups are becoming more favorable, whereas advocacy groups
are becoming less favorable. On two of these issues, however, industry is significantly more optimistic than the other actors: genetic modifications that induce bac-
teria resistance and varieties that promote public health (for example, golden rice).
Lastly, the other actors are on the same side as advocacy groups on the two remaining issues—the so-called terminator gene technology (male sterility) and the new
stacked trait varieties—although advocacy groups are far more pessimistic.

Interestingly enough, figure 14.1 showed that advocacy groups have stronger
deliberative attitudes than industry. Therefore, advocacy groups might have
appeared more open to persuasion by industry than industry by advocacy groups.
Figure 14.2 suggests the opposite. On the three issues on which convergence has
occurred, it is industry that has come to a less favorable view, a view backed strongly
by advocacy groups on all eight issues. In other words, advocacy groups appear

more persuasive, and also more ideological, than industry groups. This finding goes against common sense, as much as against important scholarly work, which suggests systematic policy victories on the part of resourceful business groups (Coleman 1988; Olson 1965).

Figure 14.2 shows that the most important opinion swings on the part of industry and advocacy groups are on different issues. This observation can be interpreted as consistent with findings by Baumgartner et al. (forthcoming, 183–185) to the effect that interest groups with different views within any given sector talk past each other (see also Sabatier and Zafonte 2001, 11566). In fact, figure 14.2 suggests it is plausible that industry works toward focusing policy discussions on genetically modified plants promoting public health, whereas advocacy groups would prefer the spotlight to be on terminator gene technologies. This said, the policy debate agenda is not easily controlled by any of the actors. Therefore, interest groups must reflect about their positions and take part in debates on issues that they would have preferred avoiding at the outset. As the deliberative perspective would suggest, interest groups might change their policy preferences in the course of such reflections and debates. For example, it is not inconceivable that industry would have preferred avoiding policy discussions on herbicide-tolerant genetically modified cultivars. However, industry might have been pulled on this issue by policy makers who wanted to forge their opinion on the desirability of these cultivars by seeking the opinion of independent experts and various interest groups. Had industry decided to stay out of these deliberations and focus entirely on varieties to improve public health, it would have deprived itself of a chance to persuade other actors about the benefits of biotechnology. Therefore, industry participated and, unexpectedly at the outset of the deliberation, a significant number of its representatives became less favorable to herbicide-tolerant varieties. In other words, Baumgartner et al. (forthcoming) might overestimate the extent to which interest groups talk past each other and the ensuing impossibility of view convergence.

In sum, opinion change can promote opinion convergence. In the controversial agrifood biotechnology sector, the opinion swings promote a convergence of views between industry and advocacy groups on three out of eight issues. In addition, on the issues for which opinion swings increase the divergence between advocacy groups and industry, the other actors do not systematically align on the opinion of industry, the most resourceful groups. In fact, on two out of five issues about which industry and advocacy groups diverge, the other actors align with the latter groups.

CONCLUSION

This chapter began by affirming that interest groups have a bad reputation in modern democracy, and argued that this bad reputation stems from an adversarial perspective on politics, promoted in scholarly work and assumed by citizens. This perspective even acted as a self-fulfilling prophesy, increasingly providing cultural norms by which political actors behave and expect others to behave. Mansbridge (1992; 2003) argues that judgments about political legitimacy, including the political legitimacy of interest groups, largely depend on one's perspective on democracy, hence the importance of awareness about our own perspective and about alternatives. Among the alternatives is the deliberative perspective. This latter perspective values interest groups, not so much as representatives of citizens, but as contributors to policy debates. In fact, it avoids seeing policy debates as endless conflicts among interest groups. Debates or deliberations, the perspective suggests, can encourage opinion change among groups and reduce view divergence over policy options. In the deliberative perspective, a policy debate, inclusive of a wide range of views and ending in agreement, is the best guarantee one can expect that policy-making actors serve the public interest.

Mansbridge (1992) makes a normative plea in favor of the deliberative perspective, whereas the goal of this chapter was primarily to verify whether this perspective already echoes with the reality of interest groups. And it does to an extent—more among interest groups than among other policy actors, and no more no less in Canada than elsewhere. In any case, the observation of attitudes consistent with the deliberative perspective should help convince skeptics about the value of its concepts and the feasibility of its prescriptions regarding the attitude of interest groups. More important, however, such observation could convince scholars to grant the deliberative perspective a pride of place in their work, next to the adversarial perspective. In other words, scholarly work has contributed to forging the adversarial political culture and outlooks on interest groups, but it might now be time for the reality of interest groups, as described in this chapter, to inform scholars, opening them to the deliberative perspective. Such an opening on the part of scholars might contribute to changing adversarial cultural norms, thereby improving the reputation of interest groups in modern democracies.

Making space for the deliberative perspective, however, does not imply political scientists giving up on the adversarial perspective. The empirical evidence provided in this chapter suggests that it still forges the attitudes of interest groups. In addition, the empirical evidence shows that political attitudes cannot be reduced to one perspective or the other. The adversarial and the deliberative perspectives are not mutually exclusive. Several of the survey respondents indicated valuing debates in a manner consistent with the deliberative perspective. Several of these respondents also believe that debates should not prevent decision making, in a manner consistent with the adversarial perspective. On some policy issues, actors with different views, especially interest groups, can debate, change their mind, and agree on the best course of action. On several other policy issues, however, actors with different views can debate, remain convinced of the rightfulness of their initial policy preference, and sustain conflicting relationships. As Walzer (2004, 103–104) argues, it is unreasonable to expect deep political disagreements, such as those between the Left and the Right, and presumably those between biotechnology optimists and skeptics, to be resolved entirely by debates and persuasion. In short, political science needs perspectives capable of accounting for both deliberative and adversarial attitudes.

REFERENCES

Aerni, Phillip, and Thomas Bernauer. 2005. Stakeholder attitudes toward GMOs in the Philippines, Mexico, and South Africa: The issue of public trust. *World Development* 34(3): 557–575.

Amara, Nabil, Rejean Landry, and Mokter Lamari. 1999. Les déterminants de l'effort de lobbying des associations au Canada. *Canadian Journal of Political Science* 32(3): 471–497.

Bachrach, Peter, and Morton S. Baratz. 1962. The two faces of power. *American Political Science Review* 56(4): 947–952.

Baumgartner, Frank R., Jeffrey M. Berry, Marie Hojnacki, David C. Kimball, and Beth L. Leech. 2009. *Advocacy and Policy Change.* Chicago, Ill.: University of Chicago Press.

Baumgartner, Frank R., and Beth L. Leech. 1998. *Basic Interests: The Importance of Groups in Politics and Political Science.* Princeton, N.J.: Princeton University Press.

Coleman, William D. 1988. *Business and Politics: A Study of Collective Action.* Montreal: McGill-Queen's University Press.

Graham, Katherine A., and Susan D. Phillips. 1997. Citizen engagement: Beyond the customer revolution. *Canadian Public Administration* 40(2): 255–273.

Habermas, Jürgen. 1987. *Theory of Communicative Action.* Boston. Mass.: Beacon.

Halpin, Darren R. 2006. The participatory and democratic potential and practice of interest groups: Between solidarity and representation. *Public Administration* 84(4): 919–940.

Lindblom, Charles E. 1977. *Politics and Markets.* New York: Basic Books.

Mansbridge, Jane J. 1992. A deliberative theory of interest representation. In *The Politics of Interest: Interest Groups Transformed*, ed. M. Petracca, 32–57. Boulder, Colo.: Westview Press.

———. 2003. Rethinking representation. *American Political Science Review* 97(4): 515–528.

Montpetit, Éric. 2008. Policy design for legitimacy: Expert knowledge, citizens, time and inclusion in the United Kingdom's biotechnology sector. *Public Administration* 86(1): 259–278.

Mutz, Diana C. 2006. *Hearing the Other Side: Deliberative versus Participatory Democracy.* Cambridge: Cambridge University Press.

Oslon, Mancur. 1965. *The Logic of Collective Action.* New York: Schocken.

Phillips, Susan D. 1993. Of public interest groups and sceptics: A realist's reply to Professor Stanbury. *Canadian Public Administration* 36(4): 606–616.

Phillips, Susan D., L. A. Pal, and D. J. Savas. 1992. *Interest Groups in the Policy Process.* Working paper series 92–13. Ottawa: School of Public Administration, Carleton University.

Pross, A. Paul. 1986. *Group Politics and Public Policy*, 2nd ed. Toronto: Oxford University Press.

Sabatier, Paul A., and Matthew Zafonte. 2001. Policy knowledge: Advocacy organizations. In *International Encyclopedia of the Social & Behavioral Sciences*, vol .17, ed. Neil J. Smelser and Paul B. Baltes, 11563–11568. Amsterdam: Elsevier.

Scharpf, Fritz W. 1997. *Games Real Actors Play: Actor-Centered Institutionalism in Policy Research.* Boulder, Colo.: Westview Press.

Schattschneider, E. E. 1960. *The Semi-Sovereign People*. New York: Holt, Rinehart and Winston.

Schneider, Anne, and Helen Ingram. 2007. "Ways of knowing: Implication for public policy." Presented at the annual conference of the American Political Science Association, Chicago, Illinois, August 30–September 2.

Stanbury, William T. 1993. A sceptic's guide to the claims of so-called public interest groups. *Canadian Public Administration* 36(4): 580–605.

Walzer, Michael. 2004. *Politics and Passion: Toward a More Egalitarian Liberalism*. New Haven, Conn.: Yale University Press.

Young, Lisa, and Joanna Everitt. 2004. *Advocacy Groups*. Vancouver: UBC Press.

....

CHAPTER 15

PUBLIC OPINION
AND PUBLIC POLICY

....

STUART SOROKA

CHRISTOPHER WLEZIEN

A principal function of representative democracy is to provide a mechanism through which public opinion and public policy are reliably and regularly connected. There should, on the one hand, be policy representation; public preferences for policy should be reflected in policy itself. There should, on the other hand, be public responsiveness; public preferences should be informed and should react to public policy. Both dynamics are central to the theoretical work on representative democracy, from Rousseau's *The Social Contract* (1762) to Lippmann (1925), Schumpeter (1950), and Dahl (1971).

These concerns are, of course, not purely theoretical. Policy representation in particular has been a prominent theme in everyday politics, especially in recent years. As in many other advanced democracies, there has been a steady increase in disaffection with governments and leaders in Canada—particularly, an increase in the number of people who feel that government does not represent their interests (for example, Anderson and Goodyear-Grant 2006). Following the Meech Lake Accord, Canadian support for "elite accommodation" or "executive federalism" largely dissipated; constitutional accommodation through back-room negotiation was met with widespread cries for transparency and public consultation (see, for example, Cairns 1991; Watts and Brown 1990). More recently, we have seen a "decline of deference" (Nevitte 1996) in the Canadian electorate. Smiley's (1972, 201) assertion that "elites are somewhat unresponsive to popular attitudes and that the citizenry for whatever reasons has a considerable tolerance for this unresponsiveness" no longer rings true. And there has been a rise in Canadian governments' reconsideration of election systems, and efforts to tap into public opinion directly through royal commissions and citizens' assemblies (see, for example, Howe et al. 2005; Seidle 2007). This is all part of an ongoing—and increasingly prominent— concern with the representation of public preferences in Canadian governance.

Less prominent in everyday politics, but equally important where representative democracy is concerned, is the degree to which Canadian public attitudes are actually informed. Indeed, this may be the more pressing concern, and it is this problem that we focus on in this chapter. We will review the evidence on the representation of public preferences in Canadian federal policy, to be sure, but we will spend more time on the substance of preferences, especially whether and to what extent preferences adjust alongside policy itself. That is, we will consider *thermostatic public responsiveness*, where public preferences for policy change reflect (among other factors) changes in policy.

The existing literature suggests that both public responsiveness and policy representation are evident in Canada. However, there is also good reason to believe that the magnitude of each is compromised by Canada's rather complicated, overlapping federal policy structure. Federalism may make public responsiveness more difficult, and, by reducing the public's ability to monitor policy outcomes, it may also lessen the incentive to represent. The opinion—policy connection may thus be rather weak in Canada, comparatively speaking. Before we discuss this consequence of federalism, however, we review the thermostatic model of opinion—policy relationships, and the existing literature on the representation of public opinion in Canadian public policy.

THE THERMOSTATIC MODEL
OF OPINION AND POLICY

To begin, let us set out a more formal but relatively simple model of the relationship between public opinion and public policy, a model that we believe captures much of what we expect in a functioning representative democracy.[1] We begin with what is perhaps the foremost element: the representation of public preferences in policy. Put succinctly, public opinion should have an effect on public policy. When the public wants more spending on health, for instance, Canadian governments should spend more on health; when the public wants less spending, governments should provide less.[2] That this is a critical feature of representative democracy requires little justification here.

Representation depends fundamentally on a responsive public, however—a public that monitors and reacts to what government is doing. There is little benefit policywise to representing inattentive and uninformed preferences; the policy consequences could be perverse. And there is also little incentive to do so; without public attention to what policy makers do, the electoral incentive to represent would be altogether absent. Public responsiveness is consequently as vital to representative democracy as representation itself.

A responsive public behaves like a thermostat (Wlezien 1995). In short, a responsive public adjusts its preferences for "more" or "less" policy in response to what policy makers do. When policy increases, ceteris paribus, the public preference for more policy decreases; conversely, when policy decreases, ceteris paribus, the public preference for more policy increases.

What exactly is "the public preference for policy?" For expository purposes, the public can be viewed as a collection of individuals distributed along a dimension of preference for policy activity—for instance, spending on health. Consider the "public preference" to be the median along this dimension—a certain "ideal" level of health spending. Now, if the level of policy differs from the level the public prefers, the public favors a corresponding change in policy, basically, either more or less. If the preferred level is greater than policy itself, the public favors more spending than currently is being undertaken. If policy makers respond, and provide more (but not too much) for health, then the new policy position would more closely correspond to the preferred level of spending. If the public is indeed responsive to what policy makers do, then the public would then not favor as much more activity on health. It might still favor more, on balance, but not as substantially as in the prior period. If policy makers overshoot the public's preferred level of spending, it would favor less.

In effect, following the thermostatic metaphor, a departure from the favored policy temperature, *which itself can change over time*, produces a signal to adjust policy accordingly and, when sufficiently adjusted, the signal stops. In this way, the public behaves much like a thermostat. When the "policy temperature" is too low, a responsive public calls for more policy; when the "policy temperature" is too high, a responsive public calls for less. This conceptualization of public preferences has deep roots in political science, of course, including Easton's (1965) classic depiction of a political system and Deutsch's (1966) models of "control."

These expectations can be expressed formally. The public's preference for "more" policy—its relative preference, R—represents the difference between the public's preferred level of policy (P^*) and the level it actually gets (P):

$$R_t = P_t^* - P_t$$

Thus, as the preferred level of policy or policy itself changes, the relative preference signal changes accordingly. The public is expected to respond currently to actual policy change when put into effect (at t). This is straightforward, at least in theory. It is, of course, less straightforward in practice, as we shall see.

Note that this model is a general one, and we do not expect it to work in all policy domains, in all countries. Public responsiveness and policy representation are likely to reflect the political importance (or "salience") of the different domains, if only because of possible electoral consequences. Indeed, we expect the pattern of representation to be symmetrical to the pattern of public responsiveness. When the public notices and responds to policy in a particular domain, policy makers will notice and respond to public preferences themselves; when the public does not respond to policy, policy makers will not represent public preferences (Wlezien 2004). This symmetry plays an important role later, as we consider the implications of federalism for public responsiveness and, by implication, representation as well. First, however, we review the state of the literature on policy representation in Canada.

Policy Representation and Parliamentary Government

The relationship between opinion and policy has received considerable academic attention in the United States.[3] In Canada, research has been considerably more limited. There is a small, related body of work focused on issue attentiveness in Canadian public opinion and government. This research suggests that there is indeed a regular connection between the issues Canadians care about and the issues receiving attention in Parliament (for example, Howlett 1998; Penner et al. 2006; Soroka 2002). At any given time, this work suggests, the issues most important to Canadians are likely to be prominent in the legislative arena as well. This is an important finding; as we have outlined, attentiveness is critical to the opinion—policy relationship.[4] It is different from the opinion—policy relationship sketched out earlier, however, which focuses not just on whether government is paying attention to issues, but whether they are actually enacting policy in line with public preferences.

The small body of work that directly addresses this opinion—policy relationship is thus, we believe, critical. Francois Petry and Matthew Mendelsohn have examined the relationship between public preferences for change and policy change in Canada during different periods and across different domains (Petry 1999; Petry and Mendelsohn 2004). Their work uses a "policy consistency" approach, comparing the distribution of responses from single survey questions with existing, proximate changes in policy.[5] It suggests, first, that consistency between preferences for change and policy change is more likely when the consensus for change in opinion is greater. That is, policy is more likely to exhibit change in a direction consistent with preferences when the distribution of preferences clearly supports that change. In short, the magnitude of public support matters; government responsiveness is proportional to the magnitude of public preferences for change. Note that although the mode of analysis is quite different, these findings are roughly consistent with the thermostatic model outlined earlier, where an x-unit shift in preferences is expected to have a y-unit effect on policy outcomes.

The second major finding in work by Petry and Mendelsohn is that policy consistency has varied across (1) governments and (2) policy domains. Where governments are concerned, the Mulroney era exhibits a greater degree of policy consistency than either the Trudeau or the Chrétien eras. This finding reminds us that representation can vary over time. It can vary across policy domains, as well. These authors suggest that government responsiveness is more likely in higher profile domains. That is, as outlined earlier, governments are more likely to appear responsive to opinion in those domains in which the public is paying attention.

Proportional government responsiveness to opinion and the effect of issue salience on representation are also evident in our own work (Soroka and Wlezien 2004), which tests directly the thermostatic model in Canada. This work draws on time series data of public preferences for spending and actual government spending, and in so doing captures the dynamic, reciprocal relationship between opinion and policy. Analyses find evidence of opinion representation in Canada; federal budgetary policy in major domestic policy domains regularly follows public preferences for policy change. That said, there is variance across domains. In particular, representation is stronger for highly salient domains such as welfare and health than for less salient domains such as environment and transportation.

Policy representation in Canada is also limited in several ways. First, the magnitude of representation in Canada is somewhat more limited than in the United States. In short, to the extent that directly comparable models are available (see Soroka and Wlezien 2005; Wlezien 2004), the effect of a given shift in preferences on policy appears smaller in Canada. Second, representation in Canada appears more "global" than domain specific. In the traditional characterization of representation, politicians respond to public opinion within particular areas (see, for example, Monroe 1979; Page and Shapiro 1992). In some cases, however, representation may be more collective. Governments may respond to a component of preferences that is common across domains. Rather than having specific preferences for each policy domain, citizens may have preferences "over the general contours of government activity" (Stimson et al. 1995; see also Stimson 1991), and it may be that governments may respond to these more "global" preferences. Of course, preferences (and representation) need not be entirely global or domain specific, but rather some combination thereof. Past work shows this to be true. It also suggests that representation in Canada—to the extent that it exists—is largely to this global component. The implication is that, even where Canadian politicians do attend to public preferences, they do so mostly in a general way. Preferences for more or less spending, generally speaking, may be represented across several domains, but the component of preferences that is specific to health, or education, may not.

Why is policy representation in Canada comparatively limited in magnitude and largely "global" in focus?[6] Political institutions likely play a role here. The U.S. presidential system may be more conducive to policy representation than the Canadian parliamentary system, for instance. Scholars have long noted the dominance of cabinets over parliaments (see, for example, the classic statements by

Bagehot [1867] and Jennings [1959]; also see Cox [1987], Laver and Shepsle [1996], and Tsebelis [2002]). These scholars portray a world in which cabinet governments exercise substantial discretion, where the cabinet is the proposer—it puts legislation to the Commons—and the legislature ultimately has only a limited check on what the government does. Indeed, where the legislature and executive are fused, the need for a government to hold the confidence of the legislature can result in relatively strong party cohesiveness, or "party discipline" (Diermeier and Feddersen 1998; Huber 1996). Strøm (2003) concludes that parliamentary government deals much better with "adverse selection" than it does "moral hazard." Once established, the cabinet is difficult to control on a recurring basis. This is certainly evident in Canada. Through control over members' of Parliament career opportunities, party discipline is extraordinarily high in Canada (Carty et al. 2000; Docherty 1997). And the system is regarded as increasingly centralized, with little space for meaningful participation by the legislature, at least on an ongoing basis (Franks 1987; Savoie 1999).

This almost certainly has implications for government responsiveness. When there are differences between what the cabinet and parliament want, the latter cannot effectively impose its own contrary will. That is, the legislature cannot consistently undertake "error correction," adjusting the government's position where it may be going too far or not far enough given public preferences. This is of particular relevance given the independence of individual ministers, and prime ministers, in the policy-making process (Laver and Shepsle 1996). Some may be more conservative than others, some more liberal. All can make mistakes. The process of amendment and veto is thus crucial. In parliamentary systems, however, this can be somewhat compromised, at least by comparison with Madisonian presidential systems. In the latter, the executive cannot act effectively without the legislature, at least with respect to statute. The legislature is the proposer, and although the executive can veto legislation, the legislature can override the veto. Most changes in policy require agreement between the executive and legislature, or else a supermajority in the latter. This is likely to reduce disjuncture between public opinion and policy change.[7]

The lack of a horizontal separation of powers may consequently make the Canadian parliamentary system less reliably responsive to public opinion over time. This concern is evident in work on Canada, certainly. Consider J. R. Mallory's (1974, 208) observation that "the mass of citizenry is perhaps as far away from the real decisions of government as they were two hundred years ago, and the cabinet system provides strong institutional barriers to the development of more democratic ways of doing things." Even so, we expect representation in the Canadian system; Canadian governments may be held accountable for their actions more easily than governments in a presidential system, as responsibility is far clearer come election time. In between elections, however, there is little to make Canadian cabinets accountable except for the prospect of a future electoral competition.[8] Although important, the electoral incentive is imperfect.

PUBLIC RESPONSIVENESS AND FEDERALISM

The magnitude and nature of public responsiveness should matter to policy representation as well. As discussed earlier, representation is, to some degree (and perhaps to a considerable degree), dependent on public responsiveness. A monitoring public is the critical incentive to represent, after all. It is for this reason that issue salience—in work by Petry and Mendelsohn (2004), as well as by Soroka and Wlezien (2004)—matters to representation. Looking across domains, representation in policy is more likely when the public notices policy change.

How informed are Canadian policy preferences? And what information do they reflect? The literature suggests a glass-half-full/glass-half-empty story. On the one hand, there is evidence of rationality on the part of the Canadian public. In a comparatively early but very detailed study of Canadian public opinion on policy, Johnston (1986) reveals a structure to Canadian attitudes on, for instance, the distribution of powers, levels of taxation, and a wide range of policy priorities. In a study modeled after Page and Shapiro's (1992) work in the United States, Bélanger and Petry (2005) also find considerable stability in Canadian public opinion over time; and when opinion change is apparent, they suggest that change is typically gradual and in response to other real-world and political trends.

Of course, stability in opinion may not be a good thing. As Bélanger and Petry (2005, 209) note, opinion change might be critical to functioning democracy, and stability may reflect complacency. For instance, our own work finds limited public responsiveness to policy change (Soroka and Wlezien 2004). The public responds thermostatically to policy change in welfare and health, but other domains exhibit less consistent responsiveness. Responsiveness appears to be largely "global" in focus as well. To the extent that public responsiveness to policy is evident, it tends to be focused on the trend in spending common across different social domains, rather than changes in spending that are unique to each domain.

That the structure of public responsiveness across domains is symmetrical with policy representation is, of course, exactly as we would expect. Representation is conditioned by responsiveness; the magnitude and focus of public responsiveness will in most cases be directly connected to the magnitude and focus of policy representation. And this should be true not just across domains, but across countries. The political institutions that facilitate responsiveness may, by implication, enhance representation. Institutions that inhibit responsiveness may similarly depress representation.

Perhaps most critically in the Canadian case, there is a growing body of literature suggesting that federalism inhibits public responsiveness. Public responsiveness requires that the people acquire accurate information about what policy makers are doing. This depends on the supply of information and on the clarity of that information. More precisely, it depends on the extent to which responsibility for policies is clear, and this is in part a function of how government itself is

organized. Federalism increases the number of different governments making policy and thus makes less clear what *government* is doing (see, for example, Downs
1999). Put differently, the government policy signal (*P*) may be confused—or,
rather, there may be different signals from multiple sources—at least in policy
domains for which different governments have responsibility. This may well
dampen public responsiveness.

Consider a unitary system, where there is but one government making policy in
all areas. In such a system, there is no mistaking the source of policy change. The
signal is clear. We thus would expect a comparatively high level of public responsiveness. (Of course, this doesn't mean that the public doesn't ignore or mistake the
policy signals in the many low-salience policy domains.) Now, consider a federal
system. Here we have multiple governments, and there are consequently multiple
sources of policy making and policy information. There may still be considerable
variance among federal systems, admittedly, indeed across policy domains within a
single system. Regardless, and fundamentally, these federal arrangements will lead
to greater or lesser degrees of clarity of responsibility (Powell and Whitten 1993; see
also Anderson 2006).

This concern has been voiced in the Canadian literature. In his classic account
of the self-sustaining behavior of Canadian provincial governments, for instance,
Alan Cairns (1977, 707) argues: "The institutionalization of government, the construction of a sphere of political and bureaucratic existence differentiated from
other spheres of collective life, automatically reduces the relative importance of
nongovernment groups, interests and individuals in policy making." Cairns suggests, in sum, that the increasingly complex maze of intergovernmental relationships makes it increasingly difficult for the public to hold governments accountable.
Donald Smiley (1979) highlights the same deficiency, in what is perhaps the best-
titled critique of Canadian executive federalism thus far: "An Outsider's Observations
of Intergovernmental Relations among Consenting Adults." Simeon and Cameron
(2002) argue that federalism poses a real problem for government responsiveness,
transparency, and accountability; Cutler (2004) presents a particularly valuable
discussion of the problems that federalism poses for the Canadian citizen.

The degree to which there is a clear policy signal to which the public can respond
will depend, in large part, on the particular federal institutional and fiscal structure,
of course. One principal difference is the extent to which governments have "exclusive" versus "concurrent" legislative powers (Watts 1999). Under "exclusive legislative powers," different governments have different responsibilities and there are no
interactions between layers. Much like the unitary system, there is no mistaking the
source of policy in each policy area; it is just that the source differs. We thus might
expect a comparatively high level of responsiveness on the part of the public in
politically important domains, regardless of which level of government is in charge.
This does presume that the availability of information about the behavior of governments is fairly equal across levels of government, however, and this may not be
true for at least two reasons: (1) the behavior of the national government may receive
more attention than lower level governments and (2) the flow of information about

lower level governments may vary meaningfully geographically—for example, across counties, states, and municipalities. Information on policy making in a federal system may thus be more available in some domains than others, depending on which government is responsible, and responsiveness may vary accordingly.

In many instances, the Canadian system is one of de facto "concurrent legislative powers" in which different governments share responsibilities.[9] (Canadian federalism is discussed in chapters 5 and 7 in this volume, so we review only the most relevant details here.) In most major domestic policy domains in Canada, there is some combination of (1) direct involvement by multiple levels of government and (2) direct involvement by one level of government, funded through fiscal transfers from another. In the former arrangement, there are different sources of policy change and implementation, which can create fairly obvious complications for the public, especially if policy change over time is not parallel across levels of government.[10] The latter is scarcely any better. Decisions made by one level of government are constrained, at least in a general way, by the budgetary policy of another. Both forms of concurrent powers, then, blur the policy signal citizens receive.[11]

What are the likely implications for public responsiveness? It may not be that the public is less informed about the sum of policy across levels of government, although this is a possibility. (It also may not be that the public is less sophisticated than in unitary systems, where little sophistication is required of citizens.) There is very good reason to think that the public will be less informed about the behavior of specific levels, however, because this would require keeping what is happening at each level perfectly straight. That is, where there are overlapping jurisdictions, we expect a dampening of public responsiveness of preferences for policy *at any particular level of government*. For instance, we might expect that individuals' preferences for more policy at the national level are less responsive to changes in national policy, independent of state, provincial, and local policy. We would expect the same at these lower levels of government as well.

Consider the following, more concrete, Canadian example: In the 1988–2005 period, for instance, roughly 61% of all welfare spending was direct spending by the federal government; the remaining 39% was spent by a combination of provincial and municipal governments. Some of that 39% was also federal funds, however, transferred to provinces through block transfers (including Established Programs Financing, the Canada Health and Social Transfer, the Canada Social Transfer). How can we reasonably expect a citizen to distinguish between policy changes that are the consequence of one government or another? Welfare policies may have grown significantly in one province, but does this mean we want the national government to do less? Or do we think that provincial government should do less? Or both? Indeed, the truth might be that we *should* think that the national government needs to do less and the provincial government more. Making such an assessment is likely rather difficult. Citizens simply cannot tell which government is principally responsible for a given shift in spending.

In short, public responsiveness is much more difficult in domains in which governments have concurrent jurisdiction, or where policies are funded through transfers between governments. And the combination of concurrent jurisdictions and fiscal transfers—as in many major domestic domains in Canada—likely makes public responsiveness especially hard. In this situation, it will very often not be clear to the public which government is responsible for which policy. (For more information on concurrency, see chapter 7, this volume).[12]

This has implications for opinion representation itself. As we already have discussed, there is good reason to think that we will have clear policy responsiveness only when we observe clear public responsiveness to policy. Note that some have argued that federalism actually increases net representation of broad policy preferences, because multiple levels of government provide greater opportunity (for example, Downs 1999; Trudeau 1968). This possibility is perfectly consistent with our conjecture regarding representation at particular levels of government. It may be that the representation of opinion at each level of government is lower even as representation across all levels of government is higher. Given lower public responsiveness, however, the pressure for representation at each level of government may be reduced.[13]

Policy and Opinion in Canada:
An Expository Analysis

What can existing data tell us about the relationship between policy and public preferences in Canada? As an expository analysis, we look here at public opinion and government spending on welfare, or "social assistance," for the period 1988–2006. Spending data are from Statistics Canada and include social assistance spending by (1) the federal government; (2) provincial, territorial, and local governments (referred to here as *provincial*); and (3) consolidated federal, provincial, territorial, and local governments (referred to here simply as *consolidated*).[14] Our measure of public preferences for welfare policy is based on the following question: Keeping in mind that increasing services could increase taxes, do you think the federal government is spending too much, just the right amount, or should be spending more on each of the following… [for example, welfare]?"[15] Following previous research, we create a percentage difference measure by subtracting the percentage of people who think we are spending too much from the percentage of people who think we are spending too little in each domain. The resulting measure of net support thus captures the degree to which the public wants more or less spending over time; it captures both direction and magnitude. Note, also, that this measure of public preferences is based on a survey question that identifies the federal government. That the question is specific about a level of government is important for our current purposes; it allows us to explore the degree to which preferences for federal spending actually respond to federal spending.

Figure 15.1 shows the resulting spending and preferences series. Note first that there are differences between the federal and provincial spending series. There are

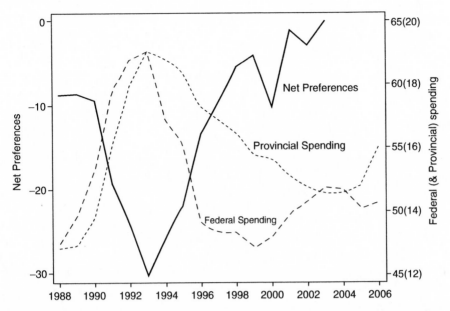

Figure 15.1 Net preferences and government spending on welfare. Spending is in millions of fiscal year 2000 dollars. Figures for provincial spending are in parentheses.

years in which the two move together, certainly, but other years in which they move in different directions. And even in years when the series are moving together, they do not necessarily move up or down the same amount (even taking into account the relative size of the federal and provincial budgets). The correlation between the two series is .59; for annual changes in spending (the policy *change* central to the thermostatic model) it is .68. This implies that spending at the two levels is more dissimilar than similar. Canadians clearly experience varying degrees of welfare commitment. And these data conceal the additional variance that results from the various provincial policies. The average bivariate correlation between the ten provincial data series (data not provided) is .42. So if federal welfare spending preferences are codetermined by federal and provincial policies, then national public preference will be the product of different, and sometimes quite disparate, provincial policy trends.[16]

Figure 15.1 hints at a thermostatic response in public opinion; when spending increases, net preferences for spending decrease, and vice versa. This is confirmed in regression models (shown in the appendix). Ceteris paribus, Canadian preferences for welfare spending respond thermostatically (negatively) to federal welfare spending. But, paradoxically, Canadian preferences for federal welfare spending also respond to provincial spending series. This is true not just when federal and provincial data are considered separately. Even when both are included in the same model, there is responsiveness to spending at both levels of government.[17] (This is somewhat apparent in figure 15.1 in the post-2000 period, when preferences continue to rise alongside declining provincial spending, even as federal welfare spending increases.) Given that part of what provinces spend on welfare comes from the federal government, we might expect federal spending preferences to be, at least in part, conditioned by provincial spending. However, for ostensibly "federal" welfare preferences to be affected by provincial spending, nevertheless highlights a potential weakness of the Canadian system. It suggests that the Canadian public is not readily able to distinguish between what one or the other level of government is doing.

There are other explanations for the patterns we observe—ones that do not assume that the public fails to differentiate between the source of spending. First, respondents may simply not think much about the word *federal* in survey questions, and their responses consequently lump together preferences for both federal and provincial spending. Second, and more substantively, we should not forget that a good deal of provincial spending in the social domains comes from the federal government. Citizens may quite reasonably adjust preferences for federal spending in reaction to provincial spending, because the latter actually is driven in large part by the former. Third, given that multiple governments are making policy in a single domain, citizens might base their preferences for one government's policy, at least in part, on what the other governments are doing as well. Again, this is entirely reasonable. If a desire for more spending at the federal level can be appeased through increased spending at the provincial level, for instance, then preferences for federal policy should shift in response to provincial policy change.

These are interesting possibilities, and ones that may help us understand the microlevel story behind our aggregate-level results. They may not matter where the relationship between responsiveness and federalism is concerned, however. Regardless of whether citizens readily distinguish between levels of government or simply choose not to, responsiveness in the Canadian federal context is not clearly directed at the policy-making behavior of any single level of government. As we have seen elsewhere, and discussed earlier, this responsiveness also is weaker than what we see in the United States and, especially, the United Kingdom.

This diminished (or opaque) public responsiveness dampens the incentive for Canadian governments to represent preferences in policy. It also lessens the value of doing so, even for those policy makers who are motivated to represent for other than electoral reasons, because preferences are less meaningful. This is not to say that there is no value in representing expressed public opinion in Canada, just that the value of public opinion to legislators at the federal or provincial levels will be reduced. It just is not clear to which government those preferences are responding, or even to which government those preferences are directed.

Conclusion: Responsiveness and Representation in Canada

What is the nature of the opinion—policy relationship in Canada? The story is, in a nutshell, as follows. There is evidence of policy representation in Canada; public policy does regularly follow public preferences, across a number of policy domains. Policy representation is likely limited more by a parliamentary rather than a presidential system. In the latter, Congress can act to correct errors made by the executive, whereas in the Canadian parliamentary system the Commons holds very little power, and cabinet has considerable freedom. Policy representation is likely also limited by public responsiveness. This responsiveness is the critical incentive for representation, but it requires a clear policy signal. To react to policy change, the public needs to be able to identify that policy change. The likelihood that citizens can identify policy change is lessened considerably by federalism. When there are multiple governments making policy in the same domains, spending funds that are often transferred from one level of government to another, the capacity to monitor or respond to government activities is likely reduced.

This problem is not unique to Canada, but this is a country for which the dampening effect of institutions on the opinion—policy link may be especially great. (Recall that the particularly complicated system of concurrent legislative powers in many Canadian policy domains likely makes the policy signal especially confusing.) This is not to say that Canada is not a functioning democracy, of course. It surely is. But the efficiency with which preferences are converted to policy, and policy change is then reflected in preferences, is diminished when compared with countries in which policy-making authority is more concentrated.

Grappling with the effects of federalism remains a critical task for future work on the opinion—policy link in Canada. The existing literature has paid relatively little attention to the potentially confusing effects of federalism outlined in this chapter. And we have not even begun to consider whether policy varies across provinces in ways that are systematically linked to regional differences in public preferences. We thus know little about the implications federalism has for the relationship between public opinion and policy—a relationship that is one of the most critical indicators of the success and strength of any representative democratic system.

APPENDIX

The model of public responsiveness to welfare spending used here is drawn from Soroka and Wlezien (2004), although it is estimated here using a longer time period. The model, briefly, regresses current net preferences for welfare spending on (1) spending, (2) a counter variable to capture the gradual upward trend in social spending preferences in the past few decades, and (3) lagged preferences to account for autocorrelation in the series. Results are shown in table 15.1 for models including federal spending, provincial spending, and both. The standardized coefficients for spending are included to facilitate comparison between measures with quite different variances. Even so, we need not (and should not) make too much here of the magnitude of coefficients; significance alone will suffice.

Table 15.1 Assessing Public Responsiveness to Federal and Provincial Welfare
          Spending

$\approx$	Dependent Variable: Net Preferences$_t$		
	(1)	(2)	(3)
Federal spending	−0.891 [−0.500] (0.205)		−0.523* [−0.293] (0.189)
Provincial spending		−3.176* [−0.866] (0.649)	−2.116* [−0.577] (0.647)
Net preferences$_{t-1}$	0.520* (0.125)	−0.095 (0.205)	0.046 (0.172)
Counter	0.302 (0.206)	1.252* (0.246)	0.892* (0.237)
Constant	−2.263 (1.763)	−9.388* (2.007)	−6.691* (1.884)
N	16	16	16
R^2	.892	.908	.945

*$P < .05$. Cells contain OLS regression coefficients, with standard errors in parentheses and with standardized coefficients in square brackets.

Note, then, that there is evidence of (statistically significant) public responsiveness to both federal and provincial spending, in columns 1 and 2, respectively. Even in column 3, where both spending series are included together, we see significant responsiveness to both federal and provincial spending. The implication is that the Canadian welfare preferences, captured through a question asking about the "federal" government, respond to changes in provincial spending above and beyond what the federal government is doing.

Acknowledgment. We are grateful to Fred Cutler and Patrick Fournier for comments on a previous draft.

NOTES

1. Note that the description of the thermostatic model here draws considerably on Wlezien (1995; 1996).

2. We can express policy representation more formally, as follows

$$P = f\{O\},$$

where P designates policy and O is opinion, and where we expect the relationship between the two to be positive. That is, if opinion favors more policy, governments should provide more policy; if opinion favors less policy, governments should provide less.

3. The literature is vast, but see, for example, Achen (1978), Bartels (1991), Erikson et al. (1993; 2002), Manza and Cook (2002), Page and Shapiro (1983), and Stimson et al. (1995). For reviews of the literature, see Burstein (2003) and Wlezien and Soroka (2007).

4. Also see Baumgartner and Jones (2002) on the role of attentiveness in policy making.

5. See Monroe (1979; 1998) for the archetypal example of the policy consistency approach and Wlezien and Soroka (2007) for a discussion of the different approaches.

6. Note that we observe similar patterns in the United Kingdom, another parliamentary system (see Soroka and Wlezien 2005).

7. This may be most likely when control of the different branches is divided, not unified.

8. We might distinguish between *indirect* representation, through elections, and *direct* representation, where sitting politicians actively represent current public interests. And it may be that even though presidential systems enhance direct representation, other systems may produce better indirect representation—essentially, a stronger relationship between votes and seats. Consider a parliamentary system with a proportional electoral system, for instance. Even so, given its plurality electoral system there is no reason to believe that indirect representation is particularly strong in Canada either.

9. This is not a so much a direct consequence of the Constitution Act, 1867 as it is an indirect one. That is, few concurrent powers are specified in the Constitution. Provincial governments are allocated many of what in the last century have become the major spending domains, but relatively limited powers of taxation. The federal government's "spending power" has consequently meant that many otherwise provincial domains are effectively concurrent.

10. Additionally, in both cases, citizens must navigate the credit stealing and/or blame avoidance that tends to exist in domains where multiple governments exert policy-making power (see, especially, Harrison [1996]).

11. Indeed, federalism only matters to public responsiveness if policy making is not parallel across governments. If government policies move together over time, then responsiveness to one level of government is indistinguishable from responsiveness to another level of government.

12. Note that Cutler and Mendelsohn (2004) find that Canadians have relatively realistic views of the relative responsibility of federal and provincial governments in various domains. But assessing responsibility is, of course, different from reacting to actual policy, and what we are concerned with here is Canadians' capacity to respond to policy making by federal and provincial governments.

13. Note also that federalism can make representation more difficult, not just because there can be multiple governments acting in a single domain, but because public responsiveness may be confused. Under such circumstances the supply-side advantages of federalism cannot be realized. Multiple governments may seek to represent preferences, but in representing expressed (and confused) preferences, policy makers could do more to misrepresent real preferences than represent them.

14. Note that consolidated spending can be less than the simple sum of federal and provincial spending. This is because a federal–provincial transfer marked clearly for social assistance is counted as federal social assistance spending in series 1, and then as provincial social assistance spending in series 2. These funds are not double counted in the consolidated measure, however.

15. These data are drawn from Environics' Focus Canada omnibus surveys. Focus Canada is a national omnibus poll conducted quarterly since the late 1970s. Questions on spending are usually delivered in the third quarter of the current fiscal year. For subsequent analysis, we will, in the few missing years, using linear interpolation.

16. Note also that provincial governments could be spending the same amount of money differently. This is a version of cross-provincial difference that is not captured here—and another reason why public responsiveness to policy may be difficult.

17. And this responsiveness is roughly equal in both significance and magnitude.

REFERENCES

Achen, Christopher H. 1978. Measuring representation. *American Journal of Political Science* 22(3): 475–510.

Anderson, Cameron D. 2006. Economic voting and multilevel governance: A comparative individual-level analysis. *American Journal of Political Science* 50(2): 446–460.

Anderson, Cameron D., and Elizabeth Goodyear-Grant. 2006. Conceptions of political representation in Canada: An explanation of public opinion. *Canadian Journal of Political Science* 38(4): 1029–1058.

Bagehot, Walter. 1867. *The English Constitution*. Reprint. Ithaca, N.Y.: Cornell University Press, 1966.

Bartels, Larry M. 1991. Constituency opinion and congressional policy making: The Reagan defense buildup. *American Political Science Review* 85(2): 457–474.

Baumgartner, Frank, and Bryan D. Jones, eds. 2002. *Policy Dynamics*. Chicago, Ill.: University of Chicago Press.

Bélanger, Éric, and Francois Petry. 2005. The rational public? A Canadian test of the Page and Shapiro argument. *International Journal of Public Opinion Research* 17(2): 190–212.

Burstein, Paul. 2003. The impact of public opinion on public policy: A review and an agenda. *Political Research Quarterly* 56(1): 29–40.

Cairns, Alan C. 1977. The governments and societies of Canadian federalism. *Canadian Journal of Political Science* 10(4): 695–726.

————. 1991. *Disruptions: Constitutional Struggles from the Charter to Meech Lake*. Toronto: McClelland and Stewart.

Carty, R. Kenneth, Lisa Young, and William P. Cross. 2000. *Rebuilding Canadian Party Politics*. Vancouver: UBC Press.

Cox, Gary W. 1987. *The Efficient Secret: The Cabinet and the Development of Political Parties in Victorian England*. Cambridge: Cambridge University Press.

Cutler, Fred. 2004. Government responsibility and electoral accountability in federations. *Publius: The Journal of Federalism* 34(2): 19–38.

Cutler, Fred, and Matthew Mendelsohn. 2004. Unnatural loyalties or naïve collaborationists? The governments and citizens of Canadian federalism. In *Insiders and Outsiders: Essays in Honour of Alan C. Cairns*, ed. Philip Resnick and Gerald Kernerman, 71–89. Vancouver: UBC Press.

Dahl, Robert. 1971. *Polyarchy: Participation and Opposition*. New Haven, Conn.: Yale University Press.

Deutsch, Karl W. 1966. *The Nerves of Government: Models of Political Communication and Control*. New York: Free Press.

Diermeier, Daniel, and Tim Feddersen. 1998. Cohesion in legislatures and the vote of confidence procedure. *American Political Science Review* 92(3): 611–621.

Docherty, David Campbell. 1997. *Mr. Smith Goes to Ottawa: Life in the House of Commons*. Vancouver: UBC Press.

Downs, William M. 1999. Accountability payoffs in federal systems? Competing logics and evidence from Europe's newest federation. *Publius: The Journal of Federalism* 29(1): 87–110.

Easton, David. 1965. *A Framework for Political Analysis*. Englewood Cliffs, N.J.: Prentice-Hall.

Easton, David, Michael B. MacKuen, and James A. Stimson. 2002. *The Macro Polity*. Cambridge: Cambridge University Press.

Erikson, Robert S., Gerald C. Wright, and John P. McIver. 1993. *Statehouse Democracy: Public Opinion and Policy in the American States*. Cambridge: Cambridge University Press.

Franks, C. E. S. 1987. *The Parliament of Canada*. Toronto: University of Toronto Press.

Harrison, Kathryn. 1996. *Passing the Buck: Federalism and Canadian Environmental Policy*. Vancouver: UBC Press.

Howe, Paul, Richard Johnston, and André Blais, eds. 2005. *Strengthening Canadian Democracy*. Montreal: Institute for Research on Public Policy.

Howlett, Michael. 1998. Predictable and unpredictable policy windows: Institutional and exogenous correlates of Canadian federal agenda-setting. *Canadian Journal of Political Science* 31(3): 495–524.

Huber, John D. 1996. The vote of confidence in parliamentary democracies. *American Political Science Review* 90(2): 269–282.

Jennings, Sir Ivor. 1959. *Cabinet Government*. 3rd ed. Cambridge: Cambridge University Press.

Johnston, Richard. 1986. *Public Opinion and Policy in Canada: Questions of Confidence*. Toronto: University of Toronto Press.

Laver, Michael, and Kenneth A. Shepsle. 1996. *Making and Breaking Governments: Cabinets and Legislatures in Parliamentary Democracies*. Cambridge: Cambridge University Press.

Lippmann, Walter. 1925. *The Phantom Public*. New York: Harcourt, Brace.

Mallory, J.R. 1974. Responsive and responsible government. *Transactions of the Royal Society of Canada*, Fourth Series, XII: 207–225.

Manza, Jeff, and Fay Lomax Cook. 2002. A democratic polity? Three views of policy responsiveness to public opinion in the United States. *American Politics Research* 30: 630–667.

Monroe, Alan. 1979. Consistency between constituency preferences and national policy decisions. *American Politics Quarterly* 12(1): 3–19.

———. 1998. Public opinion and public policy, 1980–1993. *Public Opinion Quarterly* 62(1): 6–28.

Nevitte, Neil. 1996. *The Decline of Deference*. Peterborough, Ont.: Broadview Press.

Page, Benjamin I., and Robert Y. Shapiro. 1983. Effects of public opinion on policy. *American Political Science Review* 77: 175–190.

———. 1992. *The Rational Public: Fifty Years of Trends in Americans' Policy Preferences*. Chicago, Ill.: University of Chicago Press.

Penner, Erin, Kelly Blidook, and Stuart Soroka. 2006. Legislative priorities and public opinion: Representation of partisan agendas in the Canadian House of Commons. *Journal of European Public Policy* 13(7): 1006–1020.

Petry, Francois. 1999. The opinion—policy relationship in Canada. *Journal of Politics* 61(2): 540–550.

Petry, Francois, and Matthew Mendelsohn. 2004. Public opinion and policy making in Canada, 1995–2001. *Canadian Journal of Political Science* 27(3): 505–529.

Powell, G. Bingham, and Guy D. Whitten (1993). A cross-national analysis of economic voting: Taking account of the political context. *American Journal of Political Science* 37(2): 391–414.

Rousseau, Jean-Jacques. [1762] 1997. *The Social Contract and Other Later Political Writings*. Ed. and trans. Victor Gourevitch. Cambridge, UK: Cambridge University Press.

Savoie, Donald J. 1999. *Governing from the Centre: The Concentration of Power in Canadian Politics*. Toronto: University of Toronto Press.

Schumpeter, Joseph A. 1950. *Capitalism, Socialism and Democracy*, 3rd ed. New York: Harper and Row.

Seidle, F. Leslie. 2007. Citizens speaking for themselves: New avenues for public involvement. In *Political Leadership and Representation in Canada: Essays in Honour of John C. Courtney*, ed. Hans J. Michelmann, Donald C. Story, and Jeffrey S. Steeves, 81–109. Toronto: University of Toronto Press.

Simeon, Richard, and David Cameron. 2002. Federalism and democracy: An oxymoron if ever there was one? In *Canadian Federalism*, ed. Herman Bakvis and Grace Skogstad, 278–295. Toronto: Oxford University Press.

Smiley, Donald V. 1972. *Canada in Question: Federalism in the Seventies*. Toronto: McGraw-Hill Ryerson.

———. 1979. An outsider's observations of intergovernmental relations among consenting adults. In *Consultation or Collaboration: Intergovernmental Relations in Canada Today*, ed. Richard Simeon, 105–113. Toronto: Institute of Public Administration of Canada.

Soroka, Stuart. 2002. *Agenda-Setting Dynamics in Canada*. Vancouver: University of British Columbia Press.

Soroka, Stuart N., and Christopher Wlezien. 2004. Opinion representation and policy feedback: Canada in comparative perspective. *Canadian Journal of Political Science* 37(3): 531–560.

———. 2005. Opinion—policy dynamics: Public preferences and public expenditure in the United Kingdom. *British Journal of Political Science* 35: 665–689.

Stimson, James A. 1991. *Public Opinion in America: Moods, Cycles, and Swings (Transforming American Politics)*. Boulder, Colo.: Westview Press.

Stimson, James A., Michael B. MacKuen, and Robert S. Erikson. 1995. Dynamic representation. *American Political Science Review* 89(3): 543–565.

Strøm, Kaare. 2003. Parliamentary democracy and delegation. In *Delegation and Accountability in Parliamentary Democracies*, ed. Kaare Strøm, Wolfgang Muller, and Torbjorn Bergman, 55–106. Oxford: Oxford University Press.

Trudeau, Pierre Elliott. 1968. *Federalism and the French Canadians*. Toronto: Macmillan.

Tsebelis, George. 2002. *Veto Players: How Political Institutions Work*. New York: Russell Sage Foundation.

Watts, Ronald L. 1999. *Comparing Federal Systems*, 2nd ed. Kingston, Ont.: McGill-Queens University Press.

Watts, Ronald L., and Douglas M. Brown. 1990. *Canada: The State of the Federation, 1990*. Kingston: Institute of Intergovernmental Relations, Queen's University.

Wlezien, Christopher. 1995. The public as thermostat: Dynamics of preferences for spending. *American Journal of Political Science* 39(4): 981–1000.

———. 1996. Dynamics of representation: The case of U.S. spending on defense. *British Journal of Political Science* 26(1): 81–103.

———. 2004. Patterns of representation: Dynamics of public preferences and policy. *Journal of Politics* 66(1): 1–24.

———. 2005. On the salience of political issues: The problem with "most important problem." *Electoral Studies* 24(4): 555–579.

Wlezien, Christopher, and Stuart Soroka. 2007. The relationships between public opinion and policy. In *Oxford Handbook of Political Behavior*, ed. Russell Dalton and Hans-Deiter Klingemann. New York: Oxford University Press.

CHAPTER 16

POLITICS AND THE MEDIA: CULTURE, TECHNOLOGY, AND REGULATION

JONATHAN ROSE

PAUL NESBITT-LARKING

WHETHER from the perspective of Canadian media theory or from historical developments of politics and the media in Canada, the Canadian experience can be expressed as a series of dialectical tensions related to particular patterns of socioeconomic and political evolution. Although the dualities anchoring each term in these tensions are familiar to the point of cliché, they remain vital to understanding the relationship between power and representation in Canada: metropolis and hinterland, civilization and nature, garrison and wilderness, individualism and communitarianism, freedom and order, space and time, cool and hot, technology and humanist ethics. Each of these dualities reflects the tensions in communication that are constitutive of Canada itself. In most polities, communications, including the media, are regarded as forces that exert an impact on citizens. In Canada, communications are intrinsic to the very construction and reproduction of Canada itself and to the very possibility of Canada. It is largely for this reason that, among the social sciences, communications and media theory stand as Canada's most distinctive and profound contributions. The analysis of communication is not just important; it is largely through the analysis of communication that understanding Canada itself becomes possible.

In the next section, we present the familiar dialectics of Canadian communication that have deep roots in Canadian media theory. Then, in the following sections we explore how they have given shape to, respectively, the political economies, regulatory regimes, and dominant ideas that characterize politics and the media in Canada. In the current era of new information and communications technologies (ICTs), our final section explores not merely the globalization of the Canadian media, but also how the Canadian media experience is becoming more universal.

CANADIAN MEDIA THEORY:
TRADITION AND LEGACY

Canadian scholars have played a significant role in the development of media theory and have contributed much to the way scholars everywhere think about the media. This section examines three thinkers who have exerted a significant impact on our understanding of the media: Marshall McLuhan, Harold Innis, and Dallas Smythe. According to Babe (2000b) these writers are part of the core of what he terms the "quintessentially Canadian" contribution to communication studies. They are significant in that each has changed conventional understandings of the media. McLuhan, the originator of the expression "the medium is the message," is likely the best known of these three. He believes that the importance of the media message lies less in its content than in its form. Innis's work, which transcends economics, history, and communications, takes the form of a lifelong treatise into the nature of empire. His work on communication traces the space and time biases of media that have facilitated the growth of empire (space) or acted to buttress the sacred, the traditional, and the local (time). Dallas Smythe's critical work on the role and functions of the corporate media subverts traditional notions of the audience as a consumer of the media and posits the audience instead as a commodity for sale.

Appropriately for a professor of English, Marshall McLuhan uses the playfulness of the English language to make his arguments. His aphorisms rely on tropes such as metaphor or chiasmus. McLuhan understands communication metaphorically as an extension of humans, arguing that the electronic media extend our central nervous systems and, most famously, that in the television age our world becomes a global village. The media are not merely carriers of information, but, more important, are vehicles that change humanity through modes of interaction with them. A newspaper is less interesting for its content than for the way its technological form conditions its readers. McLuhan writes that people do not actually read papers, they step into them like a hot bath (McLuhan as cited in Knowles 1998, 201). According to Babe (2000b), McLuhan also uses chiasmus to great effect. It is a figure of speech where two clauses are repeated but inverted, as in Kennedy's "ask not what your country can do for you but what you can do for your country." Chiasmus allows McLuhan to assert rhetorically that virtue could become a vice, and that electronic media result in an implosion of information instead of explosion. Challenging us to "flip" our notions of cause and effect, McLuhan argues that the electronic media no longer extend the range of empire, but rather negate existing centers of power (Babe 2000b).

McLuhan's aphorism that the medium is the message prompts us to regard as important not what is written in a newspaper or viewed on television, but rather the effect that our engagement with these media has upon us. Literate cultures that rely on linear texts will generate different practices and values than cultures that rely on visual images, or preliterate cultures that depend on oral communication. In a telling and pertinent critique, McLuhan wrote that "political scientists have been quite unaware of the effects of the media anywhere at any time simply because nobody has been willing to study the personal and social effects of media apart from their 'content' " (McLuhan 1966, 328).

In conceptualizing categories of "hot" and "cool" media, McLuhan set in place a dialectical model of how media "work us over" (McLuhan 1967, 26). His metaphor of the temperature of media can be understood as measuring degrees of participation as well as degrees of information. Hot media are characterized by a dominant sense (such as aural or visual) and are "high definition" or information rich. Rather than engage us, they condition and direct us. Cool media engage several senses, are "low definition" or lacking in information, and require the active participation of the audience.

Although the application of McLuhan's work to Canadian political science remains underdeveloped, its orientation and its insights might be brought to bear on certain critical research questions. McLuhan's concept of the global village sensitizes us to the simultaneous and apparently contradictory forces of universalist dissemination and particularist retrenchment that have characterized the spread of global communications in recent decades. McLuhan's theory that any new technoculture enhances, obsolesces, retrieves, and reverses existing technological practices is able to enlighten our consideration of emerging new technologies as they affect the political process. Nowhere is McLuhan more relevant today than in the analysis of politics and the Internet.

McLuhan was greatly influenced by the writings of Harold Innis, whose expansive thoughts on technology, media, and the impact of communications in creating empire make him one of the most significant historians of media technology. In *The Bias of Communication*, Innis (1971) points out that technology itself can be a medium (Babe 2000a, 71). Communication technologies are situated between two poles: those that are biased toward space and those that have a bias toward time. Space-biased communication is information that is easily mobile and therefore allows for the expansion of empire and control, but, as a result of this, lacks permanence and is more transient than time-biased communication. Time-biased communication is that which emphasizes continuity and tradition and, although durable, is inflexible and immobile and therefore makes state expansion more difficult. Time-biased cultures privilege the oral over the written and are therefore confined by geography and the distinctiveness of language or dialect that makes them more parochial.

According to Innis (1971), the contemporary world has evolved in a highly space-biased direction as a result of the historical succession of a series of empires.

There is less regard for oral tradition or continuity with the past and we are more linear, more rational, and bureaucratic than in the world of antiquity. If time-biased cultures are marked by their slow adaptability, space-biased cultures are so adaptable that permanence is eschewed for continual change and planned obsolescence. As for the effects of media, this means the sources of information are mobile and multiple, and are able to be break down the barriers of space; they are also ephemeral and "thin" in cultural terms.

Media, for Innis, are technologies that synthesize human intentions in communication with available material resources and, through a process of transformation, give life to cultures and discourses. These media go on to assume a dominant monopolistic position in a society, shaping its interests and concerns in the media's own form. The interests of society become the interests of the media, and those interests are determined by their space or time bias. For Innis, Canada itself is a technological miracle, an ostensibly absurd artificial creation—a quasi-autonomous and privileged outpost—necessitated by the exigencies of empire, space, and capitalism despite the traditions of Aboriginal and early-settler cultures of time and tradition. The continuing tension between time and space is integral to the Canadian experience (Nesbitt-Larking 2007, 191). In the current era of globalization, in which imperialist hegemonies encounter global counterhegemonies of resistance, the ambivalent character of the Canadian experience is emerging as increasingly relevant to global politics. Innis's model establishes the complexities of space and time, and thereby opens up the exploration of how it is possible for the strategic spatial spread of bureaucratic global empires to be undermined by tactical maneuvers from the time-biased, sacred, and traditional interstices and margins.

If Innis and McLuhan regard the media of communications as conditioning cultures and ideologies, Dallas Smythe adopts a more materialistic approach, and argues that the media are principally in the business of selling audiences to advertisers. For Smythe (1981, 233), the audience commodity is the most important product of the mass media. In his radical view of media, Smythe explains that audiences are engaged in work on behalf of advertisers. The "work" of the audience is the task of training themselves through media exposure to be good consumers. The free lunch (Smythe 1977, 5) or inducement that audiences get consists of the programs that broadcasters produce to attract audiences to advertisements and thereby deliver them to advertisers. For Smythe (1978, 124) the free lunch of "stories, stars, songs and films are passed from one to another medium and there cross-blended with the dictates of advertisers." Advertisers are willing to "buy the services of audiences with predictable specifications who will pay attention in predictable numbers and at particular times to particular means of communication (TV, radio, newspapers, magazines)" (Smythe 1977, 4).

For Smythe, the media create audiences that are socialized to be consumers and therefore conditioned to believe in the sanctity of private property, the capitalist system, and a limited role of government. Second, the media produce consumers who define themselves by what they own, and respect the highly profitable large corporations. Smythe borrows C. B. Macpherson's (1975) theory of "possessive individualism" in explaining this culture of identity through ownership. Third, the media produce a quiescent public whose capacity to question the state is moderated by its consumerism. Smythe argues that the power to control information flows is the basis of political power in Canada (Babe 2000a, 137). Although Smythe is a materialist, he also recognizes that media are important agencies of socialization. Indeed, his work specifies that distinctive forms, genres, and channels operate to reproduce different audiences.

As with McLuhan's and Innis's ideas, Smythe's work is wide open to critique. Nonetheless, like them, he opens up lines of enquiry that are both highly useful in contemporary Canadian political analysis and are as yet underdeveloped. The political economy of "coping" that Smythe explains in detail in his work describes the role of the media, in collaboration with the state and the corporations, in nurturing and maintaining a credit economy in which consumers are encouraged to borrow against their own future and therefore the entire future of the capitalist system and are trapped in a personal world of anxious acquisitiveness that sets limits to their political consciousness. Of relevance today, Smythe's theory explains why websites are able to give away content for free. Like TV news programs, websites provide free content to create an audience to sell to advertisers. Smythe might say that websites are places for advertising banners and what they put around those banners (what we might call content) is less important than the ads.

THE POLITICAL ECONOMY OF THE CANADIAN MEDIA

As businesses, Canadian news and information media share in common the well-known characteristics of other enterprises in the era of rapid globalization. They are subject to growing pressures to accumulate, innovate, consolidate, and diversify in a transnational and increasingly liquid context. A major political consequence of these trends is to be found in the growing commodification of the news product, evident in shrinking and deskilled staffs, a growing dependency on the dominant wire services, an increasing resort to "pack journalism," the expansion of "infotainment" and tabloid reductionism, and the homogenization of the news genre. Such trends have been as apparent in Canada (Taras 1999) as they have in the United States (Bennett 2005). Mobility of capital has resulted in pressures toward deregulation that have opened up a range of technological and labor innovations based upon economies of scale, scope, and specialization. Flexible specialization in the labor process has resulted in the decline of the news media professional as cross-media synergies, technological convergences, and corporate conglomerations have blurred the boundaries between information and entertainment, news and opinion, and fact and fantasy. These dominant trends toward impoverished and generic news content have been further aggravated through perceptions of risk (Beck 1999) as well as global moral panic conditioned by antiterrorist discourses. The impact of global economic forces is readily apparent in recent developments in Canadian media. Apart from increasing pressures on the Canadian federal and provincial states to deregulate and divest themselves of public-sector media, there has been increasing pressure on the federal state to relax regulations on foreign ownership of the Canadian media (Skinner and Gasher 2005). After decades of resistance to cross-media ownership, the federal government relented in 1996 with its Convergence Policy Statement (Canada, Industry Canada 2008) and, beginning in 2000, three major corporate takeovers rapidly reshaped the media landscape. CanWest Global, with holdings in broadcast media, purchased the Southam-Hollinger chain of newspapers; Bell Canada acquired CTV and the *Globe and Mail* newspaper; while newspaper giant Quebecor took over cable company Videotron, the *Sun* chain of newspapers, and the TVA television network (Nesbitt-Larking 2007, 100, 117; Skinner and Gasher 2005, 52). In the case of each of these convergences, the principal players made the argument that for media in Canada to survive in a hostile and competitive global media environment, they needed to be able to expand their enterprises and operate in a less regulated climate, even to the extent of establishing made-in-Canada oligopolies.

Despite the global forces of contemporary capitalism, media enterprises in Canada have emerged within the context of a unique political economy, and it is important to note the Canadian specificities. These continue to shape media enterprises in Canada today. Notable is the relationship with American economy and society. Canada's media policy throughout the nineteenth and twentieth centuries was grounded in the ever-present reality that, because of the asymmetry of power, American culture and cultural products were so dominant within Canada that if Canadian federal and provincial states did nothing, they might become overwhelming. The liberal creed in the United States meant that it could adopt a *laissez-faire* attitude regarding culture and culture industries, including the media. The more strongly communitarian Canadian political values were necessary to meet the vast challenges of geography and ethnolinguistic divisions, and for the very existence of the country itself. These values, enshrined in public policies, survive in a complex web of foreign ownership regulations, media regulatory agencies, and a prominent public sector in broadcasting, reflecting Canada's distinctive political economy tradition.

An open and vibrant democracy thrives on the expression of diverse viewpoints and upon a serious and sustained public dialogue regarding matters of common concern. The importance of creating a vibrant civic forum was long ago recognized as an important element in democracy. The clearest exposition of this comes from Jürgen Habermas (1989), who writes about the importance of a public sphere where citizens can engage the state and each other in an informed manner. This exchange needs to be rooted in genuine conversation informed by good argumentation and bounded by a model of trust and reciprocity. In this ideal, the media can provide the equivalent of the Athenian *agora*—a place to talk, debate, and exchange ideas. Habermas believes that a shift from real to virtual communication, changing media ownership patterns, and the growing influence of advertisers have weakened this function.

Capitalism places the capacity to conduct those conversations and to express diverse views in the exclusive hands of private media owners. The 1981 Royal Commission on Newspapers (the Kent Commission) argued that "freedom of the press should continue to mean the freedom of the proprietor to do what he likes with his newspaper" (Canada 1981, 246), and yet also claimed that "freedom of the press is not a property right of owners. It is a right of the people" (Canada 1981, 1). Although Kent defended the principles of private enterprise and the narrow rights of owners, he also expressed support for a broader public interest in promoting dialogue and protecting the *agora*. The commission had been established in the aftermath of a huge and dramatic exchange of media properties between two media corporations, and the commission regarded with concern the impact of increased corporate concentration on the articulation of a diversity of viewpoints in the news media. Along with other cultural critics, the commission was concerned that as media organizations consolidated and became more oligopolistic, editorial quality would be compromised and sacrificed with a view to profit, accountability to audiences would be reduced, and the diversity of views expressed would become narrower. An oligopoly would not have to work so hard to attract and retain audiences and could remain profitable through the purchase of cheaper material to fill the news hole.

Canadian scholars had already considered that in a free market, the audience would not accept poor and declining editorial material and would seek alternative sources. This has become a vital question in the new millennium of major cross-media convergence and conglomerate takeovers in Canada. The consequences of these recent convergences have included slashed editorial staffs in newsrooms and the recycling of materials across various media. The new corporations have also taken to the mass circulation of highly opinionated editorializing from a small number of mostly conservative commentators and have largely abandoned local news and views. A small and demoralized skeleton news staff now operates in many newspapers across Canada and attempts to sustain the professionalism of its product while its labor process is increasingly deskilled. In this context, how have audiences responded?

A common response emerges from elite theorists. They argue that owners, often in collaboration with the state elites, impose their political wills through editorializing and sanctioned media texts. Media elites propagandize through their willful imposition of conservative and probusiness editorializing and biased news reporting. Such are the views of Chomsky and Herman (1988) and James Winter (2002) in Canada. Elites further their agenda through the production and distribution of mind-numbing distractions, infotainment, and cheap "gotcha" journalism that serve to entertain the masses and keep them from critical thinking and therefore political discontent. Audiences end up cynical, disillusioned, and depoliticized. David Taras (1999) regards with deep concern the trivialization of political and other media content in the Canadian media.

On a superficial level, citizens are exposed to a greater range of programming options than ever before. The Internet, online newspapers, and television programming provide a universe of news content unimaginable to our forefathers. On the other hand, this diversity has created what Taras (1999) calls "fragmentation bombs"—that is, diverse channels speak to specific communities defined by gender, hobby, age, religion, or other category. Although there may be a multiplicity of news, many authors question the genuine diversity of viewpoints expressed.

In terms of corporate control, James Curran (2005) persuasively argues that in our current age of media conglomeration, where a few media outlets control print and electronic media, the likelihood of a press that is independent of corporate control is slim. In some cases, there is even active collusion between the press and government. Italy's Silvio Berlusconi is one such example. Using his own media empire to propel him to the office of prime minister, he then used them to back his government's legislation in support of his own private fortune. In the United States, Fox News has been a virtual adjunct of the Republican Party, being criticized as "rabid proponents of the president's position and going out of their way to crush any critical opposition to it" (McChesney and Hackett 2005, 241). In other cases, "nonaggression pacts" are made between government and media, as was the case between then-Prime Minister Tony Blair and Rupert Murdoch, the head of the largest media corporation in the United Kingdom (Curran 2005, 125).

A cursory scan of recent developments in the Canadian media reveals sufficient instances of deliberate actions by media elites to lend support to the theory. This includes the growing tendency for some high-profile Canadian journalists to abandon their role as supposedly independent political observers to become highly paid public relations practitioners for governments and cabinet ministers. Also relevant here is the highly publicized firing of *Ottawa Citizen* editor Russell Mills, by the Aspers, Canada's leading media magnates. In defiance of the Aspers, Mills had written an editorial critical of then-Prime Minster Chrétien. Despite the heavy-handed interventions of Conrad Black and the Aspers in their newsrooms (Shade 2005), more probing accounts of the political content and editorial style of the media go beyond these voluntaristic and instrumentalist explanations and establish how structures of ownership and control as well as regulatory frameworks and dominant discourses give daily shape to the media texts that are produced. This more critical approach to the media and politics is evidenced in the work of Mosco (1996) and Magder (1989, 284), who adopt more complex and nuanced structuralist approaches, and Hackett (1986), Dyer-Witheford (2005), and Clarke (2005), who insist on the capacity of audiences to reduce, refuse, and recycle media content.

THE STATE AND REGULATION
OF THE MEDIA IN CANADA

In any capitalist economy, the state is powerfully shaped by the workings of the market, both within its territorial borders and beyond. However, the state is always much more than a result of economic forces. Nowhere is this more evident than in

Canada, which from its earliest origins was a political society whose very character-istics were powerfully shaped and conditioned by its federal and provincial states. Nonetheless, globalization has called into question the apparent certainties of the modern (Westphalian) model of the nation-states everywhere, including Canada. Matters of sovereignty, legitimacy, boundaries, and citizenship are increasingly in question. The very boundaries between state and civil society are far less certain than they were in the past.

Into this complex world of the Canadian federal and provincial states and global politics, the media in Canada are situated in a regulatory environment that is some-where between a state-centric past and an increasingly deregulated and globally flexible future. The background is best expressed in the comparable historical expe-riences of two waves of nation building: the national policy era of the 1870s and '80s, and the birth of the Canadian Broadcasting Corporation (CBC) in 1936 and the National Film Board (NFB) in 1939. More important, both eras were characterized by the strong federal state forging a pan-Canadian structure of communications to promote the very possibility of the Canadian nation. In the era of the national pol-icy, the principal bonds of communication linking the prairies to central Canada were the railroads, grain elevators, and telegraph lines. In the era of the CBC and the NFB, the bonds of communication were the radio stations, traveling documentary film projectionists, and powerful radio transmitter stations, beaming Canadian content in relay across an enormous and sparse landmass. Each of these eras of nation building can be characterized by the dominance of the Canadian state as sponsor and builder of the communications infrastructure in an interventionist, paternalistic, and cautious manner. The tenor of the role of the state in promoting and preserving Canadian communications, including the media, is evident in vari-ous commissions and documents that reveal the vision of a succession of political and corporate leaders, from the Aird Report of 1928 to the Report of the Parliamentary Committee on Canadian Heritage, *Our Cultural Sovereignty* (Canada 2003). The existence and continuity of Canada could never be taken for granted. In terms of its geopolitics, Canada was and continues to be an act of will in which the state played a key role in forging bonds of communication across the vast expanses of inhospi-table emptiness. To become a political reality, Canada needed to break from Britain and to avoid the almost overwhelming pressures to become an annex of the United States. Much of the character of media regulation, and the consequent structure and content of the Canadian media themselves, is the result of the constant need to counter the powerful political, economic, and cultural presence of the United States. The existence of a viable public media in Canada and the framework of regulations designed to protect Canadian ownership, talent, and content in the media are a consequence of the American presence.

Although it is becoming increasingly difficult to declare in any definitive way the boundaries of the state, and although it has always been a challenge to dis-cern the extent to which social organizations such as the media are within or beyond the state, it is possible to identify certain state structures and practices that operate to regulate the media. In Canada, a series of ten definable policy instruments and roles can be said to have influenced the operations of the media. As a *proprietor*, the state owns a series of important corporations and agencies including the CBC and the NFB, to which it devolves certain decision-making powers. As a *custodian*, the state owns museums and archives. The custodian role has important, if largely indirect, effects on the media of communication. The state is a *regulator* through its legislative authority to set standards and define property rights as well as through the work of its regulatory agencies, notably the Canadian Radio-television Telecommunications Commission (CRTC). Certain state laws and regulations, such as the Criminal Code, the Security of Information Act, and the Emergencies Act, enable the state to act as *censor*. The state also uses a range of softer policy instruments, acting as *patron* through its control of the purse, offering grants and prizes, and acting as a *catalyst* in stimulating media through tax incentives, subsidies, and other incentives. Finally, state institutions and practices themselves are objects of interest and routinely interact with the media. The state is a central *actor*, a supplier of important news material. It is authoritative and, in a political economy of declining story resources and inadequate investigative news professionals, state institutions and personnel generate dramatic and cheap copy on a routine basis and with the appearance of objectivity. In the Canadian media, state elites routinely establish the agenda. On the basis of elite theory, the state can also be regarded as *ideologue* and even *conspirator*, and its personnel and their staffs can be seen to spin and privilege certain interpretations of fact as news *masseurs*.

In the language of neoliberalism, the Social Investment State (Giddens 1998) brings substantial pressure on the state to reduce its role as proprietor, custodian, patron, and regulator. Budgets for the CBC and the NFB have been substantially reduced, whereas staffs, programs, and bureaus have been cut (Nesbitt-Larking 2007, 129). A series of public–private initiatives in patronage, such as Telefilm Canada, have developed, and the federal and provincial states and their agencies have been under great pressure to deregulate. As Mosco (1996, 201) points out, however, a diminution in state regulation does not mean a reduction in regulation of the media as such. Instead, it implies a corresponding increase in market regulation of the media, and this has direct consequences for news and informational content as well as other decisions of channel, carriage, and content. Moreover, deregulation of the private sector has been accompanied by incremental losses of independence among the various agencies, boards, and commissions established, ostensibly at arm's length, from the government. The CBC, Telefilm Canada, the NFB, and the CRTC have increasingly been micromanaged and placed under scrutiny and pressure from governments.

An increasingly important element of in-state regulation of the media in Canada is the judicial system (Martin 2003). This is particularly critical in the post–September 11 condition of information control, surveillance, and secrecy. Freedom of the press, enshrined in section 2 (b) of the Charter, has been entrenched as a right in Canada since 1982. However, media freedom has never been an absolute right. The various counterbalances that have been established throughout the decades reflect a complex of factors that are grounded in the need to maintain order and the desire to promote equality. The right of the public to know, so proudly entrenched in the First Amendment to the U.S. Constitution, has traditionally taken a back seat to the self-assigned duty of elites to maintain peace, order, and good government, and to administer sober and discreet justice. Canada's Security of Information Act (2001) and its predecessor, the Official Secrets Act (1939), have been potential bludgeons on the statute books to be used at the discretion of the state to prevent the dissemination of a broad range of matters that they deem to be of importance to national security (Siegel 1996, 63–69). Elements of the law have been invoked to silence professional journalists in Canada. In November 2004, the Royal Canadian Mounted Police used section 4 of the Security of Information Act to raid the home of *Ottawa Citizen* foreign affairs correspondent Juliet O'Neil, confiscating her computers, papers, and files. Following a series of appeals, Ontario Superior Court Judge Ratushny struck down section 4 of the Security of Information Act, ruling that it was "unconstitutionally vague" and that it unreasonably limited freedom of expression. Despite this partial redress in favor of media freedom, the existence of laws and regulations of such generality condition journalists to exercise caution and self-censorship. To the extent that the state can sustain a climate of risk, fear, and ambiguity, the routine tasks of maintaining order and legitimating dominant discourses are undertaken by those who are objects of state surveillance, rather than by the institutions and personnel of the state itself. The tentacles of the state can be said to take control of media professionals themselves, who then become (indirectly) a part of the apparatus of government (Rose 1999). To the extent that the climate of risk and fear escalates into an apprehended threat to the state itself, so the agency of media professionals is drawn closer into the service of censorship and agitational propaganda (Compton 2004; Peers 1973, 323).

The media are essential to democracy just as are political parties, open and free elections, and the rule of law. A free press is vital in a democracy for a very basic reason. It keeps the state's power in check and expose abuses of authority. In eighteenth-century Britain, where power resided with the estates of the clergy, the nobility, and elected commons, Edmund Burke famously observed that "yonder there sat a Fourth Estate more powerful far than they all" (attributed to Burke in Carlyle [1907], 228). Robert Hackett and Yuezhi Zhao (1998, 1) suggest that "journalism is arguably the most important form of public knowledge in contemporary society. The mass media…have become the leading institution of the public sphere." The task of the media is nothing less than providing the requisite information to citizens so that they can fulfill the demands of democracy and understand the world around them. According to Pippa Norris (2000, 12), the functions of the media are to create a civic forum to encourage public debate, to act as watchdogs against abuses of state power, and to mobilize the public to learn about politics and become active in the political process.

Culture, Ideology, and Discourse: The Cultivation of Knowledge and Value in Canada

The media are key actors in the production and reproduction of ideas and ideals in a polity. Media organizations, their key personnel, and the texts they generate are profoundly important agencies in the promotion of knowledge, insight, and viewpoint. For this reason, a great deal of media research in Canada and beyond explores the politics of gatekeeping, agenda setting, framing, and priming (Nesbitt-Larking 2007, 331–337). Gatekeeping describes the propensity of news professionals to tame the information tide by reducing the enormous floods of news stories to manageable trickles of media content, thereby determining what gets into the news. Agenda setting refers to correlations between the issues reported in the media and those that media consumers find most important (McCombs and Shaw 1972). By focusing on certain issues (and therefore ignoring others) the media shape what citizens believe to be significant. The impact of agenda setting is influenced by a number of different factors, such as how abstract or concrete a story is, whether it is dramatic, if readers had prior knowledge of it, and how long the story lasts. Framing describes the way media professionals construct a news story through context, background, and orientation, thereby privileging certain readings and constructions. Priming refers to standards that people use to evaluate leaders, governments, parties, or issues (Iyengar and Kinder 1987) and is a consequence of agenda setting. Scholars such as Linda Trimble (2005), who write about women in politics, remind us that the media prime the public through the use of sexist stereotypes to frame female politicians in a manner that identifies successful political role models with males.

Media organizations and personnel operate in a field of societal ideas in which they are both senders and receivers, and in which it is often impossible to distinguish among the multiplicity of voices. Contemporary social theory uses the concept of discourse to express the range of more or less coherent systems of belief and value that are available to social actors. To engage in discourse is to contribute to the production and reproduction of texts. Texts can be spoken or written, and they can assume almost any symbolic form. What these symbolic forms share is the capacity—more or less opaque—to render or represent the world. Less obvious, but of equal importance, is the capacity of discourses to shape, condition, and change the world. Discourses use a range of narrative forms in which to encode symbols and render them expressive. Discourses are operational across a range of sociopsychological settings—from media texts through dialogue and deliberation, and the reproduction of symbols to the internal argumentation of the process of thinking (Billig 1991, 14). In their very invocation and use, discourses exert material effects on the worlds in which they are at play. As primary definers of political reality, the media clearly have a critical role to play in the reproduction of organizations, institutions, ideals, policies, and practices.

Discourses are the symbolic outcomes of arguments and as such are ideologically constituted entities. Discourses privilege certain readings of the world and prefer certain interpretations. To infuse a discourse with particular patterns of ideas that purport to explain and justify the world—ostensibly in the interests of all, but actually to the advantage of specific communities—is to engage in ideological work. Ideologies themselves are the consequence of the deliberate selection and shaping of ideas and ideals found in a broadly available political culture. Agents promoting an ideological orientation adopt one or more generic elements in the diffuse culture and then represent them in a more or less coherent view of the world. Discourses are the ideal site in which to unearth the work of ideology in shaping and privileging aspects of the broader culture through the subjective and intersubjective work of reception.

Although there is an impressive tradition of research on the ideological character of Canadian media content (Grenier 1991; Winter 2002), much of it is articulated around an instrumentalist view of ideology as the imposition of "false consciousness" and of mass audiences as passive recipients. Recent Canadian scholarship is now adopting a more balanced and better informed view of media audiences (Clarke 2005; Dyer-Witheford 2005), one that takes into account the capacity of media audiences to discriminate, to decode, to seek out counterdiscourses, and to deconstruct. The mainstream media may indeed prefer and privilege certain discourses, and in the context of global corporate convergence deliver conservative, stereotyped, and sensationalist material. Graham Knight (1991) explains how, through its skills in manipulating television conventions to look "real," tabloid television has been able to win and maintain large audiences. Using a variety of techniques and tapping into a range of broadly accepted cultural conventions, tabloid television has been able to win our trust and in so doing reproduce cynical and righteous conservative discourses that reproduce fear and contempt through constant portrayals of greed and corruption on the part of the elites, and violent, unpredictable rage on the part of social deviants. The news anchors and hosts of tabloid television set themselves up as the righteous voice of reason and the bearers of commonsense decency. Tabloid television does not have to explain itself or its promotion of certain ideological values, because as a genre its codes and conventions actually index whatever it is they purport to be displaying.

Tabloid television is clever and innovative, but it struggles to stay ahead of the discursive sophistication of its audiences. In the contemporary setting of multiple sources of political information and opinion, and of increasingly critical and discriminating audiences, cheap, sensationalized, clichéd, and ideologically slanted media texts may satisfy some of the people, some of the time. Not, however, younger and better educated Canadians, who have either turned off or are tuning into the reinvention of political journalism that is taking place on late-night comedy–news shows, or engaging themselves in cyberactivism.

Public journalism, also known as *civic journalism*, is a movement designed to put the media back in the center of the public debate. Public journalism asks journalists to address citizens as participants, not spectators; seeks to help the public to go beyond mere learning and act on its problems; and attempts to improve the climate of public discussion (Rosen 1999, 262). This is achieved through town hall meetings and creating opportunities for meaningful deliberation and debate. Public journalism initiatives are a further expression of informed citizens with the will to act as their own gatekeepers and agenda setters free from both the impoverishing impact of the corporate media and regulation from the state and media professionals. In conclusion, although it is true to say that Canadian states appear to be decreasingly capable of regulating media corporations, neither states nor corporations can keep up with the increasingly daunting challenge of regulating audiences.

CONCLUSION: THE FUTURE OF THE MASS MEDIA?

The emerging research on new ICTs and Canadian politics tends to support Small's (2007) thesis that the use of cyberspace adds little that is new to existing modes of communication and that the Internet is basically used "to amplify traditional methods of campaigning." In McLuhan's terms, our initial use of any new medium is conditioned by expectations that have been generated through the use of the old medium. Just as TV was initially used in a "radiolike" manner, so our use of the Internet by established political actors is struggling to move beyond TV mode. In its Canadian context, the Internet is embedded in the sociocultural, economic, and political realities already outlined in this chapter. The familiar dialectical tensions and the forces and relations that have shaped the national experience will therefore inform the character of whatever new ICTs emerge. At the same time, ICTs open up a plethora of new possibilities.

Much has been written on the decline of traditional media and the impact of the Internet on both the business side as well as the consumption side of mass media. Although it is true that network news viewing is losing share to the Internet (Davis 1999; Tremayne 2007), the implications of the Internet on news reporting, dissemination, and production are not clear. Some see the Internet as a great democratizing influence, creating multiple channels and allowing anyone with a computer to be a creator and consumer of news. Others see the Internet as further evidence that serious journalism is on the decline.

On the news-reporting side, it is clear that blogs have changed the nature of news reporting. Although the vast majority of blogs are about personal expression, several prominent ones, such as those of Americans Matt Drudge and Ariana Huffington, and Canadians Warren Kinsella, Andrew Coyne, and Garth Turner, have a devoted and influential audience on political matters. The blurring of the boundary lines between casual opinion and news professionalism marks a late-modern development in information flow that some regard with concern and others find liberating. Whether they are a new outlet for the corporate media, a soapbox for the disaffected and marginalized, or a voice for average citizens, blogs offer easy access to potentially large audiences.

Rapid dissemination is both the greatest strength and the profoundest weakness of blogs. A strong ideologically driven network of independent bloggers is most effective in responding to a story in the mainstream media. This allows for easy and effective mobilization of issue publics but means that those quality checks and constraints that are imposed on the professional media are absent. The range of diversity of quality among blogs makes them more akin to the penny press of the nineteenth century than to what remains of traditional journalism today. In this regard, the future of the media may in some ways approximate its past, with the reemergence of an uncontrolled mélange of fact, opinion, gossip, and vitriol.

The Internet has already had a dramatic effect on the way citizens consume the news. According to Ahlers (2006, 34), "the concept of single media use is fading." One study found that there is very little difference in the minds of consumers between online news and its hard-copy version and that consumers do not see these as competition to one another but rather as complementary. Contemporary modes of media consumption are both multichannel and multimedia. Younger users in particular report listening to the radio while online (47%), while 33% watch TV while online and 44% talk on the phone while on the Internet (Ahlers 2006, 34). The new realities of ICTs in the Canadian mediascape have done little to shift the fundamentals of media and politics in Canada that we have outlined. However, certain trends are emerging that suggest important developments in the future. The dialectics of those Canadian dualities that constructed Canada as an outpost of empire long ago resulted in a distinctive balance between technology and nature and a polity of cautious expansionism, giving rise to a constant tension between danger and opportunity. In the era of globalization, this Canadian experience has found increasing resonance through the emerging identity struggles of late-modern political movements worldwide. To the extent that ICTs are changing the Canadian political landscape, it is through the agency of new audiences. Audiences are much more active in the creation of political information than they ever have been. The multimedia environment, blogs, and other innovations in ICTs, such as ubiquitous cameras and instant messaging, are reshaping political consciousness and political cultures. In so doing, they are setting limits to the possibilities of any ideological forces that might emerge. Corporate conglomerates remain powerful and continue to move toward oligopoly through mergers and convergences. Canadian states retain their legitimacy and their coercive force. However, the role of the media in Canadian politics depends in the end upon what Edwin Black (1982, 149) said long before the rise of the new ICTs: "In much of the heated debate about the power of the mass media, one critical factor is neglected: the audience. Is anybody paying attention?"

REFERENCES

Ahlers, Douglas. 2006. News consumption and the new electronic media. *International Journal of Press/Politics* 11(1): 29–52.

Babe, Robert. 2000a. *Canadian Communication Thought: Ten Foundational Writers.*
    Toronto: University of Toronto Press.
———. 2000b. Foundations of Canadian communication thought. *Canadian Journal of
    Communication* 25(1): 19–37.
Beck, Ulrich. 1999. *The Reinvention of Politics: Rethinking Modernity in the Global Social
    Order.* Cambridge: Polity Press.
Bennett, W. Lance. 2005. *News: The Politics of Illusion*, 6th ed. New York: Pearson Longman.
Billig, Michael. 1991. *Ideology and Opinions: Studies in Rhetorical Psychology.* London: Sage
    Publications.
Black, Edwin. 1982. *Politics and the News: The Political Functions of the Mass Media.*
    Toronto: Butterworths.
Canada. 1981. *Report of the Royal Commission on Newspapers.* Royal Commission on
    Newspapers (The Kent Commission). Ottawa: Supply and Services Canada.
———. 2003. *Our Cultural Sovereignty: The Second Century of Canadian Broadcasting.*
    Standing Committee on Canadian Heritage. Ottawa: Communications
    Canada—Publishing.
Canada, Industry Canada. 2008. Convergence policy statement. March 22. http://www.ic
    .gc.ca/epic/site/smt-gst.nsf/en/sf05265e.html.
Carlyle, Thomas. [1841] 1907. *On Heroes, Hero-Worship and the Heroic in History.* Boston,
    Mass.: Houghton Mifflin Company.
Chomsky, Noam, and Edward Herman. 1988. *Manufacturing Consent: The Political
    Economy of the Mass Media.* New York: Pantheon.
Clarke, Debra. 2005. Bourdieu's "show and hide" paradox reconsidered: Audience experiences
    of convergence in the Canadian mediascape. In *Converging Media, Diverging Politics:
    A Political Economy of News Media in the United States and Canada*, ed. David Skinner,
    James R. Compton, and Michael Gasher, 165–186. Lanham, Md.: Lexington Books.
Compton, James. 2004. *The Integrated News Spectacle: A Political Economy of Cultural
    Performance.* New York: Peter Lang.
Curran, James. 2005. Mediations on democracy. In *Mass Media and Society*, 4th ed., ed.
    James Curran and Michael Gurevitch, 122–153. London: Oxford University Press.
Davis, Richard. 1999. *The Web of Politics.* New York: Oxford University Press.
Dyer-Witheford, Nick. 2005. Canadian cyberactivism in the cycle of counterglobalization
    struggles. In *Converging Media, Diverging Politics: A Political Economy of News Media
    in the United States and Canada*, ed. David Skinner, James R. Compton, and Michael
    Gasher, 267–290. Lanham, Md.: Lexington Books.
Giddens, Anthony. 1998. *The Third Way: The Renewal of Social Democracy.* Cambridge: Polity.
Grenier, Marc, ed. 1991. *Critical Studies of Canadian Mass Media.* Toronto: Butterworths.
Habermas, Jürgen. 1989. *The Structural Transformation of the Public Sphere: An Enquiry into
    a Category of Bourgeois Society.* Cambridge, Mass.: MIT Press.
Hackett, Robert. 1986. For a socialist perspective on the news media. *Studies in Political
    Economy* 19: 141–156.
Hackett, Robert, and Yuezhi Zhao. 1998. *Sustaining Democracy: Journalism and the Politics
    of Objectivity.* Toronto: Garamond Press.
Innis, Harold. 1971. *The Bias of Communication.* Toronto: University of Toronto Press.
Iyengar, Shanto, and Donald Kinder. 1987. *News That Matters: Television and American
    Opinion.* Chicago, Ill.: University of Chicago Press.
Knight, Graham. 1991. The reality effects of tabloid television news. In *Communication For
    and Against Democracy*, ed. Marc Raboy and Peter Bruck, 111–129. Toronto:
    Butterworths.

Knowles, Elizabeth, ed. 1998. *The Oxford Dictionary of Twentieth Century Quotations.* Oxford: Oxford University Press.

Macpherson, C. B. 1975. *The Political Theory of Possessive Individualism: Hobbes to Locke.* London: Oxford University Press.

Magder, Ted. 1989. Taking culture seriously: A political economy of communications. In *The New Canadian Political Economy*, ed. Wallace Clement and Glen Williams, 278–296. Kingston: McGill Queens University Press.

Martin, Robert. 2003. *Media Law*, 2nd ed. Toronto: Irwin Law.

McChesney, Robert, and Robert Hackett. 2005. Beyond wiggle room: American corporate media's democratic deficit, its global implications, and prospects for reform. In *Democratizing Global Media: One World, Many Struggles*, ed. Robert Hackett and Yuezhi Zhao, 225–267. Lanham, Md.: Rowman and Littlefield.

McCombs, Maxwell, and Donald Shaw. 1972. Agenda-setting function of mass media. *Public Opinion Quarterly* 36(2): 176–187.

McLuhan, Marshall. 1966. *Understanding Media: The Extensions of Man.* New York: McGraw-Hill.

———. 1967. *The Medium Is the Massage.* London: Penguin.

Mosco, Vincent. 1996. *The Political Economy of Communication: Rethinking and Renewal.* London: Sage.

Nesbitt-Larking, Paul. 2007. *Politics, Society and the Media*, 2nd ed. Peterborough: Broadview.

Norris, Pippa. 2000. *A Virtuous Circle: Political Communications in Postindustrial Societies.* Cambridge: Cambridge University Press.

Peers, Frank. 1973. *The Politics of Canadian Broadcasting, 1920–1951.* Toronto: University of Toronto Press.

Rose, Nikolas S. 1999. *Powers of Freedom: Reframing Political Thought.* Cambridge: Cambridge University Press.

Rosen, Jay. 1999. *What Are Journalists For?* New Haven, Conn.: Yale University Press.

Shade, Leslie Regan. 2005. Aspergate: Concentration, convergence, and censorship in Canadian media. In *Converging Media, Diverging Politics: A Political Economy of News Media in the United States and Canada*, ed. David Skinner, James R. Compton, and Michael Gasher, 101–116. Lanham, Md.: Lexington Books.

Siegel, Arthur. 1996. *Politics and the Media in Canada*, 2nd ed. Toronto: McGraw-Hill Ryerson.

Skinner, David, and Mike Gasher. 2005. So much by so few: Media policy and ownership in Canada. In *Converging Media, Diverging Politics: A Political Economy of News Media in the United States and Canada*, ed. David Skinner, James R. Compton, and Michael Gasher, 51–76. Lanham, Md.: Lexington Books.

Small, Tamara. 2007. Canadian cyberparties: Reflections on Internet-based campaigning and party systems. *Canadian Journal of Political Science* 40(3): 639–657.

Smythe, Dallas. 1977. Communications: Blindspot of western Marxism. *Canadian Journal of Political and Social Theory* 1(3): 1–27.

———. 1978. Rejoinder to Graham Murdock. *Canadian Journal of Political and Social Theory* 2(2): 120–126.

———. 1981. On the audience commodity and its work. In *Media and Cultural Studies: Keyworks*, ed. Meenakshi Gigi Durham and Douglas M. Kellner, 230–256. Malden, Mass.: Blackwell.

Taras, David. 1999. *Power and Betrayal in the Canadian Media.* Peterborough: Broadview.

Tremayne, Mark, ed. 2007. *Blogging, Citizenship, and the Future of Media.* London: Routledge.

Trimble, Linda. 2005. "Who framed Belinda Stronach? National newspaper coverage of the
    Conservative Party of Canada's 2004 leadership race." Presented at the 2005 Canadian
    Political Science Association Conference, University of Western Ontario, London,
    Ontario, June 2–4.
Winter, James. 2002. *Media Think*. Montreal: Black Rose Books.

PART V

CANADIAN SOCIETY

CHAPTER 17

....

ETHNIC, LINGUISTIC, AND MULTICULTURAL DIVERSITY OF CANADA

....

WILL KYMLICKA

THE past twenty years have witnessed growing pessimism around the world about the effects of ethnic diversity. Study after study has suggested that ethnic heterogeneity is a "problem" along multiple dimensions. Studies seem to show, for example, that countries with higher levels of ethnic heterogeneity are likely to be less peaceful, less democratic, have lower economic growth, and lower levels of social spending to help the needy.[1] High levels of ethnic diversity, in short, are widely seen as dangerous and dysfunctional for modern societies. Moreover, this threat is said to be exacerbated by the increasing tendency of ethnic minorities to mobilize politically for public recognition in the form of multiculturalism and minority rights. In an era of "identity politics," the effects of ethnic heterogeneity have become more pronounced.

Against this background, Canada stands out as an important exception. It contains very high levels of diversity—indeed, it is a statistical outlier among western democracies in its level of ethnic, linguistic, and religious diversity (Laczko 1994). Moreover, Canada has actively embraced the politics of multiculturalism and minority rights, giving public recognition and accommodation to its ethnic and linguistic diversity in a wide range of public institutions. Yet, it remains a peaceful and prosperous democracy, with a reasonably well-developed welfare state.

For this reason, Canada is often invoked as a "counternarrative" to the "master narrative" of ethnic heterogeneity's pernicious effects (Banting 2005). The Canadian experience suggests that the effects of ethnic diversity and identity politics are not predetermined, and that an explicitly multicultural form of democratic citizenship is viable. Not surprisingly, academic experts and policy makers from around the world have become interested in understanding the Canadian experience, and in exploring its relevance for other countries. As a recent *Globe and Mail* article put it, "Pluralism: The world wonders how we pull it off" (Ibbitson 2004).

Yet this "Canadian model" has its own share of stresses and controversies. Many commentators worry that Canada has gone too far in accommodating diversity, and that current policies are unsustainable. In this chapter, I will outline the basic features of the Canadian approach to ethnic diversity, and identify some of the controversies and challenges it faces.

MAPPING DIVERSITY IN CANADA

Issues of accommodating diversity have been central to Canada's history. In the seventeenth and eighteenth centuries, the earliest European settlers had to reach a modus vivendi with Aboriginal peoples; in the eighteenth and nineteenth centuries, the British colonial administrators had to learn to live with the long-settled French population; and in the nineteenth and twentieth centuries, Canada has had to accommodate successive waves of immigration. At each step along the way, Canada's stability and prosperity—and indeed its very survival—depended on being able to respond constructively to new forms of diversity, and to develop new relationships of coexistence and cooperation, without undermining the (often-fragile) accommodations of older forms of diversity, which are themselves continually being contested and renegotiated.

This long history of diversity has resulted in a "palimpsest" of federal laws and policies, with new layers continually being added on top of the old (Green 2005). Recent multiculturalism policies for ethnic groups formed by immigration overlay earlier linguistic and territorial accommodations of French Canadians, which overlay earlier historical agreements and settlements with Aboriginal peoples.[2]

If we look carefully at these policies, however, they appear not so much as three horizontal layers, but rather as three vertical silos (Kymlicka 2007a). One striking aspect of these accommodations is how disconnected they are from each other, legally and administratively. These policies not only have different historical origins, but are embodied in different pieces of legislation, administered by different federal government departments, enshrined in different sections of the Constitution, and are articulated and negotiated using different concepts and principles. As a result, each forms its own discrete silo, with very little interaction among them.

To oversimplify, we can say that in the case of Aboriginal peoples, the historic roots lie in the Royal Proclamation of 1763; the framework piece of legislation is the Indian Act; the key constitutional provisions are sections 25 and 35 of the Constitution Act, 1982; the main federal department responsible for administering and coordinating Aboriginal issues is Indian and Northern Affairs; and the guiding concepts used in articulating claims include treaty rights, Aboriginal rights, common-law title, sui generis property rights, fiduciary trust, indigeneity, self-government, and self-determination.

In the case of the French Canadians, the historic roots lie in the Quebec Act of 1774 and the British North America Act (BNA Act) of 1867; the framework piece of legislation is the Official Languages Act; the key constitutional provisions are sections 16 to 23 of the Charter; the coordinating federal government agencies are Intergovernmental Affairs (within the Privy Council Office) and the Commissioner for Official Languages; and the main concepts used in articulating claims include bilingualism, duality, (asymmetrical) federalism, distinct society, and nationhood.

In the case of immigrant/ethnic groups, the historic touchstone is the 1971 parliamentary statement of multiculturalism, the framework legislation is the Multiculturalism Act, the key constitutional provision is section 27 of the Charter, the coordinating federal government departments are Canadian Heritage and Citizenship and Immigration, and the key concepts include multiculturalism, citizenship, integration, tolerance, ethnicity, diversity, and inclusion.

Whenever claims relating to the accommodation of ethnocultural diversity are made (or contested) in Canada, the political engagement almost invariably takes place within one of these three silos. Each silo has its own well-established entry points and opportunity structures, and anyone who wishes to participate effectively in these political debates must use these access points, and master the relevant laws, constitutional provisions, and terminology. Given this tripartite structure, it is misleading to talk of *the* Canadian model of diversity, as if there was one overarching policy on diversity from which policies regarding Aboriginal peoples, francophones, and immigrant/ethnic groups are derived. There are just the three silos, with their own separate histories, discourses, legal frameworks, and governance structures.

EVOLVING FORMS OF ACCOMMODATING DIVERSITY

Although each of these three silos has a long history, there have been dramatic changes over the past forty years in relation to all three, moving in the direction of greater recognition of diversity. Let me start with the case of immigrant/ethnic groups.

Immigrant/Ethnic Groups

The terms *ethnic groups* and *immigrant groups* are often used interchangeably in Canada to refer to those who are neither indigenous nor colonizers, but were admitted under Canada's immigration policy. However, the term *immigrant group* is potentially misleading, because many of the group's members may be second, third, or fourth generation. This is obviously true of those ethnic groups, such as the Ukrainians, Poles, or Jews, who have been in Canada for more than one hundred years. By contrast, other ethnic groups such as the Vietnamese or Somalis are more recent—having arrived only in the past thirty years—and many of their members are still foreign-born immigrants.

Ethnic groups are a major element in Canadian society. First-generation immigrants—in other words, the foreign-born population—formed more than 18% of the overall population according to the 2001 Census. If we add the descendants of earlier waves of immigration, the percentage of Canadians who have origins other than British, French, or indigenous rises to around 50%.[3] So the issue of the status and treatment of ethnic groups has been an important and long-standing one in Canada.

In the past, Canada, like the other major British settler societies (the United States, Australia, New Zealand), had an assimilationist approach to immigration. Immigrants were encouraged and expected to assimilate to the preexisting British mainstream culture, with the hope that over time they would become indistinguishable from native-born British Canadians in their speech, dress, recreation, and way of life in general.[4] Indeed, any groups that were seen as incapable of this sort of cultural assimilation (such as Asians and Africans) were prohibited from emigrating to Canada or from becoming citizens.

This racially discriminatory and culturally assimilationist approach to ethnic groups was slowly discredited in the postwar period, but was only officially repudiated in the late 1960s and early '70s. There were two related changes. First, the adoption of race-neutral admissions criteria (the "points system"), so that immigrants to Canada are increasingly from non-European (and often non-Christian) societies. This change was completed by 1967. Second, the adoption of a more "multicultural" conception of integration, one that expects that many immigrants will visibly and proudly express their ethnic identity, and that accepts an obligation on the part of public institutions (like the police, schools, media, museums, and so forth) to accommodate these ethnic identities. This second change was formalized in 1971, with the adoption of the multiculturalism policy by the federal government.

The original goals of the policy were fourfold:

1. To "assist all Canadian cultural groups that have demonstrated a desire and effort to continue to develop a capacity to grow and contribute to Canada"
2. To "assist members of all cultural groups to overcome cultural barriers to full participation in Canadian society"
3. To "promote creative encounters and interchange among all Canadian cultural groups in the interest of national unity"
4. To "assist immigrants to acquire at least one of the Canada's official languages in order to become full participants in Canadian society"[5]

There have been various changes to the policy since 1971, primarily in the relative emphasis given to these four goals. Over time, starting in the mid 1970s, the second and third goals have increasingly received the lion's share of funding under the program. However, the core ideas have remained fairly stable: recognition and accommodation of cultural diversity, removing barriers to full participation, promoting interchange among groups, and promoting acquisition of the official languages. The policy was reaffirmed and given a statutory basis in the Canadian Multiculturalism Act of 1988. It was "renewed" again in 1997, after twenty-five years of operation, after a major policy review.[6]

Multiculturalism is best known as a policy of the *federal* government in Canada, and the Canadian Multiculturalism Act only covers federal departments and agencies. However, versions of the policy have been adopted as well by provincial and municipal governments, and even by businesses and civil society organizations, which is a testament to multiculturalism's "long march through the institutions," as socialists used to put it. Standing at the apex of this field of multiculturalism policies is the multiculturalism clause of the Constitution Act, 1982. Section 27 of the Constitution Act states that the Charter of Rights and Freedoms will be "interpreted in a manner consistent with the preservation and enhancement of the multicultural heritage of Canadians." This clause does not guarantee that multiculturalism policies will exist in perpetuity in Canada, or that the funds available for these programs will not be cut, but it does provide some symbolic affirmation of the public commitment to the goals of multiculturalism, and serves to place it above the fray of partisan politics.

This, then, is a brief outline of the basic contours of Canada's policy toward immigrant/ethnic diversity, and the shift from racial exclusion and cultural assimilation to race-neutral admissions and multicultural integration. This shift was remarkably quick, given the breadth of changes involved. The initial demands by ethnic groups for a "multiculturalism" policy arose in the mid 1960s, it was declared official public policy in 1971, and the administrative framework for implementing the program had been worked out by the mid 1970s. So the new contours of this first diversity silo essentially took shape between 1965 and 1975. Although the policy was (and remains) contested, for reasons I discuss later, it quickly became so embedded in Canadian political life that it was seen as appropriate to enshrine a multiculturalism clause in the Constitution in 1982. In short, multiculturalism went from being the bold idea of a few ethnic organizations in 1965 to being part of the supreme law of the land in 1982, and has since been reaffirmed in 1988 and 1997 with only minor changes in emphasis.

Aboriginal Peoples

The second set of policies concerns the rights and status of the Aboriginal peoples of Canada—the Indians, Inuit, and Métis. In the past, Canada, like all British settler states, had the goal and expectation that its indigenous peoples would eventually disappear as distinct communities, as a result of dying out, intermarriage, emigration into the cities, and cultural assimilation. Various policies were adopted to speed up this process, such as stripping indigenous peoples of their lands; encouraging residential schooling of children away from their communities; restricting the practice of their traditional culture, language, and religion; requiring cultural assimilation as a condition of acquiring citizenship; and undermining their institutions of self-government (Armitage 1995; Cairns 2000). Any laws that gave Aboriginal people a separate legal or political status, such as the system of treaties and reserves, were seen as temporary paternalistic protections for a vulnerable population unable to cope with the rigors of modern life, until such time as they were ready to stand on their own as equal and undifferentiated Canadian citizens.

However, there has been a dramatic reversal in these policies, a change that started in 1969 in response to the federal government's white paper on Indian policy (Government of Canada 1969). The white paper declared (in effect) that the need for paternalistic protections had passed, and that it was time for Aboriginal people to trade in their special status for the common rights of citizenship as individual Canadians. It therefore proposed to abolish existing treaties with Indians on the grounds that it was inappropriate and anachronistic for the state to stand in a treaty relationship with a section of its own citizens. It also proposed eliminating any special legal status of Indians on the grounds that this was inconsistent with norms of equality. In response, Aboriginal peoples engaged in massive political mobilization to protect their Aboriginal lands, treaties, and rights. They argued that these provisions were not inherently or originally paternalistic. On the contrary, they arose as a result of the exercise of Aboriginal autonomy (in other words, they reflected solemn and consensual agreements between Aboriginal peoples and Europeans), and formed the legal and material basis for ongoing Aboriginal autonomy into the future.

The federal government quickly backed down, and the Aboriginal position was subsequently strengthened by a string of developments in the early 1970s, including the Supreme Court's recognition of Aboriginal title in the 1973 Calder decision;[7] the 1974 Mackenzie Valley pipeline inquiry's conclusion that resource development must respect Aboriginal interests and Aboriginal consent (Berger 1977); and the 1975 James Bay Agreement with the Quebec Inuit and Cree, affirming both land rights and self-government powers.

It is difficult to exaggerate the shift in thinking about Aboriginal policy that took place in these few years. In 1969, the federal government was proposing to abolish existing treaties and denying that Aboriginal peoples should be seen as having any distinctive political status. By 1975, the government was not only promising to uphold old treaties, it was starting the process of signing new treaties and agreements, because treaties appropriately reflect the distinctive status of Aboriginal communities as self-governing peoples. Since then we have seen a battery of legal and political processes (land claims commissions, self-government negotiations, constitutional conferences, parliamentary committees, royal commissions) attempting to work out the implications of this new approach. Important moments include the constitutional entrenchment of Aboriginal rights in sections 25 and 35 of the Constitution Act, 1982, which not only affirmed "existing treaty and Aboriginal rights" but also extended constitutional protection to any land claims settlements or treaty rights that would be acquired in the future; the House of Common's Penner Report in 1983, which formally endorsed the principle of an Aboriginal right to self-government (Canada 1983); and the inclusion of the principle of an Aboriginal right to self-government in the 1992 Charlottetown Accord. Although the referendum on the Accord failed, the federal government has since declared that it will operate on the assumption that a right to self-government is implicit in the "existing Aboriginal rights" affirmed in the Constitution. This position was affirmed by the massive five-volume *Report of the Royal Commission on Aboriginal Peoples* in 1996 (RCAP 1996), and underpins the creation of Nunavut in 1999.

This, then, is a brief sketch of the Canadian approach to Aboriginal peoples, and the shift from paternalism/assimilation to self-government. The Canadian government today accepts, at least in principle, the idea that Aboriginal peoples will exist into the indefinite future as distinct societies within Canada, and that they must have the land claims, treaty rights, cultural rights, and self-government rights needed to sustain themselves as distinct societies. As with multiculturalism, the changes involved were dramatic and quick. The new contours of this second diversity silo were provisionally sketched out between 1969 and 1975. This shift was (and remains) contested in Canada. [8] But, as with multiculturalism, it quickly became so embedded in Canadian political life that it was felt appropriate to entrench it in the Constitution in 1982, and subsequent reports and constitutional proposals have reaffirmed it.

Francophones/Québécois

The third set of policies concerns the "French fact" in Canada—in other words, the status of the French-speaking communities that were initially established during the period of French colonialism, centered in Quebec and New Brunswick, but with long-standing settlements in many parts of Canada. When the British defeated the French to gain control over "New France," they were faced with the question of what to do with a long-settled French Canadian population that was accustomed to operating within its own full set of legal, political, and educational institutions, and that was deeply attached to these institutions. These institutions were shaped by the distinct language, culture, and religion of the French Canadians, and served to reproduce a distinct national identity. In short, the British were confronted with the challenge of a "nation within"—in other words, a historically settled and regionally concentrated group with members who conceive of themselves as a "nation" within a larger state, and who give (varying levels of) support to nationalist movements that mobilize to defend their autonomous institutions and to achieve recognition of their distinct national identity.

The British rulers were nervous about the existence of such a "nation within." The presence of such a group has been seen by most states as a threat, putting into question the legitimate authority of the state to speak for and govern all of its citizens and territory. As a result, western countries historically have attempted to suppress these forms of substate nationalism, through restricting minority language rights, abolishing traditional forms of local or regional self-government, and encouraging members of the dominant group to settle in the minority group's territory so that the minority becomes outnumbered even in its traditional homeland.

The British, too, tried this strategy in relation to French Canadians, first under the Royal Proclamation of 1763, and then again under the Act of Union of 1841, in the hope that the French would be swamped by, or assimilated into, a British settler society. But it failed miserably in both cases, and by the time of Confederation, it was clear that the national aspirations of the French would have to be accommodated through a framework of federalism and bilingualism. Federalism involved (re)establishing the French-majority province of Quebec as a political space within Canada where the French would be masters of their own home and could sustain their own institutions. Bilingualism guaranteed the use of the French language not only in Quebec, but also in the federal Parliament and courts to ensure equal opportunities for the French at the federal level.

This basic framework of provincial autonomy and federal bilingualism remains in place today, and in that sense the third diversity silo has longer historical roots than either Aboriginal rights or immigrant multiculturalism policies. However, this apparent continuity is potentially misleading, for here, too, there have been dramatic changes in the past forty years. By the early 1960s, it had become clear that the sort of provincial autonomy and federal bilingualism available under the BNA Act was inadequate. Bilingualism in the federal government, for example, had not enabled equal opportunities for francophones. On the contrary, bilingualism was largely token—the federal government operated almost exclusively in English and, as a result, French Canadians were seriously underrepresented in the federal civil service. Similarly, provincial autonomy had not enabled the French to be masters in their own home. On the contrary, they were second-class citizens in their own province, economically subordinate to the English elite that had been privileged under British rule, and relegated to the lower rungs of the economy. The accommodations built into the BNA Act were sufficient to prevent assimilation, and to avoid the "Louisianization" of Quebec, but were not sufficient to ensure either linguistic equality or national autonomy.

Faced with this situation, modernizing elites in Quebec in the 1960s engaged in a twofold struggle: (1) to acquire and exercise the powers of provincial autonomy needed to improve the educational and economic opportunities for the francophone majority within Quebec, and to make the French language a language of opportunity and mobility in society; and (2) to achieve real, as opposed to merely token, linguistic equality within the federal government. In both cases, there was the implicit (and sometimes explicit) threat that if these goals were not achieved, secession was the likely result. If equality and autonomy could not be achieved within Canada, they would be achieved outside Canada, as two equal sovereign states.

The basic legitimacy of these two goals was accepted by the federal government's Royal Commission on Bilingualism and Biculturalism, established in 1963, and a series of reforms were enacted to help achieve them. On the bilingualism front, the key reform was the 1969 Official Languages Act, which created one of the strongest systems of federal bilingualism in the world, in terms of the duties it imposes on the federal government to accommodate the use of both languages in its administration and public services. This commitment to full linguistic equality was enshrined in sections 16 through 20 and 23 of the 1982 Constitution, reaffirmed in the 1988 revision to the Official Languages Act, and strengthened once again in the 2003 Action Plan for Official Languages.

On the provincial autonomy front, a series of intergovernmental agreements have been signed to strengthen Quebec's autonomy, starting with the 1964 agreement to allow Quebec to run its own pension scheme (which was crucial in enabling the modernization of the economy), and the 1977 Cullen-Couture agreement to allow Quebec to run its own immigration program (which was crucial in ensuring that immigration was a benefit, not a threat, to Quebec's francophone majority). This commitment to honoring Quebec's distinctive needs for provincial autonomy is also implicitly reflected in the 1982 Constitution, with its constitutional guarantees for compensation in case of transfer of jurisdiction over language and culture (section 40), and its reservation concerning education in Quebec so as to protect Bill 101 (section 59). Since then, further intergovernmental agreements have been reached with Quebec to protect and expand its autonomy, most recently the 2004 health care agreement. The federal government has also made other efforts to affirm Quebec's distinctiveness and protect its autonomy, such as the 1995 parliamentary resolution recognizing Quebec as a "distinct society," the 1996 Constitutional Amendments Act granting Quebec a veto over future constitutional changes, and the 2006 parliamentary resolution recognizing Quebec as "a nation." As a result of these developments, Canada today has one of the most decentralized federal systems in the world, ensuring Quebec a high level of autonomy that it has effectively used to improve the status and opportunities of its historically disadvantaged francophone majority.

There remain disagreements within the federal government about how best to satisfy Quebec's aspirations for autonomy. Some have endorsed "asymmetrical" agreements that would grant powers to Quebec that are not available to other provinces; others have argued that any powers offered to Quebec must be offered to other provinces. Some have endorsed amending the Constitution to confirm Quebec's increased autonomy (as occurred with the 1964 pension agreement); others have argued that nonconstitutional intergovernmental agreements are sufficient to satisfy Quebec's legitimate interests. But despite these disagreements about strategy, there has been a broad consensus, from 1964 to today, that the federal government must not be seen to be trampling on Quebec's autonomy and must be willing to negotiate a more "cooperative," "flexible," or "renewed" federalism in response to Quebec's aspirations.

This, then, is a brief outline of Canada's approach to "the French fact," and the shift from second-class citizenship to full linguistic equality and strong provincial autonomy to accommodate the national(ist) aspirations of a "distinct society" within the state. Here again, this shift was fairly quick. The new contours of this third diversity silo were essentially put in place between 1964 and 1977. This shift was (and remains) contested. But as with multiculturalism and Aboriginal rights, it quickly became so embedded in Canadian political life that core elements of this package were included in the 1982 Constitution, and subsequent developments have largely affirmed it.

The extent to which this model has been constitutionalized is more contested than in the first two cases. Official bilingualism is explicitly enshrined in the Charter, and sections 40 and 59 are clearly a response to Quebec's concerns about provincial autonomy. But attempts to include a reference in the Constitution to Quebec's distinctiveness, as proposed in both the 1987 Meech Lake Accord and 1992 Charlottetown Accord, have been decisively rejected by Canadians. The idea of formally entrenching in the constitution any principle of "asymmetry," "special status," or "distinct society" (let alone "nationhood") for Quebec remains wildly unpopular in most of Canada.

Despite these constitutional rebuffs, the federal government has declared that its approach to federal–provincial relations will be premised on the assumption that Quebec is a "nation" and a "distinct society" within Canada, thereby confirming what is clear to any observer. Whatever the constitutional niceties, the federal government has understood the need to negotiate Quebec's claims for autonomy, particularly when these are seen as essential to Quebec's national project, if only because refusing to do so would likely increase support for secession.

Even more striking, the Supreme Court said, in its 1998 Secession Reference, that Quebec's distinctness must be taken into account in interpreting the Constitution, that protecting its distinctness is one of the justifications for federalism in Canada, and that failure to honor this constitutional value could provide legitimate grounds for secession. This is as close as one could come to the de facto constitutionalization of the third diversity silo.[9]

EXPLAINING THE CANADIAN MODEL

This overview of the three diversity silos is highly schematic, ignoring a multitude of advances and retreats in response to shifting political coalitions and public opinion. The funding for multiculturalism programs goes up and down, the federal government toughens and relaxes its bargaining position when negotiating Aboriginal land claims, the commitment to strengthen federal bilingualism waxes and wanes, as does the openness to negotiate new agreements with Quebec.

However, these short-term variations should not obscure the fact that there has been a dramatic shift in the baseline from which these advances and retreats are made. The federal government may play hardball when negotiating Aboriginal land claims, for example, but the obligation to negotiate land claims is now constitutionally entrenched, as are the principles of multiculturalism and bilingualism. There is no route back to the 1969 Indian white paper, or to the Anglo-conformity model of immigrant incorporation, or to the days when francophone Quebecers were hewers of wood and drawers of water and were excluded from the corridors of power.

In short, there has been a tidal wave of reform in the field of diversity policies. Canada's current policies are, in large part, the result of a wave of reform that was concentrated essentially in a single decade, from 1965 to 1975. For all three types of diversity, this wave overturned the presuppositions of earlier policies, and defined the basic parameters of multiculturalism, Aboriginal self-government, and bilingualism/provincial autonomy that remain with us today.

What explains this wave of reform? I believe that the answer lies in a broader process of liberalization. The decade between 1965 and 1975 was the most concentrated period of social and political liberalization that Canada has witnessed. That decade witnessed liberalizing reforms across virtually the entire range of social policy—liberalizing abortion laws, access to contraception, and divorce laws; abolishing the death penalty; prohibiting gender and religious discrimination; and decriminalizing homosexuality, among many other such reforms. This era is often characterized as reflecting a "human rights revolution" in Canada, and indeed it witnessed the establishment of human rights commissions in virtually every province, and at the federal level in 1977. Others have characterized it as the triumph of a "rights-based liberalism," or a "civil rights liberalism," in Canada. The reform of diversity policies, I believe, is simply one more example of this liberalization, inspired by the same liberal ideals and principles, and enacted by the same liberal reformist coalitions.

Indeed, Canada's diversity policies must be understood in the context of the global human rights revolution. In 1948, through the adoption of the Universal Declaration of Human Rights (UDHR), the international order decisively repudiated older ideas of a racial or ethnic hierarchy, according to which some peoples were superior to others and thereby had the right to rule over them. It is important to remember how radical this postwar commitment to ethnic and racial equality is. Assumptions about a hierarchy of peoples were widely accepted throughout the West up until World War II, when Hitler's fanatical and murderous policies discredited them. Indeed, the whole system of colonialism was premised on the assumption of a hierarchy of peoples, and it was the explicit basis of both domestic policies and international law throughout the nineteenth century and first half of the twentieth century (such as Canada's racially exclusionary immigration laws).

Since 1948, however, we live in a world where the idea of human equality is unquestioned, at least officially, and this has generated a series of political movements designed to contest the lingering presence or enduring effects of older ethnic and racial hierarchies. We can identify a sequence of such movements. The first was decolonization, from roughly 1948 to 1966. Some western countries that signed the UDHR did not believe that endorsing the principle of the equality of peoples would require them to give up their colonies (for example, France, Spain, Portugal), but this position was unsustainable. The second stage was racial desegregation, from roughly 1955 to 1965, initiated by the African American civil rights struggles. When the United States signed the UDHR in 1948, it did not believe that this would require abandoning its segregationist laws, but this position, too, became unsustainable. The African American civil rights struggle subsequently inspired historically subordinated ethnocultural groups around the world to engage in their own forms of struggle against the lingering presence of ethnic and racial hierarchies. We can see this in the way indigenous peoples adopted the rhetoric of "Red Power," or in the way national minorities (such as the Québécois, or Catholics in Northern Ireland) called themselves "white niggers" (Vallières 1971), or in the way Caribbean immigrants to the United Kingdom adopted the rhetoric and legal strategies of American blacks (Modood 2003). All these movements were profoundly influenced by American ideas of civil rights liberalism, and its commitment to defend equality for disadvantaged and stigmatized minorities through the enforcement of countermajoritarian rights.

However, as civil rights liberalism spread, it also had to adapt to the actual challenges facing different types of minorities around the world. For American theorists, the very idea of "civil rights" and "equality" have been interpreted through the lens of antidiscrimination in general and racial desegregation in particular. For most American theorists, the sorts of countermajoritarian rights that civil rights liberalism must defend are therefore rights to undifferentiated citizenship within a "civic nation" that transcends ethnic, racial, and religious differences.

In most countries, however, the sorts of minorities needing protection are different, and so, too, are the sorts of civil and political rights they require. African Americans were involuntarily segregated, solely on the basis of their race, and excluded from common institutions that they often wanted to join. Many minorities, however, are in the opposite position; they have been involuntarily assimilated, stripped of their own language, culture, and self-governing institutions. They, too, have faced oppression at the hands of their cocitizens and have had their civil rights denied to them, often with the enthusiastic backing of large majorities, on the grounds of their inferiority or backwardness. They, too, need countermajoritarian protections. However, the form these protections take is not solely antidiscrimination and undifferentiated citizenship, but rather various group-specific accommodations. In the Canadian context, as we have seen, these include bilingualism and provincial autonomy (for the Québécois), land claims and treaty rights (for Aboriginal peoples), and various multicultural accommodations (for immigrant/ethnic groups). The struggle for these differentiated minority rights in Canada must be understood, I believe, as a local adaptation of civil rights liberalism, and hence as a third stage in the unfolding of the human rights revolution in the sphere of ethnic and racial relations.

Viewed this way, Canada's diversity policies are centrally concerned with the constructing of liberal democratic citizens in a multiethnic state. They are forms of "citizenization," in sociological jargon. They start from the reality that ethnocultural and religious diversity in Canada has historically been defined by a range of illiberal relationships—including relations of conqueror and conquered, colonizer and colonized, settler and indigenous, racialized and unmarked, normalized and deviant, civilized and backward, ally and enemy, master and slave—and that this complex history will inevitably generate group-differentiated ethnopolitical claims. However, they seek to transform this catalog of uncivil relationships into relations of liberal—democratic citizenship, both in terms of the vertical relationship between the members of minorities and the state, and the horizontal relationships among the members of different groups. This project of citizenization is inspired and guided by the global postwar trends in human rights and civil rights liberalism.

Of course, this immediately raises a puzzle. If Canada's diversity policies are rooted in global trends regarding human rights and political liberalization, why do we not see the same trends in other countries that have similarly been influenced by the human rights revolution? Why is Canada so distinctive in its commitment to accommodating diversity?

The short answer is that Canada is less distinctive than it appears. All three of the trends are replicated across the western democracies. For example, all western democracies that contain indigenous peoples have moved in the direction of greater recognition of land rights and self-government (for example, for Native American tribes in the United States, Maori in New Zealand, Aboriginal people in Australia, Sami in Scandinavia, Greenlanders in Denmark). Similarly, most western democracies that contain substate nationalist movements have accorded autonomy and language rights to their substate national groups (for example, Catalonia and the Basque Country, Flanders, Scotland and Wales, South Tyrol, Puerto Rico). And with respect to immigrant groups, all of the traditional countries of immigration, like Australia, New Zealand, the United States, and Britain, have shifted from discriminatory to race-neutral admissions and naturalization policies, and from an assimilationist to a more multicultural conception of integration.[10] In all these cases, broader processes of liberalization and human rights reform have pushed countries in the direction of acknowledging minority rights, creating a global wave of minority rights reforms (Kymlicka 2007b).

What distinguishes Canada, therefore, is not primarily the adoption of diversity policies, but rather the centrality that these policies have come to play in Canada's collective life and collective identity. For one thing, Canada is unusual in having to deal with all three forms of diversity. Australia and New Zealand, for example, have been grappling with issues of immigration and indigenous peoples, but have no substate nationalist movements. Belgium, Switzerland, Spain, and Britain, by contrast, have been grappling with issues of both substate nationalism and immigration, but have no indigenous peoples. Canada is unusual in having to confront all three issues at the same time.

Moreover, and more important, Canada is distinctive in the extent to which it has not only legislated but also *constitutionalized* its practices of accommodation. Its commitment to multiculturalism is enshrined not only in statutory legislation, but also in section 27 of the Constitution Act. No other western country has constitutionalized multiculturalism. Similarly, Canada's commitments to Aboriginal and treaty rights are constitutionalized in a stronger or more explicit fashion than most western countries. That has been the case as well with Canada's commitments to federalism and official language rights.

This decision to constitutionalize practices of accommodation is one example of a more general feature of the Canadian experience—namely, the decision to highlight these practices in the national identity and national narratives. Although the actual practices of accommodation in Canada may not be that distinctive, Canada is unusual in the extent to which these practices have been built into its symbols and narratives of nationhood. Canadians tell each other that accommodating diversity is an important part of the Canadian identity, a defining feature of the country. This is quite unlike the United States, for example. In practice, the United States accords self-government and treaty rights to Native Americans, regional autonomy and language rights to Puerto Rico, and multicultural accommodations to immigrant groups, but these are peripheral to the self-conception of most Americans and are not considered defining features of the American national narrative. Americans accommodate diversity in practice, but they do not shout that fact from the rooftop, the way Canadians often do.[11]

Indeed, it is precisely this fact—the centrality of diversity to Canada's national identity—that is the source of such interest internationally. Many countries have experimented with policies to accommodate ethnic minorities, but rarely have these policies become part of the *majority's* self-identity. Policies of multiculturalism, bilingualism, and Aboriginal rights are no longer seen by mainstream Canadians as policies that are adopted solely for "them," but rather are seen as part of who "we" are. To be sure, it would be a mistake to exaggerate the depth of support for these policies, or to ignore the potential for backlash and retreat. But in comparison with most other countries, Canada's diversity policies appear to have taken root in a deeper way. This is attested not only by the higher level of public support for multiculturalism and minority rights in Canada compared with other countries, or the higher levels of expressed comfort with ethnic and racial diversity (Adams 2007), but also by the cross-party consensus on these matters. Most of the key decisions regarding reforms to diversity policies over the past forty years have been endorsed by all three major national parties, on the Left (New Democrats), center (Liberal), and Right (Conservative). None of these parties has attempted in recent years to win votes by "playing the race card" or by adopting antiminority political platforms.

This contrasts with the intense partisan manipulation of issues of race, immigration, and diversity in most other countries. Across the western democracies, antiminority parties and movements have been able to draw significant support from members of the majority who feel threatened by the increasing diversity of their societies. As a result, even when other countries have adopted diversity policies that are similar in some respects to Canada's, they have often been subject to greater public backlash. The dramatic retreat from multiculturalism in the Netherlands is a case in point, as are the significant if less dramatic retreats in the case of Britain and Australia.

Explanations differ regarding why there has been less "white backlash" against diversity in Canada. Some attribute it to a long-standing ethos of tolerance in Canada, dating back to the colonial-era habits of coexistence among Aboriginal peoples, French, and British. Others argue that the reform of diversity policies in the 1960s happened to coincide with a time when English Canada was casting off its earlier self-conception as a loyal outpost of the British Empire, and was looking for a new way of asserting its distinctness and independence from both the United States and the United Kingdom. In this context, the idea of "multiculturalism within a bilingual framework" provided English Canadians with a new national identity and national purpose that could anchor feelings of pride and belonging. [12] And yet others attribute the absence of backlash to a range of contingent factors relating to Canada's distinctive economic and geopolitical context.[13]

FUTURE CHALLENGES

Whatever the explanation, it seems clear that the adoption of diversity policies, and their inclusion into the national narrative, has been a smoother process in Canada than in most other countries. What is less clear, however, is whether this apparent national consensus on diversity policies is stable. The 2007 provincial election in Quebec—where the Action démocratique du Québec played the anti-immigrant card with some success—has been interpreted as the first signs that the "white worriers" who have mobilized against diversity in other countries remain a potent potential force in Canada as well.[14]

There are indeed many sources of anxiety about the future of diversity policies in Canada. I cannot address them all here. Because Aboriginal peoples and Quebec are addressed in other chapters in this book, let me focus on two unresolved issues regarding immigrant multiculturalism. The first concerns the relationship between multiculturalism and human rights liberalism. As I noted earlier, the initial impetus for multiculturalism emerged as part of a larger human rights revolution in Canada, aimed at challenging inherited ethnic and racial hierarchies. In this sense, it was seen as a progressive and emancipatory cause, and was supported by the same left-Liberal segment of public opinion that also championed the rights of women or gays. But it has become clear that the idea of multiculturalism can also be used (or abused) to try to defend cultural practices that are oppressive rather than emancipatory—for example, practices of forced arranged marriages, or female genital cutting, or the imposition of gender-biased religious family law. Multiculturalism, in short, can be invoked not to contest inherited hierarchies and inequalities between immigrants and the mainstream society, but rather to defend inherited hierarchies *within* the immigrant community in the name of cultural authenticity or religious orthodoxy. This concern became particularly prominent in Ontario in 2005, with the proposal for recognition of sharia-based family law arbitration.

In reality, attempts to invoke multiculturalism to defend such illiberal practices have been uniformly rejected in Canada. The multiculturalism policy is clearly framed as part of a larger human rights agenda, and principles of gender equality and human rights are clearly articulated within the policy. From a legal point of view, there is no possibility that multiculturalism can be invoked to justify abridging the rights of women or children within immigrant communities. But determining the precise "limits of tolerance" remains a difficult and unresolved issue, in Canada as in all western democracies.

A second concern is that multiculturalism is more about the symbolic recognition of diversity, rather than any genuine inclusion of immigrants into the larger economic and political structures in Canada. This is a long-standing criticism of multiculturalism—that it is a "feel-good" policy that leaves untouched the real hierarchies of power. Indeed, critics argue this is precisely why so many white English Canadians endorse diversity policies, because these policies have left their real power untouched (Day 2000).

There is indeed growing evidence that recent immigrants are having difficulty in the labor market, that nonwhite Canadians continue to face an "ethnic penalty" in comparison with white Canadians who have similar credentials and work experience, and that many second-generation visible minority Canadians continue to experience discrimination (Reitz and Banarjee 2007). So Canada is far from a utopia for many immigrant/ethnic groups, and multiculturalism by itself seems unable to remedy these obstacles to inclusion.

On the other hand, there is also growing evidence that immigrants integrate into the political process more quickly and effectively in Canada than in other countries. In an interesting recent study entitled *Becoming a Citizen*, Irene Bloemraad (2006) compared the political integration of Portuguese and Vietnamese immigrants in Toronto and Boston, and noted that those in Toronto are having more success in "becoming a citizen," not just in the legal sense of naturalizing, but in the substantive sense of participating and feeling a sense of political efficacy. She attributes this differential result in large part to Canada's multiculturalism policy, which encourages and funds the self-organization and self-representation of ethnic groups, and helps nurture a cadre of effective community leaders.

This illustrates my earlier comment that Canada's diversity policies are fundamentally about "citizenization." I think we can find comparable evidence of citizenship building from the Aboriginal and French silos as well, where diversity policies have enhanced the political participation of groups that were previously excluded or underrepresented politically (Kymlicka 2007a). In short, diversity policies are not a panacea for the full range of economic and social disadvantages that ethnic minorities suffer in Canada, nor are they simply a matter of feel-good symbolic recognition.

At their best, they help to construct new relations of democratic citizenship, which in turn create the political space for ongoing contestation about the future of ethnic relations in Canada.

NOTES

1. More recent research has cast doubt on some of these claims about the negative effects of ethnic heterogeneity. For overviews, see Fearon and Laitin (2003), Alesina and LeFerrara (2005), and Fish and Brooks (2004).

2. There are no universally accepted terms to designate different types of ethnocultural groups. In this chapter, I am distinguishing (1) ethnocultural groups with roots in Canada that predate European colonization ("Aboriginal peoples"), (2) ethnocultural groups rooted in projects of European colonizing settlement (French and British), and (3) ethnocultural groups that have emerged in Canada as a result of immigration. In Canadian discourse, the term *ethnic groups* is often reserved for the latter category, although all of them qualify as ethnic groups as that term is defined by most academic social scientists. It would be more accurate, therefore, to describe this third category as "ethnic groups formed through immigration." As shorthand, I will use the term *immigrant/ethnic group*, although it is important to emphasize that many members of these groups may be second-, third-, or fourth-generation descendants of the original immigrants.

3. See 2001 Census figures in Statistics Canada 2003a. A more detailed breakdown of ethnic origins was done as part of the 2002 Ethnic Diversity Survey, summarized in Statistics Canada 2003b.

4. This is often called the *Anglo-conformity model* of immigration. Historically, only a small number of immigrants integrated into the French-speaking society in Quebec, and prior to the 1970s, immigration was not seen as a tool of nation building in Quebec the way it was viewed in English Canada.

5. These are taken from Prime Minister Trudeau's statement to Parliament declaring the multiculturalism policy in 1971 (Trudeau 1971, 8546).

6. For the origins of the multiculturalism policy, see Jaworsky (1979) and Day (2000). For the twenty-five-year review, see Brighton Report (1996) and commentary in Kordan (1997). For the most recent annual report on the operation of the multiculturalism policy, see Government of Canada 2007.

7. As Borrows (2001, 18) puts it, this decision invited Canadians to "seriously contemplate the possibility that aboriginal peoples would be a permanent part of the political and legal landscape."

8. For a critique of this shift, see Flanagan (2000), who argues that the increasing recognition of Aboriginal group rights is both a violation of liberal principles of equal citizenship and a counterproductive strategy, condemning Aboriginal peoples to poverty and marginalization.

9. In the Secession Reference, the Supreme Court laid down the principles and procedures that should apply in the event of an attempt by Quebec to secede from Canada. Although denying that Quebec has a unilateral right to secede, the Court stated that the underlying values of the Constitution generate a duty on the part of the federal government to negotiate in good faith regarding the aspirations of Quebecers.

10. There are differences in how formal this shift to multiculturalism has been. In Australia and New Zealand, as in Canada, this shift was officially marked by the declaration of a multicultural policy by the central government. But even in the United States, we see similar changes on the ground. The United States does not have an official policy of multiculturalism at the federal level, but if we look at lower levels of government, such as states or cities, we will find a broad range of multiculturalism policies. State-level policies regarding the education curriculum, for example, or city-level policies regarding policing or hospitals, are often indistinguishable from the way provinces and cities in Canada deal with issues of immigrant ethnocultural diversity. As Glazer (1997) puts it, "we are all multiculturalists now." It is important to note, however, that multiculturalism has not taken hold in countries that do not view themselves as "immigrant countries," such as most countries in continental Europe. These countries may contain large numbers of "foreigners," in the form of illegal economic migrants, asylum seekers, or guest workers, but these groups were not initially admitted as part of an immigration policy or as future citizens. As a mode of "citizenization," multiculturalism only becomes a meaningful option when migrants are seen as citizens, not foreigners.

11. As Joppke (2002, 250) puts it, countries can adopt diversity policies without this being "written on the forehead of the state."

12. See McRoberts (1997) for an analysis of how bilingualism and multiculturalism, although primarily intended to encourage minorities to feel a sense of attachment to Canada, have in fact become sources of pride and identification among majority English Canadians, in part as a replacement for an obsolete British identity.

13. For example, the fact that Canada is economically dependent on immigration, the fact that Canada is not threatened by neighboring enemies who seek to destabilize the state by encouraging disloyal minorities, the fact that Canada does not face the threat of large-scale illegal immigration, and so on. I explore these explanations in Kymlicka (2004).

14. After the 2007 election, a commission established by the Quebec government held a series of public town hall meetings to discuss the issue of the "reasonable accommodation" of cultural differences. These meetings of the Consultation Commission on Accommodation Practices Related to Cultural Differences—also known as the Bouchard-Taylor Commission—revealed a high level of anxiety about the growing diversity of Quebec society. In its final report, however, released in May 2008, the Commission defended the need to accommodate diversity and rejected calls for a retreat from existing practices of accommodation (Quebec 2008). For discussions of the "white backlash" and "white worrier" phenomenon in other countries, see Hewitt (2005) and Bulbeck (2004).

REFERENCES

Adams, Michael. 2007. *Unlikely Utopia: The Surprising Triumph of Canadian Pluralism.* Toronto: Viking.

Alesina, Alberto, and Eliana LeFerrara. 2005. Ethnic diversity and economic performance. *Journal of Economic Literature* 43(3): 762–800.

Armitage, Andrew. 1995. *Comparing the Policy of Aboriginal Assimilation: Australia, Canada, New Zealand.* Vancouver: UBC Press.

Banting, Keith. 2005. The multicultural welfare state: International experience and North American narratives. *Social Policy and Administration* 39(2): 98–115.

Berger, Thomas. 1977. *Northern Frontier, Northern Homeland: Report of the Mackenzie Valley Pipeline Inquiry*. Ottawa: Supply and Services.

Bloemraad, Irene. 2006. *Becoming a Citizen: Incorporating Immigrants and Refugees in the United States and Canada*. Berkeley: University of California Press.

Borrows, John. 2001. Uncertain citizens: Aboriginal peoples and the Supreme Court. *Canadian Bar Review* 80(1–2): 15–41.

Brighton Report. 1996. *Strategic Evaluation of Multiculturalism Programs*. Ottawa: Corporate Review Branch, Department of Canadian Heritage, Government of Canada.

Bulbeck, Chilla. 2004. The "white worrier" in South Australia: Attitudes to multiculturalism, immigration and reconciliation. *Journal of Sociology* 40(4): 341–361.

Cairns, Alan. 2000. *Citizens Plus: Aboriginal Peoples and the Canadian State*. Vancouver: UBC Press.

Calder v. Attorney-General of British Columbia (1973) S.C.R. 313.

Canada. 1983. *Indian Self-Government in Canada: Report of the House of Commons Special Committee on Indian Self-Government*. Ottawa: Supply and Services.

Day, Richard. 2000. *Multiculturalism and the History of Canadian Diversity*. Toronto: University of Toronto Press.

Fearon, James, and David Laitin. 2003. Ethnicity, insurgency and civil war. *American Political Science Review* 97(1): 75–90.

Fish, Steven, and Robin Brooks. 2004. Does diversity hurt democracy? *Journal of Democracy* 15(1): 154–166.

Flanagan, Tom. 2000. *First Nations, Second Thoughts*. Montreal: McGill-Queen's University Press.

Glazer, Nathan. 1997. *We Are All Multiculturalists* Now. Cambridge: Harvard University Press.

Globe and Mail. 2004. Canada's welcome mat. *Globe and Mail*. May 31, A12.

Government of Canada. 1969. *Statement of the Government of Canada on Indian Policy*, tabled on June 25, 1969, by Jean Chrétien, Minister of Indian Affairs and Northern Development.

Government of Canada. 2007. *Annual Report on the Operation of the Canadian Multiculturalism Act 2006–7*. Ottawa: Department of Canadian Heritage, Public Works and Government Services.

Green, Joyce. 2005. Self-determination, citizenship, and federalism: Indigenous and Canadian palimpsest. In *Reconfiguring Aboriginal–State Relations*, ed. Michael Murphy, 329–352. Kingston: Institute for Intergovernmental Relations.

Hewitt, Roger. 2005. *White Backlash and the Politics of Multiculturalism*. Cambridge: Cambridge University Press.

Ibbitson, John. 2004. Pluralism: The world wonders how we pull it off. *Globe and Mail*, February 6, A21.

Jaworsky, John. 1979. *A Case Study of the Canadian Federal Government's Multiculturalism Policy*. Masters thesis, Department of Political Science, Carleton University.

Joppke, Christian. 2002. Multicultural citizenship. In *Handbook of Citizenship Studies*, ed. Bryan Turner, 245–258. London: Sage.

Kordan, Bohdan. 1997. Multiculturalism, citizenship and the Canadian nation. *Canadian Ethnic Studies* 29(2): 135–143.

Kymlicka, Will. 2004. Marketing Canadian pluralism in the international arena. *International Journal* 59(4): 829–852.

———. 2007a. Ethnocultural diversity in a liberal state: Making sense of the Canadian model(s). In *Belonging? Diversity, Recognition and Shared Citizenship in Canada*, ed. Keith Banting, Thomas Courchene, and Leslie Seidle, 39–86. Montreal: Institute for Research on Public Policy.

———. 2007b. *Multicultural Odysseys: Navigating the New International Politics of Diversity*. Oxford: Oxford University Press.

Laczko, Leslie. 1994. Canada's pluralism in comparative perspective. *Ethnic and Racial Studies* 17(1): 20–41.

McRoberts, Kenneth. 1997. *Misconceiving Canada: The Struggle for National Unity*. Toronto: Oxford University Press.

Modood, Tariq. 2003. Muslims and the politics of difference. In *The Politics of Migration*, ed. Sarah Spencer, 100–115. London: Blackwell.

Quebec. 2008. *Building the Future: A Time for Reconciliation. Report of the Consultation Commission on Accommodation Practices Related to Cultural Differences*. Quebec City: Government of Quebec.

RCAP (Royal Commission on Aboriginal Peoples). 1996. *Report of the Royal Commission on Aboriginal Peoples*. Ottawa: Minister of Supply and Services.

Reitz, Jeffrey, and Rupa Banerjee. 2007. Racial inequality, social cohesion and policy issues in Canada. In *Belonging? Diversity, Recognition and Shared Citizenship in Canada*, ed. Keith Banting, Thomas Courchene, and Leslie Seidle, 489–546. Montreal: Institute for Research on Public Policy.

Statistics Canada. 2003a. *Ethnocultural Portrait of Canada: Highlight Tables, 2001 Census*. Ottawa: Minister of Industry. http://www12.statcan.ca/english/census01/products/highlight/Ethnicity/Index.cfm?Lang=E.

Statistics Canada. 2003b. *Ethnic Diversity Survey: Portrait of a Multicultural Society*. Ottawa: Minister of Industry. http://www.statcan.gc.ca/pub/89-593-x/89-593-x2003001-eng.pdf

Trudeau, Pierre. 1971. *Statement to the House of Commons on Multiculturalism*. House of Commons, Official Report of Debates, 28th Parliament, 3rd session, October 8, 1971, 8545–8546.

Vallières, Pierre. 1971. *White Niggers of America*. Toronto: McClelland and Stewart.

CHAPTER 18

WOMEN IN CANADIAN POLITICS

BRENDA O'NEILL
LISA YOUNG

THE scholarship on women in politics in Canada is diverse in both method and perspective, ranging from feminist critiques of public policy to highly quantitative analyses of gender differences in opinion and political behavior. Although the study of women in politics has not become fully mainstream within the Canadian political science literature, it is a thriving subfield in the discipline. In an effort to reflect the sense of some of this literature and to provide an overview of Canadian women's political orientations and participation, this chapter provides an overview of women's collective action via organized feminism, and then turns to women's participation in the Canadian political process as individual citizens and voters. The chapter then turns to the formal political arena and traces the scholarly effort to explain women's persistent numerical and substantive underrepresentation in Canadian legislatures. Finally, the chapter turns to an overview of public policy in a number of policy fields that affect women's social and economic equality.

It must be noted at the outset that Canadian women are a diverse group with political interests and loyalties that vary widely. Although all Canadian women have historically faced legislative and economic discrimination, women belonging to minority ethnic groups, Aboriginal women, and economically marginalized women, among others, have frequently faced much greater legal, political, and economic obstacles. In addition, Canada's decentralized federal structure means that public policies on matters of significance to women as well as the political opportunities available to women vary significantly from province to province. Moreover, there is no unanimity of opinion among Canadian women on matters of public policy or politics.

INSTITUTIONAL CONTEXT

Four elements of the Canadian institutional framework are particularly salient for understanding women's activism and political participation in Canada. First, Canada's relatively decentralized federalism (discussed in chapter 5, this volume) has posed a challenge for women's political activism, because it has required poorly resourced advocacy organizations to divide their attention between federal and provincial governments. In many of the policy areas of particular interest to women, both levels of government have some jurisdiction, and two-pronged lobbying strategies have been required. Within the Canadian federation, Quebec stands out as distinctive in linguistic, cultural, and political dimensions (see chapter 6, this volume). This distinctiveness has presented a particular challenge in the formation of a national women's movement organization.

Second, the Westminster parliamentary system, (discussed in chapter 9, this volume), has evolved in Canada in a manner that has made Canadian parliamentary parties highly disciplined. This in turn hinders the development of cross-party legislative coalitions on issues of particular concern to women. Third, the single-member plurality electoral system predictably renders efforts to increase the number of women elected to provincial and national legislatures more challenging, thereby affecting the potential for women to be represented within the powerful national and provincial cabinets. Finally, the entrenchment of the Canadian Charter of Rights and Freedoms in the Constitution Act, 1982 (see chapters 2 and 4, this volume) has opened up a new avenue for women's efforts to achieve legal equality, and judicial review has influenced public policy on a range of public policy issues of significance to women, including legislation governing access to abortion, regulation of pornography, and treatment of victims of sexual assault in criminal proceedings.

WOMEN'S MOVEMENTS AND COLLECTIVE ACTION

Women's participation in Canadian politics cannot be meaningfully discussed without reference to organized feminism. The women's movement was a significant actor in twentieth-century Canadian politics, playing a key role in winning political rights for women, influencing public policy, and constructing the numerical under-representation of women in elected office as a salient political issue.

The first "wave" of feminist mobilization in Canada began early in the twentieth century, and centered on the fight for women's right to vote. First-wave feminist activism was motivated largely by concern for a range of social ills brought about by urbanization and industrialization. These maternal feminists accepted the definition of women's roles as wives and mothers, arguing that extending the vote to women would improve the moral tenor of the formal political arena and further the reformist agenda they espoused. Women won the right to vote in several western provinces in 1916, and nationally in 1919 (Cleverdon 1974). Of course, the franchise in Canada at the time was not universal, so it was denied to many women because of their ethnicity or other characteristics. Beyond the extension of suffrage, the primary accomplishment of first-wave feminism was the prohibition of alcohol for a relatively short period after women won the right to vote. Another occurred in 1929 when five women launched a legal challenge to the notion that women were not considered "persons" under Canadian law and were therefore not eligible to be appointed to the Senate. Britain's Judicial Committee of the Privy Council ruled in their favor, paving the way for the appointment of women to the upper house. Although organized feminism did not disappear after the "Persons Case" (*Edwards v. A.G. of Canada* 1930) was won, it was certainly less prominent, particularly in English Canada. In Quebec, women were denied the right to vote in provincial elections until 1940. During the 1930s, when English Canadian feminism was relatively inactive, Quebec feminists were engaged in a prolonged political struggle for the extension of political suffrage. The delay in the extension of the franchise to most Quebec women has been linked to the strong *idéologie de conservation* that existed in the province at the time and that argued against women's political participation on the grounds of their roles as guardians of the French Canadian culture and language, and of the Catholic faith (Tremblay 1997).

The emergence of the American women's movement in the early 1960s was echoed in Canada, launching the "second wave" of feminist mobilization. This mobilization encompassed an increased emphasis on women's equality within traditional women's organizations, a more feminist orientation within existing women's peace and leftist organizations, and the formation of American-influenced radical feminist groups (Vickers et al. 1993, chap. 1). By the mid 1960s, a variety of women's organizations, both traditional and more radical in orientation, joined together to call on the Pearson government to launch a formal inquiry into the status of women in Canada. The federal government ultimately heeded this call, and established the Royal Commission on the Status of Women (RCSW) in 1967. The RCSW held hearings across the country and heard from a wide variety of groups. These hearings, and the publicity surrounding them, resulted in widespread public discussions and debates, placing the role of women in the family, the workplace, and government on the policy agenda. The RCSW's report made 167 recommendations for government action on the status of women, with an emphasis on employment equity, development of public child care programs, access to birth control, decriminalization of abortion, and the reform of family law.

Women's organizations that had lobbied for the formation of the RCSW came together in 1972 to form the National Action Committee on the Status of Women (NAC). The new organization's explicit mandate was to lobby the federal government to enact the recommendations of the RCSW. The National Action Committee on the Status of Women was constituted as a national umbrella organization, meaning that only women's groups, not individual women, could join. With its focus on the federal government, its clear lobbying mandate, and its umbrella structure, NAC quickly became the most prominent women's organization in Canada, and for a time became an influential player on the Canadian political landscape.

The National Action Committee on the Status of Women's umbrella structure fostered a relatively peaceful coexistence of multiple strands of feminism within the Canadian women's movement. In the first two decades of mobilization, the dominant strand was liberal feminism, tempered with a strong presence of both socialist and radical feminism. Vickers et al. (1993, 37) describe the dominant ideology within the movement as "radical liberalism" characterized by a commitment to the ordinary political process, a confidence in the efficacy of state action and the welfare state, and a belief that change is possible, that dialogue with those who differ may be useful, and that helping others is a valid contribution to change. This ideology was instrumental in shaping both the lobbying strategy used by the movement as well as its internal organization and processes.

Through the 1970s and early '80s, feminists' faith in the state was fostered by the federal government's willingness to consult with women's organizations. Armed with the RCSW report and bolstered by changing public attitudes regarding the appropriate role of women in the workplace, the family, and Canadian society, NAC was able to serve in a consultative capacity to the federal government and was able to influence public policy on a range of issues. During this period, state structures also favored consultation with women's organizations, as the federal government had established an arm's-length advisory council on the status of women as well as Status of Women Canada, an agency of the powerful Privy Council Office.

Feminists's connections to the federal government were also nurtured by government funding provided to women's organizations. In response to the report of the RCSW, the federal government began offering funding to women's organizations to assist them in bringing their claims to the state. The National Action Committee on the Status of Women and many smaller, local feminist organizations became heavily reliant on operational funding from the federal government from the outset. This had several consequences for the path of feminist organization in Canada. First, it maintained English Canadian feminists's focus on the federal, rather than provincial, governments. Second, when coupled with the umbrella structure of NAC, it meant that no national individual membership organization of women (comparable with the American National Organization of Women [NOW]) was formed. This left the Canadian women's movement highly vulnerable to reductions to or elimination of state subsidies. In fact, NAC teetered on the brink of bankruptcy in the late 1990s and has subsequently been a less significant force in Canadian politics. Finally, reliance on government funding precluded formal alliances between feminist organizations and political parties (Young 2000).

The story of second-wave feminism in Canada is inextricably intertwined with the country's "constitutional odyssey" of the 1980s and early '90s (see chapter 2, this volume). With its focus on the federal government and its centralist orientation, significant elements of the English Canadian women's movement perceived the efforts to patriate and subsequently amend the Canadian Constitution as opportunities to further a feminist policy agenda by having protections for women's equality constitutionally entrenched. The first and most successful intervention came in 1980, when a national network of feminists mobilized to ensure that the new Canadian Charter of Rights and Freedoms would guarantee women's equality. Although the preliminary version of the proposed Charter included section 15, which guaranteed equality before the law and freedom from discrimination based on sex and a range of other characteristics, many women were concerned that these provisions would be inadequate. They mobilized an unprecedented campaign that ultimately led to the inclusion of section 28 of the Charter, which guarantees that "notwithstanding anything in this Charter, the rights and freedoms referred to in it are guaranteed equally to male and female persons." Feminist mobilization also ensured that section 28 was not subject to the potential legislative override that could be used on section 15. Dobrowolsky (2000, 74) observes that even though many women doubted that formal guarantees of equality would yield real policy gains for women, the "taking of section 28" was significant because "through the efforts of particular individuals and groups in the women's movement, feminist concerns were worked into a constitutional agenda that had hitherto excluded or disregarded them."

Having mobilized successfully around the Charter, liberal feminist elements of the English Canadian women's movement remained protective of the Charter, intervening in opposition to the Meech Lake Accord in an effort to ensure that the Charter remain paramount. Even those English Canadian feminists not enamored of the Charter tended to oppose the Meech Lake Accord on the grounds that its decentralizing potential would erode the Canadian welfare state and prevent the creation of new national programs, including a national child care program (Dobrowolsky 2000). Among Quebec feminists, support for the constitutional recognition of Quebec as a distinct society was strong, and English Canadian feminists's fears that the distinct society clause would allow the government of Quebec to trample on the rights of Quebec women were seen as patronizing and indicative of a lack of understanding of Quebec politics and society. After the Meech Lake Accord failed, the debate over the Charlottetown Accord introduced even deeper rifts into feminist organizations, as NAC opposed the agreement because of its potential effect on social programs and concerns about the equality of Aboriginal women under the Accord, but many prominent liberal feminists supported it as necessary for national unity.

From 1993 on, organized feminism in Canada faced hard times. Government funding for women's organizations was significantly reduced to approximately half the level provided in the 1980s (Newman and White 2006, 143), greatly reducing the capacity of groups to engage in discussions of public policy. In addition, political and public receptivity to feminist claims declined as the focus of Canadian politics shifted toward deficit reduction and the retrenchment of the welfare state (Bashevkin 1998; Newman and White 2006, 144–145). As governments pulled back from funding social programs, many programs and services used by women were reduced or eliminated. In the mid 1990s, the federal government addressed its budgetary

difficulties by reducing and restructuring fiscal transfers to the provincial governments, resulting in significant reductions in provincial government funding for
provincially funded programs, including social assistance, women's shelters, and
home care services for disabled women (Burt 2004).

Compounding these difficulties, from the mid 1990s on, feminist organizations
have struggled with internal conflicts over issues of diversity. Women of color and
Aboriginal women contested the leadership roles that middle-class white women
had played within feminist organizations, resulting in much greater diversity within
the movement's leadership as a whole, but also shifting the movement's focus
inward. The National Action Committee on the Status of Women's own history
notes that this period was characterized by "much resistance [from white feminists]
and downright acrimony, which in many instances masked the progressive work
that was being done in NAC" (Newman and White 2006, 88).

Despite these difficulties, the constitutional entrenchment of the Charter had
created a window of opportunity for feminist activists, opening up the possibility of
achieving policy change via judicial review of legislation. One of the most vibrant
Canadian feminist organizations in the post-1993 period has been the women's Legal
Education and Action Fund, or LEAF, which focuses its efforts on challenges to legislation under the Charter (Manfredi 2004). Unlike other feminist organizations,
organizations focused on Charter litigation remained financially viable because they
could continue to access public funds via the Court Challenges program, which subsidized litigation costs until it was terminated by the federal government in 2007.
Arguably, LEAF's strategy of achieving public policy change through litigation has
been more successful than the more traditional lobbying route over the past decade.

WOMEN AS INDIVIDUAL POLITICAL ACTORS

Since winning the legal rights of democratic citizenship, Canadian women's political
participation has increasingly come to mirror that of men's. That said, it would be a
mistake to conclude that gender is irrelevant to political attitudes and behavior. Research
has shown that gender "gaps" in voting and in political opinions continue to be recorded
and that women's political engagement differs from men's in several respects.

As is the case in many established democracies, Canadian women are more
likely to support parties on the Left and Canadian men are more inclined to support
parties on the Right (Erickson and O'Neill 2002; Gidengil et al. 2005). This gap has
been as large as 10 percentage points; in the 2000 election, for example, roughly 27%
of women outside of Quebec voted for the Right of center Canadian Alliance
whereas almost 40% of men did the same (Gidengil et al. 2005). It is the case, however, that "brokerage politics, the multiparty system, and politics in Quebec have
complicated Canada's political landscape and hence the way gender has played out
in the voting booth" (Erickson and O'Neill 2002, 387).

When seeking to explain these persistent gender gaps in voting, political scientists point to situational and structural factors. Women's greater reliance on the state as welfare beneficiaries and as public-sector employees, their concentration in pink-collar occupational ghettos, and the role of feminism in politicizing women all contribute to gendered voting patterns. Beyond this, gender differences in values and beliefs have been identified as key determinants of women's and men's vote choices. Regardless of occupation and income, women are more likely to adopt a statist view than men, are less likely to favor a punitive approach to dealing with questions of law and order, and are less socially conservative than men—factors that help to explain their weaker support for Canadian parties on the Right (Gidengil 1995; Gidengil et al. 2003; 2005).

Gender gaps in public opinion have been fairly consistent on a range of issues. Table 18.1 shows that Canadian women are less likely to support the use of military force and the use of nuclear energy than Canadian men; they are less supportive of free enterprise and more supportive of a strong welfare state. They are also more morally permissive than men; they are, for example, more likely to support gay marriage. Additionally, women are more likely than men on average to see crime as an important issue but are less likely to argue for tougher penalties.

The absence of a strong gender gap on some issues is particularly interesting; on the question of abortion, for example, significant gender differences have failed to be recorded (O'Neill 2001). Support for feminism additionally reveals an interesting pattern; women are consistently found to be less sympathetic to feminism than men but often more supportive of its principles (Gidengil et al. 2003; O'Neill 2003). This "I'm not a feminist but..." phenomenon is much more pronounced among younger Canadian women (O'Neill 2003).

Table 18.1 Gender Gaps in Attitudes, 2000 Canadian Election Study

Issues (% agreeing with statement)	Women	Men
Everyone benefits when businesses make a lot of money	28	37
Social welfare is a very important issue	44	31
Health care is a very important issue	90	78
Sympathetic to feminism	60	65
Feminist movement just tries to get equal treatment for women	63	53
Lack of women members of Parliament is a serious problem	41	30
Should not allow gay marriage	35	48
Should be difficult to get an abortion	35	33
Crime is a very important issue	76	68
Tougher sentences for young offenders	43	53

All differences significant at $P < .01$ except for abortion issues, where $P < .10$ applies.

Source: Gidengil, Elisabeth, André Blais, Neil Nevitte, and Richard Nadeau. 2003. Women to the Left? Gender differences in political beliefs and policy preferences. In *Women and Electoral Politics in Canada*, ed. Manon Tremblay and Linda Trimble, 145. Don Mills: Oxford.

Similar to explanations advanced for gender gaps in voting, structural and situational factors help to explain gender gaps in attitudes. Women continue to earn lower incomes than men and to be found in occupations that have traditionally been filled by women (Statistics Canada 2006). As such, women's support for the social safety net reflects their greater reliance on the welfare state, their employment in the public sector, and their employment status. The impact of the feminist movement on attitudes has also been identified as a factor influencing gender gaps in opinions in Canada (Everitt 1998).

Research examining gender differences in political engagement reveals that Canadian women are less interested in politics, pay less attention to politics, and discuss politics less often than men. They also possess "smaller stocks of political information" (Gidengil et al. 2004, 174). These gaps remain after accounting for income and educational differences and are most pronounced among the youngest generation of Canadians, suggesting that this is a persistent phenomenon (Gidengil et al. 2004, 23). Despite these gaps, women are as likely to vote as men. Gidengil et al. (2004, 130) attribute this to women's greater reported religiosity and sense of duty, which together are sufficient to overcome their weakened interest in politics.

Canadian women are as likely as men to belong to an interest group, but slightly less likely to join a political party (Gidengil et al. 2004, 130). Twenty percent of men and 17% of women surveyed in 2000 reported having joined a party at some point in their lives. This small difference means that men make up a majority of party members, although the share of women does increase in parties on the Left of the political spectrum (Cross and Young 2004). Once a member of a party, however, women appear to be as active as men (Young and Cross 2003).

Women and men in Canada reveal similar levels of associational activity, a level that is relatively high compared with many western democracies, but the types of organizations that they join and to which they volunteer their time differ significantly (Gidengil et al. 2004, 153). Women are more likely to be members of religious and community service organizations as well as women's groups; men, on the other hand, are much more likely to join sports, business, and labor groups. Women's involvement in religious organizations is associated with volunteer activity and acts as a stimulus for political engagement more broadly (O'Neill 2006a). Women's associational activities do, however, reinforce woman traditional gender roles, as women's activities tend to be "related to kin ties, care activities, and the domestic sphere, while men's organizations and interpersonal experiences tend to revolve around economic and recreational activities" (Gidengil et al. 2006, 264).

WOMEN'S POLITICAL REPRESENTATION

In comparative terms, Canada lags behind many democracies in the proportion of women elected at all levels of government. At the federal level, the proportion of women in the lower house (the House of Commons) remained constant at just more than 20%

for the past decade, earning Canada the rank of forty-seventh highest internationally, behind all of Scandinavia, much of western Europe, as well as emerging democracies such as Rwanda, Argentina, and Afghanistan (Inter-Parliamentary Union 2007). Canada does, however, have slightly higher rates of women's representation than either the United Kingdom or the United States. At the provincial level, results are similar, with the proportion of women in legislatures ranging from 13% in New Brunswick to just more than 30% in Manitoba (Equal Voice 2007). And women comprise just more than 20% of elected officials in Canadian municipalities (Federation of Canadian Municipalities 2007). The rates of women's representation are set out in table 18.2.

The numerical underrepresentation of women has consequently been a perennial focus of academic inquiry within the "women in politics" subfield. Cross-national analyses of rates of women's representation indicate that the most important determinants of women's legislative representation are the electoral system (Rule 1987), the presence of representational quotas (Dahlerup 2006), the efforts of parties to recruit women (Caul Kittilson 2006), and gender ideology in the society (Paxton and Kunovich 2003).

Canadians are generally accepting of women's social and legal equality, which means that this is an unlikely culprit for persistently low rates of women's representation. The first three factors do, however, help to explain the pattern of legislative underrepresentation. Certainly, the proportion of women in Canadian legislatures is similar to that in other countries that use single-member plurality electoral systems, suggesting a partial explanation for the limited representational gains

Table 18.2 Women in Canadian Legislatures (as of October 31, 2007)

Jurisdiction	Women in Legislature (% of total)	Women in Cabinet (% of total)
Federal	20.7	21.8
Alberta	15.7	21.0
British Columbia	21.5	21.7
Manitoba	31.6	33.3
New Brunswick	12.7	10.5
Newfoundland	20.8	28.0
Nova Scotia	17.3	17.6
Nunavut	10.5	25.0
Northwest Territories	16.0	14.0
Ontario	27.0	32.0
Prince Edward Island	25.9	20.0
Quebec	25.6	50.0
Saskatchewan	19.0	15.7
Yukon	11.1	28.6

At the federal level, the figure is for the lower house only.

Source: Equal Voice. 2007. Fast Facts: Women in Provincial Politics. www.equalvoice.ca.

Canadian women have made since the 1980s (MacIvor 2003). Compounding this is the absence of any legislated representational quotas for women. The Anglo-American liberal political culture in Canada is highly resistant to legislative measures that would guarantee women seats, perceiving such measures as discriminatory, insulting to women, and overly interventionist.

There is little question that Canadian parties are key players in the recruitment of women into Canadian politics. When women first mobilized around the issue of women's numerical representation, parties were relatively unreceptive. Through the 1970s and early '80s, parties' candidate selection processes appeared unfavorable to the nomination of women. There was also ample evidence that parties tended to nominate women disproportionately in ridings where the party was unlikely to win (Brodie 1985). As the women's movement pressed for the election of more women, however, this pattern changed. For roughly a decade, from 1984 to 1993, all three major federal parties were committed to increasing women's representation and adopted a variety of efforts designed to recruit women.

In 1993, however, the Canadian party system changed. The Progressive Conservative party was largely replaced by the right-populist Reform party and the sovereigntist Bloc québécois. Simultaneously, support for the left-of-center New Democratic Party waned. The Reform Party and its successors—the Canadian Alliance and the Conservative Party—are ideologically opposed to the idea of representational guarantees for women. The Conservatives have made no systematic efforts to increase the representation of women in its caucus, currently at 11%. The advent of the post-1993 party system in Canada, coupled with growing public resistance to the principle of affirmative action, effectively dampened any upward trend in the number of women elected (Young 2006, 58).

Although political parties' "demand" for female politicians has played a role in the persistent underrepresentation of women, there is little question that the "supply" of women putting their names forward also factors into the equation. The reasons for this limited supply of women are complex. As noted earlier, Canadian women are less likely than their male counterparts to express interest in politics and are generally less knowledgeable about the formal political arena. Research in the United States indicates that women in the professions from which politicians are usually recruited are less likely to harbor political ambitions or to see themselves as qualified to run for political office (Fox and Lawless 2004).

The prime minister and provincial premiers enjoy greater control over the proportion of women appointed to their cabinets than they do the number of women elected, although the number of women in caucus necessarily serves as a constraint. As of 2007, the proportion of women in Canadian cabinets ranged widely, from a low of 11% in Alberta to a high of 50% in Quebec. The provincial average is just less than 23%, indicating that women, once elected, are slightly more likely than their male counterparts to be appointed to cabinet (Equal Voice 2007). Given the strength of party discipline in Canada and the centralization of power within cabinet, women's appointment to provincial and national cabinets is a significant element of their political representation and influence.

The "apex of power" in Canadian politics lies in the office of the first minister—the prime minister and provincial premiers. Although several women have been elected leaders of their political party at the provincial or federal level, only one—Catherine Callbeck of Prince Edward Island—led her party to electoral victory and became premier. Two other women have served as first ministers after winning their party's leadership, but both went on to subsequent electoral defeat. Rita Johnston was elected leader of the Social Credit Party in British Columbia and briefly served as premier before going on to electoral defeat. In a similar situation, Kim Campbell was elected leader of the governing, but unpopular, Progressive Conservative Party in 1993 and served as prime minister for a brief period before she led the party to a spectacular electoral defeat later that year.

The small number and electoral travails of women party leaders has made the gendered media treatment and public assessments of party leaders a significant focus of attention within the Canadian women and politics literature in recent years. Much of this scholarship examines media coverage of female party leaders, and concludes that women are not treated fairly by the mainstream media (Gidengil and Everitt 2003; Sampert and Trimble 2003). O'Neill and Stewart (forthcoming) subject the assumption that parties led by women are destined for an almost certain defeat to systematic analysis and conclude that female leaders are no more likely than their male counterparts to lead their party to electoral defeat. They are, however, more likely to be removed as party leader or to step down, making their average time at the helm of the party shorter.

The bulk of the academic study of women's participation in electoral politics in Canada focuses on issues surrounding numeric representation, or the inclusion of women in the Canadian political elite. A second concern in the women-in-politics literature casts attention on the substantive representation of women's interests, asking whether the election of women to legislatures or the appointment of women to cabinets affects public policy outcomes on issues of importance to women. Although studies of women's participation in legislative debates in various Canadian jurisdictions have found evidence of a relationship between the presence of women as legislators and the discussion of women's experiences and policy interests, the overall conclusion drawn from these studies is that "the diverse experiences and policy needs of women have hardly been a matter of great concern to legislators, even in the presence of a 'critical mass' of women" (Trimble 2006, 125).

POLICY INFLUENCE AND KEY POLICY ISSUES

The general conclusion regarding the ability of women's activism to influence public policy in Canada is that although there have been periods of heightened influence and some high-profile successes, overall the political system has not been particularly responsive to women's demands. Women's policy influence has varied with NAC's political influence, although as mentioned earlier, groups such as LEAF have also had success in shaping policy outcomes.

Early Childhood Education and Care

Programs providing for early childhood education and care (ECEC) are crucial to the achievement of women's equality. In comparative terms, Canadian women do not fare well on this issue. A 2006 study reveals that Canada spends the lowest percentage—0.25% of its gross domestic product (GDP) for children between the ages of zero and six years of fourteen Organisation for Economic Cooperation and Development countries evaluated; by comparison, the United States and United Kingdom spend just less than 0.5% of their GDP whereas Denmark and Norway spend between 2.0% and 1.5% (Friendly et al. 2007, 241). There are currently thirteen separate jurisdictions for ECEC in Canada—each of the ten provinces and three territories—resulting in variation in programs, costs, and quality (Friendly et al. 2007). Adding to this variation, the federal government assumes responsibility for a number of programs and funding (largely, tax expenditures) related to care and education programs. The result has been described as "a patchwork of dismal programs that offers basic babysitting but not much more" (CBC 2004, cited in Newman and White 2006, 239). Agreements between the federal and provincial governments in the early 2000s to improve and expand services were subsequently terminated after the election of a new federal government in early 2006.

Although estimates suggest that there exist regulated child care spaces for 17.2% of children age zero to twelve across Canada in 2006, this percentage varies from a high of 34.8% in Quebec to a low of 5.9% in Saskatchewan (Friendly et al. 2007, 204). The variation reflects the funding that is allocated to ECEC across jurisdictions, which ranges from a high of $4,644 per regulated child care space in Quebec in 2005–2006 to a low of $1,093 per space in Alberta (Friendly et al. 2007, 208), as well as the priority assigned to the issue across jurisdictions. Quebec remains a leader on this issue: More than 40% of Canada's regulated child care spaces are said to exist in the province that accounts for roughly 24% of Canada's overall population (Organisation for Economic Cooperation and Development 2004, 5). It is the only province that provides a publicly funded universal program for ECEC.

Abortion

Women's access to safe and legal abortion is integral to their ability to achieve equality. Two dates are important in this regard: 1969 and 1988. In 1969, the Criminal Code (a federal government responsibility) was amended to allow for legal abortion access in qualified hospitals (a provincial responsibility) following the approval of the hospital's Therapeutic Abortion Committee (comprised of three doctors). To grant approval, the committee had to believe that continuing the pregnancy would endanger the life of the fetus or the mother. As such, abortion services were decriminalized but access remained difficult; not all hospitals agreed to perform the services and they could only be obtained "to protect the mother's health or life" (Haussman 2001, 68). The legislation led to social action, most notably the 1970 Abortion Caravan that traveled from Vancouver to Ottawa to raise awareness of the issue (Newman and White 2006, 269).

In 1988, the Supreme Court struck down the 1969 Criminal Code amendments as a violation of "security of the person" guarantees in section 7 of the Charter. More important, the ruling did not suggest that women had a right of access to abortion services; instead, the ruling argued that if abortion services were to be provided to women, then they needed to be offered in a relatively easily accessible and consistent manner across the country (Newman and White 2006, 270–272). An attempt by the federal government to recriminalize abortion in 1989 died after a tie vote in the Senate.

The result is a policy vacuum; although legal restrictions to abortion no longer exist, procuring the service remains relatively difficult, especially for women outside of Canada's major urban centers and for low-income women, as a result of fees and travel costs (O'Neill 2006b). Although abortions performed in hospitals are funded, those performed in clinics may or may not be funded, depending on the province in question. It is also the case that relatively few hospitals across the country perform the service, and in one Canadian province in particular, Prince Edward Island, no hospitals perform the service.

Employment and Pay Equity

The increase in number of women in the workforce has been "one of the most significant social trends in Canada in the past quarter century" (Statistics Canada 2006, 103). In 1976, women accounted for 37% of employed Canadians; by 2001 this figure had risen to 47% (Statistics Canada 2006, 103). Women's workplace struggles have included discrimination in the workplace and the "double burden" (in other words, responsibility for the home and children in addition to working for pay) (Phillips and Phillips 2000). Whether to maintain family income levels, to pursue a career, and/or to gain independence, women's labor force participation has led to the double burden, in that they continue to assume greater responsibility for the unpaid work that is required in the home. This often leaves women with less free time available for engaging in activities directly related to politics or that can act as a springboard for political activities.

Despite Canadian women's increased labor force participation, they continue to earn lower incomes than men and continue to be found in occupations that have traditionally been filled by women (Statistics Canada 2006). Discrimination in the workplace has been argued to be one of the causes of the continuing wage gap; women who worked full-time, for the full year in 2003, earned only 71% of the income of men similarly employed (Statistics Canada 2006, 139). The wage gap also reflects the fact that women compose the vast majority of part-time workers—seven in ten in 2003, a figure that has not really changed since the mid 1970s (Statistics Canada 2006, 109). Women are more likely than men to choose part-time work because of child care, family, and/or personal responsibilities. The Canadian labor force continues to be segregated by gender; in 2004, "67% of all employed women were working in teaching, nursing and related health occupations, clerical or other administrative positions, and sales and service occupations" (Statistics Canada 2006, 14).

In the 1970s, government began to move toward ensuring that women had equal access to employment (referred to as *employment equity*) and to pay equity (equal pay for work of equal value) (Burt 2004). Both issues had been highlighted in the report of the Royal Commission on the Status of Women released in 1970. It was not until 1986, however, after the 1983 Royal Commission on Equality in Employment, that the federal government passed the Employment Equity Act requiring employers to collect workforce data on four designated groups (women, Aboriginal peoples, visible minorities, and the disabled) and to set hiring goals and targets for these groups. Such programs had received constitutional recognition under section 15 of the Charter. The program's limited reach (applying only to federal employees and federally regulated employers) and the lack of strong enforcement mechanisms have limited its effectiveness. Revised and strengthened in 1995, the legislation continues to be relatively ineffective, in part because it fails to address the systemic barriers to employment that women face, such as limited access to child care and the double burden (Timpson 2001).

Pay equity legislation, which attempts to ensure that roughly comparable occupations receive roughly comparable pay, exists in several jurisdictions in Canada and has resulted in some significant gains for Canadian women. At the federal level, pay equity provisions were first introduced in 1977 and are now embodied in the Canadian Human Rights Act (1985). Several provinces have similar legislation, including Manitoba, Quebec, Ontario, New Brunswick, Nova Scotia, and Prince Edward Island; all provinces have human rights legislation in place, however, that can be used to address wage discrimination. Women's gains in the area of pay equity have largely come as a result of litigation on the part of unions and women's nongovernmental organizations rather than governments' willing compliance with regulation (Cornish and Faraday 2004). Recent action on the part of governments in Canada to repeal or amend pay equity legislation, and their unwillingness to settle pay equity rulings in times of fiscal restraint, suggests that the policy is losing ground (Newman and White 2006, 229). In 2004, the Supreme Court underscored the difficulties of implementing pay equity when it upheld a decision dismissing a union grievance for nonpayment of pay equity provisions by the Newfoundland government on the grounds that women's right to equal pay had to be balanced with the ability of governments to maintain their own fiscal health (Newman and White 2006, 229). Like employment equity legislation, the effectiveness of pay equity provisions in Canada have been constrained by their limited reach into the labor force and their reliance on litigation to address grievances, and by limited government resources (Newman and White 2006, 229).

CONCLUSION: CANADA IN A COMPARATIVE PERSPECTIVE

A review of existing scholarship on women and politics in Canada suggests that although their participation at the individual level provides them with a certain measure of influence, the economic downturn and accompanying fiscal restraint of the late 1980s and early '90s significantly weakened the women's movement in particular, and women's nongovernmental organizations more broadly. Even though governments since then have begun to enjoy budget surpluses, the ideological shift to the Right at the federal level of government has further reduced the relative importance accorded to women and women's issues. This conclusion can be placed in a broader perspective by examining how women in Canada have fared compared with other advanced democracies. Doing so suggests that, as in a number of measures, Canadian women appear neither to lead nor to trail the pack, but rather fall somewhere in the middle.

Like most postindustrial democracies, Canada was host to a vibrant women's movement from the 1960s to the '80s. Since then, however, the movement has become more institutionalized and has lost support and momentum; it nevertheless remains a presence, albeit a more muted one, in Canadian politics. This downturn reflects internal struggles as well as cutbacks in state funding. Such struggles have not been as apparent in the U.S. women's movement, for example, where Emily's List and NOW continue to command a certain level of policy influence. Generally speaking, however, in most advanced democracies, women's and gender issues do not command the same level of political attention as they once did in the 1970s and '80s.

In the aftermath of the women's movement mobilization, women have become more active players in politics, as voters and activists. Canadian women's voting behavior and their political opinions are similar to those of women in comparable countries, in their tendency to vote for Left of center or centrist parties and in their support for state welfare programs. Gender gaps in political interest, engagement, and knowledge are also similar to those in established western democracies.

That said, women's political representation lags behind that of women in many comparable democracies. The single-member plurality system and the degree of commitment of political parties to women's equality are key factors in women's limited success in achieving electoral representation in Canada. Barring significant institutional or party changes, women's political representation will not likely surpass the 20% level in the foreseeable future. Yet this level exceeds that found in the United States and the United Kingdom, which undoubtedly are the countries most similar to Canada. Thus, although women's representation may be higher than that found in countries that closely resemble Canada, the 20% ceiling pales in comparison to the 40% and higher levels of representation achieved in Rwanda, Sweden, Finland, and Argentina.

Conclusions regarding how Canadian women compare on issues of public policy are more difficult to render because they vary with the policy in question. Despite financial and other difficulties that many Canadian women face in accessing abortion procedures, the country's policy vacuum results in a law that is relatively nonrestrictive when compared with other countries. Although Canada has led the world in adopting pay and employment equity laws, women have not fared particularly well in this regard in practice. Heavy reliance on litigation for redress exacts a heavy toll and long delays on the individual women involved in legal action, and even heavier tolls on those without access to such recourse. And on a number of measures, Canada's ECEC policies lag behind those in most countries, but especially a number of the European countries that have shown a strong commitment to publicly funded ECEC.

REFERENCES

Bashevkin, Sylvia. 1998. *Women on the Defensive: Living Through Conservative Times.* Toronto: University of Toronto Press.

Brodie, Janine. 1985. *Women and Politics in Canada.* Toronto: McGraw-Hill Ryerson.

Burt, Sandra. 2004. Women and Canadian politics: Taking (some) women's interests into account. In *Canadian Politics in the 21st Century,* ed. Michael Whittington and Glen Williams, 347–370. Toronto: Nelson Thompson.

Caul Kittilson, Miki. 2006. *Challenging Parties, Changing Parliaments: Women and Elected Office in Contemporary Western Europe.* Columbus: Ohio State University Press.

CBC (Canadian Broadcasting Corporation). 2004. Canada's Child-care System Languishing: OECD. October 25. www.cbc.ca/story/canada/national/2004/10/25/childcare_041025.html.

Cleverdon, Catherine. 1974. *The Woman Suffrage Movement in Canada,* 2nd ed. Toronto: University of Toronto Press.

Cornish, Mary, and Fay Faraday. 2004. "Litigating pay and employment equity: Strategic uses and limits: The Canadian experience." Presented at the International Pay and Employment Equity for Women Conference, Wellington, New Zealand, June 2004. http://www.cavalluzzo.com/index.html.

Cross, William, and Lisa Young. 2004. The contours of political party membership in Canada. *Party Politics* 10(4): 427–444.

Dalerup, Drude. 2006. *Women, Quotas and Politics.* London and New York: Routledge.

Dobrowolsky, Alexandra. 2000. *The Politics of Pragmatism: Women, Representation and Constitutionalism in Canada.* Don Mills: Oxford University Press.

Edwards v. A.G. of Canada (1930) A.C. 124.

Equal Voice. 2007. Fast Facts: Women in Provincial Politics. www.equalvoice.ca.

Erickson, Lynda, and Brenda O'Neill. 2002. The gender gap and the changing woman voter. *International Political Science Review* 23(4): 373–392.

Everitt, Joanna. 1998. The gender gap in Canada: Now you see it, now you don't. *Canadian Review of Sociology and Anthropology* 35(2): 191–219.

Federation of Canadian Municipalities. 2007. Women in Municipal Politics. http://www.fcm.ca/english/policy/big.pdf.

Fox, Richard L., and Jennifer L. Lawless. 2004. Entering the arena? Gender and the decision to run for office. *American Journal of Political Science* 48(2): 264–280.

Friendly, Martha, Jane Beach, Carolyne Ferns, and Michelle Turiano. 2007. *Early Childhood Education and Care in Canada 2006.* Toronto: Childcare Resource and Research Unit.

Gidengil, Elisabeth. 1995. Economic man: Social woman? The case of the gender gap in support for the Canada–US Free Trade Agreement. *Comparative Political Studies* 28: 384–408.

Gidengil, Elisabeth, André Blais, Neil Nevitte, and Richard Nadeau. 2003. Women to the Left? Gender differences in political beliefs and policy preferences. In *Women and Electoral Politics in Canada*, ed. Manon Tremblay and Linda Trimble, 140–159. Don Mills: Oxford.

——. *Citizens.* Vancouver: UBC Press.

Gidengil, Elisabeth, and Joanna Everitt. 2003. Talking tough: Gender and reported speech in campaign news coverage. *Political Communication* 20(3): 209–232.

Gidengil, Elisabeth, Elizabeth Goodyear-Grant, Neil Nevitte, and André Blais. 2006. Gender, knowledge and social capital. In *Gender and Social Capital*, ed. Brenda O'Neill and Elisabeth Gidengil, 241–272. New York: Routledge.

Gidengil, Elisabeth, Matthew Hennigar, André Blais, and Neil Nevitte. 2005. Explaining the gender gap in support for the new Right: The case of Canada. *Comparative Political Studies* 38: 1171–1195.

Haussman, Melissa. 2001. Of rights and power: Canada's federal abortion policy 1969–1991. In *Abortion Politics, Women's Movements, and the Democratic State: A Comparative Study of State Feminism*, ed. Dorothy M. Stetson, 63–86. New York: Oxford.

Inter-Parliamentary Union. 2007. Women in National Parliaments. http://www.ipu.org/wmn-e/classif.htm.

MacIvor, Heather. 2003. Women and the Canadian electoral system. In *Women and Electoral Politics in Canada*, ed. Manon Tremblay and Linda Trimble, 22–36. Don Mills: Oxford University Press.

Manfredi, Christopher P. 2004. *Feminist Activism in the Supreme Court.* Vancouver: UBC Press.

Newman, Jacquetta, and Linda A. White. 2006. *Women, Politics and Public Policy: The Political Struggles of Canadian Women.* Don Mills: Oxford University Press.

Organisation for Economic Cooperation and Development. 2004. *Early Childhood Education and Care Policy: Canada Country Note.* Paris: Organisation for Economic Cooperation and Development. http://www.oecd.org/dataoecd/42/34/33850725.pdf.

O'Neill, Brenda. 2001. A simple difference of opinion? Religious beliefs and gender gaps in public opinion in Canada. *Canadian Journal of Political Science* 34(2): 275–298.

——. 2003. On the same wavelength? Feminist attitudes across generations of Canadian women. In *Women and Electoral Politics in Canada*, ed. Manon Tremblay and Linda Trimble, 178–191. Don Mills: Oxford University Press.

——. 2006a. Canadian women's religious volunteerism: Compassion, connections, and comparisons. In *Gender and Social Capital*, ed. Brenda O'Neill and Elisabeth Gidengil, 185–211. New York: Routledge.

——. 2006b. Women's status across the Canadian provinces, 1999–2002: Exploring differences and possible explanations. In *Provinces: Canadian Provincial Politics*, ed. Christopher Dunn, 467–486. Peterborough: Broadview.

O'Neill, Brenda, and David Stewart. Forthcoming. Gender and political party leadership in Canada. *Party Politics.*

Paxton, Pamela, and Sheri Kunovich. 2003. Women's political representation: The importance of ideology. *Social Forces* 82(1): 87–113.

Phillips, Paul, and Erin Phillips. 2000. *Women and Work: Inequality in the Canadian Labour Market*, 3rd ed. Toronto: Lorimer.

Rule, Wilma. 1987. Electoral systems, contextual factors and women's opportunity for election to Parliament in twenty-three democracies. *Western Political Quarterly* 40(93): 477–498.

Sampert, Shannon, and Linda Trimble. 2003. "Wham, bam, no thank you, Ma'am": Gender and the game frame in national newspaper coverage of election 2000. In *Women and Electoral Politics in Canada*, ed. Manon Tremblay and Linda Trimble, 211–226. Don Mills: Oxford University Press.

Statistics Canada. 2006. *Women in Canada: A Gender-Based Statistical Report*, 5th ed. Ottawa: Minister of Industry.

Timpson, Annis May. 2001. *Driven Apart: Women's Employment Equity and Child Care in Canadian Public Policy*. Vancouver: UBC Press.

Tremblay, Manon. 1997. Quebec women in politics: An examination of the research. In *In The Presence of Women: Representation in Canadian Governments*, ed. Jane Arscott and Linda Trimble, 228–251. Toronto: Harcourt Brace.

Trimble, Linda. 2006. When do women count? Substantive representation of women in Canadian legislatures. In *Representing Women in Parliament: A Comparative Study*, ed. Marian Sawer, Manon Tremblay, and Linda Trimble, 120–133. New York: Routledge.

Vickers, Jill, Pauline Rankin, and Christine Appelle. 1993. *Politics as if Women Mattered: A Political Analysis of the National Action Committee on the Status of Women*. Toronto: University of Toronto Press.

Young, Lisa. 2000. *Feminists and Party Politics*. Vancouver: UBC Press.

——. 2006. Women's representation in the Canadian House of Commons. In *Representing Women in Parliament: A Comparative Study*, ed. Marian Sawer, Manon Tremblay, and Linda Trimble, 76–91. New York: Routledge.

Young, Lisa, and William Cross. 2003. Women's involvement in Canadian political parties. In *Women and Electoral Politics in Canada*, ed. Manon Tremblay and Linda Trimble, 91–108. Don Mills: Oxford University Press.

CHAPTER 19

....

BEYOND THE "INDIAN PROBLEM": ABORIGINAL PEOPLES AND THE TRANSFORMATION OF CANADA

....

DAVID R. NEWHOUSE
YALE D. BELANGER

ABORIGINAL peoples in Canada constitute distinct cultural and political communities with a set of ever-evolving rights recognized by the Supreme Court of Canada. Acknowledging that Aboriginal politics is more than the sum of three-plus decades of legal decisions, this chapter examines Aboriginal politics through the dual lenses of the "Indian problem" and the "Canada problem." It highlights key events that occurred between 1969–1995 which fostered Canada's subtle policy shift from a country promoting Indian assimilation to one embracing Aboriginal self-government. This transformative period witnessed the emergence of Aboriginal governance as a central objective of Aboriginal leaders seeking to reestablish nation-to-nation relationships between Canada and First Nations peoples and to achieve legitimacy as governments within the Canadian federation in their own right.

WHO ARE CANADA'S ABORIGINAL PEOPLE?

In the early twentieth century, Indians[1] numbered approximately 127,000, about 2% of the Canadian population. Once considered a vanishing race destined for cultural absorption into mainstream society, Aboriginal people now number 1.2 million, or 3.8% of the Canadian population (Canada 2008). An additional 1.7 million Canadians report an Aboriginal ancestry without formally identifying themselves as an "Aboriginal person." Statistics Canada estimates suggest the Aboriginal population will grow to 1.47 million people by 2017. The Aboriginal population has become more urbanized, following the overall trend of the Canadian population. In 2006, 54% of the Aboriginal population lived in urban centers compared with 80% of the Canadian population. Generally described by anthropologists and policy makers as tribes and bands, Aboriginal people tend to use nation and confederacy when describing their political models. English names that include MicMac, Maliseet, Huron, Iroquoian, Ojibway, Cree, Dene, Blackfoot, Haida, Nisga'a, among others, are slowly being replaced by cultural names, such as Mi'kmaq, Wendat, Haudenosaunee, Anishnaabe, Nehiyaw, Innu, Niitsítapi. Collective terms, such as First Nations and First Peoples, are increasingly used to denote descendants of the original inhabitants of the country, although the term *Indians* is still current, as in discussion of treaties and the Indian Act, 1876.

Aboriginal people are the only group defined in the Constitution Act, 1867 and the Constitution Act, 1982. Section 91(24) of the 1867 Act specifies that "Indians, and lands reserved for the Indians" are a federal responsibility. According to the Constitution Act, 1982—specifically, section 35(2)—Aboriginal people includes all Indian, Inuit, and Métis peoples. The Inuit (formerly the Eskimo) were deemed Indians for public policy purposes in 1939 (*Re. Eskimo* 1939). With the exception of the Alberta Métis settlements populations, Métis nationally were not the subject of special federal or provincial legislation. Furthermore, despite constitutional recognition, no definition of who the Métis are was provided. It was 2003 before the *Powley* decision (*R. v. Powley* 2003) provided guidance for policy makers on expanding the definition for Métis. In a unanimous ruling, the nine-member Court said that three broad factors identified Métis rights holders: self-identification, ancestral connection to a historic Métis community, and community acceptance.

Stressing that native people were far from disappearing as predicted, Métis historian Olive Dickason (1991, 419) claims that Indians are "more prominent in the collective consciousness of the nation than they have ever been before." Aboriginal peoples now constitute distinct cultural and political communities with an array of evolving rights defined at both the individual and collective levels through court decisions and negotiated settlements.

THE POLITICS OF ABORIGINAL PEOPLES

Aboriginal peoples' politics are shaped by the dual paradigms "the Indian problem" and "the Canada problem." Constant transformation characterizes both paradigms. From 1867 to 1971, Canada's Indian policy encouraged Indians to adopt European cultural norms leading to their cultural absorption and physical assimilation into the body politic. Indian resistance to colonial civilization and citizenship projects became known as the *Indian problem* (Dyck 1991). Starting in 1971, the assimilation policy was steadily replaced by a policy of self-government and, more recently, reconciliation in the wake of the Royal Commission on Aboriginal Peoples (RCAP) report (Canada 1996).

For Aboriginal peoples, the Canada problem consists of transforming Canada into a territory that would enable them to live a distinctive lifestyle and make decisions over the important aspects of their lives. These objectives are frequently depicted as a project to restore the nation-to-nation relationship that once existed between Aboriginal peoples and the British and French colonial powers. John Ralston Saul (1998; 2008) has argued that Canada is composed of three pillars—English, French, and Aboriginal—and that it is vital to pay attention to the oft-neglected third pillar of Canadian society.

Aboriginal leaders have regularly responded to various Indian policies by proposing revisiting the nation-to-nation ideal. Robert Williams (1997) convincingly argues that indigenous political thought may be observed in the actions of Indian leaders who wish to see relationships between peoples based upon mutual reliance and trust. To show that human beings might trust one another in a multicultural world, actions should take precedence to words. At one time, sharing a peace pipe, exchanging hostages, presenting valuable gifts like land, or allowing mutual access to hunting grounds symbolized this. Pooling resources would reduce conflict. This act was captured in the metaphor of the bowl with two spoons used to symbolize the territorial commons (Dennis 1993; Henderson 1997). The Peacemaker, founder of the Haudenosaunee Confederacy, an alliance of the Mohawk, Onondaga, Seneca, Cayuga, and Oneida nations dating back to the twelfth century, put it this way:

> We have still one matter to be considered and that is with reference to the hunting grounds of our people from which they derive their living. We shall now do this: We shall have only one dish or bowl in which will be placed one beaver's tail and we shall all have coequal right to it, and there shall be no knife, for if there be a knife in it, there would be danger that it might cut someone and blood would thereby be shed. (quoted in Williams 1997, 127)

The language of kinship (mother, father, brother, cousin) to describe the nature of the relationships among peoples remains an important element of the Aboriginal historical worldview. In a constantly changing world, one must learn to adapt to live well and with mutual respect. The environment is a sea of continually changing relationships requiring renewal and reexamination on a periodic basis. Aboriginal peoples developed political institutions to reflect these ideals. It is these political institutions Aboriginal leaders brought to the table to establish relationships with the newcomers. The Canada problem then revolves around the desire of Aboriginal peoples to create a harmonious relationship with the new entity called Canada, but a relationship that fulfills its responsibilities and obligations as when an elder brother cares for younger siblings.

Contemporary Aboriginal political action remains informed by these historical ideas, as Belanger (2006) has shown in his work on post-Confederation Aboriginal political organizations. Ovide Mercredi and Mary Ellen Turpel (1994) have proposed similar ideas as the starting point for renewing the relationship between Aboriginal peoples and Canada. The report of the Royal Commission on Aboriginal Peoples formulated an Aboriginal political vision of Canada based upon these ideas of mutual respect, responsibility, and sharing (Canada 1996). Since the 1960s, Aboriginal peoples have consistently advocated for increased self-determination and self-government, and a return to the North American nation-to-nation relationship model. And yet Aboriginal peoples are repeatedly asked, What do you want? In reply, Del Riley, President of the National Indian Brotherhood during the constitutional discussions of the late 1970s, stated:

> Indian people in Canada are experiencing a reawakening. They have come of age. Indian people are saying that we are not satisfied with someone else shaping our future and running our affairs. Instead, we want a future that will take into account our spirituality and our traditional forms of government that will allow us to live the kind of lives we desire.... We seek basic human rights. Sometimes it is termed "self-determination." Our quest for self-determination includes controlling those institutions that affect our lives. (Riley 1984, 159–160)

THE COLONIAL LEGACY

Aboriginal peoples occupy a multifaceted social, political, and legal constitutional reality linked to Canada's colonial Indian policy. This is still evident in their marginal social and economic status, low levels of education and income, poor housing, and poor health. Initially confined to reserves and remote areas, a majority now live in urban centers throughout the country (Newhouse and Peters 2003). The western provinces have the largest aggregate numbers and Ontario has the largest single provincial Aboriginal population. The colonial legacy is further demonstrated by studies that show a disproportionate number of Aboriginal people encounter problems with the justice system, leading to higher incarceration rates and, once in the system, significant levels of racism (see, for example, Nova Scotia [1989]). This is indicative of the difficult relationship that many Canadians have with the country's original inhabitants (Ontario 2008).

Another aspect of the colonial legacy that continues to dominate the discussion of Aboriginal matters is the Indian Act, passed by Parliament in 1876. Despite frequent amendments, its basic premises have not changed. According to John Tobias (1983), for 130 years Canada's Indian policy has been guided by three objectives: Indian protection, civilization, and assimilation. Each goal has spawned policy initiatives aimed at improving the condition of Indian peoples (Leslie 1982; 1999). However, each goal shared as its premise the idea that Indians were inferior to Europeans and in need of protection—curiously enough, from the civilizers. Indians were assigned special legal status, thereby justifying the implementation of protective measures, while at the same time promoting the Christian religion and the Protestant work ethic. Once achieved, historical life ways could be abandoned for the more advantageous integration into Canadian society. This was core policy until the federal government retracted the white paper in 1971. The Indian Act also affected gender relations, forcing Indian society to adopt prevailing European norms that gave primacy in law to males (Fiske 2008; Jamieson 1978). An Aboriginal women's movement arose in the 1970s to challenge this privileging of men and to recreate gender relationships based upon a combination of feminist and Aboriginal traditional ideas. The Indian Act was amended in 1985 (Bill C-31) to remove discriminatory provisions on the basis of gender.

Addressing the Indian Problem

The Hawthorn Report, 1966 and 1967

Concerned about the slow pace of assimilation, the federal government in 1960 extended to Indians their hitherto denied federal franchise and full citizenship rights, while preserving the guarantee of Indian status. In 1961, a joint parliamentary committee reported that Indians were still considered a racial minority whose time had come to "assume the responsibility and accept the benefit of full participation as Canadian citizens." Other recommendations acknowledged the need for "sufficient flexibility to meet the varying stages of development of the Indians during the transition period" (Canada 1961, 605).

Growing concerns about the new citizens' poor social and economic conditions led Parliament to launch a number of studies, the most influential being a two-volume report published in 1966 and 1967 (Hawthorn 1966 and 1967). It contains a series of recommendations that have become the foundation for modern Indian policy, among them the radical conception of Indians as "citizens plus," and rejection of the old idea of assimilation into mainstream society. "Citizens plus" implied that Indians had rights additional to those of other citizens "by virtue of promises made to them and expectations they were encouraged to hold, and from the simple

fact that they once used and occupied a country to which others came to gain enormous wealth in which the Indians shared little." The report concluded that Indians
were now to be considered "charter members of the Canadian community," and at
the same time emphasized a policy orientation that stressed both "a common citizenship as well as the reinforcement of difference" (Cairns 2000, 8). The notion of
"citizens plus" proved to be extremely powerful, so much so that the Indian Chiefs
of Alberta (ICA) adopted the name for its response to the 1969 federal Indian policy
proposals.

Hawthorn acknowledged the need for Indians to govern themselves and for the
Canadian system to accommodate Indian governments. Recommendation 67
(Hawthorn 1966 and 1967, 8), for example, states that "continuing encouragement
should be given to the development of Indian local government"; recommendation
68 (Hawthorn 1966 and 1967, 8) argues that the

> problem of developing Indian local government should not be treated in the
> either/or terms of the Indian Act or the provincial framework of local government.
> A partial blending of the two frameworks within the context of an experimental
> approach which will provide an opportunity for knowledge to be gained by
> experience is desirable. (Hawthorn 1966 and 1967, 18)

The authors further recommended that "the integration of Indian communities
into the provincial municipal framework should be deliberately and aggressively
pursued while leaving the organization, legal and political structure of Indian communities rooted in the Indian Act" (Canada 1983).

The White Paper

The 1969 Statement of Indian Policy of the Government of Canada rejected the
term *citizens plus*. Instead, guided by Prime Minister Pierre Trudeau's conception of
a just society, the white paper envisioned Indians as ordinary Canadian citizens
with neither special status nor a unique claim to distinct administrative arrangements or legal relationships. The central tenets of the proposed policy—equality
and equity—were given expression in the overall goal of enabling "Indian people to
be free to develop Indian cultures in an environment of legal, social and economic
equality with other Canadians" (Canada 1969). The white paper proposed that programs and services be transferred to and delivered by provincial jurisdictions, with
Indians becoming the responsibility of their home province and being eligible for
government services and programs from the same agencies that served all other
Canadians.

The Canadian government argued that a separate legal status for Indians "kept
the Indian people apart from and behind other Canadians" and that this "separate
road [could not] lead to full participation, to better equality in practice as well as
theory." The Indian Act was to be repealed and the Department of Indian Affairs
dismantled over a five-year period. An Indian land claims commissioner would be

appointed to deal with land claims and associated issues resulting from the treaties, which were described as "historic documents" containing only "limited and minimal promises" that had in most cases been fulfilled. Reserve lands would be transferred to Indian bands who would determine ownership among their members. In sum, the proposed policy would continue the transformation of Indians into citizens with the same legal status and rights of all Canadians, a definitive and final move away from the policy regime of protection and special rights.

ADDRESSING THE CANADA PROBLEM

The Red Paper of 1970

Indian leaders reacted volubly to the white paper. They asserted that federal officials ignored or, at the very least minimized, treaties that provided a separate legal status for Indians in favor of a future in which Indians would be part of an emerging multicultural society.

The ICA in 1970 responded with *Citizens Plus*, which quickly came to be known as the *Red Paper*. In it, the chiefs presented an Indian political vision of the nature of the Indian–Canada relationship, arguing for special status within Canada similar to Hawthorn's notion of citizens plus, albeit, in this instance, one traceable to the treaties. The preamble to the red paper states: "To Us who are Treaty Indians there is nothing more important than our Treaties, our lands and the well being of our future generation" (Indian Chiefs of Alberta 1970, 12). Ensuring justice for the original peoples was an overarching theme: "The only way to maintain our culture is for us to remain as Indians. To preserve our culture it is necessary to preserve our status, rights, lands and traditions. Our treaties are the basis of our rights" (Indian Chiefs of Alberta 1970, 53).

Concerning Indian lands, the Red Paper states that "the Indians are the beneficial (actual) owners of the lands. The legal title has been held for us by the Crown to prevent the sale and breaking up of our land. We are opposed to any system of allotment that would give individuals ownership with rights to sell." (Indian Chiefs of Alberta 1970, 94). Concerning services, the paper maintains that

> the federal government is bound by the BNA Act...to accept legislative
> responsibility for Indians and Indian Lands. In exchange for the lands...the
> treaties ensure the following benefits: (a) to have and to hold certain lands called
> "reserves" for the sole use and benefit of the Indian people forever and assistance
> in the social, economic, and cultural development of the reserves; (b) the
> provision of health services...at the expense of the Federal government; (c) the
> provision of education of all types and levels to all Indian people; (d) the right of
> the Indian people to hunt, trap and fish for their livelihood free of governmental
> interference and regulation and subject only to the proviso that the exercise of

this right must not interfere with the use and enjoyment of private property.
(Indian Chiefs of Alberta 1970, 6)

The Red Paper's philosophy guided Aboriginal leaders over the next 30 years. It was based upon indigenous notions of mutual benefit and a nation-to-nation relationship. In short, First Nations gave lands to the Crown in right of Canada in return for rights, guarantees, and services.

The Red Paper stimulated responses to the white paper. The Manitoba Indian Brotherhood's *Wahbung: Our Tomorrows* (1971, 7) best captured the emerging Aboriginal political vision: "The Indian Tribes of Manitoba are committed to the belief that our rights, both aboriginal and treaty, emanate from our sovereignty as a nation of people. Our relationships with the state have their roots in negotiation between two sovereign peoples." *Wahbung* recommended a comprehensive economic and social approach to Indian community development through three stages. Personal and community recovery projects were needed to counter the pathological consequences of poverty and powerlessness, improved policy mechanisms were needed to enhance Indian interests in land and resources, and government support was needed for human resource and cultural development.

Withdrawn in 1971, the white paper continued as a potent political icon within Aboriginal politics. It prompted Indian leaders to become politically active and organized. Consensus among Indian leaders emerged concerning the best way to recognize Indians' special rights, acknowledge historical grievances over lands and treaties, and ensure direct participation in the creation of policies affecting the future of Indians.

Buttressing this resolve was a 1973 Supreme Court of Canada decision that permanently altered Canada's political landscape. In *Calder* (1973), as the case came to be known, the Court, by a six-to-one majority, confirmed preexisting Aboriginal rights as foundationally sui generis (unique rights) that were simultaneously open to legal interpretation. Hereafter, Aboriginal rights would be legally acknowledged. *Calder* also paved the way for the renewal of the treaty process and a contemporary land claims policy (Foster et al. 2008), *and* altered the way in which Canadians would conceptualize Indian–Canada history. In its provocative conclusion, the decision observed that prior to the arrival of European settlers, "Indians were there, organized in societies occupying the land as their forefathers had for centuries" (*Calder* 1973, 145). No longer could Canadian officials deny the existence of Aboriginal rights; rather, they were forced to reflect upon the principles articulated in the Red Paper and *Wahbung* that argued for self-government as the central Aboriginal right among a potential multiplicity of as yet formally unspecified rights.

The *Calder* decision represents a turning point in how Aboriginal leaders addressed the Canada problem in that they could now utilize the courts in their pursuit of resolutions to land claims, as recourse for historical mistreatment and Crown malfeasance, and to define Aboriginal rights. The courts would, during the next two decades, produce favorable rulings at all levels that included, but are not limited to, *R. v. Sparrow* (1990), *Delgamuukw v. British Columbia* (1997), and *R. v. Marshall* (1999).

Prior to the *Calder* decision, in 1973 the Council for Yukon Indians (CYI) presented its plan in *Together Today for Our Children Tomorrow* to regain control over lands and resources that included a comprehensive approach to development. In its land claims statement to Prime Minister Trudeau, the CYI sought to "obtain a settlement in place of a treaty that will help us and our children learn to live in a changing world. We want to take part in the development of the Yukon and Canada, not stop it. But we can only participate as Indians. We will not sell our heritage for a quick buck or a temporary job" (CYI 1973, 18). The CYI demanded a land base, for

> without land Indian people have no soul—no life—no identity—no purpose. Control of our own land is necessary for our cultural and economic survival. For Yukon Indian People to join in the social and economic life of Yukon, we must have specific rights to lands and natural resources that will be enough for both our present and future needs. (CYI 1973, 31)

The Push for Aboriginal Self-Government

In the mid 1970s, self-government appeared as a promising mechanism to Aboriginal leaders seeking resolution of the Canada problem. The Federation of Saskatchewan Indians (FSI; now the Federation of Saskatchewan Indian Nations [FSIN]) was the first Aboriginal organization (1977) to articulate the principles of Aboriginal self-government, although these soon became familiar to public policy makers throughout Canada. Entitled *Indian Government*, the FSI (1977, 1) established a foundational set of beliefs and principles: "No one can change the Indian belief. We are Nations; we have Governments. Within the spirit and meaning of the Treaties, all Indians across Canada have the same fundamental and basic principles upon which to continue to build their Governments ever stronger."

It enunciated eight fundamental and basic principles: (1) Indian nations are historically self-governing; (2) section 91(24) of the Indian Act gives the federal government the authority to regulate relations with Indian nations, but not to regulate their internal affairs; (3) Indian government powers have been suppressed and eroded by legislative and administrative actions of Canada, and the Indian government is greater than is currently recognized or exercised and cannot be delegated; (4) treaties reserve a complete set of rights, including the right to be self-governing and to control Indian lands and resources without federal interference; (5) treaties take precedence over provincial and federal laws; (6) the trust relationship between the federal Crown and first nations imposes fiduciary obligations on the trustee; (7) the federal government has mismanaged this relationship; and (8) Indians have inalienable rights, including the inherent sovereignty of Indian Nations, the right to self-government, jurisdiction over their lands and citizens and the power to enforce the terms of the Treaties.

The FSI envisioned sovereignty as inherent and absolute, and it has never been surrendered through negotiations or as a result of warfare. Indian governments exercised sovereign powers, the most fundamental right being its continued governance over its people and territory according to local laws and customs. "Inherent" signified that the origin of the right to self-government resided neither in Parliament nor any branch of a foreign government. Indians have always had that right and the treaties reenforce this position. A second FSI report (1979) concluded that, between 1817 and 1929, more than twenty major international treaties were signed between the British Crown and the Indian and Dene nations. In return for these treaty rights, the nations agreed to cede certain lands for use and settlement. The FSI advanced a view of treaties as recognizing the powers of Indian nations and establishing sovereign relationships between Indian nations and Canada (FSI 1979).

With these foundational principles in place, the Indian self-government discourse broadened significantly, drawing Métis, nonstatus Indians, Inuit, and urban Aboriginal peoples into the constitutional debates of the 1980s. The terminology, notably influenced by the FSIN, shifted from self-determination to self-government to the promotion of Aboriginal peoples as self-governing nations possessed of a broad and enhanced right to self-government guaranteed by treaty. This resonated with and captured the political imagination of treaty and nontreaty Aboriginal peoples. Firmly rejecting the concept of universal citizenship articulated in the white paper, it expanded the citizens plus idea. What remained (and still remains) was to convince others of this position—in particular, the government of Canada.

The Constitution of Canada, patriated in 1982, spoke of Aboriginal peoples as Indian, Inuit (formerly Eskimo), and Métis. It affirmed existing Aboriginal rights but left unspecified their extent or definition. A series of constitutional conferences was held with the intent of having Canada, the provinces, and Aboriginal peoples determine what Aboriginal rights were and what self-government meant. The televised meetings introduced Canadians to contemporary Aboriginal leaders in conversation with members of the federal cabinet and the first ministers. The concept of self-government was hotly debated; its legitimacy and foundations questioned.

In a parallel development, the House of Commons established a special committee to study Indian self-government. The committee's report in 1983 (Canada 1983), informally known by the name of its chair, Keith Penner, advanced a view of Aboriginal government as an enhanced municipal-style government within a federal framework, but with three important differences: (1) Indian government should be treated as a distinct "order" of government within Canada with distinctive jurisdictional and fiscal arrangements, (2) Indian self-government should be acknowledged as a constitutionally entrenched right, and (3) fields of jurisdiction for Indian governments might include education, child welfare, health care, band membership, social and cultural development, land and resource use, revenue raising, economic and commercial development, justice and law enforcement, and intergovernment relations. The committee's view of the Indian problem was beginning to converge with the Aboriginal view of the Canada problem in that both dealt with the constitutional fabric of the country with the goal of recognizing Aboriginal peoples as constitutional partners.

The Penner report (as it became known) recommended a new relationship with Aboriginal peoples that echoed Prime Minister Trudeau's comments at the First Ministers' Conference on Aboriginal Constitutional Matters (Ottawa, March 1983):

Clearly, our aboriginal peoples each occupied a special place in history. To my
way of thinking, this entitles them to special recognition in the Constitution and
to their own place in Canadian society, distinct from each other and distinct from
other groups who, together with them, comprise the Canadian citizenry. (Canada
1983, 39)

The report recommended that Aboriginal self-government become the basis of a
new Canada–First Nations relationship and that

the right of Indian peoples to self-government be explicitly stated and entrenched
in the Constitution of Canada. The surest way to achieve permanent and
fundamental change in the relationship between Indian peoples and the federal
government is by means of a constitutional amendment. Indian First Nations
would form a distinct order of government in Canada, with their jurisdiction
defined. (Canada 1983, 44)

The report went on to indicate that "self government would mean that virtually the
entire range of law-making, policy, program delivery, law enforcement and adjudication powers would be available to an Indian First Nation government within its
territory" (Canada 1983, 63).

The government of Canada in March 1984 accepted the Penner report and
agreed with the need to establish a new relationship with Indian peoples. The government supported the proposal that Indian communities were historically self-
governing and that the erosion of Aboriginal self-government was a detriment to
Indians and Canadian society. It should be noted that the government did not
accept the idea of entrenching Aboriginal self-government in the Constitution, even
if a decade later it would read the Constitution in such a way as to include this very
right:

The Government of Canada recognizes the inherent right of self-government as
an existing Aboriginal right under section 35 of the Constitution Act, 1982. It
recognizes, as well, that the inherent right may find expression in treaties, and in
the context of the Crown's relationship with treaty First Nations. Recognition of
the inherent right is based on the view that the Aboriginal peoples of Canada
have the right to govern themselves in relation to matters that are internal to their
communities, integral to their unique cultures, identities, traditions, languages
and institutions, and with respect to their special relationship to their land and
their resources. (Canada 1995, 3)

The Penner report's centrality to Aboriginal self-government's continued evolution
is beyond doubt. It accepted and reinforced the FSIN argument of historic Indian
self-governing nations framed by supporting historical evidence. The report's
acceptance by the House of Commons, combined with a detailed plan leading to
the formal recognition of Aboriginal self-government, however, represented the
end of a phase in the continuing debate about Aboriginal self-government. The
central question of that phase was: Do Aboriginal peoples have the right to govern
themselves? In 1984, the federal government responded in the affirmative. However,
the anticipated governance models would come to reflect the newly evolving

bureaucratic belief in a negotiated (read "delegated") form of Aboriginal self-government (Belanger and Newhouse 2004; 2008).

Constitutional discussions in the late 1980s and 1990, directed primarily at Quebec's constitutional demands, also embraced the subject of Aboriginal self-government. Assessment of the Meech Lake and Charlottetown accords assume quite different significance when the focus is on Aboriginal self-government rather than increased autonomy for Quebec. The 1987 Meech Lake Accord, which had promised only a future conference on Aboriginal self-government, was rejected in 1990 in the Manitoba legislature when its sole Aboriginal member, Elijah Harper, voted against it. The 1992 Charlottetown Accord proposed recognition of the inherent right of Aboriginal self-government and a distinct order of Aboriginal government. It foreshadowed the recommendations of the RCAP in 1996. Self-government discussions involved the federal and provincial governments and municipalities. Provincial involvement was important particularly in discussions around natural resources, social services, and education.

Not satisfied with Canada's reluctant acceptance of Aboriginal self-government, Aboriginal leaders insisted that self-government be accepted as "existing" rather than as "delegated." More than that, they pressed for its being accepted as "inherent"— a position that found its way, in 1995, into the Federal Statement on the Inherent Right to Aboriginal Self-Government, known as the Inherent Rights Policy. Although there is now much debate about the implications of the term *inherent*, a key element of the Canada problem has, arguably, been addressed.

In the late 1980s and early '90s, Aboriginal dissatisfaction at the slow progress of self-government negotiations was one contributing factor to a handful of armed confrontations nationally. In response to the high-profile Oka standoff in Quebec in 1990, in which members of the Kahnawake First Nation barricaded their community for 79 days from construction workers seeking to expand a golf course from Oka Township into a burial ground surrounded by sacred pine trees, Brian Mulroney's Progressive Conservative government established the RCAP to "deal with an accumulation of literally centuries of injustice" (Frideres 1996, 249). This 4,000-page, five-volume report recommended that Aboriginal–Canada relationships be restructured and, at the same time, formally acknowledge this "third pillar" in addition to English and French Canada. It contains an Aboriginal political vision of Canada in which Aboriginal peoples comprise nations of distinct political communities situated within the country's governing structure, replete with defined jurisdictions and authorities augmented by a third chamber of Parliament: First Peoples House. In the spirit of *Wahbung*, the RCAP also called for the delegation of sufficient federal resources to improve Aboriginal social and economic conditions.

The RCAP model equated Aboriginal governments with "national governments" or "aboriginal public governments" or "community of interest governments." It went far beyond the limited municipal-style governments proposed by Hawthorn (1966 and 1967) or those pictured in the 1960s and early '70s. It envisioned Aboriginal governments as being informed by a distinct Aboriginal political

culture rooted in local Aboriginal traditions of governance that promoted a continuing Aboriginal–Canada Confederation with Aboriginal peoples occupying a
distinct and constitutionally protected realm. A new round of treaty making, the
commissioner's argued, would give this relationship and the associated political
models shape, form, and substance. The RCAP also embraced the notion of
Aboriginal self-government's complexity, rejecting a one-size-fits-all view of
governance.

These ideas were not developed in a vacuum. Rather, they arose out of the land
claims agreements from the previous two decades, which give concrete expression
to the idea of Aboriginal self-government: the Cree—Naskapi Act (1975), the Sechelt
Indian Self-Government Act (1986), and the Yukon Settlement (1993). Post-RCAP
agreements, such as the Nisga'a Treaty (2000), Nunavut's creation in 1999, and the
Nunavik Agreement in 2005, lent further support to the RCAP trilogy. In all, twenty-
seven land claim agreements were signed between 1975 and 2007. In addition,
numerous agreements in areas such as health, education, child care, and economic
development provide a sense of how Aboriginal governance might proceed in program and service areas. There is now a large and growing body of experience and
literature in contemporary Aboriginal governance that describes contemporary
practice and informs Aboriginal governance theory.

In British Columbia, the treaty process, facilitated by the British Columbia
Treaty Commission (formed in 1992), is a joint undertaking of Canada and the First
Nations Summit. The Treaty Commission is an independent agency that oversees
the negotiations of new treaties in a section of Canada that was never part of the
historic treaty process. In Saskatchewan, a joint federal–FSIN treaty process includes
the provincial government as an official observer and focuses on developing a contemporary interpretation of Saskatchewan's four treaties. Arising out of the lands
claim policy, as well as the Royal Proclamation of 1763, the treaty process includes
land, resource, and self-government discussions.

In summary, the ideas of self-government have broadened considerably during the past three decades, evolving from an initial conception modeled after local
municipal-style governments, to one guided by Indian Act criteria, to that of a
constitutionally protected inherent right. Its most recent expression is found in
the idea of "Aboriginal national government" as a distinct order of government
within the Canadian federation. The scope of people affected by the discussions
has also expanded considerably. The initial focus of self-government on status
Indians residing on reserves has now expanded to include Métis, Inuit, and urban
Aboriginal peoples. The basis of self-government has fundamentally changed.
Aboriginal self-government is no longer conceived of as rooted in the Indian Act,
but is seen as an inherent right, rooted in history and treaties. The scope of authority and jurisdiction for self-government has also enlarged considerably. Aboriginal
governments are now seen as more than municipalities; they encompass federal,
provincial, and municipal jurisdictions as well as some unique Aboriginal authorities. In the federal system, this means that the range of actors has enlarged. In a
short period of twenty-six years, from the white paper in 1969 to the Statement of

Inherent Right in 1995, Canada moved from an official government policy of termination and assimilation to a reluctant acceptance of the inherent right of self-government.

Post-1969 Aboriginal Society
and the Development of
Postcolonial Consciousness

The remarkable political achievements of this period unfortunately have not yet resulted in an overall improvement in the quality of life for Aboriginal peoples. Concurrent with efforts to solve the Canada problem, Aboriginal peoples have pressed for additional measures to address social and economic disparities. These aspirations are advanced in a collective and powerful fashion through Aboriginal political and civil sector organizations funded by governments. Between 1965 and 1992, for example, these organizations produced hundreds of reports containing thousands of recommendations on how to improve the Aboriginal socioeconomic conditions nationally (Graham et al. 1996a; 1996b). Today, Aboriginal issues are on the agenda of virtually every government agency, as well as the Supreme Court of Canada. Governments, civil sector organizations, and members of the private sector have had to adjust to the continuing legal presence of Aboriginal peoples. For example, in 2007, the British Columbia government created the position of Aboriginal physician as a senior public officer responsible for Aboriginal health. That same year, Ontario created a new cabinet portfolio to deal with Aboriginal affairs. *Time Magazine* on February 15, 1997, described the Canadian lands claim process as "one of the boldest experiments in social justice in Canada's history" (Purvis 1997, 18).

Political developments have been paralleled in other areas as well. There is now a recognized genre known as Aboriginal art that includes a wide variety of expression. There has been an explosion of Aboriginal music. In 2008, for example, the Canadian Aboriginal Music Awards celebrated its tenth year as part of the fifteen-year-old Canada Aboriginal Arts Festival. Aboriginal literature has similarly grown and the Canadian Broadcasting Corporation (CBC) produced two regular series featuring Aboriginal characters: *North of 60* and *The Rez*. CBC Radio 2 and Thomas King produced the *Dead Dog Café*, a weekly comedy show featuring Aboriginal peoples. In September 1999, the Aboriginal Peoples Television Network was launched and is today available on basic service in every cable viewer's home across Canada.

The National Aboriginal Achievement Foundation (formerly the Canadian Native Arts Foundation) presents annual awards to Aboriginal peoples who have made outstanding contributions to their communities. It has no difficulty in finding nominees, regularly receiving many more nominees than it can possibly confer awards. In the area of education, there is now one Aboriginal university and forty-nine Aboriginal-controlled postsecondary institutes (Aboriginal Institutes' Consortium 2005). All public schools on Indian reserves are under Indian control since the last federally operated residential school was closed in 1985 (Miller 1998; Milloy 1999).

There is an extraordinary array of service and cultural organizations serving large urban Aboriginal populations. The first edition of the Arrowfax (1996) directory of Aboriginal organizations identified close to 6,000 Aboriginal organizations split evenly between the profit and not-for-profit sectors, including First Nations governments. This number has grown every year since then and now includes about 24,000 Aboriginal businesses, nearly 3,000 Aboriginal organizations, and 117 Aboriginal friendship centers across Canada.

The emergence of a widespread healing movement that affects just about every Aboriginal person in Canada has led to the establishment of several Aboriginal health centers. Increasing number of Aboriginal people are teaching in primary, secondary, and postsecondary educational institutions. Some studies point to an emergent Aboriginal middle class (see, for example, Wotherspoon 2003). There is a strong desire to advance traditional teachings and philosophies. A new category of human knowledge—traditional indigenous knowledge—has emerged and is beginning to be taught throughout the school systems.

Aboriginal peoples have developed international linkages and worked in collaborative efforts with indigenous people around the world, helping to foster a worldwide movement aimed at gaining recognition of indigenous rights and improving the quality of indigenous lives. George Manuel, former president of the National Indian Brotherhood, now the Assembly of First Nations, founded the World Council of Indigenous Peoples (1974–1996). In September 2007, after two and a half decades of lobbying, the United Nations adopted the Declaration of the Rights of Indigenous Peoples, although without Canada's support. The Declaration states that indigenous peoples have the right to the recognition, observance, and enforcement of treaties concluded with states or their successors, a position advocated by the ICA in 1970.

Modern Aboriginal society is imbued with a postcolonial consciousness. This will be the defining force within Aboriginal society over the next generation. An engaged, educated, experienced leadership has emerged over the past two decades that knows how to push hard for what it wants. Behind that leadership are thousands of students, both young and old, who are in postsecondary education institutions across the country and who, over the next decade, will move into positions of leadership in many communities. They are determined, well educated, and see Aboriginal self-government within their grasp. They have experienced aspects of it in such fields as education, health care, and economic development, and they hope to ensure that federal and provincial policies are consistent with Aboriginal principles. For example, they secured retraction of the First Nations Governance Act in 2003, arguing strongly that it was incongruent with the foundational principles of Aboriginal self-government.

Canadians do not like to think of themselves as having a colonial past, especially one that extends into the present. It will be a challenge to foster the development of positive public attitudes toward Aboriginal peoples and their governments. The RCAP recommended the establishment of a major public education effort aimed at educating Canadian citizens about Aboriginal aspirations, cultures, communities, and ways of living.

An Angus Reid Poll commissioned by Indian and Northern Affairs in 2000 found that only 25% of Canadians believed Aboriginal peoples have a historic right to self-government and that 16% believed that Aboriginal people have "no claim to any more land in Canada." A similar percentage believed that Indian land claims were "legitimate and should be fully compensated in land, money or both." At the same time, support for honoring of treaties increased from 75% in 2006 to 80% in 2008 (Belanger 2008, 403). Beginning with Trent University's Indian Eskimo Studies Program in 1969, most Canadian universities have established indigenous studies programs.

Now that the debate about self-government has moved to include its operational details, the Indian problem and the Canada problem have shifted. Aboriginal peoples, although for the most part still poor and marginalized, have made important gains in recognition of the right to self-government and in convincing Canada to share the bounty of its riches more equitably. Canada is learning how to recognize Aboriginal self-government and build it into the country's governing structure so that Aboriginal governments can govern effectively. The Harvard Project on American Indian Development links good governance to economic development, links economic development to stewardship over resources and their effective use, and links all of this to cultural consistency. Aboriginal peoples are challenging the foundations of the nation-state, but are doing so in a way that is based upon indigenous political philosophies and one that argues for collaboration and cooperation, and seeks accommodation, coexistence, and acceptance of diversity (Borrows 2002; Tully 1995; Turner 2006).

To deal with the poor socioeconomic conditions of Aboriginal peoples, Aboriginal political leaders, and provincial, territorial, and federal leaders entered into a series of agreements in 2005 called the Kelowna Accord. It aimed at spending $5 billion over a ten-year period on Aboriginal education, employment, and other measures to improve overall living conditions. The Conservative government elected in 2006 decided not to honor the agreement. This disappointed and angered Aboriginal political leaders. The unilateral cancelation of the Accord was widely seen as a harbinger of a radical change in Aboriginal policy that threatened all the gains of the previous forty years.

Despite its lack of support for the Kelowna Accord, the Conservative government moved, in 2008, to address one of the lingering aspects of the colonial legacy: the policy of assimilation and its expression in the establishment of Indian residential schools. The government formally apologized in the House of Commons for the policy of assimilation and stated that this type of policy was never to be followed again. Aboriginal national leaders speaking from the floor of the House of Commons accepted the apology. It followed the Statement of Reconciliation proffered by the federal government in 1998 as part of its response to the Report of the Royal

Commission on Aboriginal Peoples. Both statements are foundational to the rebuilding of a new Canada as envisioned by Aboriginal peoples.

Aboriginal peoples have transformed Canada as they worked to address the Canada problem. The constitutional recognition of Aboriginal peoples and the recognition of an inherent right to self-government, even though they remain contentious in some places, have been transformative, both for Aboriginal peoples and the Canadian nation. Slowly, Canada is transforming itself into a postcolonial state—a state with foundations in the political thought of its indigenous inhabitants and a state that enables its original inhabitants to live with dignity and respect as indigenous peoples.

NOTES

1. There is no agreed-upon term to represent the collectivity comprising the original inhabitants of North America. Since contact, various terms have been used—*Savage, Indian, Aboriginal Peoples, Eskimo, Inuit, First Nations*, and *First Peoples*; and *Half-breed, Métis, métis*, and *Metis* to denote those of mixed Aboriginal and European heritage. At the same time, there is no agreed-upon term for those Canadians not of Aboriginal descent. *Other Canadians, Euro-Canadians, White, Newcomers*, and *Settlers* have been used. The contemporary terms in common use are *Aboriginal* and *nonAboriginal*, although *settler* has come to be used in some academic discourse.

REFERENCES

Aboriginal Institutes' Consortium. 2005. Aboriginal Institutions of Higher Education: A Struggle for the Education of Aboriginal Students, Control of Indigenous Knowledge, and Recognition of Aboriginal Institutions: An Examination of Government Policy. Toronto: Canadian Race Relations Foundation.

Arrowfax, Inc. 1996. *First Nations Tribal Directory*. Pembina, N.Dak.: Arrowfax, Inc.

Belanger, Yale D. 2006. *Seeking a seat at the table: A brief history of Indian political organizing in Canada, 1870–1951*. PhD diss., Trent University.

———. 2008. Future prospects for Aboriginal self-government in Canada. In *Aboriginal Self-Government in Canada: Current Trends and Issues*, 3rd ed., ed. Yale D. Belanger, 395–414. Saskatoon: Purich Publishing.

Belanger, Yale D., and David R. Newhouse. 2004. Emerging from the shadows: The pursuit of Aboriginal self-government to promote Aboriginal well-being. *Canadian Journal of Native Studies* 24(1): 129–222.

———. 2008. Reconciling solitudes: A critical analysis of the self-government ideal. In *Aboriginal Self-Government in Canada: Current Trends and Issues*, 3rd ed., ed. Yale D. Belanger, 1–19. Saskatoon: Purich Publishing.

Borrows, John. 2002. *Recovering Canada: The Resurgence of Indigenous Law*. Toronto: University of Toronto Press.

Cairns, Alan. 2000. *Citizens Plus: Aboriginal Peoples and the Canadian State*. Vancouver: UBC Press.

Calder v. The Attorney General of British Columbia (1973) 34 D.L.R. (3d) 145.

Canada. 1961. *The Report of the Joint Parliamentary—Senate Committee Hearings on Indian Affairs in Canada*. Ottawa: Queen's Printer.

———. 1969. Statement of the Government of Canada on Indian Policy, 1969. June 4. www.fcpp.org/publications/worth_a_look/spr/native.html.

———. 1983. *Special Committee on Indian Self-Government (Task Force)*. Ottawa: Queen's Printer.

———. 1995. *Federal Policy Guide Aboriginal Self Government: The Government of Canada's Approach to Implementation of the Inherent Right and the Negotiation of Aboriginal Self Government*. Ottawa: Queen's Printer.

———. 1996. Report of the Royal Commission on Aboriginal People. 5 vols. Ottawa: Canada Communication Group Publishing.

———. 2008. Statistics Canada: Aboriginal peoples in Canada in 2006: Inuit, Métis and First Nations. May 13. www12.statcan.ca/english/census06/analysis/aboriginal/urban.cfm.

Council for Yukon Indians. 1973. *Together Today for Our Children Tomorrow: A Statement of Grievances and an Approach to Settlement by the Yukon Indian People*. Whitehorse: Council for Yukon Indians.

Delgamuukw v. British Columbia (1997) 3 S.C.R. 1010.

Dennis, Matthew. 1993. *Cultivating a Landscape of Peace: Iroquois—European Encounters in Seventeenth-Century America*. New York: Oxford University Press.

Dickason, Olive P. 1991. *Canada's First Nations: A History of Founding Peoples from Earliest Times*. Toronto: McClelland and Stewart.

Dyck, Noel. 1991. *What Is the Indian Problem? Tutelage and Resistance in Canadian Indian Administration*. St. John's, Newfoundland: Institute of Social and Economic Research.

Federation of Saskatchewan Indians. 1977. *Indian Government*. Saskatoon: Federation of Saskatchewan Indians.

———. 1979. *Indian Treaty Rights: The Spirit and Intent of Treaty*. Saskatoon: Federation of Saskatchewan Indians.

Fiske, Jo-Anne. 2008. Constitutionalizing the space to be Aboriginal women: The Indian Act and the struggle for First Nations citizenship. In *Aboriginal Self-Government in Canada: Current Trends and Issues*, 3rd ed., ed. Yale D. Belanger, 309–331. Saskatoon: Purich Publishing.

Foster, Hamar, Heather Raven, and Jeremy Webber, eds. 2008. *Let Right be Done: Aboriginal Title, the* Calder *Case, and the Future of Indigenous Rights*. Vancouver: UBC Press.

Frideres, James. 1996. The Royal Commission on Aboriginal Peoples: The route to self-government? *Canadian Journal of Native Studies* 17(2): 247–266.

Graham, Katherine, Carolyn Dittburner, and Frances Abele. 1996a. Soliloquy and dialogue: The evolution of public policy discourse on Aboriginal issues since the Hawthorn report. In *For Seven Generations: An Information Legacy of the Royal Commission on Aboriginal Peoples* [CD-ROM]. Ottawa: Canada Publications Group.

———. 1996b. Summaries of reports by federal bodies and Aboriginal organizations. In *For Seven Generations: An Information Legacy of the Royal Commission on Aboriginal Peoples* [CD-ROM]. Ottawa: Canada Publications Group.

Hawthorn, H. B., ed. 1966 and 1967. A Survey of the Contemporary Indians of Canada. 2 vols. Ottawa: Queens Printer.

Henderson, Sakej Youngblood. 1997. *The Mikmaw Concordat*. Halifax: Fernwood Publishing.

Indian Chiefs of Alberta. 1970. *Citizens' Plus*. Edmonton: Indian-Eskimo Association of Canada.

Jamieson, Kathleen. 1978. *Indian Women and the Law: Citizens Minus*. Ottawa: Minister of Supply and Services.

Leslie, John. 1982. *The Bagot Commission: Developing a Corporate Memory for the Indian Department*. Canadian Historical Association, historical papers, Ottawa.

Leslie, John F. 1999. *Assimilation, integration, or termination? The development of Canadian Indian Policy, 1943–1963*. PhD diss., Ottawa, Ontario: Carleton University.

Manitoba Indian Brotherhood. 1971. *Wahbung: Our Tomorrows*. Winnipeg: Manitoba Indian Brotherhood. http://www.manitobachiefs.com/amc/history/Wahbung.pdf.

Mercredi, Ovide, and Mary Ellen Turpel. 1994. *In the Rapids: Navigating the Future of First Nations*. Toronto: Penguin Books.

Miller, J. R. 1998. *Singwauk's Vision*. Toronto: University of Toronto Press.

Milloy, John S. 1999. *"A National Crime": The Canadian Government and the Residential School System, 1879–1986*. Winnipeg: University of Manitoba Press.

Newhouse, David R., and Evelyn Peters, eds. 2003. *Not Strangers in These Parts: Urban Aboriginal Peoples*. Ottawa: Policy Research Initiatives.

Nova Scotia. 1989. *Royal Commission on Donald Marshall, Jr., Prosecution*. Halifax: Queen's Printer.

Purvis, Andrew. 1997. Whose home and native land? *Time* (Canadian ed.), February 15: 18.

R. v. Marshall (1999) 3 S.C.R. 533.

R. v. Powley (2003) 2 S.C.R. 207.

R. v. Sparrow (1990) 1 S.C.R. 1075.

Re. Eskimo (1939) S.C.R. 104.

Riley, Del. 1984. What Canada's Indians want and the difficulties getting it. In *Pathways to Self-Determination: Canadian Indians and the Canadian State*, ed. Leroy Little Bear, Menno Boldt, and J. Anthony Long, 159–163. Toronto: University of Toronto Press.

Saul, John Ralston. 1998. *Reflections of a Siamese Twin: Canada at the Beginning of the Twenty-first Century*. Toronto: Penguin Group Canada.

———. 2008. *A Fair Country: Telling Truths About Canada*. Toronto: Viking Canada.

Tobias, John L. 1983. Protection, civilization, assimilation: An outline history of Canada's Indian Policy. In *As Long as the Sun Shines and Water Flows*, ed. Ian Getty and Antoine Lussier, 39–55. Vancouver: UBC Press.

Tully, James. 1995. *Strange Multiplicity: Constitutionalism in an Age of Diversity*. Cambridge: Cambridge University Press.

Turner, Dale. 2006. *This Is Not a Peace Pipe: Towards a Critical Indigenous Philosophy*. Toronto: University of Toronto Press.

Williams, Robert A. 1997. *Linking Arms Together: American Indian Treaty Visions of Law and Peace, 1600–1800*. New York: Oxford University Press.

Wotherspoon, Terry. 2003. Prospects for a new middle class among urban Aboriginal people. In *Not Strangers in These Parts: Urban Aboriginal Peoples*, ed. David R. Newhouse and Evelyn J. Peters, 147–166. Ottawa: Policy Research Initiatives.

PART VI

CANADA IN THE WORLD

CHAPTER 20

....

CANADA AND THE WORLD: BEYOND MIDDLE POWER

....

JENNIFER M. WELSH

CANADA's experience as an independent foreign policy actor is not yet a hundred years old. Like other members of the Commonwealth, Canada adhered to the principle of British primacy in imperial foreign and defense policy for the first fifty years of its life, serving up its young soldiers to the cause of European peace from 1914 to 1918. Yet, in the relatively short time that Canada has pursued its own values and interests on the world stage, it has endeavored to project an image of distinctiveness, based around the notions of sacrifice and contribution. In other words, foreign policy making has been inextricably bound up with forging a national identity. Although this reality is not unique to Canada, the country's particular federal configuration and proximity to a superpower have given the quest for distinctiveness special impetus.

This chapter provides an overview of how Canada came to have an independent voice internationally, the delicate balancing act between globalism and continentalism that has marked its role during the post-1945 period, and how foreign policy is made within Canada's confederal system. The final part identifies the issues and challenges that occupy policy makers in this first decade of the twenty-first century—an era in which Canada's most important diplomatic partner, the United States, is experiencing a crisis in its global leadership role. In the sections that follow, I follow John Kirton (2007) in defining Canadian foreign policy in broad terms. Although such policy comprises many elements and many actors, the sum of these parts can be found in the decisions, declarations, and expenditures that governments make to manage Canada's relations with the outside world (Kirton 2007, 3). A core issue that emerges from this chapter is the growing challenge of defining a coherent Canadian "national interest," given the increased activism of provinces within the international arena, the diverse nature of Canada's population, and the demands to democratize the foreign policy process.

An assumption guiding the analysis is that Canada's role in the world is constrained by structural factors such as the distribution of global economic and military power, and prevailing norms about "appropriate" behavior in the international system.[1] However, "constrained" should not be equated with "determined." Canada retains some room for maneuvering internationally, and its distinct place in the world is shaped primarily by its history, and by the forces within its own political system and broader society that influence policy makers' responses to a changing global context. Of particular salience here is Canada's multicultural makeup and increasingly globalized population.

FROM DOMINION TO MIDDLE POWER

Until the passing of the Statute of Westminster in 1931, the Dominion of Canada was represented by the United Kingdom in the realm of diplomacy, participating in international negotiations only when critical external Canadian interests were at stake (such as the demarcation of Maritime boundaries, particularly vis-à-vis the United States).[2] And although Canada was an independent member of the League of Nations, contributing to its governing council, its preferred fallback position in the event that collective security collapsed was an alliance of English-speaking peoples who were inspired by the same democratic ideals and political institutions (MacMillan 2001, 55). The strong Canadian backing for the policy of appeasement during the late 1930s, and the subsequent speed with which Canada went to war against fascism along with its Commonwealth brethren, demonstrated that formal independence would not produce a foreign policy that strayed markedly from the priorities of the "mother country" (Lyon 1998, 298).

After 1945, Canada's other English-speaking partner and powerful neighbor, the United States, assumed the role as primary architect of the postwar international order. As part of the new Pax Americana, Canada played a significant part in the creation of the multilateral institutions that still strive to regulate much of international politics today: the United Nations (UN), the World Bank and International Monetary Fund (IMF), and the North Atlantic Treaty Organization (NATO). In fact, article 2 of the NATO treaty, which calls for the formation of a North Atlantic political and economic community, is commonly held to be "Canada's clause." This process of institutionalization at the global level, which was accompanied by the development of key welfare state structures domestically,[3] contributed to Canada's own successful development as an industrialized country after 1945.

Most important, Canada lent its resources and ideas of functionalism to the creation of the UN, a body that it believed had corrected the errors of the League system of collective security (Holmes 1979). At the San Francisco conference, Canada worked alongside other states such as Australia and Mexico to challenge the prerogatives of the great powers and to promote the status and role of small- and medium-size states (Hurd 2007, 101–104). Although its efforts to prevent procedures such as the great power veto ultimately failed, this experience of diplomacy solidified Canada's reputation as a good multilateralist and upstanding member of a new class of "middle powers" that had earned a place at the international table. As the Cold War enveloped the globe, threatening to dampen the postwar aspiration for multilateralism, it was the initiative of Canadian diplomats that helped to breathe new life into the UN, first by brokering a deal in 1953 to universalize its membership, and then by recommending the creation of the UN Emergency Force to address the crisis in the Suez Canal in 1956. The latter action earned then-Foreign Minister Lester Pearson the Nobel Peace Prize and launched what has become a long-standing interest of Canada in international peacekeeping.

These early postwar years suggested to Canadian diplomats that middle powers could affect the shape and direction of international institutions. Even though Canada did not enjoy dominance equivalent to the permanent five (P5) members of the UN Security Council, its resources and ideas gave it greater influence than smaller powers that were emerging from conflict or had only recently become independent states. During this time, Canada transformed the traditional meaning of the term *middle power* (a ranking based on relative capability[4]) into a set of behavioral principles for how states in that middle rank should conduct their foreign policy (Chapnik 2000; Kirton 2007, 41). Middle "powermanship" became the dominant descriptor of Canadian foreign policy, as the country acted as a "helpful fixer" and consensus builder on seemingly intractable problems. It also served as a mediator between opposing parties (most often the United States and the Soviet Union), preventing their conflicts from escalating and engulfing both other states and innocent civilians. Above all, Canada made a habit of collaborating with so-called like-minded states (often fellow members of the British Commonwealth), to ensure that its impact was greater than what it could have achieved on its own. Examples of middle powermanship from the 1950s and '60s include Pearson's chairmanship of the UN Special Committee on Palestine, General MacNaughton's attempt to mediate between India and Pakistan over Kashmir, Paul Martin Sr.'s negotiated settlement over Cyprus, Canada's efforts as part of the International Control Commission in Indochina, and John Diefenbaker's suggestion of a UN inspection force during the Cuban Missile Crisis.

BALANCING GLOBALISM AND CONTINENTALISM

As the superpower conflict proved less amenable to outside arbitration, and as the perception of Canada's impartiality changed (it was, after all, clearly on the side of the United States and western Europe in the battle against communism), the

Canadian vocation as the mediating middle power evolved into a more general support for multilateral institutions and the rule of law. This is evident in the consistent backing given by Canadian diplomats to efforts to reform the UN (the most recent round taking place in 2005), and the enthusiasm shown by Canada to join a broad array of other international institutions, ranging from the Commonwealth and La Francophonie, to the Organization for Security and Cooperation in Europe, the Asia Pacific Economic Council, and the Organization of American States. It is not a stretch to say that when it comes to international institutions, Canada has been a "serial joiner." More recently, Canada's commitment to multilateralism and the rule of law drove its active participation in the creation of a permanent international criminal court, and Jean Chrétien's insistence in 2003 that Canada could not contribute to the U.S.-led military campaign against Iraq unless it were authorized by the UN Security Council.

Although this advocacy of multilateralism and legalism are partly driven by ideas—the liberal principles of cooperation and the peaceful resolution of disputes—they also reflect the fact that middle-size states like Canada are better able to achieve their priorities in a world mediated by institutions and regulated by rules. To put it another way, effective governance at a global level is not a "soft" Canadian ideal, but a core aspect of the national interest. Effective multilateral institutions have enabled successive Canadian governments to participate in creating the global rules that directly affect Canadians. Without such bodies, and without a strong Canadian presence in them, Canada would risk subjecting itself to the wishes of more powerful states that may not act in accordance with its priorities.

As John Kirton (2007) has argued, the close historical association between Canada and international institutions has led many to assume that Canadian foreign policy has been all about multilateral organizations, and to overlook important policy developments in other areas. Alongside the story of Canada's global contribution as a middle power has been its complex relationship with its more powerful neighbor, the United States. Indeed, Canada's geographical realities and long history of close association with the United States are as central to its national story as the need to maintain unity between French and English Canada.

Although the subject of Canada–U.S. relations is covered in more detail elsewhere in this volume (see, in particular, chapter 22), it is crucial to note here how the need to choose between further cooperation with the United States and a set of wider international responsibilities has been a recurring theme in the postwar history of Canadian foreign policy. One of the earliest books on Canadian foreign policy, *Canada Looks Abroad* (MacKay and Rogers 1938), crystallized these two options—supporting international institutions and collective security, or retreating to the "fireproof house" in North America under the protection of the United States—for a generation of policy makers. In reality, however, Canada has pursued both strategies, sometimes simultaneously. During the years that Canada was contributing to the development of global institutions such as the UN and NATO, it was also creating a dense web of economic and security ties with the United States—most notably through the North American Aerospace Defense Command, established in 1957, and the controversial decision to accept U.S. nuclear weapons on Canadian soil in 1963. In 1988, the government of Conservative Prime Minister Brian Mulroney chose to intensify those ties even further, by bringing to completion the negotiation of the first bilateral trade agreement between Canada and the United States. In 2005, under the leadership of Paul Martin, Canada took continental cooperation to a new level (which now included Mexico), by endorsing the comprehensive Security and Prosperity Partnership of North America.

For some analysts, the imperative for Canada to "side" with the United States is embraced reluctantly as a product of U.S. hegemony and Canada's asymmetrical dependence on the American economy (Clarkson 1968; 2002; Hurtig 2002). According to this "peripheral dependence perspective" (Kirton 2007, 12), Canada is destined to exist as a penetrated satellite of the United States, gradually losing the distinctiveness of its economic, political, and social model and increasingly acquiescing to the U.S. agenda in international politics. For others, increased interdependence with the United States is a valued good—the rational continuation of a policy of free exchange, which will enhance Canadian prosperity and protect Canadian territory and citizens from new and more ominous threats (Gotlieb 2003; Hart 2002–2003). According to these latter analysts, the events of September 11, 2001, made Canada's ability to walk its historic tightrope—between support for the United States and strong backing for global institutions and rules—much less tenable. The threat of exclusion from an American-sponsored trade and security perimeter had made proclamations about the virtues of multilateralism an expensive luxury that Canadians could no longer afford.

THE MAKING OF CANADIAN FOREIGN POLICY

During the frosty decades of the Cold War, the notion of a middle power seeking to find a niche between the United States on the one hand, and the Soviet Union on the other, created opportunities for Canadian distinctiveness. It even had a degree of utility during the 1990s, as states were adjusting to the breakup of the communist bloc, further liberalizing their economies and building new forms of international collaboration. Under the stewardship of former Foreign Affairs Minister Lloyd Axworthy, Canada opted for a strategy of "niche diplomacy," focusing on a specific set of progressive policies such as the Ottawa Process on Landmines (which led to the creation of a convention to ban land mines in December 1997), the preparatory meetings for the creation of the International Criminal Court, the UN Security Council's initiative to garner a UN resolution on the protection of civilians during armed conflict, and the development of the new doctrine of the "responsibility to protect."[5] In this era, writes Andrew Cooper (1997, 282), Canada's middle power policy was driven less by relative size and more by a "tool kit of skills and reputational attributes" that enabled it to respond quickly and flexibly when opportunities presented themselves. However, developments in the international context during the early part of the twenty-first century (particularly the fallout from the events of September 11), combined with significant changes within the North American region, have bred skepticism about the middle power conception of Canada's international vocation (Kirton 2002; Welsh 2004). It is not yet clear, however, what alternative vocation should fill the void. For the first time in several decades, little consensus exists about Canada's role in the world, and foreign policy has become a crucial fault line dividing political parties in Parliament.

The National Interest

If we accept, in keeping with the Realist school of international relations (Morgenthau 2006), that the key task of foreign policy is to pursue the national interest, what priorities does this suggest for Canada? At the most basic level, Canadian foreign policy makers are entrusted with ensuring the continued survival of Canada as a sovereign state—defined in international law as an entity with a permanent population and defined territory, a government, and the capacity to enter into relations with other states.[6] In Canada's case, survival has been an ongoing challenge, as Quebec separatist movements have periodically raised the specter of state fragmentation. Early in Canada's history, there was also the threat of absorption into an expanding United States. Today, although the potency of Quebec separation has receded, there is renewed concern with maintaining Canadian control over its massive territory, particularly as climate change opens up new navigation possibilities for foreign states in the Arctic.

Moving on from this imperative of survival, the responsibility of foreign policy makers is to protect and promote the well-being of Canadians. Thus, security and prosperity take pride of place in most strategic statements of Canadian foreign policy, including the most recent International Policy Statement of 2005. At first glance, these goals appear uncontroversial, and largely in line with the concerns driving other advanced industrialized countries. Elaborating on these notions, however, is a more complex and political task. Underlying the debate between globalism and continentalism in Canadian foreign policy (discussed earlier) has been a deeper contestation over *how* Canada's national interest is best pursued. In this regard, there are four key points about the national interest worth highlighting.

To begin, it is overly simplistic to believe that a foreign policy guided by the national interest will necessarily breed coherence. Interests can sometimes conflict, as seen in the example of support for free trade. Here, Canadian policy makers must weigh the short-term imperative to protect, for example, Canadian dairy farmers from dislocation against the possibility of bringing about greater global prosperity, which will trickle down to all Canadians. This dilemma compromised Canada's reputation as a free-trading nation during the most recent "Doha Round" of global trade negotiations. A similar tension exists in the realm of energy and environmental policy, where Canada's professed commitment to a global solution to climate change (via the 1997 Kyoto Protocol) conflicts with individual provinces' plans for economic development and carbon dioxide emissions.

Second, although it is tempting to think that there is a set of enduring Canadian interests just waiting to be understood and implemented by the minister of foreign affairs, there is legitimate debate over what kinds of policies will best further the security and economic well-being of Canadians. Take, for example, the issue of further economic integration within North America. Those who suggest that Canada has an interest in pursuing trade and investment opportunities outside the United States are often criticized as acting against the clear national interest in a close Canada–U.S. relationship. However, seen from a different perspective, this call for diversification could form part of a prudent calculation of the long-term national interest. Canada is no longer the number one supplier of goods and services to the United States (the European Union [EU] and China have surpassed it). Nor is it clear that the *marginal* benefit of increased efforts to promote trade and investment in the United States is greater than it would be for similar efforts in a major developing-country market. This case highlights the importance of identifying who is pressing for a particular articulation of the national interest, and with what set of underlying principles and beliefs. National interests are constructed by particular processes, people, and institutions—some of which I outline here—and it is analytically problematic to assume that this is a neutral process (Finnemore 1996).

Third, today's international environment is throwing up diverse and daunting security challenges. For much of the post-1945 period, Canadians—unlike those in most other countries—were secure against any real possibility of invasion. Nonetheless, as a member of NATO, Canada was still susceptible to nuclear attack and was part of a strategy of "forward defense" against the Soviet threat that involved the stationing of Canadian troops on the European continent. Two decades after the end of the Cold War, developments both inside and outside of Canada are calling into question the initial hope that Canada would reap a "peace dividend" from the demise of the Soviet empire and could therefore drastically cut its defense budget. During this period, the Canadian forces—in conjunction with other government departments—have engaged in a much wider array of activities, from combating illegal fishing off Canadian coastlines, to intercepting ships carrying illegal migrants, to countering drug-smuggling operations. They have also assisted civilian authorities in responding to devastating floods, hurricanes, ice storms, and forest fires. These developments suggest that having armed forces stationed at home to address domestic emergencies and challenges to territory—as opposed to organizing them for missions overseas—is no longer a "residual" requirement (Government of Canada 2005). Within North America, there is also the continuing possibility of another terrorist strike—a vulnerability that is likely to persist as global terrorist networks explore new tactics and test out "soft" spots. Several western countries, including Canada, have been identified by terrorist movements in their public declarations, and there is compelling evidence that such groups have adherents within Canada. Furthermore, a major terrorist incident within one of Canada's continental partners would have direct consequences for the free movement of people and commerce.

Canadian foreign policy makers have therefore learned, through painful experience, that the country's greatest contemporary security challenges go far beyond the traditional case of the military forces of nation-states waging war against each other. Today's threats also come from a variety of nonstate actors and have a direct impact on innocent civilians. The other reality they have acknowledged is that countries find themselves sharing mutual interests more often than ever before. The main driver of this change is globalization—the explosion and rapid movement across borders of information, technology, people, goods and services, and knowledge. The result of these processes is a world that is smaller and more interdependent. But this has a potential dark side. Globalization has transformed the way we communicate and travel, but it has also facilitated the spread of deadly disease and given terrorists modern tools to exploit open societies—with devastating consequences.

In the contemporary era of globalization, traditional and more parochial conceptions of the national interest are difficult to maintain. As stated by the UN Secretary-General's 2004 High-Level Panel on Threats, Challenges and Change: "No State, no matter how powerful, can by its own efforts alone make itself invulnerable to today's threats" (United Nations 2004, 1). Moreover, as the challenges facing states such as Canada become more interrelated, the events and phenomena that could fall within the remit of the national interest have broadened. According to this line of argument, transnational forces such as organized crime or weapons proliferation become part of the *national* security agenda. This potential widening of the national interest has sparked a public debate about what threats Canada should take as "real" and how it should prioritize them.

For example, both Liberal and Conservative party leaders have contended that Canada's national interest dictates efforts to combat the roots of global instability at their source, wherever that might be. Thus, providing assistance to so-called failed or failing states, such as Afghanistan, is not considered an altruistic act or "war of choice." Instead, Canadian foreign policy makers have defended the country's largest combat mission since the Korean War, and biggest disbursement of bilateral aid in Canadian history, as being firmly in the Canadian national interest. In a globalized world, it is argued, it is essential for Canada to contribute to the creation of stronger and more capable states. As stated by the Independent Panel on Canada's Future Role in Afghanistan: "The haven that the Taliban gave to Al Qaeda before the 9/11 attacks showed how disorder and repressive extremism there could create a threat to the security of other countries—including Canada" (Government of Canada 2008, 21).

On the other side, however, are those who argue that terrorism is not the greatest threat facing Canadians—a contention that Canadian public opinion appears to support (Canada's World 2008)—and that missions to create stable governments in far-flung regions of the globe are both futile and detrimental to Canada's standing in the world (Byers 2007). This debate is far from resolved, and manifests itself in the divisions within public opinion over support for Canada's participation in the

Afghan war. Not since the free trade debate of the late 1980s, and the earlier controversy over the placement of U.S. nuclear weapons in Canada, has a foreign policy issue occupied such a central place in the political life of the country.

Finally, Canada's pursuit of security and prosperity is intimately connected to the question of values. Values help to forge cohesion across a huge territorial mass and diverse population, helping to make both collective action and collective judgment possible. As a result, ideals such as human rights, democracy, international cooperation, openness, and the peaceful resolution of disputes have all played a part in the articulation and realization of Canada's global agenda. Some contemporary commentators on Canadian foreign policy wish this were not so, and have condemned the "idealism" that they believe has contaminated policy makers' understanding of the national interest (Burney 2005; Gotlieb 2004; Granatstein 2003; Rempel 2006). The loud preaching of Canadian values, they warn, not only compromises Canada's diplomatic weight, but also diverts investment away from the core things needed to protect the Canadian people.

Looking at the past and present of Canadian foreign policy, however, it is clear that interests and values are not antithetical, but rather work in tandem.[7] One illustration of this is the priority placed upon building and reforming international institutions. From an interest-based perspective (outlined earlier) this policy stems from rational calculations about how Canada can best achieve its objectives in a context that involves larger powers. Furthermore, as an open liberal democracy, with dense regional and global ties, Canada's security and prosperity rely upon a stable international order—which is enhanced by effective governance. But as scholars have noted, many of the organizations of which Canada is a member have no legal charters or clear enforcement mechanisms. This suggests that something additional—perhaps a preference for connection and community—is motivating the Canadian enthusiasm for multilateralism (Kirton and Trebilcock 2004). Canada's marrying of ideals with interests would have resonated even with the archetypal realist, Hans Morgenthau, who reminded his readers that the global environment that confronted states was composed not only of the distribution of military and economic capabilities (hard power) but also of "the climate of ideas" (Thompson and Clinton 2006, xxiv).

Domestic Drivers of Foreign Policy

For those attracted to a Realist explanation of state behavior, the elaboration of Canada's interests is largely predetermined by its relative place in the international distribution of power, and much of what constitutes its foreign policy is merely a reaction to pressures operating in the external environment (Nossal 1997). But, as the previous discussion of values suggests, this kind of systemic logic can only partially account for how a state such as Canada will behave. Clearly there are factors beyond Canada's position in the hierarchy of power that explain the country's traditional propensity to cooperate in multilateral institutions and to seek the peaceful resolution of disputes. Indeed, there are other countries with a similar rank that do not exhibit these tendencies (see Stairs 1998, 270). In addition, this deterministic account of Canada as a "policy taker" gives little weight to domestic forces in shaping Canadian foreign policy. The view taken here, by contrast, is that structural factors only set the broad contours for Canada's international policy; particular individuals, groups, and organizations can have an impact on both the strategic direction a government chooses to pursue and the specific policy decisions it takes. Given the constraints of space, discussion of these factors will focus mainly on the key institutional actors responsible for Canadian foreign policy.

The starting point for this analysis is the observation that Canada has a parliamentary system of government in which the executive branch (the prime minister and his or her cabinet) have the critical part to play in all policy making. This is even truer in the context of international affairs, a policy area that has traditionally been seen as falling under federal jurisdiction. These facts of hierarchy and centralization might tempt analysts to examine the experience and belief systems of successive prime ministers and cabinet ministers to explain the major events and changes in Canadian foreign policy. Prominent examples here are Lester Pearson's pursuit of peacekeeping in Cyprus, Brian Mulroney's advocacy on the eradication of apartheid in South Africa, and former Foreign Minister Lloyd Axworthy's work on the campaign to ban land mines. But from a bureaucratic politics perspective, it is also important to consider the relative power of different government departments when examining why a particular course of action was pursued. Within the federal government, the departments that have traditionally dealt with Canadian foreign policy are foreign affairs, international trade,[8] national defense, and international cooperation (the latter being responsible for the Canadian International Development Agency). During the early postwar period, the Department of External Affairs (as it was then called) exerted a great deal of influence over Canada's active involvement in peacekeeping and collective security. It is also this department that has taken the lead in producing definitive statements of Canada's international policy, such as *Foreign Policy for Canadians* (published by the Trudeau government in 1970), *Canada in the World* (issued by Chrétien's government in 1995), and, most recently, the *International Policy Statement: A Role of Pride and Influence in the World* (released during Paul Martin's tenure as prime minister in 2005) (Government of Canada 1970, 1995, 2005).

Although, in theory, foreign affairs has a leadership role in creating foreign policy; in practice, this role has been progressively marginalized—particularly since the end of the Cold War. One contributing factor, discussed by Donald Savoie in chapter 10 (this volume), is the continued centralization of authority in the Prime Minister's Office and Privy Council Office (PCO). There are dedicated advisors on foreign policy in both of these offices, and deep capacity within the PCO to analyze the implications of different policy options. This shift of decision-making power within the civil service has diminished the influence of professional diplomats in setting Canada's international agenda. Second, changes in the nature of international conflict—such as the greater prominence of civil war, the dangers posed by weapons of mass destruction, and the rise of global terrorism—have changed the relationship between the Departments of Foreign Affairs and National Defense. More specifically, analysts have suggested that defense has taken the upper hand in policy making, most notably in the case of Canada's significant contribution to stabilizing Afghanistan (Stein and Lang 2007). Third, what counts as "foreign policy" in a globalized world has expanded, meaning that other government departments traditionally seen as domestically focused are now acting internationally. Today, the Department of the Environment is engaged in thinking about Canada's commitments to alleviate global warming, and the Department of Finance is actively involved in discussions about how to reform the World Bank and IMF. And fourth, at a political level, the nature of a government's mandate will also affect the level of influence enjoyed by the civil service. At the time of writing, Canada is governed by a minority Parliament, where political maneuvering absorbs much of the attention that would otherwise be devoted to fashioning a longer term strategy for foreign policy.

Beyond the tug-of-war over policy among federal government actors is the question of how much influence Canada's provinces have over foreign policy. Scholars of federalism have long noted the problematic nature of foreign policy making in federal systems, where there is a tension between divided internal sovereignty and the indivisibility of external sovereignty (Wheare 1963). Clear demarcations between federal and substate jurisdiction are, in practice, difficult to maintain, because the responsibilities of both levels of government expand over time until the point that they begin to overlap. For the substate level, the primary goal in assuming a role in foreign policy is to achieve the maximum degree of autonomy possible with a federal system. Officials at the center, however, have a natural tendency to resist these attempts to act independently in the international realm, because the management of relations with other countries is one of the defining features of sovereign statehood. In Canada, these general problems have taken on a particular form, making the task of articulating a coherent "national interest" all that more challenging.

The first point of note is that Ottawa shares power with the provinces in a host of areas with international content, such as immigration and the environment.[9] This means that there is considerable expertise at the provincial level that can and should be harnessed in foreign policy making. But a second fact is that Canada is comprised of highly unequal provinces and territories, some of which have conflicting international objectives to those of the federal government or other members of the federation. Cases in which friction developed over foreign policy include Alberta's clash with Ottawa concerning the commitments contained within the 1997 Kyoto Protocol, British Columbia's opposition to the federal government's acceptance of U.S. fishing practices in the Pacific, and Quebec's battles with Ottawa over ownership of international cultural policy.

As in other aspects of Canadian politics, the place of Quebec poses unique and sustained challenges to centralized foreign policy making. One Quebec commentator, Louis Baltazar, has referred to the province as "probably the most advanced case of international involvement for a non-state actor" (Rowswell 2002, 215). According to legislation passed in 2000, Quebec is "free to be bound by any treaty, convention or international agreement" in matters under its jurisdiction, and its minister of international relations may "establish and maintain relations with foreign states and international organizations" (Government of Quebec, 2000). Quebec governmental officials work in several overseas missions as part of the Canadian diplomatic corps, reporting directly to the reigning ambassador or high commissioner. Yet for the most part, as Rowswell (2002) has shown, these significant areas of overlap have not led to confrontation. Quebec has earned its international influence in part by working with, and not despite, the federal government. A confrontational relationship with the federal government over foreign policy jeopardizes Quebec's access to foreign governments, because the latter will be wary about any kind of engagement that might damage their ties with Ottawa. It is also noteworthy that where foreign policy conflict *has* occurred between Ottawa and Quebec City, it has rarely been driven by differences over the substance of policy. Although there are famous instances when Quebecers and their government have taken a different line over international affairs, such as the conscription crisis during World War II or the Parti québécois' advocacy of Canada's withdrawal from NATO in the 1970s, the more frequent cause of friction is ambiguity over who speaks for Quebecers internationally. For its part, Quebec City seeks to prove that only it can provide for Quebecers interests (thereby justifying greater autonomy within the federation), whereas Ottawa combats any move that would separate Quebec from Canada on the international stage. In both cases, governments are using foreign policy as a means to reinforce a particular collective identity (Rowswell 2002).

New Issues and Challenges

Before concluding this discussion of how Canadian foreign policy is made, it is worth asking how much Canadians—individually, or collectively organized—can affect the shape of their country's foreign policy. In the wake of democratic transformations that have occurred around the world during the past three decades, there has been greater concern for involving the publics of democratic states directly in the foreign policies of their country. In Canada, this dialogue between the federal government and the broader public is still relatively new; much of it can be traced to the election of the Liberal government of Jean Chrétien in 1993, and its red book commitment to "an open process for foreign policy making." This commitment was implemented through its 1995 review of foreign policy (noted earlier), preceded by a National Forum on Canada's International Relations. One of the recommendations of that forum was that the process of public consultation be repeated annually, through the Center for Foreign Policy Development, an office established within the Department of Foreign Affairs. Although this effort at democratization faltered,[10] the question of whether and how to engage the public in the formulation of foreign policy remains highly relevant. The reasons for this are threefold. First, the debate about international affairs in Canada is still confined to a relatively small, elite group of analysts. Second, the practice of consulting with civil society groups on the direction of Canadian foreign policy is still relatively recent, and the results of these efforts have been decidedly mixed (Stairs 2000). And third, as a 2008 study conducted by Environics Research has shown, Canadians' perceptions of themselves and their country are evolving in ways that policy makers need to take into account (Canada's World 2008).

With respect to territory, Canadians believe that their borders are more porous and that nontraditional threats—such as environmental degradation or communicable disease—are of the greatest concern. In terms of identity, Canadians are highly global in their outlook. The majority are likely to follow international news almost as frequently as they do national or provincial developments,[11] and almost half have donated money to organizations and causes that address issues in other countries. The country's multicultural makeup means that many Canadians have multiple allegiances and are significantly invested in other countries or regions of the world (the amounts are substantially greater than Canada's annual bilateral foreign aid budget). This relatively high level of global engagement has translated into higher expectations about what Canada should do on the international stage. Although the majority of Canadians admit that their country exerts "some" rather than "a lot" of influence in the world, their ideas for how Canada could contribute coalesce around leadership on the environment and global warming, confronting human rights abuses, and fighting hunger and poverty (Canada's World 2008).

The challenge for foreign-policy makers going forward is how to reconcile the aspirations of the Canadian people with a set of global realities that could frustrate Canada's potential. The lesson emerging from the roughly seventy years of Canadian experience in foreign policy is that to remain a secure and prosperous nation, Canada must foster international cooperation as well as defend its sovereignty. But in promoting collective action today, Canadian policy makers are operating in a less permissive environment.

The most visible manifestation is the transformation of multilateral peacekeeping. Although the Canadian public still largely identifies with the Pearsonian vision, peace operations no longer solely entail the separation of the warring parties and impartial surveillance, but rather now involve direct engagement in complex multiparty conflicts. Moreover, since the conflicts that erupted in Yugoslavia in the 1990s, the number and scope of international efforts to rehabilitate former zones of conflict have continued to grow. In the process, the lines between conflict prevention, peacekeeping, humanitarian reconstruction, and state building have blurred. As the current experience in Afghanistan demonstrates, western countries (including Canada) have not yet come to grips with these new demands. How Canada adapts to this new paradigm will be critical not only to the resolution of conflict but also to the more general question of what responsibilities Canadians have to "outsiders."

In addition, the traditional multilateral institutions that governed the world after 1945 are now under strain. From the disagreements produced by recent

American unilateralism to the increasing influence demanded by large developing countries, the organizations that currently exist for resolving global issues have come under heavy criticism. Although the UN continues to operate within its "One World, One UN" framework, in practice the divide between the G77 (which roughly represents developing countries) and the Organisation for Economic Cooperation and Development (which represents the developed world) currently prevents meaningful cooperation on many issues. Similarly, were we to design the IMF and World Bank today, our priorities would not be rebuilding Europe and Japan (indeed, the EU is now the world's largest aid donor). And finally, NATO's original reason for existing, a defensive alliance against the Soviet Union, has long ceased to drive the organization, and it now finds itself operating "out of area"—both geographically and in terms of its on-the-ground activities. As the legitimacy and effectiveness of these existing global institutions are increasingly questioned, the task for Canada is to collaborate with others to design and implement successful reforms. The "new multilateralism," as it has been called, must be more representative, so that nations with different cultures and capabilities can build mutually beneficial partnerships. It must also be more responsive to the new dilemmas facing the global community (such as climate change), so that problems are tackled before they become crises.

This institutional evolution will take place within a new global distribution of power. The agenda of the United States has shifted and sharpened since September 11, and its capacity and reputation have suffered as a result of its military campaign in Iraq. In particular, the economic viability of its expansive foreign policy goals is waning, given historic levels of national indebtedness and the fall-out from the recent global recession. These developments give rise to questions about the role it will play in managing international affairs in the immediate future. Although there is great anticipation that the new U.S. president will reinvigorate the country's global role, the challenges facing a post-Bush administration and the changing contours of the international system mean that we are unlikely to see a revival of the kind of U.S.-led multilateralism that characterized the early post-1945 period.

As a trusted friend with shared liberal–democratic values, Canada can collaborate internationally with the United States on issues of common concern. Indeed, whether Canadian citizens acknowledge it, many of the priorities that Canada pursues internationally (such as liberalized trade or "good governance") are inspired by the same values that animate U.S. foreign policy. But at the same time, Canadian foreign-policy makers must recognize that emerging giants, like China, India, and Brazil, are already making their presence felt. Their growing influence—particularly in the economic realm—carries significant implications for Canada. Canada's economy is currently the twelfth largest in the world, but remains smaller than those of Brazil, Korea, India, and Italy. Its defense spending, relative to gross domestic product, has fallen below such countries as Norway, Sweden, the Netherlands, and Australia, and its development assistance budget now accounts for only 3% of the global total. Even Canada's much-vaunted reputation as the world's peacekeeper has been damaged by its traumatic experience in Somalia and prolonged underinvestment in the armed forces. Although the country was once part of every

UN peacekeeping mission, and contributed 10% of the world's peacekeeping personnel, it now ranks thirty-fourth on the list of contributor countries and has had to turn down a series of requests to send its forces to war-torn countries (Cohen 2003).

If Canada stands idle in the face of these changes, its voice in international affairs will diminish. Its priority now is to reinvest in foreign policy capacity and to reach out to these emerging great powers, both by developing new bilateral ties and by reforming the global governance architecture to accommodate their needs. In so doing, Canada will ensure that the world continues to reflect Canadian values and interests.

NOTES

1. The constraints placed on state behavior by material factors are the main focus of the so-called Realist school of international relations (Waltz 1979). Recently, Constructivist theorists have demonstrated how norms and social "facts" also form part of the structure of the international system (Wendt 1999).

2. Canada formed part of the British delegation in negotiations with the United States leading to the Treaty of Washington. However, after the United Kingdom's ineffective efforts to advance Canadian territorial interests vis-à-vis Alaska, Canada negotiated directly with the United States in creating the International Joint Commissions in 1909 (Spencer et al. 1981).

3. John Ruggie (1982) has described this relationship between the Bretton Woods international economic system and the entrenching of Keynesian economic principles domestically as producing a system of "embedded liberalism."

4. One of the earliest references to middle powers was by the renaissance philosopher Giovanni Botero (1956, 8–9). He claimed: "Middle-sized states are the most lasting, since they are exposed neither to violence by their weakness nor to envy by their greatness, and their wealth and power being moderate, passions are less violent, ambition finds less support and licence less provocation than in large states" (see also Wight 1986, 30–67).

5. The International Commission on Intervention and State Sovereignty (2001) released its report, *The Responsibility to Protect*, after Axworthy had left office.

6. These four criteria are listed in the 1933 Montevideo Convention on Rights and Duties of States (Malanczuk 1997, 75).

7. This is also true for other countries, particularly the United States. The administration of George W. Bush was deeply motivated by values, giving freedom and democracy a central place in both the 2002 and 2006 National Security Strategy.

8. The bureaucratic home for international trade policy has varied throughout the years between a stand-alone department (as in the government of Paul Martin Jr.) or a joint department with foreign affairs.

9. Kirton (2007, 230) estimates that 85% of these powers are under provincial control.

10. The Center has recently been abolished.

11. The 2007 Pew Global Attitudes Project revealed that Canadians are among the top five globally engaged populations (out of a sample of forty-seven countries).

REFERENCES

Botero, Giovanni. 1956. *The Reason of State*. Trans. D. P. Waley. London: Routledge and Kegan Paul.

Burney, Derek. 2005. "Foreign policy: More coherence, less pretence." Simon Reisman Lecture in International Trade Policy, March 14. Ottawa: Carleton University, Centre for Trade Policy and Law.

Byers, Michael. 2007. *Intent for a Nation: A Relentlessly Optimistic Manifesto for Canada's Role in the World*. Vancouver: Douglas and McIntyre.

Canada's World. 2008. *The Canada's World Poll*. Toronto: Environics Research.

Chapnik, Adam. 2000. The Canadian middle power myth. *International Journal* 55: 188–206.

Clarkson, Stephen. 1968. *An Independent Foreign Policy for Canada?* Toronto: McClelland and Stewart.

——. 2002. *Uncle Sam and Us: Globalization, Neoconservatism, and the Canadian State*. Toronto: University of Toronto Press.

Cohen, Andrew. 2003. *While Canada Slept: How We Lost Our Place in the World*. Toronto: McClelland and Stewart.

Cooper, Andrew Fenton. 1997. *Canadian Foreign Policy: Old Habits and New Directions*. Scarborough: Prentice-Hall.

Finnemore, Martha. 1996. *National Interests in International Society*. Ithaca, N.Y.: Cornell University Press.

Gotlieb, Allan. 2003. The paramountcy of Canada–US relations. *National Post*, May 22, A20.

——. 2004. "Romanticism and realism in Canada's foreign policy." Toronto: C. D. Howe Institute Benefactors Lecture, November 3.

Government of Canada. 1970. *Foreign Policy for Canadians*. Ottawa: Department of External Affairs.

——. 1995. *Canada in the World*. Ottawa: Department of Foreign Affairs and International Trade.

——. 2005. *Canada's International Policy Statement: A Role of Pride and Influence in the World*. Ottawa: Department of Foreign Affairs and International Trade.

——. 2008. *Independent Panel on Canada's Future Role in Afghanistan*. Ottawa: Minister of Public Works and Government Services.

Government of Quebec. 2000. *An Act Respecting the Exercise of the Fundamental Rights and Prerogatives of the Quebec People and of the Quebec State*. Quebec: Quebec Official Publisher.

Granatstein, J. L. 2003. "The importance of being less earnest." Toronto: C. D. Howe Institute Benefactors Lecture, October 21.

Hart, Michael. 2002–03. Lessons from Canada's history as a trading nation. *International Journal* 58(1): 25–42.

Holmes, John. 1979. *The Shaping of Peace: Canada and the Search for World Order 1943–1957*, vol. 1. Toronto: University of Toronto Press.

Hurd, Ian. 2007. *After Anarchy: Legitimacy and Power in the United Nations Security Council*. Princeton, N.J.: Princeton University Press.

Hurtig, Mel. 2002. *The Vanishing Country: Is It Too Late to Save Canada?* Toronto: McClelland and Stewart.

International Commission on Intervention and State Sovereignty. 2001. *The Responsibility to Protect*. Ottawa: International Development Research Center.

Kirton, John. 2002. Canada as a principal summit power. In *Canada among Nations 2002: A Fading Power*, ed. Norman Hillmer and Maureen Appel Molot, 209–232. Toronto: Oxford University Press.

————. 2007. *Canadian Foreign Policy in a Changing World*. Toronto: Nelson.

Kirton, John, and Michael Trebilcock, eds. 2004. *Hard Choices, Soft Law: Voluntary Standards in Global Trade, Environment and Social Governance*. Aldershot: Ashgate.

Lyon, Peter. 1998. The old commonwealth: The first four Dominions. In *The Oxford History of the Twentieth Century*, eds. Michael Howard and W. Roger Louis, 292–304. Oxford: Oxford University Press.

MacKay, Bert, and E. B. Rogers. 1938. *Canada Looks Abroad*. Oxford: Oxford University Press.

MacMillan, Margaret. 2001. *Peacemakers: The Paris Conference of 1919 and Its Attempt to End War*. London: John Murray.

Malanczuk, Peter, ed. 1997. *Akehurst's Modern Introduction to International Law*. London: Routledge.

Morgenthau, Hans J. 2006. *Politics among Nations: The Struggle for Power and Peace*, 7th ed. New York: McGraw-Hill.

Nossal, Kim Richard. 1997. *The Politics of Canadian Foreign Policy*, 3rd ed. Scarborough: Prentice Hall.

Rempel, Roy. 2006. *Dreamland: How Canada's Pretend Foreign Policy Has Undermined Sovereignty*. Montreal: McGill-Queens University Press.

Rowswell, Ben. 2002. The federal context: Ottawa as padlock or partner? *The American Review of Canadian Studies* 32(2): 215–237.

Ruggie, John Gerard. 1982. International regimes, transactions, and change: Embedded liberalism in the postwar economic order. *International Organization* 36(2): 379–415.

Spencer, Robert, John Kirton, and Kim Richard Nossal. 1981. *The International Joint Commission Seventy Years On*. Toronto: Center for International Studies.

Stairs, Denis. 1998. Of medium powers and middling roles. In *Statecraft and Security: The Cold War and Beyond*, ed. Ken Booth, 270–286. Cambridge: Cambridge University Press.

————. 2000. Foreign policy consultations in a globalizing world: The case of Canada, the WTO, and the shenanigans in Seattle. *Policy Matters* 1(9).

Stein, Janice Gross, and Eugene Lang. 2007. *The Unexpected War: Canada in Kandahar*. Toronto: Viking Canada.

Thompson, Kenneth, and W. David Clinton. 2006. Foreword. In *Politics among Nations: The Struggle for Power and Peace*, 7th ed., xvii–xxxix. New York: McGraw-Hill.

United Nations. 2004. *A More Secure World: Our Shared Responsibility*. Report of the High-Level Panel on Threat, Challenges, and Change. New York: United Nations.

Waltz, Kenneth. 1979. *Theory of International Politics*. New York: McGraw-Hill.

Welsh, Jennifer. 2004. *At Home in the World: Canada's Global Vision for the 21st Century*. Toronto: HarperCollins Canada.

Wendt, Alexander. 1999. *Social Theory of International Politics*. Cambridge: Cambridge University Press.

Wheare, Kenneth C. 1963. *Federal Government*, 4th ed. London: Oxford University Press.

Wight, Martin. 1986. *Power Politics*, 2nd ed., ed. Hedley Bull and Carsten Holbraad. London: Royal Institute of International Affairs.

CHAPTER 21

CANADA–UNITED STATES RELATIONS

STEPHEN BROOKS

> Geography has made us neighbors, history has made us
> allies, and economics has made us business partners, but we
> are friends by choice.
>
> —John F. Kennedy

President John F. Kennedy made these remarks during a visit to Ottawa in 1961. Between Canada and the United States stretched 5,525 miles of what was commonly referred to as "the world's longest undefended border." The two countries had emerged from World War II as close military allies, a partnership that was deepened and institutionalized during the Cold War years of the 1950s. The value of trade across the Canada–U.S. border exceeded that of any other bilateral trading relationship in the world, and each nation was the other's largest trading partner. American investment in the Canadian economy was massive, with about one quarter of all nonfinancial assets being controlled by American owners. And although the personal relationship between President Kennedy and Prime Minister John Diefenbaker was frosty at best, relations between the Canadian and American peoples were, by and large, quite positive.

This was the era of the *special relationship*, as it came to be called, between Canada and the United States. Joined at the hip by geography, history, and economics, as President Kennedy observed, relations between the two countries during the 1950s and part of the '60s were characterized by a quiet diplomacy that relied on close personal contacts and shared understandings. The special relationship was nurtured by the intimacy of the vast network of linkages across the Canada–U.S. border, but it turned out to be a fairly brief moment in the history of Canada–U.S.

relations. The asymmetry in this bilateral relationship, the United States being the dominant partner in every significant respect, and the longstanding ambivalence of many Canadians and their elites toward the United States provided the basis for criticisms of the special relationship and quiet diplomacy. "Close, but not too close," expressed the view of most Canadians about their country's relationship to its superpower neighbor. This continues to be the prevailing view among Canadians, although there is no agreement on how close is too close.

When President George W. Bush visited Ottawa in 2004, he was greeted by pro-testers and canceled what would otherwise have been a normally scheduled address to Parliament after some Canadian legislators threatened to disrupt his speech. The special relationship between Canada and the United States seemed to belong to a distant time. But even at moments of great stress in the Canada–U.S. relationship— and disagreement over whether Saddam Hussein's Iraq should be invaded without the support of a UN resolution was one of these moments—the relationship is mainly characterized by cooperation and agreement. Conflict and acrimony will always steal the headlines, sometimes creating the misleading impression that these two countries are hardly the friends that President Kennedy declared them to be. The occasional conflict and acrimony are real, but so, too, is the dense network of public and private linkages that often goes unnoticed and that acts as a shock absorber during the rough patches in Canada–U.S. relations.

This chapter examines the broad historical and cultural background of Canada–U.S. relations. As indicated earlier, these relations have been characterized by inti-macy, asymmetry and ambivalence. The chapter concludes with some thoughts on possible future directions in a relationship that has preoccupied Canadians for more than 200 years.

INTIMACY

It is arguable that no two countries have closer ties than Canada and the United States. Indeed, the fact that they are separate countries is in some ways one of those products of historical circumstances that might well not have happened if events had unfolded in only a slightly different manner. When the thirteen colonies declared their independence from Great Britain in 1776, the northernmost British colonies did not join in the revolution. They had been invited to attend the Continental Congress, but declined to do so. The Articles of Confederation, the first constitution of the United States, included a provision (section XI) that expressly provided for the entry of Canada into the new American republic. According to Canadian historian P. B. Waite (1965, 56–57), popular sentiment among *les habitants* at the time of the American Revolution was probably in favor of joining the upstart colonies in their revolution against British rule. The idea that the French-speaking Catholic population of Quebec sought refuge behind the British Crown from the threatening tide of liberalism to the south is also questioned by political scientist Denis Monière (1981). Like Waite, Monière argues that this perception of America certainly existed among members of the French Canadian clergy, pleased as they were with the protections granted to them under the Quebec Act of 1774, but it was not shared by the *peuple* on whose behalf they claimed to speak.

The population of Quebec was overwhelmingly French speaking and Catholic. But in the case of the English-speaking founders of Canada, they spoke the same language as Americans and were not significantly different in ethnic, religious, or socioeconomic terms. However, the semiofficial narrative of Canadian history—the one that tends to be taught in schools and embraced by opinion leaders—insists that there were, nonetheless, important cultural differences and that among these was the rejection by the founders of Canada of what they saw as a foreign and undesirable value system. In other words, it maintains that these early Canadians and *canadiens* perceived the fledgling United States and Americans in a negative light and, moreover, that this hostile perception led them to create and defend a society and institutions that were self-consciously not American.

There is an element of truth in the semiofficial narrative of Canadian history, but it exaggerates both the extent of the differences that separated Canadians and Americans culturally, and the degree to which general opinion among Canadians and *canadiens*—as distinct from influential elements of elite opinion—embraced a negative image of America and Americans. Moreover, although the political paths of the United States and Canada diverged as a result of the American Revolution and the Loyalist migration to what remained of British North America, the two societies remained joined by ties of population, economics, and values.

People

For much of their shared history the border separating Canada from the United States provided little resistance to the movement of people from one side to the other. It was, in the words of one historian, more of a legal fiction than a real barrier to emigration of Americans north and Canadians south. And, indeed, these population movements were impressive, particularly during the years from the end of the American Revolutionary War to the early and even mid twentieth century. Ties of population helped generate and maintain the intimacy of Canada–U.S. relations.

Cross-border migration began with the Loyalist emigration from the United States in the 1780s. Between 30,000 and 50,000 American colonists left the newly independent United States for Canada. Despite some interpretations to the contrary, the weight of the evidence suggests strongly that these immigrants to Canada were not very different in their cultural values and beliefs from their American neighbors. Leaving this matter aside for now, it is even more striking that, by 1812, an estimated 80% of Upper Canada's population of 136,000 consisted of people who had migrated from the United States, only one in four of whom were Loyalists (Landon 1967, 19–20). These Americans had migrated primarily in response to economic factors—in this case, the prospect of cheap land in a region where the danger from Amerindians was less than at the expanding western frontier of the United States.

The War of 1812 was followed by official efforts in British North America to discourage immigration from the United States and to encourage settlement by immigrants from the British Isles. The strong American presence in Upper Canada was diluted as tens of thousands of immigrants arrived from the British Isles. However, economic forces that pulled thousands of Americans north before the War of 1812 also attracted Canadians to the United States. Randall and Thompson (2002, 53) estimate that between 1840 and 1900 about 625,000 people emigrated from Ontario to the American Midwest, New England, and California, and another 427,000 from the Maritimes, mainly to the northeast of the United States. The wave of Canadian emigrants became heavier in the second half of the nineteenth century, as a result, in large part, of a massive migration of French Canadians from Quebec to the northeastern region of the United States. By century's end, almost every French Canadian family had at least one member living in the United States, and the total number of French Canadian immigrants to the United States is estimated to have been roughly 900,000 for the period 1840 to 1930. To get a sense of the scale of this migration, it is worth noting that the total population of Quebec as of the 1901 census was roughly 1.6 million.

The last decades of the nineteenth century and the first of the twentieth were marked by an extraordinary level of cross-border migration. Hansen and Brebner estimate that the net emigration of native-born Canadians and recently arrived immigrants surpassed one million during the single decade of 1881 to 1891. Another study concludes that about two of every three immigrants to Canada during the years 1901–1921, a period during which total immigration to Canada was roughly three million, left to the United States (cited in Porter 1965, 30–31). Randall and Thompson (2002) estimate that the net migration of Canadians to the United States between 1840 and 1900 was about 1.4 million, representing about one quarter of Canada's total population at the turn of the century. Goldwin Smith (1891, 235), who famously expressed the view that the most striking thing about Canada was that it was not America, remarked that "if [Americans] do not annex Canada they are annexing the Canadians."

By 1930, the total number of Canadian-born persons who had emigrated to the United States may have been about 2.75 million (Lavoie 1972, 76–79), but the permeable border that allowed the easy and extensive movement of Canadians to the United States and Americans to Canada became a more serious barrier to entry during the Great Depression. The U.S. Congress imposed the same immigration requirements on Canadians as applied to those from other countries (the U.S. Immigration Act of 1921 had exempted Canadians from the immigration quotas that applied to others) and generally made it more difficult to move to and work in the United States. In some ways, however, these new barriers to the free movement of people were beside the point. Cross-border migration between these two countries has always been mainly a response to economic factors, and the Depression of the 1930s saw real unemployment rates in both Canada and the United States reach roughly one third of the labor force. In these circumstances, immigration to both countries from abroad plummeted and the historically high rate of cross-border migration dropped dramatically. Indeed, an estimated 100,000 Canadians returned to Canada between 1930 and 1936, in most cases because the economic incentives that had drawn them south had disappeared.

At the dawn of the Depression, Canadians constituted the third largest group of foreign-born people in the United States, surpassed only by Germans and Italians. Since then, the "mingling of peoples" that has created such an extensive network of human ties across the Canada–U.S. border has declined. The 2000 U.S. Census reported 820,771 Canadian-born persons living in the United States, less than one third of 1% of the American population, compared with 1.2 million Canadians or about 1.6% of the total population in 1900. The percentage of American born living in Canada has fluctuated around 250,000 in recent censuses, representing less than 1% of the Canadian population. These numbers understate the personal ties that exist between members of extended families that the span the border and also fail to take into account the millions of same-day, and longer, visits for work, shopping, and vacation made annually by residents of each country to the other.

Cross-border migration has continued to fluctuate in response to economic factors. In particular, the flow of Canadians to the United States has spiked at several points over the past half century, most recently in the 1980s and then again toward the end of the '90s and into the first few years of the twenty-first century. Likewise, cross-border visits continue to maintain a connective tissue of personal relations between the two countries, although these have dropped significantly since the terrorist attacks of September 11, and may continue to decrease if American measures to tighten border security, scheduled to take effect in 2009, are implemented. "It used to be that North America was the continent without borders," observes H. V. Nelles (2007). "Now it is much easier to move between the countries of Europe than it is between the nations of the Americas."

Values

The intimacy of Canada–U.S. relations is based, in large measure, on culture. There is, first of all, the obvious fact that English is the first language of large majorities on both sides of the border. This fact allows for the fairly seamless flow of cultural products across the border. Not only do most Canadians and Americans speak the same language, their lifestyles, consumption patterns, and norms of social interaction are probably as similar as between two neighboring countries anywhere in the world.

Few serious students of Canada–U.S. relations will deny these important similarities. But many, particularly on the Canadian side, will be quick to emphasize what they believe to be the important points of cultural difference between Canadians and Americans. The distinctive values and beliefs of Canadians, they argue, explain why Canadian institutions and policies differ from those of the United States. Some go so far as to maintain that Canadian values are more like those of western European societies than those of Americans, and an even greater number claim to see evidence of increasing divergence in the cultures of these two countries.

The question of how similar Canadian values and beliefs are to those of the United States is one of the two original questions asked about the Canadian condition. (The other involves relations between French- and English-speaking Canada.) In a very real sense, the origins of English Canada lie in the American Revolution and the rejection of the new American republic and its values by the tens of thousands of colonists who migrated north after the Revolutionary War. These were the Loyalists, whose rejection of the new American republic has been interpreted by some historians and political scientists on both sides of the border, including Seymour Martin Lipset (1990), as a rejection of the liberal–democratic values it represented.

This interpretation of the Loyalists and the ideological baggage that they brought with them to Canada is dismissed by most historians as containing at least as much fantasy as fact. "What the Revolution did," wrote Hansen and Brebner (1940, 78), "was to exercise a selective process upon a logical movement of North American population and thereby cast a unique romantic colour over the Loyalists which too often eclipsed the underlying [mainly economic] character of the migration in which they took an involuntary part." The selective process that Hansen and Brebner refer to involved the loyalty to the British Crown and thus rejection of the need for revolution. Although some Loyalists doubtless went further to embrace rather feudal or at least aristocratic predemocratic notions about politics and social relations, the vast majority did not. They were, in terms of their social background characteristics and political beliefs, broadly similar to the American neighbors they left behind. "Throughout the nineteenth century," wrote Bell and Tepperman (1979, 77), "the most prominent Anglophone historians were themselves Loyalists or descended from Loyalist ancestors. Along with others, they portrayed Canadian history in ways that glorified the Loyalists' aims and actions. They gave Canada myth and rhetoric." These last words—*myth* and *rhetoric*—are especially important to an understanding of Canada–U.S. relations. Contemporary tropes about the differences between these two countries and arguments for why Canadians should resist policies that are alleged to be "Americanizing" continue to be nurtured by this deep well of mythology about the ideological foundations of English Canada.

Even if one grants that the ideological differences between the Loyalists and their American neighbors involved core values—a highly dubious proposition—there remains the stubborn fact that a large share of the population of English-speaking Canada in the three decades after the Revolutionary War was American born and *not* Loyalist. As argued in the previous section of this chapter, economics had more to do with the settlement of English-speaking Canada during these years than did ideology.

Just how different are the values and beliefs of Canadians and Americans today, and does the answer to this question matter in terms of relations between the two countries? Opinions differ on these two questions. On the issue of value differences, there is little doubt that the cultures of Canada and the United States are not identical. Of course the same can be said of Alberta and Ontario or of Massachusetts and Mississippi. This is an important point because comparisons between Canada and the United States often presume a homogeneity in each that does not exist in reality. Regional differences aside, it is reasonable to speak of certain general differences between the cultures of Canada and the United States. Americans tend to be more individualistic than Canadians. They are more likely than Canadians to be churchgoers and to hold what may be described as socially conservative views. Canadians are more likely than Americans to agree that government has a responsibility to take care of the poor.

But the most striking fact is that the attitudinal differences between Canadians and Americans tend to be relatively small, certainly when compared with those between either population and the citizens of other wealthy western democracies. Although the American and Canadian populations differ significantly in their religious values and behavior, even here Canadians resemble Americans more closely than they do the French, Germans, or even the British. Canada's placement on the two axes of modernization that are used in the World Values Survey (2000) is much closer to the United States than to other wealthy democracies. Only New Zealand and Australia come as close to Canada in terms of the value orientations measured by that study. If only English-speaking Canada is included, the distance between Canada and the United States is even narrower, with the population of mainly French-speaking Quebec being somewhat closer to the western European norm on many cultural matters than is true of the rest of Canada.

Policy differences from health care, education, welfare, and taxation to matters involving protection of the environment, the use of force to resolve international conflicts, and crime and punishment are often attributed to cultural differences between the two societies. When the Canadian and American governments have been at loggerheads over Canadian policies to protect domestic cultural producers from foreign competition, to limit foreign investment, to support regime change in Iraq, or to participate in international agreements on land mines, an International Criminal Court, or global warming, these contretemps have often been attributed to differences in the values and beliefs of the two populations. Such differences are not unimportant, but they have often mattered more for elites than for the general public. For example, it is hard to square the fact of an English Canadian population whose most popular television programs, musicians, magazines, and even fiction writers have long been the same as Americans' with the idea of a people keen to protect themselves from the supposed depredations of American popular culture. Moreover, differences in national economic interests or in the Canadian state elite's perceptions of how best to protect the decision-making autonomy of their government have usually been at least as important as culture—and sometimes more—in explaining Canada–U.S. conflicts.

Interests

The intimacy that has long existed between Canada and the United States has been nurtured by ties of trade and shared security interests. The governments of these two countries have been embroiled in occasionally acrimonious and sometimes protracted conflicts over such matters as the treatment of American investment in Canada (1960s–1980s), Canadian softwood lumber exports to the United States (1980s–2006), Canada's claims to sovereignty in the Arctic (long-standing, but more relevant in recent years as a result of the rapid melting of the Arctic ice pack and thus the increased potential for an Arctic navigation passage between the Atlantic and Pacific oceans and for the profitable exploitation of natural resources in that region), and Canadian defense spending. However, the majority of their economic and security relations have been characterized by cooperation and a commonality of interests.

This was not always so. For well over a century, from before Confederation until the 1989 Canada–U.S. Free Trade Agreement, economic protectionism through tariffs and other forms of support for Canadian-based producers, including public owner-ship in some sectors, was the Canadian state's response to the competitive challenge posed by the United States. Canadian governments rejected closer economic integra-tion with the United States, preferring to promote East–West ties of trade in the face of geographical and market forces that pulled in a North–South direction. Nationalistic economic policies from the National Policy of 1879 to the National Energy Program of 1981 slowed, but did not stop, the irresistible advance of continental economic integra-tion. American investment poured into Canada, the volume of cross-border trade increased steadily, and the Canadian corporate presence in the American economy also grew, even during the 1970s and early '80s when nationalist fears resonated widely in Canada and a number of policies were adopted with the ostensible aim of reducing Canada's economic dependence on the United States.

To some degree, the Great Canadian Debate over free trade in the 1980s and the 1989 implementation of the Canada–U.S. Free Trade Agreement—reversing more than a century of official, but largely ineffectual, protectionism—may be seen as an embrace of the inevitable. The shared economic interests of the two countries had reached such a scale that their disruption by political forces on the American side of the border came to be seen by many in Canada's business and political elites as an unacceptable risk. The nature and challenges of the Canada–U.S. trade relationship are the subjects of chapter 22 in this book. Suffice it to say, that, for now, the intimacy of these economic ties is both enormous and hugely important to governments and interests on both sides of the border, if rather more on the Canadian side.

ASYMMETRY

Living next to you is in some ways like sleeping with an elephant. No matter how friendly and even-tempered is the beast, if I can call it that, one is affected by every twitch and grunt.

—Pierre Trudeau

This quotation from Canadian prime minister Pierre Trudeau on the occasion of a visit to Washington in 1969 is justly famous for encapsulating the Canadian dilemma. The relationship between Canada and the United States is far from being one between equals. On the contrary, Canadians are reminded at every turn of their dependence on the United States and of that country's enormous influence on their society. The forces of globalization that have produced a historically unprecedented level of integration across the world in recent decades have not diminished Canada's vulnerability to "every twitch and grunt" coming from the United States.

The asymmetry in the Canada–U.S. relationship is nowhere more evident than in matters of economics. Each country is the other's major trading partner (although, as of 2008, trade between the United States and China is on the cusp of overtaking and surpassing trade with Canada in the very near future), but whereas exports to the United States account for roughly one third of Canada's gross domestic product, American exports to Canada amount to less than 5% of that country's national income. American investment has been the single largest source of foreign investment in Canada for about a century, and today accounts for close to two thirds of all foreign investment. Canadian investors have an important presence in the American economy, but their investments represent only about 7% of all foreign investment in an economy that is much less dependent on foreign capital than Canada's. The enormous trading relationship between these two countries is also hugely asymmetrical, affecting Canada's vital interests far more than those of the United States.

It would be an overstatement to say that Canada has no leverage in this relationship. After all, Canada is the single largest source of energy imports to the United States and is the destination for more than half the value of all American automotive exports. The Canadian economy is extremely important, even strategically important, to the United States. However, the influence that this might otherwise give Canadian negotiators in trade disputes with Washington is diluted by Canada's far greater across-the-board dependence on the American economy. This was evident during the two-decade-long dispute over Canadian softwood exports to the United States. The Canadian media were full of stories about the imposition of American duties on Canadian lumber, but the issue received barely any attention in the American press.

The asymmetry in the Canada–U.S. economic relationship is not helped, from Canada's point of view, by the fact that Americans—from policy makers and opinion leaders to average citizens—often have little awareness of the scale of these relations and even harbor serious misconceptions about them. A *Time*/CNN poll of June 11, 2001, found that about two thirds of Americans believed that Mexico, not Canada, had more of an impact on the U.S. economy, at a time when the annual value of Canada–U.S. trade was about forty times greater than trade across the Rio Grande. For decades, it has been routine for American political leaders to overlook the importance of Canada as a trading partner, focusing instead on Japan, China, or the European Union (EU). In some ways, of course, this is testimony to the generally good nature of Canada–U.S. trade relations, allowing them to be taken for granted by American decision makers in ways that trade with other countries may not.

One of the great ironies of recent Canada–U.S. relations is that Canada's greater economic integration with the United States, under the free trade architecture of the Free Trade Agreement and North American Free Trade Agreement (NAFTA), may well have created the political space for Canada to pursue a more independent line in matters of foreign policy than was available before free trade. This is exactly opposite to the prediction of Canadian critics of free trade, who argued that the last shreds of Canadian sovereignty and policy autonomy would be vaporized by the tighter economic embrace produced by free trade. If, however, one looks at the actual record of Canadian foreign policy since the mid 1990s, there are several notable instances of Canada being at loggerheads with the United States over global warming, land mines, an International Criminal Court, continental missile defense, sovereignty in the Arctic waters, and, most important, the formal refusal of the Canadian government to join the American-led invasion of Iraq. In all of these cases, it may be argued that the Canadian refusal to side with the American government, and Canadian criticism of the American position, did not have serious and enduring consequences beyond a loss of goodwill in Washington toward Canada. This is certainly a more nebulous consequence, and one more easily repaired, than being slapped with trade duties by the U.S. Commerce Department or facing the punitive wrath of Congress.

Before free trade, Canadian governments depended on what was left of the so-called special relationship between Canada and the United States as protection against American retaliation if Canadian policies were perceived to stray far from the line Washington deemed acceptable. Free trade may have loosened the leash to some degree, because some of these forms of retaliation are no longer available to Congress and the White House or, if used, can at least be challenged under the terms of the free trade agreements.

The asymmetry in Canada–U.S. relations does not stop at trade. As a global superpower with military bases and economic interests throughout the world, and the weight of other countries' expectations on its shoulders, the United States has sometimes approached international affairs in ways that Canadians and their governments have found objectionable. One of the prominent themes running through Canadian foreign policy since the end of World War II has been multilateralism and the search for procedures and forums for international decision making that are less likely to be simple reflections of or dominated by the interests and values of a single country. To put it more bluntly, Canadian governments have had a tendency to search for counterweights to American dominance.

Chief among these counterweights has been the United Nations and its agencies. There are, however, many other multilateral organizations to which Canada belongs, including the North American Treaty Organization (NATO), the World Bank, the Organisation for Economic Cooperation and Development, the World Trade Organization, the Organization of American States, the Commonwealth, and La Francophonie. Some of these multilateral organizations are dominated by the

United States and therefore can hardly be said to serve as counterweights to its might. NATO, for example, has almost never blocked the will or modified the military objectives of American administrations. Multilateralism does not necessarily dilute American influence and may, in some circumstances, actually magnify it by providing greater political legitimacy to American goals through their association with other countries and structures of multilateral decision making. On the whole, however, the multilateral approach favored by Canadian governments clearly holds out the possibility of allowing for the representation of interests and points of view that might at least attenuate the dominance of the United States.

"One of the great foreign policy challenges facing Canada," observes Michael Ignatieff (2003, 15), "is staying independent in an age of [American] empire." This is a large part of the explanation for multilateralism's attractiveness in the eyes of many Canadians and those who govern them. Multilateralism, when it is not a convenient cover for the ambitions and interests of a single-member state, as the Warsaw Pact clearly was for the former Soviet Union or as critics say the International Monetary Fund and World Bank are of the United States' global economic power, implies that states are willing to accept some limitations on their national sovereignty. Canada's governing elites and opinion leaders, like their counterparts in Europe, "have a vision of a multilateral world in which...sovereignty is not unconditional, but limited and bound by rights agreements, or multilateral engagements which limit and constrain the sovereignty of states in the name of collective social goods" (Ignatieff 2003, 15). Ignatieff's characterization of the vision Canadians have of the world and their place in it is fundamentally correct, and even those Canadian governments that have tended to embrace the primacy of Canadian relations with the United States, such as the Conservative governments of Brian Mulroney (1984–1993) and Stephen Harper (2006–) have remained faithful to the multilateralist vision that is crucial in providing Canada with some distance from the policy preferences of its southern neighbor.

In recent years, the Canadian commitment to multilateralism has been seen in the leadership role that Canada took in the creation of the International Criminal Court and in the negotiations, known as the Ottawa Process, that led to the international treaty banning land mines. It was also evident in Canada's ratification of the Kyoto Protocol on greenhouse gas emissions and general support for the United Nations as the proper and necessary forum for the discussion of issues of war and peace, and the decision to use force to resolve international conflicts. It would be an overstatement to say that all Canadians have this multilateral vision of the world, but recent history suggests that it has broad popular support. The problem for Canada—a problem that is also experienced by many other allies of the United States, although less acutely—is that multilateralism is not embraced as enthusiastically by its major trading partner and military ally, and sometimes produces outcomes that set Canada at odds with the United States.

The emergence of terrorism as a major concern among American policy makers in the aftermath of the attacks of September 11 has exposed another dimension of asymmetry in the Canada–U.S. relationship. Canadians and their leaders have tended to be less convinced that the sorts of measures widely seen to be necessary in the United States to combat terrorism are, in fact, justified. "For Americans, living with the terrorist threat is now 'the new normal,'" observes Karlyn Bowman (2005, 6). "Security risks today mean terrorism." Canadians are considerably less likely to believe either that terrorism poses a threat to their country and its interests or that a terrorist attack on their soil is more than a remote possibility. Two years after September 11, more than half of Americans believed that another terrorist attack on the United States was "very likely," compared with only about 10% of Canadians who believed that the probability of such an attack on Canada was this great. By 2005, these numbers for Americans had dropped to one in four, but this was still about four times greater (27% vs. 6%) than the percentage of Canadians who believed that a terrorist attack was very likely (Graves 2005, 11). "For most Canadians," says Frank Graves (2005, 12), "'risk' does not simply equal terrorism."

Terrorism and national security were, of course, central issues in the 2004 American presidential election. They were once again toward the center of the American political radar screen in the 2008 election campaign. The issue was not entirely absent from the Canadian national elections of 2004, 2006, and 2008, but in a way that was refracted through Canada's relationship to the United States. It arose in the context of the Canadian government's participation in the NATO mission in Afghanistan and, in particular, whether Canadian troops should be deployed in combat roles. Public opinion was divided on Canada's involvement in Afghanistan, as were the country's political parties, unlike public opinion and political parties in the United States, where support for the mission of fighting the Taliban continued to enjoy widespread support at the same time as public support for the war in Iraq was much weaker (Bowman 2007).

President George W. Bush's repeated claim that "[t]he fight against global terrorism is the calling of our time" (State of the Union Address, January 25, 2008) did not rally all Americans behind him. However, this claim resonated far more widely in the United States than in Canada. Indeed, Canadian politicians who hewed too closely to the White House line in the "War on Terrorism" were certain to feel the bite of that perennial truth of Canada–U.S. relations: close, but not too close. Michael Ignatieff's failure to win the leadership of the Liberal Party in 2006 may well have been the result of a perception among many Liberals that he had trespassed beyond this line. His defense of the "American empire" as the best hope for the global spread of democracy and human rights, and his advocacy of Canadian combat troops in Afghanistan and the U.S. invasion of Iraq in 2003, haunted him throughout the leadership campaign and proved more than some Liberals could accept.

Ambivalence

Two Canadian interpretations of the American connection
are clearly distinguishable. One tends to stress, even to

eulogize, the harmony of a "unique partnership" between
two sovereign states; the other complains of American
arrogance, domination, neglect, or indifference. Both points
of view are easily supported by factual evidence; both are
well endowed with emotional overtones. Moreover, most
Canadians have an ambivalent attitude toward the United
States and react differently at different times, according to
immediate stimuli and the nature of the audience.

—Richard Preston (1965, 129)

These observations were made almost half a century ago, but they are as appropriate today as when historian Richard Preston made them. Ambivalence toward the
United States and Americans has always been part of the Canadian condition. From
the American side, a sort of benign indifference has been typical, uncomplicated by
much in the way of accurate information about the neighbor to the north or by
strong sentiments of any sort. The Canadian writer Mordecai Richler would occasionally tell a story about a New York publisher friend of his who once speculated
on what new books would be guaranteed to drive a publisher into bankruptcy. At
the top of his list was *Canada: Our Friendly Neighbor to the North*.

On the other hand, a book with the title *The United States: The Evil Empire to
the South*, is, at a minimum, guaranteed attention in Canada. Indeed, countless such
books, television and radio documentaries, university lectures, political speeches,
election campaign ads, and other forms of communication have been produced
over the years. Nationalist sentiment and thought in English-speaking Canada has
always been a reaction to the perception that intimacy with the United States jeopardizes important Canadian values and interests. (The fairly brief exception to this
interpretation of English Canadian nationalism involved the anti-imperial Canada
first movement in the years just after Confederation.) Canadians can lay a serious
claim to being the world's oldest—but also least dangerous—anti-Americans.

However, Canadians also tend to admire much of what they associate with the
United States and this, too, is a sentiment as old as the relationship between these
two societies. The antirepublican rhetoric that characterized the United States as a
sort of vulgar mobocracy came mainly from elites in British North America and
may have reflected their own insecurities, envy, and need to construct a plausible
and high-toned narrative explaining Canada's separate status than it did the sentiments of average citizens. Millions of these average citizens had, after all, shown
themselves to be indifferent to the border and what it supposedly represented in
cultural and political terms by migrating across it.

No national identity is as tied to an image of America as that of English-speaking
Canada. Confronted with the overwhelming economic and cultural power of the
United States, a country with which they share a border, a language, and much culture and history, English Canadian elites have understood that their status, prestige,
and prospects require various forms of defense against American competition. For
most of the country's history, the Canadian capitalist class was staunchly

protectionist, supporting high tariffs and restrictions on foreign (mainly American) investment in such sectors of the economy as banking, transportation, and communication. Canadians cultural elites have relied on the state to subsidize their livelihoods and to ensure that a supply of Canadian-made culture exists. State elites have often seen in protectionist measures the necessary means to protect their authority and relevance. "The state or the United States," has long been the mantra of English Canadian nationalists. Some of these nationalists themselves have occasionally lamented the degree to which the identity of English Canada has been so dependent on state intervention.

When a case is being made for protection or promoting some aspect of English Canadian culture, identity, or independence, a negative image of the United States is almost invariably invoked. Hostility toward America and its perceived attributes serves two important functions: It distinguishes Canada from its southern neighbor and, at the same time, validates the role and prestige of the nationalist elites who are largely dependent on a life support system of state subsidies, public agencies, and other forms of protection. But although anti-Americanism is deeply ingrained in Canadian society—produced and reproduced by successive generations of opinion leaders—it is less intense and less influential today than at its high watermark of the 1960s and '70s. Nor is there near the degree of anti-American consensus that one finds among the opinion-shaping classes in such countries as France and Germany.

Alongside the nationalist defenders of Canadian identity, culture, and institutions are the elites whose stance toward the United States is considerably warmer. Most prominent among them are the representatives of industries who believe that their business prospects would be improved, rather than threatened, by more openness and integration with the American economy. They achieved major victories with the 1989 Canada–U.S. Free Trade Agreement, and then again with NAFTA in 1993. The interests of continentally oriented business elites have found allies in some segments of the opinion-shaping classes of English Canada, such as the Fraser Institute and the C.D. Howe Institute (two market-oriented research institutions), and the CanWest Global Communications Corporation, whose newspapers tend to be more sympathetic to the United States than much of the Canadian mass media. Some prominent journalists and public intellectuals can also be counted on to criticize the motives and arguments of their anti-American colleagues.

One such voice was the late Mordecai Richler, who incurred the enmity of most of his fellow Canadian writers when he supported free trade with the United States. He argued that those who produce culture ought to do so for the world, rather than depend on and hide behind the seductive protections of the state. Similar sentiments have been expressed by Robert Fulford (2003, A16), one of Canada's leading cultural critics, who has characterized the virulence of contemporary European anti-Americanism as "almost Canadian in its odious condescension and ignorant resistance to fact." J. L. Granatstein (1997, 199), one of English Canada's foremost contemporary historians, has characterized the anti-Americanism of English Canadian cultural and political elites (and for much of the country's history, a good part of its business elite) as being both a cover behind which they could advance their own self-interest and hide their own insecurities. Canadians may be the world's oldest and most practiced anti-Americans, but their opinion leaders have always been divided in their stance toward the United States; nor have sentiments of the general population been as intense as those of the nationalists who claimed to speak on their behalf.

THE FUTURE OF CANADA–U.S. RELATIONS

The temptation to identify three possible options for the future of Canada–U.S. relations—the status quo, closer integration, and less integration—must be resisted. There really are only two options. One involves some form of the status quo, adapted to unfolding circumstances that are not entirely predictable. The other involves greater integration of various sorts between these two countries. Less integration and a more autonomous Canada whose relationship with the United States is less dependent is more likely a fantasy than a realistic and realizable scenario for the future.

The status quo would mean that Canada–U.S. relations will continue to be characterized by a dense network of economic, cultural, security, and diplomatic ties. Friction over particular issues will continue to arise from time to time for the simple reason that the relationship is so vast and many sided, and the interests and values of these countries are not identical. Moreover, their national issue agendas are asymmetrical, with American decision makers being more preoccupied in recent years by matters of national security and Canadians by the periodic trade conflicts that arise with their southern neighbor. Former U.S. Ambassador to Canada Paul Cellucci's (2007, 137) observation that "security trumps trade" was a reminder to Canadians that their priorities and perspectives on the bilateral relationship are not mirrored in Washington.

Significantly greater integration between the two countries is not out of the question, but this would require circumstances that simply do not exist today. The ambivalence that many Canadians feel about their country's relationship to the United States would have to be overcome, and their attachment to the idea of Canadian sovereignty would have to diminish rather sharply. On the American side, public opinion toward greater integration with Canada is indifferent—the question just does not arise—but at the level of political decision makers and economic elites, that country's leaders would need to be convinced that such a step would be in their own interests. This would not be a simple matter.

The idea of a big next step in Canada–U.S. integration has been moot for many years. Allan Gotlieb, Canada's ambassador to Washington from 1981 to 1989, is one of the influential voices in support of what he calls a "grand bargain" between the two countries. "Like it or not," he says, "in the U.S. political system a foreign country is just another special interest. And not a very special one at that. It lacks the clout of a domestic special interest because it cannot contribute to political campaigns or deliver votes." Gotlieb argues that tighter formal integration across the Canada–U.S. border would help protect Canadian economic interests from precisely the sort of American domestic political pressures that were at play for years during the softwood lumber dispute. "It is possible," he argues, "that a single market or customs union would enhance our interests." But, he acknowledges, Canada would have to be able to offer something in return, probably in terms of much greater cooperation and even harmonization of policies on matters of border control, terrorism, and defense issues. Gotlieb advocates what he calls a grand bargain with the United States, establishing a North American community of law. By this, Gotlieb appears to mean agreed-upon rules and institutions to enforce them. Although he is a bit vague on this, his proposals would transform the formal relationship between Canada and the United States into something along the lines of the shared decision making and diminished national autonomy that have been characteristic of the EU's trajectory toward greater integration over the last couple of decades. This, he believes, is the best hope for overcoming the unavoidable and lopsided asymmetry—both political and economic—in the Canada–U.S. relationship (Gotlieb 2003, A17).

The "grand bargain" option is advocated by, among others, the influential Canadian Council of Chief Executives, the organization whose support for Canada–U.S. free trade in the 1980s was important in the achievement of that first big step toward the institutionalization of a continental partnership. The obstacles, however, are enormous. It is, for example, difficult to imagine American decision makers accepting a harmonization of labor markets, including the free movement of workers across the Canada–U.S. border, without a prior harmonization of immigration policies. It is also hard to imagine a harmonization of environmental, food, occupational, workplace safety, and other standards, along the lines of the EU model, when these are not even standardized between Canadian provinces (there tends to be greater standardization between American states because of mandates imposed by Congress and federal agencies). The idea of a common currency and the full coordination of monetary policy would have to be on American terms, given the enormous asymmetry between the two economies. And then there is the stubborn fact that most Canadians do not perceive a compelling reason to take a next big step toward continental integration.

Pragmatic tinkering at the margins of the bilateral relationship between these two countries is probably the most likely scenario for the future. Nevertheless, another terrorist attack on the scale of September 11, leading to a renewed spike in American concern with security, could change matters dramatically. Canada's economic prosperity is too dependent on the smooth flow of trade across the border to allow for much greater friction in the movement of goods. President Kennedy's declaration that Canadians and Americans are friends by choice remains as true today as when he made it almost half a century ago. But friendship has limits, and this is a scenario that would put that friendship to the test.

REFERENCES

Bell, David, and Lorne Tepperman. 1979. *The Roots of Disunity: A Look at Canadian Political Culture*. Toronto: McClelland and Stewart.

Bowman, Karlyn. 2005. Threat perceptions in the United States and Canada. *One Issue, Two Voices*, issue 4: 2–9. Toronto: Canada Institute, Woodrow Wilson International Center for Scholars. http://www.wilsoncenter/topics/pubs/threats.pdf.

———. 2007. *America and the War on Terror*. Washington, D.C.: American Enterprise Institute.

Cellucci, Paul. 2007. *Unquiet Diplomacy*. Toronto: Key Porter Books.

Fulford, Robert. 2003. Bashing the US makes us feel good all over. *National Post*, September 22, A16.

Gotlieb, Allan. 2003. A grand bargain with the US. *National Post*, March 5, A17.

Granatstein, J. L. 1997. *Yankee Go Home! Canadians and Anti-Americanism*. Toronto: Harper Collins.

Graves, Frank. 2005. The shifting public outlook on risk and security. *One Issue, Two Voices*, issue 4. Toronto: Canada Institute, Woodrow Wilson International Center for Scholars.

Hansen, Marcus Lee, and John B. Brebner. 1940. *The Mingling of the Canadian and American Peoples*. New Haven, Conn.: Yale University Press.

Ignatieff, Michael. 2003. Canada in the age of terror: Multilateralism meets a moment of truth. *Policy Options* 24(2): 14–18.

Landon, Fred. 1967. *Western Ontario and the American Frontier*. Toronto: McClelland and Stewart.

Lavoie, Yolande. 1972. *L'Emigration des canadiens aux Etats-Unis avant 1930*. Montreal: Les Presses de l'Université de Montréal.

Lipset, Seymour Martin. 1990. *Continental Divide: The Values and Institutions of the United States and Canada*. New York: Routledge.

Monière, Denis. 1981. *Ideologies in Quebec: The Historical Development*. Toronto: University of Toronto Press.

Nelles, H. V. 2007. Review of Bukowczyk et al., *Permeable Border*. *Michigan Historical Review* 33(1).

Preston, Richard A. 1965. *Canada in World Affairs, 1959 to 1961*. Toronto: Oxford University Press.

Porter, John. 1965. *The Vertical Mosaic*. Toronto: University of Toronto Press.

Randall, Stephen J., and John Herd Thompson. 2002. *Canada and the United States: Ambivalent Allies*, 3rd ed. Montreal: McGill-Queen's University Press.

Smith, Goldwin. 1891. *Canada and the Canadian Question*. London: Macmillan.

Statistics Canada. 2009. *Census of Canada 1981* and *2001*. Ottawa. www.statcan.gc.ca.

United States Census Bureau. 2009. *Census of the United States, 1900* and *2000*. Washington, D.C. www.census.gov.

Waite, P. B., ed. 1965. *Pre-Confederation*, vol. II. Scarborough, Ont.: Prentice-Hall.

World Values Survey. 2000. www.worldvaluessurvey.org.

CHAPTER 22

TRADE, GLOBALIZATION, AND CANADIAN PROSPERITY

MICHAEL HART

National economies are more open to one another than ever before. With international trade at an unprecedented level, much of what people consume is imported and much of what they produce is exported. Businesses send huge quantities of capital to other nations...[and] must think globally about every economic decision they face. Technologies, artistic movements, business practices, musical trends and fads and fashions reach all corners of the developed world almost instantaneously. Global economy and culture form a nearly seamless web in which national boundaries are increasingly irrelevant to trade, investment, finance, and other economic activity.

—Jeffrey Frieden (2006, 1)

Jeffrey Frieden (2006) opens his survey of global capitalism with the previous words and cautions that this description of globalization could have been applied as much to the world of 1908 as to that of 2008, but not to many years in between. He is right that globalization is not a new phenomenon, but perhaps is too glib in insisting that there is little to differentiate the globalization evident a century ago from what we are experiencing today. There is a difference, one that is critical to appreciating the role of international trade and investment to Canada's current and future prosperity.

The fact that the globalization evident at the turn of the twentieth century soon collapsed and took more than half a century to rebuild is an important part of the story explaining today's global economy. Canada is very much a part of the current phase of globalization, but was much more on the periphery of the globalization that emerged in the second half of the nineteenth century. Policy choices played an important role in both cases, particularly those involving foreign trade and investment.

Canada has always been a trading nation, but Canadians have not always been keen traders. From their earliest colonial days, Canadians have had to struggle with the reality of too much geography and too little demography. They found the answer in trade. Canadians enthusiastically accepted that they would need to export their surplus resources, but they were less sanguine about importing a wide array of manufactures and other goods. Not surprisingly, the trade policy measures adopted by successive governments often suffered from a high level of internal conflict. Until well into the twentieth century, trade policy choices were further complicated by their need to serve both fiscal and economic development objectives.

Over the past half century, however, as a result of successful multilateral, regional, and bilateral negotiations, a rules-based international trade order has become a universally accepted part of both intellectual and intergovernmental discourse. Canada was an important player in the design and implementation of that order. Its success in knitting national economies into a global economy proved critical to Canada's ability to take greater advantage of the continuing process of global integration, and will remain important to its further evolution.

This chapter considers the role of trade and trade policy in conditioning Canada's participation in the modern global economy and examines emerging issues critical to Canada's continued ability to participate in globalized trade and investment. It begins with a brief survey of the role of trade and investment, and supporting policies, in shaping Canada's economic structure and development.

CANADA AND GLOBALIZATION

The ability of people to interact peacefully with one another over time and space through trade, investment, and other forms of exchange has steadily expanded throughout time. Progress was initially slow and limited to a few regions of the globe. For some 500 years, however, it has been appropriate to speak of globalization as interregional contacts reached global proportions. Throughout this period, cumulative advances in technology greatly expanded the ability of people in diverse and widely separated parts of the globe to interact and trade with one another. Dramatic decreases in transportation and communication costs have, on two occasions, allowed such interaction to expand rapidly and engage more than limited elites. Throughout the course of the second half of the nineteenth century, the introduction of steam engines, railways, steel-hulled ships, refrigeration, the telegraph, and more spurred a quantum leap in global trade and investment (Frieden 2006; O'Rourke and Williamson 1999). The legal and institutional underpinnings of that expansion, however, collapsed in the face of two global wars and a global depression, and it took another half century of painful rebuilding of a new framework to pave the way for the second quantum leap in globalization driven by even further advances in transportation and communication technologies.

Canada's discovery and development as an extension of European civilization was an integral part of the early stages of globalization. As such, the Canadian colonies existed at the periphery of European civilization, but was critically dependent on it through trade and investment. Nationhood—or, more accurately, Dominion status (1867)—added to Canadian opportunities to participate in the surge in globalization that occurred in the second half of the nineteenth century, but the decision to adopt the autarchic National Policy in 1879 ensured the truncated development of the Canadian economy for the next six decades and more. High tariffs and other customs measures encouraged the development of small, import substitution manufacturing facilities. On the export side, even modest levels of protection for processed and fabricated resource products in Europe and the United States contributed to a pattern of exploiting Canada's rich resource base by developing and exporting forest, mineral, and agricultural products at relatively low levels of processing. The result was an economy that relied on competitive, export-oriented resource sectors to offset the economic cost of uncompetitive, domestically oriented manufacturing sectors (Hart 2002, 45–84).

The National Policy was decidedly a second-best option. Subsequent historiography has emphasized its nation-building virtues. Perhaps, but for the first quarter century, efforts to strengthen East–West economic links brought meager results at best. The opening of the prairies to dry-land wheat farming after the turn of the twentieth century made the East–West orientation look more successful, but Canadians continued to pay a heavy price for the National Policy. By that time, high tariffs and similar measures on finished and intermediate goods had succeeded in stimulating the development of a thriving, high-cost manufacturing sector in central Canada. Exporters of Canadian resource products to world markets, on the other hand, found that their ability to compete at world prices was frequently undercut by the high cost of machinery and other inputs protected by the National Policy. Ordinary Canadians paid the price of lower wages, higher prices, and less choice than might have been the case in a more open economy. The National Policy may have fostered a larger economy, but as John Dales (1966) pointed out a generation ago, it retarded the development of a more prosperous one. It also contributed to keeping Canada at the periphery of globalization.

Forging an East–West economy also created sectorial and regional tensions. Ontario and Quebec became the main sites for import substitution manufacturing, and thus the principal clients of the National Policy's protection. In later years, even the agricultural output of the two central provinces became dependent on the peculiar Canadian institution of supply management, itself dependent on tight border restrictions. The Maritime and western provinces, on the other hand, continued to rely largely on resource exploitation—agriculture, fish, forest products, metals, and minerals—for international markets. Even the huge growth in U.S. demand for Canadian mineral and forest products in the middle decades of the twentieth century did not dispose the federal government to ease protection for central Canada's manufacturing output. Thus, two sets of tensions developed: between export-oriented resource sectors and import-competing manufacturers, and between the resource-rich periphery and the people-rich center.

The trade, investment, and industrialization patterns that developed in this period cast a long shadow. United States and British capital was crucial to the growth of both resource and manufacturing industries. Exports of a relatively narrow range of resource products—initially to Britain and later to the United States—paid for the import of machinery, necessities, and luxury products that could not be produced domestically—largely from the United States. For a brief period, the system of imperial preferences, developed in the first half of the twentieth century, provided Canadian manufacturers with modest export opportunities in Commonwealth markets. Small, high-cost domestic manufacturers supplied most of the goods consumed at home and ensured that Canadians would enjoy a standard of living well below that of their neighbors to the south who, although equally protectionist, enjoyed the benefits of a large continental economy.

The disaster of the Depression of the 1930s brought home to Canadian policy makers that relying on a narrow resource base for exports and a broad but small and inefficient domestic manufacturing sector was retarding Canada's long-term economic development and prosperity. Starting cautiously in the 1930s with two agreements negotiated with the United States under its Good Neighbor Policy, and continuing after World War II on the basis of the multilateral regime embedded in the new General Agreement on Tariffs and Trade (GATT), Canada adopted a policy of cautious pragmatism, gradually exposing the Canadian economy to greater international competition in return for modest but steady access to foreign markets for competitive Canadian exporters. As such, Canada was emulating the policy mix adopted by most industrialized countries. The advanced economies clustered around the North Atlantic, together with Japan, Australia, and New Zealand, cooperated with both the GATT and the Organisation for Economic Cooperation and Development in negotiating a global economic regime based on reciprocal market access commitments, a common framework of rules to guarantee those commitments, and broad steps toward ever greater domestic economic policy convergence.

This new, more economically sustainable policy mix led to steady growth in the Canadian economy's international exposure. In the years immediately following World War II, exports and imports of goods and services added up to roughly a third of the value of the Canadian economy (gross domestic product [GDP]). By the 1980s, that figure had risen to more than half of a much larger economy. The range of exportable goods had grown significantly as Canadian firms became more specialized, competitive, and actively engaged in the reemerging global economy, and Canadians' access to a much wider range of goods and services at world prices had risen in tandem. The result was a more prosperous Canada.

By the 1980s, changes in the structure of the economy over the first four post-war decades disposed the federal government, with strong support from the business sector, to pursue a free trade agreement with the United States (Canada–U.S. Free Trade Agreement [CUFTA]) and thus ensure that Canadian firms had tariff-free access to a vastly larger market. Four factors were particularly important in convincing both government and business that such a bilateral arrangement was critical to Canada's further economic development. First, Canada's continued reliance on global exports of resource-based products looked increasingly vulnerable as a result of the combined impact of new, lower cost competitors in developing countries and the higher costs of exploiting Canada's resource base. Second, the gradual reduction of import barriers had made more and more sectors of the Canadian economy open to international competition, but access to foreign markets remained sufficiently uncertain to deter investment in export-oriented Canadian firms. Third, the U.S. market—the most critical, largest, and most proximate outlet for competitive Canadian firms—seemed to be turning inward and adding to investment uncertainty. Finally, the prospect of multilateral negotiations providing Canadian firms with more certain access to the United States and other markets appeared a long shot (Hart et al. 1994, 13–35).

Trade, Investment Policy, and Globalization

The CUFTA marked a major departure in Canadian trade policy and practice. Throughout the previous fifty years, Canada's approach to trade policy making had been incremental, pragmatic, and cautious. More could certainly have been done, or done more boldly, but radical departures had, in the view of Canada's trade policy practitioners, been neither warranted nor likely to succeed. They were convinced that the basic realities within which Canadian government policies operated, including the capability and interests of Canadian firms, limited the scope for more adventurous policy paths. In Canada, trade and investment are primarily private-sector activities; governments can facilitate or frustrate these activities, but ultimately they do not trade or invest. Those areas in which governments have engaged directly in economic activity—such as Crown corporations—had not provided much comfort to those who believed that government could do better than the private sector.

The relatively small Canadian market had imposed a second limitation. Without secure access to foreign markets, it would have been unlikely that much Canadian industrial production could attain the competitive scale required to finance innovation and other desirable features. Additionally, both business leaders and experienced trade officials had developed a clear understanding of the extent to which foreign markets offered real rather than potential opportunities. In the case of Japan, for example, Canadian exporters had long faced some formidable barriers involving not only market access, but also costs, consumer interests and preferences, and institutional barriers. Even large, well-financed American and European firms, backed up by the muscle of their more powerful governments, had found the Japanese market tough sledding in areas other than those for which there were no Japanese suppliers. European and developing country markets offered their own difficulties. Over time, Canadian firms might find niches in these markets, but only if they earned enough from Canadian and U.S. markets to finance the effort.

Increasing concentration on the United States as both Canada's principal supplier and leading market thus reflected not only the reality of proximity and similar tastes and business practices, but also the impact of policy. During the first three postwar decades, Canadian officials had learned that only U.S. officials were responsive to Canadian offers and requests in reciprocal bargaining at the GATT or in bilateral deals such as the 1958 Defense Production Sharing Agreement and the 1965 Automotive Products Agreement. Belated efforts in the 1970s to seek special arrangements with the European communities and Japan had proved disappointing, and had had little impact on the trade and investment patterns that had become firmly embedded in consumer preferences, business practices, and government policies.

Within these realities, Canadian officials had used the policy instruments at their disposal to encourage trade and industrial patterns that provided Canada with growing prosperity. The desired pace of adjustment, however, was dependent on both external and domestic factors. Externally, Canada's major trading partners, particularly the United States, had to open up their markets to Canadian suppliers and accept the discipline of international rules to underwrite this market access. Domestically, governments, firms, and workers had to accept increasing levels of foreign competition and to make constant efforts to upgrade and adjust domestic production. The mutually reinforcing impact of these external and domestic dimensions has been key to the incremental nature of this strategy.

Although incremental, the results were impressive. Slowly but steadily, Canada had opened its economy to greater competition. The successful conclusion and implementation of the CUFTA in 1989, and its subsequent expansion into the North American Free Trade Agreement (NAFTA) with the inclusion of Mexico in 1994, may thus have been a major departure from the incremental past, but it provided a strong catalyst to expanding Canada's exposure to the global economy, aided and abetted by a favorable Canada–U.S. exchange rate. Negotiating and implementing the CUFTA would have been much more difficult without the base of solid experience over the previous fifty years of trade negotiations.

It also proved a successful leap. Throughout the 1990s, Canada experienced one of the strongest periods of trade-led growth in its history. Merchandise exports to all sources more than doubled at market prices. Total trade—exports and imports, goods and services—hit more than C$900 billion in 2000, rising from less than 50% to nearly 90% as a proportion of GDP. Two-way trade between Canada and the United States reached nearly C$700 billion, the equivalent of almost 70% of Canadian GDP. Various factors contributed to this surge in growth in the external sector, including the pull of the red-hot U.S. economy and a favorable exchange rate, but the adjustments induced by freer trade in both production and consumption patterns played a significant role. Adjustments in exchange rates since then have reduced the reliance on the United States for both exports and imports to some extent, whereas growth in trade slowed significantly and reduced the role of trade in the economy somewhat (table 22.1).

Investment figures for the past two decades are similarly indicative of sustained engagement and on a more balanced basis than was the case in earlier periods. In 1997, Canada's international investment position passed a historic divide: outward investment flows were larger than inward flows. Since then, Canada has maintained its position as a net outward investor (table 22.1). In addition to continued activity by foreign investors in the Canadian economy, Canadian investors have become active players in foreign markets. Foreign direct investment (FDI) has become an increasingly important part of Canada's engagement with the global economy.

Although there remain exceptions and challenges, the default position for Canada is now clearly free trade and open markets. The exceptions include well-fortified castles of protection in agriculture, even though most cross-border trade in food and agricultural products is now largely free of restrictions. There are cumbersome rules of origin requiring companies to use raw materials and parts procured in North America to benefit from free trade, rather than cheaper inputs procured offshore. Residual investment restrictions in the transportation, communications, financial services, and energy sectors prevent the achievement of full efficiencies. Old economy industries, such as steel and lumber, remain attached to antidumping, countervailing duty, and safeguard measures to hold more agile competitors at bay. There are service sectors that need further liberalization. Government procurement remains encased in myriad trade-restricting rules. This is a serious agenda worthy of concerted attention, but making progress on these issues is a small part of the challenge. The emerging agenda can only be fully appreciated by assessing the nature and extent of modern globalization and Canada's stake in that process.

GLOBALIZATION, INDUSTRIAL FRAGMENTATION, AND CROSS-BORDER INTEGRATION

The global economy that has emerged over the past half century rests on much more extensive and sophisticated institutional and structural foundations than was the case during earlier periods. International trade in the nineteenth century and well into the twentieth typically involved transactions between firms and individuals in one country and unrelated firms and individuals in another. By the middle of the twentieth century, it was dominated by the large, vertically integrated, horizontally diversified, managerially coordinated enterprise famously described by Alfred Chandler (1977; 1990). With the exception of raw materials, machinery, and luxury

Table 22.1 Canadian Trade and Investment Patterns, 2000–2006 (measured in billions of current Canadian dollars)

	2000	2001	2002	2003	2004	2005	2006
Exports of goods and services							
World	489.1	480.8	477.5	460.1	493.0	518.0	523.7
United States	394.3	387.9	384.4	364.7	387.7	405.8	398.4
European Union*	32.4	33.9	33.1	34.4	37.5	40.7	44.9
Japan	13.2	12.0	11.9	11.0	11.4	11.8	11.9
Rest of world	49.2	47.0	48.1	50.0	56.4	59.7	68.5
Imports of goods and services							
World	427.8	417.9	427.4	415.7	440.2	466.9	486.5
United States	308.6	295.6	297.5	283.8	295.7	306.8	312.1
European Union	43.7	45.8	47.3	46.9	48.8	51.6	56.1
Japan	13.8	12.7	14.7	13.4	12.8	13.6	15.2
Rest of world	61.7	63.8	67.9	72.1	82.9	94.9	103.1
Outward FDI flows							
World	66.4	55.8	42.0	32.1	56.8	40.6	51.3
United States	38.0	27.8	17.6	5.7	40.1	23.0	22.9
European Union	15.9	7.8	10.9	15.7	2.5	2.6	16.3
Japan	3.7	1.8	1.7	0.3	1.3	-0.4	-4.3
Rest of world	8.8	18.4	11.8	10.4	12.9	15.4	16.4

Inward FDI flows							
World	99.2	42.8	34.8	10.5	0.5	35.0	78.3
United States	16.5	39.2	28.4	5.2	6.7	18.4	21.0
European Union	76.9	1.3	4.4	3.8	−13.9	8.9	29.1
Japan	0.2	0.2	0.8	0.5	0.4	0.6	2.5
Rest of world	5.6	2.1	1.2	1.0	7.3	7.1	25.7
Outward FDI stocks							
World	356.5	399.3	435.5	412.2	449.0	459.6	523.3
United States	177.9	188.5	200.0	169.6	198.9	204.6	223.6
European Union	75.2	82.4	90.3	107.2	121.6	119.2	144.5
Japan	5.6	7.0	9.7	8.4	8.4	6.1	4.9
Rest of world	97.8	121.4	135.5	127.0	120.1	129.7	150.3
Inward FDI stocks							
World	319.1	340.4	356.8	373.7	383.5	407.6	448.9
United States	193.7	219.9	231.6	238.1	246.8	259.0	273.7
European Union	96.0	92.1	94.3	102.2	101.4	104.4	118.4
Japan	8.0	7.9	9.3	9.9	10.1	10.5	11.3
Rest of world	21.4	20.5	21.6	23.5	25.2	33.7	45.5

FDI, foreign direct investments.

*EU 15 for 2000 and 2001; EU 25 for subsequent years.

Source: Statistics Canada, Balance of International Payments, tables 376–0001, 376–0002, and 376–0003; and catalog 67–202–X, third quarter 2007.

products, goods and services were primarily consumed in the country in which they were produced by such firms. Goods and, to some extent, services were also produced for export but the successful penetration of a market often led to import-substituting investments and a return to the dominant pattern of domestic production for local consumption. International transactions thus largely involved sales of primary goods, machinery, and luxury goods, exports of excess production, establishment of foreign affiliates through foreign direct investment, transfers of technology through affiliates and licensing arrangements, and the provision of various supporting services such as transportation, communication, and insurance.

In response to market liberalization, particularly among industrialized countries, this pattern began to change in the 1960s and '70s. Rather than the interindustry trade patterns that were prevalent in the nineteenth and early twentieth centuries, trade increasingly involved intraindustry trade responding to, and fueled by, a major expansion in consumer preferences and industry specialization. As a result, exports steadily increased as a share of global output, rising from about 7% in 1950 to about 15% by the mid 1970s (World Trade Organization 1996; 2007).

By the 1980s, in response to developments in communications technologies and transportation facilities, and the progressive liberalization of global markets, production was being reorganized on a global basis, and the nature of extranational economic transactions reflected this change. As Paul Krugman (1995, 334) explains, "the trend in manufacturing has been to slice up the value chain—to produce a good in a number of locations, adding a little bit of value at each stage." This kind of fragmentation was originally confined to the firm and then to spatially proximate and, often, related firms. Increasingly, however, neither geography nor ownership remained as serious obstacles to the fragmentation of production and its subsequent integration. Even more pertinent to international trade, national borders were no longer significant barriers to the organization of production. Technology has allowed specific tasks in the production of goods and services to be widely separated in time, space, and organization. The global economy was being transformed into "a highly complex, kaleidoscopic structure involving the *fragmentation* of many production processes, and their *geographical relocation* on a global scale in ways which slice through national boundaries" (Dicken 2003, 9 [emphasis in original]). Between the mid 1970s and today, trade as a share of global output doubled once again as an increasing range of tasks became tradable and facilitated the further globalization of production (World Trade Organization 2007).

Relocating slices of production or tasks in the value chain and integrating them through sophisticated trade and investment strategies is one of the ways in which new technologies can be harnessed to increase productivity. Both value-chain fragmentation and the sophistication of the firms that make up the fragments have made it easier to relocate specific nodes of production and to take advantage of a range of distant factors, from low-cost labor, specialized skills, and attractive markets, to access to critical inputs and public policy considerations. As Howard Lewis and David Richardson (2001, 11) point out: "[I]t is becoming increasingly meaningless, if not outright impossible, to think of trade as something separate from cross-border investment, or of exporting as something separate from importing products and innovative ideas. All are tied together in the extended family of global commitment."

Systematic data on the extent of this integration are difficult to find, in part because official statistics still pay too little attention to trade in parts and components, and cannot capture the full value of cross-border service links or the input of services provided through proprietary and other networks (for example, design, engineering, and marketing, whether done in house, outsourced locally, or outsourced internationally) (Mandel et. al, 2006; Ridgeway 2006). Statistical agencies have no way of counting the value of Italian design and German engineering in a toilet ultimately manufactured in Mexico and imported into Canada through a U.S. distribution network. They count the computer on which this chapter was written as a Chinese import, rather than as the fruit of the design, engineering, and marketing input of the brains at Apple's Cupertino, California, campus. In a world in which tariffs are increasingly unimportant, customs officials are less interested in the origin or foreign value added of a particular cross-border transaction and are content to record its final transaction price. The data they supply to statistical agencies often severely overvalue some transactions and undervalue diverse inputs from other countries.

What is happening at the global level has a longer history at a cross-border Canada–U.S. level. Proximity, history, technology, opportunity, and policy have combined to create deep and irreversible ties between Canadian and American production and consumption patterns. As U.S. business economist Stephen Blank puts it:

> Ottawa and Washington talk about the world's largest bilateral trading relationship. But we really don't trade with each other, not in the classic sense of one independent company sending finished goods to another. Instead we make stuff together;...[we] share integrated energy markets; dip into the same capital markets; service the same customers with an array of financial services; use the same roads and railroads to transport jointly made products to market; fly on the same integrated airline networks; and increasingly meet the same or similar standards of professional practice. (Blank 2005, 1)

Philip Cross and his colleagues at Statistics Canada have calculated that the import content of Canadian exports has risen steadily over the past two decades. It was 25.5% in 1987 and peaked at 33.5% in 1998. The rapid rise in trade in the 1990s was, in large part, the result of rationalization, with imported components replacing domestic components, with the final product exported to a broader market base. More significant than the rise in exports as a share of GDP was the rise in value-added exports in GDP, which rose from 21.4% in 1987 to reach 28.8% in 1999 (Cross 2002; Cross and Cameron 1999). Economist Glen Hodgson concludes that

> trade has evolved beyond the traditional exporting and importing of goods, and has entered the next generation of trade—integrative trade. Integrative trade is driven by foreign investment and places greater weight on elements like the integration of imports into exports, trade in services and sales from foreign affiliates established through foreign investment. (Hodgson 2004)

Nowhere has this process of integration been more pronounced than between Canada and the United States.

High levels of both two-way intraindustry trade and FDI indicate continued cross-border integration and rationalization of production between Canada and the United States, as well as a deepening interdependence of manufacturing and service industries. Integration has allowed Canadian industry to become more specialized and has contributed importantly to the growth of value-added sectors. The changing intensity and composition of bilateral trade have contributed significantly to making Canadians better off both as consumers and as producers. Canadians employed in export-oriented sectors have consistently been better educated and better paid than the national average. Specialization, in turn, increases, as markets expand in response to the increased openness fostered by trade agreements.

Analysis of cross-border investment patterns indicates that much of it is trade enhancing as Canadian and U.S. firms strengthen their position in supply chains and distribution networks, whereas overseas investment is geared more to substituting for trade. McCain's, for example, invests in Europe to process locally sourced inputs while it invests in the United States to enhance its ability to distribute product from its Canadian operations. Canadian firms have become increasingly involved in cross-border mergers and acquisitions, the principal vehicle for FDI flows and for seizing the advantages of deepening integrative trade. From the beginning of 2003 through the first quarter of 2006, for example, Canadian firms acquired more than 1,000 foreign firms, whereas foreign firms acquired 373 Canadian firms (Yalden 2006).

THE EMERGING POLICY AGENDA

Canada's self-image as a trading nation and its record of active and constructive participation in international trade negotiations over more than seventy years have created the inertia that is now driving contemporary trade policy. Much of this activity, however, seems to serve little more than the interests and concerns of individual Canadian firms rather than the broader interests of the Canadian economy. In the on-again/off-again Doha Round of the World Trade Organization (WTO) negotiations, for example, Canada has found itself largely on the sidelines, unable to contribute constructively, because it now has little to contribute, or gain, from multilateral trade negotiations. The focus of these negotiations has become development and North–South issues, which may engage Canadian foreign policy interests but are peripheral to trade and development priorities. Canada's most basic economic interests are now inextricably bound up with the United States, and the slow, cumbersome, incremental process of multilateral negotiations at the WTO offers at best marginal benefits. The rules and procedures embedded in the WTO and its constituent agreements may continue to provide an essential basis for the conduct of world trade, including cross-border trade with the United States, but its role as the premier negotiating forum to govern deepening integration has been surpassed by bilateral arrangements.

Following the conclusion of the CUFTA and NAFTA by the Mulroney government, the Chrétien government concluded free trade agreements with smaller trading partners, signaling the extent to which free trade, rather than protection, had become the default position in Canadian trade policy. Experience has demonstrated, however, that it is difficult to conclude such agreements with minor partners because of small pockets of politically potent opposition.

Willingness to engage the United States, on the other hand, has been much less apparent, despite mounting evidence that Canadians are likely to benefit more from U.S. engagement than anything else, including as the gateway to global markets. Canada's involvement in the global economy is much more diversified than is commonly appreciated. As partners in North American production strategies, many Canadian-based firms trade with the world through the United States. As such, the full importance of cross-border exchange becomes clearer: As the U.S. economy moves further up the value chain, so does the Canadian economy, increasing opportunities for participants in North American value chains and investment opportunities in overseas economies. Deepening integration has allowed Canadian industry to become more specialized and has contributed importantly to the growth of value-added sectors. The changing intensity and composition of cross-border trade and investment have also contributed significantly to making Canadians better off both as consumers and as producers.

The strategic challenge facing Canadians today is whether they want their government to help or hinder accelerating cross-border economic integration. According to Aaron Sydor (2007, 68), "[t]he real challenge presented by the rise of value chains is to make Canada the location of choice for those high-value activities that are essential to maintaining and improving the standard of living of Canadians." For Canada, that environment is critically dependent on seamless access to the North American economy as a whole. The extensive network of cross-border trade arrangements has worked exceedingly well, but many of these arrangements no longer address directly the needs and circumstances in which the two countries now find themselves. It is evident that neither the WTO as a body of rules nor the Doha Round of trade negotiations provides a way to address the most pressing issues between Canada and the United States in a timely or effective way. The issues are peculiar to the relationship, do not lend themselves to multilateral solutions, and, given the determination of developing countries to shape multilateral negotiating agendas, have no possibility of finding a place even if Canada and the United States were inclined to go down that road.

A bilateral context, on the other hand, offers the chance to shape the agenda and focus uniquely on innovative instruments and institutions to address cross-border issues. A conventional new trade agreement, for example a customs union, is unlikely to yield results significant enough to justify the investment of political capital necessary to achieve success. A conventional approach would, in effect, clean up the leftovers from earlier negotiations but fail to address emerging issues flowing from deepening integration. It would provide, at best, a partial answer to the challenges and problems that flow from the deep integration that now characterizes cross-border commerce. At its most basic, it would be limited to the exchange of goods, and not address issues related to the exchange of services, capital, intellectual property rights, or the movement of people.

Reaping the full benefits of deepening cross-border economic integration will require that Canada and the United States address three fundamental and interrelated issues: reducing the impact of the border, accelerating and directing the pace of regulatory convergence, and building the necessary institutional capacity to implement the results of meeting the first two challenges. Each of these will prove difficult, and solving the problems associated with either of the first two will prove illusory without addressing the other, as well as institutional capacity.

Border Administration

The first challenge is to address the increasingly dysfunctional impact of border administration. The intensity of the cross-border relationship is apparent from the 36,000 trucks and 400,000 people who cross the border every day. Nevertheless, even after fifteen years of "free" trade, the Canada–U.S. border continues to bristle with uniformed and armed officers determined to ensure that cross-border commerce complies with an astonishing array of prohibitions, restrictions, and regulations. The list of rules and regulations for which the border remains a convenient, and even primary, enforcement vehicle has grown, rather than diminished, since the implementation of free trade, particularly in response to the new security realities created by September 11 (see chapter 27, this volume). Administering the physical border imposes high costs on the two governments, on firms and individuals who use the border frequently to conduct their affairs in the integrated North American economy, and on the two economies in terms of opportunities missed to reap the full benefits of deep integration. The result is not an integrated, single North American market, but two markets with many cross-border ties that remain hostage to the efficiency and reliability of customs and immigration clearance.

Given the extent of cross-border integration, the two governments have taken steps to address border congestion, but with limited results to date. Efforts to make the border less intrusive and more efficient were integral to the 1996 Shared Border Accord, the 1999 Canada–United States Partnership Forum, the 2001 Smart Border Accord, and the 2005 Security and Prosperity Partnership. These initiatives, however, have been limited by the decision to work within the confines of existing legislative mandates and by the lack of a strategic framework. Furthermore, they assume continued need for current levels of border administration and thus are not aimed at eliminating or limiting the impact of the border, but at making that impact more efficient.

In the years to come, the two governments are likely to look to ways to reduce the impact of the border by, for example, strengthening institutional contacts, enhancing cooperation, sharing information and intelligence gathering, and gradually focusing ever larger efforts at initial entries into North America. They may also make greater investments in infrastructure and in technology (both at ports of entry and the corridors leading to such ports). Both types of investments are critical components of any comprehensive effort at improving the management of the border and reducing its commercial impact. Such investments will rely much more on risk assessments and random inspections. Finally, the two governments may accelerate discussions about increasing the level of convergence in U.S. and Canadian policies governing such matters as cargo and passenger preclearance programs, law enforcement, and immigration and refugee determination procedures.

The cross-border exchange of services takes place, to a significant extent, without much government notice at the border. Some of it is exchanged electronically, some is eventually embedded in goods, and its extent is difficult to measure. Nevertheless, there are elements of border administration that are pertinent to trade in services, particularly professional services, entertainment services, and similar economic transactions that require the movement across the border of "natural" persons (in other words, real people). The CUFTA and NAFTA include provisions to facilitate the temporary movement of business people, but these provisions stop far short of allowing the free movement of labor. Unlike the Schengen Agreement in Europe, which allows for the free movement of people throughout the area covered by the arrangement, Canada and the United States still maintain stringent controls on the cross-border travel of each other's residents.

Reducing border administration will have beneficial effects at three levels: reducing enforcement and administrative costs for governments, reducing compliance costs for industry, and reducing trade and investment disincentives. Various attempts have been made at quantifying the extent of these benefits. As Pierre Martin (2006, 15) concludes: "[A]lthough the total costs are difficult to estimate with precision, they are significant and likely to become higher." The impact a more open border would have on either direct or indirect costs is equally difficult to estimate. Experience with the Schengen Agreement in Europe, however, suggests that the move toward more open borders both boosted commerce and reduced direct and indirect costs without any significant negative impact on security and regulatory objectives.

Regulatory Cooperation

A key component to trimming border costs and congestion will lie in meeting a second challenge: reducing the impact of regulatory differences between Canada and the United States. As Europeans learned, regulatory cooperation and reducing border formalities are two sides of the same coin. There may be a long tradition of pragmatic, informal problem solving between the regulatory authorities of the two federal governments, as well as among provincial and state governments, but deepening integration is leading governments to consider how much regulatory enforcement needs to be exercised at the border and how much could be exercised behind the border. More fundamentally, as regulatory cooperation and convergence proceed, the two governments are considering whether the time has come for a more formal, treaty-based process of regulatory cooperation aimed at eliminating to the largest extent possible what has been characterized as the tyranny of small differences (Hart 2006).

The need to produce multiple versions of the same good, for example, can increase design and production costs, and prevent firms from enjoying the economies of scale that would flow from producing to satisfy a single globally accepted standard. An ever-growing range of goods have to be tested and certified to exacting standards and regulatory requirements before they can be sold. An equally exploding range of services faces onerous and often repetitive qualification and certification requirements. Compliance with different national rules, together with the repetition of redundant testing and certification of products and providers for different markets, raises costs for manufacturers and providers operating in the integrated North American economy. Additionally, complex and lengthy product- or provider-approval procedures can slow down innovation, frustrate new product launches, and operate to protect domestic producers and providers from foreign competitors. For smaller firms, the cost of acquiring knowledge of and access to another country's regulatory regime can dissuade them from attempting to develop that market altogether.

A coherent program of cross-border cooperation is likely to strengthen Canadian regulatory outcomes. The benefits from further regulatory convergence lie in reducing costs and duplication, and is more likely to involve adoption of best practices than a race to the bottom. Lack of compatibility in various sectors from transportation and food safety, to telecommunications, pharmaceuticals, environmental protection, labor markets, and professional services adds to compliance and enforcement costs for both government and industry, continues to segment the two national markets, and requires continued border administration. Lessons from Europe and elsewhere suggest significant benefits from cooperation leading to more effective regulation, higher levels of compatibility, and reduced border administration.

For consumers, regulatory divergence is tantamount to a concealed "inefficiency tax" that citizens pay on virtually everything they purchase. This tax is the sum of the costs of duplicate regulations, border administration delays, and other regulatory impediments. For businesses, higher costs of compliance hinder their international competitiveness and complicate the most efficient deployment of scarce resources. For governments, regulatory divergence increases risk, reduces efficiency, and leads to less than optimum outcomes in achieving regulatory goals.

Initially, the two governments are likely to focus on and gain experience at the federal level, but given the federal structure of the two countries, the sooner they engage provincial and state regulatory authorities in a similar process of mandatory information exchange and consultations, the sooner the two countries will arrive at a "North American" approach to meeting their regulatory goals and objectives.

Because of the large number of jurisdictions involved, this is an area that will require some creative decision rules as well as institutions to make them work. Fortunately, at the federal level, extensive regional networks of collaboration already exist between Canadian and U.S. regulators. Any successful federal strategy on economic integration and regulatory convergence will need both to complement and to take advantage of these existing cross-border institutions.

Institutional Capacity

Integral to any progress in addressing the governance of deepening integration is the need to build sufficient institutional capacity and procedural frameworks to reduce conflict and provide a more flexible basis for dynamic rule making and adaptation for the North American market as a whole. It may well be necessary to consign traditional aversion to bilateral institution building to the dustbin and look creatively to the future. Although the European model of a complex supranational infrastructure may not suit North American circumstances, there are lessons Canadians and Americans can learn from the EU experience.

The deep integration described here has occurred in the historical absence of an institutional infrastructure for managing this complex, multifaceted relationship. As former Canadian ambassador to the United States, Allan Gotlieb (2003, A16), observes, "the world's largest bilateral economic relationship [is] managed without the assistance of bilateral institutions and procedures." Unlike other bilateral relationships enjoyed by both Canada and the United States, there is no body to provide political or policy oversight of the relationship, no regular meetings between heads of government or foreign or trade ministers, and no formal structure of committees looking at the relationship in a coherent and coordinated manner. The absence of formal structure results from a determined and largely successful effort to treat issues in the relationship vertically, rather than horizontally, and to build firewalls to prevent cross-linkages. In part, this method of management derives from Canadian fears that, as the smaller partner, Canadian interests would be overwhelmed in any more formal relationship. In part, it originates in the U.S. system of governance that makes coherence and coordination in both foreign and domestic policies extraordinarily difficult to achieve on a sustained basis.

The institutional gap is filled by inspired ad hoc solutions. The interconnected natures of the Canadian and American economies virtually require Canadian and U.S. officials to work closely together to manage and implement a vast array of similar but not identical regulatory regimes from food safety to refugee determinations. Officials and, in some cases, ministers have developed a dense network of informal cooperative arrangements to share information, experience, data, and expertise with a view to improving regulatory outcomes, reducing costs, solving cross-border problems, implementing mutual recognition arrangements, establishing joint testing protocols, and more. On any given day, dozens of U.S. and Canadian officials at federal, provincial, and state levels are working together, visiting, meeting, sharing e-mails, taking phone calls, and more. Little of it is coordinated or subject to a coherent overall view of priorities or strategic goals. Some of it is mandated by formal agreements ranging from NAFTA to less formal memorandums of understanding. More important, much of this activity is the natural result of officials with similar responsibilities and shared outlooks seeking support and relationships to pursue them. NAFTA and similar arrangements mark efforts by governments to catch up with these forces of silent integration and provide appropriate and facilitating governance.

Much will be achieved on the basis of existing networks of cooperation, with the addition as necessary of specific joint or bilateral commissions or working groups in instances when existing networks are inadequate. More will be achieved, however, if the two governments commit to the establishment of a limited number of bilateral institutions with a mandate to provide them with the necessary advice and information to effect a more integrated North American approach to regulation. An independent Canada–U.S. secretariat with a mandate to drive the agenda and report annually to the president and prime minister on progress could, for example, prove critical to overcoming bureaucratic inertia. Similarly, a joint advisory board to the president and prime minister could contribute some creative drive to the development of new bilateral initiatives. As numerous studies have demonstrated, regulatory agendas are prone to capture, geared to serving the narrow interests of regulator and regulated. Bilateral initiatives limited to regulatory authorities are unlikely to prove immune from this reality. Regular review by an independent advisory board of progress in implementing a bilateral program of "guided" regulatory convergence could thus prove a valuable addition in keeping the program focused on broader objectives.

Conclusion

Whether driven by the push of government policy or the pull of market forces, deepening integration between two or more countries disposes them to create common policies to regulate the production and distribution of goods and services and a joint approach to external trade and investment. Canada and the United States, although formally committed to no more than a free trade area, have, in reality, already implemented aspects of a customs union and even of a common market. Based on broadly shared goals and perspectives, and common needs, the two governments have developed a dense framework of informal networks and relationships that ensures a high degree of convergence in the design and implementation of a wide range of rules and regulations.

The effective market today is global and its reach is increasingly reflected in the organization of production. The United States in the nineteenth century and the EU, and to a lesser extent, Canada in the closing years of the twentieth century, saw a need to forge rules and governance structures consonant with the emergence of larger markets and more widely integrated production strategies. These efforts focused on divergent regulatory regimes that artificially segmented markets and frustrated achieving the benefits of wider markets and more efficient production structures. Today, both markets and production have gone global, whereas governance remains largely national in scope and reach.

Alan Blinder (2006, 114) suggests that "the governments and societies of developed world must face up to the massive, complex, and multifaceted challenges that offshoring [in other words, globalization] will bring. National data systems, trade policies, educational systems, social welfare programs, and politics must all adapt to the new realities." Sam Palmisano, Chair and Chief Executive Officer of IBM, puts it more constructively:

> Globalization has arrived—in all its controversial, disruptive, and historic glory. The challenge before us is to address the serious issues it raises....If we believe that the opportunities we face are greater than the dangers, then we had better demonstrate the enormous liberating and innovative potential of global integration—not just in words but in deeds. (Palmisano 2007, FP15)

For Canada, there is no better place to start then to bring the governance of Canada–U.S. trade and investment into line with the realities of deep cross-border integration and thus strengthen the ability of Canadians to reap the full benefits of globalization.

REFERENCES

Blank, Stephen. 2005. It is time for Canada to think carefully about North America. *Embassy*. www.embassymag.ca/html/index.php?display=story&full_path=/2005/september/7/blank/.

Blinder, Alan S. 2006. Offshoring: The next industrial revolution? *Foreign Affairs* 85(2): 113–128.

Chandler, Alfred. 1977. *The Visible Hand: The Managerial Revolution in American Business.* Cambridge, Mass.: Harvard University Press.

———. 1990. *Scale and Scope: The Dynamics of Industrial Capitalism.* Cambridge, Mass.: Harvard University Press.

Cross, P. 2002. Cyclical implications of the rising import content in exports. *Canadian Economic Observer* 15(12): 3.1–3.9.

Cross, P., and G. Cameron. 1999. The importance of exports to GDP and jobs. *Canadian Economic Observer* 12(11): 3.1–3.5.

Dales, John H. 1966. *The Protective Tariff in Canada's Development.* Toronto: University of Toronto Press.

Dicken, Peter. 2003. *Global Shift: Reshaping the Global Economic Map in the 21st Century*, 4th ed. London: Sage Publications.

Frieden, Jeffrey. 2006. *Global Capitalism: Its Fall and Rise in the Twentieth Century.* New York: Norton.

Gotlieb, Allan. 2003. A grand bargain with the US.*National Post*, March 5, A16.

Hart, Michael. 2002. *A Trading Nation: Canadian Trade Policy from Colonialism to Globalization.*Vancouver: University of British Columbia Press.

———. 2006. *Steer or Drift? Taking Charge of Canada–US Regulatory Convergence.* C.D. Howe Institute Commentary, no. 229. Toronto: C.D. Howe Institute.

Hart, Michael, with Bill Dymond and Colin Robertson. 1994. *Decision at Midnight: Inside the Canada–US Free Trade Negotiations.* Vancouver: University of British Columbia Press.

Hodgson, Glen. 2004. Trade in evolution: The emergence of integrative trade. *EDC Economics.* March. www.edc.ca.

Krugman, Paul. 1995. Growing world trade: Causes and consequences. *Brookings Papers on Economic Activity 1995*, no. 1: 327–377.

Lewis, Howard, III, and J. David Richardson. 2001. *Why Global Commitment Really Matters.* Washington, D.C.: Institute for International Economics.

Mandel, Michael, with Steve Hamm and Christopher J. Farrell. 2006. "Why the economy is a lot stronger than you think." *Business Week*, February 13, 62. http://proquest.umi.com/pqdlink?did=984153441&sid=1&Fmt=3-&clientId=12306&RQT=309&VName=PQD.

Martin, Pierre. 2006. The mounting costs of securing the "undefended" border. *Policy Options*27(6): 15–18.

O'Rourke, Kevin H., and Jeffrey G. Williamson. 1999. *Globalization and History: The Evolution of a Nineteenth-Century Atlantic Economy.* Cambridge, Mass.: MIT Press.

Palmisano, Samuel J. 2007. The glory of globalization. *National Post*, July 21, FP15.

Ridgeway, Art. 2006. "Data issues on integrative trade between Canada and the US: Measurement issues for supply chains." Presented at the Centre for Trade Policy and Law (CTPL) conference Integrative Trade between Canada and the United States: Policy Implications. www.carleton.ca/ctpl/conferences/index.html#tlconf.

Sydor, Aaron. 2007. The rise of global value chains. In *Canada's State of Trade 2007*, 47–70. Ottawa: Foreign Affairs and International Trade.

World Trade Organization. 1996. *International Trade Trends and Statistics.* Geneva. wto.org.

World Trade Organization. 2007. *International Trade Trends and Statistics.* Geneva. wto.org.

Yalden, Robert. 2006. Gobble means grow. *National Post*, June 28, FP23.

PART VII

MAJOR ISSUES OF THE TWENTY-FIRST CENTURY

CHAPTER 23

CONTINUITIES AND CHANGE IN THE DESIGN OF CANADA'S SOCIAL ARCHITECTURE

JANE JENSON

CANADA has always been classified in the family of liberal welfare regimes, whose defining characteristic is "a preference for market solutions to welfare problems" (Myles 1998, 342). The labor market is central, but so, too, are other markets, including those for retirement income via private pensions and for private services such as supplementary health care or child care. Despite an underlying preference for market solutions, the ways to institute them—via a mix of responsibilities among the family and community as well as markets and the state—have varied throughout time and across the several jurisdictions that share responsibility for social policy in Canada.

A second characteristic of the history and future of Canadian social policy is that it is profoundly shaped by the institutions of federalism (Banting 1987). Disputes over social policy have been a focus of intergovernmental politics for most of the country's history, and compromises settled in that area have shaped intergovernmental relations more broadly. The involvement and powers of each level of government to shape social policy has also widely varied over time. If from Confederation to World War II the provinces and their wards, the municipalities, were all powerful in the domain of income security, from the 1940s to the '80s, the federal government dominated (Banting 1987, 47). Spending by the federal government significantly shapes support for the unemployed, for seniors, and for children, but the provinces and territories retain a good deal of leeway for choices about both income transfers and services in these same domains. For example, Employment Insurance (EI) paid to unemployed workers who meet its eligibility requirements, is a federal program. Provinces and territories are responsible for training and for any benefits offered to the unemployed not eligible or no longer eligible for EI.

This chapter must, therefore, consider intergovernmental relations because it seeks to tell a general story about the shifting intersections of institutional arrangements in four key welfare-producing sectors: market, state, family, and community.[1] It will do so by focusing on policy instruments as well as program design, because it is choices about each of them that actually determine the content of social policy. In Canada's liberal welfare regime, the main goal of social policy after 1945 was to increase the economic security of all categories of the population more than it was to redistribute income from rich to poor, and therefore this chapter concentrates on income security instruments and programs (Banting 2006, 431).

Analyzing the Social Architecture

Social architecture is the term used to describe the blueprints for welfare regimes and "welfare regimes...bundle together programmes and policies which transcend the 'welfare state' narrowly conceived" (Goodin et al. 1999, 5). In his work, Gøsta Esping-Andersen (1999, 33, 35) describes three pillars of this architecture: "[T]he welfare state is one among three sources of managing social risks, the other two being family and market," and their interaction produces a "welfare triad." This vision of three institutional locales has been widely adopted. Nevertheless, it has also been criticized for failing to consider a location where much welfare is generated—that is, the "third" or nonprofit sector. For example, Adalbert Evers (1998, 162–163) describes: "the 'mixed economy' of market, state, voluntary organisations and the family," and conceptualization of a welfare diamond (Evers et al. 1994). Although remaining within the welfare regime tradition, this chapter adopts a four-sector rather than only a three-sector approach to social architecture. It looks, in other words, at the mix of responsibilities among family, market, community, and state, seeing a welfare diamond rather than triad (Jenson 2004a).

Each country makes its own choices about the shape of its welfare diamond and therefore the relationships among sectors. Across all regime types, by far the major source of welfare for most of the population is market income, earned by the individual or a family member (Esping-Andersen et al. 2002, 11). However, regimes are also structured around the assumption that there are numerous nonmarketized benefits and services provided within the family, such as parental child care, housework, and care for elderly relatives. The community is a third source of welfare in most regimes, albeit with greater variability across regime types than for the previous two sectors. This sector, with its mix of volunteers and paid workers, provides a range of services and supports, such as child care, food banks, recreation, and leisure either for free or on a nonprofit basis. Finally, in all welfare regimes some portion of welfare comes from the state, via public services (such as child care, health care, or other services for which we are not required to pay full market prices) as well as by income transfers.

Although a liberal welfare regime has a preference for market solutions, not even a liberal regime will leave everything to markets. What a liberal regime does do more than a social–democratic or conservative one, however, is both support citizens in their market choices and support markets providing certain services that in other regime types are provided as public services. For example, after World War II, Canada provided a basic public pension to all seniors, as did many countries at the time, and in the mid 1960s it added a contributory pension to the public system. However, the federal government also makes tax expenditures (in other words, forgoes taxes) to encourage the development of private retirement pensions. These tax advantages to individuals are Registered Retirement Savings Plans (RRSP), which enable tax-sheltered savings for retirement. By making such tax expenditures, the government is also fostering a large market for pension funds populated by the banks and other financial institutions that offer RRSPs to their customers.[2]

Child care provides another example. In the Canadian liberal welfare regime, public policies send parents into the market to purchase child care, providing some tax relief for their expenditures, and also shaping the market for child care via regulations identifying the kinds of services for which parents can claim a tax deduction or obtain a subsidy. The federal government provides a tax deduction for any kind of child care service as long as the provider supplies a receipt (meaning, the provider is not working "under the table" and not paying taxes), leaving parents to make the choice about whether they wish to hire an untrained baby-sitter or use a licensed child care provider. Quebec, however, made another choice about how to structure the child care market. By providing child care places at a very low flat rate, the government's policy since 1997 has included an effort to undermine the market for untrained, unlicensed, and "under-the-table" baby-sitters. It sought to encourage parents to rely on either early childhood centers or licensed family daycare providers, by making such forms so affordable that baby-sitters could not compete on price (Jenson 2002, 324).

These examples suggest that, although all types of welfare regimes may display convergence around the ideas that it is important to ensure adequate income so that retired persons may live in dignity or that families need help in balancing work and family responsibilities, liberal regimes will favor markets. However, they also illustrate that there are still significant differences among interventions to shape markets or family behavior within the category of liberal welfare regime.

Historically, social policy has relied on three policy instruments to construct its social policy architecture (Banting 1987, 7–12; Myles 1998, 350–352):

1. Public assistance, intended to address the needs of those without adequate income from any other source and using means testing as the main tool
2. Social insurance, based on labor market performance and using contributions as the tool
3. Social citizenship, using universality as the tool

Recently, a fourth instrument has gained popularity: tax-based income supplementation, which relies on income testing and is delivered exclusively through the tax system (Myles and Pierson 1997). The next sections of the chapter will tell the story of social policy in Canada, tracking the policy design and range of instruments in its social architecture over time.

THE CANADIAN WELFARE REGIME AFTER 1945

One of the first provincewide public assistance programs of the twentieth century was for poor mothers of young children who had been widowed or abandoned by their male partner. Mothers' allowances were eventually instituted in all provinces, but full coverage took thirty-three years, beginning in Manitoba in 1916 and arriving in 1949 in Prince Edward Island and Newfoundland (Boychuk 1998, 28ff). Nowhere were rates very generous, however, and therefore charity provided by churches and other agencies often supplemented the allowances.

The crisis of the 1930s revealed a depth of need that could not be satisfied by limited public assistance programs such as mothers' allowances and municipal relief for the poor. Intergovernmental relations came under particular stress from constitutional debates about who had responsibility for the unemployed. Only when the provinces accepted a constitutional amendment that surrendered some of their jurisdiction, could the federal government set up the Unemployment Insurance (UI) program in 1940 that was (and remains) under its exclusive jurisdiction (Banting 1987, 48–49).

The lessons of the Depression were not lost on policy makers planning for postwar reconstruction. There was growing recognition, at least outside of Quebec, of the advantages of pan-Canadian and cross-provincial sharing of risks. The federal government made a wartime announcement of a "grand design" for a new social security system (Boychuk 1998, 42). During the next three decades, that new system was built. Its elements were universal flat-rate family allowances (1944); contributory unemployment insurance (1940); a universal flat-rate old-age pension (Old Age Security [OAS]) and a needs-based one, the costs of which were shared with the provinces (1952); universal hospital insurance (1957); and public assistance, with federal–provincial cost-sharing of the Unemployment Assistance Act (for the unemployed not eligible for UI, 1956) and support for the blind (1951) and the disabled (1954). Mothers' allowances remained an exclusively provincial responsibility.

If social policy instruments were mixed, financing was equally mixed. Unemployment Insurance was funded by contributions from employers and employees as well as the federal government. The OAS depended on an old-age security fund created with earmarked taxes. For the rest, the federal government asserted its constitutional spending power to "make grants for any purpose" and used cost sharing as the way to shape social policy. Most provinces accepted, more or less willingly, the dollars that the federal government offered and the conditions it set on the use of those transfers for programs for the disabled, the blind, hospitals, and even for the improvement of their administration via research and experimentation (Banting 1987, 53). Without half of the costs paid by Ottawa, few provinces would have been able to create a modern system of social security; their own revenues were simply too limited.

In the mid 1960s, this piecemeal approach to addressing social risks was replaced by three major reforms. In 1966, a range of programs were combined into the Canada Assistance Plan (CAP), with which the federal government promised to match provincial social spending. The Canada Assistance Plan consolidated the Unemployment Assistance Act together with legislation providing public assistance to the physically disabled, made federal funding available for benefits for lone parents and poor families, and provided for a range of social services including daycare (Mahon 2000, 595–596). The result was a significant convergence in program design and benefit levels in social assistance across all provinces (Banting 1987, 94–96).

The Canada Pension Plan (CPP) and Quebec Pension Plan (QPP) also date from 1966. Together, they constitute a compulsory social insurance scheme that covers virtually the whole of the labor force. It requires both employees and employers to contribute toward a wage-related retirement pension at age sixty-five as well as long-term disability and survivor's benefits. An innovation in intergovernmental relations, it permitted Quebec to "opt out" of the CPP and establish its own QPP.[3] This insurance approach was complemented by the addition of a guaranteed income supplement (GIS) at the same time, and the gradual reduction to age sixty-five of the universal OAS pension.

Finally, building on the Hospital Insurance and Diagnostic Act of 1957, which had given the federal government authority to enter into agreements with the provinces to establish a comprehensive, universal plan covering acute hospital care and laboratory and radiology diagnostic services, the Medical Care Act of 1966 extended health insurance to cover doctors' services.

This consolidation of three decades of social policy action was the capstone of the system. For Rice and Prince (2000, 80) these three actions signaled the transformation of "social welfare in Canada from a system of allocating benefits on the basis of relief and means testing, to one of allocating benefits on the principles of universal entitlement, public service, and social insurance." For John Myles (1998, 351), one could say that "by the end of the period of welfare state reform in the early 1970s, the programmatic design, if not spending levels, of the Canadian welfare state was remarkably similar to that of Sweden." By this, Myles meant that design choices for programs and instruments privileged social insurance or social citizenship principles.

In these years, with their ideas as well as their actions, decision makers in both the private and public sectors were redesigning the welfare diamond. The market sector was organized around collective agreements negotiated between unions and employers that provided private health, pension, and other protections to union members and their families at a time that union membership rates were on the rise. This "private welfare state" was an especially important component of income security for the retired, and a supplement to universal health benefits. At the same time, the state sector was moving toward providing a series of new social citizenship rights (family allowances, health care, OAS) as well as redesigned social assistance programs (CAP) and contribution-based social insurance for employment, workers' compensation, and the CPP/QPP portion of pensions.

Families, too, had a major role in providing well-being. Both state and market sectors assumed that male breadwinners and female caregivers were the norm; responsibility for their elderly relatives and children remained overwhelming private with very few services, either public or private (Mahon 2000). Communities were also in the picture. Although the voluntary sector was actively involved, little attention was actually devoted to its role or contribution. The exception to this silence was in Quebec, where the Catholic Church had been responsible for delivering welfare to the francophone population (schools, hospitals, charities, and so on) until the Quiet Revolution of the early 1960s. Quebec's relatively tardy development of public spending led, in the 1960s, to a lively debate about public and private roles and responsibilities. Elsewhere, however, the fact that the Children's Aid Society was delivering virtually all child protection services in some provinces, that churches ran schools and hospitals in part with public funds, that the Victorian Order of Nurses provided publicly financed home care, or that CAP required that nonprofit community-based associations deliver much of publicly subsidized child care did not attract a great deal of attention.

Throughout all of this, preference for market solutions remained. That social policy spending should be limited was a value in itself, which helps to account for the differences in spending levels if not design between Canada and Sweden. For example, when policy makers were shown by, among others the Royal Commission on the Status of Women, that families were struggling to juggle work and family life as women's labor force participation rates rose, three new instruments were adopted. One used the contributory unemployment insurance system to provide paid maternity benefits in 1971. The second, reflecting the preference for supporting market choices, led the federal government to provide a child care expense deduction, administered through the tax system, rather than to fund universal child care services directly, as Sweden was doing at the same time. The third involved provinces using CAP funds to offer child care subsidies to low-income families so that they would be able to establish and help maintain the labor force.

This mid 1960s capstone to the social architecture was not in place very long, however, before reformers were rearranging the basic building blocks. Indeed, the GIS was a precursor of an instrument that would gain great popularity in the next decades. The GIS is available to seniors with the lowest incomes. As an income-tested benefit, it is regulated via the tax system. This new instrument soon spread to other policy areas.

REDESIGNING THE MIX:
CHANGING THE INSTRUMENTS

Michael Prince (2003, 127) identifies three periods that distinguish the federal government's actions with respect to the social architecture since 1984. Efforts to restrain costs of social programs characterized 1984–1988. From 1988 to 1997, restructuring the social role of government was the objective, under both Conservative and Liberal governments. This period brought a number of significant changes in program design and instruments. A third phase, which Prince terms "repairing the social union," opened in 1997. The federal government announced that it had tamed its deficit and could think again about investing in the social architecture and reasserting its place in the social union (the name developed at the time to describe intergovernmental relations in key areas of social policy). This third period lasted until the election of the government of Prime Minister Harper in 2006.

The Canada Assistance Plan was profoundly affected in the second phase. The basic design of CAP had remained relatively unchanged from 1966 to 1990 (Boychuk 1998, 48). Then, in what was the first volley in what would become an upheaval in intergovernmental relations in the realm of income security, the Conservative government's 1990 budget imposed a "cap on CAP." Instead of the open-ended financing in which the federal government matched the spending choices of the provinces, the federal government imposed a limit of 5% annually on any increase in transfers to the three richest provinces. "The 'cap on CAP' decapitated [CAP] and put all the provinces on notice that they too could no longer count on the same level of federal largess." (Battle 1998, 329).

Then, in 1995, CAP was ended unilaterally by the Liberal government, in the name of its politics of deficit and debt control and restructuring the social role of the government. In its place, the Department of Finance's budget announced Canada Health and Social Transfer (CHST). Using a carrot-and-stick approach, albeit more stick than carrot, the federal government released the provinces from almost all conditions on spending of the money transferred to them.[4] The exchange was that they lost billions of dollars of transfers and the guaranteed countercyclical funding that allowed them to respond to rising loads of social assistance claims during times of economic downturn (Battle 1998, 330).

The result of this reform has been significant reductions in levels of disposable income available to social assistance recipients. Looking at change over time and comparing 2005 social assistance incomes with the peak year of each province and family type, the National Council of Welfare has identified major losses. Overall, one third of all household types lost $3,000 or more in income. In Alberta, the income in real dollars of a single person on welfare decreased by almost 50% between 1986 and 2005, whereas from 1992 to 2005 in Ontario, the welfare income of a lone parent with one child decreased by almost $6,600, and a couple with two children lost just more than $8,700 (National Council of Welfare 2006, 48).

Abolition of CAP and subsequent reforms to the social assistance regime in all provinces means that social assistance is again a program intended to do little more than serve as a last-resort safety net for recipients. Given the cuts to their real incomes, which were below the poverty line at the best of times, recipients must rely increasingly on family solidarity, where it is available, and also on community support in the form of food banks and other charitable supports.

Income security for the unemployed was also restructured in 1988–1997 to restrict eligibility (although not the requirement to contribute) (Battle 1998, 332). An initial reform in 1971 had expanded the system significantly and moved it toward serving goals beyond providing insurance for temporary job loss. The expansion included, among other things, the introduction of benefits for workers not previously covered (e.g., fishing benefits) and new kinds of benefits (sickness and maternity). Taking into account regional differences in unemployment rates, it also increased the possible duration of benefits in high-unemployment regions and reduced the minimum qualifying work periods. This shift appeared to mark a "reorientation away from the logic of social insurance towards a logic of social cohesion—increasingly aimed at bridging various fault-lines including those based on region as well as relationship to the labour market, such as distinctions between primary and secondary income earners" (Boychuk 2004, 14).

Throughout the 1980s, Canada's overall unemployment rate was consistently above the Organisation of Economic Cooperation and Development (OECD) average and during the recession of the early 1990s it reached 10%. The Conservative government of the day proposed a number of adjustments (including tightening eligibility), but its major changes involved eliminating any government contribution to the UI fund and trying to reinforce the market sector by increasing its responsibility both for funding UI and for developing training programs (Campbell 1992, 32–33). It was the Liberal government elected in 1993 that undertook the most significant overhaul and redesign, however.

Its reforms, which also renamed the program Employment Insurance, signaled a shift away from the 1970s' focus on social cohesion as well as significantly reduced coverage (Banting 2006, 426). The percentage of the unemployed receiving regular benefit payments fell between 1989 and 1997 from 87% of the officially counted unemployed to 42%. In other words, well more than half the officially unemployed received no insurance payments (Battle 1998, 332). Later reforms did lengthen parental leaves benefits to twelve months and provide coverage to part-time workers. Nonetheless, complicated and restrictive eligibility rules have made conditions more stringent for certain types of part-time workers, especially part-time workers in high-unemployment areas and new entrants to the labor market working part-time (Rice 2002, 115).

The move to EI as well as the cap on CAP and the creation of the CHST all had major effects on the social architecture. The federal government and several provinces were much influenced by the ideology of neoliberalism, which advocated a smaller role for the state and much greater reliance on markets, families, and communities. Throughout these years, the programs and instruments of social citizenship in particular were criticized and lost their popular legitimacy. Thus, beyond the goal of husbanding spending overall, during the periods both of cost restraint (1984–1988) and restructuring the social role of government (1988–1997) there was pressure to use new instruments to target spending to low-income Canadians rather than making universal payments.

Such criticisms helped to legitimate the fourth instrument of social policy: tax-based income supplementation. Not much has been heard about this instrument thus far in this chapter, but John Myles and Paul Pierson (1997, 446) had this to say about the past three decades: "In Canada, the NIT/GI [negative income tax/guaranteed income] model has been firmly imprinted as the policy paradigm of choice among legislators and officials."

What is this NIT/GI model? It is based on a specific instrument: the negative income tax. It provides a guaranteed, albeit always low, income to a targeted category of the population, such as seniors, families with children younger than eighteen, or the working poor:

> The original idea, proposed by Milton Friedman in 1943, was fairly simple: In good times, workers would pay taxes to governments; in bad times governments would pay taxes to workers. Eligibility is determined exclusively by income reported in a tax return. There is no surveillance of beneficiaries or administrative discretion beyond that normally associated with the auditing of tax returns. Tax-back rates on earnings and other sources of income are always *much* less than 100 percent. One result is that benefits can reach into the ranks of the middle class, albeit at a diminishing rate. (Myles and Pierson 1997, 447 [emphasis in the original])

Canada is, of course, not alone in relying on NIT instruments in the realm of income security; however, in Canada, the NIT instrument has been used broadly to manage the income of retired seniors as well as within the unemployment insurance regime. It also was deployed to construct the replacement for the first program of social citizenship: family allowances.

The 1966 GIS was the first experiment with an NIT in Canada, and the instrument continued to be favored in the area of pension incomes. In 1975, an income-tested spouse's allowance was added to the OAS/GIS to cover those, usually women, between age sixty and sixty-four whose spouse received the minimum benefit and they themselves had no earned income. The allowance was later extended to widows and widowers of OAS/GIS recipients between sixty and sixty-four years of age. After failing to do so in 1985, because of a revolt of "gray power" well covered in the media, the federal government in 1989 finally succeeded in imposing income testing on the then-universal OAS (Battle 1998, 333).

The next big step toward a fully NIT system was supposed to be a seniors' benefit to replace OAS, GIS, and two other tax credits. This major reform, announced in 1996 and scheduled to take effect in 2001, would have "completed the transition" (Myles 1998, 448), however, the proposal came to naught and the promise the next year to extend income testing foundered, as well, on opposition from the voters and the business community. The latter feared a contraction in their markets, if individuals lost the incentive to save for their retirement in private pension plans and especially RRSPs.

Therefore, income security after retirement continues to rest on multiple instruments: the CPP/QPP contributory pension plans, the income-tested OAS/GIS, and private pensions either negotiated via collective agreements or from tax-sheltered savings. In other words, the family and the market sectors of the welfare diamond are both significantly involved in the ways Canadians obtain their retirement incomes, as is the state, which has its own programs and shapes the market conditions of the other two.

After UI was eliminated and EI took its place, a measure of income testing was introduced into the new unemployment program as well. First, the maximum benefit was capped at a quite low level of earnings; the reimbursement rate is 55% of earnings but only up to a maximum of $41,100 in earnings, although low-income unemployed workers with children (earning less than $25,921) are eligible to receive the Employment Insurance Family Supplement, which can raise the reimbursement rate to as much as 80%. In this family supplement, which uses an NIT instrument, we see the intersection of two areas of income security—that of families and that of the unemployed.

The family supplement in the unemployment insurance regime was only one example of reliance on income testing as an instrument to supplement the income of families with children. Indeed, after the first experiment with the GIS for seniors in 1966, incomes of family with dependent children emerged as the next frontier for experimenting with the NIT in Canada's social architecture. In 1970, the federal government suggested it would institute a Family Income Supplement Plan. The plan would have transformed family allowances from a universal to an income-tested program. Opposition before and during the 1972 election campaign caused the government to take another track; allowances were substantially raised, but were made subject to taxation (Banting 1987, 112–113). Subsequently, the universal family allowances were left to languish, by being only partially indexed to inflation, and new income-tested family benefits were introduced (Stroick and Jenson 1999, 79).

In subsequent periods of social policy redesign, when the social role of government was being restructured, the NIT instrument was applied without hindrance. As the federal government moved into its phase labeled that of "repairing the social union" (Prince 2003, 127), child benefits became the terrain on which experimentation occurred. Immediately after the earthquake budget of 1995, the provinces and territories announced at their annual conference (which does not include the federal government) a major process of rethinking social policy. This led the next year to the creation of the Provincial/Territorial Council on Social Policy Renewal, which the federal government was invited to join. Over the following years, until the Social Union Framework Agreement (SUFA) was signed in 1999, a number of important initiatives in the area of child and family benefits emerged from these processes of intergovernmental negotiations (Fortin et al. 2003).

Chief among these was the National Child Benefit (NCB) initiative. Its 1998 self-description clearly locates the NCB as an innovation both in the way that governments would work together and in the objectives they would pursue.

The National Child Benefit is a joint initiative of the Government of Canada and provincial and territorial governments. Goals of the initiative are to:
  • help prevent and reduce the depth of child poverty;
  • promote attachment to the work force; and
  • reduce overlap and duplication between Canadian and provincial/territorial programs.
The National Child Benefit will begin to remove child benefits from welfare, assist parents with the cost of raising children, and make it easier for low income parents to support their families through employment without resorting to welfare.[5]

The third goal announces that the NCB is about intergovernmental relations and, in particular, new methods for coordination. It includes something we can call *asterisk federalism* (Jenson 2001), in which Quebec simply does not participate in initiatives undertaken by the other twelve governments.[6] Beyond that, however, the initiative as a whole reveals a consolidation of perspectives on the objectives of a redesigned social architecture. The NCB marked the unveiling of a social investment perspective on social architecture (Banting 2006; Jenson and Saint-Martin 2003). Along with a number of other actions within the area of child and family policy, this perspective shaped most of the innovations in social policy in the last years of the twentieth century and the first half of this one.

THE SOCIAL INVESTMENT PERSPECTIVE: ACHIEVEMENTS AND CHALLENGES

For more than a decade, welfare regimes, especially liberal and social–democratic ones, have displayed convergence around ideas for modernization of social models via labor market involvement of all adults and new forms of investment, especially in human capital and early childhood education and care, and in "children" more generally (Esping-Andersen et al. 2002). International organizations have also been the carriers; a social investment emphasis was present in the analyses of the Organisation of Economic Cooperation and Development (OECD) by the mid 1990s and in "third-way" Britain by the late 1990s (Dobrowolsky and Jenson 2005). Three key features of the perspective can be identified. The first is the emphasis on education and learning to ensure that adults today and children in the future will be able to adapt to the labor market conditions of a knowledge-based economy, which demands flexibility in employment relations and supplies many precarious forms of jobs, such as part-time, temporary, and self-employment. The second is an orientation to the future. This means that there is greater concern for setting the conditions for future success, for individuals and countries as a whole, than in achieving equality in the present. Third, and last, there is the idea that successful individuals enrich our common future and that ensuring success in the present is beneficial for the community as a whole, now and into the future. These three ideas can be seen as three principles, the translation of which into social policy has consequences.

Canada's version of the social investment perspective brought an intensification of policy attention to children as well as an emphasis on fighting poverty, especially child poverty, by ensuring that as many parents as possible among low-income families would be in the paid labor force (Jenson 2004b). It also has brought little attention to improving the income security of adults without children younger than eighteen who are considered "employable." When not in the labor force, they have seen their income supports substantially reduced and benefits made much more difficult to access (Banting 2006, 424ff.).

The view of adults is also different in the social investment perspective. Adults raising children gain access to a wide range of benefits and services that adults without young children cannot access. At the same time, these programs are founded on the assumption that all adults *should* participate in the paid labor force and, therefore, they seek to promote employability and sustain participation. Caring for children as a lone mother is no longer accepted as a substitute for labor force participation.

It is in this context that the new initiative to relaunch the social union needs to be interpreted. The NCB was composed of a set of interrelated parts. The federal government's portion consists of two benefits paid directly to families with children. The first is the basic Canada Child Tax Benefit (CCTB). It is income tested and on a sliding scale, with the maximum available to those with a net income less than $37,178. The cutoff was high, with the intent being to provide some CCTB to 80% of families. The second benefit paid by the federal government is the National Child Benefit Supplement (NCBS), going to very low-income families (an annual income of less than $20,883). The result is an NIT structure that reaches both middle- and low-income families.

In some ways, however, the fanfare that accompanied the announcement of the NCB would involve a large dose of exaggeration, if it were assessed only as an income transfer. By themselves, the CCTB and NCBS did little to "reduce the depths of child poverty." Initial amounts paid out as the basic benefit and the various cutoff points for employed families were exactly the same as those made by earlier benefits (Jenson 2000, 17). Although the names changed, the emphasis on favoring employment income over that from social assistance remained, both in the official presentation of the program (quoted earlier) and in the details of its design. In the name of "removing child benefits from welfare," the NCB design legitimated provinces and territories simply treating the CCTB and NCBS as "income" and reducing social assistance payments accordingly (Banting 2006, 428). This "clawback" provoked a storm of protest among advocates for the poor and poor families.[7]

Where the NCB initiative was innovative, however, was in the notion that it would take down the "welfare wall." The basic idea is that social assistance during the years of CAP had been structured such that accepting a low-paying job and going off social assistance could be very costly for families, because they would lose valuable benefits beyond income. For example, few low-paying jobs provide supplementary health and dental benefits, but social assistance did. Therefore, the provincial portion of the NCB initiative was designed around the idea that provinces would take the money saved by not paying social assistance to cover children (now replaced by the NCBS) and "reinvest" those dollars in extended benefits to ease the transition from welfare to work. And, indeed, many of them did just that.

The social investment perspective brought several other innovations as well, in the area of child health, early learning, and so on (Jenson 2004b). The structure of intergovernmental relations in each was quite similar. The federal government would offer additional funding to the provinces to develop programs in specific areas. In particular, the federal government worked for half a decade to induce the provinces and territories to improve child care services, both in terms of quantity and quality. In 2005, just before the Liberal government was defeated by the Conservatives in January 2006, it managed to convince all ten provinces to sign agreements for using new federal funds to generate spaces for early childhood learning and care. This success was seen as a major victory by advocates for child care as well as the federal government.

The social investment perspective, with its emphasis on "making work pay," is also now the driver behind the fall in income of social assistance recipients. Although much attention went to smoothing the transition of parents from social assistance to employment, those who did not make that transition saw their incomes reduced over time, as we have seen. The gap between average incomes and those of social assistance recipients, including those with children, widened. This loss of income affected "single employables" even more than lone-parent families on social assistance (Banting 2006, 426–429). In part, these declines were the result of governments engaged in retrenchment—that is, simply reducing their expenditures—and in part from the strategy of the NCB, which was to ensure that any net benefit from the CCTB and the NCBS went only to families not receiving social assistance. Although earlier ideas about social policy had accepted "need" as a basis for receiving income transfer, by the first half of the first decade of this century, need was not sufficient. Adults had to demonstrate a willingness to engage in employment by taking a job before the advantages of this postdeficit spending would reach them.

We see in the design of the NCB and its surrounding child-focused initiatives a redesign of the welfare diamond in Canada's liberal welfare regime. The market sector has gained in importance. It is now expected to be the source of earned income for all working-age adults, with few exceptions. Only exempted from this requirement are citizens with a disability, whose social benefits have fared better in the years of cost cutting, and adults who live with another whose income is sufficiently high that they can choose to remain out of employment. Income security programs, and especially employment insurance, have been designed to ensure that there are significant incentives to stay in the labor force. In a positive direction, longer parental leaves coupled with guarantees of a return to their job give parents more time with a newborn, thereby reducing the probability that they will exit the labor force to care for the child. More difficult for many, however, have been the large-scale reductions in unemployment benefits and other work-related supports. The cuts make it much more likely for many people that a job loss or layoff will leave them without any replacement income.

At the same time, the state sector has redesigned its relationship to the market. Benefits such as the CCTB and NCBS derive from the recognition that market incomes are frequently inadequate. People may be employed full-time and full year and still be living in poverty. People who are able to find only part-time or part-year work are in a more precarious situation. Indeed, the number of working poor in Canada increased dramatically between 1981 and 1997. Working poor families went up 66% and working poor "unattached individuals" (the Statistics Canada label for working-age adults not living with family members) increased 153% (Rice 2002, 110–111). Income inequalities before and, increasingly, after taxes and transfers have increased into this decade, such that economic security has dropped, despite the increase in wealth and consumption (Banting 2006, 432).

When the federal government set about to "repair the social union" after 1997, it displayed some willingness to spend anew. However, it was only willing to commit funds to supplement the salaries of low-income earners when they had children as well as to promote provision of some low-cost services (subsidized child care, for example) so that parents could remain in the paid labor force. Although family allowances after 1945 were meant to redistribute income from those without to those with children, child benefits now directly address weak points in markets, such as low wages and high cost services. For the rest, little has changed from the choices made during the previous decade to trust in markets, families, and communities more than the state sector.

In many domains, family responsibility remains high or has even increased. Parents who follow the injunction to seek employment find themselves facing bills for child care, transportation, and other costs of employment that weigh heavy. Canadian parents outside Quebec pay a significant portion of the costs of child care, because government assumes a much smaller share than in many countries. Moreover, parents have difficulty finding reliable and quality care. Almost the first act of the Harper government in 2006 was to announce the termination of the federal–provincial accords on child care signed in 2005 and their replacement by an allowance to families with children younger than six years of age. This taxable benefit did little to cover the costs of nonparental child care while significantly slowing the opening of new services, which is what the accords had been intended to do. The year 2006 saw the smallest absolute increase in child care spaces in several years, lagging well behind the number created each year since 2001 (Childcare Research and Resource Unit 2008). In addition, families with responsibilities for caring for family members with disabilities or vulnerable elderly family have very little in the way of public support to do so.

The result is that many low-income Canadians have little choice but to turn for support to their communities. For example, reliance on food banks (in other words, free food donated for distribution by volunteers to needy persons) has grown exponentially in the past decade, increasing 91% between 1989 and 2006 (Canadian Association of Food Banks 2007). This means that many are receiving charity in the same way they relied on it before 1945.

Some of these patterns, such as favoring families with children for income transfer, follow directly from the social investment perspective. However, the other patterns just described reveal the limit of its design. Although after 1945 the goal was income security of all, the objective in the social investment perspective is narrower and its outcomes more limited. Income security in retirement meets international standards, but the social investment emphasis on children is not generating the promised results. On international measures Canada remains a laggard on child poverty and well-being, and dead last in the public provision of what a major international economic organization, the OECD, sees as a pillar of the new economy—high-quality preschool child care services (OECD 2006, 105). With these gaps in putting the model in place, Canada is at risk of having let its "preference for market solutions to welfare problems" tilt too much toward the market, with insufficient attention to solving the real welfare problems that continue to exist in any modern society.

NOTES

1. Throughout this chapter, the term *welfare* will be used in its generic sense—as a synonym for well-being and in the sense of the expression "welfare state" and "welfare regime." It should never be construed, as in U.S. usage, as a synonym for social assistance, as in the expression "welfare recipient."

2. Similar use of public funds for tax expenditures are offered to families saving for postsecondary education with a Registered Education Savings Plan (RESP).

3. Quebec, in the midst of its post-1960 nationalist Quiet Revolution, opted out of the Canada Pension Plan, establishing an independent but coordinated provincial system.

4. The Canada Assistance Plan transfers came with three conditions: provinces provide income assistance only on the basis of need, they have an appeals system in place for the use of applicants and recipients, and no minimum residence requirements would be imposed. Only the third was carried over to the CHST (Battle 1997, 331).

5. This description is from the original presentation of the NCB, June 15, 1998. www.nationalchildbenefit.ca/ncb/ncbfaq_e.shtml.

6. This is "asterisk federalism" because key documents include a footnote (originally in the form of an asterisk) that, although Quebec shares most of the goals of the initiative, it refuses to participate because to do so would be to accept an intrusion into areas of provincial competence (Jenson 2000, 16, 22). See, for example, the description of the National Child Benefit at http://www.nationalchildbenefit.ca/ncb/thenational.shtml.

7. All but New Brunswick and Newfoundland and Labrador applied the clawback. For one of many critical discussions of it, see National Council of Welfare (2006, 56ff.).

REFERENCES

Banting, Keith. 1987. *The Welfare State and Canadian Federalism*, 2nd ed. Montreal:McGill-Queen's University Press.

———. 2006. Dis-embedding liberalism? The new social policy paradigm in Canada. In *Dimensions of Inequality in Canada*, ed. David A. Green and Jonathan R. Kesselman, 417–452. Vancouver: University of British Columbia Press.

Battle, Ken. 1998. Transformation: Canadian social policy since 1985. *Social Policy and Administration* 32(4): 321–340.

Boychuk, Gerald W. 1998. *Patchworks of Purpose. The Development of Social Assistance Regimes in Canada*. Toronto: University of Toronto Press.

———. 2004. *A History of the Canadian Social Architecture: The Logics of Policy Development*. Report F|36. Ottawa: CPRN. www.cprn.org.

Campbell, Robert. 1992. Jobs…Job…Jo…J…: The Conservatives and the unemployed. In *How Ottawa Spends 1992–93. The Politics of Competitiveness*, ed. Frances Abele, 23–56. Ottawa: Carleton University Press.

Canadian Association of Food Banks. 2007. Hunger Count 2007. http://www.cafb-acba.ca/main.cfm.

Childcare Research and Resource Unit. 2008. Child Care Statistics 2007. www.childcarecanada.org.

Dobrowolsky, Alexandra, and Jane Jenson. 2005. Social investment perspectives and practices: A decade in British politics. In *Social Policy Review #17*, ed. Martin Powell, Linda Bauld, and Karen Clarke, 203–230. Bristol: The Policy Press.

Esping-Andersen, Gøsta. 1999. *Social Foundations of Industrial Economies*. Oxford: Oxford University Press.

Esping-Andersen, Gøsta, Duncan Gallie, Anton Hemerijck, and John Myles. 2002. *Why We Need a New Welfare State*. Oxford: Oxford University Press.

Evers, Adalbert. 1998. Part of the welfare mix: The third sector as an intermediate area. *Voluntas* 6(2): 159–182.

Evers, Adalbert, Marja Pilj, and Clare Ungerson, eds. 1994. *Payments for Care*. Aldershot, UK: Avebury.

Fortin, Sarah, Alain Noël, and France St-Hilaire, eds. 2003. *Forging the Canadian Social Union: SUFA and Beyond*. Montreal: Institute for Research on Public Policy.

Goodin, Robert, Bruce Headey, Ruud Muffels, and Henk-Jan Dirven. 1999. *The Real Worlds of Welfare Capitalism*. Cambridge: Cambridge University Press.

Jenson, Jane. 2000. Le nouveau régime de citoyenneté du Canada: investir dans l'enfance. *Lien social et Politiques* 44: 11–23.

———. 2001. Canada's shifting citizenship regime: Investing in Canada's children. In *The Dynamics of Decentralization: Canadian Federalism and British Devolution*, ed. Trevor C. Salmon and Michael Keating, 107–124. Montreal: McGill-Queen's University Press.

———. 2002. Against the current: Child care and family policy in Quebec. In *Child Care Policy at the Crossroads: Gender and Welfare State Restructuring*, ed. Sonya Michel and Rianne Mahon, 309–332. New York: Routledge.

———. 2004a. *Canada's New Social Risks: Directions for a New Social Architecture*. Report F|43. Ottawa: CPRN.www.cprn.org.

———. 2004b. Changing the paradigm: Family responsibility or investing in children. *Canadian Journal of Sociology* 29(2): 169–192.

Jenson, Jane, and D. Saint Martin. 2003. New routes to social cohesion? Citizenship and the social investment state. *Canadian Journal of Sociology* 28(1): 77–99.

Mahon, Rianne. 2000. The never-ending story: The struggle for universal child care policy in the 1970s. *Canadian Historical Review* 81(4): 582–615.

Myles, John. 1998. How to design a "liberal" welfare state: A comparison of Canada and the United States. *Social Policy and Administration* 32(4): 341–364.

Myles, John, and Paul Pierson. 1997. Friedman's revenge: The reform of "liberal" welfare states in Canada and the United States. *Politics and Society* 25(4): 443–472.

National Child Benefit. 1998. www.nationalchildbenefit.ca/ncb/faq_e.shtml.

National Council of Welfare. 2006. *Welfare Incomes 2005*. Ottawa: National Council of Welfare. http://www.ncwcnbes.net/en/research/welfare-bienetre.html.

Organisation of Economic Cooperation and Development. 2006. *Starting Strong II*. Paris: Organisation of Economic Cooperation and Development.

Prince, Michael. 2003. SUFA: Sea change or mere ripple for Canadian social policy? In *Forging the Canadian Social Union: SUFA and Beyond*, ed. Sarah Fortin, Alain Noël, and France St-Hilaire, 125–156. Montreal: Institute for Research on Public Policy.

Rice, James J. 2002. Being poor in the best of times. In *How Ottawa Spends 2002–03: The Security Aftermath and National Priorities*, ed. G. Bruce Doern, 102–120. Don Mills, Ont.: Oxford University Press.

Rice, James J., and Michael J. Prince. 2000. *The Changing Politics of Canadian Social Policy*. Toronto: University of Toronto Press.

Stroick, Sharon M., and Jane Jenson. 1999. *What Is the Best Policy Mix for Canada's Young Children?* Report F|09. Ottawa: CPRN. www.cprn.org

CHAPTER 24

HEALTH CARE

GREGORY P. MARCHILDON

THE political and administrative organization of health care in Canada reflects the inherent complexity and diversity of an immense territory and relatively decentralized federation. In addition to the country's original Aboriginal inhabitants and a historic French-speaking community concentrated in the province of Quebec, Canada is now a major destination for immigrants throughout the world. Most of the country's thirty-three million people live in large urban centers hugging the border with the United States, with the remainder scattered in its vast rural and remote regions.

Even when focusing on public health care, it is misleading to speak of a single health care system in Canada. Instead, there are many health care systems, often operating simultaneously within the country. All levels of government—federal, provincial, territorial, and local—are involved to varying degrees in the financing, administration, and delivery of public health care. Relative to the wealthier countries in the Organisation for Economic Cooperation and Development, the private sector in Canada has a large role in health care. Nonetheless, the appropriate line between the public and private sectors within health care has been, and continues to be, hotly disputed in the political arena.

There has always been a left–right divide on the question of the role of the state in health care in Canada. Political parties with a more conservative, market orientation, such as the Conservative Party of Canada and its provincial equivalents, tend to emphasize individual responsibility, the impact of incentives on patients, and the limits of government capacity in funding, administering, and delivering public health care. Political parties with a more social democratic ethos, such as the New Democratic Party (NDP), tend to emphasize the role of collective responsibility and the obstacles to access created by patient fees as well as the administrative efficiencies of single-payer public administration. Occupying a middle ground between the two, the Liberal Party of Canada (and its provincial equivalents) has sometimes been divided on the appropriate role of the state in public health care, although the federal Liberals, under Prime Minister Lester B. Pearson, played a key role in the introduction of national medicare in the 1960s (Bryden 1997).

In addition to this left–right ideological divide on the role of the state, there is a continuing debate concerning the appropriate role of the central government in a federation where the provinces have considerable authority and responsibility under the current Constitution and where the continuing threat of Quebec secession has pushed the federation in the direction of asymmetrical administrative arrangements in numerous social policy areas, including health care (Béland and Lecours 2007). Despite these tensions, the federal government plays an important role in both funding and setting the national dimensions of universal public health care in Canada. Indeed, more than any other single social policy, medicare has shaped the political history of Canada and is considered by many to be a defining aspect of Canadian citizenship (Canada 2007). Until medicare, Canada's health policy trajectory was almost identical to the policy trajectory of the United States (Maioni 1998). Since that time, the Canadian approach to public health care policy more resembles the universal systems of western Europe and Australasia than the categorical and welfare-based system in the United States and the rest of the Americas (Marchildon 2006; Tuohy 1999).

POLITICAL HISTORY OF MEDICARE

Medicare began with the introduction of a universal hospital insurance program in Saskatchewan in 1947. There are many possible explanations as to why Saskatchewan pioneered "hospitalization," but three facts stand out. The first is that the province suffered more than any other provinces from the Great Depression of the 1930s and therefore a disproportionately larger number of its residents experienced the impact of being unable to pay for hospital and medical services. The second fact is that the political party most supportive of universal public health care—the social–democratic Cooperative Commonwealth Federation or CCF (the forerunner of the NDP)—first won office in Saskatchewan in 1944, decades before it was able to win office in British Columbia (1972) and Manitoba (1977). It was the Saskatchewan CCF government that first implemented a working model of single-payer, universal hospitalization in 1947, followed fifteen years later by universal medical care insurance (Johnson 2004; Naylor 1986). The third fact is that government at a local level, through numerous municipal hospitals and the municipal doctor plans, had already prepared a sizeable portion of the provincial population for public-sector funding and administration of health insurance (Houston 2002).

Saskatchewan's single-payer model of public administration was exported to the rest of the country with the federal government's offer to share 50% of provincial expenditures as long as the provincial schemes met certain conditions in terms of health insurance coverage. By 1961, all provinces had universal hospital insurance.

Then, in 1964, the federal Royal Commission on Health Services, commonly known as the *Hall Commission*, recommended that the federal government use its spending power to encourage provincial adoption of universal coverage for physician services. Two years later, Parliament passed the Medical Care Act, which stipulated that the federal government would share the cost of the new program with all provinces that met the federal conditions of universality, public administration, portability, and comprehensiveness. By 1972, all the provinces and territories had implemented universal medical care insurance for inpatient and outpatient physician services (Taylor 1987).

In 1977, the federal government and the provinces agreed to replace the cost-sharing transfers for hospitalization and medical care insurance with block transfer funding. Although the Established Programs Financing (EPF) arrangement gave the provinces greater flexibility in terms of how they spent federal transfers, the federal government was able to link, and thus cap, the growth in transfers to the provinces to the growth in the economy. No longer would increases in federal funding be tied to increases in provincial funding of universal health care programs.

Although hospital user fees and extra billing of patients by physicians were not unknown before the EPF, these practices became much more commonplace afterward. As a result, the federal minister of health ordered an external review by Emmett Hall, the previous chair of the 1964 Royal Commission on Health Services. Hall's report in 1980 recommended amending federal legislation to discourage user fees and extra billing as an unreasonable impediment to access. As the minister of health and welfare in the Trudeau Liberal government, Monique Bégin piloted the Canada Health Act through Parliament, and the legislation was ultimately supported by all political parties in the federal Parliament when it became law in 1984. Under section 20, the federal government was required to deduct, dollar for dollar, from federal transfers, the value of extra billing or user fees imposed by any physician or hospital in a given province. At the same time, however, Ottawa made it clear that those provinces that eliminated such fees within three years of the introduction of the law would have their deductions reimbursed at the end of the period. By 1988, extra billing and user fees had been virtually eliminated for medically necessary or required hospital and physician services (Bégin 1988; Taylor 1987). The Canadian model of medicare, discussed in depth later in this chapter, had become an established part of the country's political landscape.

CONTEMPORARY POLITICAL ORGANIZATION OF HEALTH CARE

Canada is a federal state with authorities and responsibilities divided between federal and provincial governments. With the important exception of provincial jurisdiction over hospitals and similar institutions, the authority over health or health

care was never explicitly addressed in the constitutional division of powers as originally drafted in the 1860s. However, based on a number of nonhealth-specific provisions in the Constitution as well as judicial interpretation over time, it can be
inferred that the provinces have primary (but not exclusive) jurisdiction over health
care (Braën 2004; Leeson 2004). The provinces have the authority to finance and
administer most public health care in Canada, ranging from single-payer hospital
and medical care services to publicly supported long-term care and home care as
well as programs, education, and infrastructure for public health, health promotion, illness prevention, and prescription drug therapies.

Through its general powers, the federal government is responsible for protecting the health and security of all Canadians. This includes Health Canada's regulation and approval to introduce new prescription drugs and natural health products
to the market. Through its jurisdiction over patents, the government of Canada is
responsible for prescription drug patent protection as well as retail price regulation
through an administrative tribunal—the Patent Medicine Prices Review Board. The
federal government is responsible for the health services of First Nations people living on reserves, the Inuit (who mainly live in the far north), members of the armed
forces and veterans, the Royal Canadian Mounted Police, and inmates incarcerated
in federal penitentiaries. As illustrated in figure 24.1, the federal government funds
health research through the Canadian Institutes of Health Research (formerly the
Medical Research Council) and collects health data on a national basis through
Statistics Canada. Although the federal government is constitutionally responsible

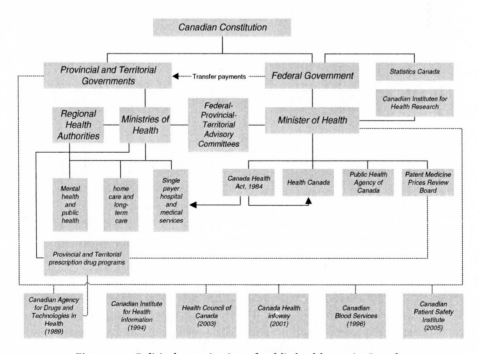

Figure 24.1 Political organization of public health care in Canada.

for health care in Canada's three northern territories and continues to provide the lion's share of funding, it has delegated most of the administration of public health care to the governments of Yukon, Northwest Territories, and Nunavut (Marchildon 2006).

Through its spending power, defined as the ability to spend in areas that go beyond jurisdictional competence, the federal government also sets some of the national dimensions of provincial "medicare"—the universally available hospital and medical care services that come under provincial and territorial single-payer administration. It does this through its enforcement of the Canada Health Act and its five principles—public administration, universality, accessibility, comprehensiveness, and portability. The Canada Health Act of 1984 replaced older legislation— the Hospital Insurance and Diagnostics Services Act of 1957 and the Medical Care Act of 1966—that had dealt with hospital and physician care services separately.

Universal medicare in Canada has four distinguishing design features. The first is that it is highly decentralized in both political and administrative terms. Not only do individual provincial and territorial governments administer medicare, the actual provision of services is in the hands of private not-for-profit or public arm's-length health organizations as well as physicians, the majority of whom work in private-for-profit physician practices on fee-for-service schedules negotiated with provincial and territorial governments (Deber 2004).

The second feature is that medicare coverage is "narrow but deep." Although universal coverage is largely limited to those hospital and medical care services deemed medically necessary or required (as shown in fig. 24.2), all such services are freely available to all Canadians at the point of service. The Canada Health Act dis-

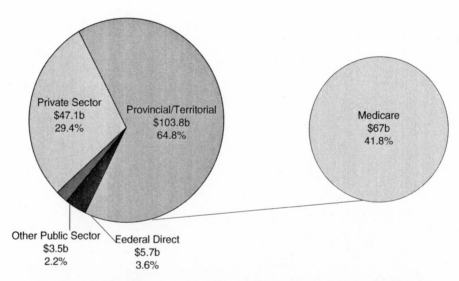

Figure 24.2 Medicare as a share of total health care in Canada, 2007. Hospital and physician expenditures are used as a proxy for medicare expenditures. Reprinted with permission from Canadian Institute for Health Information (2008 106–107).

courages user fees by requiring the federal government to withdraw, dollar for dollar, federal transfer funding to provinces or territories that permit health facilities or physicians within their jurisdictions to charge patients for any medicare service. Of course, provinces and territories can impose user fees or other patient charges on nonmedicare public health care services or products.

The third feature of medicare is single-payer administration. Each province or territory is the single source of payment for medicare services. This system allows for the effective control of hospital and physician expenditures as exemplified in the way that provincial and territorial governments constrained medicare costs during the early to mid 1990s (Tuohy 2002). Compared with multipayer systems involving multiple private insurance companies, single-payer government administration has lower overhead and administrative costs (Hussey and Anderson 2003; Reinhardt 2007). Despite the fact that medicare constitutes less than 42% of total health care expenditures in Canada (see fig. 24.2), per capita administrative costs on all health care are only about one third those in the United States, because of the efficiencies derived from single-payer administration (Woolhandler et al. 2003).

The fourth feature is that private insurance for medicare is prohibited or discouraged by the provinces through varying laws and regulations. As a consequence, there is nothing similar in Canada to the duplicative private health insurance for medicare offered in countries such as the United Kingdom, Australia, New Zealand, and Ireland (Flood 2007; Flood and Archibald 2001). It should be noted, however, that beyond medicare, multipayer insurance is the norm. For example, prescription drugs therapies are covered by both private (largely employment-based) insurance plans and public drug plans (Marchildon 2007).

FEDERAL–PROVINCIAL COLLABORATION AND CONFLICT

As a result of high degree of health policy interdependence and, at times, competition among the federal, provincial, and territorial governments, there is considerable emphasis on the intergovernmental mechanisms required for constructive collaboration (Adams 2001). As illustrated earlier in figure 24.1, these intergovernmental mechanisms fall into two main groups. The first is controlled directly by the federal, provincial, and territorial ministers of health. Along with a mirror committee of deputy ministers and a myriad of subcommittees and working groups, ministers of health along with their senior officials work on their priorities without the aid of a permanent secretariat. Agreement is based on consensus rather than majority decision rules (O'Reilly 2001).

Over time, this work has become so time-consuming that more specialized intergovernmental organizations with permanent bureaucracies (shown at the bottom of fig. 24.1) have been created by health ministers in recent years to facilitate and coordinate policy and program areas. Although funded by all governments, these not-for-profit corporations have varying degrees of governance and managerial autonomy. For example, the Canadian Agency for Drugs and Technologies in Health conducts a major health technology assessment program for a broad range of prescription drugs, medical devices, and other health technologies to assist all jurisdictions in decisions concerning the inclusion of new drugs on formularies and the purchase of new health technologies on the basis of both clinical and cost-effectiveness.

The Canadian Institute for Health Information was created to coordinate the gathering and dissemination of administrative and other health data previously defined and gathered in isolation by the provincial, territorial, and federal governments. Canadian Blood Services was set up by the provinces and territories in response to a major "tainted blood" controversy surrounding the safety of the country's blood supply as managed by the Canadian Red Cross in the mid 1990s (Wilson et al. 2004). Canada Health Infoway emerged out of the desire of federal, provincial, and territorial ministers of health to accelerate the development of electronic health records. The Health Council of Canada's mandate is to provide an assessment of progress in priority areas of health reform as well as make recommendations for future health reforms on a national basis. The Canadian Patient Safety Institute's mandate is to provide systematic evidence on medical errors and initiate change to improve patient safety throughout Canada.

This federal–provincial institution building has clashed with the preference of successive governments in Quebec to create their own "national" health institutions rather than participate as one province among many in pan-Canadian institutions. As a result, Quebec has decided, on a case-by-case basis, the nature of its association with these organizations, ranging from participation in the case of Canada Health Infoway (which the province joined in 2004) and observer status (its official position in the majority of organizations), to overt hostility in the case of the Health Council of Canada. In this last case, Quebec was joined by Alberta, which also refused to participate, because it shares the view that the provinces alone are responsible for deciding the direction of public health care policy.

Overall, however, the relationship among the various levels of government in these new intergovernmental organizations has been mainly collaborative relative to the long-standing conflict between the provinces and the federal government over transfer funding and the conditions of the Canada Health Act. In a dispute that can be traced to unilateral decisions by the federal government to cap or reduce transfer funding since the 1980s, the provinces long insisted that the central government was not living up to its original commitment to fund one half of the costs of medicare. When the federal Liberal government under Prime Minister Jean Chrétien slashed federal transfers to the provinces as part of its fiscal austerity package in 1994–1995, provincial premiers began to deflect public criticism of their own cuts to health care in the early 1990s onto the federal government. Citing the need to reinvest in health care, the premiers urged a restoration of federal transfers. The debate over the level of transfers became the centerpiece of a series of first minister conferences beginning with the Social Union Framework Agreement meeting of February 1999 and ending with the first ministers' meeting on health care in 2004 (Marchildon 2004).

At the same time, some provinces set up commissions and task forces to review their health systems and recommend future directions. In Alberta, the Mazankowski Task Force recommended the introduction of some patient–user payments (a violation of the accessibility condition under the Canada Health Act) and an expert panel to review and delist health services if they are found to be no longer medically necessary (Alberta 2001). In the face of public opposition, the Alberta government ultimately chose not to implement the more controversial recommendations in the Mazankowski report.

By 2001, the federal government had established its own Royal Commission led by former Saskatchewan premier Roy Romanow. In his report, he recommended against the introduction of user fees and in favor of expanding medicare to a defined list of home care services and, eventually, prescription drugs. He also recommended that the federal government increase the level of its federal transfers to make up for the cuts of the 1980s and '90s in return for a strengthening of the Canada Health Act (Canada 2002). Although the provinces agreed that the federal government should increase transfers to fill what they dubbed the "Romanow Gap," most provinces wanted fewer rather than more conditions attached to the transfers. After the release of the Romanow report in 2003, the first ministers' meeting again turned on the issue of federal transfers, with two provinces—Quebec and Alberta—refusing to join the Romanow-inspired Health Council in Canada, in part because of their disappointment over the final federal offer on transfers (Lazar and St-Hillaire 2004; Marchildon 2004). The debate over transfers came to a head the following year when Prime Minister Paul Martin agreed to an enormous transfer increase, thereby securing agreement in the "Ten-Year Plan to Strengthen Health Care." By this time, however, the debate on health care had shifted from federal transfers to the ultimate fiscal sustainability of medicare and the changing role of private delivery and private insurance.

The Sustainability Debate

In public finance, sustainability can be defined by the extent to which its revenue stream is sufficient to fund ongoing government expenditures, including public health care services. For the individual who must pay for both public and private health expenses, however, sustainability is defined by the extent to which household income is sufficient to pay for expected medical expenses as well as unexpected expenses caused by unpredictable disease or injury. Public budgets can always be made more sustainable simply by offloading public health care expenditures onto individual households. The result could be neutral in terms of total health care expenditures, but if public budget cutting generates more administrative overhead, discourages access to primary health care (thereby increasing the likelihood of more expensive acute care), or lowers the overall health status of the population by reducing public health services and infrastructure, savings to the public purse may be more than offset by increased societal costs. For this reason, sustainability should take into consideration total (private as well as public) health care costs and compare these with the rate of growth of the economy in question, which can be used as a rough proxy for the growth of both public revenue and private income (Evans 2004).

On the revenue side, medicare and other public health care services are almost entirely funded out of the general taxation revenues of the provinces, territories, and the federal government. As can be seen in table 24.1, virtually no funding comes from taxation at the municipal (local) level of government. Although municipalities—in particular, larger urban governments—remain responsible for some public health and safety measures, provincial governments through regional health authorities have largely absorbed the responsibility for funding a large array of public health and illness prevention services. The SARS outbreak of 2003 in Toronto highlighted deficiencies in Canada's public health infrastructure— particularly in terms of epidemic surveillance and control—as well as the lack of intergovernmental communication among municipal, provincial, and federal

Table 24.1 Total Health Expenditures by Source of Finance, 1975, 1990, and 2007 (percent distribution)

Year	Provincial Government (after federal transfers)	Federal Government Direct	Municipal Government	Social Security Funds	Total Public Sector	Private Sector
1975	71.4	3.3	0.6	1.0	76.2	23.8
1990	69.6	3.2	0.6	1.1	74.5	25.5
2007	64.8	3.6	0.8	1.4	70.6	29.4

The year 2007 is a forecast. The Provincial Government column also includes territorial governments. Federal Government Direct refers to federal government spending through Health Canada, the Public Health Agency of Canada, as well as arm's-length agencies and intergovernmental bodies, payments for health care services for responsible groups (for example, First Nations on reserve, Inuit, the armed forces), as well as expenditures for health research, health protection and promotion, and pharmaceutical and health products regulation. Municipal Government depicts expenditures in public health and capital construction and equipment expenditures by cities, as well as dental services provided by municipalities in Nova Scotia, Manitoba, and British Columbia. Social Security Funds are social insurance programs that involve compulsory contributions by employees, employers, or both, such as workers' compensation and Quebec's mandated drug plan.

Source: Canadian Institute for Health Information. 2007. *National Health Expenditure Trends, 1975–2007.* Ottawa: Canadian Institute for Health Information.

governments. In the aftermath of the crisis, the National Advisory Committee on SARS recommended the establishment of a more effective federal presence, and the Public Health Agency of Canada was created in 2004 (Health Canada 2003; Wilson et al. 2004).

In the past, many provinces also collected flat tax "health premiums" (poll taxes) to supplement regular tax revenues, but most jurisdictions have eliminated these nominally earmarked taxes in favor of relying exclusively on general tax revenues to fund public health care. Today, only one province—British Columbia—continues to collect premiums that, in any event, constitute a modest portion of the funds needed to finance public health care programs in the province.

The argument concerning the unsustainability of public health care in Canada is simple. The growth in provincial health care expenditures has been outstripping provincial revenue growth since the latter part of the 1990s, and if growth trends continue, spending on health care will crowd out key social and educational expenditures (MacKinnon 2004). Although there is little or no empirical evidence supporting the crowding-out theory (Landon et al. 2006), it is indisputable that health care expenditures have grown faster than the growth of the economy as a whole for decades. There are at least two explanations for this. On the supply side, health care is a leading sector of the economy that is rapidly incorporating new technologies, new research, and new knowledge. We are paying more but we are also getting much more for what we pay, because medical products and services are constantly being improved. In the case of the United States, Nordhaus (2002) calculated that health care spending contributed at least as much to the American economy as all other expenditures combined in the twentieth century.

On the demand side, health care is what economists term *a superior good*—that is, both individually and collectively, we tend to spend progressively more on health care than most other goods and services as our income increases. As we become wealthier, we strive to live longer and we tend to demand a higher quality of life. In fact, higher income (measured by gross domestic product [GDP] per capita) is the single most important factor determining higher levels of both public and private health spending (Gerdtham and Jönsson 2000; Reinhardt et al. 2002). In Canada, private health spending has been growing more rapidly than public health spending and currently constitutes almost 30% of total health expenditures relative to the mid 1970s, when private expenditures made up only 24% of total health expenditures (see table 24.1).

However, as shown in table 24.2, medicare expenditures have grown more slowly than other public and private health care expenditures in Canada, and indeed they have grown more slowly than the GDP in the past thirty years. Hospital and physician services (which lie at the core of medicare) have shrunk in importance relative to other forms of health care. At the same time, because of the single-payer mechanism, during the budget cutting of the early to mid 1990s, provincial and territorial governments were able to constrain medicare costs much more effectively than their respective expenditures on long-term care, home care, and prescription

Table 24.2 Trends in Health Expenditure, Five-Year Averages and Entire Period (1976–2005)

	1976–1980	1981–1985	1986–1990	1991–1995	1996–2000	2001–2005	Entire Period
THE as percentage of GDP	7.0	8.0	8.5	9.6	9.0	10.0	8.7
Medicare as percentage of GDP	4.1	4.5	4.7	5.0	4.2	4.3	4.5
Non-medicare as percentage of GDP	2.9	3.5	4.7	4.6	4.9	5.7	4.4
Mean real annual growth rate in THE	3.3	4.2	4.0	1.6	4.0	5.2	3.7
Mean real annual growth rate in medicare	2.2	4.0	3.3	-0.5	2.1	4.3	2.6
Mean real annual growth rate in non-medicare	4.9	4.5	4.8	3.9	5.7	5.9	5.0
Mean real annual growth rate in GDP	3.6	3.1	2.3	2.0	4.3	2.5	3.0

Real gross domestic product (GDP) figures are expenditure-based, seasonally adjusted, chained 1997 dollars. Real health expenditures are in constant 1997 dollars, calculated using the health component of the Consumer Price Index. THE, total health expenditure.

Source: Canadian Institute for Health Information. 2007. *National Health Expenditure Trends, 1975–2007.* Ottawa: Canadian Institute for Health Information; Marchildon, Gregory P. 2006. *Health Systems in Transition: Canada.* Toronto: University of Toronto Press.

drugs. Indeed, drug plans constitute the most rapidly escalating sector of health care costs. The reality is that, unlike medicare, provinces are limited in terms of regulatory and price control mechanisms to address costs that are growing well over double the rate of revenue growth. Although the federal government has the authority to regulate numerous aspects of prescription drugs from their introduction to the Canadian market to their retail prices, Ottawa does not manage any major drug plan except a noninsured health benefits prescription drug plan for First Nations people on reserves and Inuit (Marchildon 2007).

The arguments concerning sustainability can be divided into two rival camps. The first argues that private funds are needed to supplement public funding to solve the sustainability crisis. This was the argument posited by the Mazankowski and Castonguay task forces in Alberta (2001) and Quebec (2008). The logic is that the growth in public health care funding is outstripping government revenue growth and that an increasing share of future funding for health care will have to come from private sources. The second—best represented by the Fyke Commission in Saskatchewan (2001) and the federal Romanow Commission (Canada 2002)—argues that effective health reform and administrative improvements can reduce the rate of growth in public health care expenditures whereas changes to financing, especially the introduction of user fees for medicare services, will cause severe damage to universal access without producing any long-run savings.

Despite the fact that the real (inflation-adjusted) growth of medicare has actually been below the real rate of economic growth—a very good proxy for the rate of public revenue growth—the debate continues to focus on medicare rather than private health care and other forms of public health care, such as prescription drug plans. Despite this, the federal government, even after the election of a minority government under Conservative Prime Minister Stephen Harper in 2006, has shown little desire to weaken the conditionality of the Canada Health Act. And despite musings to the contrary, no provincial government has chosen to introduce user fees or other forms of patient participation in direct payment for medicare services.

Aside from the absence of user fees, the other notable feature of the Canadian model relates to the way in which opting out of medicare is permitted by the provinces. Patients can get treatment from physicians or surgical facilities that are officially not part of medicare but they must pay for such treatment out-of-pocket; they cannot purchase insurance for medicare services within Canada (Flood and Archibald 2001). In fact, opting out by physicians and health facilities has been rare (Madore and Tiedemann 2005), despite the fact that four of ten provinces have never banned the purchase of private health insurance for medicare services. Nonetheless, the Supreme Court of Canada's landmark decision in *Chaoulli v. Quebec (Attorney General)* (2005) appeared to open the door to the future possibility of opting out of the public system in favor of a parallel private system. At the time of the decision, Quebec was one of the six provinces that legally prohibited private health insurance for medicare services.

CHAOULLI AND THE PUBLIC–PRIVATE DEBATE

A Montreal physician and antimedicare activist, Dr. Jacques Chaoulli of Montreal was a long-time supporter of a parallel private tier who had, at various times, opted out of Quebec's medicare system. Along with his patient, Georges Zeliotas, he sued the Quebec government for the time Zeliotas spent on a public waiting list for knee replacement surgery as an infringement of the right to life and personal security under the Quebec Charter of Human Rights and Freedoms and as contrary to the right to life, liberty, and security of the person under the Canadian Charter of Rights and Freedoms. After losing in the Quebec courts, Chaoulli and Zeliotas appealed to the Supreme Court of Canada. In a four-to-three decision, the majority ruled that the Quebec government's ban on private medicare insurance was contrary to the Quebec Charter in a situation in which the province's quality and timeliness of medicare services was unreasonable. However, when one of the four majority judges found that it was unnecessary to determine whether provincial prohibitions on private medicare insurance were also contrary to the Canadian Charter of Rights and Freedoms, the ruling was not applied beyond Quebec (Flood et al. 2005).

In February 2006, in response to the decision, the Quebec government changed its law to allow the purchase of private insurance for hip, knee, and cataract surgeries. Except for these three types of elective treatment, the provincial government maintained its prohibition on private insurance for all other medicare services and continued to prevent opted-out physicians from treating medicare patients. The government also decided that if Quebec residents waited longer than six months for surgery, they had a right for immediate treatment at any public facility in the province, and if patients wait longer than nine months, they can obtain treatment outside the province or at a private clinic within the province, at public expense (Flood 2007; Prémont 2007).

Although no market for private health insurance for elective medicare services has yet emerged in Quebec, *Chaoulli* continues to have considerable political impact. Previous to the decision, there was little debate about the single-payer principle and provincial prohibitions or regulatory restrictions on private medicare insurance. Not only had the Romanow Commission concluded that the single-payer, single-tier dimension was one of the Canadian model's greatest strengths, but the standing senate committee studying health care in Canada, chaired by Michael Kirby, also ended up supporting the principle and practice of a single payer (Canada 2002; Senate 2002). Disheartened by both reports, the small minority of critics of the single-payer system was given a new lease on life with *Chaoulli*. Of great note is the shift of the Canadian Medical Association (CMA) to a more oppositional position toward medicare in the wake of *Chaoulli*. At its annual meeting in 2005, the CMA passed a resolution that "when timely access to care cannot be provided in the public health care system patients should have access to private health insurance to reimburse the cost of care obtained in the private sector" (quoted in Lemmens and Archibald 2005, 323).

Well before the Supreme Court decision in *Chaoulli*, wait lists for elective surgery and advanced diagnostic tests, as well as overcrowded hospital emergency rooms and the delays involved in getting certain types of physician care, had become a major political issue in Canada. With opposition parties and the media regularly criticizing ministries of health, a number of provincial governments responded to the pressure by spending more on advanced diagnostics and human resources, particularly physicians. They also changed wait list management practices in an effort to reduce wait times and the level of public anxiety (McIntosh 2007). More controversially, a few provinces began to permit the contracting out of some services to private for-profit clinics and surgical facilities.

In Alberta, the Progressive Conservative government under Premier Ralph Klein set up a framework for this type of contracting out through the Health Care Protection Act of 2000. The legislation sets the criteria (including consistency with the principles of the Canada Health Act) under which regional health authorities can purchase services from private clinics. Since that time, the Calgary Health Region in particular has contracted with private for-profit surgical clinics, which are permitted to serve both medicare and nonmedicare patients. Both the Calgary Health Region and the Alberta government claim that the use of these private facilities has reduced patient waiting times for relatively simple surgeries and freed up operating room space for lengthier, more complex procedures in public hospitals. Opponents have argued that these arrangements open up the possibility of queue jumping by nonmedicare patients, allow the private sector to skim the least problematic and therefore the most profitable patients and procedures from the public sector and, by luring away physicians, nurses, and other key professionals, make health human resource shortages even more acute in the public sector (Shrybman 2007).

Conclusion

Medicare in Canada represents a political compromise between provider (especially physician) autonomy from government control on the one hand and equitable access to health care on the other, neatly summed up as "private practice, public payment" by David Naylor (1986). At the heart of this compromise is the single-payer system of administration. Although it was vigorously fought during medicare's formative stages, the principle of single payer became accepted by all political parties after it was implemented on a national scale. Only recently has this principle come into question, led not by a political party, but by the judicial activism of the courts in response to the presence of surgical wait times.

Although no provincial government has chosen to break with the Canada Health Act, and no federal administration has yet weakened the law or dispensed with the federal transfers that underpin the law, there is pressure at the edges to relax the principles. At the same time, there is little willingness to move in the oppo-site direction. Despite the recommendations of the Romanow Commission, the federal, provincial, and territorial governments have shown no willingness to expand the ambit of medicare in even the most incremental and most cost-effective manner. In part, this is a consequence of concerns about the fiscal sustainability of public health care services beyond medicare, but it also reflects ideological and fis-cal assumptions about the limits of government involvement in health care. And, in part, this is the result of a federal government less willing than in the past to use its influence with the provinces, through the spending power, to shape health care programs with national dimensions.

Acknowledgment. I thank Tom McIntosh for his very helpful critique of this chapter.

REFERENCES

Adams, Duane. 2001. Canadian federalism and the development of national health goals and objectives. In *Federalism, Democracy and Health Policy in Canada*, ed. Duane Adams, 61–105. Montreal: McGill-Queen's University Press.

Alberta. 2001. *A Framework for Reform: Report of the Premier's Advisory Council on Health.* Mazankowski report. Edmonton: Premier's Advisory Council on Health.

Bégin, Monique. 1988. *Medicare: Canada's Right to Health.* Ottawa: Optimum Publishing.

Béland, Daniel, and André Lecours. 2007. Federalism, nationalism and social policy decentralization in Canada and Belgium. *Regional and Federal Studies* 17(4): 405–419.

Braën, André. 2004. Health and the distribution of powers in Canada. In *The Governance of Health Care in Canada*, ed. Ton McIntosh, Pierre-Gerlier Forest, and Gregory P. Marchildon, 25–49. Toronto: University of Toronto Press.

Bryden, P. E. 1997. *Planners and Politicians: Liberal Politics and Social Policy, 1957–1968.* Montreal: McGill-Queen's University Press.

Canada. 2007. *Building on Values: The Future of Health Care in Canada.* Romanow Commission report. Saskatoon: Commission on the Future of Health Care in Canada.

Canadian Institute for Health Information. 2007. *National Health Expenditure Trends, 1975–2007.* Ottawa: Canadian Institute for Health Information.

Chaoulli v. Quebec (Attorney General) (2005) 1 S.C.R. 791.

Deber, Raisa B. 2004. Delivering health care: Public, not-for-profit or private? In *The Fiscal Sustainability of Health Care in Canada*, ed. Gregory P. Marchildon, Tom McIntosh, and Pierre-Gerlier Forest, 233–298. Toronto: University of Toronto Press.

Evans, Robert G. 2004. Financing health care: Options, consequences, and objectives. In *The Fiscal Sustainability of Health Care in Canada*, ed. Gregory P. Marchildon, Tom McIntosh, and Pierre-Gerlier Forest, 139–196. Toronto: University of Toronto Press.

Flood, Colleen M. 2007. *Chaoulli's* legacy for the future of Canadian health care policy. In *Medicare: Facts, Myths, Problems, Promise*, ed. Bruce Campbell and Gregory P. Marchildon, 156–191. Toronto: James Lorimer.

Flood, Colleen M., and Tom Archibald. 2001. The illegality of private health care in Canada. *Canadian Medical Association Journal* 164(6): 825–830.

Flood, C. M., Kent Roach, and Lorne Sossin, eds. 2005. *Access to Care, Access to Justice: The Legal Debate over Private Health Insurance in Canada*. Toronto: University of Toronto Press.

Fyke, Kenneth J. 2001. *Caring for Medicare: Sustaining a Quality System*. Regina: Commission on Medicare.

Gerdtham, Ulf-G, and Bengt Jönsson. 2000. International comparisons of health expenditure: Theory, data and econometric analysis. In *Handbook of Health Economics*, vol. 1A, ed. Anthony J. Culyer and Joseph P. Newhouse, 11–53. New York: Elsevier.

Health Canada. 2003. *Learning from SARS: Renewal of Public Health in Canada*. Ottawa. Health Canada.

Houston, C. Stuart. 2002. *Steps on the Road to Medicare: Why Saskatchewan Led the Way*. Montreal: McGill-Queen's University Press.

Hussey, Peter, and Gerard Anderson. 2003. A comparison of single- and multi-payer health insurance systems and options for reform. *Health Policy* 66(3): 214–228.

Johnson, A. W. 2004. *Dream No Little Dreams: A Biography of the Douglas Government of Saskatchewan, 1944–1961*. Toronto: University of Toronto Press.

Landon, S., M. L. McMillan, V. Muralidharan, and M. Parsons. 2006. Does health-care spending crowd out other provincial government expenditures? *Canadian Public Policy* 32(2): 121–141.

Lazar, Harvey, and France St-Hilaire, eds. 2004. *Money, Politics and Health Care: Reconstructing the Federal–Provincial Partnership*. Montreal: Institute for Research on Public Policy.

Leeson, Howard. 2004. Constitutional jurisdiction over health and health care services in Canada. In *The Governance of Health Care in Canada*, ed. Tom McIntosh, Pierre-Gerlier Forest, and Gregory P. Marchildon, 50–82. Toronto: University of Toronto Press.

Lemmens, Trudo, and Tom Archibald. 2005. The CMA's *Chaoulli* motion and the myth of promoting fair access to health care. In *Access to Care, Access to Justice: The Legal Debate over Private Health Insurance in Canada*, ed. Colleen M. Flood, Kent Roach, and Lorne Sossin, 323–346. Toronto: University of Toronto Press.

MacKinnon, Janice C. 2004. The arithmetic of health care. *Canadian Medical Association Journal* 171(6): 603–604.

Madore, O., and M. Tiedemann. 2005. *Private Health Care Funding and Delivery under the Canada Health Act*. Parliamentary information and research service report PRB 05–52E. Ottawa: Library of Parliament.

Maioni, Antonia. 1998. *Parting at the Crossroads: The Emergence of Health Insurance in the United States and Canada*. Princeton, N.J.: University of Princeton Press.

Marchildon, Gregory P. 2004. *Three Choices for the Future of Medicare*. Ottawa: Caledon Institute of Social Policy.

———. 2006. *Health Systems in Transition: Canada*. Toronto: University of Toronto Press.

———. 2007. Federal Pharmacare: Prescription for an ailing federation? In *Medicare: Facts, Myths, Problems, Promise*, ed. Bruce Campbell and Gregory P. Marchildon, 268–284. Toronto: James Lorimer.

McIntosh, Tom. 2007. *Wait Times without Rhetoric: Lessons from the Taming of the Queue*. Ottawa: Canadian Policy Research Networks.

Naylor, C. David. 1986. *Private Practice, Public Payment: Canadian Medicine and the Politics of Health Insurance, 1911–1966*. Montreal: McGill-Queen's University Press.

Nordhaus, William. 2002. *The Health of Nations: The Contribution of Improved Health to Living Standards*.NBER working paper no. 8818. Cambridge, Mass.: National Bureau of Economic Research.

O'Reilly, Patricia. 2001. The federal/provincial/territorial health conference system. In
    Federalism, Democracy and Health Policy in Canada, ed. Duane Adams, 17–59.
    Montreal: McGill-Queen's University Press.
Prémont, Marie-Claude. 2007. Bill 33: The fallout from the *Chaoulli* decision in Quebec
    and its impact on equity in health care. In *Medicare: Facts, Myths, Problems, Promise*,
    ed. Bruce Campbell and Gregory P. Marchildon, 192–196. Toronto: James Lorimer.
Quebec. 2008. *Getting Our Money's Worth: Report of the Task Force on the Funding of the
    Health System*. Castonguay Task Force report. Quebec: Government of Quebec.
Reinhardt, Uwe E. 2007. Styles of rationing health care: The United States vs. Canada. In
    Medicare: Facts, Myths, Problems, Promise, ed. Bruce Campbell and Gregory
    P. Marchildon, 65–81. Toronto: James Lorimer.
Reinhardt, Uwe E., P. Hussey, and G. F. Anderson. 2002. Cross-national comparisons of
    health systems using OECD data, 1999. *Health Affairs* 21(3): 169–188.
Senate. 2002. *The Health of Canadians: The Federal Role. Volume Five: Principles and
    Recommendations for Reform*. Ottawa: Standing Senate Committee on Social Affairs,
    Science and Technology.
Shrybman, Steven. 2007. P3 hospitals and the principles of medicare. In *Medicare: Facts,
    Myths, Problems, Promise*, ed. Bruce Campbell and Gregory P. Marchildon, 197–211.
    Toronto: James Lorimer.
Taylor, Malcolm G. 1987. *Health Insurance and Canadian Public Policy: The Seven Decisions
    That Created the Canadian Healthcare System*, 2nd ed. Montreal: McGill-Queen's
    University Press.
Tuohy, Carolyn H. 1999. *Accidental Logics: The Dynamics of Change in the Health Care
    Arena in the United States, Britain, and Canada*. New York: Oxford University Press.
———. 2002. The costs of constraint and prospects for health care reform in Canada.
    Health Affairs 21(3): 32–46.
Wilson, Kumanin, Jennifer McCrea-Logie, and Harvey Lazar. 2004. Understanding the
    impact of intergovernmental relations on public health: Lessons from reform
    initiatives in the blood system and health surveillance. *Canadian Public Policy* 30(2):
    177–194.
Woolhandler, Steffie, Terry Campbell, and Daniel U. Himmelstein. 2003. Costs of health
    care administration in the United States and Canada. *New England Journal of Medicine*
    349(8): 768–775.

CHAPTER 25

··

SCIENCE AND TECHNOLOGY: POLITICIANS AND THE PUBLIC

··

GRACE SKOGSTAD

IN early 2008, American and European government officials separately announced that food from cloned animals was safe. Critics of animal cloning immediately denounced the regulators' verdict and consumer advocates publicly reminded their governments that most North Americans and Europeans oppose animal cloning and do not want to eat food from cloned animals. On both sides of the Atlantic, government officials declared that cloned meat would continue to be withheld from the market, pending further consultation with the public about the animal safety risks and the ethical appropriateness of the novel technology. As such consultations proceed, it is safe to predict that they will be controversial.

The politics of science and technology regulation have acquired heightened importance across industrialized democracies, including Canada. Like their counterparts elsewhere, Canadian citizens and their governments have long looked to scientific and technological innovations to improve the quality of human life. Historically, and with a few exceptions, such innovations have elicited little controversy in Canada. Nor do most technological advancements do so today. Information and communication technologies, for example, are welcomed by most Canadians. So are technological advancements that promise a more environmentally sustainable way to exploit Canada's rich natural resources and energy sources. However, we appear to be in a new era in terms of the role that science and technology play in the lives of individuals and the potential for some technologies to elicit controversy.[1]

First, and as the example of cloning illustrates, some contemporary scientific and technological innovations are challenging fundamental ontological under-standings and core values. Scientific advancements in the life sciences—notably modern biotechnology procedures that entail genetic interventions and manipula-tions—challenge cultural beliefs regarding what is "natural" and what is not. As Chalmers explains:

> By going to the creation of life itself through the production, manipulation or transformation of DNA, they break the traditional dichotomy in Western thought between nature and society and go to the human capacity not merely to control and regulate the environment, but also to make it and own it. (Chalmers 2005, 663)

Not surprisingly, then, a novel technology like biotechnology often elicits heated—and probably irreconcilable—public debates about not only its risks, but also its ethical appropriateness.

Second, governments across industrialized societies view scientific and techno-logical innovations as providing a competitive edge in domestic and foreign mar-kets. A 2007 policy document of the Canadian government declared: "Scientific and technological innovations enable modern economies to improve competitiveness and productivity, giving us the means to achieve an even higher standard of living and better quality of life" (Government of Canada 2007, 1). This view of science and technology led Canadian governments in the late twentieth and early twenty-first centuries to expand their financial assistance to scientific research organizations and high-technology sectors. The belief that scientific and technological innovation is a source of competitiveness has also given Canadian governments strong incen-tives to encourage the rapid implementation of new technologies.

Third, even as governments look to technological innovations to render their economies more competitive, some industrialized democracies are also experienc-ing a cultural shift in attitudes toward science and technology. This transition includes both a decline of faith in science and technology as forces of progress, as well as lesser willingness to accord authority to scientists and other experts to decide the acceptability and regulation of new technologies (Canadian Food Inspection Agency 2001, sect. 1.1.5). These attitudinal changes occur as the role of public insti-tutions in the production of scientific knowledge has declined and that of private firms increased. In addition, intellectual property regimes—to attract investment by granting the inventor a patent or monopoly right to produce, use, or sell the invention for a period of time—often guarantee confidentiality of private research data. These developments, along with governments entering partnerships with pri-vate technology developers, diminish governments' autonomy to define public research priorities independently of private interests (Doern and Reed 2000; McHughen 2000). Critics of a situation in which governments and the public are reliant, to a large degree, on the science of industry fear the neglect of public con-cerns about scientific and technological innovations, especially those of a social and ethical nature.

Fourth, this spotlight on the politics of technology regulation occurs alongside diminished trust by citizens—in Canada and elsewhere—in politicians and democratic institutions to act in the public interest (on Canada, see Bricker and Greenspon 2001; Canadian Food Inspection Agency 2001, sect. 1.1.4). To restore it, there are calls for democratic reforms. They include mechanisms of direct citizen engagement to open up regulatory processes to a broader constituency of social actors, greater respect for principles of transparency and accountability in decision making, and more opportunities for the concerns of citizens to be aired and heeded in institutions of representative democracy.

The forgoing developments render the politics of technology regulation more complex, contentious, and politically salient. As Jasanoff (2006, 758) phrases it: "[T]echnology, once seen as the preserve of dispassionate engineers committed to the unambiguous betterment of life, now has become a feverishly contested space in which human societies are waging bitter political battles over competing visions of the good and the authority to define it." Even if not all countries are "waging bitter political battles" over new technologies, in the current international political economy one country's domestic regulatory politics often transcend its borders to affect the politics and policy options of other countries.

A central governing challenge of contemporary democracies is thus to find ways to mediate controversies between those who have faith in science and are willing to take the risks of a technological innovation, and those who do not. Governments' strategies to mediate these differences, including through the provision of vehicles for public representation, participation, and deliberation, provide important insight into the quality of democratic governing in the polity. If, as Jasanoff (1995, 311) states, the regulation of technological enterprises "is a kind of social contract that specifies the terms under which state and society agree to accept [its] costs, risks and benefits," what do the processes of constructing this contract, and its terms, tell us about contemporary governing in Canada?

This chapter addresses this question by examining the politics of the regulation of biotechnology in the health and life sciences in Canada. Biotechnology is one of four areas of science and technology identified by the government of Canada as priorities. The other three are information and communications, natural resources and energy, and the environment (Government of Canada 2007).

The first section of the chapter begins theoretically, delineating two constitutive elements of regulatory political cultures with respect to novel technologies. These constitutive elements are, first, ideas and institutional practices regarding how collective knowledge of the risks and benefits of a novel technology is produced and validated; and, second, the formal and informal methods of ensuring accountability and legitimacy in decision making with respect to the technology. On the basis of these two dimensions, political cultures can be distinguished in terms of whether they are deferential or precautionary, and whether they adhere to fiduciary or agency accountability principles. When deferential cultures and fiduciary norms dominate, the result is likely to be technocratic regulatory politics that gives a privileged role in regulatory decision making to scientists and other experts. When precautionary cultures and agency norms of accountability dominate, there is a greater possibility for participatory regulatory politics.

The second section examines Canada's regulatory political culture and politics. It documents the Canadian political culture of deference to science and technology. As a whole, Canadians accept most new technologies and are prepared to defer to the judgments of scientists and other experts regarding both their risks and the appropriate measures to mitigate these risks. Canada's deferential regulatory political culture, which has tended to lessen, but not eliminate, controversy around Canadian regulatory politics for science and technology, can be attributed primarily to two factors. The first is the country's historical dependence on natural resource extraction, and by extension, on technological advancements to extract material benefits from these resources. The second is the predominance of liberalism as an economic and political ideology. The deferential regulatory culture favors a fiduciary model of accountability, as do the Westminster parliamentary system and judicial deference to parliamentary sovereignty and delegated authority.

The third and fourth sections of the chapter examine the politics of the regulation of biotechnology in Canada, as illustrated by, first, genetically modified (GM) crops and foods (also called *plant biotechnology*), and, second, assisted reproductive technologies (ART). Although the regulation of GM crops and foods illustrates the dominance of a technocratic politics of regulation, the second, ART, reveals a more participatory regulatory politics. The case of GM product regulation suggests that technocratic politics is apt to prevail when a new technology is seen to provide appreciable economic benefits, and regulators are confident that its safety risks can be gauged and regulated. The second, more participatory and more democratic model revealed by the regulation of ART does not eschew an important role for elites in regulatory policy processes, but provides more avenues for a broader array of social groups to participate. The ART example suggests that participatory politics are likely to coincide with regulation of a new technology that raises ethical issues on which societal divisions occur. The final section of the chapter provides a summary and conclusion.

POLITICAL CULTURES OF SCIENCE AND TECHNOLOGY

Regulatory political cultures establish the parameters within which governments regulate scientific and technological innovations. The regulatory political culture of a political community includes its amalgam of ideas and institutional practices that pertain to the roles of science, experts, the state, and the public in decision making (Jasanoff 1995; 2005). Two dimensions of regulatory political cultures are particularly important. The first is how collective knowledge of the risks and benefits of a novel technology is produced and validated. The second is the formal and informal methods of ensuring accountability and legitimacy in decision making with respect to the technology (Jasanoff 2005, 21).

Producing and Validating Knowledge: Deferential versus Precautionary Political Cultures

Governments everywhere turn to scientists and other experts to produce knowledge about the risks of a novel scientific or technological enterprise (a process known as *risk assessment*) and to advise on measures to mitigate them and to ensure the safety of a new technology (a process known as *risk management*). However, scientific risk assessments are rarely definitive, at least in the early stage of a new technology's development, when both the probability of a hazard occurring and its consequences are necessarily probabilistic. In addition to the uncertainties that could be reduced in principle with more empirical research, there are other unknown uncertainties with a probability that cannot be theoretically or empirically calculated because they are rooted in the technology's novelty, complexity, and variability in different contexts.

Even when scientists agree on the nature and degree of risk of new technologies, there are always additional questions about the social value of a technology. Medical researchers are called upon to explain the potential health benefits of embryonic stem cell research, and bio-ethicists to clarify the ethical issues that surround creating and destroying human embryos in pursuit of medical understanding of the causes of and treatments for serious medical conditions such as Parkinson's and Alzheimer's diseases, spinal cord injuries, and diabetes. The normative judgments of scientists regarding the desirability of embryonic stem cell research, including its use in therapeutic or reproductive cloning, are always important in helping governments and the public to appraise the efficacy of regulatory practices.

Despite their similarity in giving an important place to expert advice in regulatory policy making, regulatory political cultures divide epistemologically on their understandings of how knowledge regarding the risks, costs, and benefits of scientific discoveries and technological innovations is produced and validated. In a *deferential political culture*, scientific experts predominate in the production of such knowledge and are assumed to be best positioned to characterize both the nature of the hazards posed by a technology and the appropriate interventions or regulations to reduce and manage these risks. This epistemological understanding often coexists with a positivist view of science—that is, a belief in science as capable of producing neutral and universal facts. A deferential political culture is most likely in political communities that have a positive orientation toward technology and science, and equate scientific discoveries and technological innovations with societal benefits and progress. In a deferential political culture, neither citizens nor governments are likely to regard the "everyday" knowledge of the public as an effective substitute for effective policy making. The deferential political culture is also often described as *technocratic* political culture of risk regulation, given its assumption that risks and benefits are quantifiable by technical experts (Jasanoff 2006).

In a *precautionary political culture*, by contrast, there is greater skepticism that technological developments represent progress and more emphasis on the uncertain risks, rather than the potential benefits, posed by new technologies. The limits of scientific knowledge are stressed, and scientific claims are viewed as indeterminate, uncertain, and not necessarily reliable. Because the expert knowledge of scientists is never, then, certain (when it comes to appraising the hazards of a new technology), a precautionary political culture is more likely than a deferential culture to err in rejecting technologies with initially uncertain risks that are later found to be safe, rather than accept technologies with initially uncertain risks that are later determined to render the product unsafe. In precautionary political cultures, lay citizens are also likely to be given a larger role in the production and validation of knowledge regarding how best to regulate novel technologies.

Rule and Norms of Accountable and Legitimate Regulatory Decision Making

A fundamental principle of democracies is that the people or their representatives should control decision making. Mechanisms of democratic accountability must, therefore, be built into regulatory processes to legitimize regulatory outcomes as desirable and appropriate. These accountability mechanisms are ideally built into the processes of *formulating* regulatory policy frameworks as well as into *implementing* these frameworks. At the policy formulation stage, accountability norms typically require conformity to an *agency* model of accountability—that is, regulatory policies that are consistent with the preferences of citizens, as expressed either by citizens directly or indirectly through their elected representatives as their delegated agents (Majone 2001). Policy formulation processes consistent with an agency model of accountability can vary enormously in their inclusiveness. Those wherein governments consult only with those they designate stakeholders provide a less participatory regulatory politics than those that provide forums of public debate, including hearings of legislative committees.

In the implementation of regulatory policy frameworks, *fiduciary* principles of accountability vie with agency accountability principles. A fiduciary model of accountability entrusts delegated regulatory agents—typically at arms' length from governments and with expertise credentials—with considerable independence to act for the benefit of those who have delegated them authority (Majone 2001). The accountability of the fiduciary rests, in large part, on its performance—upholding the delegate's best interests—but also on procedural controls, like judicial and peer review, and requirements of reason giving, that limit its discretionary behavior (Majone 1996, 292).

Depending upon the breadth of societal actors consulted and the array of issues addressed in regulatory policies, the politics of novel technology regulation can be described as either *technocratic* or *participatory*. *Technocratic* regulatory politics describe regulatory politics wherein the considerations of experts prevail, including when disagreements about the risks/costs and benefits of novel technologies arise between laypersons and experts. *Participatory* regulatory politics prevail when the public not only has opportunity to air its view on regulatory policy with respect to a novel technology, but these views are also reflected in the substance of the policies themselves. Fiduciary principles of accountability and technocratic regulatory politics are likely to pass tests of democratic legitimacy in a deferential regulatory political culture toward science and technology. By contrast, legitimation norms in a precautionary political culture are likely to require agency principles of accountability and participatory regulatory politics.

THE POLITICAL CULTURE OF REGULATING INNOVATIVE TECHNOLOGIES IN CANADA

Secondary accounts and survey data lend support to characterizing Canada's political culture as deferential toward the role of scientists and other experts in producing knowledge about technology. Among the set of values and beliefs shared by Canadians is a faith in science and technology. Writing in the late 1960s, George Grant (1969) described Canada and the United States as "technological societies." Thirty years later, survey data support his characterization. A 1989 survey of 2,000 Canadians concluded that "substantial majorities" of Canadians shared a belief with Europeans and Americans "in the promise of science and technology" (Miller et al. 1997, 110). Canadians have faith in science and technology despite their "relatively low" level of understanding of "basic scientific concepts" (Miller et al. 1997, 109). Survey data gathered in 2000 showed rising levels of support for science and technology, with more than three out of five Canadians believing that more emphasis on the development of technology and scientific advances would benefit mankind (Nevitte and Kanji 2004, 86–87). This favorable view was confirmed in a 2006 survey that found that Canadians generally approve of many key areas of emerging technology. They expect nanotechnology, bioproducts, and stem cell research to improve their lives over the next twenty years, and believe the benefits to society of these technologies outweigh their risks.

Canadians' enthusiasm for technological innovations is not, however, universal. Rather, it is contingent upon the perceived benefits of the new technology exceeding its perceived risks (Government of Canada 2004a, 8). The 2006 study found that Canadians were not supportive of GM animals, food, and fish; all were seen to have more risks than benefits (Industry Canada 2006).

Two factors in particular explain Canadians' deferential political culture with respect to most technological innovations. The first, according to Grant (1969, 114), is the predominance of liberalism and its central assumption "that man's essence is his freedom and therefore that what chiefly concerns man in this life is to shape the world as we want it." In Grant's view, technology and liberalism support each other as "the governing faith of the society" (Grant 1969, 28). More recently, Ronald Manzer (1994, 267–268) has coined the term "technological liberalism" to capture the currently dominant view that material well-being and human progress are overwhelmingly dependent upon technological innovation and scientific creativity.

Second, historically, and even today, the economic fortunes of many Canadians have been closely tied to technology. Technological advancements enabled the exploitation of the country's natural resources, be it for the production of cheap food, or the extraction of valuable minerals, oil, and gas. Given this direct link between technology and their own economic well-being, it is not surprising that so many Canadians have faith in technology.

Canadians' deferential or permissive attitudes toward science and technology lend support to the second feature of Canada's regulatory political culture: regulation of novel technologies based on fiduciary principles of accountability. Survey data gathered by the government of Canada reveal that "most Canadians" believe that decisions with regard to biotechnology products should be "science based and expert" rather than based on the views of average citizens or moral and ethical issues (Government of Canada 2004b, 3; see also Gaskell and Jackson 2005). Furthermore, "[i]n general, Canadians seem to have assumed a casually watchful and mostly neutral stance [on biotechnology], relying on science to sort things out" (Government of Canada 2004b, 5). However, the same survey data also show that there is "a considerable minority" of Canadians with "some doubts about the legitimacy of the sound science approach" and who want regulatory processes to provide more opportunities for the views of average citizens to be taken into account (alongside scientific evidence), and for the moral and ethical issues of new technologies like stem cell research and GM foods to be considered (Gaskell and Jackson 2005, 75).

Principles of decision making in Canada's political institutions lend support to a fiduciary model of novel technology risk regulation. Canada's system of Westminster parliamentary government vests considerable political authority in the executive even while adhering to principles of responsible government that make the executive (cabinet ministers) responsible in the legislature to the electorate. The principle of responsible government allows a government to delegate responsibility for the implementation of regulatory frameworks to a regulatory agency as long as elected officials answer to Parliament and the Canadian electorate for the delegated agency's performance.

The fiduciary model of accountability has also been upheld by Canadian courts. They have traditionally deferred to the decisions of regulatory agencies on matters on which they have expertise and will intervene in regulatory decisions only when those decisions can be shown to be unreasonable (Sossin 2003).[2] Canadian courts have been unwilling to play the activist role of their American counterparts in the regulation of biotechnology. The case of the Harvard oncomouse—a mouse genetically modified to produce mice susceptible to cancer—is instructive. Although the U.S. Supreme Court ruled in *Diamond v. Chakrabarty* (1980) that higher life forms (the oncomouse) could be patented, the Canadian Supreme Court was not prepared to do so. In *President and Fellows of Harvard College v. Canada (Commissioner of Patents)* (2002) the Canadian court observed that the 133-year-old Canada Patent Act was not adequate to address the complex ethical and legal issues raised by the GM mouse. However, it deemed it inappropriate for the courts to fill the legislative void. The majority of the Court said the complexity of the issue demanded that Parliament deal with it by engaging in a public debate on the issue, balancing the competing social interests around it, and drafting appropriate legislation on patenting higher life forms.

Institutional differences between Canada and the United States, including Canadian judicial deference versus American judicial activism, have had an impact on the regulatory politics of technology and science. Although Americans share Canadians' faith in technology as an instrument of progress, their regulatory politics with respect to new technologies are often more contested. The American institutional separation of powers makes Congress reluctant to delegate rule-making discretion to executive agencies, and the courts have been given strong powers to ensure that administrative agencies both carry out and do not exceed their mandate. As a result, courts have come to play a prominent role in U.S. regulatory governance, with court battles over the scope of regulation often turning on the quantitative and scientific data of contending parties. The result is frequently a contest of scientists—a phenomenon that works to undermine an image of science as objective and universal. By contrast, and as noted earlier, scientific experts continue to enjoy a high reputation in Canadian regulatory politics around novel technologies.

With courts playing a far less role in the regulation of novel technologies, the political arena in Canada becomes a crucial site for mediating conflicts about appropriate regulatory frameworks to capture their benefits and mitigate their costs/risks. Writing in 1994, Harrison and Hoberg were pessimistic about the efficacy of the political arena as a site for a participatory regulatory politics. They argued that science-based regulation in Canada did not exclude cooperation with regulated actors, but it closes the regulatory process to public scrutiny and offers far fewer institutionalized opportunities to participate in regulatory policy making than exist for the American public. The politics of regulating GM crops and foods, and ART provide support for their view, but they also reveal important differences in patterns of technocratic and participatory regulatory politics.

REGULATING GENETICALLY MODIFIED CROPS AND FOODS: TECHNOCRATIC REGULATORY POLITICS

Genetically modified plants are produced when a (pest- or herbicide-resistant) gene is transferred from one plant to another. Their expected economic benefits include increased crop yields as a result of the GM plant's protection from pests and diseases, and the environment benefits from less use of chemical pesticides. The potential human health risks of GM plants/foods include allergenicity or toxicity. Genetically modified crops' potential environmental risks include harm to other plant or insect life, and adverse effects on biodiversity. Aside from these safety considerations, there are social and economic issues raised by GM crops and foods that include the distribution of the benefits and risks of the technology, biotechnology developers' structural power over farmers, and consumers' rights to avoid GM products.

The content and the process that led to Canada's 1993 Regulatory Framework for Biotechnology is consistent with Canadians' deferential political culture toward science and technology and technocratic regulatory politics. In keeping with the insistence of biotechnology developers that GM products not be discriminated against, Canada's framework regulates GM plants the same way it regulates all plants with *novel* traits—that is, with characteristics that are neither familiar nor substantially equivalent to those of existing cultivated species. Scientific analyses of the degree of risk posed by a GM product trigger its degree of regulation. Genetically modified plants and foods are approved in Canada by the Canadian Food Inspection Agency solely on a risk assessment of their safety. Other social, economic, and ethical issues raised by the novel technology are not addressed within the regulatory framework.

In arriving at this framework, Canadian government officials sought information and advice from scientific networks and advisory committees in developing the GM policy and regulatory framework (Moore 2000). There was limited opportunity for a public debate on plant biotechnology. Existing legislation was used to regulate GM products, thereby eliminating the parliamentary debate that ordinarily accompanies policy innovation. Subsequently, multistakeholder consultations and workshops allowed for some public input into regulations and policy guidelines. Although some of these consultations in the early and mid 1990s were ostensibly designed to elicit feedback on the social and ethical dimensions of plant biotechnology, critics say they failed to realize this objective (Abergel and Barrett 2002). After the regulatory framework was in place, it provided little opportunity for public input and little transparency on the decision to approve particular GM crops/foods. Nor was there an opportunity to appeal regulatory decisions. Even so, until the late 1990s, there was very little public debate or controversy in Canada about both this regulatory framework and GM foods and crops.

When controversy around GM crops and foods arose in the late 1990s—as the media covered the rejection of plant biotechnology in Europe—the government of Canada turned to science to bolster the legitimacy of existing regulations. In November 1999, it asked scientists external to the government of Canada, in the Royal Society of Canada, to provide advice on scientific issues of GM foods. As discussed further later, this strategy backfired when the expert panel of the Royal Society produced a damning critique in January 2001 of the scientific integrity of Canada's risk regulatory framework and recommended a more precautionary approach.

The Canadian government also took initiatives toward more participatory plant biotechnology regulatory politics. It created the Canadian Biotechnology Advisory Committee (CBAC) in 1999 to provide advice to a ministerial committee on the social, ethical, regulatory, economic, health, environmental, and scientific considerations of biotechnology policy. The CBAC was also given a mandate to enhance public awareness of biotechnology and to provide opportunities for Canadians to voice their views on those biotechnology matters that fell within CBAC's advisory remit.[3] Twenty-one experts external to government and drawn from diverse backgrounds served on the CBAC. They devised a consultation document, in concert with various stakeholder groups (industry, agricultural producers, a nutritionist, and an environmental group), to focus discussion in a series of multistakeholder workshops and Internet discussions in 2001 on GM food.[4]

The success of this consultative exercise was impaired when the vast majority of environmental and public interest nongovernmental organizations decided to boycott the consultations on the grounds that the CBAC's remit was too narrow and it lacked independence from government. The CBAC observed the lack of a mechanism by which to incorporate nonscientific (principally social and ethical) factors into discussion of plant biotechnology policy development, and urged the government of Canada to engage in a further dialogue with the Canadian public (Canadian Biotechnology Advisory Committee 2002). At the same time, it reiterated that GM crops and food should continue to be approved solely on the basis of scientific assessments.

There is little evidence that the CBAC's initiatives engaged the Canadian *public* in a discussion about the broader issues raised by biotechnology. Furthermore, it is difficult to determine whether the CBAC had an impact on the substance of Canadian plant biotechnology policy.

As noted earlier, the Canadian government stumbled in its efforts to bolster support for its GM regulatory framework by appealing to the faith Canadians have in science. The report of the Royal Society expert panel, titled *Elements of Precaution: Recommendations for the Regulation of Food Biotechnology*, found significant and numerous deficiencies in existing risk regulatory procedures and concluded they failed to conform to scientific standards (Royal Society of Canada 2001, 214). The panel's report targeted provisions in existing regulations that protected developers' confidentiality and compromised the public transparency of scientific data and the scientific rationales on which regulatory decisions are based. It criticized the absence of independent review of data and the inadequate consultation of the expert scientific community in the design and execution of testing regimes for GM organisms. The panel concluded that GM plants were being approved without sufficient research to appraise their environmental impacts, and that the existing regulatory system did not warrant Canadians' confidence (Royal Society of Canada 2001, 132, 215).

These criticisms of the Royal Society panel can be read as an indictment of practices that undermined fiduciary principles of accountability in the regulation of GM products. So can its criticisms of conflicts of interest that "compromise the integrity of regulatory science and decision making" (Royal Society of Canada 2001, 212). These conflicts of interest stem, first, from the dual mandate of regulatory agencies to promote the development of agricultural biotechnology as well as to regulate it; and, second, "the increasing domination of the research agenda by private corporate interest" that makes it difficult for scientists to be disinterested (Royal Society of Canada 2001, ix).

A report two years later by the CBAC can also be understood as urging a more robust fiduciary model of accountability (Canadian Biotechnology Advisory Committee 2002). It called for greater scientific rigor and transparency in Canadian regulatory policies by more involvement of outside experts in risk assessments of GM products, clearer information on how GM products are regulated, and public disclosure of the data on which safety assessments are made. And like the Royal Society expert panel, the CBAC urged clarification of the mandates of government agencies involved in plant biotechnology to avoid responsibilities for regulation overlapping with other functions like economic development and trade promotion.

The recommendations of the Royal Society panel and the CBAC were consistent with a more precautionary political culture of regulating the products of genetic engineering. A shift in this direction by the government of Canada has not occurred—at least not completely. In a 2006 analysis, Andrée (2006, 377) concluded that although the government of Canada had taken some efforts to implement recommendations consistent with such a precautionary approach, it "continues to fall short of meeting the [Royal Society of Canada] Panel's expectations in key areas, including food safety, environmental assessment, peer review, transparency, and monitoring and surveillance."

In sum, and to quote Isaac (2002, 200), the Canadian plant biotechnology regulatory process is "narrow and judicious...limited to traditional actors and experts" and provides "limited say" to citizens, consumer, and environmental organizations. These features have diminished its legitimacy among the Canadian public. Public opinion data reveal that four in ten Canadians believe the biotechnology regulatory system is too lax, and another two in ten say they are uncertain about it. Three fifths of Canadians believe the government "probably does not do enough" to study and manage the risks associated with biotechnology (Industry Canada 2006, 12).

In contrast to the technocratic politics of regulating GM products, a more participatory politics characterized the process that led to regulation of ARTs in Canada.

REGULATING ASSISTED REPRODUCTIVE TECHNOLOGIES: PARTICIPATORY POLITICS

Assisted reproductive technologies are biomedical procedures and practices used to assist conception and pregnancy. They include assisted insemination, in vitro fertilization, embryo research, and surrogacy. Survey data indicate that Canadians are supportive of ART; for example, more than four fifths of Canadians approve the use of stem cell research, providing that it is regulated and controlled at "the usual" or tighter levels (Gaskell and Jackson 2005, 73). Canadians' support for stem cell research is undoubtedly linked to their belief that it will improve their lives (Industry Canada 2006, 3).

An ART regulatory framework that was consistent with Canada's deferential political culture of science and technology and a technocratic regulatory politics would allow a wide range of ART, providing that rules were in place to monitor their use and conditions of access (Rothmayr et al. 2004). Such a regulatory framework would be consistent with beliefs that (medical) science benefits human beings and "that the medical community and researchers know best, and that regulation should be left to professional organizations" (Rothmayr et al. 2004, 232–233). It would also be consistent with the preference of the medical professionals and researchers for autonomy (in quest of scientific knowledge) and self-regulation. By contrast, a public that has apprehensions about ART, and a polity that ascribes to a precautionary approach to technology/science, would demand a more rigorous regulatory framework that discriminates among practices and put limits on ART.

The process that led to the adoption of the Assisted Human Reproduction Act in March 2004 displays features of a democratic and participatory politics, but one with an outcome that, nonetheless, is consistent with the same deference to elites that is characteristic of a technocratic model of regulation. The process of designing an ART framework began in 1989 when a Royal Commission on reproductive technologies was set up in response to demands from a coalition of Canadian women's groups who believed a regulatory framework was needed. The Royal Commission held public hearings in seventeen Canadian cities, and, after wide input, produced a 1993 report that recommended that some ART practices, such as human cloning, be prohibited and that a regulatory commission be established to oversee permitted ART practices.

On its receipt of the Royal Commission's report, the federal Liberal government drafted legislation on ART to put a moratorium on human cloning and commercial surrogacy. In a deviation from legislative practice, the health minister presented a parliamentary committee with a bill that had received first, but not second, reading in the House of Commons. The departure from standard practice suggested that the government was prepared to pay more than customary heed to the testimony heard by the parliamentary committee. The responsible minister subsequently withdrew the draft bill from the parliamentary committee when it was determined, says Montpetit (2003, 104), that government officials had not "adequately consulted" Canadians before its introduction.

Although Montpetit's (2003) argument suggests respect for a participatory model of novel technology regulation, this initial legislative attempt drew criticisms from the organizations with expertise on the issue, including the Canadian Medical Association, the Canadian Bar Association, and the National Association of Women and the Law. The government's withdrawal of its legislation in face of their opposition suggests deference to elite stakeholder groups in society. Even so, the fact that the government persisted with its strategy of legislating a framework for ART regulation meant that this debate conformed more to participatory democratic processes by being conducted in the transparent forum of the national Parliament and media coverage.

The substantive features of the regulatory framework incorporated in the Assisted Human Reproduction Act adopted in 2004 also supports a more democratic regulatory model of process design in that it "complies largely with the recommendations of the Royal Commission on New Reproductive Technologies" (Montpetit 2007, 84) and enjoyed the support of major Canadian scientific and research bodies, patient advocacy groups, and Canadian feminist organizations (Darnovsky 2003). Consistent with the Royal Commission's recommendations, the Act prohibits creating embryos for research or cloning them to obtain stem cells. Canadian researchers are limited to using embryos left over from the process of in vitro fertilization treatments.[5] The ban on human cloning, to recall, had been opposed by organizations representing the medical profession. This outcome suggests limits to the influence of scientific elites and the influence of feminist groups in particular (Darnovsky 2003).

The implementation of ART regulatory policies is consistent with fiduciary principles of accountability. The Act established a regulatory body, the Assisted Human Reproduction Agency of Canada, and gave it authority to license, regulate, and monitor clinics that engage in ART practices. Insofar as the Act itself failed to specify the purposes for which embryo research could be conducted, the agency was seen to have considerable discretion on this matter. Both the agency's mandate, and the preponderance of medical experts on its board of directors, are consistent with a fiduciary and technocratic regulatory model.

CONCLUSION

The politics of the regulation of technological and scientific innovations are complex and often controversial. When public disputes flare around new technologies, governments can face difficult tradeoffs between advancing technologies that promise benefits—economic and medical, for example—but that are resisted by society. Governments' strategies to mediate such societal divisions and create acceptable compromises reflect their political cultures of novel technology regulation.

Canada's deferential or permissive political culture toward science and technology has joined with principles of fiduciary accountability to ease Canadian decision makers' task of interest mediation. Having determined that it is only a minority that is skeptical of plant biotechnology, Canadian governments have not only licensed it without imposing onerous regulatory requirements, but also made limited efforts to depart from their technocratic and fiduciary regulatory model. Canadian governments have not, for instance, seen the necessity of undertaking direct democracy initiatives—consensus conferences, referenda, nationwide consultative exercises—that have occurred in countries like Denmark, Austria, and England, where the public has been more hostile to genetically engineered crops and foods and insisted on a more precautionary approach. Nor have Canadian governments seen fit to heed the strong preference of the Canadian public—at least as voiced in survey polling—for mandatory labels on foods that contain or are made from GM products. Instead, Canadian governments have supported voluntary labeling by food manufacturers.

The scope that Canada's deferential political culture provides for technocratic regulatory decision making should not be exaggerated. Even if Canadians assess the benefits of new technologies overwhelmingly on the basis of their risks and benefits (cloning is the exception where ethical reasons are important in Canadians' aversion to it), and regard experts' judgments about risks and benefits as the basis of good regulation, they nonetheless expect the formulation of regulatory frameworks to be more consistent with agency principles of democratic accountability (Government of Canada 2004a, 26). The demand for a more participatory regulatory politics of public consultation and transparent policy processes was heeded more fully in the formulation of an ART regulatory policy.

The design of ART regulatory policy made Parliament and parliamentary committees a venue for the representation of the full spectrum of views. Does this example then mean that Parliament is an effective forum in which to define the terms of the social contract under which society agrees to accept the costs, risks, and benefits of a novel technology? Yes and no. On the yes side, the very publicness of Parliament (and the publicity the media gives its business) can allow it to play an important role in helping to define the stakes of a novel technology. This function is arguably better performed when governments have a minority in the Parliament than when their governing position is secured by a majority. On the no side, Parliament and parliamentary committees are adversarial chambers that normally have little incentive and limited capacity to engage in the kind of deliberation often needed to build understanding across those who hold divergent values. Nor can parliamentarians necessarily be relied upon to represent majority public opinion. For example, although survey data indicate "almost universal support" among Canadians for research that uses embryos left over from fertility clinics (Industry Canada, 2006, 25), several members of Parliament argued during the ART legislation debate that the public supported a ban on embryonic stem cell research (Caulfield and Bubela 2007). In the case of GM food, the House of Commons Standing Committee on Agriculture recommended the voluntary labeling of GM food products even while survey data show that a majority of Canadians prefer mandatory labeling.

Canadian decision makers have often opted for multistakeholder consultations as a supplement to, or replacement for, consultations by parliamentary committees. When stakeholder consultations serve only to provide a second opportunity for the very groups that appear before elected and appointed officials to reiterate their positions, they add only modestly to the creation of a participatory politics of regulation. However, the potential of stakeholder consultations to strengthen participatory politics and agency principles of accountability is much greater if and when they are structured to allow dialogue and learning across societal groups—as representatives of the diverse public—as well as across societal and government officials. We have too little information to know how many stakeholder consultations in Canada realize this outcome. Indeed, as long as the majority of Canadians have faith in technology and support science-based decision making around novel technologies, governments are likely to have few incentives to reshape regulatory processes more fully on participatory politics lines.

Finally, Canada's regulatory culture and politics for novel technologies can be an asset in the contemporary political economy. They enable the ready embrace of new technologies that are perceived to render Canada's economy more competitive in the domestic and international economy. At the same time, Canada's political culture of deference to science is consistent with the rules of international trade agreements. Both the North American Free Trade Agreement and the World Trade Organization agreements rely on scientific risk assessments to differentiate between legitimate and illegitimate regulatory measures that restrict trade on the grounds of protecting human, animal, and plant health and safety. These economic and political developments, combined with technological advancements like cloned animals, ensure that the politics of the regulation of novel technologies will continue to be politically charged for some time to come.

Acknowledgment. I gratefully acknowledge the research assistance of Evan Sotiropoulos, MA, University of Toronto.

NOTES

1. Science encompasses all the natural, social, humanities, health, and engineering disciplines that generate knowledge about nature, human beings, and artifacts and systems. Technology refers both to knowledge and artifacts in the form of goods, services, organizations, methods, and tools. Technology (computers) can contribute to science and science to technology.

2. Chief Justice McLachlin's decision in *Dr. Q. v. B.C. College of Physicians and Surgeons* (2001), 198 D.L.R. (4th) 250 (B.C.C.A.), para. 29, is the clearest statement of the deferential approach.

3. The CBAC has been disbanded and replaced by the Science, Technology and Innovation Council, but information on it can be obtained at http://cbac-ccb.ca.

4. A discussion of the process that led to the dialogue tool and its purpose can be found at http://cbac-cccb.ca/epic/site/cbac-cccb.nsf/vwapj/backgrounder_nov14. doc/$FILE/backgrounder_nov14.doc.

5. Available public opinion data suggest the government's prohibition on creating embryos in the laboratory for the purpose of extracting stem cells is consistent with the far

lesser degree of public support for this method of obtaining stem cells than for the using embryos left over from fertility clinics (see Industry Canada 2006, 25).

REFERENCES

Abergel, Elisabeth, and Katherine Barrett. 2002. Putting the cart before the horse: A review of biotechnology policy in Canada. *Journal of Canadian Studies* 37(3): 135–161.

Andrée, Peter 2006. An analysis of efforts to improve genetically modified food regulation in Canada. *Science and Public Policy* 33(5): 377–389.

Bricker, Darrell, and Edward Greenspon. 2001. *Searching for Certainty: Inside the New Canadian Mindset.* Toronto: Doubleday.

Canadian Biotechnology Advisory Committee. 2002. Improving the regulation of genetically modified foods and other novel foods in Canada. http://www.cbac.gc.ca/epic/site/cbaccab.nsf/vwapj/Improving_Regulation_GMFoodAug02.pdf/$FILE/Improving_Regulation_GMFoodAug02.pdf.

Canadian Food Inspection Agency. 2001. *Risk Communication and Government: Theory and Application for the Canadian Food Inspection Agency (CFIA).* Ottawa: Government of Canada. http://www.inspection.gc.ca/english/corpaffr/publications/riscomm/riscomme.shtml.

Caulfield, Timothy, and Tania Bubela. 2007. Why a criminal ban? Analyzing the arguments against somatic cell nuclear transfer in the Canadian parliamentary debate. *The American Journal of Bioethics* 7(2): 51–61.

Chalmers, Damian. 2005. Risk, anxiety and the European mediation of the politics of life. *European Law Review* 30(15): 649–674.

Darnovsky, Marcy. 2003. *Canada Considers Comprehensive Legislation on Assisted Reproduction Techniques.* Oakland, Calif.: Center for Genetics and Society. http://geneticsandsociety.org/article.php?id=2734&&printsafe=1.

Diamond v. Chakrabarty (1980) 447 U.S. 303.

Doern, G. Bruce, and Ted Reed. 2000. Canada's changing science-based policy and regulatory regime: Issues and framework. In *Risky Business: Canada's Changing Science-Based Policy and Regulatory Regime*, ed. G. Bruce Doern and Ted Reed, 3–28. Toronto: University of Toronto Press.

Gaskell, George, and Jonathan Jackson. 2005. A comparative analysis of public opinion: Canada, the USA and the European Union. In *First Impressions: Understanding Public Views on Emerging Technologies*, 63–75. Ottawa: Canada. CBS_Report_FINAL-ENGLISH2495fd-922005–5696.pdf.

Government of Canada. 2004a. *Genomics, Health and Society: Emerging Issues for Public Policy.* Symposium report. March 24–25. Ottawa: Policy Research Initiative. http://policyresearch.gc.ca/doclib/Genomics_final_E2.pdf.

———. 2004b. Summary of public opinion research into biotech issues in Canada. http://www.biostrategy.gc.ca.

———. 2007. Mobilizing science and technology to Canada's advantage. http://www.ic.gc.ca/cmb/welcomeic.nsf/vRTF/PublicationST/$file/S&Tsummary.pdf.

Grant, George. 1969. *Technology and Empire.* Toronto: House of Anansi.

Harrison, Kathryn, and George Hoberg. 1994. *Risk, Science, and Politics.* Montreal: McGill-Queen's University Press.

Industry Canada. 2006. Emerging technologies tracking research. http://www.biostrategy/
    gc.ca/english/View.asp?pmiid=524&x=837.

Isaac, Grant E. 2002. *Agricultural Biotechnology and Transatlantic Trade: Regulatory Barriers
    to GM Crops*. London: CABI Publishing.

Jasanoff, Sheila. 1995. Product, process or programme: Three cultures and the regulation of
    biotechnology. In *Resistance to New Technology*, ed. Martin Bauer, 311–331. Cambridge:
    Cambridge University Press.

———. 2005. *Designs on Nature: Science and Democracy in Europe and the United States*.
    Princeton, N.J.: Princeton University Press.

———. 2006. Technology as a site and object of politics. In *The Oxford Handbook of
    Contextual Political Analysis*, ed. Robert E. Goodin and Charles Tilly, 745–763. Oxford:
    Oxford University Press.

Majone, Giandomenico. 1996. *Regulating Europe*. London: Routledge.

———. 2001. Two logics of delegation: Agency and fiduciary relations in EU governance.
    European Union Politics 2(1): 103–121.

Manzer, Ronald. 1994. *Public Schools and Political Ideas: Canadian Educational Policy in
    Historical Perspective*. Toronto: University of Toronto Press.

McHughen, Alan. 2000. The regulation of GM foods: Who represents the public interest?
    International Journal 4: 624–632.

Miller, Jon D., Rafael Pardo, and Fujio Niwa. 1997. *Public Perceptions of Science and
    Technology: A Comparative Study of the European Union, the United States, Japan and
    Canada*. Chicago, Ill.: The Chicago Academy of Social Science.

Montpetit, Éric. 2003. Public consultations in policy network environments: The case of
    assisted reproductive technology policy in Canada. *Canadian Public Policy* 29(1):
    95–110.

———. 2007. The Canadian knowledge economy in the shadow of the United Kingdom
    and the United States. In *The Politics of Biotechnology in North America and Europe*, ed.
    Éric Montpetit, Chistine Rothmayr, and Frederic Varone, 83–102. Lanham, Md.:
    Lexington.

Moore, Elizabeth. 2000. *Science, Internationalization, and Policy Networks: Regulating
    Genetically-Engineered Food Crops in Canada and the United States, 1973–1998*. PhD
    diss., University of Toronto.

Nevitte, Neil, and Mebs Kanji. 2004. New cleavages, value diversity, and democratic
    governance. In *Canadian Politics*, ed. James Bickerton and Alain-G. Gagnon, 79–97.
    Peterborough: Broadview Press.

President and Fellows of Harvard College v. Canada (Commissioner of Patents) (2002) 4
    S.C.R. 45.

Rothmayr, Christine, Frederic Varone, Uwe Serdult, Arco Timmermans, and Ivar Bleiklie.
    2004. Comparing policy design across countries: What accounts for variation in ART
    policy? In *Comparative Biomedical Policy: Governing Assisted Reproductive Technologies*,
    ed. Ivar Bleiklie, Malcolm L. Goggin, and Christine Rothmayr, 228–253. London:
    Routledge.

Royal Society of Canada. 2001. *Elements of Precaution: Recommendations for the Regulation
    of Food Biotechnology in Canada*. Ottawa: Royal Society of Canada. http://www.agbios.
    com/docroot/articles/2001035-A.pdf.

Sossin, L. 2003. Empty ritual, mechanical exercise or the discipline of deference? Revisiting
    the standard of review in administrative law. *The Advocate's Quarterly* 27(4): 478–501.

CHAPTER 26

....

CANADIAN ENVIRONMENTAL POLITICS AND POLICY

....

MICHAEL HOWLETT
SIMA JOSHI-KOOP

THE environment has become one of the defining political issues of the early twenty-first century in Canada, as in many other countries. The growing transboundary character of environmental issues combined with advances in communications technology and international trade have put pressure on Canadian policy makers to pursue environmental policies and processes compatible with those across other political regimes, especially the United States. At the domestic level, concrete and observable ecological degradation, economic restructuring, and increasing demands for inclusion from environmental nongovernmental organizations (ENGOs) and Aboriginal groups have widened and reshaped the politics of the environment in Canada (Howlett 2001). Altogether, these changes present challenges for Canadian governments, both in how they understand environmental issues as well as in the types of policy instruments they can use to address them.

In light of this changing political context, the chapter will reexamine government engagement on environmental issues in Canada since the 1950s, focusing on the changes that have occurred since then at the federal level. This discussion will be undertaken with a view to updating existing understandings of how and why environmental policy is made in this country. In particular, the chapter will highlight the diminishing capacity, and willingness, of Canadian governments to direct policy outcomes by means of traditional policy instruments, such as regulation and laws, and the consequence that has followed: increased reliance on complex procedural instruments, which only indirectly determine policy outcomes by altering the relations between and resources and interests held by participants in the policy process. As evidenced by activities undertaken in the first decade of the twenty-first century, Canada's governments have begun to develop a new style of environmental policy making very different from that developed in the 1960s, when issues such as pollution and waste management first appeared on government agendas.

We begin this chapter by identifying the domestic context for environmental issues and, specifically, key features and drivers of environmental politics and policy in Canada. From there we move to an examination of how environmental issues enter onto governmental agendas and are typically addressed (or not) by subsequent government action. A review of environmental policies over the past half century demonstrates that, although Canadian environmental politics has often translated into a cycle of policy action followed by policy retreat, at another level, environmental politics lurch forward, backward, and sideways, both in the types of instruments proposed to address environmental issues and how those environmental issues come to be understood by key political actors.

THE CONTEXT OF CANADIAN
ENVIRONMENTAL POLITICS

Canada's environmental politics are complex and multifaceted. The environment is both symbolically and materially important for Canadians. They take pride in their geography: the abundance of fresh water and the ample forests, the world's longest coastline, the Canadian Rockies, and the mythological North "untouched by civilization." For Canada's First Nations, too, the environment holds both productive and nonproductive value, with material, cultural, and political significance for these communities (Hessing and Howlett 1997; Poelzer 2002). The country's vast and diverse landmass underpins a significant portion of its economic activity. With 175 billion barrels of "economically viable" oil reserves (in the Athabaska Oil Sands), a figure the Canadian Association of Petroleum Producers (2007) claims is "enough oil to meet the world's energy needs for 500 years," Canada stands second only to Saudi Arabia as the world's largest source of recoverable oil. In addition, the country possesses immense deposits of nickel, uranium, and zinc. Furthermore, it can claim 20% of the world's freshwater and almost 16% of world trade in forest products (Natural Resources Canada 2008; Parks Canada 2004).

Despite the salience of the environment to the economic and cultural life of Canada, scholars have lamented the absence of comprehensive government action on long-term environmental protection and resource management, notwithstanding what at times has amounted to immense public pressure, and, even, ambitious legislation (Harrison 1996; McKenzie 2002; Toner 2002). Several explanations are commonly cited for this failure. First, environmental issues constitute a shared authority under the Constitution Act, 1867, resulting in political entanglement and jurisdictional confusion about which problems can or should be attacked by which level of government: federal or provincial, or even local. The provinces are vested with power over natural resource development and exploration, but the federal government enjoys jurisdiction over fisheries, shipping and navigation, criminal law, federal lands, and interprovincial and international trade. Furthermore, the federal government has the potential for even wider authority over the environment under the "Peace, Order, and good Government" clause of section 91 of the Constitution Act. Arguably, throughout the course of Canadian history, these divisions of power have been an infrequent source of conflict between the two orders of government, because the federal government initiated environmental legislation only in the past forty years. Nonetheless, when the federal government did assert itself in this area, provincial governments were quick to protest the "intrusion." One consequence of jurisdictional overlap and sensitivity about the environment, has been checkerboard public policies and failure to develop comprehensive efforts for environmental protection (McKenzie 2002, 105).

In addition to the constitutional problems, environmental issues also suffer from administrative complexity. At one time it may have been appropriate to channel environmental issues into a single federal department—Environment Canada—for resolution. However, in an age of challenges such as climate change and global warming, it is impractical to look to individual departments to be champions of entire policy sectors. It is inadequate because most, if not all, such environmental issues are interconnected with social, economic, health, and security issues as well. Efforts made by Environment Canada to reduce greenhouse gas emissions are futile if policies developed by an industry bureau of the federal government or by a provincial government have the unintended consequence of increasing them.

Between the 1970s and late '90s, administrative structures were created in Canada to foster interdepartmental and intergovernmental cooperation around environmental policy and other issues (Skogstad and Kopas 1992). However, as new dimensions to environmental issues have been recognized, previously excluded societal actors such as Aboriginal peoples and environmentalists have also gained greater access to policy making. In sum, not only are environmental issues today more multidimensional and interconnected with other issues than in the past, but the types of actors that must be included in the policy process for the government's policy decisions to be considered legitimate has expanded (Howlett 2002).

Complications for environmental governance in Canada do not stop there, however. At the broader level, and across policy sectors, government departments have also struggled to maintain a high level of policy capacity in the context of declining policy resources. As a result of government retrenchment, many policy units, including federal advisory councils on a number of environmental issues, were dismantled in the 1990s, leaving much of the comprehensive policy analysis critical to long-term policy development in the hands of research centers attached to universities (Prince 2007). Under the Liberal government's 1993–1997 program review, Environment Canada alone suffered a 25% reduction in staff, of which 250 full-time equivalent employees were cut from its policy branch, a pattern repeated in most provinces during the same decade (Savoie 1998; Toner 1996).

Thus, for reasons both internal and external to government, policy influence over the state of the environment in Canada today is more diffuse than it was in the past. As governments continue to prefer "leaner" departments, as policy issues demand greater technical knowledge, as more policy work occurs outside of the state, and as a wider variety of environmental actors proliferates in "civil society," environmental issues require increased cooperation and collaboration between state and nonstate actors in order for government's formal policy responses to be effective. Politicians and public servants no longer enjoy a monopoly over the direction and content of public policy. They no longer possess all the technical information needed to make effective decisions, nor can they ignore the ever-widening array of nonstate actors demanding input into decision-making processes (Prince 2007).

At the same time that governments must work with multiorganizational networks of state and nonstate actors on environmental issues, they must also be prepared to look beyond short-term policy horizons. Because environmental issues often manifest themselves as long-term problems, governments require long-term approaches to deal with them effectively. Forward-looking environmental policies in areas such as climate change adaptation often entail narrowly distributed short-term costs with broadly enjoyed and in-the-distant-future benefits, such as limiting oil and gas production in Alberta to help preserve the atmosphere. However, for politicians with, at most, a five-year electoral mandate, such long-term policy horizons are politically unrewarding. In addition, politicians realize that the general public has a limited attention span for environmental issues. Because these issues are rarely seen by the public to have a measurable impact on their well-being, they tend to attract limited and only indirect public attention (Soroka 2002). As a consequence, politicians may believe they can safely ignore environmental issues in the absence of concerted media coverage of ecological studies, events, and disasters, or of political action on the part of environmental groups, either of which may successfully focus public concern. This distinguishes the environment from other issues (such as taxation or unemployment) that do not require media coverage to be considered important to voters, because their effects are felt directly by individuals on a daily basis.

The Cyclical Nature of Canadian Environmental Politics

As a result of these political properties, environmental issues are highly cyclical in nature and highly susceptible to fluctuations in political attention. In his 1972 article, Anthony Downs focused on this characteristic to develop the concept of an issue–attention cycle as a means to understand American environmental policy and politics. Kathryn Harrison (1996) has used Downs's issue–attention cycle model to portray the failures of environmental policy making in Canada between the 1960s and '90s. She has argued that ambitious initiatives on the environment in Canada have almost always been followed by their abandonment at the stage of policy implementation. Although the federal government introduces legislation in Parliament when polls show strong public interest in the environment, subsequent attention to the subject frequently declines, with the result that implementation of environmental policies tends to be half-hearted, if followed through at all (Harrison 1996). Governments desire to be credited by electorates for their action on the environment during peak attention to the issue at the same time that they want to avoid imposing large costs on powerful industrial sectors and antagonizing other governments who retain a jurisdictional stake in natural resources (Hoberg and Harrison 1994). Thus, the issue in Canada regarding environmental politics may be summarized as one of how to secure genuine and sustained commitment from governments for action in the absence of strong electoral incentives to do so.

Although the issue–attention cycle significantly clarifies Canada's history of failures around the implementation of environmental protection policies, it is important to note that the content of environmental politics and the processes by which it has developed have not remained static throughout the past half century. Scholars have written extensively in recent years about the "hollowing out" of state capacity and its growing dependence on societal actors for the delivery of public services. They have further noted the proliferation of policy analysis and advice outside of government since the 1960s, increased demands from citizens to be consulted since the 1980s, and the rise of networks of interorganizational actors as venues for policy formation in the 1990s (Dunn and Kelly 1992; Rhodes 1994). These changes have not been without implications for the content and processes of politics and many areas of policy. In particular, in many sectors including the environment, governments have increasingly relied on indirect procedural rather than substantive policy instruments to realize their goals (Buuren and Klijn 2006; de Bruijn and ten Heuvelhof 1995; Klijn et al. 1995).

Canada's contemporary environmental politics thus has three interrelated components. The first is political commitment, which Harrison (1996) demonstrates has fluctuated between active and passive political pressure and policy making. The second is the policy processes of government, which now include increased use of contracts, partnerships, public advisory commissions, stakeholder consultation, and funding to nongovernmental organizations (NGOs) to affect indirectly the resources, interests, and relations among environmental policy stakeholders (Howlett 2001). The third is the principal mechanism by which substantive changes on the ground have been made by governments when direct action has been taken. These can range from the creation of regulatory agencies to the use of public enterprise, exercise of financial incentives, and the practice of "moral suasion" (Peters and Nispen 1998). The environmental sector in Canada has increasingly featured privatization and downsizing of government agencies, deregulation, and a shift toward an emphasis on "voluntary regulation" (Gibson 1999).

Although environmental policy in Canada has featured cycles of policy activism and neglect, Canada's governments have succeeded in constructing three relatively long-lasting sets of institutional arrangements for dealing with environmental issues. The following section will examine the environmental sector through the lens of the three environmental policy regimes that have been constructed by Canadian governments throughout recent decades. It will highlight the interaction between political commitment to the environment and the policy instruments selected by governments to address environmental issues.

Three Regimes of Environmental Policy in Canada

Canadian environmental policy can be understood as a cyclical process of active policy selection and passive policy implementation in the context of two significant mitigating forces: a shifting understanding of environmental problems, and an expanding and changing policy tool kit available to address them. In particular, Canada has moved away from aggressive substantive instruments designed to address policy issues and has simultaneously embraced bolder procedural instruments designed to mollify public concerns, with the effect that environmental issues are dealt with more collaboratively and inclusively but also less directly than in the past. This section will trace the government's engagement on environmental issues throughout the past half century to demonstrate both the cyclical and evolutionary natures of environmental politics and policy in Canada.

Private Law Environmental Protection, Pre-1960s

Before the 1960s, environmental concerns in Canada were few and were primarily addressed through private property rights enforcement by the country's common and civil (in Quebec) law systems. To the extent that environmental policy existed, it was primarily developed and enforced through limited provincial government activities to protect property owners from some of the negative effects of polluting activities on the part of others and was encapsulated in the record of court cases related to adjudication of property rights issues. Canada's courts heard mainly private actions concerning negative environmental effects during this period, and only to the extent that these grievances involved financial losses for individual claimants (Elder 1973; Jeffreys 1984). Actions under this private law regime provided some protection for private property from ecological damage, but it fell short of a comprehensive policy for environmental protection, excluding as it did both publicly owned property and collective issues related to large-scale problems such as air and water pollution.

Other jurisdictions had better success in adapting their legal systems to accommodate emerging environmental concerns with industrial pollution and wildlife depredations, but even here, the results were not necessarily more effective. In the United States, for example, the courts began, in the 1930s, to allow citizens legal redress, under the notion of a "public trust," in particular air and coastal lands as shared resources neither owned privately nor protected publicly but henceforth open to judicial protection (Sax 1971). In Canada, stronger adherence to British common-law practices concerning torts, such as negligence and malfeasance, resulted in only very restricted standing for persons seeking legal remedies for environmental damage. Canadian courts were adamant that recourse already existed for the protection of natural resources through legislation by public authorities and private action by aggrieved individuals (Hunt 1981). "Class action" lawsuits in Canada proved extremely difficult to mount because of strict criteria for eligibility—for instance, claimants had to be individually identifiable and they had to maintain nearly identical claims. As a result, it was very difficult to litigate public trust and collective pollution issues (Chester 1981). The logic of the Canadian judicial system meant that if initiatives to protect the "common good" were to be taken, it was up to government to act, primarily through legislative statutes (Miller 1977).

This initial divergence between Canada and the United States on environmental protection was compensated for in the case of private legal actions by the fact that Canadian penalties for violation of private property rights were more severe than in the United States. U.S. plaintiffs had greater access to the courts as a result of a more expansive definition of the term *court action;* however, the remedies handed down in that country were more limited than in Canada. Courts in the United States did recognize the right of private individuals to act on behalf of the public, but common-law torts had largely been stripped of their deterrent effect after a series of prodevelopment decisions handed down in the mid-nineteenth century that limited damages received by plaintiffs in these actions (Howlett 2000). In sum, although Canada adopted weaker procedural instruments for environmental protection than the United States, its substantive instruments—in terms of the scope of the decisions handed down by the courts—were simultaneously stronger than the ones existing in the United States. As a consequence, the level of environmental protection in the two countries remained roughly congruent.

Public Law Regulatory Regime, 1960–1990

This private law approach to environment policy in both countries, however, proved sorrowfully inadequate as a protective shield, especially when environmental issues expanded during the last half of the twentieth century, as both countries experienced rapid population and economic growth after World War II. By the 1960s, it was no longer practical to think of environmental protection in terms of grievances against individual owners of private property. On the contrary, emerging environmental problems were increasingly public, and later global, in scale (Paehlke 2000). This demanded an approach that would recognize the collective nature of environmental damage—in other words, an approach that supplemented common law legal devices with a public law regulatory apparatus. In addition, many of the environmental issues that ignited public attention during the 1960s were ill-suited to the kind of ex post mitigative or compensatory policy treatment offered through court action. Environmental disasters, including well-publicized poisonings of local populations by industrial pollutants found in water supplies and food chains, wildlife extinctions, and resource shortages caused by overharvesting precipitated public concern for preventative mechanisms to avoid these problems ex ante. This included high-profile environmental degradation caused by major tanker wrecks and oil spills off the coasts of England (1967) and Nova Scotia (1970), as well as realization of the devastating environmental impact of DDT and other pesticides. The publication of Rachel Carson's *Silent Spring* in 1962 succeeded in mobilizing public awareness to environmental issues, although it would take ten years of concerted political effort for this initial concern to translate into concrete political action, with the banning of DDT in the United States in 1972 (Paehlke 1997).

The surge in public concern for the environment from across Canada in the 1960s sent a signal to the federal government that it could no longer maintain that it lacked jurisdiction on the environment, and to provincial governments that more action was needed to supplement existing private law environmental protection regimes. For the first time, Canada's federal government entered into the environmental policy fray, initially through bilateral government–industry accords (Schrecker 1984; 1990) and then in 1969 passing several acts: The Clean Air Act, the Amendments to Fisheries Act, the Northern Inland Waters Act, the Arctic Waters Pollution Prevention Act, and the Canada Water Act, which ushered in a new era of public protection of the environment (Cotton and McKinnon 1993).

Dissecting these new environmental policy initiatives into their procedural and substantive components reveals that, despite an ambitious posture, these federal actions had mixed results. On the one hand, the federal government had enacted new and progressive laws. In some instances, however, they included standards that affected provincial jurisdiction over national resources. This represented unilateral activity that was uninvited and unwelcome by provincial governments with a primary concern of retaining virtually unfettered control over economic development of natural resources (Fafard 2000). Yet, on the other hand, several of the Acts contained clauses mandating consultation with the provinces and rejected the notion of uniform national standards (Harrison 1996). Regulation through public law had become the primary *substantive* policy instrument for environmental protection; yet, the content of this instrument was achieved through a *process* of consultation with industry groups and eleven major governments. In particular, the enactment, implementation, and compliance levels of environmental standards were developed through closed bargaining between government and industry representatives (Emond 1985; Estrin 1975; Schrecker 1984; Swaigen 1980; Thompson 1980). As a result, the assertiveness of the federal government's new regulations was moderated so much that the implementation of the legislation failed to realize the promised effect.

Despite these contradictions between stated government policy aims and their implementation, heightened concern for the environment in the 1960s and early '70s had direct effects on government institutions and societal organizations. It was at this time that Canada's first national ENGOs and its most successful international one (Greenpeace) were founded, followed by ministries for the environment within both orders of government (Paehlke and Torgerson 1990). Environmental assessments, the first tool developed in Canada to try to anticipate and mitigate environmental damage before it happened, were also created and mandated during this period (Rolf and Thompson 1985). By the time of the 1972 federal election economic issues had come again to monopolize the attention of the electorate. It would not be until the late 1980s and early '90s, however, when environmental issues would again reappear on the public agenda and receive renewed governmental interest (Harrison 1996; Parson 2001).

Collaborative Government, Post-1990

In a second wave of policy reform, beginning in 1988, Parliament passed the Canadian Environmental Protection Act (CEPA), signaling the return to a more active federal government in the field. CEPA differed from previous federal Acts in several important ways. First, it emphasized national standards through strict equivalency conditions and annual reporting. Federal ambivalence to "regulating the provinces," which had been the sentiment conveyed in statutes from the previous era, had disappeared. Second, it included new powers for the federal government—not contemplated in previous Acts—to promote life cycle management of pollutants and to deal with chemical substances and associated health and environmental risks. Third, the assertion of mandatory compliance in CEPA's companion document, the *CEPA Enforcement and Compliance Policy* (Environment Canada 2001), was "nothing short of a 'radical shift in philosophy' from the traditional approach of gradual, negotiated compliance" (Harrison 1996, 140). In the past, as we have seen, the federal government had been prepared to pass legislation on the environment, but struggled to make good on its promises to *implement* the Acts through regulations and enforcement procedures. Most legislation did not contain clauses obliging governments to implement their terms. The fact that such an article could be found in CEPA set the Act apart from all other federal environmental activities to date.

A year after CEPA, the federal government also found itself coerced into further environmental activism by courts and environmental groups as a result of problems with the technical wording of the Environmental Assessment and Review Process (EARP) rules, which used the word *shall* rather than *may* with respect to the responsibility of government to conduct many types of environmental assessments. Although the EARP regulation had existed since 1984, it was not until a few years later that environment groups achieved the degree of professionalism necessary to cite the mandatory language of the EARP statutes in court to force governments to implement the guidelines. Equipped with legal knowledge, environmental groups brought several cases before Canada's courts, arguing that the federal government was bound by the EARP guidelines to perform environmental assessments in the *Rafferty-Alameda* and *Oldman Dam* cases in Saskatchewan and Alberta, respectively (Hoberg 1997; Howlett 1994). After these victories, the number of environmental assessments skyrocketed, with benefits for the environment, perhaps, but not for relations between the federal and provincial governments, already strained as a result of intensive constitutional discussions throughout these years (Harrison 1996). At the same time, federal participation in the negotiation of international treaties and agreements to reduce emissions (the Convention on Long-Range Transboundary Air Pollution), phase out ozone-depleting substances (the Montreal Protocol), and establish global objectives on climate change and biodiversity (such as the Earth Summit in Rio de Janeiro in 1992) exacerbated federal–provincial tensions.

As a result, in the late 1980s and early '90s, Canada began to experiment with new procedural instruments designed to ease government-to-government and government-to-ENGO conflicts. Closed, bilateral consultations between industry groups and government, which characterized Canadian environmental policy making in the previous era, were gradually replaced with less formalized intergovernmental, multistakeholder processes, including the creation of federal and provincial Round Tables on the Environment and Economy, the Commons Standing Committee on the Environment, the Environmental Management Framework Agreement, the Canada-Wide Accord on Environmental Harmonization, and other local and provincial initiatives (Howlett 1990). Industry groups and provincial governments benefited the most in terms of increased standing, although ENGOs did improve their access to the policy process somewhat. The increasing emphasis on wider consultation within international bodies such as the Brundtland Commission and the 1992 Earth Summit also could not be ignored by governments in their domestic politics.

These new and more inclusive and collaborative processes to align economic and environmental goals better ushered in yet another Canadian environmental policy regime—the third since the early 1960s. However, it did not directly translate into greater environmental protection. On the contrary, the procedural instruments used under this strategy to improve consultation were those that many argued had been the least effective at environmental protection (Howlett 2002; Muldoon and Nadarajah 1999; Winfield 2001). Concerns abound that multilateral agreements and consultations with industry representatives led to the dominance of voluntary arrangements over other more stringent policy instruments (Gibson 1999; Parson 2001; VanNijnatten 1999). Scholars have noted that these new procedural instruments conveniently emerged at a time when political priorities had again taken a sharp turn away from environmental awareness toward deficit reduction, and that they fitted with the then-prevailing do-more-with-less philosophy of federal and provincial agencies (Howlett 2002). In the end, few of the announced voluntary environmental programs were ever implemented in Canada, and even fewer efforts have been made since then to expand those that were (Antweiler and

Harrison 2007; Howlett 2002, 36). By 1998, environmental politics in Canada had returned to the familiar pattern of federal–provincial cooperation with the ratification of the Canada-wide Accord on Environmental Harmonization. The Accord, signed by the federal government, all provinces (except Quebec), and the territories, sought to delineate the roles of the federal and provincial governments with respect to environmental policy. Its ultimate goal was to reduce overlap and the potential for duplication through ongoing and formal consultations between governments, although its immediate effect was to dilute earlier federal government initiatives in this area (Winfield 2001).

There are some important differences about this recent period of environmental politics in Canada when compared with the past. Undoubtedly, all three regimes have featured novel policy approaches—the 1969 regulatory framework, CEPA in 1988 and its enforcement and compliance policy, the 1999 Canada-wide Accord on Environmental Harmonization, and the 2002 Species at Risk Act and its associated stakeholder working group—even if many of these policies were tempered in their implementation. What is particularly striking about the more recent governmental policy responses to the environment, however, is the process by which they have been developed. Environmental policy making has become a collaborative activity, and a multiplicity of stakeholders enjoy standing throughout this process, including other governments, industry groups, and representatives of civil society. Although the content of environmental policy could once be ascertained through the (bilateral) negotiations between the federal government and with provincial or industry representatives alone, more recently, the content of environment policy is influenced by entirely nongovernmental and extragovernmental interactions as well, such as those of the Species at Risk Working Group. This change is responsible for at least part of the pattern of the ebb and flow of the policy and the cycles of regulation and implementation characteristic of Canadian environmental politics since the 1960s.

THE CANADIAN COMMONS IN THE TWENTY-FIRST CENTURY: THE CASE OF CLIMATE CHANGE

In 2002, a student of public policy made the prediction that increased demands from an environmentally attentive public combined with international pressures would, once again, "make it difficult for the federal government to *not* play a more active role" in environmental policy in the future (Winfield 2001, 136 [emphasis added]). And, indeed, efforts at greater federal–provincial coordination and collaboration with a wider array of stakeholders have continued through the present decade.

Many of these initiatives now center on the effort to combat global climate change as a result of Canada's accession to the Kyoto Protocol on greenhouse gases in 2002. This includes the federal climate change secretariat, which in 2000 unveiled the national Climate Change Action Plan (including the National Implementation Strategy and the National Business Plan on Climate Change), signed by all provinces (except Ontario) and the territories. Notwithstanding this progress, all such plans have revealed the continuing weaknesses associated with implementation in Canadian environmental policy (Lee and Perl 2003). Through its promotion of research and awareness, the National Business Plan on Climate Change, like the Liberal government's Green Plan before it,[1] eschews the regulatory approaches of the 1970s and '80s, as well as the new market-based instruments (such as the carbon tax, tradable permits) that have been increasing in popularity in Europe and some American jurisdictions (Toner 2002). Perhaps the most noteworthy achievement of the federal government over the past few years was the passing of Canada's Species at Risk Act in 2002, and the collaborative processes leading up to it that included proposed amendments from the Species at Risk Working Group, composed of Forest Products Association of Canada, the Canadian Nature Federation, the Mining Association of Canada, the Sierra Club of Canada, and the Canadian Wildlife Federation (Donihee 2000).

Between 2006 and 2007, as the discussion of global warming and climate change accelerated, the environment again not only topped the public agenda in major opinion polls, but international pressures also bore down on the Conservative minority government led by Stephen Harper to meet its Kyoto commitment and to endorse absolute emissions reductions. These had been sanctioned by all countries at the Commonwealth Summit and all but two other countries (Japan and China) at the United Nations Framework Conference on Climate Change, both in 2007. Despite domestic public pressure, binding international commitments, and recent calls from the international community, Canada's federal government explicitly declined to support stricter environmental measures—the Kyoto protocol generally, and binding absolute emissions targets specifically.

To understand the federal government's lack of environmental activism in the face of public and international pressure requires reflection on the policy mix that has won favor with Canadian governments since the mid 1990s. On its own, an issue–attention cycle of public opinion does not explain the government's record on the environment in the twenty-first century, because strong and sustained media and public attention to the environment has not always resulted in ambitious policy legislation but, rather, has been tempered by the constraints of federalism and the fortunes of political actors.

This became apparent in the case of the Harper government soon after it came to office in 2006. In the First Session of the Thirty-seventh Parliament, for example, the Conservative government's approach to addressing climate change—the Clean Air Act—was so ill-received by opposition parties that it was sent to committee before its second reading, where its regulatory content was so significantly strengthened that it no longer resembled the government's initial bill. As a consequence of the prime minister's decision to close the parliamentary session early, the amended bill died on the floor and was not revived. In December 2007, the federal government re-introduced a piece of the original Clean Air Act as a government bill: The Renewable Fuels Act. The wording of the Renewable Fuels Act confirmed the federal government's intent on preserving its original and less restrictive regulatory measures.[2]

Although this may contradict the surge in public interest in environmental issues, it certainly falls within the purview of a government intent on taking a flexible approach based on consultation with industry groups and governments. It is also consistent with a federal government attracted to the achievement of environmental protection through procedural rather than substantive instruments. Further evidence of this approach was again seen after 2007, when the Conservative government announced a $225 million dollar partnership with the Nature Conservancy of Canada to work with organizations such as Ducks Unlimited Canada to provide matching funds for the purchase of "ecologically sensitive lands" from private landowners in return for the retention of their hunting rights (Office of the Prime Minister 2007).

The Harper government's emphasis on "emission's intensity" targets as "the best way to engage major polluters such as the U.S. and China" (Curry 2007, A1) failed to fit with the approach advocated by almost all other western countries. The government of Canada claims that emission intensity targets warrant a different rubric for success than those applied to the capping of greenhouse gas emissions at absolute levels, although it is not entirely clear how different those measures for success should be and whether this can be justified against the government's overarching goal of reducing *absolute* emissions by between 45% and 65% by 2050. (Department of the Environment et al. 2006)

The Harper government's emphasis on medium- and long-term emissions reductions was heavily criticized by other political parties, the media, and NGOs. Canada's National Round Table on the Economy and the Environment (NRTEE), by contrast, backed up the government's approach. In particular, the NRTEE expressed the importance of medium- and long-term thinking on climate change policy, and criticized both the Kyoto Protocol for its shortsightedness and regulatory measures for their false appeal under the "myth" that they lead to deeper substantive emissions reductions[3] (National Round Table on the Economy and the Environment 2007, 14). This demonstrates the declining yet lingering presence of elements of previous policy regimes, which emphasized regulation. At the same time as it confirms the broadening of the procedural policy tool kit to which federal governments can increasingly turn when addressing environmental issues. (Dudek and Golub 2003).

Can the current Canadian regime, centered as it is on the use of indirect procedural instruments, offset its soft substantive measures so that its overall environmental policy can be considered an ambitious one? The answer is as yet uncertain. As policy making takes place today increasingly by and through collaborative networks, procedural policy instrument use will continue to provide opportunities and impediments to environmental protection in Canada. Unfortunately, it is not yet clear whether the political rhetoric behind the federal government's emphasis on procedural instruments amounts to a genuine desire for a more realistic commitment to major current environmental issues such as climate change, or if it functions simply as a politically compatible partner to lagging substantive policy implementation at home.

As others have suggested, the effectiveness of procedural instruments is difficult to evaluate because their effects on policy outcomes are less direct, although their impact should not automatically be discounted. Although procedural instruments are more limited in scope and less visible in their outcomes than substantive instruments, they are important tools for policy change and are increasingly significant tools for governments that must now operate in the context of complex interorganizational networks of societal actors that may be particularly resistant to the use of many more traditional substantive policy instruments like subsidies and regulation (Buuren and Klijn 2006; Howlett 2000).

CONCLUSION

This chapter has argued that although environmental policy in Canada may appear to amount to little more than recurring federal–provincial turf wars or the cynical response to periodic bursts of public interest in ecological issues, the federal government has used different procedural and substantive instruments in the pursuit of evolving environmental goals throughout at least three different stages in Canadian history. Canadian environmental policy is thus better understood as a cyclical process of active policy selection and passive policy implementation, *but* in the context of significant mitigating forces. As environmental policy issues have become more multifaceted, they have become less amenable to ex post resolution through the courts and have moved to ex ante anticipation and mitigation through statutory provisions.

The ever-widening array of stakeholders in the policy process has contributed further to the complexity of environmental politics and policy issues. It brings more perspectives and concerns to the issues, necessitates an even greater and broader involvement of actors, and demands the increasing adjustment of procedural instrument responses. All of this occurs in the context of a federation with divided jurisdictions, where continual adjustments are required to laws and processes through intergovernmental bargaining and negotiation. As a result, the current Canadian environmental policy regime features novel procedural instruments. The Species at Risk Working Group and the National Areas Conservation Program have increased the standing of environmental groups and provincial governments in national policy making, although they also tend to displace substantive policy tools (regulation) in favor of "softer" instruments such as information campaigns, subsidies to NGOs, and voluntary approaches for environmental protection.

Looking ahead, it is clear that the new century will provide even further challenges for countries on environmental issues. Regarding the particularly big current topic—climate change—it appears that a new era of international politics has begun, one in which developing countries, such as China and India, are shaking up previously held notions regarding what to do about the global greenhouse gas emissions problem. Although most developed countries have expressed a preference for "continuing the Kyoto path" of binding absolute emissions targets for western nations, the Harper government chose to play the role of the black sheep on the international stage by deviating substantially from this sentiment and advocating a "beyond Kyoto" approach. As a result, it emphasized certain principles in its approach: flexibility, inclusion, long-term targets, and an economically realistic approach. These were at odds with most of the international community, although consistent with the views of the administration in Washington led by George W. Bush (Brennan 2007; Fuller and Gelling 2007; York 2007).

On balance, it is neither accurate to condemn Canada's government on its recent environmental policy intentions nor to congratulate it on its policy initiatives. What is clear is that Canada has continued to move further away from substantive instruments and more toward procedural ones. The substantive instruments it has enlisted (emissions intensity caps) appear to be somewhat weak (Dudek and Golub 2003).

Canada's current procedural approach, characterized by (1) industry consultation, (2) funding to ENGOs, and (3) long-term multilateral agreements could be—but has not yet proved to be—effective at environmental protection. On the one hand, procedural instruments offer flexibility, have the potential for cost-effectiveness, and can engage a wider array of critical actors and harness their collective capabilities while offering a better fit with interconnected and cross-cutting policy issues than regulation through vertically integrated government departments (Klijn et al. 1995). On the other hand, procedural instruments can lead to less stringent measures for environmental protection through a process of harmonization around the weakest policies; the neglect of implementation, monitoring, and reporting; and the compromise of democratic accountability resulting from closed-door government–industry deals (Harrison 1996; Parsons 2001; Winfield 2001).

NOTES

1. Although cited as the most ambitious and comprehensive framework for action on sustainable development ever witnessed in Canada, the majority of the Green Plan's initiatives were not implemented, including the voluntary agreements. As Hoberg and Harrison (1994, 120) argued, the Green Plan demonstrated the federal government's greater affinity for research and information dissemination than it did for regulation, an approach they argued was simply "not consistent with the instrument choices of a government motivated to take immediate and direct action to protect the environment."

2. Although the portion of the Clean Air Act covering motor vehicle fuel consumption standards was rewritten by legislative committee in 2006 to *mandate* rather than *allow* the government to prescribe regulations for fuel consumption standards, the federal government's Renewable Fuels Act retains the word *may,* rather than *shall,* thus making no binding commitments on the minister of the environment for environmental standards.

3. Under the Kyoto Protocol Implementation Act, the NRTEE is required to assess the likelihood of the government's plans to meet its stated objectives, without passing any judgment on the merit of these objectives themselves. This Act is the result of a Liberal-sponsored bill that was passed in the first session of the thirty-seventh Parliament under Canada's Conservative minority government, which requires the NRTEE to make a formal response to the federal government's climate change plan, which is also required under the Act.

REFERENCES

Antweiler, Werner, and Kathyrn Harrison. 2007. Canada's voluntary ARET program: Limited success despite industry co-sponsorship. *Journal of Policy Analysis and Management* 26(4): 755–773.

Brennan, Richard. 2007. Harper defiant on climate change: PM insists nations, not just developed ones, must work together to reduce gas emissions. *Toronto Star*, November 26, A21.

Buuren, Arwin van, and Klijn, Erik-Hans. 2006. Trajectories of institutional design in policy networks: European interventions in the Dutch fishery network as an example. *International Review of Administrative Sciences* 72(3): 395–415.

Canadian Association of Petroleum Producers. 2007. Industry facts and information, oil sands, research and production. December 12. http://www.capp.ca/default.asp?V_DOC_ID=1162.

Canadian Wildlife Federation Inc. v. Canada (Minister of the Environment) (1989) 3 F.C. 309.

Carson, Rachel. 1962. *Silent Spring.* Boston: Houghton Mifflin.

Chester, Simon. 1981. Class actions to protect the environment: A real weapon or another lawyer's word game? In *Environmental Rights in Canada*, ed. John Swaigen, 60–151. Toronto: Butterworths.

Cotton, Roger, and Kelley M. McKinnon. 1993. An overview of environmental law in Canada. In *Environmental Law and Business in Canada*, ed. Geoffrey Thompson, Moira L. McConnell, and Lynne B. Huestis, 1–30. Aurora: Canada Law Book.

Curry, Bill. 2007. PM wants hard caps scrapped in next green deal. *Globe and Mail*, September 26, A1.

de Bruijn, Johan A., and Ernst F. ten Heuvelhof. 1995. Policy networks and governance. In *Institutional Design*, ed. David L. Weimer, 161–179. Boston: Kluwer Academic Publishers.

Department of the Environment, Department of Health, Department of Natural Resources, and Department of Transport. 2006. Notice of intent to develop and implement regulation and other measures to reduce air emissions. *Canada Gazette*, 141(42), s. 9.3.

Donihee, John. 2000. The New Species at Risk Act and Resource Development. *Resources* 70: 1–7.

Downs, Anthony. 1972. Up and down with ecology: The issue–attention cycle. *The Public Interest* 28: 38–50.

Dudek, Daniel, and Alexander Golub. 2003. Intensity targets: Pathway or roadblock to preventing climate change while enhancing economic growth? *Climate Policy, Supplement* 3(2): 21–28.

Dunn, William, and Rita Kelly, eds. 1992. *Advances in Policy Studies Since 1950.* New Brunswick: Transaction Publishers.

Elder, P. S. 1973. Environmental protection through the common law. *University of Western Ontario Law Review* 12: 107–171.

Emond, D. P. 1985. Environmental law and policy: A retrospective examination of the Canadian experience. In *Consumer Protection, Environmental Law and Corporate Power,* ed. Ivan Bernier and Andrée Lajoie, 89–179. Toronto: University of Toronto Press.

Environment Canada. 2001. *Compliance and Enforcement Policy for the Canadian Environmental Protection Act, 1999 (CEPA 1999).* Ottawa: Minister of Public Works and Government Services Canada.

Estrin, David. 1975. Environmental law. *Ottawa Law Review* 7(2): 397–449.

Fafard, Patrick C. 2000. Groups, government and the environment: Some evidence from the Harmonization Initiative. In *Managing the Environmental Union: Intergovernmental Relations and Environmental Policy in Canada,* ed. Patrick Fafard and Kathryn Harrison, 81–101. Montreal: Institute of Intergovernmental Relations, Saskatchewan Institute of Public Policy.

Friends of the Oldman River Society v. Canada (Minister of Transport) (1992) 1 S.C.R. 3.

Fuller, Thomas, and Peter Gelling. 2007. Deadlock stymies global climate talks. *New York Times,* December 12. http://www.nytimes.com/2007/12/12/world/12climate.html?em&ex=1197694800&en=618463e0c990c94c&ei=5087%0A.

Gibson, R. B. 1999. *Voluntary Initiatives: The New Politics of Corporate Greening.* Peterborough: Broadview Press.

Harrison, Kathryn. 1996. *Passing the Buck: Federalism and Canadian Environmental Policy.* Vancouver: University of British Columbia Press.

Hessing, Melody, and Michael Howlett. 1997. *Canadian Natural Resource and Environmental Policy.* Vancouver: University of British Columbia Press.

Hoberg, George. 1997. Governing the environment. In *Degrees of Freedom: Canada and the United States in a Changing World,* ed. Keith Banting, George Hoberg, and Richard Simeon, 341–386. Montreal: McGill-Queen's University Press.

Hoberg, George, and Kathryn Harrison. 1994. It's not easy being green: The politics of Canada's Green Plan. *Canadian Public Policy* 20(2): 119–137.

Howlett, Michael. 1990. The Round Table experience: Representation and legitimacy in Canadian environmental policy making. *Queen's Quarterly* 97(4): 580–601.

———. 1994. The judicialization of Canadian environmental policy 1980–1990: A test of the Canada–U.S. convergence hypothesis. *Canadian Journal of Political Science* 27(1): 99–127.

———. 2000. Managing the "hollow state": Procedural policy instruments and modern governance. *Canadian Public Administration* 43(4): 412–431.

———. 2001. Complex network management and the governance of the environment: Prospects for policy change and policy stability over the long term. In *Governing the Environment: Persistent Challenges, Uncertain Innovations,* ed. Edward A. Parson, 303–344. Toronto: University of Toronto Press.

———. 2002. Policy instruments and implementation styles: The evolution of instrument choice in Canadian environmental policy. In *Canadian Environmental Policy: Context and Cases*, ed. Debora L. VanNijnatten and Robert Boardman, 25–45. Oxford: Oxford University Press.

Hunt, Constance D. 1981. The public trust doctrine in Canada. In *Environmental Rights in Canada*, ed. John Swaigen, 151–194. Toronto: Butterworths.

Jeffreys, M. I. 1984. Environmental enforcement and regulation in the 1980's: *Regina v. Sault Ste. Marie* revisited. *Queen's Law Journal* 10(1): 43–70.

Klijn, Erik-Hans, Joop Koppenjan, and Katrien Termeer. 1995. Managing networks in the public sector: A theoretical study of management strategies in policy networks. *Public Administration* 73: 437–454.

Lee, Eugene, and Anthony Perl. 2003. *The Integrity Gap: Canada's Environmental Policy and Institutions*. Vancouver: University of British Columbia Press.

McKenzie, Judith I. 2002. *Environmental Politics in Canada: Managing the Commons into the Twenty-first Century*. Oxford: Oxford University Press.

Miller, Arthur. 1977. *An Overview of Federal Class Actions: Past, Present and Future*. Washington D.C.: Federal Judicial Center.

Muldoon, Paul, and Ramani Nadarajah. 1999. A sober second look. In *Voluntary Initiatives: The New Politics of Corporate Greening*, ed. R. B. Gibson, 51–65. Peterborough: Broadview Press.

National Round Table on the Economy and the Environment. 2007. *Response of the National Round Table on the Economy and the Environment to Its Obligations under the Kyoto Implementation Protocol Act*. Ottawa: Government of Canada.

Natural Resources Canada. 2008. Canadian Forestry Service. Government of Canada. January 28. http://cfs.nrcan.gc.ca/index/forestindustryincanada.

Office of the Prime Minister. 2007. PM announces support for national land conservation program. Government of Canada. March 30. http://pm.gc.ca/eng/media.asp?id=1573.

Paehlke, Robert. 1997. Green politics and the rise of the environmental movement. In *The Environment and Canadian Society*, ed. T. Fleming, 251–274. Toronto: ITP Nelson.

———. 2000. Environmentalism in one country: Canadian environmental policy in an era of globalization. *Policy Studies Journal* 28(1): 160–175.

Paehlke, Robert, and D. Torgerson. 1990 *Managing Leviathan: Environmental Politics and the Administrative State*. Peterborough: Broadview Press.

Parks Canada. 2004. International Year of Freshwater. Government of Canada. January 21. http://www.pc.gc.ca/nature/eaudouce_freshwater/itm2-/index_e.asp.

Parson, Edward A. 2001. Environmental trends: A challenge to Canadian governance. In *Governing the Environment: Persistent Challenges, Uncertain Innovations*, ed. Edward A. Parson, 3–30. Toronto: University of Toronto Press.

Peters, B. Guy, and Frans K. M. van Nispen, eds. 1998. *Public Policy Instruments. Evaluating the Tools of Public Administration*. Cheltenham: Edward Elgar Publishing.

Poelzer, Greg. 2002. Aboriginal peoples and environmental policy in Canada: No longer at the margins. In *Canadian Environmental Policy: Context and Cases*, ed. Debora L. VanNijnatten and Robert Boardman, 87–106. Oxford: Oxford University Press.

Prince, Michael J. 2007. Soft craft, hard choices, altered context: Reflections on twenty-five years of policy advice in Canada. In *Policy Analysis in Canada: The State of the Art*, ed. Laurent Dobuzinskis, Michael Howlett, and David Laycock, 163–185. Toronto: University of Toronto Press.

Rhodes, Ron A. W. 1994. The hollowing out of the state. *Political Quarterly* 65(2): 138–151.

Rolf, Carole A., and Andrew R. Thompson. 1985. Environmental protection alternatives in the 1980s. In *Environmental Protection and Resource Development: Convergence for Today*, ed. B. Sadler, 79–100. Calgary: University of Calgary Press.

Savoie, Donald. 1998. Towards a different shade of green: Program review and Environment Canada. In *Managing Strategic Change*, ed. P. Aucoin and Donald J. Savoie, 71–97. Ottawa: Canadian Center for Management Development.

Sax, Joseph L. 1971. *Defending the Environment: A Strategy for Citizen Action*. New York: Alfred A. Knopf.

Schrecker, Ted. 1984. *Political Economy of Environmental Hazards*. Ottawa: Law Reform Commission of Canada.

———. 1990. Resisting environmental regulation: The cryptic pattern of business–government relations. In *Managing Leviathan: Environmental Politics and the Administrative State*, ed. R. Paehlke and D. Torgerson, 165–199. Peterborough, Ont.: Broadview Press.

Skogstad, Grace, and Paul Kopas. 1992. Environmental policy in a federal system. In *Canadian Environmental Policy: Ecosystems, Politics, and Process*, ed. R. Boardman, 43–60. Toronto: Oxford University Press.

Soroka, Stuart. 2002. Issue attributes and agenda-setting by media, the public, and policymakers in Canada. *International Journal of Public Opinion Research* 14(2): 264–285.

Swaigen, John. 1980. Environmental law 1975–1980. *Ottawa Law Review* 12(2): 439–488.

Thompson, Andrew R. 1980. *Environmental Regulation in Canada: An Assessment of the Regulatory Process*. Vancouver: Westwater Research Centre.

Toner, Glen. 1996. Environment Canada's continuing roller coaster ride. In *How Ottawa Spends, 1996–97*, ed. G. Swimmer. Ottawa: Carleton University Press.

———. 2002. Contesting the green: Canadian environmental policy at the turn of the century. In *Environmental Politics and Policy in Industrialized Countries*, ed. Uday Desai, 71–120. Cambridge, Mass.: MIT Press.

VanNijnatten, Debora L. 1999. Participation and environmental policy in Canada and the United States: Trends over time. *Policy Studies Journal* 27(2): 267–287.

Winfield, Mark S. 2001. Environmental policy and federalism. In *Canadian Federalism: Performance, Effectiveness and Legitimacy*, ed. Herman Bakvis and Grace Skogstad, 124–137. Toronto: Oxford University Press.

York, Geoffrey. 2007. Ottawa gains key allies to "move beyond Kyoto." *Globe and Mail*, December 6, A1.

CHAPTER 27

DEFENSE AND SECURITY

ELINOR SLOAN

SURROUNDED by oceans and bordering only one country, a friendly superpower to the south, Canada has historically felt little threat to its territory. To the extent that a potential security threat has existed, it has been an economic one, and the Canadian government's imperative for decades now has been to ensure the country maintains its access to the American market. The absence of a direct military threat in the post–World War II period, apart from ballistic missiles, against which it was deemed there was no defense, allowed Canada to focus more broadly on international peace and security. Canada's internationalist perspective was expressed in its contribution to collective defense as a founding member of the North Atlantic Treaty Organization (NATO), and collective security as a firm advocate of the United Nations (UN). Its membership in and support of these organizations reflected, in part, a general sense that Canada, as a trading nation, benefits from and is dependent on a peaceful global environment. However, it also reflected a more self-interested understanding that participation in multinational organizations would give Canada a stronger voice in world affairs than would otherwise be the case, and that it would prevent Canada from being completely overwhelmed and consumed (figuratively at least) by the United States.

Many of these themes continue in the twenty-first century. Canada's security and prosperity is still most directly dependent on access to the American market, which is the end point of at least 80% of Canadian exports in any given year. Although America remembers September 11, Canada remembers September 12 as well—the day that all cross-border traffic came to a halt, causing millions of dollars in lost revenues for Canadian businesses. The Canadian political and military leadership also continues to be internationalist in nature, placing a great value on UN and NATO membership, and taking as its starting point the long-standing perspective that the "best defense is a good offense" (in other words, that threats to Canada are best met as far from Canadian borders as possible). Yet there are some subtle changes. Abroad, Canada's Cold War emphasis on peacekeeping missions under UN auspices changed, from about the mid 1990s onward, to more robust operations under NATO leadership. Although previously Canada participated in almost all UN missions, now Canada is prioritizing where it sends its troops. At home, an eclectic mixture of possible terrorist threats to Canada, a concern that Canada not be a base for terrorist threats against the United States, and a melting polar ice cap is forcing the government to place greater emphasis on domestic and continental security concerns than has historically been the case.

This chapter touches on all of these themes. The first section centers on homeland security, drawing out the measures Canada has taken since September 11 to ensure its border with the United States remains secure but open to trade. The second section focuses on defense, first highlighting the historical evolution of Canadian defense priorities, and then looking more closely at current Canadian defense policy. The concluding section discusses future issues and challenges for Canada with respect to defense and security, with a particular emphasis on the Canadian forces.

HOMELAND SECURITY

One meaning of security is the absence of a threat to values. A threat to national security is best understood as an action or sequence of events that could drastically and, over a brief period of time, hold those values at risk. Some of these threats will require a military response, but many will not. Homeland security refers to civilian-led measures to protect the people, property, and infrastructure of a country.

Although it is tempting to date Canada's (and America's) increased focus on homeland security to September 11, in fact, conceptually and rhetorically, it began much earlier. After the euphoria of the end of the Cold War wore off and it became clear that the new world order, although less dangerous than the old order, was still filled with conflict, U.S. analysts began to think about the next threat to the United States and its allies. The lesson America's adversaries took from the 1991 Gulf War, it was argued, was that they could not compete against the United States on the traditional, conventional battlefield. Instead, potential adversaries would have to develop "asymmetrical" approaches to target America's vulnerabilities and weaknesses, including terrorism and the use of weapons of mass destruction. Although American forces and facilities overseas faced these threats, it was felt that the American homeland was especially vulnerable. An increased threat to the homeland figured prominently in the Pentagon's May 1997 Quadrennial Defense Review, and also in the bipartisan congressional Report of the National Defense Panel later that year. It was not long before this thinking permeated north of the border. By 1998, Canada's defense analysts, too, were focusing in their research on the asymmetrical threat to Canada and North America.

Canada's proximity to the United States, as well as its open society and multi-ethnic population, make it attractive as a terrorist "safe haven" to launch attacks against the United States. Already in the mid to late 1990s, the counterterrorism program of the Canadian Security Intelligence Service (CSIS) was focusing on the Sunni Islamic terrorist threat to Canada (CSIS 2002). The Canadian Security Intelligence Service was tracking a change in the nature of terrorist activity in Canada. No longer used solely for logistical or support activities, Canada had become a staging area to launch attacks. This was exhibited most vividly with the case of Ahmed Ressam, a terrorist residing illegally in Montreal who was caught just before millennium celebrations trying to enter the United States to carry out a terrorist strike on the Los Angeles airport. After September 11, the threat has further transformed such that there may also be a direct terrorist threat to Canadian territory. Newspaper accounts indicate the Royal Canadian Mounted Police (RCMP) has disrupted numerous terrorist plots against Canada over the past several years, most notably the 2006 arrest of seventeen suspected terrorists accused of planning attacks in southern Ontario.

During the late 1990s, the United States took some measures to respond to the asymmetrical threat to the homeland. U.S. president Bill Clinton issued, for example, presidential decision directives on critical infrastructure protection and combating terrorism.[1] However, it was not until after September 11 that America initiated major organizational changes to address such threats, creating, most notably, the Department of Homeland Security (DHS) in March 2003. Canada's response in the immediate aftermath of the attacks was to increase funding to organizations like CSIS and the Communications Security Establishment (CSE) to bolster its intelligence-gathering capability. This remained its focus until a change of Liberal prime ministers in December 2003, at which time Canada created an organization broadly parallel to DHS—Public Safety and Emergency Preparedness Canada, renamed Public Safety Canada (PSC) by the new Conservative government in early 2006.

Just as DHS in the United States is built on the old Federal Emergency Management Agency, so, too, in Canada is PSC built on emergency preparedness (previously a component of the Department of National Defense). The federal government works with the provinces to ensure they can respond to an emergency, whether it is a terrorist incident or a natural disaster. At the hub of its effort is a government operations center, created in 2004 and functioning on a 24/7 basis, which serves to coordinate and monitor communications during an emergency so that all agencies involved are "in the loop." The protection of Canada's critical infrastructure—which may include anything from electrical, water, and energy supplies to financial, telecommunications, and transportation systems—is also a central mandate of PSC. In this domain, PSC works closely with industry to promote both cyber and physical protective measures.

In some cases, an emergency response could involve a military contribution, although civilian organizations are the first responder. Municipal, provincial, and finally federal government levels are responsible for the safety and security of the Canadian population, and they are the lead agencies in responding to security threats on Canadian territory. But under the National Defense Act, as revised in 1950, provinces may also seek "assistance to civil authorities" in the event of a "national emergency" (Morton 1995, 138). Such calls have come on numerous occasions in the post–Cold War period in response to weather-related emergencies like floods, snowstorms, and an ice storm. In addition, on two occasions in recent memory Canadian forces (CF) has been called out in "aid of the civil power"—the 1970 FLQ Crisis (discussed later) and the 1990 Oka Crisis. The key distinction between the CF "assisting civil authorities" and acting in "aid of the civil power" is that, in the latter instance, the CF temporarily becomes the lead agency, because it is beyond the power of civil authorities to suppress, prevent, or deal with the situation (Sloan 2005, 84).

One crisis scenario that would almost certainly require the assistance of the Canadian military, in either a supporting or lead role, is the terrorist use of a weapon of mass destruction against a major population center. Such an event has been a leading concern of Canadian security and intelligence agencies in the post–September 11 period. The CF has a number of units with the skills to address such threats, including Joint Task Force 2, which is Canada's special operations force, and a Canadian Incident Response Unit. In 2006, the incoming Conservative government announced it would increase Canada's emergency response capability by stationing "territorial response battalions" made up of a mix of regular and reserve forces at fourteen locations across the country. This ultimately proved unfeasible because of the personnel demands of Canada's ongoing commitment to Afghanistan (discussed later in this chapter). However the CF has developed a force employment structure designed to mobilize Canada's existing land force reserves in six major Canadian cities in a crisis situation.

Beyond emergency preparedness and infrastructure protection, PSC encompasses three organizations central to Canadian security: CSIS and the RCMP, which were previously part of the solicitor general organization, and a newly created (in late 2003) Canada Border Services Agency (CBSA). The RCMP is responsible for law enforcement, whereas CSIS is a domestic security intelligence-gathering organization akin to Britain's MI5. For many years, the intelligence-gathering function was part of the RCMP, as continues to be the case with the Federal Bureau of Investigation in the United States, which also has significant law enforcement responsibilities. However, in the early 1980s, a Royal Commission on national security and intelligence (the Inquiry into Certain Activities of the RCMP) determined that intelligence gathering and law enforcement were not compatible functions. As a result, the two were separated with the creation of CSIS in 1984. Although CSIS has liaison officers at some of Canada's overseas embassies to gather information directly related to threats on Canadian soil, the organization is not permitted to gather foreign intelligence about other countries, in the manner of the Central Intelligence Agency in the United States. Canada's only foreign intelligence agency is CSE, which since the end of World War II has been collecting foreign electronic intelligence. An ongoing and as yet unresolved debate within Canada is whether the country should create its own foreign intelligence-gathering agency, with some arguing Canada is too reliant on its allies for human intelligence, and others making the case that it would simply be too expensive, and would divert valuable and overstretched CSIS resources at home. The final key component of Canada's public safety apparatus is the CBSA. Encompassing the security-related components of three previously existing organizations—the intelligence interdiction and enforcement program from Citizenship and Immigration Canada, the port-of-entry program from the Canadian Food Inspection Agency, and the customs program from the Canada Customs and Revenue Agency (now renamed the Canada Revenue Agency)—the CBSA is charged with facilitating and managing the smooth flow of people and goods across the border.

The CBSA is on the "front lines" of addressing Canada's long-standing security interest in maintaining access to the U.S. market. When first created, its mission was essentially to implement the Smart Border Accord, negotiated between Canada and the United States within months of the September 11 attacks. The Accord's thirty-two-point action plan included a range of measures, from high-tech preclearance cards to expedite trucks going through the land border, to the establishment of integrated border enforcement teams made up of U.S. and Canadian agencies to respond to threats. Some twenty integrated border enforcement teams are in place across the continent, and all other elements of the Smart Border Accord have also been implemented. Since 2005, the CBSA and its counterpart organization in the United States, the Bureau of Customs and Border Protection, have been responsible for implementing the Security and Prosperity Partnership (SPP). Essentially a follow-on to the Smart Border Accord, the security component of the SPP encompasses measures to secure North America from external threats (for example, compatible procedures at foreign ports), prevent and respond to threats within North America (such as port and airline security), and further streamline the secure movement of low-risk travelers across the border (for example, technological upgrades to Smart Border technology).

These agencies and activities are described in *Securing an Open Society: Canada's National Security Policy* (Privy Council Office 2004). Released in 2004, the policy marked the first time in history the Canadian government had explicitly stated the country's approach to guaranteeing its security. Unlike the United States, which produces a national security strategy every four years, Canada has no such tradition. In the post–World War II period, successive Canadian governments pursued security policies for Canada, but until 2004, these were always implicit in government actions and choices, rather than explicitly stated.[2]

Securing an Open Society sets out what it calls an integrated approach to security (Privy Council Office 2004, vii). It encompasses measures as wide ranging as more effectively conducting threat assessments through the establishment of an integrated threat assessment center housed in the CSIS, increasing federal–provincial emergency preparedness coordination with the creation of a government operations center, better addressing health pandemics through the creation of a new Public Health Agency, keeping the Canada–U.S. border open through the Smart Border Accord and follow-on initiatives, and strengthening marine security through the creation of Maritime Security Operation Centers. These latter organizations, which are located in Halifax and Esquimalt, are a good example of the integrated, interagency or "whole-of-government" approach Canada has adopted. Led by the Canadian navy, they include representation from Transport Canada, the CBSA, the Canadian Coast Guard, and the RCMP, bringing together the information each of these organizations collect relating to the security of Canada's maritime approaches.

The September 11 attacks increased U.S. security concerns that terrorists could enter the United States by way of Canada. As a result, Canada renewed its pledge, first stated by Prime Minister Mackenzie King in 1938, that Canada would ensure that no enemy forces could "pursue their way either by land, sea or air, to the United States across Canadian territory" (Eayrs 1965, 183). This concern is reflected in the National Security Policy's priorities. Although its first priority is to protect Canada and Canadians at home and abroad, its second is to "ensur[e] that Canada is not a base for threats to our allies" (read, the United States). Canada's homeland security efforts are designed both to safeguard Canada *and* to reassure the United States. Although the National Security Policy's third priority is to contribute to international security, initiatives of this nature were not elaborated until a separate international policy statement was released a year later (discussed later). *Securing an Open Society* (Privy Council Office 2004), hastily produced under Paul Martin's Liberals, remained in place as Canada's national security policy under the new Conservative government.

DEFENSE

The Historical Evolution of the Canadian Defense Policy

Defense is part of the broader concept of security and pertains to those aspects of security that are best addressed through military means. Since the end of World War II, Canada has produced seven defense policy statements: *Canada's Defense* (Department of National Defense 1947), *White Paper on Defense* (Department of National Defense 1964), *Defense in the '70s* (1971), *Challenge and Commitment: A Defense Policy for Canada* (Department of National Defense 1987), *Defense White Paper* (Department of National Defense 1994), *Canada's International Policy Statement: Defense* (Department of National Defense 2005), and *Canada First Defense Strategy* (CFDS) (Department of National Defense 2008). The 1947 document set out what would become the familiar parameters of Canada's defense priorities throughout the following decades: to defend Canada against aggression, to assist the civil power in maintaining law and order within the country, and to carry out any undertakings which Canada might assume in cooperation with friendly nations or under any effective plan of collective action under the United Nations. A more refined statement of these priorities came to be (1) the protection of Canada and Canadian sovereignty, (2) the defense of North America in cooperation with the United States, (3) contributing to collective defense through NATO, and (4) contributing to international peace and security through the UN. In his study of Canadian defense policy, Douglas Bland (1997, 3–4) has called the first two priorities—defending Canada and defending North America—"strategic imperatives" in Canadian defense policy, whereas contributions abroad through NATO or the UN have historically been "strategic choices."

Although the exact wording has varied, these themes have remained consistent throughout time. That said, the relative emphasis placed on each priority has varied in response to the government of the day's perception of the security environment. The 1964 defense white paper actually reversed the order of priorities, placing UN activities first, followed by NATO, North America, and the defense of Canada. This may have reflected a government view at the time that there was little or no direct threat to Canadian territory. It was also no doubt influenced by the internationalist perspective of then-Prime Minister Lester B. Pearson, who is best known as the recipient of the 1957 Noble Peace Prize for his role in developing the concept of peacekeeping while he was Canada's secretary of state for external affairs (in other words, foreign minister). During the 1950s and '60s, often heralded as Canada's "golden age" of international involvement, Canada stationed 10,000 troops in Germany as its commitment to NATO, and contributed forces to every UN peacekeeping mission established. The 1960s also marked a period of significant defense reorganization as Pearson's minister of defense, Paul Hellyer, initiated and carried out the integration and unification of the Royal Canadian Navy, the Canadian Army, and the Royal Canadian Air Force into the CF.

In the wake of the 1969 transit through the Northwest Passage of the U.S. supertanker *Manhattan*, and the 1970 October crisis during which the Front de Liberation du Quebec (FLQ) carried out terrorist activities on Canadian soil, the government of Pierre Elliott Trudeau brought the emphasis back to defense imperatives. *Defense in the '70s* not only emphasized the threat to Canada and Canadian sovereignty, but also cut Canada's troop commitment to NATO by half and questioned the value of international peacekeeping. Informed by détente, the government downplayed the Soviet threat, but over the next decade—as East–West relations deteriorated and the "second Cold War" emerged—the government changed course, restating the importance of NATO. This renewed Cold War perspective formed the organizing principle of the next defense white paper, *Challenge and Commitment: A Defense Policy for Canada*. Released in 1987, after the government of Prime Minister Brian Mulroney had been in office for almost three years, the paper stressed the need for strategic defense against ballistic missiles, firmly supported North American Aerospace Defense Command (NORAD) and NATO, and committed Canada to the peaceful settlement of international disputes, including peacekeeping. However, the paper is best remembered for its call for a three-ocean naval capability (Pacific, Atlantic, and Arctic). Although this capability was explicitly linked to Soviet submarines coming through the Arctic and close to Canadian waters, the call was also driven by renewed concerns about Canadian sovereignty in the north after American icebreaker *Polar Sea* transited the Northwest Passage in summer 1985.

The end of the Cold War quickly rendered the 1987 white paper obsolete. After four decades of Cold War, defense planners were faced with a "blank sheet of paper" that proved daunting to fill. Some important decisions were made, such as the Mulroney government's 1992 decision to end Canada's long-standing Cold War commitment of stationed forces in Germany (in fact, most of these forces simply went to Bosnia). But it was not until December 1994, well into the post–Cold War era and after the formation of a Liberal government under Jean Chrétien, that Canada issued a new defense white paper. When it did, the familiar themes remained in place, with the order of the chapters indicating defense priorities: the Protection of Canada, Canada–United States Defense Cooperation, and Contributing to International Security. The range of operations the white paper outlined, from preventative deployments and traditional peacekeeping, to enforcing the will of the international community, defending allies, and postconflict peace building, were meant to respond to what it described as a period of unpredictable conflicts and risks. The outlook was Pearsonian in nature and focused on the ability to conduct operations around the world, even as resources were cut back dramatically in recognition of the post–Cold War peace dividend.

The 2005 Defense Policy Statement

After the September 11 attacks, many argued that the security environment had changed and that there was a need for a new defense white paper. However, the Chrétien government made the case that the 1994 white paper's emphasis on an unpredictable security environment aptly described the post–September 11 world, and thus that the policy remained relevant. Ultimately, it was not until the Liberal leadership changed, with the Liberals now led by Paul Martin, that Canada received a new defense policy. Canada's International Policy Statement of April 2005 comprised four separate documents, including one on defense that was soon dubbed the Defense Policy Statement (DPS).

The DPS marked Canada's response, in military and defense terms, to the post–September 11 security environment. Consistent with its predecessors, the policy focuses on defending Canada and North America, and contributing to international security. But in rhetorical and, to a certain degree, concrete terms, it placed a greater emphasis on the "home game" than any Canadian defense policy since the sovereignty-oriented *Defense in the '70s*. Abroad, the primary focus was on failed and failing states as the area in which Canada could best "make a difference." The document draws out the notion of a "three-block war" in which Canada may be involved in a humanitarian effort, a stabilization and reconstruction mission, and a combat or counterinsurgency operation, all within a space no bigger than three city blocks. Responding to these challenges required an efficient expeditionary capability, as well as the ability to sustain forces overseas. At home, the emphasis was on the ability to conduct the surveillance of Canada's vast territory, airspace, and maritime approaches, and to respond to asymmetrical threats like the terrorist use of a weapon of mass destruction on Canadian territory, perhaps in a major Canadian city. Specific mention was also made of pressing sovereignty and security demands in the North as climate change led to greater diamond mining opportunities and therefore criminal activity, and melting ice enabled increased shipping and traffic.

The combined demands of needing an efficient expeditionary capability and placing a greater emphasis on homeland defense led to the most extensive reorganization of the CF since its creation in the late 1960s. In early 2006, the CF established four new command structures: Canadian Expeditionary Forces Command (CEFCOM), Canada Command, Canadian Operational Support Command (CANOSCOM), and Canadian Special Operations Forces Command (CANSOFCOM). Previously, all operations had been the responsibility of one (overworked) deputy chief of defense staff (DCDS); under the new structure, operations abroad and operations at home are divided between CEFCOM and Canada COM, respectively, with CANOSCOM and CANSOFCOM supporting both of the "geographical" commands.

Consistent with the post–September 11 environment, the DPS stressed the necessity of taking the defense of Canada into greater consideration. "In the past, Canada has structured its military primarily for international operations, while the domestic role has been treated as a secondary consideration.... Clearly, this approach will no longer suffice" (Department of National Defense 2005, 18). In place of previous ad hoc arrangements, the CF established Canada Command as a single integrated (sea, land, and air assets) structure to address threats to Canadian territory, much as the United States created Northern Command in October 2002 to create—for the first time—a single structure responsible for the defense of the United States. Canada Command is also charged with coordinating with PSC for civil support missions (as is Northern Command with respect to DHS). In addition, the new Canadian organizational arrangements include the creation of six regional headquarters across the country reporting to Canada Command.

But the DPS's rhetorical and organizational emphasis on the defense of Canada was not matched with personnel and equipment commitments. Since summer 2003, Canada had had some 2,000 military personnel in Kabul, Afghanistan, as part of the International Security Assistance Force (ISAF). Canada's contribution to this NATO-led mission is consistent with the change in the nature of its participation in international operations. During the Cold War, Canada was a major contributor of military forces to UN peacekeeping missions. Most of these operations, now known as "traditional peacekeeping operations," were not very dangerous because they had the consent of the parties to the dispute. However, in the first post–Cold War decade, such missions became more dangerous; the UN was faced with nonstate actors that may or may not consent to the international presence. In early 1996, the leadership of the international mission in Bosnia moved from the UN to NATO, which as a military alliance was better suited to addressing the new conflicts. Canada's participation adjusted as well; today, the vast majority of Canada's military forces deployed abroad are operating under NATO, not UN, leadership.

When ISAF's mandate expanded to encompass not just operations in the north and west of Afghanistan, but also in the south and eventually the east, so, too, did the nature of Canada's involvement change. Beginning in summer 2005, CF commitment to Afghanistan increased to 2,500 troops and moved southward to Kandahar, where by early 2006, Canada took over responsibility for the American-run Provincial Reconstruction Team. New equipment projects initiated during this time, such as air-to-surface precision-guided munitions and targeting pods for Canada's C-18 fighter aircraft, reflected an overseas emphasis, as did discussions (and, later, exercises) surrounding the creation of a Standing Contingency Task Force, centered on the acquisition of an amphibious landing ship, for the rapid deployment of CF units overseas.

One issue the Martin government was forced to address was that of ballistic missile defense (BMD). The question of Canada's participation in a U.S.-led BMD system dates back almost to the launch of Sputnik in 1957. The orbit of this tiny Soviet satellite around the earth provided the first concrete evidence that American territory could be threatened by ballistic missiles, and sparked a half-century-long search for technology that could defend against such threats. The technological difficulty of "hitting a bullet with a bullet" proved so daunting that the United States all but abandoned it in the 1970s. America signed the Anti-Ballistic Missile Treaty with the Soviet Union in 1972, which limited each country to one ballistic missile site apiece, and then decommissioned its only BMD site in 1976. Less than a decade later, after U.S. president Ronald Reagan announced a Strategic Defense Initiative (SDI) to make ballistic missiles "impotent and obsolete," the United States reinvigorated its search for BMD technology. However, this proved equally elusive and, with the end of the Cold War, U.S. president George H. W. Bush scaled back the program to one of Global Protection Against Limited Strikes. The Clinton administration further restricted the search to a National Missile Defense, but Congress, out ahead on the issue, committed the United States to deploying a BMD system "as soon as technologically feasible." After the September 11 attacks, the administration of George W. Bush withdrew America from the ABM Treaty and, after its Missile Defense Agency had a number of successes in testing ballistic missiles, in 2004 the United States announced it would begin deploying a BMD system.

Canada has historically hesitated to be part of a BMD system for fear that it would intensify the East–West arms race and lead to the weaponization of space. When the 1958 NORAD treaty was renewed in 1968, Canada actually insisted a clause be inserted stating it would not be obliged to participate in a BMD system. But in the 1981 renewal, with the ABM Treaty in place and BMD seemingly a dead issue, the clause was removed—just two years before Reagan's famous SDI speech. When, in 1985, America's allies were formally approached to participate in "Star Wars," Prime Minister Mulroney sidestepped the issue, rejecting government-to-government participation yet allowing Canada's defense industry to compete for contracts. This on-the-fence approach remained in place for the next two decades. The 1994 defense white paper stated only that Canada was "interested gaining a better understanding of missile defense through research and consultation with like-minded nations" and that any potential future role in BMD would be determined in conjunction with "possible NATO-wide aerospace defense arrangements" (Department of National Defense 1994, 25).

The post–September 11 security environment, America's withdrawal from the ABM Treaty, technological advances in BMD, and, ultimately, America's decision to deploy a BMD system finally forced Canada to state its position. In August 2004, the two countries signed an agreement that allowed NORAD threat assessment information pertaining to ballistic missiles to be shared with U.S. Northern Command, which was given the BMD responsibility for North America. The arrangement ensured that Canada would continue to be part of the surveillance, threat assessment, and warning aspects of BMD, as it had been ever since NORAD moved from strictly air warning and defense to a combination of aerospace warning and air defense around 1960. But would Canada be part of decisions surrounding the actual response to an incoming ballistic missile? This required full Canadian participation in America's nascent but now—for the first time—physically existing BMD system. In the face of opposition among the Canadian public and especially within the ranks of the Liberal party, in early 2005 the Martin government stated that Canada would not join America's BMD system, a position that Canada's next, Conservative, government did not seek to reverse.

Canada First Defense Strategy

Like DPS before it, the CFDS promises to increase the relative attention paid to Canada's traditional defense "imperatives." The CFDS, formally released in June 2008 by the Conservative government of Stephen Harper, sets out six core missions for the CF: conduct daily domestic and continental operations, including in the Arctic and through NORAD; support a major international event in Canada (like the Olympics); respond to a major terrorist attack (on Canadian soil); support civilian authorities during a crisis in Canada like a natural disaster; lead or conduct a major international operation for an extended period; and deploy forces in response to crises elsewhere in the world for shorter periods.

The CFDS is a unique document in that the government discussed many of its broad tenets, and announced many of its associated equipment acquisitions, over the course of about two years before the strategy was actually released. Under the slogan "Stand Up for Canada," during the 2005–2006 election, the Conservatives promised to enhance Canada's military presence in the Arctic as part of a "Canada First" defense strategy. Originally, this was to include three "armed icebreakers," but after extensive internal debate this proved politically and financially unfeasible. In 2007, the government formally announced a number of initiatives directly related to the defense of the Arctic: the construction of a deepwater port and refueling station in Nunavut, the establishment of an army Arctic training center also in Nunavut, and the purchase of between six and eight arctic offshore patrol vessels, capable of going through fresh ice one meter thick. Although less robust than the icebreakers would have been, the patrol vessels will still significantly boost CF capability in the north, once they arrive in the mid 2010s, because none of the navy's current vessels are ice capable. In 2008, the Harper government also announced the purchase, over a ten-year period, of a new Polar-class icebreaker for the Canadian Coast Guard.

Despite the Conservatives' rhetorical focus on Canada, the arctic-related pronouncements were not the first made by the government. In 2006 it announced that Canada would purchase three new joint support ships to replace the navy's aging supply ships (something Martin's Liberals had also announced); four C-17 strategic lift air transporters, giving Canada an entirely new capability (historically only the United States and the Soviet Union had strategic airlift); new tactical lift planes to replace Canada's 1960s-era Hercules C-130s; new military trucks; and battlefield helicopters, a crucial capability Canada has not had since the early 1990s. As part of the actual release of the CFDS in spring 2008, the government further announced Canada would invest in fifteen ships to replace the navy's destroyers and frigates, ten to twelve maritime patrol aircraft, sixty-five next-generation fighter aircraft, and a family of land combat vehicles.

This extensive list of planned acquisitions is the result of relatively few defense equipment purchases in the first dozen years after the end of the Cold War. Both the Liberals under Paul Martin and the Conservatives under Stephen Harper had to grapple with the consequences of severe defense budget cuts during Jean Chrétien's ten years in power. From 1993 to 1998 the Canadian defense budget was cut by some 30%. In subsequent years it stabilized and began to increase marginally, but even the "security" budget of December 2001 focused primarily on civilian security measures like increased support to CSE and the CSIS, as well as on increasing the size of the CF's special operations forces. The upshot has been aging military equipment in increasing disrepair or, in some cases, capabilities that are completely nonexistent.

Many of the capital acquisitions the Conservative government has promised are at least a decade away. The C-17 strategic lift aircraft have already arrived, as have most of the trucks. A contract has been signed for the tactical lift aircraft, which will begin arriving in 2010, and it is likely a contract will soon be signed for battlefield helicopters. However, in a defense procurement process that includes five stages spread over about ten years—(1) the CF defines the requirement; (2) a request for proposals goes out to companies; (3) companies submit their proposals; (4) the government awards the contract, including timelines; and (5) the equipment arrives—all other commitments are only at stage one or two.

Issues for the Future

Costs and Budget

The cost of rebuilding the CF is likely to pose a significant challenge for the CF and the Canadian government in the years to come. Historically, NATO countries have set an informal goal of allocating no less than 2% of their country's gross domestic product to its military forces. This goal was actually met by Canada in the late 1970s and '80s, but it declined throughout the 1990s, and in the post–September 11 period it hovered around 1.2%, only beginning to increase in 2007 (NATO International Staff 2007, 7). Some critics argue Canada should strive to meet the 2% target, whereas others make the case that the target is less important than absolute values. Canada stands about sixth among NATO members in terms of overall defense spending.

When the Harper government came to power, Canada's annual defense budget was about $14.5 billion (all values Canadian dollars), slightly above the low of roughly $12 billion reached at the turn of the century. In 2005, the Martin government announced a significant increase in the defense budget of about $15 billion over five years to 2010, and a year later the Harper government announced an additional increase of about $5 billion, again over five years. This put the fiscal year 2011–2012 defense budget at about $20 billion. A centerpiece of the 2008 defense strategy announcement was the government's commitment to long-term and stable funding throughout the life of the CFDS, which is intended as a twenty-year plan. To this end, the federal budget of February 2008 stated that beginning in fiscal year 2011–2012, the automatic annual increase in defense spending would be 2% per year until 2028.

Not all of this money can be used for equipment. Far from it. Every year the annual defense budget is divided into three components: personnel costs, operations and maintenance, and capital acquisitions. The latter includes the whole range of purchases, from ships, aircraft, and tanks to military satellite communications and advanced technologies for command and control. In any given year, personnel costs take up more than half the defense budget. After that, there are significant expenditures on operations and maintenance, particularly if the CF is engaged extensively in overseas operations. The remaining portion is allocated to capital expenditures; however, if operational costs go above the original allocation, then the capital expenditure budget is the first to be "raided."

Although the Conservative government has guaranteed a certain level of defense spending for the next twenty years, a new government could just as easily overturn these guarantees. Nonetheless, if this commitment were to remain in place, and if the capital budget is not "raided," the CF will have about $60 billion to spend on capital acquisitions in the period 2008–2028, according to the CFDS (Department of National Defense 2008, 12). This is sufficient in terms of the total amount of money that is needed to purchase the range of platforms announced under the CFDS and, after they arrive, to maintain them until 2028. However, the difficulty is in the timing. Reduced investments in defense in the 1990s have led to a situation in which a whole range of major military platforms—supply ships, destroyers, maritime patrol aircraft, fighters, battlefield helicopters, light armored vehicles—must be replaced within the same window: the decade of the 2010s. As a result, a far larger proportion of the funds will be needed sooner, rather than later. Not surprising, many members of the Canadian defense community have argued that the CFDS funding formula is unlikely to meet the CF's reinvestment requirements.

Recruitment

One of the biggest challenges the CF faces in the future is recruiting. At the end of the Cold War, the size of Canada's regular force stood at about 85,000 troops, but by the mid 1990s it had declined to 60,000, as called for in the 1994 defense white paper. The drawdown actually began under the Conservative government of Brian Mulroney, as Canada, like most of its allies, responded to the end of the Cold War with force reductions. Although the mandated level was 60,000, in fact the effective strength of the CF stood at about 53,000 throughout the late 1990s and early 2000s. And yet the CF was far busier than it had ever been during the Cold War, deploying forces to Somalia, Cambodia, Bosnia, Haiti, Kosovo, and Afghanistan, among other places. In 2004, the Martin government announced it would add 5,000 troops to the CF, and when the Conservatives came to power two years later, they stated a further increase of 10,000 personnel for an overall mandated force level of some 75,000 troops.

Increasing the size of the CF has proved to be very difficult. Part of the issue is finding enough suitable recruits. The CF, like all major organizations in Canada and the western world, is struggling with an aging population and a decreasing pool of young people from which to recruit. Moreover, those with the technological skills that the CF needs are also in high demand in the civilian world. Nonetheless, a steady number of young Canadians have demonstrated their interest in joining the CF; the army, for example, has several thousand personnel who have completed the recruiting process and are awaiting training.[3] A greater challenge for the CF has been to ensure there are enough highly trained personnel to train the new recruits. The ongoing Canadian commitment to Afghanistan has meant that many of these trainers are away on deployment or are conducting exercises in preparation for going overseas. This, in turn, has slowed the CF's ability to absorb new recruits, forcing the Conservatives to scale back their original force size goal. The CFDS states a regular force-level objective of 70,000, with no specific time frame regarding when this will be achieved.

Military Command Structure

Canada's future military leadership may also need to reexamine Canada's military command structure. Implementing the new organization, which was the vision of former Chief of Defense Staff General Rick Hillier, has not been without its problems. In part, the issue is that navy, army, and air force personnel who otherwise would have been deployed on operational missions have been assigned to fill new headquarters positions, thereby contributing to the difficulty the CF is facing in sustaining its military commitment abroad. The chief of the land staff, especially, has drawn attention to the detrimental effect the new command structure has had on the army's trained effective strength (Leslie 2008, 3). But also, with responsibility for Canada's military operations divided between CEFCOM and Canada Command, it can be difficult to prioritize resources. Should the available Hercules transport aircraft be allocated to Canada Command to fight forest fires in British Columbia, or to CEFCOM to ferry supplies into Afghanistan? These sorts of decisions, which under the previous organization would have been made by the DCDS, must now filter up to an increasingly pressed chief of defense staff.

Tricommand Arrangements

A further issue concerns the future relationship among Northern Command, Canada Command, and NORAD. Created as a Canada–U.S. binational command for air defense, and subsequently for aerospace warning and control, for more than half a century NORAD has been responsible for addressing air threats to North America. In 2002, the United States created Northern Command as a single locus of authority for defending the United States, including all of the sea, land, and air dimensions, and Canada did the same with the creation of Canada Command in 2006. Since both NORAD and Northern Command are headquartered at Peterson Air Force Base in Colorado Springs, the United States was able to accommodate the fact that air defense was already the responsibility of a preexisting organization by "double-hatting" the commander of NORAD as the commander of Northern Command. Although the deputy commander of NORAD is always a Canadian, a similar double-hatting arrangement is not feasible for Canada. Apart from the fact that Canada Command is located in Ottawa, the Canadian public would not accept the person responsible for defending Canada reporting to an American general. Already the two new geographical commands have developed extensive ties; the establishment of Canada Command appears to have simplified and streamlined the Canada–U.S. defense relationship. Future arrangements are still being examined regarding how NORAD will relate to Northern Command and Canada Command, with one possibility being that NORAD will become a subcommand that reports to the commanders of Northern Command and Canada Command.

Future Focus

In the not too distant future the Canadian government will also need to rethink the balance it finds between missions at home and missions abroad. As its title would indicate, the CFDS—both as discussed during and after the 2005–2006 election and in its formal iteration of June 2008—placed significant emphasis on missions at home. However, the actual actions of the Conservative government during its years in power have not reflected this emphasis. Far from scaling back CF commitment to southern Afghanistan that it had inherited from the Liberals, the Conservatives expressed even greater support. The government extended the mission twice, first to 2009 and then to 2011. Almost all equipment purchases that have actually taken place have related to overseas missions, including new Leopard tanks, precision-guided artillery howitzers, and the C-17 transporters (although these would also be useful for missions across the vast expanses of Canada).

Already the government is starting to look beyond Afghanistan. The end date of 2011 is appearing to be increasingly firm, although it is more likely that the commitment will be scaled back rather than eliminated altogether. And future projects like the acquisition of a high- or medium-altitude unmanned aerial vehicle are being examined in the context of their contribution to overseas missions and to conducting the surveillance of Canada's East, West, and Arctic shores. Historically, events like the *Manhattan* and *Polar Sea* transits have sparked an increase in government concern for Canadian sovereignty, but this has always faded within a short period of time as attention returned to missions abroad.

The difference today is the onward march of climate change and the melting polar ice cap. Experts note that the Arctic's perennial ice is retreating much more quickly than originally expected. Within the not too distant future there is likely to be an increase in shipping traffic, because routes through Canada's Northwest Passage and Russia's Northern Sea cut thousands of miles off the voyage between various destinations around the world (Borgerson 2008, 66, 69). Moreover, what are believed to be substantial oil and gas reserves under the Arctic Ocean floor are likely to become more accessible, and this could set off a "scramble for resources" among Arctic countries (Boswell 2008). The almost certainty of an open Arctic ocean for at least part of the year, and the inevitability that activity in the north will increase, means that future Canadian governments will have no choice but to accord greater attention to Canada's defense imperatives.

CONCLUSION

Canada, like all countries, frames its defense and security policy in the context of its geopolitical position. These considerations have historically included a peaceful neighborhood dominated by a friendly superpower, little or no direct threat to Canadian territory, an economic security interest in maintaining access to the American market, a political interest in participating in international organizations—both to assist in maintaining international peace and security, and to have a voice separate from that of the United States—and a resulting military tradition of contributing to overseas operations.

The twenty-first century has brought both change and continuity in these themes. In the area of civilian-led security measures, the Canadian government has instituted numerous organizational changes and allocated significant resources. This has been done, in part, to protect Canadians, but also to ensure Canada does not pose a security threat to the United States, and therefore that it maintains access to the American market. The Canadian military, too, has undergone a major reorganization designed to defend Canada better. However, recent governments have continued to commit most of Canada's concrete defense resources to the overseas dimension of defending Canada. Most Canadians still see little direct threat to their country, and this is reflected in the government's actions, if not its stated priorities. This emphasis is likely to shift as climate change and the melting Arctic inevitably bring greater activity in and around Canada's northern approaches. Canada's neighborhood is changing, and so, too, must the balance it finds in providing for its defense and security.

NOTES

1. The full titles are Presidential Decision Directive 62: Protection Against Unconventional Threats to the Homeland and Americans Overseas and Presidential Decision Directive 63: Critical Infrastructure Protection.
2. For a discussion of Canada's historically implicit international security policy, see David Dewitt and David Leyton-Brown (1995).
3. Lieutenant-General Andrew Leslie, Chief of the Land Staff, presentation to the Conference of Defense Associations, Ottawa, June 3, 2008.

REFERENCES

Bland, Douglas L. 1997. *Canada's National Defence, Vol. I: Defence Policy*. Kingston, Ont.: Queen's University School of Policy Studies.

Borgerson, Scott G. 2008. Arctic meltdown. *Foreign Affairs* 87(2): 63–77.

Boswell, Randy. 2008. EU report warns of trouble over Arctic resources. *Ottawa Citizen*, March 11, A8.

Canadian Security Intelligence Service. 2002. *2001 Public Report*. Ottawa: Government of Canada.

Department of National Defence. 1947. *Canada's Defence*. Ottawa: Government of Canada.

———. 1964. *White Paper on Defence*. Ottawa: Government of Canada.

———. 1971. *Defence in the 70s*. Ottawa: Government of Canada.

———. 1987. *Challenge and Commitment: A Defence Policy for Canada*. Ottawa: Government of Canada.

———. 1994. *Defence White Paper*. Ottawa: Government of Canada.

———. 2005. *Canada's International Policy Statement: Defence*. Ottawa: Government of Canada.

———. 2008. *Canada First Defence Strategy*. Ottawa: Government of Canada.

Dewitt, David, and David Leyton-Brown. 1995. Canada's international security policy. In *Canada's International Security Policy*, ed. David Dewitt and David Leyton-Brown, 1–30. Scarborough, Ont.: Prentice Hall.

Eayrs, James. 1965. *In Defence of Canada: Appeasement and Rearmament*. Toronto: University of Toronto Press.

Leslie, Andrew. 2008. *Chief of Land Staff Level 1 Business Plan*. Ottawa: Department of National Defence.

Morton, Desmond. 1995. "No more disagreeable or onerous duty": Canadians and military aid of the civil power, past, present, and future. In *Canada's International Security*

Policy, ed. David Dewitt and David Leyton-Brown, 129–152. Scarborough, Ont.: Prentice Hall.

NATO International Staff. 2007. *NATO–Russia Compendium of Financial and Economic Data Relating to Defense*. Brussels: NATO.

Privy Council Office. 2004. *Securing an Open Society: Canada's National Security Policy*. Ottawa: Government of Canada.

Sloan, Elinor. 2005. *Security and Defence in the Terrorist Era*. Montreal: McGill-Queen's University Press.

CHAPTER 28

DEMOCRATIC REFORM: THE SEARCH FOR GUIDING PRINCIPLES

F. LESLIE SEIDLE

EACH year since 1972, Freedom House, a respected nongovernmental organization, has published a report on the state of freedom around the world as experienced by individuals. In 2008, Canada, along with ten other Organisation for Economic Cooperation and Development (OECD) countries, was given the highest rating possible for the following subcategories of the survey: electoral process, political pluralism and participation, and functioning of government.[1] It is thus perhaps not surprising that Canadian officials and nongovernmental organizations are regularly asked to advise other governments on democratization. As for Canadians' own perceptions of the state of their democracy, there is little reason to think many find it seriously wanting. This does not mean they are uncritical of certain aspects of their democratic processes and institutions. They have been, and still are—as will be demonstrated in this chapter.

Although some theorists have defined democracy as a process by which citizens choose their political leaders, others look beyond the electoral process. For Giovanni Sartori (1987, 113), conceiving voting as participation "leaves us with a weak and overly diluted meaning of the term." Robert Dahl (2005, 188–189) stipulates that representative democratic government requires the following institutions:

- Elected officials
- Free, fair, and frequent elections
- Freedom of expression
- Access to alternative sources of information

- Associational autonomy
- Inclusive citizenship

Taken together, these items constitute what Dahl labels "polyarchal: democracy (rule by the many)." As Charles Tilly (2007, 10) has noted, this definition goes beyond the process of choosing leaders to include "regularized interactions among citizens and officials."

Focusing on democracy as an ongoing process places the bar higher. This explains in part why, during the past four decades, commissions, legislative committees, academics, and others have produced a legion of proposals to reform Canada's political institutions. As we shall see, some called for major changes in the ground rules by which representative government functions. Others wanted to integrate regional interests more effectively into national policy making. Still others sought ways to better reflect Canada's growing demographic diversity. The following section explores briefly some of the objectives underlying pressures for democratic reform. The core of this chapter is an analysis of various measures to reform the Senate, the electoral system, and the regulation of political finance and related matters. One of the purposes of the analysis is to explore the main objectives reform advocates hoped to achieve. The concluding section discusses why, despite considerable effort, change has not come about in the first two of these areas and ends with some suggestions for advancing democratic reform in the future.

Objectives of Democratic Reform Proposals

Four objectives have been central to one or more of the democratic reform thrusts analyzed in this chapter: enhanced government legitimacy, more representative legislatures, greater responsiveness in governance, and probity and accountability of legislators. In this section, some of the theoretical grounds of these objectives are briefly discussed as a backdrop to the review of the various measures.

Enhanced Government Legitimacy

The degree to which citizens find the decisions of political leaders acceptable depends in good measure on the leaders' legitimacy. In this regard, David Beetham (1991, 94) contends that political legitimation must be *mass* legitimation: "[T]he expression of consent has in principle to be available to all, whether they take advantage of it or not." Such consent confers moral authority and, according to Beetham, one of the principal ways it is expressed is through the choice of government through elections.

In light of ratings such as that of Freedom House, it may not be immediately clear why the concept of legitimacy is included in the present analysis. Although the concept may not have been as prominent as the others reviewed later, it has figured in many Senate reform proposals. The argument most often runs as follows: Appointment of senators, nominated by the prime minister alone, constrains the degree to which they can use the second chamber's legislative powers (which are virtually equal to those of the House of Commons), particularly when this would lead to conflict with the democratically elected House of Commons. Although not all reform advocates have favored direct election of the Senate, most consider its lack of legitimacy a major flaw within Canada's system of government (see chapter 9, this volume).

Issues of legitimacy have also arisen when the governing party has elected very few or no members from a certain region. For example, in 1980, the Liberals elected only two members of Parliament (MPs) from western Canada—both from Manitoba. To secure cabinet representation for the three other western provinces, Prime Minister Trudeau appointed three senators to cabinet. When the government later introduced the National Energy Program, staunchly opposed in western Canada (particularly, Alberta), its legitimacy was challenged on several grounds, among them the Liberals' paltry elected representation from the region.

More Representative Legislatures

Canadian democratic reform debates have reflected a concern with what Hanna Pitkin (1972) has labeled "descriptive" or "mirror" representation. This concept places a high value on "a representative body [being] distinguished by an accurate correspondence or resemblance to what it represents" (Pitkin 1972, 60). Most of those who subscribe to this view do not call for a completely accurate correspondence between a legislature and those who are being represented. Nevertheless, they have pointed out, with considerable justification, that the membership of the House of Commons and provincial legislative assemblies is often a long way from resembling the electorate.

One critique, *unfairness in party representation*, has been directed at a number of tendencies of the single-member plurality (SMP) electoral system that are not unique to Canada (these are discussed further in the next section). In response, some have advocated a new electoral system that would lead to a more proportional party breakdown among MPs, both nationally and within regions. Some others, notably the Royal Commission on the Economic Union and Development Prospects for Canada (Macdonald Commission), have preferred Senate reform as a corrective. In its 1985 report, the commission recommended the Senate be elected by proportional representation. The rationale was that the parties represented in the Senate would probably have at least some senators from all regions; some of them could then be named to cabinet (as is the practice in Australia) and would be seen as legitimate spokespersons for their regions.

The *representation of demographic groups* highlights another aspect of the reflection of difference. For Anne Phillips (1995), concern for the gender and racial composition of legislatures is an extension of the twentieth century's progress toward universal citizenship. She emphasizes the "politics of presence," and not merely for symbolic reasons: "When policies are worked out *for* rather than *with* an excluded community, [those in power] are unlikely to engage with all relevant concerns (Phillips 1995, 13 [emphasis in original]). However, Phillips does not argue that presence should prevail over the representation of ideas (primarily through political parties). Rather, she writes that "[i]t is in the relationship between ideas and presence that we can best hope to find a fairer system of representation" (Phillips 1995, 25).

Greater Responsiveness in Governance

Another aspect of Pitkin's conceptual framework underlines the importance of "acting in the interest of the represented, in a manner responsive to them" (Pitkin 1972, 209). Applying this to political institutions, Pitkin stipulates that the government is required to respond to the wishes of the represented unless there are good reasons to the contrary. She nevertheless sees some limits: "There need not be a constant activity of responding, but there must be a constant condition of respon*siveness*, of potential readiness to respond" (Pitkin 1972, 23 [emphasis in original]).

In reality, legislators are pressured to respond to a range of interests, both in their constituency and elsewhere; but one of these, the political party to which they belong, invariably overwhelms the others. Indeed, this is one of the most long-standing criticisms of representative government in Canada. Despite various parliamentary reforms intended to allow MPs and provincial legislators to be more responsive to their constituents and to contribute more meaningfully to policy development, party discipline is stronger than ever, at least for the governing party caucus (Docherty 2005, 6). Independent action is further hampered by the powers of the prime minister, which recent research suggests are stronger than in most other advanced democracies (O'Malley 2007).

For a time, another avenue, referendums and other direct democracy measures (including recall and initiative processes) attracted considerable interest as a way of allowing citizens to have their own say (Mendelsohn 1996). Direct democracy was one of the core policies of the Reform Party, founded in Alberta in 1988. The influence of Reform's antielite stance and its leader, Preston Manning, were part of the reason that first ministers' decided to put the 1992 Charlottetown Constitutional Accord to a national referendum before proceeding with ratification by Parliament and the legislative assemblies. Direct democracy advocates also had some impact at the provincial level. For example, under the Social Credit government in British Columbia, the Recall and Initiative Act was adopted in 1994. Even before the Canadian Alliance (the successor to the Reform Party) merged with the Progressive Conservatives in 2003, political interest in direct democracy processes had waned, and such measures are absent from the Conservative Party platform. For these reasons, this chapter does not review the direct democracy options that Reform and others advanced a number of years ago.

Financial Probity of Political Parties and Office Holders

Citizens expect legislators to carry out their duties honestly and openly. Criminal law has long banned such flagrant abuses as accepting bribes from those seeking to advance their interests through legislation and regulation. More recently, measures such as conflict-of-interest codes and registration of lobbyists have been adopted to keep a check on more subtle attempts at influence on legislators and other office holders through various regulations, including public reporting. However, concerns about the potential impact of money also extend to party and election finance. In this context, John Rawls (1972, 225) wrote that "the principle of participation" risks losing much of its value "whenever those who have greater private means are permitted to use their advantages to control the course of public debate." Such concerns are reflected in election spending limits, which (as we shall see later) have quite a long history in Canada; and, to a certain degree, in limits on the size and source of political contributions.

DEMOCRATIC REFORM MEASURES:
OBJECTIVES AND OUTCOMES

This section reviews major attempts to reform the Senate, the electoral system, and the regulation of political finance and legislators' accountability. A focus is placed on the main objectives of the various measures, particularly as they relate to the theoretical considerations discussed earlier. A key question is: Why, despite so much effort to correct evident weaknesses in Canada's democratic system, has significant change occurred only in the third area?

The Senate

The Senate has long presented a conundrum: how to transform an institution that does not pass most people's test of legitimacy when broad agreement about even the objectives of reform is lacking. This explains, in part, why the constitutional provisions on the Senate remain, in virtually every respect, as they were in 1867 (the 1965 reduction of senators' term from life to age seventy-five is one exception). There has been fairly broad agreement that a reformed second chamber should continue to carry out legislative review, which most acknowledge the current Senate does fairly well (Franks 2003; Smith 2003, 110–117). The more contentious objectives have related to representation, including the number of senators per province, whom senators should represent, and to what end.

Senate reform was not initially central to the federal–provincial constitutional negotiations that began in 1968 in response to political developments in Quebec. Prime Minister Trudeau's priorities were to entrench a charter of rights (with strong protection for the English and French official languages) and to "patriate" the constitution from the United Kingdom, along with a domestic amending formula. The election of the Parti québécois led Trudeau to attempt a broader set of constitutional changes, which were set out in Bill C-60 (1978). These included the establishment of a "House of the Federation," with half its members named by the House of Commons and the other half by provincial legislatures, in both cases to reflect parties' vote shares in the previous election. According to the federal government, this model took account of the reality that federal and provincial legislators and parties represent different interests and would allow differing views to be expressed openly (Seidle 1992, 97–98). A number of provincial governments objected to Trudeau's move, and the matter was referred to the Supreme Court of Canada. In its 1980 decision, the court ruled that changes that would alter the Senate's "essential characteristics" could not be enacted by Parliament alone (Supreme Court of Canada 1980, para. 49).

A different model was put forward in 1979 by the Task Force on Canadian Unity (created in July 1977). Its wide-ranging report advocated extensive decentralization and (among other changes) replacing the Senate by a "Council of the Federation." The latter, inspired by the German *Bundesrat*, would be composed of delegations named by provincial governments. Here, the intent was to ensure that the views of provincial governments would be taken into account before action that would have "an impact upon areas of legitimate provincial concern occurs, thus inducing more harmonious federal–provincial relations" (Task Force on Canadian Unity 1979, 99). This institutional expression of interstate federalism was a radical departure, as the Task Force acknowledged. Trudeau was not pleased with the report's decentralist thrust, and it went nowhere. The principle of provincial appointment of a reformed second chamber was nevertheless endorsed by some other bodies (Seidle 1992, 99).

Starting in the mid 1980s, direct election—an option consistent with intrastate federalism (representing regional interests within federal institutions)—began to receive serious consideration. In fact, a western Canadian variant, termed *Triple E* (elected, effective, equal provincial representation), became a rallying cry for that region's demands for greater influence. Triple E was first articulated in a 1981 Canada West Foundation report that proposed an equal number of senators per province be directly elected using the single transferable vote. It was claimed this would provide "the most direct way for the effective articulation of regional concerns within the national government" (McCormick et al. 1981, 108).

Support for the Triple E model grew, in part through the efforts of the Canadian Committee for a Triple E Senate led by Albertan Bert Brown. However, when first ministers signed the Meech Lake Accord in 1987, the focus on the conditions presented by Quebec to accept the Constitution Act, 1982 (see chapters 2 and 6, this volume) meant that Senate reform was not included. Rather, the Accord stipulated that, following ratification of the amendments, first ministers would address the issue at annual constitutional conferences. The Alberta government was under pressure and, in 1988, introduced the Senatorial Selection Act, by which Albertans would "elect" persons to fill Senate vacancies. In 1989, the first such exercise took place, and Stan Waters received the most votes. Prime Minister Mulroney initially refused to appoint him, calling the Alberta move an infringement of his exclusive right to recommend nominees to the governor general. However, in 1990, after the failure of the Meech Lake Accord, Mulroney reconsidered and proposed Waters for appointment as a senator.

The harsh reaction in Quebec to the death of the Accord led Mulroney to try again. Months of intergovernmental discussions led to the August 1992 Charlottetown Accord, a broad package, which this time included equal provincial representation in the Senate and relatively modest but significant powers for the reformed second chamber (Stilborn 2003, 48–49). On selection, provincial governments could have chosen between direct election and selection by the provincial legislature. The second option, included late in the negotiations at Quebec's insistence, did not specify that appointees would reflect party diversity. As Jack Stilborn (2003, 35) has pointed out, "placing the power to select entirely in the hands of a government majority could result in senators more closely akin to proxies of the provincial government." The relative clarity of early Triple E proposals had been lost to the imperatives of intergovernmental negotiations.

First ministers made a further concession to Quebec: a guarantee the province would have 25% of House of Commons seats in perpetuity. Despite this, the Senate reform elements contributed to the vote against the Accord in Quebec in the October 1992 referendum. The concession to Quebec on House of Commons seats was very unpopular in the rest of the country, and support for the Senate model was only slightly higher there than for the status quo (Johnston et al. 1996, 78–79). The Accord's rejection, by a vote of 55% to 45% in referendums on the Accord, meant more than the closing of a chapter in the constitutional reform saga; it led governments to a shared view that returning to the table would inevitably pull them back into the maw of what Peter Russell has labeled "megaconstitutional politics"— something they should avoid at all costs.

The Liberals, in power from 1993 to 2006, deflected calls to revisit Senate reform by claiming the country had no appetite to return to constitutional negotiations. After becoming prime minister in 2006, Stephen Harper launched what was described as a "staged approach," with the following elements:

- Senate Appointment Consultations Act: This bill would allow for a provincewide "consultation" in conjunction with a federal or provincial general election. A variation of the single transferable vote electoral system would apply. Voters would indicate their preference among a list of "nominees," and a list of "selected nominees" would be determined according to a formula included in the bill (Bédard 2007, 10–12). The assumption was that the nominee who placed first would be appointed to the Senate. Harper and government ministers nevertheless repeatedly stated that the way senators are *appointed* would not change, and that the measure did not require approval under the general amending formula (two thirds of the provinces representing at least 50% of the population). However, a number of provincial governments indicated their opposition to the attempt to make such a potentially significant change without their involvement. The Quebec intergovernmental affairs minister even stated that if Parliament enacted the bill, his government would challenge the legislation in court. A House of Commons committee held hearings on the bill but did not report prior to the 2008 general election.

- Senate Tenure Act: A second bill proposed that the term of newly appointed senators be reduced to eight years. Again, the government's position was that provincial government consent was not required. This was contested during two sets of Senate committee hearings (Special Senate Committee on Senate Reform 2006) and, in June 2007, the Senate adopted a motion, sponsored by the Liberal majority, stating that the bill should not proceed to third reading until the Supreme Court had ruled on its constitutionality.
- Moratorium on Senate appointments unless nominee chosen by popular vote: Harper has taken the position that Senate vacancies will only be filled if a provincewide "consultation" is first held. Following such a vote in Alberta, Bert Brown was appointed a senator in July 2007. However, this position did not stop Harper from appointing a senator for Montreal and naming him to cabinet after the Conservatives elected no one from the city in the 2006 election. By September 2008, Senate vacancies had risen to sixteen. Harper could nevertheless point to a May 2008 announcement from the Saskatchewan government that it planned to introduce legislation along the lines of Alberta's and a statement from the Manitoba government the same month that it would consult the public on the matter. This could be seen as progress toward Harper's end game—namely, that as so-called elected senators became increasingly numerous, pressure would mount for full-fledged Senate reform (Flanagan 2007).

The Conservative government's reform initiative began with a strong commitment from Harper, who even took the unusual step of appearing before a Senate special committee on September 7, 2006. However, its will to press forward later flagged, although the jibes directed at the Liberal Senate majority did not. If Harper gained a parliamentary majority in the 2008 election and the House of Commons passed legislation to reduce senators' term, it would be more difficult for the Senate to reject it. As for Harper's other measure, even a Commons majority might not be sufficient. Although some experts consider the bill to be legal, a number do not. Among the latter, Ron Watts (2008) has stated that attempting to reform the Senate "on the sly through the use of ordinary legislation constitutes an anticonstitutional process." Moreover, acting in the face of outright opposition from Quebec's National Assembly could have significant political repercussions.

Harper did have public opinion behind him. For example, in a May 2008 national survey, 64% of respondents said they agreed with the proposal to limit appointed senators to eight-year terms. Although the survey did not ask respondents about the Conservatives' Senate consultation legislation, 60% supported "allowing Canadians to directly elect their senators" (Angus Reid Strategies 2008).

Finally, the stated objectives of the Harper initiative were somewhat myopic. The preamble of the Senate appointment consultation and tenure bills stated that "the Government of Canada has undertaken to explore means to enable the Senate better to reflect the democratic values of Canadians and respond to the needs of Canada's regions" (Senate of Canada 2006). However, Harper and the lead ministers said little about what this meant. Just how would a transformed Senate respond to regional needs? Are these the only needs that merit the Senate's attention? Would it be justifiable for the Senate, with enhanced legitimacy, to retain its current, very significant legislative powers? These and other questions remained unanswered. This underlines the need, as a first step, to develop publicly supported guiding principles about the role of the reformed second chamber within Canada's system of government and the ways its work would benefit citizens. Democratic reform cannot really be credible if this requirement is paid only lip service.

Electoral System

Although electoral reform became a lively issue only in the past several years, work by academics, commissions, and other public bodies dates from the late 1970s (Seidle 1996, 292–300). The critique of the SMP voting system, currently used for all federal, provincial, and territorial elections,[2] has consistently focused on *unfairness in party representation*, including the following tendencies:

- The leading party usually wins a majority of seats with less than 50% of the popular vote.
- The party with the most votes often wins many more seats than its vote share.
- Other parties, except those with votes that are regionally concentrated, are usually underrepresented.

There has also been a particular concern about federal parties' regional representation:

- Regionally focused parties often elect considerably more members than their share of the vote, sometimes giving the impression they are the region's "voice" in the House of Commons.
- Despite receiving a significant share of the vote in certain regions, the governing party sometimes elects virtually no MPs from those areas, thus weakening its claim to act legitimately on behalf of all parts of the country.

As noted in the previous section, the 1980 federal election gave rise to the latter phenomenon. Some electoral reform proposals put forward around that time addressed the problem. This has been less the case more recently, as even the Liberals have been able to elect members from all or virtually all provinces.

Fewer democratic reform proposals have focused on the *underrepresentation of demographic groups*, although this was a leitmotif of the 1991 report of the Royal Commission on Electoral Reform and Party Financing (Lortie Commission). On the basis of Pitkin's (1972) "descriptive representation" criterion, Parliament and the provincial legislative assemblies do not fare very well. For example, after the 2006 election

- Women accounted for 21.3% of the members of the House of Commons
- A total of 7.8% of MPs[3] were from visible minorities (in 2006, people from visible minorities accounted for 16.2% of the Canadian population)
- A total of 1.6% of MPs were Aboriginal (3.8% of the population in 2006)

The projected growth rate for the last two groups is expected to exceed the Canadian average for quite some time, so their underrepresentation may become a more pressing concern.

This section discusses three electoral reform proposals presented between 2004 and 2007 by the Law Commission of Canada (LCC) (2004), the British Columbia Citizens' Assembly on Electoral Reform (2004), and the Ontario Citizens' Assembly on Electoral Reform (2007). As with the review of Senate reform measures, the focus will be on their objectives. In the case of Ontario and British Columbia, the citizen-focused process used to develop their proposals will also be covered.

The report of the LCC was the fruit of an ambitious program of research and consultations that began in 2001. The initiative had strong backing from the LCC's president, Nathalie Des Rosiers, who spoke frequently at public forums about the issue. The report explored the range of representational dynamics summarized earlier, as well as related issues, including youth involvement and the decline in turnout. The recommendations centered on a mixed-member system:

- Two thirds of MPs would continue to be elected by SMP.
- The remaining one third would be elected from provincial and territorial party lists.
- Voters would have two votes: one for a constituency MP and one for a party list (for the latter, they could endorse the party "slate" or indicate a preference for a candidate on the list).

The LCC report listed the "potential benefits" of a different electoral system (Law Commission of Canada 2004, 139), including that most of the vote/seat distortions associated with SMP would be corrected (table 28.1). Greater numbers of women and minority candidates would be elected, but this would result primarily from the efforts of political parties, to whom the report directed several recommendations. To increase female representation in Parliament, for example, the report recommended that parties consider a range of issues, including parity on party lists,

Table 28.1 Objectives of Electoral Reform Proposals

	Law Commission of Canada	British Columbia Citizens' Assembly	Ontario Citizens' Assembly
Party representation			
Fairer representation for parties in legislature	√	√	√
Facilitate representation for new/ emerging parties	√		
Reduce chances of "wrong winner"		√	
Retain links between electors and local member		√	√
Demographic representation			
Women	√		√
Ethnocultural and linguistic minorities	√		
Aboriginal people	√		
Youth	√		
Voting procedure			
Voter choice		√	√
Simplicity			√
Governance			
More consensual government	√	√	√
More power for elected members		√	√
Government stability			√

Sources: Law Commission of Canada (2004); British Columbia Citizens' Assembly on Electoral Reform (2004); Ontario Citizens' Assembly on Electoral Reform (2007).

the use of quotas for party lists and constituency nominations, and campaign finance measures to enhance access to candidacy. Similar measures were also proposed to promote greater representation of Aboriginal people (Law Commission of Canada 2004, 112–113, 122–123). In addition, the report suggested the new system "might result in high voter turnout."[4] Finally, the LCC report addressed the implications for governance. It was acknowledged that the proposed voting system could lead to shorter-lived governments. However, the report disputed the claim that coalition governments would not be able to make tough decisions, and cited research suggesting that countries with proportional representation do not necessarily fare less well economically than those with majoritarian systems (Law Commission of Canada 2004, 143).

Neither the Liberals, who were in power when the LCC report came out, nor the Conservatives had any interest in pursuing electoral system reform. In fact, some of their members criticized the LCC study, claiming the issue should be left to MPs. Although the New Democratic Party (NDP) made some attempts to advance the issue during the Martin minority government (2004–2006), it remains a marginal concern at the federal level.

In 2004, British Columbians came very close to endorsing a new voting system. Electoral reform had attracted some public attention for a number of years, in part through the efforts of a small advocacy group: Fair Voting BC. Significant distortions in party representation were the main reason Premier Gordon Campbell decided to establish a citizens' assembly to examine electoral reform.

The citizens' assembly exercise, which began in January 2004, was notable in a number of respects, including (1) the 160 members, half women and half men, were chosen through a random selection process; (2) political parties were excluded from membership and kept a distance from the assembly; and (3) the assembly's work, which included learning, consultation, and deliberation phases, lasted almost ten months (see Ratner 2005). The assembly recommended a form of the single transferable vote (BC-STV), with electoral districts of two to seven members. Its report suggested this would further three broad principles: fair election results, effective local representation, and greater voter choice (table 28.1). Regarding the last item, some assembly members argued that allowing voters to rank candidates of their preferred party (or even more than one party) was more democratic and could allow citizens to challenge candidates favored by party elites (Seidle 2007, 309). Governance issues received limited attention in the report, although it was stated that the new system would put an end to majority governments and that "[c]oalition governments, and the more consensual decision making they require, are normal in most western democracies" (British Columbia Citizens' Assembly on Electoral Reform 2004, 7).

The Campbell government announced that the assembly's eventual recommendation would be put to a referendum on May 17, 2005, and that a supermajority threshold would apply. The proposal would have to receive at least 60% of the votes across the province, as well as a majority of the votes in at least 60% of the constituencies. During the campaign, the STV proposal benefited from having been developed by a nonpartisan body of citizens. In addition, quite a number of citizens' assembly "alumni" canvassed for a yes vote. However, in the absence of public funding, both sides' educational efforts were hampered by limited resources. The Liberals and the opposition NDP remained officially neutral. The yes side nearly obtained the necessary supermajority: 57.4% of those who voted endorsed BC-STV, and it had majority support in all but two constituencies.

In the face of the result, which many saw as an endorsement of change, Campbell announced a second referendum would be held in conjunction with the 2009 election (the threshold will be the same) and that, in the interim, maps of the province according to BC-STV and the current system would be prepared. Perhaps this second vote will lead to change in Canada's westernmost province. However, it is difficult to imagine that, with the positive experience of the citizens' assembly several years in the past, voters will be more inclined than in 2005 to endorse BC-STV.

Unlike British Columbia, Ontario had virtually no public debate about the electoral system until quite recently. The Ontario Liberals' 2002 election platform included a commitment to democratic renewal, and a number of changes have been instituted. These included the adoption of fixed dates for elections and timely disclosure of political donations. The platform also called for the creation of a citizens' assembly on electoral reform, but this did not take place until September 2006.

The ground rules for the Ontario Citizens' Assembly on Electoral Reform were based closely on those of the British Columbia pioneer: The 103 members, one for each constituency, were randomly selected; fifty-two were female and fifty-one male; and the work was divided into learning, consultation, and deliberation phases. The Ontario assembly chose a different model from that recommended in British Columbia, a mixed-member proportional (MMP) system. Its main features were as follows:

- Ninety members would be elected from constituencies and thirty-nine from closed party lists.
- The legislative assembly would be increased from 103 to 129 members.
- Voters would have two votes: one for a constituency candidate and the second for a party.
- The list seats would be compensatory, and any party that obtained 3% of the provincial vote would be eligible for list seats.

The assembly's report included three "priority objectives": voter choice, fair election results, and strong local representation (Ontario Citizens' Assembly on Electoral Reform 2007, 5–6). It also made an unsubstantiated claim that its proposed system was "more likely than the current one to increase the participation of women and other underrepresented citizens in the legislature" (Ontario Citizens' Assembly on Electoral Reform 2007, 9). On governance, the report stated: "The likelihood of coalitions in a Mixed Member Proportional system may make the environment in the legislature less adversarial than it is now. Parties within a coalition government will need to work together to manage the affairs of the province effectively" (Ontario Citizens' Assembly on Electoral Reform 2007, 11). No potential drawbacks were discussed.

During the October 10, 2007, referendum campaign, the governing Liberals remained neutral; the opposition Progressive Conservatives had no official position, but the party leader, John Tory, criticized the model; the leaders of the NDP and the Green Party supported the reform. Fair Vote Ontario focused on "fair representation" concerns and said little about governance. Opponents tapped into antipolitician sentiment by arguing that the proposed increase in seats was unwarranted and that members elected from lists would, in effect, be appointed by parties. Premier McGuinty had set the same threshold as in British Columbia. When the votes were counted, only 36.9% had supported change. Observers agreed that Ontarians were not well informed, and some reform advocates blamed Elections Ontario's public education campaign. However, Laura Stephenson and Brian Tanguay (2008, 23) have observed that the parties did little to encourage a full debate and that "Ontario's flirtation with electoral reform [proceeded] without general support."

Electoral reform has been on the public agenda in three other provinces (Seidle 2007). After a series of public consultations, Prince Edward Island held a referendum in November 2005 on an MPP system. The result, 36.4% in favor, was almost the same as Ontario's. In Quebec, the Liberal government in 2004 tabled draft legislation providing for an MMP model. However, after extensive hearings by a National Assembly committee, the initiative went no further; opposition within the Liberal caucus was a key factor. In New Brunswick, a Commission on Legislative Democracy recommended MMP as part of a broad package in its well-documented 2004 report. A few modest changes were made, but there has been no action on the voting system.

Taking stock of the recent provincial debates, several points emerge. First, except in British Columbia and Quebec, advocacy groups have not greatly broadened public interest in electoral reform. In contrast, groups played an active role in promoting electoral reform in New Zealand, where MMP was introduced in 1996, and adopting a mixed system for the new Scottish Parliament (Seidle 2002, 13–15). Second, political leadership did not really extend beyond launching a consultation process. Examining electoral reform outside the partisan arena may be appropriate and can have advantages—for example, encouraging citizen "buy-in," as occurred in British Columbia. However, the approach allowed most party leaders to skirt the issue during the referendum campaigns, perhaps contributing to low citizen awareness (at least in Ontario and Prince Edward Island). Third, the various reports and advocacy groups did not adequately address the governance implications. Almost all the reports presented a rather rosy view of coalition government (the presumed result of adopting the recommended voting system), but said little about the potential impact on public policy—for example, that a broader range of party and other interests might be taken into account. Finally, except perhaps in British Columbia, public opinion is ambivalent. A report from a 2007 national survey noted that Canadians are not "disenchanted" with the electoral system and added: "They see flaws, especially with respect to fairness, and they are open to change, but they are not calling for it" (Compas and Frontier Centre for Public Policy 2007, 75). This suggests that, when the issue returns to the public agenda, fairer party representation arguments need to be bolstered by others, including the potential for more responsive governance.

Political Finance and Office Holders' Accountability

In contrast to the lack of real change in the two areas reviewed here, significant measures to regulate campaign finance and the accountability of federal office holders have been put in place since the mid 1970s. The changes have been championed by political leaders and, in most cases, had all-party support.

Financial scandals, the rising costs of elections, and the example provided by Quebec's 1963 reform[5] led the Pearson Liberal government to establish the Committee on Election Expenses in 1964. Its 1966 report recommended spending limits for candidates (but not parties), partial reimbursement of candidates' media advertising costs, disclosure of parties' and candidates' revenue and spending, and a tax credit for contributions to parties and candidates. Although continued escalation of election costs, particularly television advertising, was the main reason the Trudeau Liberal government introduced political finance legislation several years later, there was also spillover from the Watergate scandal in the United States (Seidle and Paltiel 1981, 229, 232).

The 1974 Election Expenses Act was adopted with all-party agreement during the minority 1972–1974 Parliament. It introduced a broad framework governing party and election finance with three main pillars: (1) *spending limits* for registered political parties and candidates; (2) *public reporting* of registered parties' revenue and expenses (annually), and parties' and candidates' election expenses and contributions; and (3) *public funding* through reimbursements for registered parties and candidates, and an income tax credit for political contributions. Although some adjustments were made during the ensuing twenty-five years, the main lines remained as is. The rules governing party registration and spending by other interveners (often referred to as *third parties*) were nevertheless modified as a result of court challenges.

In 2003, responding to the initial revelations from what became known as the sponsorships scandal (discussed later in this chapter and in chapter 10, this volume), the Chrétien Liberal government launched a major reform of political finance. Bill C-24 was directed at perceptions of undue influence on the part of large donors, and a major shift took place through the introduction of limits on the source and size of political contributions. All parties supported the bill except the Canadian Alliance (which opposed the increased public funding for parties). The main changes, which came into effect on January 1, 2004, were the following:

- Contribution limits that allowed individuals only to donate a total of $5,000 a year to a registered party and its constituency associations, candidates, and nomination contestants (persons seeking nomination as a candidate); individuals could also give up to $5,000 in total to the contestants for a registered party's leadership. Corporations and trade unions could contribute up to $1,000 in total each year to the local entities of a registered party (constituency associations, candidates, and nomination contestants).
- To compensate for national parties' loss of revenue from business and unions, public funding was increased through a new annual allowance, paid quarterly to parties that qualify for reimbursement; an increase in the value of the reimbursements; and more generous rules for the income tax credit.
- Registered parties that receive an annual allowance must file quarterly reports of their contributions.
- Registered electoral district associations, which were not previously covered, must file annual reports of their contributions and expenses.
- Nomination contestants must respect a spending limit equal to 20% of the limit for candidates within that electoral district.

- Leadership contestants of a registered party must, for the four-week period prior to the vote, submit weekly reports of contributions; and a full report on contributions and expenses six months after the leadership contest. No limit on leadership contestants' spending was enacted.

The principle of probity at the heart of the 1974 framework was thus extended considerably by adding a fourth pillar—the contribution limits—applying reporting and related requirements to a much broader range of entities, and expanding public funding.

The changes did not stop there, however. Details continued to emerge about questionable payments the federal government made to Quebec advertising agencies and other bodies under its sponsorships program (which had been established after the 1995 Quebec referendum to improve the federal government's visibility and image in the province). Following further revelations and a scathing report from the auditor general, Chrétien's successor, Paul Martin, appointed a commission of inquiry chaired by Justice John Gomery of the Quebec Superior Court. His preliminary report portrayed a web of fraudulent payments to Liberal-friendly firms, in some cases for little or no work, and negligence on the part of the public servants who administered the program. Discredited by the revelations, the Liberals were reduced to a minority in the 2004 election and lost the January 2006 election to the Conservatives.

Acting on an election promise, the Harper government subsequently introduced an omnibus measure, Bill C-2—the Accountability Act. It reflected the view that "Canadians have every right to expect that public office holders and public-sector employees will be guided by the highest standards of ethical conduct" (Government of Canada 2006). One element of the bill was a tightening of the contribution limits. As of January 1, 2007,

- Individuals were allowed to give a maximum of $1,000 a year to a national party
- At the constituency level, businesses, unions, and other organizations were barred from making political contributions
- An individual's contributions to the local entities of a registered party (candidates, electoral district associations, and nomination contestants) were limited to an aggregate of $1,000 a year
- Individuals can also give a maximum of $1,000 to a leadership candidate or candidates (all the limits are adjusted annually for inflation)

According to the government, these and related changes to the Canada Elections Act "would increase transparency, reduce opportunities to influence politicians with contributions, and help Canadians feel more confident about the integrity of the democratic process" (Government of Canada 2006). The government could expect to receive some credit for extending the ban on business and union donations to the local level. In a survey conducted during the 2006 election, 59.5% of respondents agreed that the ban on such donations at the national level was a "good thing" and only 4.8% though it was a "bad thing."[6] Partisan interest was not absent, however. By tightening the contribution limits, Harper hoped to hamper Liberal Party fund raising.

Bill C-2, which all parties supported, also provided for enhanced public reporting by a range of political and public service officer holders, stricter rules on lobbying, and extensive new constraints on contracting and other financial transactions. Although many of the changes were directed at the public service, others applied to ministers, MPs, and senators. For example, the powers of the conflict of interest and ethics commissioner were strengthened, and an ethics officer for the House of Commons and another for the Senate were given considerable statutory authority. Some have suggested the Accountability Act was an overreaction to the sponsorships scandal and that one of its results has been to complicate many processes within an already risk-averse public service. Although this may be true, it is too early to draw firm conclusions about the overall impact on government administration.

As for the effects on the democratic process, the Harper legislation needs to be considered along with the Chrétien bill. Although some leading Liberals argued that lowering the contribution limits was excessive, Bill C-24's restrictions on the *source* of party donations has caused them much greater difficulty (in 2003, the last year businesses and unions could donate to national parties, the Liberals received 62% of their contributions from business). As the Liberal Party struggled to adapt to the citizen-based regime,[7] the Conservatives have far outpaced it in fund-raising. In 2007, the Conservative Party received $16,983,630 in donations, compared with $4,471,903 for the Liberals.

Although debate about the impact of the Chrétien and Harper reforms will continue, the fundamental rules governing almost all aspects of federal political financing and the conduct of office holders are firmly anchored. In this domain, political leaders have been highly responsive to public concern about ethics in politics. The guiding principles have not always been explicit, but it is clear that the objectives of probity and transparency now underpin many important aspects of the federal democratic process. It remains to be seen whether and how the goal posts can be advanced to further the objectives of representativeness and responsiveness in governance.

CONCLUSION

Reform of the Senate and the electoral system has proved difficult, in part, because of the level of consent required. Regarding the Senate, the amending formula places the bar quite high. Moreover, on the only occasion that all governments agreed on reform, the amendments were put to a referendum along with the rest of the Charlottetown Accord and were rejected. Taking another tack, the Harper government has attempted to change the way senators are selected through simple legislation, but this has been criticized as skirting the amending formula. As for the electoral system, in British Columbia, Prince Edward Island, and Ontario, the government set the level of approval required in the referendum vote on changing the voting method at 60%. In the latter two provinces, the result was well below 50%, but in British Columbia the 57% yes vote indicated a relatively strong desire for change.

Political leadership has also been exercised less decisively in these two areas with regard to political finance and accountability legislation. Despite the Senate's evident lack of legitimacy, the federal government added Senate reform to the constitutional agenda only when it became a popular issue in western Canada through promotion of the Triple E model. As for the voting system, even in the five provinces where the issue was actively considered between 2004 and 2007, few political leaders went beyond establishing a consultation process. Although not taking a public position on a voting system reform proposal can be defended on certain grounds, it is not surprising that (except in British Columbia) the issue attracted insufficient attention and many voters were uninformed. In contrast, prime ministers Chrétien and Harper personally championed the important bills on political finance and other matters that were directed, in part, at hampering undue influence by private interests.

Looking to the future, it is difficult to be optimistic about the likelihood of significant institutional reform. When even a modest change such as reducing senators' terms to eight years cannot be enacted, one is tempted to conclude that, at least for the shorter term, Senate reform is unattainable. Changing the electoral system does not require provincial consent, but the issue will not be advanced at the federal level until, as happened in the five provinces, there is the will to launch a consultation process. This prognosis does not mean that advocates of more representative and responsive legislatures should abandon their efforts. Progress in advancing these objectives can, and should, be made through other channels, while not abandoning the ultimate objective of structural reform.

Regarding representativeness, one avenue for change is through political parties. Although most of the national parties have processes to promote the election of women, women often become candidates in nonwinnable constituencies. As for visible minorities and Aboriginal people, their concentration in certain constituencies has helped diversify somewhat the membership of the House of Commons. In light of these groups' increasing share of the population and the need to have their voices heard within federal politics, parties should consult widely and develop new approaches that will increase their presence. Political leadership can also have an impact through direct action and/or by encouraging cultural change. When Premier Jean Charest decided to name an equal number of men and women to the Quebec cabinet after the 2007 provincial election, he did not need to have legislation adopted. His move was applauded, and this has apparently had an impact on how cabinet decisions are made (Séguin 2008).

As for responsiveness, members' capacity to act—and to be seen to act—for those they represent is hampered by two related maladies that afflict the House of

Commons: excessive partisanship and unyielding party discipline. Although minority parliaments (starting in 2004) might have provided an opportunity for inter-party cooperation in the work of committees, under the Harper government many of them degenerated into partisan conflict resembling the circus of the House itself. Past efforts at parliamentary reform have been directed at enhancing committees' role in public policy development. The procedural changes achieved little, and further such moves will founder unless party leaders demonstrate a real commitment to values different from those of sports teams and begin to encourage a cultural change that will allow members to play a more meaningful role in their various activities. Political parties outside Parliament can also contribute to responsiveness in governance by devoting more energy to policy development, particularly through innovative processes that may draw in youth and other groups that are not very active in party politics.

Finally, there is a need to be clear about guiding principles. Institutional reform proposals have sometimes been supported by overly ambitious claims. If the power of the prime minister and party discipline remained as strong as they have been, would an elected Senate with a suspensive veto have significantly increased the impact of regional interests in federal policy making? Would women's representation improve through voting system reform proposals that do not include specific rules about how party lists would be constructed (for example, through the "zipping" [alternation] of women and men candidates)? Would the Senate better reflect the democratic values of Canadians, as the Harper bills claimed (without defining them), if senators continued to be appointed but for shorter terms?

Pursuing democratic reform, whether formally or through political leadership and the actions of parties, requires a clear-sighted and realistic view of the potential benefits. As this chapter has suggested, two guiding principles—greater representativeness and enhanced responsiveness—need to be pursued with renewed vigor. This will require explicit political commitment and a willingness to listen to other parties and to citizens. Above all, there is a need for new and creative approaches. These may emerge if there are clear signals that they will be given serious consideration. Political leaders would do well to join the process and demonstrate that they, too, want to participate in reforming Canada's democratic institutions.

Acknowledgments. I thank Jean-Simon Farrah for his research assistance and Peter Aucoin for his perceptive comments on an earlier version of this chapter.

NOTES

1. The survey consists of an extensive set of questions used to rate the extent of political and civil rights in the various countries. There are four other subcategories: freedom of expression and belief, associational and organizational rights, rule of law, and

personal autonomy and individual rights. The 2008 survey covered 193 countries and fifteen "related and disputed territories" (Freedom House 2008).

2. Three provinces have had experience with alternative voting systems. In Manitoba, the single transferable vote (STV) was enacted for the Winnipeg provincial constituencies in 1920, and the alternative vote (AV) for rural ridings in 1924; both were repealed in 1955. In 1924, Alberta adopted STV for urban constituencies and AV for rural ridings; both were repealed in 1956. British Columbia used the alternative vote for the 1952 and 1953 elections, but then reverted to SMP.

3. Information provided by Jerome Black of McGill University (personal communication, May 30, 2008).

4. The report cited research showing that turnout was five to six points higher in countries with proportional or compensatory mixed electoral systems, while noting that turnout had dropped in most OECD countries during the previous decade, including a number of countries with full proportional systems (Law Commission of Canada 2004, 39–40).

5. In 1963, Quebec was the first jurisdiction in Canada to introduce spending limits (for parties and candidates) and public funding through reimbursements to candidates.

6. The question was part of the 2006 Canadian Election Study's campaign period survey; only 4.8% of respondents said the ban was a "bad thing" and 35.6% had no opinion or did not know (Canadian Election Study 2006).

7. The Liberals' fund-raising effort was long hampered by the absence of a single national membership list (the provincial and territorial wings each kept their own lists). This was rectified at the party's 2006 convention, but it will take some time before the Liberals can develop a sophisticated data base and other tools to rival those of the Conservatives.

REFERENCES

Angus Reid Strategies. 2008. Canadians welcome Saskatchewan's proposal to elect Senators. May 28. http://angusreidstrategies.com/uploads/pages/pdfs/2008.05.28_Senate.pdf.

Bédard, Michel. 2007. Legislative summary: Bill C-20: Senate Appointment Consultations Act. December 13. http://www.parl.gc.ca/39/2/parlbus/chambus/house/bills/summaries/c20-e.pdf.

Beetham, David. 1991. *The Legitimation of Power*. Atlantic Highlands, N.J.: Humanities Press International.

British Columbia Citizens' Assembly on Electoral Reform. 2004. *Making Every Vote Count: The Case for Electoral Reform in British Columbia*. Final report. December.

Canadian Election Study. 2006. 2006 Data Set. http://ces-eec.mcgill.ca/surveys.html#2006.

Compas and Frontier Centre for Public Policy. 2007. Public Consultations on Canada's Democratic Institutions and Practices: A Report for the Privy Council Office. http://www.democraticreform.gc.ca/grfx/docs/1.Public%20Consultations%20Report.pdf.

Dahl, Robert. 2005. What political institutions does large-scale democracy require? *Political Science Quarterly* 120(2): 187–197.

Docherty, David. 2005. *Legislatures*. Vancouver: UBC Press.

Flanagan, Tom. 2007. Rebuilding the Senate, one block at a time. *The Globe and Mail*, April 23, A19.

Franks, C. E. S. 2003. The Canadian Senate in modern times. In *Protecting Canadian Democracy: The Senate You Never Knew*, ed. S. Joyal, 151–188. Montreal: McGill-Queen's University Press.

Freedom House. 2008. *Freedom in the World 2008*. Washington, D.C.: Freedom House. http://freedomhouse.org/template.cfm?page=351&ana_page=342&year=2008.

Government of Canada. 2006. Federal accountability action plan. http://www.faa-lfi.gc.ca/docs/ap-pa/ap-pa02-eng.asp.

Johnston, Richard., André Blais, Elisabeth Gidengil, and Neil Nevitte. 1996. *The Challenge of Direct Democracy: The 1992 Canadian Referendum*. Montreal: McGill-Queen's University Press.

Law Commission of Canada. 2004. *Voting Counts: Electoral Reform for Canada*. Ottawa: Law Commission of Canada.

McCormick, Peter, Ernest C. Manning, and Gordon Gibson. 1981. *Regional Representation: The Canadian Partnership*. Calgary: Canada West Foundation.

Mendelsohn, M. 1996. Introducing deliberative direct democracy in Canada: Learning from the American experience. *American Review of Canadian Studies* 26(3): 449–468.

O'Malley, Eoin. 2007. The power of prime ministers: Results of an expert survey. *International Political Science Review* 28(1): 7–27.

Ontario Citizens' Assembly on Electoral Reform. 2007. *One Ballot, Two Votes: A New Way to Vote in Ontario*. May 15.

Phillips, Anne. 1995. *The Politics of Presence*. Oxford: Clarendon Press.

Pitkin Hannah F. 1972. *The Concept of Representation*. Berkeley: University of California Press.

Ratner, R. S. 2005. The BC Citizens' Assembly: The Public Hearings and Deliberation Stage. *Canadian Parliamentary Review* 28(1): 24–33.

Rawls, John. 1972. *A Theory of Justice*. Oxford: Clarendon Press.

Sartori, Giovanni. 1987. *The Theory of Democracy Revisited*. Chatham, N.J.: Chatham House Publishers.

Séguin, Rhéal. 2008. Charest's angels and his surprising rise in popularity. *Globe and Mail*, April 26, F3.

Seidle, F. Leslie. 1992. Senate reform and the constitutional agenda: Conundrum or solution? In *Canadian Constitutionalism 1791–1991*, ed. Janet Ajzenstat, 91–122. Ottawa: Canadian Study of Parliament Group.

———. 1996. The Canadian electoral system and proposals for reform. In *Canadian Parties in Transition*, 2nd ed., ed. A. Brian Tanguay and Alain-G. Gagnon, 282–306. Toronto: Nelson Canada.

———. 2002. *Electoral System Reform in Canada: Objectives, Advocacy and Implications for Governance*. Ottawa: Law Commission of Canada.

———. 2007. Provincial electoral systems in question: Changing views of party representation and governance. In *Canadian Parties in Transition*, 3rd ed., ed. Alain-G. Gagnon and A. Brian Tanguay, 303–334. Peterborough, Ont.: Broadview Press.

Seidle, F. Leslie, and K. Z. Paltiel. 1981. Party finance, the Election Expenses Act and campaign spending in 1979 and 1980. In *Canada at the Polls, 1979 and 1980*, ed. Howard R. Penniman, 227–279. Washington, D.C.: American Enterprise Institute.

Smith, David. 2003. *The Canadian Senate in Bicameral Perspective*. Toronto: University of Toronto Press.

Senate of Canada. 2006. Bill S-4 (An Act to amend the Constitution Act, 1867 (Senate tenure). Ottawa: Public Works and Government Services Canada.

Special Senate Committee on Senate Reform. 2006. *Report on the Subject-matter of Bill S-4, An Act to Amend the Constitution Act, 1867 (Senate tenure)*. October. Ottawa: Public Works and Government Services Canada.

Stephenson, Laura, and Brian Tanguay. 2008. "The Ontario electoral system referendum: Information, interest, and democratic renewal." Presented at the annual meeting of the Canadian Political Science Association, Vancouver, June 5, 2008.

Stilborn, Jack. 2003. Forty years of not reforming the Canadian Senate: Taking stock. In *Protecting Canadian Democracy: The Senate You Never Knew*, ed. Serge Joyal, 31–66. Montreal: McGill-Queen's University Press.

Supreme Court of Canada. 1980. *Authority of Parliament in Relation to the Upper House.* 1 S.C.R. 54.

Task Force on Canadian Unity. 1979. *A Future Together: Observations and Recommendations.* Ottawa: Minister of Supply and Services Canada.

Tilly, Charles. 2007. *Democracy*. Cambridge: Cambridge University Press.

Watts, Ronald. 2008. Bill C-20: Faulty procedure and inadequate solution. Testimony before the legislative committee on Bill C-20. May 7. http://www.queensu.ca/iigr/working/senate/papers/2008–11.pdf.

INDEX

....

Page numbers in bold indicate figures or tables.